SECOND EDITION

ISSUES IN TERRORISM AND HOMELAND SECURITY

SELECTIONS FROM CQ RESEARCHER

Los Angeles | London | New Delhi
Singapore | Washington DC

For information:

SAGE Publications, Inc.
2455 Teller Road
Thousand Oaks, California 91320
E-mail: order@sagepub.com

SAGE Publications Ltd.
1 Oliver's Yard
55 City Road
London, EC1Y 1SP
United Kingdom

SAGE Publications India Pvt. Ltd.
B 1/I 1 Mohan Cooperative Industrial Area
Mathura Road, New Delhi 110 044
India

SAGE Publications Asia-Pacific Pte. Ltd.
33 Pekin Street #02-01
Far East Square
Singapore 048763

Printed in the United States of America

Library of Congress Cataloging-in-Publication Data
Issues in terrorism and homeland security : selections from CQ researcher.—2nd ed.
      p. cm.
Includes bibliographical references.
ISBN 978-1-4129-9201-5 (pbk.)
   1. Terrorism—United States. 2. Terrorism—United States—Prevention. 3. Terrorism—Government policy—United States. 4. National security—United States. 5. Terrorists—United States. 6. Terrorism. I. CQ researcher.

HV6432.I87 2011
363.3250973—dc22   2010029244

This book is printed on acid-free paper.

15   16   17   18   19   10 9 8 7 6 5 4 3 2

Acquisitions Editor:	Jerry Westby
Editorial Assistant:	Nichole O'Grady
Production Editor:	Laureen Gleason
Typesetter:	C&M Digitals (P) Ltd.
Cover Designer:	Candice Harman
Marketing Manager:	Erica DeLuca

Contents

Annotated Contents

of leftists who demonized capitalism, or those who resented America's unrelenting cultural influence — what some call the McGlobalization of the world. Now, anti-Americanism seems epidemic, especially in the Muslim world but also in Europe, Asia and Latin America. In European intellectual circles it has even become a badge of honor. Ironically, while resentment of the U.S. simmers, people seeking economic opportunity continue to emigrate to the U.S.

Religious Fundamentalism:
Does It Lead to Intolerance and Violence?

People around the world are embracing fundamentalism, a belief in the literal interpretation of holy texts and, among the more hard-line groups, the desire to replace secular law with religious law. At the same time, deadly attacks by religious extremists in India, Uganda, Somalia and Nigeria are on the rise — and not just among Muslims. Meanwhile, political Islamism — which seeks to install Islamic law via the ballot box — is increasing in places like Morocco and in Muslim communities in Europe. Christian evangelicalism and Pentecostalism — the denominations from which fundamentalism derives — also are flourishing in Latin America, Africa, Central Asia and the United States. Ultra-Orthodox Jewish fundamentalists are blamed for exacerbating instability in the Middle East and beyond by establishing and expanding settlements on Palestinian lands. And intolerance is growing among Hindus in India, leading to deadly attacks against Christians and others. As experts debate what is causing the spread of fundamentalism, others question whether fundamentalists should have a greater voice in government.

Hate Groups: Is Extremism on
the Rise in the United States?

National crises create opportunities for extremists. Today the global economic crisis now wreaking havoc on millions of American households is hitting while the first black president is in the White House and the national debate over illegal immigration remains unresolved. Already, some far-right extremists are proclaiming that their moment is arriving. Indeed, an annual tally by the Southern Poverty Law Center shows 926 hate groups operating in 2008, a 50 percent increase over the number in 2000. And the Department of Homeland Security

concludes that conditions may favor far-right recruitment. But a mix of conservatives and liberal free-speech activists warn that despite concerns about extremism, the administration of Barack Obama should not be intruding on constitutionally protected political debate. Some extremism-monitoring groups say Obama's election showed far-right power is waning, not strengthening. But that equation may change if the economic crisis deepens, the experts caution.

Nuclear Proliferation and Terrorism:
Can "Rogue" States and Terrorists
Acquire Nuclear Weapons?

The recent discovery of a global black market in nuclear weapons and related technology has intensified concerns that so-called rogue nations and terrorist organizations like Osama bin Laden's al Qaeda network might acquire nuclear bombs. The network run by the "father" of Pakistan's atomic bomb, A.Q. Khan, sold nuclear-weapons materials to Iran and North Korea, which have refused to sign the Nuclear Non-Proliferation Treaty (NPT). Virtually all the other nations of the world are signatories. President Bush responded to the revelations about Khan's network with a plan to strengthen international anti-proliferation efforts, including calling on the U.N. Security Council to require all states to criminalize proliferation of components that could be used to make weapons of mass destruction. While arms experts commended the president for focusing on proliferation, some said his proposals did not go far enough.

Terrorism and the Internet: Should Web Sites That
Promote Terrorism Be Shut Down?

A decade ago, terrorist organizations operated or controlled only about a dozen Web sites. Today there are more than 7,000. Terrorist groups use the Internet for many activities, ranging from raising funds to explaining how to build a suicide bomb. They find the Internet appealing for the same reasons everyone else does: It's cheap, easily accessible, unregulated and reaches a potentially enormous audience. As terrorist content spreads to chat rooms, blogs, user groups, social networking sites and virtual worlds, many experts, politicians and law enforcement officials are debating how government and industry should respond. Some want Internet companies to stop terrorists from using the Web, while others say

ANNOTATED CONTENTS **xi**

that is not the role of Internet service providers. As governments enact laws based on the belief that the Internet plays a significant role in promoting terrorism, critics say the new measures often overstep free-speech and privacy rights.

TERRORIST ENVIRONMENTS

Understanding Islam:
Is Islam Compatible With Western Values?

With more than 1 billion adherents, Islam is the world's second-largest religion after Christianity. Within its mainstream traditions, Islam teaches piety, virtue and tolerance. Ever since the Sept. 11, 2001, terrorist attacks in the United States, however, many Americans have associated Islam with the fundamentalist groups that preach violence against the West and regard "moderate" Muslims as heretics. Mainstream Muslims and religious scholars say Islam is wrongly blamed for the violence and intolerance of a few. But some critics say Muslims have not done enough to oppose terrorism and violence. They also contend that Islam's emphasis on a strong relationship between religion and the state is at odds with Western views of secularism and pluralism. Some Muslims are calling for a more progressive form of Islam. But radical Islamist views are attracting a growing number of young Muslims in the Islamic world and in Europe.

Crisis in Pakistan:
Can the Fragile Democracy Survive?

South Asia experts warn that Pakistan — recently dubbed "the new center of the war against terrorism"— could become the world's first nuclear-armed "failed state." The Muslim country's new president faces a spike in terrorist bombings, rising Islamic fundamentalism, a weakened democracy and a faltering economy. Already, more people have been killed in suicide bombings in Pakistan during the first eight months of 2008 than in Iraq or Afghanistan. And Indian authorities suspect that Islamic terrorists from Pakistan-controlled Kashmir perpetrated the 2008 Mumbai terrorist attacks that killed 173 people. Another challenge for President Asif Ali Zardari and his relatively young nation: growing resentment about recent U.S. military incursions into terrorist-infested Pakistani tribal territories. Although the country has weathered many storms since

its founding in 1947, experts wonder if recent developments threaten its survival. As the new administration tries to hold the disparate nation together, a strong military — with a long history of usurping civilian rule — is poised to take over once again. The world watches with growing concern to see if the fragile democracy can survive or if Pakistan — with its nuclear arsenal — will devolve into chaos.

Radical Islam in Europe:
Are Terrorists Expanding Their Recruiting Efforts?

The recent spate of foiled terrorist plots by Muslim extremists in Great Britain, Germany and Denmark is a grim reminder that radical Islam continues to pose a serious threat in Europe. Some experts warn that Europe could export its brand of terrorism to the United States, since many of Europe's 15 million Muslims carry European passports that give them easy access to this country. European capitals like London have provided a haven for terrorists to organize, some critics say, because countries like Britain have failed to integrate Muslims into mainstream society. But other experts blame international terrorist networks, which recruit from a small minority of estranged European Muslims. Others argue that in fighting terrorism at home, countries like France have gone too far in curbing Muslims' civil liberties. Concerned that their secular Western values are under threat from conservative Muslims, some European countries are considering limiting immigration and requiring new citizens to adopt the national language and beliefs.

Global Jihad: Does a Terrorist
Movement Threaten the West?

President Bush declared in early October that the war in Iraq is a key front in the war with terrorist jihadists. But the president's critics insist that the war actually serves as a recruiting tool for jihadists. Since the Sept. 11, 2001, attacks that made Osama bin Laden and the al Qaeda terrorist organization notorious — and celebrated — worldwide, jihadists have struck more than 107 times in more than a dozen countries — a figure that doesn't include hundreds of attacks on civilians and American soldiers in Iraq. The global terror offensive points to the existence of a unifying jihadist ideology. But much is unknown about the terrorists. Are their goals political or strictly religious? Do they operate under a unified command or through a loose network of organizations and cells? Meanwhile, evidence is mounting that al Qaeda remains strong enough to have played a role in the subway and bus bombings in London on July 7, 2005.

Human Rights Issues: Are They a Low Priority Under President Obama?

Human rights advocates are voicing disappointment with what they have seen so far of President Obama's approach to human rights issues in forming U.S. foreign policy. They applaud Obama for working to restore U.S. influence on human rights by changing President George W. Bush's policies on interrogating and detaining terrorism suspects. But they also see evidence that the Obama administration is reluctant to challenge authoritarian governments for clamping down on political dissidents or rigging elections. As one example, these critics complain that Obama should not have tried to curry favor with the Chinese government by postponing a meeting with the Dalai Lama until after the president visits China in November. Administration officials insist Obama is devoted to human rights and democratization and cite among other moves the decision to join the United Nations Human Rights Council. Conservative critics, however, say the council is a flawed institution and the United States should have stayed out.

KEEPING THE HOMELAND SECURE

Homeland Security: Is America Safe From Terrorism Today?

Following the Sept. 11, 2001, terrorist attacks, the U.S. government created the Department of Homeland Security, giving it stepped-up power to shadow and detain terrorism suspects. Then-President George W. Bush credited these measures — and intelligence and military operations abroad — with preventing new attacks on U.S. soil in the nearly eight years since 9/11. But some intelligence experts argue that the new department failed to coordinate the nation's many turf-conscious intelligence agencies, and that continued U.S. military pressure has rendered Osama bin Laden's al Qaeda terrorist network incapable of mounting new attacks within the United States. Moreover, jihadist cells

that have wreaked havoc in Europe lack counterparts in the U.S., where Muslims are far less alienated, experts say. Still, the danger of a new attack remains. According to an emerging school of thought, Americans should learn to live with the possibility of an eventual attack, rather than expecting government to eliminate all danger.

Port Security: Are New Anti-Terrorism Measures Adequate?

The controversy over an Arab company's plan to operate terminals at six U.S. seaports put port security at the top of lawmakers' agenda. But some security experts say the firestorm over the ill-fated Dubai Ports World deal masks a bigger problem: the failure of the United States to invest enough in security — including infrastructure upgrades, advanced radiation-detection equipment and manpower — to prevent terrorists from smuggling radioactive bombs or other dangerous materials into one of the more than 360 U.S. seaports. Only 5 percent of the 11.3 million shipping containers arriving at U.S. seaports last year were examined, leading some members of Congress to call for inspections of all U.S.-bound containers. The Bush administration defends its port security strategy and vows to install more radiation-detection devices at U.S. and overseas ports and to expand programs that ask U.S. businesses and foreign governments to voluntarily heighten security overseas.

Policing the Borders: Can the United States Guard Against Terrorists?

To keep America safe from terrorists, customs and immigration agents must monitor 7,500 miles of land and sea borders, dozens of airports and 300 official ports of entry. They also monitor the 11 million trucks, 2.2 million rail cars and 7,500 foreign-flag ships that enter the country each year. And they oversee the 31 million non-citizens — mostly tourists — who visit each year. After Sept. 11, President Bush formed the Office of Homeland Security, and Congress passed sweeping legislation giving police and intelligence agencies more power to monitor U.S. borders. But experts disagree over which security steps would be most cost-effective and least disruptive to trade and Americans' daily lives. And civil libertarians warn that some proposed measures — such as linking driver's licenses to a national database and targeting certain ethnic groups — would undermine civil liberties.

Interrogating the CIA: Should Its Role in Terrorism Cases Be Reexamined?

Attorney General Eric H. Holder Jr. has asked a career federal prosecutor to reexamine evidence of possible abuses by Central Intelligence Agency operatives years ago in the questioning of "high-value" terrorism suspects. The CIA's role in interrogating detainees has been controversial because the agency used so-called "enhanced" techniques, including waterboarding. Under President George W. Bush, the Justice Department approved the harsh measures even though many critics said some amount to torture. President Obama has now barred the use of the techniques, but former Vice President Dick Cheney is among those who say the practices yielded valuable intelligence that helped keep the country safe after the Sept. 11 terrorist attacks in 2001. A newly released internal CIA report documents several apparent abuses during the interrogation program. The release of the report is said to be hurting morale at the CIA even as it prompts renewed calls for a broad investigation of the Bush administration's policies in the war on terror.

Torture Debate: Is the U.S. War on Terror Legitimizing Torture?

Countries around the globe — including the United States — are using coercive interrogation techniques in the fight against terrorism that critics say amount to torture. Despite international laws banning the practice, authoritarian nations have long abused prisoners and dissidents, and a handful of democracies have used torture in recent decades against what they considered imminent threats. Republican presidential candidates say they would authorize torture to prevent impending terrorist attacks. U.S. soldiers in Iraq say they would torture suspects to save the lives of their comrades. Human rights advocates worry the use of torture by the United States is legitimizing its use globally and destroying America's moral authority to speak out against regimes that abuse prisoners in far worse ways. U.S. officials credit "enhanced interrogation" methods with averting terrorist attacks. But many experts say information gained by torture is unreliable.

Treatment of Detainees: Are Suspected Terrorists Being Treated Unfairly?

The Supreme Court recently struck down the Bush administration's system for holding and trying detainees at the U.S. Naval base at Guantánamo Bay, Cuba. The administration had maintained that the Geneva Conventions did not protect alleged terrorists captured in Afghanistan and other battlefields in the five-year-old war on terror, and critics say that policy led to the use of abusive interrogation methods, such as "waterboarding" and sleep deprivation. The critics, including top military lawyers, successfully argued that the United States was violating the laws of warfare. They also opposed military commissions the administration has proposed for conducting detainee trials. Bush said the war on terrorism required the commissions' streamlined procedures, which deny some rights guaranteed by the conventions. The court's decision leaves Congress with two options: require detainees to be tried under the military's existing court-martial system or create a new, legal version of the administration's commissions.

Prosecuting Terrorists: Should Suspected Terrorists Be Given Military or Civil Trials?

President Obama is under fierce political attack for the administration's decision to try Khalid Sheikh Mohammed, the alleged mastermind of the Sept. 11 attacks, and Umar Farouk Abdulmutallab, the so-called Christmas Day bomber, in civilian courts instead of military tribunals. Republican lawmakers argue that the defendants in both cases should be treated as "enemy combatants" and tried in the military commissions established during the Bush administration. Administration officials and Democratic lawmakers say criminal prosecutions are more effective, having produced hundreds of convictions since 9/11 compared to only three in the military system. And they insist that Abdulmutallab is providing useful information under interrogation by FBI agents. But the administration is reconsidering Attorney General Eric Holder's original decision to hold Mohammed's trial in New York City and considering making greater use of military commissions with other terrorism cases.

Preface

Why is there controversy over a definition of terrorism? What motivates someone to become a terrorist? What can be done to stop new terrorist groups from forming and to protect us from those that roam the globe today? These questions and many more are addressed in a collection of articles for debate offered exclusively through *CQ Researcher*, CQ Press and SAGE. With a focus on articles that bring students up-to-date on timely global issues, this reader promotes in-depth discussion and helps students formulate their own positions on critical issues. Furthermore, it helps bring pressing issues into the classroom for any course on terrorism and homeland security.

This second edition includes eighteen up-to-date reports by *CQ Researcher,* an award-winning weekly policy brief that brings complicated issues down to earth. This collection was carefully crafted to cover a range of issues relevant to criminology, criminal justice, public administration and public policy studies, and it will help students gain a deeper, more critical perspective on many of the wide-ranging issues and debates in our ongoing analysis of terrorism and homeland security.

CQ RESEARCHER

CQ Researcher was founded in 1923 as *Editorial Research Reports* and was sold primarily to newspapers as a research tool. The magazine was renamed and redesigned in 1991 as *CQ Researcher.* Today, students are its primary audience. While still used by hundreds of journalists and newspapers, many of which reprint portions of the reports, the *Researcher's* main subscribers are now high school, college and public libraries. In 2002, *Researcher* won the American Bar Association's coveted Silver Gavel award for magazine excellence for a series of nine reports on civil liberties and other legal issues.

Researcher staff writers — all highly experienced journalists — sometimes compare the experience of writing a *Researcher* report to drafting a college term paper. Indeed, there are many similarities. Each report is as long as many term papers — about 11,000 words — and is written by one person without any significant outside help. One of the key differences is that writers interview leading experts, scholars and government officials for each issue.

Like students, staff writers begin the creative process by choosing a topic. Working with the *Researcher's* editors, the writer identifies a controversial subject that has important public policy implications. After a topic is selected, the writer embarks on one to two weeks of intense research. Newspaper and magazine articles are clipped or downloaded, books are ordered and information is gathered from a wide variety of sources, including interest groups, universities and the government. Once the writers are well informed, they develop a detailed outline, and begin the interview process. Each report requires a minimum of ten to fifteen interviews with academics, officials, lobbyists and people working in the field. Only after all interviews are completed does the writing begin.

CHAPTER FORMAT

Each issue of *CQ Researcher,* and therefore each selection in this book, is structured in the same way. Each begins with an overview, which briefly summarizes the areas that will be explored in greater detail in the rest of the chapter. The next section chronicles important and current debates on the topic under discussion and is structured around a number of key questions, such as "Does religious fundamentalism lead to intolerance and violence?" "Are terrorists expanding their recruiting efforts?" or "Is the U.S. war on terrorism legitimizing torture?" These questions are usually the subject of much debate among practitioners and scholars in the field. Hence, the answers presented are never conclusive but detail the range of opinion on the topic.

Next, the "Background" section provides a history of the issue being examined. This retrospective covers important legislative measures, executive actions and court decisions that illustrate how current policy has evolved. Then the "Current Situation" section examines contemporary policy issues, legislation under consideration and legal action being taken. Each selection concludes with an "Outlook" section, which addresses possible regulation, court rulings, and initiatives from Capitol Hill and the White House over the next five to ten years.

Each report contains features that augment the main text: two to three sidebars that examine issues related to the topic at hand, a pro versus con debate between two experts, a chronology of key dates and events and an annotated bibliography detailing major sources used by the writer.

ACKNOWLEDGMENTS

We wish to thank many people for helping to make this collection a reality. Tom Colin, managing editor of *CQ Researcher,* gave us his enthusiastic support and cooperation as we developed this edition. He and his talented staff of editors and writers have amassed a first-class library of *Researcher* reports, and we are fortunate to have access to that rich cache. We also wish to thank our colleagues at CQ Press, a division of SAGE and a leading publisher of books, directories, research publications and Web products on U.S. government, world affairs and communications. They have forged the way in making these readers a useful resource for instruction across a range of undergraduate and graduate courses.

Some readers may be learning about *CQ Researcher* for the first time. We expect that many readers will want regular access to this excellent weekly research tool. For subscription information or a no-obligation free trial of *CQ Researcher,* please contact CQ Press at www.cqpress .com or toll-free at 1-866-4CQ-PRESS (1-866-427-7737).

We hope that you will be pleased by this edition of *Issues in Terrorism and Homeland Security.* We welcome your feedback and suggestions for future editions. Please direct comments to Jerry Westby, Publisher, SAGE Publications, 2455 Teller Road, Thousand Oaks, CA 91320, or jerry.westby@sagepub.com.

—The Editors of SAGE

Contributors

Brian Beary, a freelance journalist based in Washington, D.C., specializes in European Union (EU) affairs and is the U.S. correspondent for *Europolitics,* the EU-affairs daily newspaper. Originally from Dublin, Ireland, he worked in the European Parliament for Irish MEP Pat "The Cope" Gallagher in 2000 and at the EU Commission's Eurobarometer unit on public opinion analysis. A fluent French speaker, he appears regularly as a guest international-relations expert on television and radio programs. Beary also writes for the *European Parliament Magazine* and the *Irish Examiner* daily newspaper. His most recent report for *CQ Global Researcher* was "Race for the Arctic."

Mary H. Cooper specializes in defense, energy and environmental issues. Before joining *The CQ Researcher* as a staff writer in 1983, she was Washington correspondent for the Rome daily newspaper *l'Unitá.* She is the author of *The Business of Drugs* (CQ Press, 1990) and holds a BA in English from Hollins College in Virginia. Her recent reports include "Exporting Jobs," "Weapons of Mass Destruction" and "Bush and the Environment."

Sarah Glazer, a London-based freelancer, is a regular contributor to the *CQ Researcher.* Her articles on health, education and social-policy issues have appeared in *The New York Times, The Washington Post, The Public Interest* and *Gender and Work,* a book of essays. Her recent *CQ Researcher* reports include "Increase in Autism" and "Gender and Learning." She graduated from the University of Chicago with a BA in American history.

Kenneth Jost graduated from Harvard College and Georgetown University Law Center. He is the author of the *Supreme Court Yearbook* and editor of *The Supreme Court from A to Z* (both CQ Press). He was a member of the *CQ Researcher* team that won the American Bar Association's 2002 Silver Gavel Award. His previous reports include "Closing Guantánamo" and "The Obama Presidency" (with *CQ Researcher* staff). He is also author of the blog *Jost on Justice* (http://jostonjustice.blogspot.com).

Peter Katel is a *CQ Researcher* staff writer who previously reported on Haiti and Latin America for *Time* and *Newsweek* and covered the Southwest for newspapers in New Mexico. He has received several journalism awards, including the Bartolomé Mitre Award for coverage of drug trafficking from the Inter-American Press Association. He holds an AB in university studies from the University of New Mexico. His recent reports include "Mexico's Drug War" and "Future of the Military."

Robert Kiener is an award-winning writer whose work has appeared in the *London Sunday Times, The Christian Science Monitor, The Washington Post, Reader's Digest, Time Life Books, Asia Inc.* and other publications. For more than two decades he lived and worked as an editor and correspondent in Guam, Hong Kong, England and Canada and is now based in the United States. He frequently travels to Asia and Europe to report on international issues. He holds a MA in Asian Studies from Hong Kong University and an MPhil in International Relations from Cambridge University.

Samuel Loewenberg, now based in Berlin, is an award-winning freelance writer who has reported on global issues for *The New York Times, The Economist, The Washington Post* and *Newsweek* among others. He covered the terrorist bombings in both Madrid and London, as well as the anti-globalization movement in Brazil. He is a former Columbia University Knight-Bagehot Journalism Fellow.

Barbara Mantel is a freelance writer in New York City whose work has appeared in *The New York Times,* the *Journal of Child and Adolescent Psychopharmacology* and *Mamm Magazine.* She is a former correspondent and senior producer for National Public Radio and has won several journalism awards, including the National Press Club's Best Consumer Journalism Award and the Front Page Award from the Newswomen's Club of New York. She holds a BA in history and economics from the University of Virginia and an MA in economics from Northwestern University.

Patrick Marshall, a *CQ Researcher* contributing writer, is the reviews editor at *Federal Computer Week* and a technology columnist for the *Seattle Times;* he is based in Bainbridge Island, Washington. His recent reports include "Policing the Borders" and "Three-Strikes Laws." He holds a bachelor's degree in anthropology from the University of California at Santa Cruz and a master's in foreign affairs from the Fletcher School of Law and Diplomacy.

Pamela M. Prah is a *CQ Researcher* staff writer with several years previous reporting experience at Stateline.org, *Kiplinger's Washington Letter* and the Bureau of National Affairs. She holds a master's degree in government from Johns Hopkins University and a journalism degree from Ohio University. Her recent reports include "Disaster Preparedness," "Eating Disorders" and "Coal Mining Safety."

Seth Stern is a legal-affairs reporter at the *CQ Weekly Report.* He has worked as a journalist since graduating from Harvard Law School in 2001, including as a reporter for the *Christian Science Monitor* in Boston. He received his undergraduate degree at Cornell University's School of Industrial and Labor Relations and a master's degree in public administration from Harvard's Kennedy School of Government. He is co-authoring a biography of Supreme Court Justice William J. Brennan Jr.

Re-examining 9/11

Could the Terrorist Attacks
Have Been Prevented?

Kenneth Jost

1

National security adviser Condoleezza Rice defended the Bush administration's anti-terrorism policies in April 2004 before the commission investigating the Sept. 11, 2001, attacks. Former U.S. counterterrorism coordinator Richard A. Clarke generally praised the Clinton administration's policies in his testimony but sharply criticized Bush's anti-terrorism record.

AFP/Paul Richards (Rice) and Luke Frazza

From *CQ Researcher*,
June 4, 2004.

When President Bush's national security adviser, Condoleezza Rice, agreed after weeks of pressure to testify before the independent commission investigating the Sept. 11, 2001, terrorist attacks, relatives of victims filled the first three rows immediately behind her.

Many listened on April 8 with a mixture of frustration and anger as Rice fended off questions about the administration's anti-terrorism policy in the months before the attacks.

"To listen to her not recall things, to hear those kinds of statements was very frustrating," says Carie Lemack, whose mother was on the first plane that crashed into the World Trade Center. "It was all very surreal."

Rice stoutly defended the administration's anti-terrorism policy, saying that the White House was working overtime to develop a comprehensive strategy to eliminate the al Qaeda terrorist organization. She also discounted the importance of an intelligence briefing that Bush had received on Aug. 6 warning of Osama bin Laden's intention to attack within the United States — possibly an airline hijacking.[1]

The so-called Presidential Daily Brief, or PDB, was "historical information based on old reporting," Rice said. "There was no new threat information."

After more than three hours, Rice stepped down from the witness stand, embracing some 9/11 family members on her way out. But Lemack kept her distance. "Accountability, ma'am, accountability," Lemack shouted at her.

"That's the word that resonates with me: accountability," Lemack explains today. "If my mother was the CEO of a company, and somebody messed up, at the end of the day it was her fault. She would be accountable."[2]

Can Separate, Secret Agencies Learn to Share?

The U.S. intelligence community "was not created and does not operate as a single, tightly knit organization," a congressional commission wrote in 1996. "It has evolved over nearly 50 years and now amounts to a confederation of separate agencies and activities with distinctly different histories, missions and lines of command."

As a result, there is no single place where intelligence-gathering can be coordinated and collected information can be analyzed. In the wake of hearings by the independent Sept. 11 commission, some lawmakers say the intelligence network should be restructured.

DOMESTIC INTELLIGENCE AGENCIES

HOMELAND SECURITY DEPARTMENT

Secret Service — Primary duties are protecting the president and stopping counterfeiters.

Customs Service — Inspecting cargo coming into the country by land, sea and air.

Border Patrol — Identifying and stopping illegal aliens before they enter the country.

Coast Guard Intelligence — Processing information on U.S. maritime borders and homeland security.

JUSTICE DEPARTMENT

Federal Bureau of Investigation — Lead agency for domestic intelligence and operations. Has offices overseas.

Drug Enforcement Administration — Collects intelligence in the course of enforcement of federal drug laws.

DEPARTMENT OF ENERGY

Office of Intelligence — Key player in nuclear weapons and non-proliferation, energy security, science and technology.

TREASURY DEPARTMENT

The Office of Intelligence Support — Collects and processes information that may affect fiscal and monetary policy.

STATE AND LOCAL POLICE AGENCIES

Coordinate with the FBI through joint counterterrorism task forces.

Trying to Pull It All Together

Several agencies were created before and after the Sept. 11 terrorist attacks primarily to analyze and integrate intelligence data. Among them:

Terrorist Threat Integration Center — Created by President Bush in 2003, this analysis center located in the CIA is designed to assess all terrorism-related information from U.S. and foreign intelligence sources.

Counterterrorist Center — CIA unit that coordinates counterterrorist efforts of the intelligence community; feeds information to the Terrorist Threat Integration Center.

Information Analysis and Infrastructure Protection Directorate — Part of the Department of Homeland Security created in 2002 to analyze terrorist-related intelligence and assess threats to critical infrastructure.

Terrorist Screening Center — A multi-agency center administered by the FBI to develop a watch-list database of suspected terrorists.

The Intelligence Community

As director of the CIA, George J. Tenet is the titular head of the U.S. intelligence community, a network of 15 departments and agencies. These agencies conduct both domestic and international intelligence-gathering.*

* Tenet abruptly resigned "for personal reasons" on June 10, 2004, just after this report went to press. President Bush said Tenet had done a "superb job for the American people" and that CIA Deputy Director John McLaughlin will become acting director after Tenet's resignation takes effect in mid-July.

Lemack helped found one of the major 9/11 survivors' groups, the Family Steering Committee, which vigorously lobbied a reluctant Bush administration in 2002 to create the independent National Commission on Terrorist Attacks upon the United States, the so-called 9/11 commission.[3] Family groups have kept up the pressure since then. Most recently, they forced an equally reluctant House Speaker J. Dennis Hastert, R-Ill., to give the commission more time to complete its report; it is now due on July 26.

INTELLIGENCE AGENCIES OPERATING OVERSEAS

CIVILIAN AGENCIES

Central Intelligence Agency (CIA) — Lead agency for collecting and analyzing foreign intelligence, including information on terrorism. Briefs the president daily.

Department of State Counterterrorism Office — Coordinates efforts to improve counterterrorism cooperation with foreign governments.

Bureau of Intelligence and Research — Analyzes and interprets intelligence on global developments for secretary of State.

MILITARY AGENCIES

National Security Agency (NSA) — Collects and processes foreign signal intelligence from eavesdropping and signal interception. Also charged with protecting critical U.S. information security systems.

Defense Intelligence Agency (DIA) — Provides intelligence to military units, policymakers and force planners. It has operatives in many U.S. embassies.

National Geospatial-Intelligence Agency (NGA) — The intelligence community's mapmakers, able to track movements of people and machines or changes in topography.

National Reconnaissance Office (NRO) — Builds and maintains the nation's spy satellites. Provides information to the Defense Department and other agencies.

Army Intelligence

Navy Intelligence

Marine Corps Intelligence

Air Force Intelligence

TAKING STEPS TO IMPROVE COORDINATION

The weakest link in the intelligence campaign against terrorism has been the analysis and sharing of millions of bits of raw data swept up by government agencies operating in the United States and abroad.

The original plan for correcting this flaw after the Sept. 11 attacks was to centralize analysis in the Department of Homeland Security, which Congress created in 2002. After the law was passed, however, President Bush changed tack. By executive fiat in early 2003 — no written executive order was issued — Bush created the Terrorism Threat Integration Center (TTIC), housed in the Central Intelligence Agency, to coordinate terrorism-related analysis.

Except for a passage in Bush's 2003 State of the Union speech and an address to FBI employees, the administration did not formally outline the roles and responsibilities of agencies participating in the center. A memorandum signed in 2003 by Attorney General John Ashcroft, Director of Central Intelligence George J. Tenet and Homeland Security Secretary Tom Ridge explained the information-sharing responsibilities of the center's participants.

It was not until an April 13, 2004, letter from Tenet, Ridge, FBI Director Robert S. Mueller III and TTIC Director John O. Brennan to several members of Congress that the administration made clear that terrorism-related intelligence would be analyzed by the threat center Bush had created.

The letter was sent in response to a series of inquiries dating to February 2003 from Susan Collins, R-Maine, chairwoman of the Senate Governmental Affairs Committee, and Carl Levin of Michigan, the panel's second-ranking Democrat.

The letter said Brennan's unit controls "terrorism analysis (except for information relating solely to purely domestic terrorism)," which is the province of the FBI. Homeland Security manages information collected by its own components, such as the Coast Guard and Secret Service, and is responsible for analyzing material "supporting decisions to raise or lower the national warning level."

— *Justin Rood*

CQ Graphic/Marilyn Gates-Davis

Judging by questions from the 10 commission members and from several "staff statements" already released, the panel's final report is likely to fault the anti-terrorism policies of both Bush and his Democratic predecessor, Bill Clinton.[4] For Bush, the report is likely to intensify the political problems generated by legal attacks on the administration's post-9/11 detention policies and the recent, high-profile disclosures — including shocking photographs — of Iraqi prisoners being abused by U.S. servicemembers.[5]

The commission gained most attention with its reconstruction of events immediately leading up to the four hijackings of Sept. 11, which ultimately took some 3,000 lives. The actions of the 19 hijackers also have been dissected to try to understand how they eluded detection by immigration, law enforcement and aviation-security personnel on Sept. 11 and in the days, months and years beforehand.[6]

In its first interim report, released on Jan. 26, 2004, the commission staff documented numerous holes in immigration procedures that allowed some of the hijackers to enter or remain in the United States despite detectable visa violations. Another staff report released the same day reconstructed how the hijackers exploited "publicly available vulnerabilities of the aviation-security system" to pass through checkpoint screening and board their flights.[7] (*See sidebars, pp. 6, 14.*)

"I would not say that 9/11 was preventable, but I would certainly say we had a chance," says Amy Zegart, an assistant professor of public policy at UCLA who specializes in national security issues. "We could have been better organized than we were. Whether that could have made a difference, we'll never know."

The commission is also examining how the Clinton and Bush administrations dealt with al Qaeda since its first attack: the 1993 truck-bomb explosion at the World Trade Center that killed six persons and injured more than 1,000.

In sharply critical statements in April, the commission staff said the Central Intelligence Agency (CIA) failed through the 1990s to develop a "comprehensive estimate" of al Qaeda. In a second report, the staff said the FBI had failed to go beyond its law enforcement role to try to detect and prevent possible terrorist incidents. That report also criticized Bush's attorney general, John Ashcroft, for giving terrorism a low priority in the months before 9/11.[8]

Officials from both the Bush and Clinton administrations testified before the panel to defend their actions, including CIA Director George J. Tenet,* who served in both administrations; FBI Director Robert S. Mueller III and his Clinton administration counterpart, Louis Freeh; and Ashcroft and his predecessor, Janet Reno.

The parade of high-ranking officials came after the commission's most dramatic witness before Rice's appearance: Richard A. Clarke, a career civil servant whom Clinton named in 1998 as the nation's first national

counterterrorism coordinator and who continued in that position under Bush for more than two years, though with downgraded status.

Clarke appeared before the panel after publication of his first-person account, *Against All Enemies*, which paints a fairly positive picture of the Clinton administration's counterterrorism policies but sharply criticizes the Bush administration's record. Bush "failed to act prior to Sept. 11 on the threat from al Qaeda despite repeated warnings," Clarke writes. He goes on to blame Bush for having launched "an unnecessary and costly war in Iraq that strengthened the fundamentalist, radical Islamic terrorist organization worldwide."[9]

Zegart, who is writing a book on U.S. intelligence agencies' response to terrorism, faults both the CIA and the FBI for organizational deficiencies and "cultural" blind spots in dealing with the problem.[10] But she also criticizes policymakers in both the Clinton and Bush administrations. "It seems fairly clear that terrorism was not a high enough priority for either administration," she adds.[11]

Under widespread pressure, Bush himself agreed to submit to questioning by the commission, but only after insisting that Vice President Dick Cheney accompany him and that no recording or transcript be made of the closed-door session. (The commission had earlier heard separately from Clinton and former Vice President Al Gore.) The April 29 meeting with Bush and Cheney lasted more than three hours. Afterward, the commission said Bush and Cheney had been "forthcoming and candid." Bush described the meeting as "very cordial."

As the 9/11 commission continues its hearings and deliberations, here are some of the major questions being considered by the panel and by policymakers, experts and the public:

Did the Clinton administration miss good opportunities to take action against al Qaeda?

The CIA's Counterterrorism Center knew enough about bin Laden's role in financing and directing al Qaeda that it created a special "Issue Station" in January 1996 devoted exclusively to tracking his activities. But the unit's "sense of alarm" about bin Laden was not widely shared, according to the 9/11 commission staff. "Employees in the unit

9/11 Commission Bucked White House

The special commission created to investigate the 9/11 terrorist attacks has clashed with the Bush administration ever since its creation.

Congress approved creating the 10-member National Commission on Terrorist Attacks upon the United States on Nov. 15, 2002, a month after the White House had blocked a version passed by both the House and the Senate that summer. President Bush signed the bill into law on Nov. 27 and immediately named former Secretary of State Henry Kissinger to chair the commission.[1]

Congressional Democrats chose former Senate Majority Leader George Mitchell of Maine as the vice-chair of the panel. But both men resigned from the posts barely two weeks later: Mitchell cited the time demands of the job; Kissinger refused ethics requirements to disclose the clients of his international consulting firm.

Bush then picked former New Jersey Gov. Thomas F. Kean to chair the panel on Dec. 16. Kean, currently president of Drew University, is well regarded as a political moderate but lacks any foreign policy experience. In the previous week, congressional Democrats had tapped former Rep. Lee Hamilton of Indiana as vice chair. Hamilton had extensive foreign affairs experience during 34 years in the House and was widely respected.

The law creating the commission required it to complete its work within 18 months — by May 27, 2004. The timetable, insisted on by the White House, was aimed at getting the commission's report published before the 2004 presidential campaign. By late 2003, however, the commission was saying that it needed more time to complete its work. House Speaker J. Dennis Hastert, R-Ill., opposed the request, but finally agreed in late February 2004 to a 60-day extension for the commission's report — now due on July 26.

The commission said it needed more time in part because federal agencies — chiefly, the Defense and Justice departments — had responded slowly to requests for information. The commission also tangled with the White House over access to intelligence briefings Bush received on terrorism issues — including the now famous Aug. 6 "Presidential Daily Brief" warning of Osama bin Laden's interest in attacking the United States.

Bush eventually bowed to the commission's demands. He also agreed under pressure in April 2004 to meet and answer questions from all 10 members of the commission.

AFP Photo/Timothy A. Clary

Commission Chairman Thomas Kean, left, and Vice Chairman Lee Hamilton.

The commission now states on its Web site that it has had access to every document and every witness it has sought, and that Bush has yet to assert executive privilege on any document request.

Kean and Hamilton have maintained the appearance of bipartisan unity in public statements and hearings. However, Attorney General John Ashcroft complained that Jamie Gorelick, deputy attorney general under President Bill Clinton, should have recused herself from discussions of Justice Department guidelines limiting information sharing between intelligence agencies and the FBI. Both Kean and Hamilton defended Gorelick.

Other Democrats on the panel include Richard Ben-Veniste, a former Watergate prosecutor; former Sen. Bob Kerrey of Nebraska; and former Rep. Timothy Roemer of Minnesota. Besides Kean, the Republican panel members are Fred Fielding, White House counsel under President Ronald Reagan; former Sen. Slade Gorton of Washington; former Navy Secretary John F. Lehman; and former Illinois Gov. James R. Thompson.

---

[1] The legislation was part of the Intelligence Authorization Act for Fiscal Year 2003, Public Law 107-306. The text of the law is on the commission's Web site: www.9-11commision.gov.

Improved Aviation Security Still Has Gaps

The American airline industry was virtually brought to its knees on Sept. 11, 2001, by 19 men with box cutters like those available at any hardware store.

The federal government's response to the hijackings — creation of a massive, new security agency with 45,000 passenger screeners — created a more secure atmosphere at U.S. airports. But two years after its creation, the Transportation Security Administration (TSA) finds itself consistently criticized by politicians and the public. Occasional security gaffes — including a North Carolina college student's efforts last October to expose security glitches by hiding box cutters on two Southwest Airlines flights — have not helped the agency's image.

Moreover, lawmakers have complained the TSA is understaffed at some airports and overstaffed at

Weapons confiscated from passengers at Los Angeles International Airport last year include a knife hidden inside a belt.

AFP Photo/Robyn Beck

others. For example, Rep. Harold Rogers, R-Ky., pointed out at a March hearing that the tiny Rutland, Vt., airport had seven screeners to handle just seven passengers a day.[1]

In addition, those lawmakers who in 2001 opposed the idea of taking airport security away from private contractors and making it a federal responsibility remain critical of the agency. Rep. John Mica, R-Fla., chairman of the Aviation Subcommittee of the House Transportation and Infrastructure Committee, believes more and more private companies should be given the opportunity to take screening back from the government in order to prove that businesses can do as good a job as the government in keeping terrorists off airplanes.

"Private screening companies are required to meet the same rigorous security standards as . . . federal screeners," Mica said. "As long as the highest-level security standards are

---

told us they felt their zeal attracted ridicule from their peers," the staff's March 24, 2004, statement said.[12]

The skepticism even among intelligence professionals about targeting bin Laden was one of many difficulties the Clinton administration faced in confronting al Qaeda in the late 1990s. Clinton today gets some credit, even from political conservatives, for recognizing the threat. But he is also criticized for failing to mobilize support in or outside the government for strong action or to make effective those initiatives he was willing to authorize — most significantly, an Aug. 20, 1998, cruise missile attack against an al Qaeda base in Afghanistan aimed at killing bin Laden after he was linked to the Aug. 7, 1998, bombings of embassies in Kenya and Tanzania.

Moreover, many of the intelligence agencies' missteps occurred on Clinton's watch — most notably, the CIA's and FBI's mutual failure in 2000 to track two al Qaeda operatives into the United States and their eventual roles as 9/11 hijackers. Many experts fault Clinton for adopting

a law enforcement approach toward al Qaeda — focusing on criminal prosecutions inside the United States — instead of a military approach using armed force.

"They continued to have largely a criminal-justice model for al Qaeda rather than a military model, rather than a counterinsurgency model," says John Pike, director of GlobalSecurity.org, an Alexandria, Va., think tank.

Mark Riebling, editorial director at the conservative Manhattan Institute and author of a history of the relationship between the CIA and the FBI, says it was "patently absurd" for Clinton to designate the Justice Department as the lead agency in his 1995 Presidential Decision Directive on terrorism. Both men, however, say Clinton's approach matched what Riebling calls the "conventional wisdom" of the time.

Some other experts are less forgiving of what they regard as the Clinton administration's misdirection. "There was a strategic failure to understand the magnitude of the threat — that the 1993 World Trade Center met or exceeded, how that is accomplished should be determined by those most closely involved."[2]

But a recent investigation of five airports still using private security firms gave private screeners a mixed review. Clark Kent Ervin, inspector general of the Department of Homeland Security (DHS), said private contractors and the TSA performed "equally poorly."[3] But he blamed the problem largely on the slow hiring and screening process, which is still overseen by the TSA, even for the few airports still using private screeners.

As the summer travel season unfolds and the commercial airline industry continues its financial recovery, the TSA is nearing a crossroads.[4] In November, airports will be able to "opt out" of the federalized screening programs and outsource the work to private contractors. Mica predicts up to 25 percent of the nation's airports will opt out, primarily out of frustration with the TSA's bureaucracy.

About the same time, controversial passenger database programs like the Computer Assisted Passenger Pre-screening System (CAPPS II) and the entry-exit immigration tracking system known as US VISIT will be in place at many airports, adding a new layer of scrutiny while raising questions about privacy.

TSA executives insist they have made the skies safer, noting that there have been no terrorist attacks on airlines since 9/11. In addition, the agency has confiscated 1.5 million knives and incendiary devices and 300 guns, just since last October, said TSA Deputy Administrator Stephen J. McHale.[5]

Despite the progress, several security gaps still exist in passenger aviation: There are no shields to protect commercial airliners from attacks with shoulder-fired missiles, and there is no mandatory screening of air cargo. Rep. Jim Turner, D-Texas, the top Democrat on the House Homeland Security Committee, has introduced a bill that would require cargo screening and hardened cockpit doors on foreign airliners flying in U.S. airspace.

"There are still some security gaps. We need to do more, faster on this troubled system. It's not foolproof," Turner says. "But the good news is that it is clearly more difficult for a terrorist to use an airplane as a weapon."

— *Martin Kady II*

---

[1] Martin Kady II, "TSA Shouldn't Expect an Easy Ride From This Appropriations Cardinal," *CQ Today*, March 12, 2004, p. 1.

[2] Quoted in *CQ Today*, April 23, 2004, p. 3.

[3] Testimony to House Transportation and Infrastructure Committee's Subcommittee on Aviation, April 22, 2004.

[4] Although some older airlines are still struggling, overall revenues for the industry have recovered somewhat since 9/11. See Eric Torbenson, "Airlines Get Lift from Rise in Revenue," *The Dallas Morning News*, May 21, 2004.

[5] Testimony to House Transportation and Infrastructure Committee Subcommittee on Aviation, May 13, 2004.

---

bombing and the other incidents were part of a larger campaign," says Steven Aftergood, a senior research analyst at the liberal-oriented Federation of American Scientists.

But Aftergood also says the administration's attitude coincided with the public's. "There was a kind of post-Cold War relaxation that did not properly assess the rising hostility in parts of the Islamic world," he says. "It seems to have been a blind spot."

On the other hand, Richard Betts, a professor at Columbia University and member of the Hart-Rudman commission on terrorism in the late 1990s, says Clinton could have done more to mobilize public support for stronger action against al Qaeda. "There would have been political support for much more decisive military action" after the embassy bombings in Africa, Betts says.

Pike gives the administration credit for the strike against the al Qaeda camp in Afghanistan. Stronger action — an invasion of Afghanistan — was unrealistic at the time, he says. "I don't think they could have convinced anybody even if they had convinced themselves," he says.

In any case, Betts notes that Clinton faced personal and political problems in trying to overcome the military's reluctance to go after al Qaeda. "Clinton, being Clinton, had no moral authority to challenge the military on anything," Betts says.

"The other problem is that there was that whole impeachment business," Pike adds. "The last two years of the administration, they were politically paralyzed."

Intelligence experts also emphasize that the administration inherited a decades-old lack of CIA and FBI coordination. "The problem was deeply structural," says Greg Treverton, a RAND Corporation senior research analyst who has held intelligence-related positions in government. "We built these agencies to fight the Cold War. But they set us up to fail in the war on terror."[13]

The "most stunning" of the agencies' missteps, Zegart and others say, was the lack of effective follow-up after two of the eventual hijackers — Nawaf al Hazmi and Khalid al Mihdhar — were observed at an al Qaeda meeting in Kuala Lumpur, Malaysia, in 2000. After receiving pictures of the two from Malaysia's security service, the CIA tracked both men into the United States. Subsequent events are bitterly disputed by the agency and FBI.[14]

In one version, the CIA never told the FBI about the two men; in the other, the FBI had access to the information but failed to act on it. In any event, the two men were never put on a terrorism "watchlist" and lived openly in San Diego — under their real names — until the hijackings. The 9/11 commission staff says the episode illustrates the failure "to insure seamless handoffs of information" among intelligence agencies — including the ultrasecret National Security Agency.[15]

Was the CIA or the FBI more to blame for the foul-up? "There's plenty of blame to go around," Zegart says bluntly.

Clinton left office with actions against al Qaeda again under discussion after the bombing of the *USS Cole* off Yemen in August 2000. But delays in linking the bombing to al Qaeda and reluctance to engage in a quick tit-for-tat response combined to quash any proposals to retaliate. Instead, Clinton and his national security team told incoming President Bush that he should put al Qaeda at the top of the list of national-security problems.

Did the Bush administration miss telltale clues that might have prevented the 9/11 attacks?

Intelligence agencies picked up a high volume of al Qaeda-related "threat reporting" in summer 2001. More than 30 possible overseas targets were identified in various intercepted communications. Officers at the CIA's Counterterrorism Center felt a sense of urgency, but some felt administration policymakers were too complacent. In fact, two veteran officers "were so worried about an impending disaster that . . . they considered resigning and going public with their concerns."[16]

Their frustration further buttresses the damning picture of the Bush administration's view of al Qaeda drawn by Clarke. He says in his book that his initial briefing on al Qaeda in January 2001 was greeted with sharp skepticism from Paul Wolfowitz, the deputy secretary of Defense. "I just don't understand why we are beginning by talking about this one man bin Laden," Clarke quotes Wolfowitz. Moreover, he describes Wolfowitz as linking the 1993 trade center bombing and other incidents to

"Iraqi terrorism" — a theory Clarke says was "totally discredited."[17]

Experts representing a range of political views say Clarke's account rings true. "They took a long time to get off the mark studying this," the Manhattan Institute's Riebling says.

The American Federation of Scientist's Aftergood agrees: "In its first eight months, the Bush administration received warnings [about al Qaeda], but nevertheless moved at a leisurely pace until the crisis was upon us."

RAND's Treverton says the new administration apparently regarded state-sponsored terrorism as a greater threat than al Qaeda, and thus discounted Clinton officials' warnings. "It's pretty plain that terrorism — particularly, the brand represented by al Qaeda — was not quite on their radar scope," he says.

Some experts are less critical, acknowledging the difficulties that a new administration faced in taking office and setting policies on a range of foreign-policy and national-security issues. "Six months into a new administration, they were still getting their sea legs," says Pike of GlobalSecurity.org.

In both interviews and her sworn testimony before the 9/11 commission, national security adviser Rice insisted Bush understood the threat posed by al Qaeda. She told the commission on April 8 the administration was seeking to develop "a new and comprehensive strategy to eliminate" al Qaeda.

"I credit the administration with recognizing that at some point they were going to have to make really hard strategic choices," says James Jay Carafano, senior research fellow for defense and homeland security at the conservative Heritage Foundation. "That's a real testament to the administration."

Still, Carafano and others say the administration would have been hard-pressed to take stronger action against al Qaeda before 9/11. "Can you imagine if Bush had walked in the door and said let's invade Afghanistan?" Carafano asks. Pike says there were "missed opportunities, but they probably were not attainable, not realistic opportunities that you could have convinced people to implement."

The debate over the administration's response has come to focus on the now-famous PDB warning that bin Laden was "determined" to strike in the United States. The two-page document was first described in press accounts in May 2002, but the White House refused to provide it to the joint inquiry by House and Senate Intelligence

CHRONOLOGY I: THE CLINTON YEARS

1993-2000 *Al Qaeda grows into worldwide terrorist organization under Osama bin Laden; U.S. attacked at home and abroad; Clinton administration tries but fails to stunt group's growth and kill or capture bin Laden.*

Feb. 26, 1993 Truck bomb at World Trade Center kills six, injures more than 1,000; conspirators are later identified, indicted and some convicted.

June 1995 Presidential Decision Directive 39 labels terrorism a "potential threat to national security," vows to use "all appropriate means" to combat it; FBI designated lead agency.

January 1996 CIA's Counterterrorism Center creates special "Issue Station" devoted exclusively to bin Laden.

May 1996 Bin Laden leaves Sudan for Afghanistan.

June 25, 1996 Attack on Khobar Towers, U.S. Air Force residential complex, in Saudi Arabia kills 19 servicemembers.

April 1998 Taliban declines request to turn bin Laden over to United States.

May 1998 Presidential Decision Directive 62 lays out counterterrorism strategy; Richard A. Clarke named first national director for counterterrorism.

August 1998 U.S. embassies in Kenya and Tanzania bombed on Aug. 7; Clinton orders cruise missile strike ("Operation Infinite Reach") on al Qaeda base in Afghanistan; Aug. 20 strike hits camp, but after bin Laden had left. . . . Plan for follow-up strikes readied ("Operation Infinite Resolve") but not executed; Pentagon opposed.

December 1998 Plans prepared to use Special Operations forces to capture leaders of bin Laden network, but never executed; strikes readied after bin Laden possibly located, but intelligence deemed not sufficiently reliable, and strikes not ordered.

February, May 1999 Bin Laden located in February and again on several nights in May, but no strike ordered due to risk of killing visiting diplomats from United Arab Emirates (February), doubts about intelligence (May).

Summer 1999 High volume of threat reporting tied to Millennium celebrations.

July 1999 Clinton imposes sanctions on Taliban; U.N. sanctions added in October; through end of year, administration debates diplomatic vs. military approach but comes to no conclusion.

January 2000 Al Qaeda unsuccessfully tries to bomb *USS The Sullivans*; plot undisclosed until after attack on *USS Cole*. . . . Two future 9/11 hijackers tracked by CIA from al Qaeda meeting in Malaysia to United States; CIA and FBI trade accusations later over failure to place them on terrorism watch list.

Oct. 12, 2000 Attack on *Cole* kills 17 sailors; after the attack is linked to al Qaeda, strikes readied, but not ordered.

committees investigating 9/11 and declassified it on April 10 only under pressure from the 9/11 commission.[18]

The brief describes bin Laden as wanting to retaliate "in Washington" for the 1998 missile strike in Afghanistan. It also quotes a source as saying in 1998 that a bin Laden cell in New York "was recruiting Muslim-American youths for attacks." Since that time, the brief continues, the FBI had noticed "patterns of suspicious activity" in the U.S. "consistent with preparations for hijackings or other types of attacks." Rice, in her testimony, described the brief as "historical," and Bush later insisted that it contained no "actionable intelligence."

Some experts agree. "That does not seem to me to be a case of something that was egregiously overlooked and that should have prompted a response that could have made a difference," says Columbia University's Betts. "I don't think that was politically realistic before the fact."

Aftergood is more critical. "The fact that Bush received the Aug. 6 PDB while on vacation in Texas tells us something," he says. "What it tells us is that more could have been done; greater vigor could have been exercised." As one example, Bush named Cheney on May 8, 2001, to head a task force to look into responding to a domestic attack with biological, chemical or radioactive weapons. The task force was just getting under way in September.

CHRONOLOGY II: THE BUSH YEARS

2001-Present *Bush administration developing anti-terrorism policies on eve of 9/11 attacks; president rallies nation, launches invasion of Afghanistan to eliminate haven for al Qaeda; later, investigations by congressional committees, independent commission focus on missed clues, possible reforms.*

January 2001 President Bush takes office Jan. 20; administration officials briefed on *USS Cole* attack, but no strikes ordered; national security adviser Condoleezza Rice retains Richard A. Clarke in White House post but has him report to lower-level officials and asks him to draft new counterterrorism strategy.

March-July 2001 Various options for Afghanistan discussed at deputies level.

May 8, 2001 Bush names Vice President Dick Cheney to head counterterrorism task force; it was just getting organized in September.

Summer 2001 Increased threat reporting prompts concern by Clarke, CIA Director George J. Tenet.

June 2001 Draft presidential directive circulated by deputy national security adviser Stephen Hadley calls for new contingency military plans against al Qaeda and Taliban.

July 2001 Federal Aviation Administration issues several security directives; agency is aware that terrorist groups are active in United States and interested in targeting aviation, including hijacking. . . . Internal FBI memo urges closer scrutiny of civil aviation schools and use of schools by individuals who may be affiliated with terrorist organizations.

Aug. 6, 2001 Bush receives Presidential Daily Brief (PDB) warning, "Bin Ladin Determined to Strike in U.S."; two-page brief notes interest in hijacking; no immediate follow-up.

Late August 2001 Immigration and Naturalization Service arrests Zacarias Moussaoui in Minnesota after FBI lawyer raises suspicions about his enrollment in flight school; FBI headquarters rejects bid to search his computer.

Sept. 4, 2001 Top officials approve draft directive on terrorism for submission to Bush, calling for covert action, diplomacy, financial sanctions, military strikes.

Sept. 10, 2001 Three-phase strategy on Afghanistan agreed on at interdepartmental meeting of deputies.

Sept. 11, 2001 Hijackers fly airliners into World Trade Center and Pentagon as well as field in Pennsylvania; 3,000 persons killed; nation reacts with shock, anger.

October-December 2001 U.S.-led coalition ousts Taliban regime in Afghanistan.

2002 House, Senate Intelligence committees launch joint investigation of 9/11; under pressure, Bush administration also agrees to separate probe by independent commission.

2003 CIA, FBI, other intelligence agencies sharply criticized in report by joint congressional intelligence committees; panels call for intelligence overhaul, including new director of national intelligence.

2004 9/11 commission's interim staff reports fault CIA, FBI, other agencies for pre-9/11 lapses; Clarke book blasts Bush administration as slow and weak on terrorism; Bush, aides rebut criticisms; commission due to report in late July.

In line with existing procedure, the Aug. 6 PDB was not disseminated outside the White House. So, the Federal Aviation Administration (FAA) was given no special reason to step up airport security. Perhaps more significantly, the Justice Department never received the warning about possible domestic airline hijackings — which might have heightened attention to concerns raised by FBI agents in Phoenix and Minnesota in the months before Sept. 11.

In Minnesota, FBI lawyer Coleen Rowley had raised suspicions about a French-Algerian man, Zacarias Moussaoui, who attended flight school without being able to identify who was paying his tuition. But FBI

officials in Washington said Rowley did not have enough information to justify searching his computer. Moussaoui is now charged with conspiracy in the attacks. Meanwhile, an FBI counterterrorism agent in Phoenix had become suspicious of the number of Arab men taking flight lessons, but FBI headquarters also rejected his request for an investigation.

Are intelligence reforms needed to better guard against future terrorist attacks?

After weeks on the defensive following publication of Clarke's book and the 9/11 commission hearings, the

Bush administration sought to regain control of the agenda by leaking word in mid-April of possible plans to back major changes in intelligence gathering. The White House was said to be considering a longstanding proposal from the intelligence community to create a new "director of national intelligence" with budgetary and operational control over all of the government's 15 intelligence agencies. In addition, the White House was said to be eyeing the creation of a new FBI domestic-intelligence unit.[19]

The proposed organizational changes draw mixed reactions. Some experts say the changes are long overdue, others that they would be ill-advised. Several say the greater need is for changes in procedures and attitudes better adapted to confronting the threat of terrorism in an age of instant global communication.

"I'm skeptical of large institutional changes," says Aftergood. Instead, he favors "steady, incremental reform and learning directly from experience, including, above all, learning from mistakes."

The proposal for a director of national intelligence, or DNI, at first seems simply a new title for the current director of central intelligence, or DCI. The 1947 National Security Act empowers the DCI to coordinate all the intelligence agencies with overseas operations.

In practice, however, the DCI has had no control over individual agency's budgets or other matters. "Almost every major study of the intelligence agencies has recommended bolstering the authority of the DCI," UCLA's Zegart says.

She would prefer to increase the DCI's power instead of creating a new position. "George Tenet needs more power over the entire community," she says. In particular, Zegart says the preponderant role of the military units — with around 80 percent of the estimated $40 billion intelligence budget — skews priorities in favor of identifying and locating military targets ("tactical intelligence") at the expense of broader research and analysis ("strategic intelligence").

Other experts, however, envision a DNI with a broad analytical role and no operational authority. "A director of national intelligence is probably a pretty good idea," RAND's Treverton says. "Someone looking across the spectrum and asking how we're spending the money, and what we're getting for it."

"You have to break up the two hats that Tenet wears," says Melvin Goodman, a former CIA officer who teaches at the National War College. "To be director of central

intelligence and director of the CIA is an impossible task."

Tenet told the 9/11 commission, however, that he opposed separating the DCI's overall role from operational control of the CIA. The Defense Department has also resisted taking the military intelligence agencies' budgets out of the Pentagon. "Politically, it would be a very bloody fight to bring it about," says Columbia University's Betts, "and [very] expensive."

Proposals to reorganize the FBI reflect the view that the bureau's historic law enforcement role short-changes intelligence collection and analysis. The methodical collection of evidence for use in courtroom prosecutions is "not quick enough" to prevent terrorist incidents, Zegart says. In addition, she says the FBI's "culture" is ill-suited to intelligence work.

Mueller says he is reorienting FBI policies and procedures to deal with the problems. "That kind of cultural change takes a long time," says a dubious Zegart. But Pike is more optimistic. "I found the argument compelling that the FBI has the matter in hand," he says.

In any event, Pike and other experts strongly oppose one widely discussed proposal: To create a freestanding domestic-intelligence unit comparable to Britain's MI-5. "We're citizens; we are not subjects," Pike remarks.

The Heritage Foundation's Carafano calls it "a really bad idea. We don't need another intelligence organization. We probably have too many now."

Zegart acknowledges the criticisms and suggests a "semiautonomous" domestic-intelligence unit within the FBI might be the answer. Other experts, however, say leadership is more important than organizational change. "If you've got a director who has a mission to reorient [the agency's priorities], it's not absolutely clear to me that a reformed FBI might not be able to do the job," Betts says.

Apart from organizational issues, several experts say 9/11 exposed above all the need for better information sharing. Much of the debate has focused on the "wall" — guidelines restricting the CIA's ability to provide intelligence to the FBI or other domestic agencies.

Several other experts, however, say cultural and organizational barriers may be more significant. "We have a CIA that is very much focused on secrets," Treverton says. The problem, he says, is "getting people to talk to people more."

Aftergood agrees. "The age of central intelligence is behind us," he says. "What we need to move toward is distributed intelligence" — making information more readily accessible for use in enhancing security and preventing terrorist incidents.

In any event, he says, organizational changes alone will not solve the problems. "Institutional arrangements are all less important than the ability of the people who are engaged," he says.

BACKGROUND

Dysfunctional Systems?

The 9/11 attacks disclosed huge gaps in the ability of U.S. intelligence, law enforcement and security systems to detect or prevent terrorist incidents at home. In hindsight, government agencies gave too little attention to domestic terrorist attacks, while airlines and the government agency that regulated them were lax in instituting and enforcing security measures. In addition, both the CIA and the FBI were constrained by reforms instituted after surveillance abuses by both agencies against domestic political groups in the 1960s and '70s.

Neither the CIA nor the FBI was created with counter-terrorism in mind.[20] The FBI was established within the Justice Department by President Theodore Roosevelt. It first drew critical scrutiny during and after World War I for its aggressive investigations of sedition, espionage and anti-draft cases. A public and congressional backlash prompted Attorney General Harlan Fiske Stone in 1924 to appoint J. Edgar Hoover, then the bureau's assistant director, as director with a charge to professionalize the organization.

Hoover gained national celebrity by leading the FBI's anti-gangster efforts in the 1930s. With the Cold War, however, the bureau again turned its attention to suspected subversives. Hoover also directed FBI investigations of civil rights groups — notably, by eavesdropping on the Rev. Dr. Martin Luther King Jr. Investigations by journalists and congressional committees in the late '60s and early '70s uncovered a wide-ranging counterintelligence program — known as COINTELPRO — that used illegal or dubious practices to investigate or disrupt domestic political groups.

The Central Intelligence Agency traces its origins to the famed World War II Office of Strategic Services (OSS),

which combined research and analysis functions with espionage, counterespionage, sabotage and propaganda. In late 1944, OSS chief Gen. William J. Donovan outlined to President Franklin D. Roosevelt a plan for a centralized peacetime civilian intelligence agency.

After Roosevelt's death, President Harry S Truman in 1946 created a weak coordinating body called the "Central Intelligence Group." A year later, the National Security Act created the CIA in its present form to coordinate and evaluate intelligence affecting national security.

The CIA became notorious for Cold War covert operations against communist or anti-American regimes in the 1950s and '60s. It toppled leftist governments in Iran and Guatemala, supported anti-Castro rebels in Cuba and encouraged U.S. entry into the war in Southeast Asia. The Watergate scandals under President Richard M. Nixon in the early 1970s led to evidence of illegal domestic political spying by the agency.

Despite its prominence, the CIA is actually dwarfed by Department of Defense intelligence agencies. The biggest is the National Security Agency (NSA), which grew from World War II codebreaking into intensely secretive, electronic surveillance worldwide. Another DoD unit, the National Reconnaissance Office, manages satellite-collection systems, and the National Geospatial Intelligence Agency processes images gleaned from the satellites. Each of the military services also has its own intelligence unit.

The Pentagon also has its own analytical office: the Defense Intelligence Agency, which — like the State Department's Bureau of Intelligence and Research — provides assessments and policy advice independent of, and often at variance with, CIA conclusions. Coast Guard Intelligence and the Department of Homeland Security's (DHS) Information Analysis and Infrastructure Protection Directorate have been added to the intelligence community since 9/11.

Aviation safety is the province of the Federal Aviation Administration (FAA). Hijacking and sabotage emerged gradually as a major FAA concern after hijackings of planes to and from Cuba became common in the early 1960s. After the first passenger death in a U.S. hijacking in 1971 and a rash of violent hijackings, the agency began scanning carry-on baggage and passengers for potential weapons in December 1972.[21] Additional security measures were adopted after other deadly incidents in the 1980s: air marshals in 1985 and X-raying of checked baggage following the bombing of Pan Am Flight 103 over Lockerbie, Scotland, in 1988.

During the '90s, there were no hijackings or aircraft bombings within the United States, possibly leading to increased security laxness. Two Department of Transportation reports in 1999 and 2000 faulted airport-security procedures — specifically for failing to control access to secure areas.

Meanwhile, several studies in 2000 and early 2001 found overall counterterrorism policies deficient.[22] The reports drew attention for short periods but then largely disappeared from the national agenda.

Frustrating Initiatives

Terrorism became a major domestic concern for the United States in the 1990s, but al Qaeda became a major focus of that concern only slowly. The deadly 1995 bombing of the federal office building in Oklahoma City turned out to be the work of domestic rather than international extremists. Meanwhile, bin Laden's buildup of his organization into a wide-ranging, paramilitary operation largely escaped attention — even from intelligence agencies — until the middle of the decade. Even after al Qaeda was linked to the 1998 bombings of two U.S. embassies in Africa, bin Laden remained little known to Americans.

Bin Laden began his path to international terrorism as a "freedom fighter" in Afghanistan in the 1980s, seeking to undo the Soviet invasion of the predominantly Islamic country.[23] He founded al Qaeda (Arabic for "the base") in 1987 to mount a global Islamic crusade. The son of a wealthy Saudi family, he turned against the Saudi government — and the United States — after the Saudis allowed U.S. troops on the Arabian peninsula during and after the Persian Gulf War (1991).

Bin Laden was known at the time only as a "terrorist financier" working from Sudan.[24] Clarke, who handled counterterrorism at the National Security Council (NSC) early in President Bill Clinton's first term, pressed the CIA for more information. In 1996, according to Clarke's account, the CIA got its first big break when a top aide to bin Laden defected. Jamal al-Fadl described bin Laden as the mastermind of a widespread terrorist network with affiliate groups or sleeper cells in 50 countries. By this time, bin Laden had moved his base of operations to Afghanistan.

The administration had tried without success while bin Laden was in Sudan to persuade Saudi Arabia to take him into custody for prosecution and trial. Once bin Laden was in Afghanistan, the Counterterrorism Security Group that Clarke headed drew up plans to abduct him — plans never executed because of logistical difficulties.

When al Qaeda was linked to the 1998 embassy bombings, however, Clinton authorized cruise missile strikes at an al Qaeda base in Afghanistan; they missed bin Laden by minutes.*

Tasked by Clinton, Clarke then designed a strategy to eliminate al Qaeda, including diplomatic efforts to eliminate its sanctuary in Afghanistan; covert action to disrupt terrorist cells; financial sanctions beginning with the freezing of funds of bin Laden-related businesses; and military action to attack targets as they developed.

In his book, Clarke voices great frustration with efforts to put the plan into effect — particularly the military's reluctance to get engaged. The 9/11 commission staff says the strategy "was not formally adopted" and that Cabinet-level officials have "little or no recollection of it."

Clarke writes that Clinton also approved assassinating bin Laden. Tenet told the 9/11 commission, however, that the agency considered the instructions unclear, at best. Clarke writes that he viewed the CIA's demurrals as an "excuse" for its inability to carry out the mission. Efforts to enlist the FBI's help in counterterrorism also proved difficult, according to the commission's staff report. Clinton's national security adviser, Samuel R. Berger, told the panel that despite regular meetings with Attorney General Reno and FBI Director Freeh, the FBI "withheld" terrorism information, citing pending investigations.

In Clinton's final year in office, al Qaeda was viewed as an increasing threat in the United States and overseas. Al Qaeda had been linked to plans to disrupt celebrations of the new Millennium: A plot to plant bombs at Los Angeles International Airport was foiled when an Algerian man later linked to al Qaeda was stopped at the U.S.-Canadian border on Dec. 18, 1999, driving a car filled

---

* Clinton also approved a missile strike against a pharmaceutical plant near Khartoum, Sudan, suspected of manufacturing precursors of chemical weapons. The Sudanese government denied that the factory had any connection to chemical weapons — denials credited today by many U.S. intelligence experts.

Reorganizing Immigration Triggers Growing Pains

Rep. Harold Rogers, R-Ky., was so fed up with the Immigration and Naturalization Service's efforts to stop illegal immigrants from crossing the borders that he introduced a bill to abolish the agency. The 2000 measure went nowhere.

But the Sept. 11, 2001, terrorist attacks accomplished what Rogers could not: They ushered in the demise of the INS. The agency had spectacularly failed to track the comings and goings of the 19 hijackers, some of whom were in the United States on student visas — allowing them to operate without fear that the government would realize they had overstayed their visas.

The Homeland Security Act of 2002 broke up the old INS into separate pieces and assigned its duties to different divisions within the newly created Department of Homeland Security (DHS). Immigration investigations and administration were assigned to the new Bureau of Immigration and Customs Enforcement, while border enforcement became the responsibility of Customs and Border Protection.

However, reorganizing the INS has not come without bureaucratic growing pains. According to a May 11 General Accounting Office report, the department lacks adequate long-term estimates of the cost of its proposed US VISIT program, a multibillion-dollar computer system designed to track the entry and exit of every foreign visitor.[1] Meanwhile, the so-called "visa waiver" program, which allows citizens of 27 U.S.-friendly countries to travel in the United States without visas, is underfunded and poorly organized, according to an April report by the DHS's inspector general. That report also noted that DHS has not adequately tracked lost or stolen foreign passports to determine whether they were used to enter the country.

By October 2004, the passports of visitors without visas must include biometric data, such as fingerprint or facial recognition, to make them less susceptible to fraud. All 27 countries — which include England, France and Japan — will likely miss the deadline, according to DHS Secretary

The Department of Homeland Security's US VISIT program uses digital cameras and computers to track immigrant entries and exits at airports.

AFP Photo/Robyn Beck

Tom Ridge and Secretary of State Colin L. Powell, who both asked Congress to extend the deadline.

"Rushing a solution to meet the current deadline virtually guarantees that we will have systems that are not operable," Powell said in April 21 testimony before the Senate Judiciary Committee's Subcommittee on Immigration. Sen. Saxby Chambliss, R-Ga., has introduced a bill to extend the deadline.

U.S. citizens will not be exempt from such biometric identities. This fall, the State Department will begin a pilot project to equip U.S. passports with biometric identifiers, with nationwide production of biometric passports beginning some time next year.

— Martin Kady II

---

[1] U.S. General Accounting Office, "First Phase of Visitor and Immigration Status Program Operating, but Improvements Needed," GAO-04-586 (May 11, 2004).

with bomb-making materials. Clarke reported afterward that al Qaeda "sleeper cells" might have taken root in the United States.[25]

In March, officials approved a four-part agenda that included disruption, law enforcement, immigration enforcement and U.S.-Canadian border controls. The

White House also approved Predator aircraft attacks on al Qaeda bases — or on bin Laden himself. But CIA opposition to the flights derailed the plan. And Clinton left office in January 2001 with retaliation for al Qaeda's role in the October 2000 attack on the *Cole* still under consideration.

Postmortems

The Bush administration gave little visible attention to counterterrorism before 9/11. Bush drew wide public approval for rallying the nation immediately after the attacks and then leading a broad international coalition in ousting the pro-al Qaeda Taliban government in Afghanistan. But both the Clinton and Bush administrations have come under critical scrutiny since then — first from a joint inquiry by two congressional committees and now from the 9/11 commission.

Both administrations were blamed for not better coordinating the various agencies involved in counterterrorism. The Bush administration is also faulted for failing to appreciate the gravity of the threat that al Qaeda posed and for missing potential opportunities to disrupt or prevent the 9/11 attacks.

Clarke briefed Rice on al Qaeda during the transition period in January 2001. He writes that Rice seemed ill-informed about al Qaeda and voiced doubts about the need for a 12-person NSC unit devoted to counterterrorism. Rice told the 9/11 commission that Bush's national security team fully appreciated the threat from al Qaeda and wanted to make sure there was "no respite" in the fight against the organization. She says she took "the unusual step" of retaining Clarke and his staff despite the change in administrations. But Clarke says his position was downgraded so that he reported to deputies rather than to Cabinet-level "principals."

Rice directed Clarke to prepare a new counterterrorism strategy. Clarke says the work proceeded slowly, even with the spike in "threat reporting" in summer 2001. But Rice stressed in her testimony that the final document — approved by Cabinet-level officials on Sept. 4 — was the administration's first major national-security policy directive.

The multipart strategy parallels Clarke's unacted-on 1998 plan: diplomacy, financial sanctions, covert actions and military strikes. But Rice stressed to the 9/11 commission one difference: Whereas Clinton had called for bringing terrorists from Afghanistan to the United States for trial, the Bush plan directed the Pentagon to prepare for military action in Afghanistan itself.

When the war in Afghanistan ended, Congress in 2002 decided to examine the events leading up to 9/11. The House and Senate Intelligence committees completed their joint investigation in December 2002, but the 900-page report was not released until July 24, 2003 — while the Bush administration reviewed the document for classified material.

When finally released, the report painted a sharply critical portrait of both the CIA and the FBI. Prior to 9/11, intelligence agencies had received "a modest, but relatively steady, stream of intelligence reporting" indicating the possibility of terrorist attacks in the United States, but they "failed to capitalize on both the individual and collective significance" of the information, the panels reported. Intelligence agencies were "neither well organized, nor equipped, and did not adequately adapt" to meet the threats posed by global terrorism.[26]

The intelligence committees laid out ambitious recommendations, beginning with the proposal — periodically recommended by the intelligence community — to create a powerful director of national intelligence (DNI) over the entire intelligence apparatus. The Cabinet-level position would be separate from the CIA director. The panels also called for Congress and the executive branch to "consider promptly" whether the FBI should retain responsibility for domestic intelligence or whether "a new agency" should take over those functions.

The 16-page laundry list included a host of other recommended changes — less visible but equally or even more important, including developing "human sources" to penetrate terrorist organizations; upgrading technology to "better exploit terrorist communications"; maximizing "effective use" of covert actions; and developing programs to deal with financial support for international terrorism.

The panels also called for "joint tours" for intelligence and law enforcement personnel in order to "broaden their experience and help bridge existing organizational and cultural divides" between the different agencies.

In addition, the committees asked that the 9/11 commission study Congress's own record in monitoring the intelligence community, including whether to replace the separate House and Senate oversight panels with a single committee and whether to change committee membership rules. Currently, members are limited to eight-year terms, but many say the restriction prevents them from developing sufficient expertise on intelligence agencies before they are forced to leave the panel.[27]

CURRENT SITUATION

Ground Zero

Police, firefighters and other emergency personnel were universally celebrated for their rescue efforts on Sept. 11 once the World Trade Center towers had been turned into raging infernos. However, in emotional hearings on May 18 and 19 — punctuated by angry outbursts from several victims' family members in the audience — the 9/11 commission sharply criticized the Police and Fire departments' overall management of the disaster.

Inadequate planning, poor communications and interdepartmental rivalries significantly hampered rescue efforts, the commission staff suggested in two interim reports.[28] The critique — and barbed comments from some commissioners during the hearing — drew sharp retorts from current and former city officials. Former Mayor Rudolph W. Giuliani conceded "terrible mistakes" were made, but he denied any problems of coordination.[29]

But the staff reports said longstanding rivalry between the Police and Fire departments led each to consider itself "operationally autonomous" at emergency scenes. "The Mayor's Office of Emergency Management had not overcome this problem," the report said. Commissioner John Lehman called the command-and-control system "a scandal" and the city's disaster-response plans "not worthy of the Boy Scouts."

The staff reports also said 911 and Fire Department dispatchers had inadequate information and could not provide basic information to callers inside the buildings about the fires. "The 911 operators were clueless," said Commissioner Slade Gorton. The staff report also suggested that fire officials were slow to recognize the likelihood of the towers collapsing and therefore slow to order the buildings evacuated.

Thomas Von Essen, the fire commissioner at the time, called Lehman's remark "outrageous." For his part, Giuliani said firefighters were "standing their ground" in the building in order to get civilians out. Giuliani, who now runs his own security-consulting firm, called for Lehman to apologize. The former Navy secretary declined.

The staff reports also criticized the World Trade Center's owner, the Port Authority of New York and New Jersey. Despite biannual fire drills, civilians were not directed into stairwells or given information about evacuation routes, the report said. Civilians were "never instructed not to

evacuate up" or informed that rooftop evacuations "were not part of the . . . evacuation plan." The report also noted that evacuation drills were not held and participation in fire drills "varied greatly from tenant to tenant."

The emergency response at the Pentagon, on the other hand, was "generally effective," the staff reports said, praising the "strong professional relationships and trust" established among emergency responders and "the pursuit of a regional approach to response" by departments from different jurisdictions.

New York's current mayor, Michael Bloomberg, told the commission on May 19 that the city was taking steps to "improve communications within and between the Police and Fire departments." Earlier, however, the commission's vice chairman, Lee H. Hamilton, had described the city's plan as a "prescription for confusion."

Bloomberg also criticized the allocation of post-9/11 federal emergency-preparedness assistance, saying that New York ranked 49th out of 50 states in per-capita funding received despite its prominence as a terrorist target. Homeland Security Secretary Tom Ridge told the commission the Bush administration had been trying to get Congress to change the allocation formulas, but he also said it was important to help each state.

In his appearance, Giuliani was asked about the significance of federal officials' failure to tell the city about the threat warnings described in Bush's Aug. 6 intelligence briefing. "I can't honestly tell you we would have done anything differently," Giuliani said. "We were doing, at the time, all that we could think of that was consistent with the city being able to move and to protect the city."

High Court Review

As President Bush was taking flak for his actions before Sept. 11, the administration was also awaiting Supreme Court rulings on the legality of aggressive detention policies adopted in the post-9/11 war on terrorism.

The justices will decide whether the government has crossed constitutional bounds by denying judicial review to some 600 foreign nationals detained at Guantánamo Bay Naval Base in Cuba since being captured in Afghanistan and Pakistan and to two U.S. citizens held as "enemy combatants" in the United States. One was captured in Afghanistan; the other was arrested at the Chicago airport in May 2002 and charged with conspiring to explode a radioactive bomb somewhere in the United States.

Should Congress create the new position of director of national intelligence?

YES
Sen. Dianne Feinstein, D-Calif.
Ranking Minority Member,
Subcommittee on Terrorism,
Technology and Homeland Security

Written for *The CQ Researcher,* May 2004

Intelligence failures on Iraq's weapons of mass destruction and in the months prior to Sept. 11, 2001, have made clear the need for reform within our nation's intelligence community. The place to start with this reform effort is at the top. We should begin by establishing a single director of national intelligence with the statutory and budgetary authority to truly oversee our nation's intelligence-gathering efforts.

The lack of coordination between intelligence agencies is well known. This disunity was described thoroughly in last summer's report by the Senate-House Inquiry into Sept. 11 and was echoed in the recent 9/11 commission hearings. Our intelligence-gathering efforts are plagued by territorial battles and reluctance among agencies to work together — reluctance that has caused the misreading of threats and endangered our nation.

This post-Cold War era of non-state, asymmetric threats demands cooperation among intelligence agencies. In an age when we must be prepared for the dangers of suitcase nukes, dirty bombs and bioterrorism, our entire government must share information to keep us safe.

The current intelligence structure is inadequate to address the threats posed by al Qaeda and other terrorist organizations. With 15 separate agencies, offices and departments charged with collecting or analyzing intelligence — including such little-known bodies as the National Reconnaissance Office and the National Geospatial-Intelligence Agency — our intelligence community is fragmented and inefficient.

The intelligence leadership structure exacerbates these divisions. The director of central intelligence (DCI) is charged with overseeing an agency while also acting as the leader of the entire intelligence community — two widely divergent functions that limit his effectiveness.

The DCI is further hampered by the fact that he oversees a mere one-fifth of the intelligence budget while the secretary of Defense controls most of the remaining 80 percent.

The best way to address this structural defect is to establish a single director of national intelligence with the statutory and budgetary authority to concentrate full time on coordinating intelligence resources, setting priorities and deciding strategies for the intelligence community and advising the president on intelligence matters.

Referring to the way we gather and analyze intelligence, 9/11 commission member and former Navy Secretary John Lehman recently said, "A revolution is coming."

Serious threats to our national security remain. We cannot afford to wait any longer to reform our intelligence community.

NO
Harold Brown
Counselor/Trustee, Center for
Strategic and International Studies,
Secretary of Defense (1977-1981)

Written for *The CQ Researcher,* May 2004

The present structure of the intelligence community is not working well. We need better connections between the various intelligence agencies. But there are reasons to be careful about inserting an additional position called director of national intelligence (DNI).

One suggestion is to have the DNI be a staff person in the White House. But that would merely add another layer to dealing with intelligence issues. If a referee among departments and agencies with intelligence functions is needed, the president's national security adviser or a deputy can do that.

Another suggestion is to have a DNI with line authority, budget authority and personnel authority over all of the intelligence agencies, including both CIA and those in the Department of Defense. But intelligence support is so important to military operations that any functions taken out of the Pentagon's control would likely be duplicated. And further centralizing of intelligence analysis would suppress alternative views and estimates, which recent history shows to be a mistake.

A DNI who is also director of the CIA cannot be an impartial overseer of the other agencies. But if there is a separate, subordinate, CIA head, the DNI will be too remote from the sensitive area of covert operations. Burying those further down the chain would provide more opportunity for uncontrolled activity.

Perhaps the biggest gap revealed by 9/11 is that between the FBI and the CIA. Discussion about the scope of DNI control usually omits the national security section of the FBI. If the Defense Department is recalcitrant about transferring large segments of its intelligence activities, that's nothing compared to the resistance from the Department of Justice and the FBI to taking away their national security functions.

Some suggestions for better organization can be found in the report of the Commission on the Roles and Capabilities of the U.S. Intelligence Community, which I headed in the mid-1990s. We suggested "double-hatting" heads of the separate intelligence agencies, so that they would report both to the secretary of Defense and the director of central intelligence. That's awkward, but it does correspond to the need for the DCI and the secretary of Defense to thrash out differences, which is necessary in any structure of intelligence. That report also proposed giving the DCI additional budgetary authority and training responsibility.

I would move in the direction of assuring better coordination of planning and operations, including across the sensitive boundary between domestic and foreign intelligence operations, but cautiously. Most of the proposals that have been suggested so far would likely make things worse, not better.

The mother of a World Trade Center victim reacts angrily to former New York Mayor Rudolph W. Giuliani's testimony before the 9/11 commission in May 2004. While conceding "terrible mistakes" were made, Giuliani denied any problems of coordination between the Police and Fire departments. Commissioner John Lehman had called the city's disaster-response plans "not worthy of the Boy Scouts."

Civil-liberties and human-rights organizations say the lack of access to courts is inconsistent with the U.S. Constitution and international law. But the government argues courts have very limited authority to review the president's authority as commander in chief to detain enemy combatants.

The justices seemed divided along their usual conservative-liberal fault line during arguments in the three cases in late April: Justices Sandra Day O'Connor and Anthony M. Kennedy, moderate-conservatives who often hold the balance of power on the court, gave mixed signals.

In the first case to be argued, a former federal appeals court judge told the justices on April 20 that the government had created "a lawless enclave" at Guantánamo by blocking the foreigners from going to court to challenge their detention. "What's at stake in this case is the authority of the federal courts to uphold the rule of law," said John Gibbons, a lawyer in Newark, N.J., and former chief judge of the federal appeals court in Philadelphia.[30]

Most of the 600 detainees being held at Guantánamo were captured during operations against al Qaeda or the Taliban in Afghanistan or Pakistan. The high court case stemmed from *habeas corpus* petitions filed by Kuwaiti, British and Australian nationals, all of whom claimed they had not been fighting the United States. Two lower federal courts dismissed the petitions, saying Guantánamo was outside U.S. jurisdiction.

In his argument, Solicitor General Theodore Olson noted that the United States was still fighting in Afghanistan and warned that judicial review of the detainees' cases would invite legal challenges to combat-zone treatment of captured enemy soldiers. "Judges would have to decide the circumstances of their detention, whether there had been adequate military process, what control existed over the territory in which they were kept," Olson said.

The administration urged a similarly broad view of executive authority in the cases of the two citizens, argued on April 28.[31] Deputy Solicitor General Paul Clement told the justices it was "well established and long established that the government has the authority to hold both unlawful enemy combatants and lawful prisoners of war captured on the battlefield to prevent them from returning to the battle."

Lawyers representing the two detainees, however, insisted the government's position amounted to authorizing "indefinite executive detention." Frank Dunham, a federal public defender, told the justices, "We could have people locked up all over the country tomorrow without any due process, without any opportunity to be heard."

Dunham was representing Yaser Hamdi, an American-born Saudi seized in Afghanistan. The second case involved José Padilla, a Chicagoan arrested at O'Hare Airport on May 8, 2002, after a flight originating in Pakistan. Both men were held at a Navy brig in Charleston, S.C., without charges and without access to lawyers. The federal appeals court in Richmond, Va., upheld Hamdi's detention, while the federal appeals court in New York ordered the government to charge Padilla or release him.

The cases raise legal questions that the high court has not considered since two pro-government rulings in World War II-era cases: One involved German saboteurs captured in the United States and later executed and the other German soldiers captured in China and later tried by military tribunals.[32]

The administration argued that both decisions supported its position in the current cases, while the detainees' attorneys maintained the rulings were factually and legally distinguishable. Decisions in the current cases are due before the justices' summer recess at the end of June.

OUTLOOK

Law of Averages?

Could 9/11 happen again? Federal officials warn that a new terrorist attack could come this summer or during the presidential campaign this fall. And they concede that despite tightened security measures, there is no assurance that an attack could be thwarted.

"Those charged with protecting us from attack have to succeed 100 percent of the time," national security adviser Rice told the 9/11 commission. "To inflict devastation on a massive scale, the terrorists only have to succeed once, and we know they are trying every day."

"I tend to be somewhat fatalistic about surprise attacks," says Columbia University's Betts. "We're dealing with a problem of batting averages. You're never going to bat 1,000."

The terrorist attacks have already brought about significant changes in the federal government and in Americans' daily routines. In Washington, the new Department of Homeland Security in 2002 consolidated existing border and transportation security functions and emergency preparedness and response under one department. And Americans in all walks of life have grown accustomed to tighter security, while aviation experts are warning of long security lines this summer. Meanwhile, many employers have increased their fire and evacuation drills.

Intelligence reorganization has emerged as the most significant issue in the two official investigations of 9/11. Leading Democratic members of the House and Senate Intelligence committees have proposed creating a new "director of national intelligence" with budget authority over all 15 intelligence agencies and who would no longer head the CIA itself.

A bill by Rep. Jane Harman, D-Calif., ranking member of the House panel, would give the proposed DNI substantial budgetary authority over the intelligence community but leave responsibility for "execution" with the Pentagon or other departments that house existing agencies. The DNI would serve at the pleasure of the president, while the bill would give the director of the CIA a 10-year term — the same as the FBI director. Senate Intelligence Committee member Dianne Feinstein, D-Calif., has sponsored similar legislation since 2002. Her current bill is somewhat less detailed than Harman's and does not give the CIA director a fixed term.[33]

Neither Feinstein nor Harman has any Republican cosponsors. Harman says there is "no reason" Republicans should not support the measure. "This is not a partisan bill," she says. GOP staffers on the Intelligence panels say Republican members are taking a wait-and-see approach. For its part, the administration has given no additional specifics since Bush said in mid-April that the intelligence agencies need to be overhauled.

"We will see no major reforms before another major catastrophic attack," says UCLA's Zegart. "Even then, I don't put the odds better than 50/50. The barriers to intelligence reform are exceptionally high."

The National War College's Goodman is more optimistic but sees the 9/11 commission report as the key to any significant changes. "The only hope is that this 9/11 report will be so strong and so shocking that people will suddenly say, 'Stop. Something's got to be done.'"

Commission Chairman Kean has repeatedly said he hopes the panel's final report will be unanimous. But some commission members are saying the panel may be divided on such major issues as intelligence reorganization. "Unanimity is a nice goal, but it isn't going to be a necessary goal," former Sen. Slade Gorton said.[34] A divided report is assumed likely to have less impact than a unanimous one.

Proposals to reorganize the FBI seem unlikely to advance, largely to allow time to evaluate the changes being put into effect by Director Mueller. Meanwhile, Rep. Christopher Cox, R-Calif., chairman of the House Select Homeland Security Committee, plans to give DHS's intelligence unit more authority over terrorism intelligence in the department's authorization bill. Cox says he is concerned that the unit — known as the Information Analysis and Infrastructure Protection Directorate — is not playing the role intended when the DHS was created.

As for local emergency preparedness, Homeland Security Secretary Ridge told the 9/11 commission his department has disbursed $8 billion to states, regions and cities to train and equip first responders. Noting the communications problems in New York City, Ridge also said the department was working to make communications and equipment "interoperable" between different departments and jurisdictions. Democrats have criticized the administration for not spending enough money to strengthen local emergency preparedness.

Republican and Democratic lawmakers are also squaring off already over renewing the USA Patriot Act, which Congress passed after 9/11 to strengthen law enforcement powers in anti-terrorism cases. Bush is urging Congress to extend the legislation this year, but Democrats are criticizing some of its provisions and questioning the need for action now. Some of the provisions expire in 2005.

Many observers fear that no matter how hard the government tries, the threat of terrorism cannot be eliminated. "There are going to be terrorist attacks, and there are going to be successful terrorist attacks," says the Heritage Foundation's Carafano. "We're never going to be immune from terrorism."

NOTES

1. For background, see David Masci and Kenneth Jost, "War on Terrorism," *The CQ Researcher*, Oct. 12, 2001, pp. 817-848.

2. Some eyewitness material taken from David Lightman, "A Frustrating Day for 9/11 Families," Knight Ridder/Tribune News Service, April 8, 2004.

3. The Family Steering Committee's Web site can be found at www.911independentcommission.org. For other victims' organizations, see Families of Sept. 11 (www.familiesofseptember11.org) and World Trade Center United Family Group (www.wtcufg.org).

4. The commission maintains a thorough and well-organized Web site: www.9-11commission.gov.

5. For background, see Kenneth Jost, "Civil Liberties Debates," *The CQ Researcher*, Oct. 24, 2003, pp. 893-916, and David Masci and Patrick Marshall, "Civil Liberties in Wartime," *The CQ Researcher*, Dec. 14, 2001, pp. 1017-1040.

6. For background, see Martin Kady II, "Homeland Security," *The CQ Researcher*, Sept. 12, 2003, pp. 749-772.

7. Staff Statement No. 1 (immigration), Jan. 26, 2004. Staff Statement No. 3 (aviation security), Jan. 27, 2004.

8. Staff Statement No. 11 (intelligence community), April 14, 2004. Staff Statement No. 9 (law enforcement), April 13, 2004.

9. Richard A. Clarke, *Against All Enemies: Inside America's War on Terror* (2004), p. x. See also Masci, *op. cit.*

10. For an overview, see the Intelligence Community's Web site: www.intelligence.gov.

11. Zegart's book is tentatively titled *Stuck in the Moment: Why American National Securities Agencies Adapted Poorly to the Rise of Terrorism After the Cold War* (Princeton University Press, forthcoming 2005). Zegart notes as disclosure that Condoleezza Rice, President Bush's national security adviser, was her dissertation adviser at Stanford University.

12. Staff Statement No. 7 (intelligence policy), March 24, 2004.

13. For background, see Brian Hansen, "Intelligence Reforms," *The CQ Researcher*, Jan. 25, 2002, pp. 49-72.

14. See Michael Isikoff and Daniel Klaidman, "The Hijackers We Let Escape," *Newsweek*, June 10, 2002; and David Johnston and James Risen, "Inquiry Into Attack on the Cole in 2000 Missed Clues to 9/11," *The New York Times*, April 11, 2004, Section 1, p. 1.

15. Staff Statement No. 2 ("Three 9/11 Hijackers: Identification, Watchlisting, and Tracking") Jan. 26, 2004.

16. Staff Statement No. 7, *op. cit.*

17. Clarke, *op. cit.*, pp. 231-232.

18. The document is appended to Staff Statement No. 10.

19. See Douglas Jehl, "Administration Considers a Post for National Intelligence Director," *The New York Times*, April 16, 2004, p. A1.

20. Background drawn from entries in George T. Kurian (ed.), *A Historical Guide to the U.S. Government* (1998).

21. History drawn from undated "Aviation Security" entry on Web site of U.S. Centennial of Flight Commission: www.centennialofflight.gov/essay/Government_Role/security/POL18.htm.

22. See Scott Kuzner, "U.S. Studied Terrorist Threat for Years," in David Masci and Kenneth Jost, *op. cit.*, p. 840.

23. For a compact biography, see Charles S. Clark, "Bin Laden's War on America," in Masci and Jost, *op. cit.*, pp. 824-825.

24. Remainder of section drawn from 9/11 commission Staff Statement No. 8; Clarke, *op. cit.*, pp. 134-154, 181-204.

25. For background on computer-related Millennium problems, see Kathy Koch, "Y2K Dilemma," *The CQ Researcher*, Feb. 19, 1999, pp. 137-160.

26. House Permanent Select Committee on Intelligence/Senate Select Committee on Intelligence, Report of the Joint Inquiry into Intelligence Community Activities before and after the Terrorist Attacks of Sept. 11, 2001, December 2002 (S. Rept. 107-351, H. Rept. 107-792; www.gpoaccess.gov/serialset/creports/911.html).

27. See Dana Priest, "Congressional Oversight of Intelligence Criticized," *The Washington Post*, April 27, 2004, p. A1.

28. Staff Statements Nos. 13 (emergency preparedness and response), May 18, 2004, and 14 (crisis management), May 19, 2004.

29. Some quotes taken from coverage in *The New York Times*, May 19-20.

30. The case is *Rasul v. Bush*, 03-334. For information, including a transcript of the oral argument, see the Supreme Court's Web site: www.supremecourtus.gov.

31. The cases are *Hamdi v. Rumsfeld*, 03-6696, and *Rumsfeld v. Padilla*, 03-1027.

32. The decisions are Ex parte Qirin, 323 U.S. 283 (1944) (saboteurs), and *Johnson v. Eisentrager*, 339 U.S. 763 (1950) (POWs).

33. Harman's bill is HR 4104, Feinstein's S 190. Feinstein's legislation was also incorporated in a broad intelligence reorganization measure (S1520) introduced July 31, 2003, by Sen. Bob Graham, D-Fla.

34. Quoted in Philip Shenon, "9/11 Panel May Not Reach Unanimity on Final Report," *The New York Times*, May 26, 2004, p. A19.

BIBLIOGRAPHY

Books

Bamford, James, *Body of Secrets: Anatomy of the Ultra-Secret National Security Agency from the Cold War Through the Dawn of a New Century,* **Doubleday, 2001.**

Published before 9/11, this informative general history of the NSA has two index entries for Osama bin Laden. Includes detailed notes.

Benjamin, Daniel, and Steven Simon, *The Age of Sacred Terror, Random House,* **2002.**
Former National Security Council staffers in the Clinton administration provide a comprehensive account of the rise of al Qaeda. Benjamin is a senior fellow at the Center for Strategic and International Studies in Washington and Simon is an assistant director of the International Institute for Strategic Studies in London. Includes glossary, detailed notes.

Clarke, Richard A., *Against All Enemies: Inside America's War on Terror, Free Press,* **2004.**
The former national coordinator for security, infrastructure and terrorism under both Clinton and Bush offers his controversial first-person account of the government's anti-terrorism efforts leading up to the 9/11 attacks.

Lowenthal, Mark M., *Intelligence: From Secrets to Policy* **(2nd ed.),** *CQ Press,* **2003.**
This updated overview of the structure, role and operations of the various agencies in the nation's intelligence community was written when Lowenthal worked with a security-consulting firm. He is now assistant director of central intelligence for analysis and production. Includes suggested readings, Web sites and other appendix material.

Riebling, Mark, *Wedge: From Pearl Harbor to 9/11. How the Secret War Between the FBI and CIA Has Endangered National Security, Touchstone,* **2002 (originally published, 1994).**
The director of the Manhattan Institute for Policy Research provides a detailed history of policy differences and bureaucratic rivalry between the CIA (and its precursors) and the FBI. An epilogue and afterword in the paperback edition relate continuing tensions between the agencies through 9/11. A 14-page list of sources is included; sources for the epilogue and afterword are posted at secretpolicy.com/wedge/epilogue.

Treverton, Greg, *Reshaping National Intelligence for an Age of Information, Cambridge University Press,* **2001.**
A RAND Corporation expert argues for a "sweeping" reshaping of national intelligence to make it more open and decentralized in the post-Cold War information age.

Articles

Dlouhy, Jennifer A., and Martin Kady II, "Lawmakers Eager to Weigh In on Overhaul of Intelligence," *CQ Weekly*, April 17, 2004, pp. 902-905.
Overview of lawmakers' views on various proposals to reorganize the U.S. intelligence community.

Gup, Ted, "The Failure of Intelligence," *The Village Voice*, April 13, 2004.
A veteran journalist and author provides a critical overview of terrorism-related intelligence collection and analysis before 9/11. Gup is now a journalism professor at Case Western Reserve University.

Johnston, David, and Eric Schmitt, "Uneven Response Seen to Terror Risk in Summer '01," *The New York Times*, April 4, 2004, Section 1, page 1.
The author reconstructs the Bush administration's limited follow-up to increased threat reporting during summer 2001; includes chart detailing some of the 33 intercepted messages with threat warnings.

Paltrow, Scot J., "Detailed Picture of U.S. Actions on Sept. 11 Remains Elusive," *The Wall Street Journal*, March 22, 2004, p. A1.
The reporter provides a meticulous reconstruction of the government's actions on Sept. 11, with some evidence contradicting previous official accounts.

Reports and Studies

***House Permanent Select Committee on Intelligence/ Senate Select Committee on Intelligence, Report of the Joint Inquiry into Intelligence Community Activities before and after the Terrorist Attacks of September 11, 2001*, December 2002 (S. Rept. 107-351, H. Rept. 107-792; www.gpoaccess.gov/serialset/creports/911.html).**
The 900-page report includes a summary of major findings and conclusions and a list of 17 recommendations. The report is dated December 2002 but was released in July 2003 following executive branch review for redaction of classified material.

***National Commission on Terrorist Attacks upon the United States* (www.9-11commission.gov).**
The 9/11 commission's extensive Web site includes testimony and transcripts from all hearings and interim reports by the commission or staff. The commission's final report is scheduled to be released on July 26; the report will be published by W.W. Norton on the day of release and available for $10.

For More Information

Center for Strategic and International Studies, 1800 K St., N.W., Washington, DC 20006; (202) 887-0200; www.csis.org.

Families of September 11, 1560 Broadway, Suite 305, New York, NY 10036-1518; (212) 575-1878; www.families ofseptember11.org.

Federation of American Scientists, 1717 K St., N.W., Suite 209, Washington, DC 20036; (202) 546-3300; www.fas.org.

National Commission on Terrorist Attacks Upon the United States, 301 7th St., S.W., Room 5125, Washington, DC 20407; (202) 331-4060; www.9-11commission .gov.

World Trade Center United Family Group, P.O. Box 2307, Wayne, NJ 07474-2307; (973) 216-2623; www.wtcufg .org.

2

Anti-Americanism

Is Anger at the U.S. Growing?

Samuel Loewenberg

President George W. Bush lands on the aircraft carrier *USS Abraham Lincoln* in May 2003 and declares the formal end to combat in Iraq. Many critics abroad blame Bush and the Iraq War — now entering its fifth year — for the decline in U.S. prestige.

AFP Photo/Stephen Jaffe

From *CQ Global Researcher*,
March 2007.

S oon after the Sept. 11, 2001, terrorist attacks, the cover of *Newsweek* pictured a turbaned child holding a toy machine gun. The headline read: "The Politics of Rage: Why Do They Hate Us?"[1]

Since then, versions of that question — simultaneously plaintive and rhetorical — have been repeated throughout the U.S. media. The most common answer often reflected the views of Harvard scholar Samuel P. Huntington, who described an inevitable schism between Christianity and Islam in his seminal 1993 essay, "Clash of Civilizations."[2]

But America's critics are far more diverse, and their criticisms more differentiated, than can be explained away by a simple East vs. West conflict. Today not only radical Eastern Islamists but also more and more Latin Americans and former close allies in Europe are finding America and its policies reprehensible.

Some of the most outspoken voices come from Europe, where dismissive attitudes about the mixing bowl of people in the New World have long been a staple of intellectual preening. Since the 17th century, America has been depicted as a haven for uncouth debauchers, religious zealots and puffed-up nationalists. Only after World War II, when America emerged into a position of military and economic might, did it became an object of both desire and envy.

As the United States flexed its muscles over the subsequent decades, others began to perceive it as a threat to their own national sovereignty and identity. America was too big, too influential, too sure of its virtues. Protesters around the world began to attack all three facets of American influence — economic, political and cultural. By the end of the Cold War, the United States was the only remaining superpower, and even more vulnerable to accusations of arrogance and bullying.

In 1999 this sole superpower was symbolically attacked on a much smaller — and non-lethal — scale than it was on Sept. 11, 2001, when French protesters dismantled a McDonald's restaurant in the town of Millau, turning farmer and union leader José Bové into an international hero.[3]

"Look," Bové said later, "cooking is culture. All over the world. Every nation, every region, has its own food cultures. Food and farming define people. We cannot let it all go, to be replaced with hamburgers. People will not let it happen."[4]

That act of cultural theater preceded many others, and by 2003, as the United States led the invasion into Iraq, America was regularly being pilloried as an international villain, damned for its military excursions and held up as a convenient target for all sorts of global discontent.[5]

The indictment against America, writes Andrei S. Markovits, a Romania-born professor of comparative European politics at the University of Michigan, "accuses America of being retrograde on three levels":

- Moral: America is viewed as the purveyor of the death penalty and of religious fundamentalism, while Europe abolished the death penalty in favor of rehabilitation and adheres to an enlightened secularism;
- Social: America is viewed as the bastion of unbridled "predatory capitalism," as former German Chancellor Helmut Schmidt put it, while Europe is the home of the considerate welfare state; and
- Cultural: America is viewed as common, prudish and prurient, Europe as refined, savvy and wise.[6]

Those bleak assessments of the United States have played out in innumerable protests in recent years. When tens of thousands of leftist protesters from around the world gathered in Porto Alegre, Brazil, during the World Economic Forum in February 2002, they waved signs declaring "No blood for oil," and "Bush is #1 Terrorist." Raucous anti-globalization protests have followed the meetings of the World Trade Organization and the G8 from Doha to Davos to Seattle.

When 70,000 protesters gathered in Berlin's Alexanderplatz in March 2003, a banner proclaimed: "We Aren't Allowed to Compare Bush to Hitler. Too Bad!"[7]

When 2,000 Pakistanis in Islamabad rallied against Danish cartoons that had caricatured the Prophet Muhammad in 2006, they also shouted "Death to America!" and torched an effigy of President George W. Bush, as if Bush himself had commissioned the works.[8]

This was a long way from the moment after the 9/11 attacks, when the globe was in brief solidarity with the United States, as epitomized by the famous banner headline in the French newspaper *Le Monde*, "We are all Americans."[9]

Something had changed.

In just a few years, what once seemed to be a clash of two halves of the globe had metastasized into a clash between America and the rest of the world. These sentiments were not coming from isolated pockets of religious fundamentalists but from America's longstanding allies throughout the world. In Europe, anti-U.S. sentiment had reached record levels.

The Iraq invasion "did not create anti-Americanism but it increased it and gave it form," according to Professor Gérard Grunberg, deputy director of Sciences Po, a political institute in Paris.[10]

Many clearly think that negative attitudes toward the United States are now at an all-time high. "Anti-Americanism is deeper and broader now than at any time in modern history. It is most acute in the Muslim world, but it spans the globe," according to a recent survey by the Pew Research Center for People & the Press.[11] In another Pew poll, Europeans gave higher approval ratings to China than to the United States.[12]

Yet much of the anti-American hostility disguises the fact that many of the most vociferous European critics really don't know much about the USA. As British scholar Tony Judt, director of the Remarque Institute at New York University, points out, Europeans complain about their own governments' policies by saying they have been influenced by America.[13]

But on both sides of the Atlantic, says Judt, even in the supposed age of "globalization," there is a massive ignorance about the reality of politics, and of everyday life. "We don't actually understand each other any better than we did in the 1930s."

How did America go, in the eyes of many, from being the symbol of democracy, freedom and opportunity — an ideal to strive for — to an example to be avoided? Judt calls anti-Americanism the "master narrative" of the current age, in which declared opposition to the United States became a uniting factor for disparate critics of economic, cultural and foreign policies around the globe. In America they had found "a common target."

But these days, the overwhelming source of anti-American sentiment, not only in Europe but also throughout the world, is U.S. foreign policy, especially the Bush administration's pursuit of the war in Iraq.

Resentment of the policies and personalities in the Bush administration cannot be overstated. Even President Richard M. Nixon's transgressions were mostly identified as domestic problems (the Watergate scandal), while the Vietnam War was seen as part of larger Cold War politics and did not evoke the same strong anti-American sentiment as Iraq does today.

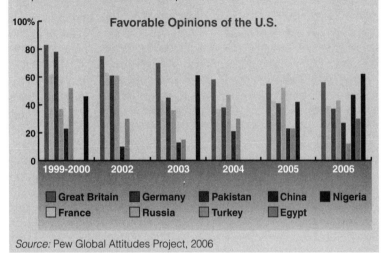

America's Global Image Slips

Since the beginning of the Bush administration in 2001, favorable opinions of the United States have declined in many countries. In Great Britain — an ally in the war in Iraq — approval levels fell from 83 percent in 1999-2000 to 56 percent in 2006.

Source: Pew Global Attitudes Project, 2006

Although there certainly was European criticism about the American war in Vietnam, Americans did not hear about it on a daily basis, as they do with criticisms of the war in Iraq. Instant television reporting and the Internet bring the war as well as its critics into homes every hour. Now, says Judt, "Whatever catastrophes the Americans are involved in overseas are immediately visible, with no time lag."

Another foreign conflict strongly identified with the United States and a recurrent theme at anti-war protests around the globe is the Israeli-Palestinian stalemate. European and Middle Eastern criticism of U.S. support of Israel ranges from humanitarian concerns about Palestinian rights to demagoguery invoking a Jewish-American-capitalist conspiracy.

"This didn't come from nothing," says Markovits. In his new book, *Uncouth Nation: Why Europe Dislikes America*, he traces the origins of anti-American sentiment to the 19th century, when European elites feared the pugnacious, young country.

For Americans, it is easy to dismiss criticism of U.S. policies as simply an irrational ideology, Markovits writes. But the term "anti-Americanism" is misleading,

he says, because it lumps together rational criticisms, whether one agrees with them or not, with a disembodied, ideological opposition to an idea of America, in which the country stands as a symbol for a variety of foreign, cultural and political discontents.

As Markovits notes, "Anti-Americanism is a particularly murky concept because it invariably merges antipathy toward what America does with what America is — or rather is projected to be in the eyes of its beholders." In contrast to classical stereotypes, which usually depict powerless minorities, the United States does, in fact, have great political, economic and cultural power. This makes it especially difficult to disentangle the perception from the reality. Critics of America assume that the expansion of this power, rather than a more benign exercise of it, is always the top priority of the American government. This is particularly true when it comes to the view, shared by much of the globe, that the United States is too tightly connected to Israel.

As Beirut's *Daily Star* said after the United States deposed Saddam Hussein: "Having waged an 'illegitimate' war on Iraq that has stoked anti-American feelings around the world, challenged and ignored international

AFP/Getty Images/Eric Cabanis

French activist and farmer José Bové has a following in Solomiac, France, after attempting to rip up a crop of genetically modified maize. Bové gained fame for destroying a French McDonald's restaurant in 1999.

law and the United Nations . . . the Bush administration is not about to 'offer Iraq on a golden platter to an opposition group or to the U.N. Security Council.'

"It will deny others a say in shaping post-war Iraq, and it won't withdraw its forces on request . . . . Israel, of course, will be an exception, and is the only U.S. partner whose participation in shaping post-war Iraq is 'guaranteed.' That is because Israel was the main reason for which the war was waged."[14]

Trying to sort out real criticisms of the United States from the political symbolism that makes up much anti-Americanism is a daunting task. But for America's many critics around the globe, the daily carnage in Iraq has confirmed that America, having found no weapons of mass destruction in Iraq, is now on a reckless crusade.

In the week after the Sept. 11, attacks, Bush declared, "this crusade, this war on terrorism, is going to take a while."[15] While the term "crusade" went largely unnoticed in the United States, it alarmed many around the world with its evocation of the ancient wars between Christianity and Islam.

As Americans seek to understand global criticism of the United States, here are some of the key issues being debated:

Is the United States the primary force behind globalization policies that harm other countries?

Before there was anti-Americanism there was anti-globalization. For many critics, they are mostly the same.[16]

Globalization is the umbrella term for the rapidly increasing social, technological, cultural and political integration of nation-states, corporations and organizations around the world.

Its supporters believe that globalization is a positive engine of commerce that brings increased standards of living, universal values, multiculturalism and technology to developing countries. Globalization's critics claim it is a slave to corporate interests, harms the environment and tramples human rights and the economic and ethical claims of the poor and working classes.

It's no surprise, then, that America has become the country most vilified by the anti-globalization movement. After all, U.S. brands like McDonald's, Marlboro and Nike are among the most recognized in the world.

Globalization does have its defenders, and at least one links the movement to an old socialist tradition in Europe. "Globalization simply means freedom of movement for goods and people," wrote the late French journalist and philosopher Jean-Francois Revel, "and it is hard to be violently hostile to that.

"But behind the opposition to globalization lies an older and more fundamental struggle against economic liberalization and its chief representative, the United States. Anti-globalism protests often feature an Uncle Sam in a stars-and-stripes costume as their supreme scapegoat."

Lashing out at America through targeting its products had roots in the Cold War. For example, some Eastern Bloc countries prohibited Coca-Cola but not Pepsi, because Coke was so strongly identified with the United States. But the movement reached its peak at the turn of the 21st century with global protests against the World Trade Organization, against the incursion of McDonald's and Starbucks and against acceptance of genetically modified foods from the United States.[17]

Championing the pure-food cause was Great Britain's Prince Charles. In 1999, after representatives of 20 African countries had published a statement denying that gene technologies would help farmers to produce the food they needed, Charles came to their defense: "Are we going to allow the industrialization of life itself, redesigning the natural world for the sake of convenience?

Or should we be adopting a gentler, more considered approach, seeking always to work with the grain of nature?"[18]

Reluctance to accept American products and economic power has brought together critics from the left and the right. For both, "America represents the ideal of unfettered capitalism itself," says Fernando Vallespin, director of the Sociological Research Centre of Spain, a nonpartisan think tank in Madrid. "For those on the left, the concern is for labor exploitation. For those on the right, it is the loss of national sovereignty."

Resentment of the American economic model is particularly strong in Europe, which is currently confronting painful and unpopular adjustments to its own long-held social-welfare state model. Politicians, unions and disenfranchised workers in France, Italy and Spain say they do not want to adopt the "Anglo-Saxon" model, a reference not to Germany or England but to the United States. Spaniards are vociferous critics of the American way of life, says Vallespin, "but on the other hand we are probably one of the most American in terms of our patterns of consumption."

Cost-cutting proposals that seem to erode Europe's time-honored cradle-to-grave welfare privileges — such as fees for seeing a doctor or reducing the meal allowances of factory workers — have been denounced as "American." But in truth, most policies are still far from American-style capitalism.

In Germany, American business interests are seen as a double threat. After a recent buying spree of distressed companies by hedge funds, most of them American, German Vice Chancellor Franz Muentefering said the funds "fall like a plague of locusts over our companies, devour everything, then fly on to the next one."

Muentefering's statement was widely scrutinized, with some critics suggesting that the image of locusts preying on German companies evoked sentiments that were not only anti-American but also anti-Semitic.

There is no doubt the United States has been leading the current charge to deregulate markets, but it is still wrong to blame it for the world's economic inequalities, says Charles Kupchan, a professor of international affairs at Georgetown University and the former director for European affairs at the National Security Council during the Clinton administration.

He points out that large corporations in nearly every European country have been globalizing. In fact,

AFP/Getty Images

Yankee mice Mickey and Minnie reign at Disneyland Paris during Disney's 100th anniversary. Despite protests against American cultural imports by French intellectuals, more people visit the Paris theme park than any other Disney attraction in the world.

the precursor to modern globalization was not the commercial efforts of the United States but European imperialism of the past 500 years. A large part of that was the economic domination and exploitation of Latin America and Africa.

The remnants of Europe's imperialist past continue to earn big profits for European countries, with Spain holding powerful telecom and banking concessions in Latin America, and the French profiting off mining and agricultural interests in their former colonies in Africa. Yet, curiously, the focus of the anti-globalization debate continues to revolve around the United States.

"There is an unjustifiable equation between globalization and Americanization," says Kupchan.

Spanish Blame Bombing on War in Iraq

Spain's support of U.S. seen as critical factor

On the morning of March 11, 2004, a coordinated bomb attack on four rush-hour trains in Madrid killed 191 people and injured more than 1,700.

Spain had lived through decades of terrorism from the Basque separatist group ETA, but these bombers were not seeking independence; they were attempting to intimidate the Spanish government. In February 2007, Spanish authorities put 29 men on trial for the bombings, claiming they belonged to a local cell of Islamic militants aligned with al Qaeda.

In sharp contrast to the American reaction after the Sept. 11, 2001, terrorist attacks, Spanish citizens did not view the assault as part of a war between Islam and the West. Instead, many turned their anger toward the United States and their own government, which had supported the U.S.-led invasion of Iraq.

"We didn't want to go to war, but we did because of [former Prime Minister José Maria] Aznar," said Miguel Barrios, a 45-year-old maintenance worker who was in one of the bombed trains. "They didn't pay attention to the anti-war movement."[1]

It became clear that in an effort to stay aligned with the interests of the United States, the world's sole superpower, the Spanish government had run against the will of its own people. In the wake of the railroad attacks that Spanish government was voted out. The new prime minister, José Luis Rodriguez Zapatero, withdrew Spain's 1,300 troops from Iraq within weeks, risking a rupture of the close alliance Spain had enjoyed with the U.S.

"Mr. Bush and Mr. Blair will reflect on our decision," said Zapatero. "You cannot justify a war with lies. It cannot be."

People felt the war in Iraq had never been Spain's business, said Miguel Bastenier, a columnist for *El Pais*, Spain's largest newspaper. "Aznar was doing what Bush wanted without any particular reason for Spain to be there.

"There was undoubtedly the feeling that Spain was being punished for its association with the aggressive policies of the United States," and that "their country had been targeted by Muslim terrorists because it was now seen as being allied with the Jewish state."

In 2002, when war in Iraq was still only imminent, millions of Spaniards had taken to the streets to protest the coming invasion; polls showed more than 80 percent opposed to supporting the United States.

"Bush wants to go into Iraq to get the oil," said Virgilio Salcedo, a 29-year-old computer programmer who came to the rally in Madrid with his parents. "Everybody knows

At the same time, the U.S. government, under both the current Bush administration and the Clinton presidency, pushed often and hard on behalf of U.S. business interests.

The most famous attempt, which failed spectacularly, was the U.S. attempt to open Britain to bioengineered foods. The lobbying attempt, led by former Clinton U.S. Trade Representative Mickey Kantor, ran up against deeply held British attitudes of reverence for pristine nature.

"These senior executives thought they could just walk in and buy [British officials] a glass of champagne and charm them," said Evie Soames, a British lobbyist who represented the U.S. company Monsanto, which was attempting to sell its genetically modified seeds in England for several years.[19]

More recent American lobbying efforts have borne fruit. In 2001 the European Union tried to impose a strict safety-testing regime on chemical manufacturers; the Bush administration mounted a massive lobbying campaign that mobilized American embassies across Europe and Asia. The final, much scaled-back, version of the testing regime will save U.S. chemical companies billions of dollars.

Perhaps the biggest global concern about U.S. economic interests has been the perception that the U.S.-led invasion of Iraq was driven by America's thirst for petroleum. Notably, the most ubiquitous slogan, "No blood for oil," popped up at protests in the United States and abroad during the first Persian Gulf War in 1991 as well as the current war.

In a scathing commentary about President Bush's belief that he is on a direct mission from God, Henry that he doesn't want to help the people there."

"We think our president has sold out the country to the Americans," said Susanna Polo, a 30-year-old economist.

"Aznar is Bush's dog," added Raquel Hurtado, a 19-year-old economics student.[2]

Even for those most deeply affected by 9/11, like 53-year-old Rosalinda Arias, whose sister died in the World Trade Center attacks, U.S. motives were suspect. "It is all business. They want petroleum; they want to bring U.S. imperialism," said Arias, owner of a restaurant in Madrid.

For the many older people attending the rally, memories of the Franco dictatorship were still fresh, including America's support of the fascist regime in the 1930s. Now they had little faith in Bush administration claims that America was going to liberate Iraq.

"There are lots of dictatorships that have been backed by the USA," said Carlos Martin, a 67-year-old

A tear rolls down a girl's cheek during a rally in Madrid following terrorist bombings in March 2004 that killed nearly 200 people. Her message: "Peace, not terrorism."

Getty Images/Ian Waldie

translator of Italian literature. "I can't imagine how the Iraqi people are feeling now. They were bombed in 1991, then they had 12 years of horrible sanctions, and now they are being bombed again. I can't imagine they will look at the Americans as liberators."

Some of the protesters' worst fears were realized as the U.S. Coalition Forces invaded and subdued Baghdad in 2003, then settled into the current quagmire.

But Spain did not seek revenge against the killing of 191 of its citizens. A 40-year-old teacher named Valeria Suarez Marsa gave a softer voice to the public mood. "It is more important then ever to call for peace," she said. "The bombs reminded us of that urgency."

---

[1] The author covered the Madrid protests in 2002.

[2] Quoted in Samuel Loewenberg, "A Vote for Honesty," *The Nation*, March 18, 2004.

A. Giroux, a professor of communications at Canada's McMaster University, wrote: "Surrounded by born-again missionaries . . . Bush has relentlessly developed policies based less on social needs than on a highly personal and narrowly moral sense of divine purpose."[20]

In the months before the invasion of Iraq in March 2003, *The Economist* summed up the anti-Bush sentiment: "Only one thing unsettles George Bush's critics more than the possibility that his foreign policy is secretly driven by greed. That is the possibility that it is secretly driven by God . . . . War for oil would merely be bad. War for God would be catastrophic."[21]

Is the United States threatening other cultures?

Any American who has traveled abroad for any length of time will be familiar with the following exchange: "Oh,

you're American. I hate Americans." Or, the rhetorical litmus-test question: "What do you think of your president?" This, however, is soon followed by "I love New York" or "Have you ever been to Disneyland?"

For decades, America's most influential export has not been cars or televisions, but culture. This can be mass media like Hollywood movies and hip-hop music, fast-food restaurants that are often seen as crass and objectionable, or soft drinks such as Coca-Cola.

While these cultural products have long been embraced on a worldwide scale, they have also raised concerns that their appeal would diminish traditions and habits that other cultures hold dear. This love-hate relationship with American popular culture and consumerism was reflected in a 2005 Pew study that found "72 percent of French, 70 percent of Germans and 56

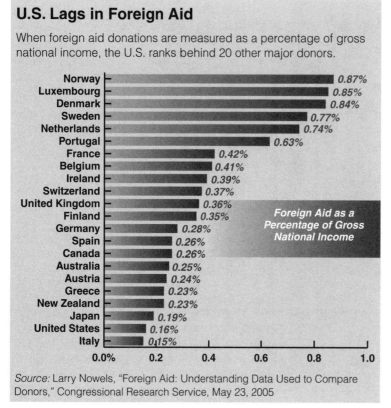

U.S. Lags in Foreign Aid

When foreign aid donations are measured as a percentage of gross national income, the U.S. ranks behind 20 other major donors.

Foreign Aid as a Percentage of Gross National Income

Country	Percentage
Norway	0.87%
Luxembourg	0.85%
Denmark	0.84%
Sweden	0.77%
Netherlands	0.74%
Portugal	0.63%
France	0.42%
Belgium	0.41%
Ireland	0.39%
Switzerland	0.37%
United Kingdom	0.36%
Finland	0.35%
Germany	0.28%
Spain	0.26%
Canada	0.26%
Australia	0.25%
Austria	0.24%
Greece	0.23%
New Zealand	0.23%
Japan	0.19%
United States	0.16%
Italy	0.15%

0.0%   0.2   0.4   0.6   0.8   1.0

Source: Larry Nowels, "Foreign Aid: Understanding Data Used to Compare Donors," Congressional Research Service, May 23, 2005

percent of Britons regard the spread of American culture negatively. In all of these countries, paradoxically, large majorities of respondents — especially young people — say they like American movies and other cultural exports."[22]

The University of Michigan's Markovits says resentment of U.S. culture has deep roots among European elites. "Many of the components of European anti-Americanism have been alive and well in Europe's intellectual discourse since the late 18th century," he writes. "The tropes about Americans' alleged venality, mediocrity, uncouthness, lack of culture and above all inauthenticity have been integral and ubiquitous to European elite opinion for well over 200 years. All of these 'Americanizations' bemoan an alleged loss of purity and authenticity for Europeans at the hands of a threatening and unwelcome intruder who — to make matters worse — exhibits a flaring cultural inferiority."[23]

"The fear is that what's happening in America will happen in Europe, and that left to their own devices

people will go to vulgar theme parks and shop at Wal-Mart," says Nick Cohen, a liberal British columnist. At its roots, this strain of anti-Americanism is a conservative ideology, he says. European elites were concerned that Americans had forsaken the church and the social hierarchy, according to Cohen, the author of a book reassessing European social liberals, *What's Left? How Liberals Lost Their Way.*

Nowhere is the ambivalence toward American culture more apparent than in France. When a Walt Disney theme park opened near Paris in 1994, French critics called it "a cultural Chernobyl." Yet today it rivals the Eiffel Tower as the country's most popular tourist destination. Without doubt, the biggest symbol of American cultural effrontery for the French is McDonald's. Yet the French are the biggest consumers of Big Macs in Europe.[24]

When France was making a national celebrity of farmer-activist Bové in 1999, the quality of McDonald's cheeseburgers was not the big issue; the enemy was the corporation. But food in France has deep and sentimental roots.

At a protest gathering on Bové's behalf, *The New York Times* interviewed a 16-year-old French lad who had come mostly for the carnival atmosphere. "But my father was a farmer," he said, "and I am here representing my family, too. We believe in what Mr. Bové believes in. We don't want the multinationals to tell us what to eat."[25]

In the 19th and early 20th centuries, when millions of Europeans sought their fortunes in the United States, American culture promised relief from the restrictions of European social hierarchies. "America was a hope, especially for the lower classes, in those times," says Detlev Claussen, a professor of social theory, cultural studies and sociology at Germany's Leibniz Hannover University. In the wake of World War I, Germans embraced American jazz, literature and art.

Nazi propaganda enthusiastically portrayed Americans as evil capitalists during World War II, but attitudes mellowed after the war when, despite the continued presence of the American military, the U.S. Marshall Plan helped rebuild Europe. Even in the 1960s and '70s, Germans were enthralled by American history and pop culture and established hundreds of re-enactment clubs that staged "Wild-West" shootouts and sympathetic portrayals of Indians.

The positive view of America began to change only in the Vietnam War era of the late 1960s, says Claussen. Even then, Germans made a distinction between disdain for American policies and adoration of cultural icons like Bob Dylan and the Rev. Martin Luther King Jr.

Now even those distinctions are eroding. The new anti-Americanism, Claussen says, stems from a sense of disappointment in the American utopia, tinged with envy of its political and economic power. Many Germans, he says, have simply given up on the idea of a virtuous America as a land of promise.

"When you can make no distinction between politics and culture, when you say, 'I don't like America, full stop,' that's real anti-Americanism," he says.

Is the "American Century" over?

On Feb. 7, 1941, in an editorial in *Life* magazine entitled "The American Century," media magnate Henry Luce advocated that the United States enter World War II and begin a global crusade on behalf of the values of freedom, opportunity, self-reliance and democracy.[26]

The concept of the "American Century," a potent ideal even before Luce's epochal essay, encompasses the modern history of American dominance, from the Spanish-American War to World War II, the Cold War and America's emergence as the world's only superpower in the 1990s.

These days, many are questioning whether the United States has squandered its position atop the global hierarchy. Rivals have emerged, even as the Soviet Union, once a contender, has dissolved. The European Union has been revitalized by the membership of new former Soviet-bloc countries. China and India, with their massive populations, are rapidly becoming developed countries. Perhaps the American "empire," like the Roman Empire and others before it, is already locked into inevitable decline.

Time recently devoted a cover story to China that concluded that, "in this century the relative power of the U.S. is going to decline, and that of China is going to rise. That cake was baked long ago."[27]

For the time being, however, the United States is the world's richest country and leading economy, with a gross domestic product (GDP) of $13 trillion. Its armed forces are stationed in 40 countries, its corporations and its charities operate throughout the globe and its technology arguably remains the most innovative. America is still a magnet for millions around the world, but its image has been badly tarnished by the Iraq War.

"There is a perception in the rest of the world that the U.S. is no longer capable of being the global leader that it once was," says Julia E. Sweig, director of Latin America studies at the Council on Foreign Relations and author of the 2006 book *Friendly Fire: Losing Friends and Making Enemies in the Anti-American Century.*

For many, that would be no great loss. No one likes the king of the hill for long. America (at least as a concept) is genuinely unpopular. A Pew survey found that "favorability ratings for the United States continue to trail those of other major countries. In Europe, as well as in predominantly Muslim countries, the U.S. is generally less popular than Germany, France, Japan and even China. In Western Europe, attitudes toward America remain considerably more negative than they were in 2002, prior to the Iraq War."[28]

"The tendency now is to view the U.S. as a threat to international stability," says Georgetown University's Kupchan.

Muslims in Southeast Asia, for example, no longer look up to the United States, says Farish A. Noor, a history professor at the Centre for Modern Oriental Studies in Berlin. "That's gone. It's completely erased now. An entirely new image of America has been constructed by the Islamists."

Of course, the damage to America's status did not begin with the invasion of Iraq. Still alive is the memory of the war in Vietnam, as well as America's Cold War support of totalitarian regimes, such as Augusto Pinochet's in Chile and Saddam Hussein's in Iraq (when Iraq was fighting Iran). In Latin America, many blamed the United States for encouraging the "dirty war" of the 1970s and '80s in Argentina and for supporting right-wing paramilitary squads in Nicaragua against the Marxist Sandinista junta.

At the same time, the United States cut back many "soft power" programs in cultural, economic and humanitarian

C H R O N O L O G Y

1700s-1800s *Europeans express disdain over U.S. independence.*

1768 Dutch philosopher Cornelius de Pauw describes America as "a Moronic Spirit" and the people "either degenerate or monstrous."

1776 English radical Thomas Day decries American hypocrisy: "If there be an object truly ridiculous in nature, it is an American patriot, signing resolutions of independency with the one hand, and with the other brandishing a whip over his affrighted slaves."

1842 British writer Charles Dickens lambastes oppressive Northern cities, Southern ignorance and Mississippi River pollution in *American Notes*.

1901-1980 *U.S. industrial power helps win world wars; Cold War begins.*

1919 Allies defeat Germany in World War I after U.S. enters war in 1917.

June 6, 1944 American forces lead invasion of Europe on D-Day; millions extend thanks to GIs.

August 1945 U.S. drops atomic bombs on Hiroshima and Nagasaki, forcing Japan to surrender. . . . Post-war U.S.-funded Marshall Plan provides development assistance to war-ravaged Europe.

1961 U.S. involvement in Vietnam begins, sparking anti-U.S. sentiment.

1967 Israel wins Six-Day War against Egypt, Jordan and Syria, begins occupation of West Bank and Gaza Strip. U.S. support for Israel feeds anti-Americanism.

1979 Shah overthrown in Iran. U.S. declared "The Great Satan."

1980s-1990s *Soviet Union collapses. U.S. involvement in Central America misfires. Resentment of world's sole superpower grows.*

1981 U.S.-trained Salvadoran soldiers massacre 800 women and children and elderly people in the country's bloody civil war; U.S. blamed.

Nov. 9, 1989 Berlin Wall falls. Citizens of newly reunited German capital dance to American TV star David Hasselhoff's "Looking for Freedom."

1989 U.S. arrests former American ally Gen. Manuel Noriega of Panama for drug trafficking.

1999 Negotiations conclude for Kyoto global warming pact; U.S. signs but Congress refuses to ratify.

1999 Farmer José Bové destroys a McDonald's in southern France as a consumer protest. Protests are held against globalization, multinational corporations and U.S. products.

2000s *President George W. Bush begins a unilateralist foreign policy, alienating allies.*

Sept. 11, 2001 Terrorists hijack four airplanes and crash three into the World Trade Center and the Pentagon. . . . In October a worldwide, U.S.-led coalition invades Afghanistan.

2002 In France, Thierry Meyssan's bestseller *L'Effroyable Imposture* (*The Terrible Fraud*) alleges the U.S. was behind the Sept. 11 attacks. . . . Venezuelan strongman Hugo Chavez, temporarily toppled in an aborted coup, accuses Bush administration of backing the revolt. . . . American companies abroad are vandalized.

2003 Millions march in Europe to protest U.S-led invasion of Iraq. . . .

2004 U.N. Secretary-General Kofi Annan calls Iraq invasion "illegal." . . . Abu Ghraib prison abuses shock the world. . . . Terrorists bomb Madrid trains.

2005 U.S. sends disaster aid to Indonesia and Pakistan, gaining goodwill. . . . Terrorists bomb London buses.

2006 British television airs a mock documentary about the imagined assassination of President Bush.

Feb. 10, 2007 Russian President Vladimir Putin denounces U.S. expansionism and military spending.

March 8, 2007 President Bush begins five-nation Latin American tour, sparking protests across the region.

aid in Latin America. Many of these were replaced with aggressive law-and-order programs that were part of the American government's war on drugs, and, after Sept. 11, the "war on terror."

And even before al Qaeda's 9/11 attacks, foreigners were critical of the U.S. rejection of global treaties, including the Kyoto Protocol for climate change, the creation of the International Criminal Court and rules for curbing biological weapons. Some of these treaties were actually rejected during the Clinton administration. The impression was strong that the United States would go it alone, because it thought it could.

It was at that point that many nations began to view the United States as "a delinquent international citizen."[29]

Some analysts wonder if the end of the American Century will begin in the Americas. Stepping into the hemispheric leadership vacuum, leftist President Hugo Chavez of Venezuela mocks President Bush as "the little gentleman" from the North and works at consolidating the region under his own oil-rich leadership.

American involvement in Latin America, long treated as a vast raw-material commodities mart by U.S. businesses, had already alienated many South and Central American countries, and, more recently, many Latin Americans have blamed U.S.-backed free-market economic policies for destabilizing their economies.

In 2005 Chavez even attempted to turn old-style American "soft power" on its head, offering and delivering 17 million gallons of heating oil to low-income families in New York and New England.

President Bush's March 2007 diplomatic swing through Latin American was intended to soothe feelings, but his administration's neglect, says Sweig, "has ripped off the Band-Aid that had covered up latent wounds for a long time."

As Bush was addressing an audience in Uruguay on March 10, Chavez led a counter rally in Argentina in which he called Bush a "political corpse." Alluding to the fact that he had previously called Bush "the devil" at the United Nations, Chavez bragged that, "He does not even smell of sulfur anymore; what [smells] is the scent of political death, and within a very short time it will become cosmic dust and disappear."[30]

In Muslim nations, the fiery rhetoric of the Bush administration's war on terror sparked a new depth of hostility. Among predominantly Islamic countries in Southeast Asia, which had previously looked on the U.S. as liberators, the Bush administration "squandered five decades of goodwill," says Noor. "So much of this has been personalized in Bush. He is like an icon of everything that is bad about the U.S."

Because of the war in Iraq and the festering Palestinian question, hatred for America on the Arab "street," as well as among Islamists, is raw and without nuance. But it is instructive to hear voices from a recent *New York Times* report about a new al Qaeda training camp for jihadists at a Palestinian refugee camp north of Beirut.

" 'The United States is oppressing a lot of people,' the group's deputy commander, Abu Sharif, said in a room strewn with Kalashnikovs. 'They are killing a lot of innocents, but one day they are getting paid back.'

" 'I was happy,' Hamad Mustaf Ayasin, 70, recalled in hearing last fall that his 35-year-old son, Ahmed, had died in Iraq fighting American troops near the Syrian border. 'The U.S. is against Muslims all over the world.'

"On the streets of the camp, one young man after another said dying in Iraq was no longer their only dream."

It was suicide.

" 'If I had the chance to do any kind of operation against anyone who is against Islam, inside or outside of the U.S., I would do the operation,' " said 18-year-old Mohamed.[31]

In England, *The Guardian* noted the continuing concern about the United States' use of its power during the months leading up to the invasion of Iraq. "Of course, enemies of the U.S. have shaken their fist at its 'imperialism' for decades," the paper editorialized. "They are doing it again now, as Washington wages a global 'war against terror' and braces itself for a campaign aimed at 'regime change' in a foreign, sovereign state.

"What is more surprising, and much newer, is that the notion of an American empire has suddenly become a live debate inside the U.S. And not just among Europhile liberals either, but across the range — from left to right."[32]

BACKGROUND

The Ungrateful Son

The story begins in Europe. The roots of antagonism toward the New World grew among the nations that first

At a Berlin Café, Musing About America

"We were hoping America would not elect Bush"

*P*renzlauer Berg was once on the gritty side of town, in East Berlin, when Berlin was a divided city. The Berlin Wall was torn down nearly 20 years ago, and few signs of it remain.

Prenzlauer Berg is now fashionable, but there's still a certain working-class feel to it. On a rainy afternoon last February three friends met for coffee at the Wasser und Brot (Water and Bread), a barely decorated neighborhood café frequented mostly by local workmen, artists, students and retirees.

Baerbel Boesking is a 45-year-old actress, originally from Lower Saxony; Robert Lingnau, 33, is a composer and writer. Petra Lanthaler, 30, is a psychologist. She came to Berlin four years ago from northern Italy.

They sipped tea and coffee and smoked, musing about the United States, George Bush and the future of relations with those increasingly alienating Americans:

Is America different from other countries?

ROBERT: America is very powerful so it has more impact on us than any other country. All of the oil stuff, all of the pollution, the politics.

BAERBEL: Since the student protests here in the 60s, many people still think of the United States as an imperialist, capitalist power. People think Americans are just

superficial, and Bush has only made that worse. But I know that not all Americans are superficial, like [filmmaker] Michael Moore, for instance.

PETRA: I don't think the American people are superficial. As far as I know, there are also many people in the United States who are rebelling against Bush.

Did your impression of America change after Sept. 11?

ROBERT: I think that the American government in some way participated or co-arranged for 9/11, or at least they knew certain things in advance and didn't act to prevent it. They wanted to install the Patriot Act, so that the government could take more control over people's lives. With the terrorist threat, people let the Patriot Act go through. Meanwhile, Bush is cutting billions from Medicare but putting more and more money into the war in Iraq.

BAERBEL: I often hear things like this from my friends. Many of them have the opinion that this whole thing, 9/11, was self-done by the U.S. itself. These are really educated people, it's horrible. This is an unbelievable point of view, like people who believe that the landing on the moon was just a Hollywood production.

ROBERT: I have two degrees actually. I think the Americans landed on the moon, but I don't think the

colonized it. America was the repository of the old world's disenfranchised and discontented, after all.

It was 18th-century British author Samuel Johnson who famously declared, "I am willing to love all mankind except an American." And another Briton, the 19th-century playwright George Bernard Shaw, quipped that "an asylum for the sane would be empty in America." Austria's Sigmund Freud, the father of psychoanalysis, was not enamored of the United States either. "A mistake," he called it, "a gigantic mistake."[33]

While some Americans might take pride in being loathed by European intellectuals, most have been mystified by, if not indifferent to the barbs. European anti-American feeling, argues the University of Michigan's Markovits, stems from the Europeans' sense that they have lost their own power and influence, and the subsequent search for a

contemporary identity in a differently aligned global pecking order.

"Unlike elsewhere in the world," he said, "at least until very recently, America represented a particularly loaded concept and complex entity to Europeans precisely because it was, of course, a European creation."

The son, in other words, had rejected the father; America had "consciously defected from its European origins," Markovits says.

European conservatives and elites were miffed at America's rejection of the strictures of European class and religious hierarchies, the very things that people rebelled against when they emigrated to America.

One of the first Anti-American sentiments was the "degeneracy hypothesis," the belief that humidity and other atmospheric conditions in America created weak and government did their best to prevent what happened. I don't think they wrote the script for what happened, but in a way they participated in order to get the Patriot Act through and for what came after.

PETRA: I don't want to believe that a government would do that. It's true that after 9/11 the U.S. took advantage of these fears of terrorism.

Anti-war demonstrators sometimes have signs comparing Bush to Hitler.

BAERBEL: Bush is not equal to Hitler. You can't compare somebody to Hitler.

ROBERT: You can compare Stalin to Hitler, but not Bush.

BAERBEL: You can compare Mao, this new guy in Korea and Saddam Hussein, but it is crazy to say that Bush is like Hitler.

BAERBEL: I was watching a television debate between Bush and [Sen. John] Kerry [D-Mass.], and Bush said that his role model was Jesus. He's got a long way to go. I don't think Jesus would have started a war with Iraq. I'm a Christian, too.

What do you think about American culture?

PETRA: The first words that come into my mind are big size. The shops are much bigger, the portions are much bigger, everything is bigger. People are bigger. But I know that's a really superficial answer because I've never actually been to America. I am impressed by their

scientific research. They think much more globally than Europeans do.

ROBERT: They don't seem to think globally about pollution and global warming. For me, there are two things that constitute my everyday life: that's jazz music and Apple Macintosh. That's what I think of when I think about U.S. culture. Both native American art forms.

BAERBEL: I had an American boyfriend once. From Kansas.

Do you think relations between America and Europe will improve with a new president in 2008?

BAERBEL: Yes, if it's a Democrat. It's really good you have term limits in the United States. We had Helmut Kohl for 16 years.

ROBERT: But if Jeb Bush gets elected, this is like 16 years of Kohl.

PETRA: All of my friends, most everybody I knew, we were really hoping that America would not elect Bush for the second term. It was really disappointing.

ROBERT: My hope for the next president is that he didn't study at Yale and that he hasn't been a member of Skull and Bones [the exclusive secret society].

It was still raining and cold when the friends left the smoky warmth of the Wasser und Brot. It wasn't their anti-Americanism that stood out but how much they knew about America and American life. And it begged the question: Would Americans know half as much about Germany, even the name of the chancellor?

morally inferior animals and human beings. The court philosopher to Frederick II of Prussia, Cornelius de Pauw, argued in 1768 about Americans that, "the weakest European could crush them with ease."[34]

As American industry rose in the late 19th century, the speed of American life became a major threat to European traditions of craftsmanship. "The breathless haste with which they work — the distinctive vice of the new world — is already beginning ferociously to infect old Europe and is spreading a spiritual emptiness over the continent," observed the German philosopher Friedrich Nietzsche.[35]

The notion that the mixing of races was bringing down the level of capability in Americans was another major thrust of anti-Americanism. Blacks and "low quality" immigrants, it was said in European salons, would lead to ultimate dissolution.

Arthur de Gobineau, a French social thinker, declared that America was creating the "greatest mediocrity in all fields: mediocrity of physical strength, mediocrity of beauty, mediocrity of intellectual capacities — we could almost say nothingness."[36]

After World War I, allies of the United States, France and Great Britain, found themselves massively in debt to the brash and newly powerful Americans, which generated resentment. These sentiments spread during the Great Depression. Sometimes the bias took on anti-Semitic overtones, including the widely held theory that the American government was ruled by a Jewish conspiracy.[37]

After World War II, the U.S. Marshall Plan helped rebuild Europe. Yet as American power grew while Europe licked its wounds, the United States became a scapegoat for an increasing sense of weakness among those nostalgic

AFP/Getty Images/Rizwan Tabassum

Pakistani protesters burn the American flag and a mock Israeli flag to protest the Israeli attack on southern Lebanon in August 2006. Anti-American sentiment often ties the U.S. and Israel together as partners in the exploitation and humiliation of other countries.

for their former empires. It was then that the global spread of American cultural, economic, and political power — rock 'n' roll, McDonald's and U.S. military bases — established the United States as a symbol of global authority, and one to be resisted.

Religious Differences

The staying power of American religiosity created another divide between Europe and the United States. Historian Huntington's "clash of civilizations" theory postulated that the big divide was between Christianity and Islam. But one of the deepest rifts between Europe and the United States centered on the relationship between religion and government.

Europeans had begun abandoning churchgoing in the 1950s and no longer felt that religion should play a role in political affairs.[38] But a large majority of Americans not only continued to go to church but also maintained the belief that religious tenets should provide moral direction to their elected leaders.

Many Europeans have been aghast at what they viewed as American religious fervor, particularly when it has seemed to influence government policy. "An American president who conducts Bible study at the White House and begins Cabinet sessions with a prayer may seem a curious anachronism to his European allies, but he is in tune with his constituents," write Judt and French scholar Denis Lacorne.[39]

Even in Spain, which has one of the most conservative religious establishments in Europe, American evangelicals'

penchant for focusing on sexual issues does not resonate. In 2005, for example, a large majority of the Spanish population voted to legalize gay marriage, a key moral issue to some conservative American Christians.

Policies and traditions that regularly mix church and state in the United States — prayer in schools, God in the Pledge of Allegiance and the open displays of faith by President Bush — "were really shocking to the average Spaniard," says Charles Powell Solares, a deputy director at the Elcano Royal Institute, a think tank in Madrid. He says that 90 percent of Spaniards are in favor of a radical separation between church and state.

On the other hand, polls in Indonesia, Pakistan, Lebanon and Turkey reveal that the majority of people in Muslim countries believe the United States is secular and ungodly.[40]

Foreign Affairs Bully?

Muslims and Americans have not always been adversaries. The United States, after all, supported Islamists in Afghanistan in their fight against the Soviet Union in the 1980s, as well as Bosnian Muslims against Christian Orthodox Serbia in the 1990s.

Moreover, the United States maintains strong relationships with Saudi Arabia, Jordan and Egypt, and Muslim immigrants continue to flow into America — from Pakistan, Bangladesh, Afghanistan, India and even Iraq.

In Indonesia and Malaysia, home to some of the world's largest Muslim populations, anti-Americanism is a recent phenomenon. For most of the postwar 20th century, the United States was seen as an anti-colonial power because of its role in liberating those countries from Japan.

"It's not a coincidence that the Malaysian flag looks like the American flag," says Noor of Berlin's Centre for Modern Oriental Studies.

The advance of high-speed communications has been a key factor in the attitude shift in Southeast Asia. "New media, especially satellite television and the Internet, reinforce negative images of the U.S. through a flood of compelling, highly graphic images," said Steven Simon, a Middle East scholar at the Council on Foreign Relations. "Some of these images present the Muslims as victims; others as victors. All tend to frame events as segments of an ongoing drama between good and evil."[41]

This "us vs. them" dynamic had its genesis in Europe. "Many of these originated outside the Muslim world entirely," Simon told the House International Relations Committee. They were "introduced to the region by Nazi and Soviet propaganda in mid-20th century."

Most notoriously, the British-appointed mufti of Jerusalem, Haj Amin al-Husayni, made a pact with the German government in the 1930s and spread ill will throughout the region against the Western allies, including the United States. Great Britain, of course, was already an object of scorn and resentment for its heavy-handed colonial administration of Muslim territory.

Simon also noted that after Britain pulled out of the Middle East in the 1940s and America began to vie for influence during the Cold War, the United States inherited the animosity that Muslim countries had against Britain, their former conquerors. "The substitution of American power in the region for British authority was bound to tar the U.S. with the imperialist brush," Simon said.

American Exceptionalism

Americans' self-image has been rooted in the certitude that their country is different — a beacon of personal, political and economic freedom in the world. This idea really came of age during World War II, when American industrial power, along with Soviet manpower, liberated Europe. Then the Yanks were cheered and admired, but some scholars believe that the roots of anti-American feelings by many Europeans stem from this U.S. "salvation."

A residue of that feeling remains in France, which truly had been liberated. Germany, however, had been the enemy, and even during the height of the Cold War in the 1960s and '70s, many West Germans deeply resented the presence of American military bases.

Even though the American army's airlift of supplies had saved West Berlin, few thought of the United States as having saved them from the Nazis or the Soviets, says Claussen, at Leibniz Hannover University, and West German politicians were loath to suggest that "America has liberated us."

Spain until recently was America's closest ally in continental Europe, but enmity toward the United States has existed since the 1950s, says Powell Solares, at Madrid's Elcano Royal Institute. Spain never viewed America as a liberator because the country was largely uninvolved with World War II. Instead, they tend to condemn the U.S. for supporting fascist Gen. Francisco Franco as part of its Cold War policy.

A female U.S. Army soldiers frisks a Kurdish woman at a checkpoint in Ramadi, Iraq, in October 2004. Several people had been killed in clashes between rebels and U.S. troops. The War in Iraq underlies much of the spiraling anti-American sentiment around the world today.

AFP/Getty Images/Patrick Baz

"And that means that Spaniards have never associated the U.S. with freedom and democracy," says Powell Solares, citing polls from the 1960s and '70s in which Spaniards viewed the United States as a bigger threat to world peace than the Soviet Union.

After the collapse of the Soviet Union in 1991 the former republics of the Soviet Union and its satellite nations emerged with more solidarity with the United States than most of the countries of Western Europe. Except for Great Britain, Eastern European nations have contributed more troops per capita to the Coalition Forces in the invasions of Afghanistan and Iraq. Several have allegedly allowed controversial secret CIA prisons on their soil.

When U.S. Secretary of Defense Donald Rumsfeld distinguished between the "Old Europe" and "New Europe" in 2003, he was paying homage to the willingness of the newly liberated nations to aid the United States, in contrast to the recalcitrance of Germany and France — Old Europe.[42] French officials labeled the secretary's bluntness as "arrogance."

Anti-Americanism got only a short reprieve in the aftermath of the 9/11 attacks.

"Initially, there was a spontaneous outpouring of sympathy and support for the United States," Pew researchers found. "Even in some parts of the Middle East, hostility toward the U.S. appeared to soften a bit. But this reaction proved short-lived. Just a few months after the attacks, a Global Attitudes Project survey of opinion leaders around

Disapproval of American Policies Is Widespread

More than half of the 26,000 people surveyed in 25 countries disapprove of the United States' role in several foreign-policy areas. Fifty-six percent disagree with the U.S. approach toward global warming, while nearly three-quarters are critical of the war in Iraq.

Do you agree or disagree with U.S. handling of:

North Korea's nuclear program	Global warming	Iran's nuclear program	Israeli-Hezbollah war	War in Iraq
16% / 30% / 54%	17% / 27% / 56%	12% / 28% / 60%	14% / 21% / 65%	7% / 20% / 73%

○ Approve   ● Disapprove   ◐ No opinion

Source: The poll was conducted for BBC World Service by the international polling firm GlobeScan; 26,381 people in Asia, Africa, Europe, South America, the Middle East and the United States were interviewed between Nov. 3, 2006, and Jan. 9, 2007.

the world found that, outside Western Europe, there was a widespread sense that U.S. policies were a major cause of the attacks."

In Venezuela, President Chavez cynically suggested, "The hypothesis that is gaining strength . . . is that it was the same U.S. imperial power that planned and carried out this terrible terrorist attack or act against its own people and against citizens of all over the world. Why? To justify the aggressions that immediately were unleashed on Afghanistan, on Iraq."[43]

CURRENT SITUATION

Missteps and Failures

Because of their self-proclaimed virtues and their emphasis on human rights, Americans are often held to higher expectations on the world stage than are other nations. When they fail to perform to those standards, they are doubly condemned. Many who see U.S. foreign policy floundering are as disappointed as they are angry.

Some of the criticisms of the United States — such as the allegations that the government was behind the 9/11 attacks — are so irrational that there is no way to answer them. But there are inescapable realities that will not go away.

America's credibility on human rights has been severely damaged by prisoner abuse at Abu Ghraib, the U.S.-run Baghdad prison for terrorism suspects, and alleged mistreatment at the Guantanamo Bay detention camp in Cuba, as well as by CIA renditions and secret detention camps in Eastern Europe.[44] Its reputation for competence has been trampled by revelations that Iraq's alleged weapons of mass destruction had been trumped up by an overeager White House yearning for battle. Most jarring of all is the bloodshed in Iraq that has claimed at least 34,000 Iraqis and more than 3,000 American troops.[45]

After the revelations at Abu Ghraib, Patrick Sabatier of the French newspaper *Liberation* wrote, "One can lose a war in places other than battlegrounds. The torture that took place in the Abu Ghraib prison is a major defeat for the U.S. The photographs fan the fires of anti-American hate in the Arab world. Elsewhere they trigger reactions of disgust, and take away from the coalition's small dose of moral legitimacy, gained by toppling Saddam's regime."[46]

Even Americans themselves no longer defend the U.S position in Iraq, Pew researchers found. "As to whether the removal of Saddam Hussein from power made the world a safer place," the survey said, "views are also lopsidedly negative. In no country surveyed, including the

Will anti-Americanism wane after President Bush leaves office?

YES

Dr. Farish A. Noor
Professor of history, Centre for Modern Oriental Studies, Berlin

Written for *CQ Global Researcher*, March 2007

It is undeniable that the image of the United States of America has declined significantly in Southeast Asia during President George Bush's term. Over the past two years I have witnessed more than two-dozen anti-American demonstrations in Malaysia and Indonesia, where the issues ranged from Malaysia's protracted negotiations with the USA on the Free Trade Agreement to America's actions in Afghanistan and Iraq. At almost all of these demonstrations effigies of George Bush and Condoleezza Rice were paraded and sometimes set alight.

Historically America was seen as a liberator and savior in the Southeast Asian region, especially in its role against the Japanese imperial army during the Second World War and its efforts to prevent the Western European colonial powers (Britain, France and the Netherlands) from recolonizing their former colonies Malaya, Indonesia, Vietnam, Burma and the Philippines.

Admiration for America, the American way of life and American values was at its peak during the postcolonial developmental era of the 1960s to 1980s, when Southeast Asian countries sent tens of thousands of students to the U.S. for further education. The American economic model became the framework for the postcolonial economies of the region; and America was doubly thanked for helping to keep the region safe from communism.

Yet, America today is seen as the enemy of Islam, and for Muslim-majority countries like Malaysia, Indonesia and Brunei this poses new problems for bilateral relations. One major factor that has worsened the situation was the use of bellicose rhetoric by the Bush administration in its unilateral "war on terror," which was couched in terms of a "crusade." Subsequent actions and misjudgments (such as the invasion of Iraq without sufficient consultation with Muslim countries) and the deteriorating security condition in Iraq and Afghanistan have merely compounded the problem even more.

Much of the damage, however, is due to the unilateralist character of a Bush administration that was seen as cavalier, gung-ho and insensitive to Muslim concerns. Thanks in part to the overreach and over-projection of the image of Bush in this campaign, however, much of the controversy surrounding the war on terror, the invasion of Afghanistan and Iraq, etc. has been associated with President Bush himself on a personal level.

There is every reason to believe that some of the anti-Americanism we see in Southeast Asia today will wane with a change of administration. But this also depends on whether the next U.S. government can bring the campaigns in Afghanistan and Iraq to a close with minimum loss of life.

NO

Manjeet Kripalani
*Edward R. Murrow Press Fellow, Council on Foreign Relations;
India Bureau Chief,* BusinessWeek

Written for *CQ Global Researcher*, March 2007

The favorability rating of the U.S. in the eyes of the world has fallen precipitously since the Iraq invasion, and continues to decline as the war wears on.

Will America ever recover its lost reputation? Perhaps, but it will take years. The perception of the U.S. is that of a power in descent, a nation spent in the ignominious and outmoded task of building Empire. The ideals and positive force that the U.S. represented have been discredited since 2003, given the fundamentalist fervor with which they have been pursued.

That's not the best option in an increasingly complex world. Getting a global consensus on crises like Darfur, trade imbalances, terrorism and Middle East peace in a world without the powerful moral authority of the U.S. will be more difficult. But it has created space for other leadership to step up to the task.

This ascendant world comprises powers like Russia, but more widely the countries of Asia — notably China, India and even Japan. As the beneficiary of past American ideals, Japan has developed goodwill over decades through aid, anti-war sensitivities and the potential to be the stable "America" in Asia.

China and India are both poor, developing countries — but much of today's world looks more like them than it does the U.S.-dominated developed world. Their experiences are being closely watched by their peers, with whom there are centuries-old cultural and historic ties.

In this new world order, the U.S.' tarnished image really doesn't matter. America is still a powerful country, and these same ascendant nations are meshed with it economically and politically. China is in a tight economic embrace with America. Japan is still militarily protected by the U.S. and is its strongest, staunchest ally in Asia.

India, after years of hostile relations with the U.S., has turned pragmatic. Since 2001, America's popularity in India has been on the rise. That's because Indians, affected by terrorism for decades, view Washington as fighting their war for them. And despite domestic pressure, President Bush has continued to support the outsourcing of back-office jobs to India. The signing of the nuclear deal last December is surely good for U.S. business and Indian consumers. But its symbolism is far greater: Its confidence in India's non-proliferation record has ensured that democratic India will wholeheartedly embrace the U.S. economically, technologically and politically.

This ensures that in the future, no matter how much moral authority the U.S. loses, its wagon is hitched firmly to the stars of these ascendant nations — and vice versa.

AFP/Getty Images/Stephane De Sakutin

Political theater plays out in Paris as orange-jump-suited Amnesty International protesters call on the United States to close the Guantánamo Bay, Cuba, prison camp.

United States, does a majority think the Iraq leader's overthrow has increased global security."[47]

Another strike against the American war in Iraq is its duration — longer now than World War II. And the carnage can be seen daily on television. "If the war had had a quick or favorable ending, people would have forgotten about it. But it is in the news every day," says Vallespin, at the Sociological Research Centre of Spain.

Support for Israel

For many Americans and Europeans, Israel cannot be forsaken. It is a place of immense historical and spiritual importance, and was established to right grievous historic wrongs. This is felt not only by America's 3 million Jews but also by an overwhelming number of the country's Christians.

Muslim nations, however, and many other non-Muslim countries, see Israel as a regional bully propped up by the United States. Pew surveys found that many people "suspect the United States of deliberately targeting Muslim nations and using the war on terror to protect Israel," as well as to gain control of Middle East oil.[48]

Clear evidence of a biased relationship was seen in the fact that the United States announced a $10 billion military-aid package to Israel on the same day that the U.S. military began its assault on Iraq in 2003.

"To announce this package on the same day that Iraq is bombed is as stupid as it is arrogant," said Nabeel Ghanyoum, a military analyst in Syria. "This is effectively telling the Arab world, 'Look we are bombing Iraq as we please, and we are giving Israel as much financial aid [as] it wants.' "[49]

In his study of the links between anti-Israeli sentiment and anti-Americanism, the University of Michigan's Markovits found that the crucial link was made after the Israeli victory in the 1967 war, while America was embroiled in Vietnam.

"Israel became little more than an extension of American power to many, especially on Europe's political left," he wrote. "Israel was disliked, especially by the left, not so much because it was Jewish but because it was American. And as such it was powerful."[50]

A Good Neighbor?

There have been positive moments in the past few years. The Council on Foreign Relations' Simon says that there was an upsurge in America's standing in 2004, when it provided substantial aid in the wake of the devastating Southeast Asian tsunami. The perception that this aid was "unconditional," he said, had a "sharply positive effect" on perceptions of the United States.

Noor at the Centre for Modern Oriental Studies in Berlin disagrees. He says he visited storm-damaged areas of Indonesia and Pakistan after the disaster and perceived even this seemingly altruistic venture was a public-relations disaster for the United States.

"They showed up on aircraft carriers and other warships," he says, "and the soldiers sent to help the victims were still wearing their combat fatigues from the Iraq War." It would have been far wiser to send civilian aid workers rather than the military, he says, who were regarded by many storm victims as emissaries of the imperial United States. "America is now seen [there] as something alien."

The Remarque Institute's Judt says that the U.S. government's disdain for international institutions has had a lasting negative effect, particularly among America's longtime allies. The Bush administration created an "in-your-face America," he says, that conveyed the message: "Not only do the things we do annoy you, but we don't care. We are going to do what we do, and you can take it or leave it."

For example, during his short stint as U.S. envoy to the United Nations, Ambassador John Bolton was criticized — and also praised — for his straight-from-the-shoulder diplomacy, including his disparagement of the United Nations itself. "The Secretariat building in New York has 38 stories," he famously once said. "If it lost 10 stories, it wouldn't make a bit of difference."[51] Bolton was blamed by some U.N. officials for quietly sabotaging the organization's reform initiative by stirring differences between poor and rich countries.

"He sometimes makes it very difficult to build bridges because he is a very honest and blunt person," said South Africa's ambassador, Dumisani Shadrack Kumalo, chairman of a coalition of developing nations. He said it sometimes appeared that "Ambassador Bolton wants to prove nothing works at the United Nations."[52] Bolton resigned in December 2006.

In addition, both Noor and Latin America expert Sweig at the Council on Foreign Relations say the U.S. reputation for generosity has been hurt by drastic cuts in foreign-assistance programs under the U.S. Agency for International Development (AID), as well as cuts in funds for libraries, scholarships and other cultural activities. Private giving by Americans remains the highest per capita in the world, and American foreign-development aid is the highest in the developed world in pure dollar terms, but the level of aid sinks very low when measured as a percentage of GDP.[53]

Such aid programs in many cases were replaced by "War on Terrorism" initiatives, including a $300 million propaganda campaign from the Pentagon. The psychological-warfare operation included plans for placing pro-American messages in foreign media outlets without disclosing the U.S. government as the source.[54]

Alarmist rhetoric is a poor substitute for help, says Noor, because the United States no longer has people on the ground in Muslim countries who know the cultures and the languages. When they were in effect and fully funded, he says, U.S. aid programs were so successful that Islamist movements in those countries have mimicked them. "They borrowed the tactics of the Peace Corps."

Missed Opportunities

By linking Israel and the United States into a single, fearsome conspiracy, anti-American activists have created strange bedfellows: fundamentalist Muslims, socialists and Western pacifists. Left-leaning groups used to find common cause in socialist ideals. Now, "anti-Americanism is the glue that holds them together, and hatred of Israel is one aspect," said Emmanuele Ottolenghi, a research fellow at the Centre for Hebrew and Jewish studies at Oxford University in England.[55]

While America's close relationship with Israel was often questioned outside the United States, the U.S. role in opposing the Soviet Union during the Cold War more

Venezuelan President Hugo Chavez fulminates about the United States at Miraflores Palace, Caracas, in 2006. Chavez, who is attempting to form an alternative coalition of South American countries opposed to the United States, insults and belittles the American president at every opportunity.

than outweighed it, says Georgetown University's Kupchan. Now, he says, the old bonds don't count for so much.

"The World War II generation is dying off; the reflexive support of the transatlantic partnership of that generation is disappearing. You have a new generation of Europeans for whom the United States is not the savior from the Nazis and the Soviets that it was for their parents," says Kupchan.

Meanwhile, even with a new U.S. presidential election nearing, fears remain strong in Europe about the actions of the Bush administration in its remaining months. Of particular concern is the possibility of a dangerous new U.S. offensive against Iran, which says it will continue developing nuclear energy.

"We think that the growing tensions between the two countries are made more dangerous by George Bush's detachment from the electorate: There's a real risk that he may strike at Iran before he leaves power," John Micklethwait, editor of *The Economist,* recently wrote.[56]

OUTLOOK
Lasting Damage?

When prosecutors in Munich decided in January to charge CIA counterterrorism operatives with kidnapping a German citizen, Khalid el-Masri, the newspaper *Sueddeutsche Zeitung* declared: "The great ally is not allowed to simply send its thugs out into Europe's streets." Indeed,

Craig Whitlock reported, the decision "won widespread applause from German politicians and the public."[57]

In the wake of such incidents, many at home and abroad are asking how — and even if — the United States can repair its image and its relations with its allies. Some analysts believe that the coming new presidential administration, whether Republican or Democratic, can do it through diligent cooperation and outreach. Others say the damage is so severe that it would take decades.

"When Bush goes, assuming that there isn't a war with Iran, it will be possible for the next president to exercise damage control," says Remarque Institute Director Judt.

Sweig of the Council on Foreign Relations sees a longer road ahead. "It will be the work of a generation to turn this around," she says.

Gerard Baker, U.S. editor for the *Times of London*, posits a more complex future. "Somewhere, deep down," he writes, "tucked away underneath their loathing for George Bush, in a secret place where the lights of smart dinner-party conversation and clever debating-society repartee never shine, the growing hordes of America-bashers must dread the moment he leaves office.

"When President Bush goes into the Texas sunset, and especially if he is replaced by an enlightened, world-embracing Democrat, their one excuse, their sole explanation for all human suffering in the world will disappear too. And they may just find that the world is not as simple as they thought it was."[58]

Critics agree that as long as the United States remains the world's greatest economic and military force, it will often be blamed for its negative impact on other countries, and seldom thanked for positive contributions. The inferiority complex that the University of Michigan's Markovits says drives Europe's brand of anti-Americanism will probably continue to fester until the EU can learn to assert itself in global affairs when humanitarian as well as military demands are compelling.

The Israeli-Palestinian conflict also will remain a problem and a source of agitation against U.S. policy, as long as Israel insists on occupying Palestinian land, America supports its right to do so and Palestinian politicians are unable to bring their angry streets to a compromise solution for statehood. The problem is multi-faceted.

But, as Powell Solares at Madrid's Elcano Royal Institute points out, much of the global public sees only one thing: "The perception that the main problem with the Arab-Israeli conflict is that the U.S. will always back Israel."

Iraq looms over all questions about the future. "The U.S. presence in Iraq will seriously impede American efforts to influence hearts and minds," Simon, the Middle East expert at the Council on Foreign Relations, told a House subcommittee last September. "Our occupation will reinforce regional images of the United States as both excessively violent and ineffectual."[59]

But what will follow the "American Century" in the near future if the United States has lost the trust of the world?

"It may be that the United States has not shown itself worthy or capable of ensuring the unity of a civilization whose laws have governed the world, at least for the last few centuries," writes Jean Daniel in *Le Nouvel Observateur* in Paris.

"But since a united Europe capable of taking over this mission hasn't yet emerged," Daniel continues, "all we can do is hope that the American people will wake up and rapidly call a halt to these crude interventionist utopias carelessly dredged out of the Theodore Roosevelt tradition. Utopias that, in the words of an American diplomat, have made George W. Bush and his brain trust 'lose their intelligence as they turned into ideologues.' "[60]

NOTES

1. See Fareed Zakaria, "The Politics of Rage: Why Do They Hate Us?" *Newsweek*, Sept. 24, 2001.

2. Samuel P. Huntington, "The Clash of Civilizations?" *Foreign Affairs*, summer 1993; www.foreignaffairs .org/19930601faessay5188/samuel-p-huntington/ the-clash-of-civilizations.html.

3. James Keaten, "French Farmer José Bové Leads New McDonald's Protest," The Associated Press, Aug. 13, 2001; www.mcspotlight.org/media/press/mcds/ theassociatedpr130801.html.

4. Quoted in David Morse, "Striking the Golden Arches: French Farmers Protest McDonald's Globalization," *The Ecologist*, Dec. 31, 2002, p. 2; www.socsci.uci.edu/~cohenp/food/frenchfarmers .pdf.

5. For background, see Mary H. Cooper, "Hating America," *CQ Researcher*, Nov. 23, 2001, pp. 969-992.

6. Andrei S. Markovits, "European Anti-Americanism (and Anti-Semitism): Ever Present Though Always Denied," Working Paper Series #108. Markovits is Karl W. Deutsch Collegiate Professor of Comparative Politics and German Studies at the University of Michigan.

7. Paul Hockenos, "Dispatch From Germany," *The Nation*, April 14, 2003; www.thenation.com/doc/20030414/hockenos.

8. "Pakistani Cartoon Protesters Chant Anti-American Slogans," FoxNews.com, Feb. 21, 2006; www.foxnews.com/story/0,2933,185503,00.html.

9. Jean-Marie Colombani, "We Are All Americans," *Le Monde*, Sept. 12, 2001.

10. Quoted in Denis Lacorne and Tony Judt, eds., *With Us or Against Us: Studies in Global Anti-Americanism* (2005).

11. "Global Opinion: The Spread of Anti-Americanism," *Trends 2005*, p. 106; Pew Research Center for People and the Press, Jan. 24, 2005; http://people-press.org/commentary/display.php3?Analysis ID=104.

12. "U.S. Image Up Slightly, But Still Negative American Character Gets Mixed Reviews," Pew Research Center for People and the Press, June 23, 2005; http://pewglobal.org/reports/display.php?Report ID=247.

13. Lacorne and Judt, *op. cit.*

14. "War in Iraq: Winning the Peace," *The* [Beirut] *Daily Star*, April 6, 2006, from Worldpress.com; www.worldpress.org/Mideast/1041.cfm.

15. Peter Ford, "Europe Cringes at Bush 'Crusade' Against Terrorists," *The Christian Science Monitor*, Sept. 19, 2001.

16. For background, see "Brian Hansen, "Globalization Backlash," *CQ Researcher*, Sept. 28, 2001, pp. 961-784.

17. For background, see Sarah Glazer, "Slow Food Movement," *CQ Researcher*, Jan. 26, 2007, pp. 73-96, and David Hosansky, "Food Safety," *CQ Researcher*, Nov. 1, 2002, pp. 897-920.

18. Quoted in *The Daily Mail*, June 1, 1999, BBC Online Network; http://news.bbc.co.uk/2/hi/uk_news/358291.stm.

19. Quoted in Sam Loewenberg, "Lobbying Euro-Style," *The National Journal*, Sept. 8, 2001.

20. Henry A. Giroux, "George Bush's Religious Crusade Against Democracy: Fundamentalism as Cultural Politics," *Dissident Voice*, Aug. 4, 2004; www.dissidentvoice.org/Aug04/Giroux0804.htm.

21. "God and American diplomacy," *The Economist*, Feb. 8, 2003.

22. Pew Research Center, *op. cit.*, Jan. 24, 2005.

23. Markovits, *op. cit.*

24. "Burger and fries à la française," *The Economist*, April 15, 2004.

25. Suzanne Daley, "French Turn Vandal Into Hero Against US." *The New York Times*, July 1, 2000.

26. Henry Luce, "The American Century," *Life*, Feb. 7, 1941.

27. Michael Elliott, "China Takes on the World," *Time*, Jan. 11, 2007.

28. "America's Image Slips, But Allies Share U.S. Concerns Over Iran, Hamas; No Global Warming Alarm in the U.S., China," Pew Research Center for People and the Press, June 13, 2006; http://pewglobal.org.

29. Lacorne and Judt, *op. cit.*

30. "Hugo Chavez: Latin America Rises Against the Empire," March 10, 2007, from audio transcript on TeleSUR; http://latinhacker.gnn.tv/blogs/22178/Hugo_Chavez_Latin_America_Rises_Against_the_Empire.

31. Souad Mekhennet and Michael Moss, "New Face of Jihad Vows Attacks," *The New York Times*, March 16, 2007.

32. "Rome AD . . . Rome DC?" *The Guardian*, Sept. 18, 2002; www.guardian.co.uk/usa/story/0,12271,794163,00.html.

33. Quoted in Judy Colp Rubin, "Is Bush Really Responsible for Anti-Americanism Around the World," Sept. 27, 2004, George Mason University's History Network; http://hnn.us/articles/7288.html.

34. Cornelius de Pauw, "Recherches philosophiques sur les Américains ou Mémoires interessants pour servir à l'histoire de l'espèce humaine," London, 1768.

35. Friedrich Nietzsche, *The Gay Science*, sec. 329 (1882).
36. Arthur Gobineau, (Count Joseph Arthur de Gobineau) and Adrian Collins [1853-55] 1983. *The Inequality of Human Races*, Second edition, reprint.
37. Barry Rubin and Judith Colp Rubin, *Hating America: A History* (2004).
38. Lacorne and Judt, *op. cit.*, p. 26.
39. *Ibid.*
40. Pew Research Center, *op. cit.*, June 23, 2005.
41. Testimony before House International Relations Committee, Sept. 14, 2006.
42. Quoted in "Outrage at 'Old Europe' Remarks," BBC Online, Jan. 23, 2003.
43. "Theory That U.S. Orchestrated Sept. 11 Attacks 'Not Absurd,' " The Associated Press, Sept. 12, 2001, www.breitbart.com/.
44. For background, see Peter Katel and Kenneth Jost, "Treatment of Detainees," *CQ Researcher*, Aug. 25, 2006, pp. 673-696.
45. For background, see Peter Katel, "New Strategy in Iraq," *CQ Researcher*, Feb. 23, 2007, pp. 169-192.
46. Patrick Sabatier, Liberation, Paris, Quoted in WorldPress.com, "Iraq Prisoner Abuse Draws International Media Outrage," May 12, 2004; www.worldpress.org/Mideast/1861.cfm.
47. Pew Research Center, *op. cit.*, June 23, 2005.
48. Pew Research Center, *op. cit.*, Jan. 24, 2005.
49. Firas Al-Atraqchi, "Disillusion, Anger on the Arab Street," *Dissident Voice Online*, March 21, 2007; www.dissidentvoice.org/Articles3/Atraqchi_Arab Street.htm.
50. Markovits, *op. cit.*
51. Quoted in Anne Applebaum, "Defending Bolton," *The Washington Post*, March 9, 2005, p. A21.
52. Quoted in Peter Baker and Glenn Kessler, "U.N. Ambassador Bolton Won't Stay," *The Washington Post*, Dec. 6, 2006, p. A1.
53. "Review of the Development Cooperation Policies and Programmes of United States," Organization for Economic Cooperation and Development, 2006.
54. Matt Kelley, "Pentagon Rolls Out Stealth PR," *USA Today*, Dec. 14, 2005.
55. Glenn Frankel, "In Britain, War Concern Grows Into Resentment of U.S. Power; Anxiety Over Attack on Iraq Moves to Political Mainstream," *The Washington Post*, Jan. 26, 2003, p. A14.
56. John Micklethwait, "Letter to Readers," *The Economist*, Feb. 8, 2007.
57. Craig Whitlock, "In Another CIA Abduction, Germany Has an Uneasy Role," *The Washington Post*, Feb. 5, 2007, p. A11.
58. Gerard Baker, "When Bush Leaves Office," *Times of London*, TimesOnline, March 2, 2007.
59. Testimony before International Relations Subcommittee on the Middle East, Sept. 14, 2006.
60. Jean Daniel, "Our American 'Enemies,' " *La Nouvel Observateur*, Sept. 23, 2003, quoted on WorldPress.org.

BIBLIOGRAPHY

Books

Cohen, Nick, *What's Left? How Liberals Lost Their Way, Fourth Estate,* **2007.**
A well-known liberal British columnist for *The Observer* and *The New Statesman* gives a scathing critique of anti-Americanism among the British Left, the anti-globalization movement and intellectuals who have become apologists for militant Islam.

Garton Ash, Timothy, *Free World: America, Europe and the Surprising Future of the West, Random House,* **2004.**
In an engaging critique of anti-American sentiment, a former journalist who runs the European Studies Centre at Oxford University argues that in the post-Cold War world, America is the "other" against which Europeans try to define their own identity.

Joffe, Josef, *Uberpower: The Imperial Temptation of America, W. W. Norton,* **2006.**
The editor and publisher of *Die Zeit,* a German weekly, and a fellow in international relations at the Hoover Institution, provides a European intellectual's insight into the envy at the heart of anti-Americanism and its parallels with classical anti-Semitism.

Katzenstein, Peter, and Robert Keohane, eds., *Anti-Americanisms in World Politics,* **Cornell University Press, 2006.**

Two international-relations scholars bring together the insights of historians, social scientists and political scientists.

Kohut, Andrew, and Bruce Stokes, *America Against the World: How We Are Different and Why We Are Disliked,* **Times Books, 2006.**

Kohut, director of the Pew Research Center for the People and the Press, and Stokes, international economics columnist for *National Journal,* provide a comprehensive survey of public opinions about America from around the world.

Kupchan, Charles, *The End of the American Era: U.S. Foreign Policy and the Geopolitics of the Twenty-first Century,* **Vintage, 2003.**

A former National Security Council staffer and a senior fellow at the Council on Relations argues that with the rise of China and the European Union America can no longer afford to have a unilateralist foreign policy.

Lacorne, Denis, and Tony Judt, eds., *With Us or Against Us: Studies in Global Anti-Americanism,* **Palgrave Macmillan, 2005.**

Essays by 11 scholars analyze anti-American sentiment in Western and Eastern Europe, the Middle East and Asia.

Markovits, Andrei S., *Uncouth Nation: Why Europe Dislikes America,* **Princeton University Press, 2007.**

A professor of comparative politics and German studies at the University of Michigan, Ann Arbor, writes provocatively about the anti-Americanism in everyday European life.

Revel, Jean-Francois, *Anti-Americanism,* **Encounter Books, 2003.**

Revel, a leading French intellectual, castigates his countrymen for pointing their fingers at America when they should be dealing with their own current and historical problems.

Sweig, Julia, *Friendly Fire: Losing Friends and Making Enemies in the Anti-American Century,* **Public Affairs, 2006.**

The director of Latin American studies at the Council on Foreign Relations argues that American policies in Latin America, including sponsoring dictators and condoning human-rights violations, set the stage for the current animosity toward the U.S.

Articles

Judt, Tony, "Anti-Americans Abroad," *The New York Review of Books,* **May 2003.**

The director of the Remarque Institute at New York University examines the rage for new books in France attacking America.

Reports and Studies

"America's Image Slips, But Allies Share U.S. Concerns Over Iran, Hamas," *Pew Research Center,* **2006; http://pewglobal.org/reports/display.php?ReportID=252.**

The latest poll by the Pew Global Attitudes Project finds that while anti-Americanism had dipped in 2005, it began rising again.

"Foreign Aid: An Introductory Overview of U.S. Programs and Policy," *Congressional Research Service, Library of Congress,* **2004; http://fpc.state.gov/documents/organization/31987.pdf.**

This study of American foreign aid includes data on humanitarian, military and bilateral-development aid.

"Worldviews 2002," *German Marshall Fund of the United States and The Chicago Council on Foreign Relations,* **2002; www.worldviews.org.**

A comprehensive survey of contrasting European and American public opinion following the Sept. 11 terrorist attacks finds that Europeans believed U.S. foreign policy contributed to the attacks.

For More Information

Centre for Modern Oriental Studies, Kirchweg 33, 14129 Berlin, Germany; +49-(0)-30-80307-0; www.zmo.de. German think tank conducting comparative and interdisciplinary studies of the Middle East, Africa, South and Southeast Asia.

Council on Foreign Relations, 58 E. 68th St., New York, NY 10065; (212) 434-9400; www.cfr.org. Promotes a better understanding of the foreign-policy choices facing the United States and other governments.

Elcano Royal Institute, Príncipe de Vergara, 51, 28006 Madrid, Spain; +34-91-781-6770; www.realinstitutoelcano

.org. Non-partisan Spanish institution generating policy ideas in the interest of international peace.

Pew Global Attitudes Project, 1615 L St., N.W., Suite 700, Washington, DC 20036; (202) 419-4400; www .pewglobal.org. Assesses worldwide opinions on the current state of foreign affairs and other important issues.

USC Center on Public Diplomacy, USC Annenberg School, University of Southern California, 3502 Watt Way, Suite 103, Los Angeles, CA 90089-0281; (213) 821-2078; http://uscpublicdiplomacy.com. Studies the impact of government-sponsored programs as well as private activities on foreign policy and national security.

Religious Fundamentalism

Does It Lead to Intolerance and Violence?

Brian Beary

Burqas enshroud women in Kabul, Afghanistan's capital, reflecting life under strict Islamic regimes like the Taliban. Overthrown in 2001, the radically fundamentalist Taliban has regained control in some parts of the country. In addition to requiring the burqa, it restricts women's movements, prevents men from shaving or girls from being educated and prohibits singing and dancing.

From *CQ Global Researcher*, February 2009.

L ife is far from idyllic in Swat, a lush valley once known as "the Switzerland of Pakistan." Far from Islamabad, the capital, a local leader of the Taliban — the extremist Islamic group that controls parts of the country — uses radio broadcasts to coerce residents into adhering to the Taliban's strict edicts.

"Un-Islamic" activities that are now forbidden — on pain of a lashing or public execution — range from singing and dancing to watching television or sending girls to school. "They control everything through the radio," said one frightened Swat resident who would not give his name. "Everyone waits for the broadcast." And in case any listeners in the once-secular region are considering ignoring Shah Duran's harsh dictates, periodic public assassinations — 70 police officers beheaded in 2008 alone — provide a bone-chilling deterrent.[1]

While the vast majority of the world's religious fundamentalists do not espouse violence as a means of imposing their beliefs, religious fundamentalism — in both its benign and more violent forms — is growing throughout much of the world. Scholars attribute the rise to various factors, including a backlash against perceived Western consumerism and permissiveness. And fundamentalism — the belief in a literal interpretation of holy texts and the rejection of modernism — is rising not only in Muslim societies but also among Christians, Hindus and Jews in certain countries. (*See graph, p. 48.*)

Religious Fundamentalism Spans the Globe

Fundamentalists from a variety of world religions are playing an increasingly important role in political and social life in countries on nearly every continent. Generally defined as the belief in a literal interpretation of holy texts and a rejection of modernism, fundamentalism is strongest in the Middle East and in the overwhelmingly Christian United States.

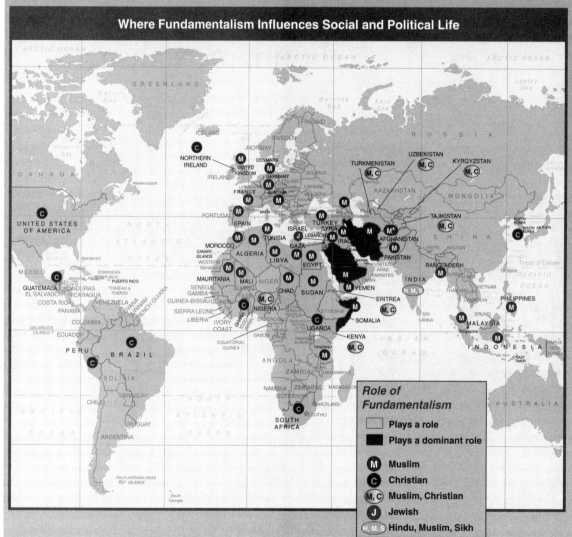

Where Fundamentalism Influences Social and Political Life

* The ultra-conservative Taliban ruled from 1996-2001 and are fighting to regain control.

Sources: U.S. National Counter Terrorism Center, Worldwide Incidents Tracking System, http://wits.nctc.gov; David Cingranelli and David Richards, Cingranelli-Richards (CIRI) Human Rights Dataset, CIRI Human Rights Project, 2007, www.humanrightsdata.org; The Association of Religious Data Archives at Pennsylvania State University, www.thearda.com; Office of the Coordinator for Counterterrorism, Country Reports on Terrorism, United States Department of State, April 2008, www.state.gov/documents/organization/105904.pdf; Peter Katel, "Global Jihad," *CQ Researcher*, Oct. 14, 2005

Islamic fundamentalism is on the rise in Pakistan, Afghanistan, the Palestinian territories and European nations with large, often discontented Muslim immigrant populations — notably the United Kingdom, Germany, Denmark, Spain and France, according to Maajid Nawaz, director of the London-based Quilliam Foundation think tank.

In the United States — the birthplace of Christian fundamentalism and the world's most populous predominantly Christian nation — 90 percent of Americans say they believe in God, and a third believe in a literal interpretation of the Bible.[2] Perhaps the most extreme wing of U.S. Christian fundamentalism are the Christian nationalists, who believe the scriptures "must govern every aspect of public and private life," including government, science, history, culture and relationships, according to author Michelle Goldberg, who has studied the splinter group.[3] She says Christian nationalists are "a significant and highly mobilized minority" of U.S. evangelicals that is gaining influence.[4] TV evangelist Pat Robertson is a leading Christian nationalist and "helped put dominionism — the idea that Christians have a God-given right to rule — at the center of the movement to bring evangelicals into politics," she says.[5]

Although the number of the world's Christians who are fundamentalists is not known, about 20 percent of the 2 billion Christians are conservative evangelicals, according to the World Evangelical Alliance (WEA).[6] Evangelicals reject the "fundamentalist" label, and most do not advocate creating a Christian theocracy, but they are the socially conservative wing of the Christian community, championing "family values" and opposing abortion and gay marriage. In recent decades they have exercised considerable political power on social issues in the United States.

Many Religions Have Fundamentalist Groups

Religious fundamentalism comes in many forms around the globe, and many different groups have emerged to push their own type of fundamentalism — a handful through violence. The term "Islamist" is often used to describe fundamentalist Muslims who believe in a literal interpretation of the Koran and want to implement a strict form of Islam in all aspects of life. Some also want to have Islamic law, or sharia, imposed on their societies.

Christian Fundamentalists

- Lord's Resistance Army (LRA), a rebel group in Uganda that wants to establish a Christian nation — **violent**
- Various strands within the evangelical movement worldwide, including the U.S.-based Christian nationalists, who insist the United States was founded as a Christian nation and believe that all aspects of life (including family, religion, education, government, media, entertainment and business) should be taken over by fundamentalist Christians — **rarely violent**
- Society of St. Pius X, followers of Catholic Archbishop Marcel Lefebvre, who reject the Vatican II modernizing reforms — **nonviolent**

Islamic Fundamentalists

- Jihadists, like al Qaeda and its allies across the Muslim world — **violent***
- Locally focused Islamist groups Hezbollah (Lebanon) and Hamas (Gaza) — **violent**
- Revolutionary Islamists, like Hizb ut-Tahrir (HT), a pan-Islamic Sunni political movement that wants all Muslim countries combined into a unitary Islamic state or caliphate, ruled by Islamic law; has been involved in some coup attempts in Muslim countries and is banned in some states — **sometimes violent**
- Political Islamists, dedicated to the "social and political revivification of Islam" through nonviolent, democratic means. Some factions of the Muslim Brotherhood — the world's largest and oldest international Islamist movement — espouse using peaceful political and educational means to convert Muslim countries into sharia-ruled states, re-establishing the Muslim caliphate. Other factions of the group have endorsed violence from time to time.
- Post-Islamists, such as the AKP, the ruling party in Turkey, which has Islamist roots but has moderated its fundamentalist impulses — **nonviolent**

Judaism

- Haredi, ultra-orthodox Jews — **mostly nonviolent**
- Gush Emunim, aim to reoccupy the biblical Jewish land including Palestinian territories — **sometimes violent**
- Chabad missionaries, who support Jewish communities across the globe — **nonviolent**

Indian subcontinent

- Sikh separatists — **sometimes violent**
- Hindu extremists, anti-Christian/Muslim — **sometimes violent**

* For an extensive list of global jihadist groups, see "Inside the Global Jihadist Network," pp. 860-861, in Peter Katel, "Global Jihad," *CQ Researcher*, Oct. 14, 2005, pp. 857-880.

Sources: *Encyclopedia of Fundamentalism;* "Foreign Terrorist Organizations," U.S. Department of State

Christians Are a Third of the World's Population

About 20 percent of the world's 2 billion Christians are evangelicals or Pentecostals — many of whom are fundamentalists. But statistics on the number of other fundamentalists are not available. Christians and Muslims together make up more than half the world's population.

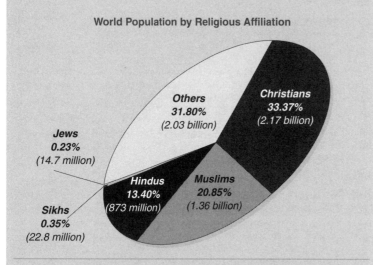

World Population by Religious Affiliation

Others 31.80% (2.03 billion)
Christians 33.37% (2.17 billion)
Jews 0.23% (14.7 million)
Hindus 13.40% (873 million)
Muslims 20.85% (1.36 billion)
Sikhs 0.35% (22.8 million)

Major Concentrations of Religious Denominations
(in millions)

Christians		Hindus		Jews	
United States	247	India	817	United States	5.3
Brazil	170	Nepal	19	Israel/Palestine	5.3
Russia	115	Bangladesh	15	France	0.6
China	101	Indonesia	7	Argentina	0.5
Mexico	100	Sri Lanka	2.5	Canada	0.4

Muslims		Sikhs	
Indonesia	178	India	21
India	155	United Kingdom	0.4
Pakistan	152	Canada	0.3
Bangladesh	136	United States	0.3
Turkey	71	Thailand	0.05

Sources: World Christian Database, Center for the Study of Global Christianity, Gordon-Conwell Theological Seminary, www.worldchristiandatabase.org/wcd/home.asp; John L. Allen Jr., "McCain's choice a nod not only to women, but post-denominationalists," National Catholic Reporter, Aug. 30, 2008, http://ncrcafe.org/node/2073

Christian evangelicalism is booming in Africa — especially in Anglophone countries like Kenya, Uganda, Nigeria, Ghana and South Africa.[7] "We are all — Pentecostals,

Anglicans and Baptists — very active in evangelizing," says James Nkansah, a Ghanaian-born Baptist minister who teaches at the Nairobi Evangelical Graduate School of Theology in Kenya. "Even the Catholics are doing it, although they do not call themselves evangelists." A similar trend is occurring in Latin America, especially in Brazil, Guatemala and Peru among the Pentecostals, who stress the importance of the Holy Spirit, faith healing and "speak in tongues" during services.

Both evangelicals and Catholics in Latin America have adopted the basic tenets of U.S.-style evangelicalism, according to Valdir Steuernagel, a Brazilian evangelical Lutheran pastor who is vice president at World Vision International, a Christian humanitarian agency. Like U.S. evangelicals, South American evangelicals passionately oppose gay marriage and abortion, but they do not use the term "fundamentalist," says Steuernagel, because the word "does not help us to reach out to the grassroots."

South Korea also has a thriving evangelical community. A visiting U.S. journalist describes a recent service for about 1,000 people at a popular Korean evangelical church: "It was part rock concert and part revival meeting," with the lead guitarist, "sometimes jumping up and down on the altar platform" like Mick Jagger, recalls Michael Mosettig.[8] Elsewhere in Asia — the world's most religiously diverse continent — Christian missionaries in China have grown their flocks from fewer than 2 million Christians in 1979 to more than 16 million Protestants alone in 2008.[9] It is unknown how many of those are fundamentalists.

Among the world's 15 million Jews, about 750,000 are ultra-Orthodox "Haredi" Jews who live in strict accordance with Jewish law. Half of them live in Israel, most of the rest in the United States, while there are small pockets in France, Belgium, the United Kingdom, Canada and Australia. About 80,000 live in the Palestinian territories on Israel's West Bank because they believe it is God's will.[10] The flourishing fundamentalist Chabad movement — whose adherents would prefer to live in a Jewish theocracy governed by religious laws — sends missionaries to support isolated Jewish communities in 80 countries.

"We accept the Israeli state, but we would have liked the Torah to be its constitution," says Belgian-based Rabbi Avi Tawil, an Argentine Chabad missionary. "But we are not Zionists, because we do not encourage every Jew to go to Israel. Our philosophy is, 'Don't run away from your own place — make it better.'"

In India, Hindu fundamentalists insist their vast country should be for Hindus only. In late 2008, a sudden upsurge in fundamentalist Hindu attacks against Christian minorities in the state of Orissa in eastern India ended with 60 Christians killed and 50,000 driven from their homes.[11] (*See p. 71.*)

Besides their rejection of Western culture, the faithful embrace fundamentalism out of fear of globalization and consumerism and anger about U.S. action — or inaction — in the Middle East, experts say. Some also believe a strict, religiously oriented government will provide better services than the corrupt, unstable, secular regimes governing their countries. Religious fundamentalism also thrives in societies formerly run by repressive governments. Both Christian and Muslim fundamentalism are spreading in Central Asian republics — particularly Uzbekistan, Kyrgyzstan and Tajikistan — that were once part of the repressive, anti-religious Soviet Union. (*See sidebar, p. 62.*)

Many fundamentalists — such as the Quakers, Amish and Jehovah's Witnesses — oppose violence for any reason. And fundamentalists who call themselves "political Islamists" pursue their goal of the "social and political revivification of Islam" through nonviolent, democratic means, according to Loren Lybarger, an assistant professor of classics and world religions at Ohio University and author of a recent book on Islamism in the Palestinian territories.[12]

In recent years radical Islamic extremists have perpetrated most violence committed by fundamentalists. From January 2004 to July 2008, for instance, Muslim militants killed 20,182 people, while Christian, Jewish and Hindu extremists together killed only 925, according to a U.S. government database.[13] Most of the Muslim attacks were between Sunni and Shia Muslims fighting for political control of Iraq. (*See chart, p. 53.*)[14]

Asmaa Abdol-Hamiz, a Muslim Danish politician and social worker, questions the State Department's statistics. "When Muslims are violent, you always see them identified as Muslims," she points out. "When Christians are violent, you look at the social and psychological reasons."

In addition, according to Radwan Masmoudi, president of the Center for the study of Islam and Democracy, such statistics do not address the "more than one million innocent people" killed in the U.S.-led wars in Iraq and Afghanistan, which, in his view, were instigated due to pressure from Christian fundamentalists in the United States. (*See "At Issue," p. 69.*)

Nevertheless, some radical Islamists see violence as the only way to replace secular governments with theocracies. The world's only Muslim theocracy is in Iran. While conservative Shia clerics exert ultimate control, Iranians do have some political voice, electing a parliament and president. In neighboring Saudi Arabia, the ruling royal family is not clerical but supports the ultra-conservative Sunni Wahhabi sect as the state-sponsored religion. Meanwhile, in the Palestinian territories, "there has been a striking migration from more nationalist groups to more self-consciously religious-nationalist groups," wrote Lybarger.[15]

Experts say Muslim militants recently have set their sights on troubled countries like Somalia and nuclear-armed Pakistan as fertile ground for establishing other Islamic states. Some extremist groups, such as Hizb ut-Tahrir, want to establish a single Islamic theocracy — or caliphate — across the Muslim world, stretching from Indonesia to Morocco.

Still other Muslim fundamentalists living in secular countries such as Britain want their governments to allow Muslims to settle legal disputes in Islamic courts. Islamic law, called sharia, already has been introduced in some areas in Africa, such as northern Nigeria's predominantly Muslim Kano region.[16]

In the Wake of Fundamentalist Violence

Two days of fighting between Christians and fundamentalist Muslims in December destroyed numerous buildings in Jos, Nigeria, (top) and killed more than 300 people. In India's Orissa state, a Christian woman (bottom) searches through the remains of her house, destroyed during attacks by fundamentalist Hindus last October. Sixty Christians were killed and 50,000 driven from their homes.

Muslim extremists are not the only fundamentalists wanting to establish theocracies in their countries. The Jewish Israeli group Kach, for instance, seeks to restore the biblical state of Israel, according to the U.S. State Department's list of foreign terrorist organizations. Hindu fundamentalists want to make India — a secular country with a majority Hindu population that also has many Muslims and Christians — more "Hindu" by promoting traditional Hindu beliefs and customs.

While militant Christian fundamentalist groups are relatively rare, the Lord's Resistance Army (LRA) has led a 20-year campaign to establish a theocracy based on the Ten Commandments in Uganda. The group has abducted hundreds of children and forced them to commit atrocities as soldiers. The group has been blamed for killing hundreds of Ugandans and displacing 2 million people.[17]

In the United States, most Christian fundamentalists are nonviolent, although some have been responsible for sporadic incidents, primarily bombings of abortion clinics. "The irony," says John Green, a senior fellow at the Washington-based Pew Forum on Religion and Public Policy, "is that America is a very violent country where the 'regular' crime rates are actually higher than they are in countries where global jihad is being waged."

Support for violence by Islamic extremists has been declining in the Muslim world in the wake of al Qaeda's bloody anti-Western campaigns, which have killed more Muslims than non-Muslims. U.S. intelligence agencies concluded in November 2008 that al Qaeda "may decay sooner" than previously assumed because of "undeliverable strategic objectives, inability to attract broad-based support and self-destructive actions."[18]

But fundamentalist violence, especially Islamist-inspired, remains a serious threat to world peace. In Iraq, fighting between Sunni and Shia Muslims has killed tens of thousands since 2003 and forced more than 4 million Iraqis to flee their homes. And 20 of the 42 groups on the State Department's list of terrorist organizations are Islamic fundamentalist groups.[19] No Christian or Hindu fundamentalists are included on the terrorist list.

However, Somali-born writer Ayaan Hirsi Ali — herself a target of threats from Islamic fundamentalists — says that while "Christian and Jewish fundamentalists are just as crazy as the Islamists . . . the Islamists are more violent because 99 percent of Muslims think Mohammad is perfect. Christians do not see Jesus in as absolute a way."

As religious fundamentalism continues to thrive around the world, here are some of the key questions experts are grappling with:

Is religious fundamentalism on the rise?

Religious fundamentalism has been on the rise worldwide for 30 years and "remains strong," says Pew's Green.

Fundamentalism is growing throughout the Muslim and Hindu worlds but not in the United States, where its growth has slowed down in recent years, says Martin Marty, a religious history professor at the University of Chicago, who authored a multivolume series on fundamentalism.[20] Christian fundamentalism is strong in Africa and Latin America and is even being exported to industrialized countries. Brazilian Pastor Steuernagel says "evangelical missionaries are going from Brazil, Colombia and Argentina to Northern Hemisphere countries like Spain, Portugal and the United Kingdom. They are going to Asia and Africa too, but there they must combine their missionary activities with aid work."

Islamic fundamentalism, meanwhile, has been growing for decades in the Middle East and Africa. For example, in Egypt the Muslim Brotherhood — which seeks to make all aspects of life in Muslim countries more Islamic, such as by applying sharia law — won 20 percent of the seats in 2005 parliamentary elections — 10 times more than it got in the early 1980s.[21] In Somalia, the Islamist al-Shabaab militia threatens the fragile government.

More moderate Muslims who want to "reform" Islam into a more tolerant, modern religion face an uphill battle, says Iranian-born Shireen Hunter, author of a recent book on reformist voices within Islam. Reformers' Achilles' heel is the fact that "they are often secular and do not understand the Islamic texts as well as the fundamentalists so they cannot compete on the same level," she says.

In Europe, secularism is growing in countries like France and the Netherlands as Christian worship rates plummet, but Turkey has been ruled since 2002 by the Justice and Development Party, which is rooted in political Islam. Though it has vowed to uphold the country's secular constitution, critics say the party harbors a secret fundamentalist agenda, citing as evidence the

Radical Muslims Caused Most Terror Attacks

More than 6,000 religiously motivated terrorist attacks in recent years were perpetrated by radical Muslims — far more than any other group. The attacks by Christians were mostly carried out by the Lord's Resistance Army (LRA) in Uganda.

Religious Attacks, Jan. 1, 2004-June 30, 2008

	Killed	Injured	Incidents
Christian	917	371	101
Muslim*	20,182	43,852	6,180
Jewish	5	28	5
Hindu**	3	7	6
Total	**21,107**	**44,258**	**6,292**

* More than 90 percent of the reported attacks on civilians by Sunni and Shia terrorists were by Sunnis. Does not include the Muslim attacks in Mumbai, India, in December 2008, allegedly carried out by Muslim extremists from Pakistan.

** Uncounted are the Hindu extremist attacks on Christian minorities in late 2008 in India, which left more than 60 Christians dead.

Note: Perpetrators do not always claim responsibility, so attributing blame is sometimes impossible. Also, it is often unclear whether the attackers' motivation is purely political or is, in part, the result of criminality.

Sources: National Counter Terrorism Center's Worldwide Incidents Tracking System, http://wits.nctc.gov; Human Security Research Center, School for International Studies, Simon Fraser University, Vancouver, www.hsrgroup.org.

government's recent relaxation of restrictions on women wearing headscarves at universities.[22]

In Israel, the ultra-Orthodox Jewish population is growing thanks to an extremely high birthrate. Haredi Jews average 7.6 children per woman compared to an average Israeli woman's 2.5 children.[23] And ultra-Orthodox political parties have gained 15 seats in the 120-member Knesset (parliament) since the 1980s, when they had only five.[24] Secularists in the United States saw Christian fundamentalists grow increasingly powerful during the presidency of George W. Bush (2001-2009). Government policies limited access to birth control and abortions, and conservative religious elements in the military began to engage in coercive proselytizing. "From about 2005, I noticed a lot of religious activity: Bible study weeks, a multitude of religious services linked to public holidays that I felt were excessive," says U.S. Army Reserve intelligence officer Laure Williams. In February 2008, she

Moderate Islamist cleric Sheik Sharif Ahmed became Somalia's new president on Jan. 31, raising hope that the country's long war between religious extremists and moderates would soon end. But the hard-line Islamist al-Shabaab militia later took over the central Somali town of Baidoa and began imposing its harsh brand of Islamic law.

AFP/Getty Images/Simon Maina

recalls, she was sent by her superiors to a religious conference called "Strong Bonds," where fundamentalist books advocating sexual abstinence, including one called *Thrill of the Chaste*, were distributed. Williams complained to her superiors but did not get a satisfactory response, she says.

In the battle for believers among Christian denominations, "Conservative evangelicals are doing better than denominations like Methodists and Lutherans, whose liberal ideology is poisonous and causing them to implode," says Tennessee-based Southern Baptist preacher Richard Land. "When you make the Ten Commandments the 'Ten Suggestions,' you've got a problem."

However, the tide may be turning, at least in some quarters, in part because the next generation appears to be less religious than its elders. Some see the November

2008 election of President Barack Obama — who got a lot of his support from young voters in states with large evangelical populations where the leaders had endorsed Obama's opponent — as evidence that the reign of the Christian right is over in the United States.

"The sun may be setting on the political influence of fundamentalist churches," wrote *Salon.com* journalist Mike Madden.[25] In fact, the fastest-growing demographic group in the United States is those who claim no religious affiliation; they make up 16 percent of Americans today, compared to 8 percent in the 1980s.[26]

And in Iran, while the Islamic theocracy is still in charge, "the younger generation is far less religious than the older," says Ahmad Dallal, a professor of Arab and Islamic studies at Georgetown University in Washington, D.C.

Moreover, support for fundamentalist violence — specifically by al Qaeda's global terrorist network — has been declining since 2004.[27] For example, 40 percent of Pakistanis supported suicide bombings in 2004 compared to 5 percent in 2007.[28] Nigeria is an exception: 58 percent of Nigerians in 2007 said they still had confidence in al Qaeda leader Osama bin Laden, who ordered the Sept. 11, 2001, terrorist attacks on the United States. Notably, al Qaeda has not carried out any terrorist attacks in Nigeria. Support for al Qaeda has plummeted in virtually all countries affected by its attacks.[29]

And while the Muslim terrorist group Jemaah Islamiyah remains active in Indonesia — the world's most populous Muslim-majority country — claims of rampant fundamentalism there are overstated, according to a report by the Australian Strategic Policy Institute. The study found that 85 percent of Indonesians oppose the idea of their country becoming an Islamic republic.[30]

Although there has been a "conspicuous cultural flowering of Islam in Indonesia," the report continued, other religions are booming, too. In September 2008, for example, authorities overrode Muslim objections and approved an application for a Christian megachurch that seats more than 4,500 people.[31]

Is religious fundamentalism a reaction to Western permissiveness?

Religious experts disagree about what attracts people to religious fundamentalism, but many say it is a response to rapid modernization and the spread of Western multiculturalism and permissiveness.

"Fundamentalism is a modern reaction against modernity," says Jerusalem-based journalist Gershom Gorenberg. "They react against the idea that the truth is not certain. It's like a new bottle of wine with a label saying 'ancient bottle of wine.' "

Peter Berger, director of the Institute on Culture, Religion and World Affairs at Boston University, says fundamentalism is "an attempt to restore the taken-for-grantedness that has been lost as a result of modernization. We are constantly surrounded by people with other views, other norms, other lifestyles. . . . Some people live with this quite well, but others find it oppressive, and they want to be liberated from the liberation."[32]

Sayyid Qutb, founder of Egypt's Muslim Brotherhood, was repulsed by the sexual permissiveness and consumerism he found in the United States during a visit in 1948.[33] He railed against "this behavior, like animals, which you call 'Free mixing of the sexes'; at this vulgarity which you call 'emancipation of women'; at these unfair and cumbersome laws of marriage and divorce, which are contrary to the demands of practical life. . . . These were the realities of Western life which we encountered."[34]

A similar sentiment was felt by Mujahida, a Palestinian Islamic jihadist who told author Lybarger she worried that her people were losing their soul after the 1993 peace agreement with Israel. "There were bars, nightclubs, loud restaurants serving alcohol, satellite TV beaming American sitcoms, steamy Latin American soap operas [and] casinos in Jericho" to generate tax and employment.[35]

And opposition to abortion and gay rights remain the primary rallying call for U.S. evangelicals. In fact, the late American fundamentalist Baptist preacher Jerry Falwell blamed the 9/11 Islamic terrorist attacks in the United States on pagans, abortionists, feminists and homosexuals who promote an "alternative lifestyle" and want to "secularize America."[36]

In her account of the rise of Christian nationalism, journalist Goldberg said the things Islamic fundamentalists hate most about the West — "its sexual openness, its art, the possibilities for escaping the bonds of family and religion, for inventing one's own life — are what Christian nationalists hate as well."[37]

Pew's Green agrees fundamentalists are irritated by permissive Western culture. "There has always been sin in the world," he says, "but now it seems glorified."

But others say the U.S.-led invasion of Iraq in March 2003 triggered the global surge in violent Islamic militancy. The average annual global death toll between March 2003 to September 2006 from Muslim terrorist attacks jumped 237 percent from the toll between September 2001 to March 2003, according to a study published by Simon Fraser University in Canada.[38]

Moreover, when bin Laden declared war on the United States in a 1998 fatwa, he never mentioned Western culture. Instead, he objected to U.S. military bases in Saudi Arabia, the site of some of Islam's holiest shrines. "The Arabian Peninsula has never — since God made it flat, created its desert and encircled it with seas — been stormed by any forces like the crusader armies now spreading in it like locusts, consuming its riches and destroying its plantations." Bin Laden also railed against Israel — "the Jew's petty state" — and "its occupation of Jerusalem and murder of Muslims there."[39]

Some believe former President George W. Bush's habit of couching the "war on terror" in religious terms helped radical Islamic groups recruit jihadists. *An-Nuur* — a Tanzanian weekly Islamic magazine — noted: "Let us remember President Bush is a saved Christian. He is one of those who believe Islam should be destroyed."[40]

Nawaz, a former member of the revolutionary Islamist Hizb ut-Tahrir political movement, says fundamentalists' motivation varies depending on where they come from. "Some political Islamists are relatively liberal," says the English-born Nawaz. "It's the Saudis that are religiously conservative. The problem is their vision is being exported elsewhere."

Indeed, since oil prices first skyrocketed in the 1970s, the Saudi regime has used its growing oil wealth to build conservative Islamic schools (madrasas) and mosques around the world. As *New York Times* reporter Barbara Crossette noted, "from the austere Faisal mosque in Islamabad, Pakistan — a gift of the Saudis — to the stark Istiqlal mosque of Jakarta, Indonesia, silhouettes of domes and minarets reminiscent of Arab architecture are replacing Asia's once-eclectic mosques, which came in all shapes and sizes."[41]

Pew Forum surveys have found no single, predominant factor motivating people to turn to Islamic fundamentalism. Thirty five percent of Indonesians blame immorality for the growth in Islamic extremism; 40 percent of Lebanese blame U.S. policies and

What Is a Fundamentalist?

Few claim the tarnished label

With the word fundamentalism today conjuring up images of cold-blooded suicide bombers as well as anti-abortion zealots, it is hardly surprising that many religious people don't want to be tarred with the fundamentalist brush.

Yet there was a time when traditionalist-minded Christianity wore it as a badge of honor. Baptist clergyman Curtis Lee Laws coined the term in 1910 in his weekly newspaper *Watchman-Examiner*, when he said fundamentalists were those "who still cling to the great fundamentals and who mean to do battle royal for the faith."[1] Several years earlier, Christian theologians had published a series of pamphlets called "The Fundamentals," which defended traditional belief in the Bible's literal truth against modern ideas such as Charles Darwin's theory of evolution.

Essentially a branch within the larger evangelical movement, the fundamentalists felt that the Christian faith would be strengthened if its fundamental tenets were clearly spelled out. Today, while one in three U.S. Christians considers himself an evangelical, "a small and declining percentage would describe themselves as fundamentalist," says

Southern Baptist minister Richard Land of Nashville, Tenn. "While most evangelicals support fundamentalist principles, it is unfair to compare them to the Islamists who take up arms and kill people," he says.

Although some may see the label "fundamentalist" as synonymous with radical Islamic extremists, Ahmad Dallal, a professor of Arab and Islamic Studies at Georgetown University in Washington, D.C., notes that the Arabic word for fundamental — *usul* — was never used in this context historically. "There is some logic to applying the word 'fundamental' in an Islamic context, however," he says, because "both the Muslim and Christian fundamentalists emphasize a literal interpretation of the holy texts."

Traditionalist Catholics do not call themselves fundamentalists either. But Professor Martin Marty, a religious history professor at the University of Chicago and author of a multivolume series on fundamentalism, says Catholic followers of French Archbishop Marcel Lefebvre are fundamentalists because they refuse to accept reforms introduced by the Second Vatican Council in 1965. But "theocons" — a group of conservative U.S. Catholic intellectuals — are

influence; 39 percent of Moroccans blame poverty and 34 percent of Turks blame a lack of education.[42]

Then there are those who just want to regain their lost power, notes Iranian-born author Hunter. "In Iran, Turkey, Tunisia and Egypt, there was a forced secularization of society," she says. "Religious people lost power — sometimes their jobs, too. They had to develop a new discourse to restore their standing."

Religious fundamentalists in Nigeria are largely motivated by anger at the government for frittering away the country's vast oil supplies through corruption and mismanagement. "When a government fails its people, they turn elsewhere to safeguard themselves and their futures, and in Nigeria . . . they have turned to religion," asserted American religion writer Eliza Griswold.[43]

Many Christian and Muslim leaders preach the "Gospel of prosperity," which encourages Nigerians to better themselves economically. But Kenyan-based Baptist preacher Nkansah says that "while the Gospel

brings good health and prosperity," the message can be taken too far. "There are some people in the Christian movement who are too materialistic."

Nkansah argues that evangelism is growing in Africa because "as human beings we all have needs. When people hear Christ came onto this planet to save them, they tend to respond."

But a journalist in Tajikistan says poverty drives Central Asians to radical groups like the Hizb ut-Tahrir (HT). "In the poor regions, especially the Ferghana Valley on the Kyrgyz-Tajik-Uzbek border, HT is very active," says the journalist, who asks to remain unnamed for fear of reprisals. "Unemployment pushes people to find consolation in something else, and they find it in religion."

Should religious fundamentalists have a greater voice in government?

Religious fundamentalists who have taken the reins of government — in Iran (since 1979), Afghanistan not fundamentalists, he says, because they accept the so-called Vatican II changes. Theocon George Weigel, a fellow at the Ethics and Public Policy Center in Washington, eschews the word "fundamentalist" because he says it is "a term used by secular people with prejudices, which doesn't illuminate very much."

Neither are religious Jews keen on the term. Rabbi Avi Tawil, director of the Brussels office of the Chabad Jewish missionary movement, says "fundamentalism is about forcing people. We don't do that. We strictly respect Jewish law, which says if someone would like to convert then you have to help them."

Jerusalem-based writer Gershom Gorenberg notes that unlike Christians and Muslims, fundamentalist Jews do not typically advocate reading holy texts literally because their tradition has always been to have multiple interpretations. The

Al Qaeda leader Osama bin Laden hails the economic losses suffered by the United States after the Sept. 11, 2001, terrorist attacks. "God ordered us to terrorize the infidels, and we terrorized the infidels," bin Laden's spokesman Suleiman Abu Ghaith said in the same video, which was broadcast soon after the attacks that killed nearly 3,000 people.

AFP/Getty Images/MBC

term is even harder to apply to Hinduism because — unlike Christianity, Judaism and Islam — whose "fundaments" are their holy texts, Hinduism's origins are shrouded in ancient history, and its core elements are difficult to define.[2]

Yet fundamentalists are united in their aversion to modernism.

As Seyyed Hossein Nasr, an Islamic studies professor at George Washington University, noted: "When I was a young boy in Iran, 50 or 60 years ago . . . the word fundamentalism hadn't been invented. Modernism was just coming into the country."[3]

[1] Brenda E. Brasher, *Encyclopedia of Fundamentalism* (2001), p. 50.

[2] *Ibid.*, p. 222.

[3] His comments were made at a Pew Forum discussion, "Between Relativism and Fundamentalism: Is There a Middle Ground?" March 4, 2008, in Washington, D.C., http://pewforum.org/events/?EventID=172.

(1996-2001) and the Gaza Strip (since 2007) — have either supported terrorism or have instituted repressive regimes. Grave human rights abuses have been documented, dissenters tortured, homosexuals hanged, adulterers stoned, music banned and education denied for girls.

Ayaan Hirsi Ali — a Somali-born feminist writer, a former Dutch politician and a fellow at the conservative American Enterprise Institute who has denounced her family's Muslim faith — says fundamentalists should be able to compete for the chance to govern. "But we must tell them a system based on Islamic theology is bad," she says. "The problem is that Muslims cannot criticize their moral guide. Mohammad is more than a pope, he is a king. As a classical liberal, I say not even God is beyond criticism."

However, Danish politician Abdol-Hamid, whose parents are Palestinian, argues that because most countries won't talk to Hamas, the ruling party in the Gaza Strip, because of its terrorist activities, "we failed the Palestinians

by never giving Hamas a chance." In Denmark, she continues, "We have Christian extremists, and I have to accept them." For instance, she explains, the far-right Danish Peoples Party (DPP) wants to ban the wearing of Muslim headscarves in the Danish parliament, and DPP member of parliament Soren Krarup, a Lutheran priest, says the hijab and the Nazi swastika are both symbols of totalitarianism. Abdol-Hamid hopes to become the first hijab-wearing woman elected to the parliament.

After interviewing Hamas's founding father, Sheikh Ahmed Yassin, Lebanese-born journalist Zaki Chebab wrote that Yassin "was confident that . . . Israel would disappear off the map within three decades," a belief he said came from the Koran.[44]

A Christian fundamentalist came to power in Northern Ireland without dire consequences after the Rev. Ian Paisley — the longtime leader of Ulster's Protestants, who established his own church stressing biblical literalism and once called the pope the "antichrist" — ultimately

Many Voice Concern About Islamic Extremism

A majority of respondents in nine out of 10 Western countries were "very" or "somewhat" concerned about Islamic extremism in a 2005 poll. Islam was playing a greater role in politics in five out of six Muslim nations, according to the respondents, and most blamed U.S. policies and poverty for the rise in Islamic extremism.

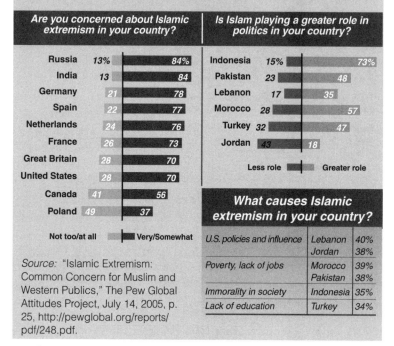

Are you concerned about Islamic extremism in your country?		
Russia	13%	84%
India	13	84
Germany	21	78
Spain	22	77
Netherlands	24	76
France	26	73
Great Britain	28	70
United States	28	70
Canada	41	56
Poland	49	37

Not too/at all — Very/Somewhat

Is Islam playing a greater role in politics in your country?		
Indonesia	15%	73%
Pakistan	23	48
Lebanon	17	35
Morocco	28	57
Turkey	32	47
Jordan	43	18

Less role — Greater role

What causes Islamic extremism in your country?		
U.S. policies and influence	Lebanon	40%
	Jordan	38%
Poverty, lack of jobs	Morocco	39%
	Pakistan	38%
Immorality in society	Indonesia	35%
Lack of education	Turkey	34%

Source: "Islamic Extremism: Common Concern for Muslim and Western Publics," The Pew Global Attitudes Project, July 14, 2005, p. 25, http://pewglobal.org/reports/pdf/248.pdf.

"It is a delicate game," says fundamentalism expert Marty. "If you have a republican system with a secular constitution, then, yes [fundamentalists must be allowed to have a voice], because they have to respect that constitution. But it's very much a case of 'handle with care.'"

Conservative Catholic theologian George Weigel, a senior fellow at the Ethics and Public Policy Center in Washington, says religious people are entitled to be involved in politics, but "they should translate their religiously informed moral convictions into concepts and words that those who don't share their theological commitments can engage and debate. This is called 'democratic courtesy.' It's also political common sense."

Indeed, religious Muslims not only have the right but also the duty to participate in government, according to Rachid Ghannouchi, a Tunisian-born Islamic thinker. Denouncing countries like Tunisia and Algeria that repress Islamic fundamentalism, Ghannouchi said, "the real problem lies in convincing the ruling regimes...of the right of Islamists — just like other political groups — to form political parties, engage in political activities and compete for power or share in power through democratic means."[46]

But ex-Islamist Nawaz warns: "We should not be encouraging Islamists, because every terrorist group has grown out of a nonviolent Islamist group."

Israeli journalist Gorenberg also notes that radical Jewish fundamentalists have repeatedly resorted to violence, citing the case of Baruch Goldstein, a U.S.-born Israeli doctor and supporter of the Kach party who killed 29 Muslims at the tomb of Abraham in Hebron in 1994.

Washington-based Turkish journalist Tulin Daloglu is anxious about her country's future under the ruling Justice and Development Party. "Women are starting to cover their hair in order to get jobs in government," she claims. "The case is not at all proven that Islam and

reconciled his lifelong differences with Northern Irish Catholic leaders and has served amicably with them in government after they offered him political power.[45]

Kenyan-based evangelical Nkansah says "politics is part of life." If a religious person is called into politics in Kenya, he explains, "they should go because that is their vocation." He supports Kenya's model, in which many clergy members, including bishops, enter politics, even though the constitution bans parties based on religion. But evangelical pastor Steuernagel says that in Brazil, religious leaders are increasingly going into politics. "I do not think it is healthy," he says, "but it is happening."

In Central Asia, Islamic parties are only allowed in Tajikistan. But while the Islamic Revival Party has become a significant force there, the party "is neither dangerous nor radical," according to the Tajik journalist, and "does not dream about having a state like Iran."

democracy can live in harmony. Turkey is a swing state" in that regard.

Meanwhile, in some Asian and African countries where the rule of law is weak — Pakistan and Somalia for example — many are clamoring for Islamic law. Often the existing government is so dysfunctional that the quick, decisive administration of Islamic law, or sharia, is attractive. In Pakistan, says British journalist Jason Burke, "the choice between slow, corrupt and expensive state legal systems and the religious alternative — rough and ready though it may be — is not hard." Even educated, relatively wealthy women are demanding sharia, he said.[47]

For example, the Taliban has been able to seize control in Pakistan's Swat region because of "an ineffectual and unresponsive civilian government, coupled with military and security forces that, in the view of furious residents, have willingly allowed the militants to spread terror deep into Pakistan."[48]

BACKGROUND

'Great Awakening'

Christian fundamentalist movements trace their origins to the emergence of Protestantism in 16th-century Europe, when the German monk Martin Luther (1483-1546) urged people to return to the basics of studying the Bible.[49] In 1620 a group of fundamentalist Protestants known as the Pilgrims fleeing persecution in England settled in North America and, along with the Puritans who arrived shortly afterwards, greatly influenced the course of Christianity in New England.

In the 1700s, as science began to threaten religion's preeminence, North Americans launched a Protestant revival known as the "Great Awakening," from which the evangelical movement was born. Revivals held throughout the American colonies between 1739 and 1743, offered evangelical, emotionally charged sermons — often in open-air services before large groups — that stressed the need to forge a personal relationship with Jesus Christ. Leaders in the movement included preachers George Whitfield, Gilbert Tennent and Jonathan Edwards.[50]

A similar revival movement — the Sunday school movement — began in the late 18th century, becoming a

Evangelicals from Uganda's Born Again Church are spiritually moved last August while listening to a sermon by Pastor Robert Kayanja, one of Uganda's most prominent evangelical preachers. While Uganda has long been heavily Christian, many churchgoers have switched from mainstream to Pentecostal sects in recent years.

primary vehicle for evangelism.[51] The term "fundamentalist" originated in the United States when the first of a 12-volume collection of essays called *The Fundamentals* was published in 1910, outlining the core tenets of Christianity.[52] In 1925 fundamentalists were the driving force in the trial of Tennessee schoolteacher John Scopes, who was convicted of breaking a Tennessee law that forbade the teaching of evolution instead of the Bible's version of how the world was created. Even though the fundamentalists won the case, they were lampooned in the popular press, and their credibility and esteem suffered. They withdrew from the limelight and formed their own subculture of churches, Bible colleges, camps and seminaries.

By 1950, the charismatic American Baptist preacher Billy Graham had begun to broaden the fundamentalists' base, and they became masters at harnessing the mass media, especially radio and television. The 1973 U.S. Supreme Court's *Roe v. Wade* ruling legalizing abortion further galvanized evangelicals, leading Baptist preacher Falwell in 1979 to establish the Moral Majority — a conservative political advocacy group.

After his unsuccessful run for president of the United States in 1988, television evangelist and Christian nationalist Robertson formed the Christian Coalition to fight for "family-friendly" policies — specifically policies against homosexuality and abortion. By the mid-1990s

CHRONOLOGY

A.D. 70-1700s *The three great, monotheistic, text-based religions — Christianity, Islam and Judaism — spread worldwide.*

70 Romans destroy the second Jewish temple in Jerusalem, causing Jews to scatter across the globe.

319 Christianity becomes the official religion of the Roman Empire; pagan sacrifices are outlawed.

632 Mohammad dies in Medina, Arabia. . . . Islam begins to spread to the Middle East, Africa, India, Indonesia and Southern Europe.

1730s-40s Evangelical movement is born in the United States in a religious revival known as the "Great Awakening."

1800s-1920s *Fundamentalist impulses are triggered in reaction to scientific developments, modernization and — in the case of Islam — Western colonization.*

1859 British biologist Charles Darwin presents theory of evolution in *On the Origin of Species*, casting doubt on the Bible's account of creation.

1906 African-American evangelist William J. Seymour launches the Azusa Street revival in Los Angeles, sparking the worldwide Pentecostal movement.

1910 American Christian oil magnates Lyman and Milton Stewart commission The Fundamentals, promoting fundamentalist Protestant beliefs that the Bible contains no errors.

1921 Jailed Hindu nationalist Vinayak Damodar Savarkar writes *Hindutva: Who is a Hindu?* — laying the foundation for movements promoting Hindu identity, including the radical Bajrang Dal.

1928 Hasan al-Banna, a schoolteacher in Cairo, Egypt, establishes the Muslim Brotherhood, which calls for all Muslims to make their societies more Islamic.

1940s-1970s *Fundamentalism becomes a significant force in politics and society.*

1948 Israel declares independence, causing millions of Jews — both secular and religious — to return to their spiritual homeland.

1967 Fundamentalist Jews settle in Palestinian territories occupied after the Six-Day War, triggering an explosion in Islamic fundamentalism among disgruntled Arabs.

1973 U.S. Supreme Court's *Roe v. Wade* ruling legalizes abortion, galvanizing Christian fundamentalists into political activism.

1979 Islamists overthrow the Shah of Iran and install the world's first Islamic theocracy in modern times.

1980s-2000s *Fundamentalists increasingly endorse violence to further their goals — especially in the Muslim world.*

1984 Indian government storms a Sikh temple, which Sikh militants had occupied, leading two of Prime Minister Indira Gandhi's Sikh bodyguards to murder her.

1994 American Jewish fundamentalist Baruch Goldstein kills 29 Muslims praying at a mosque in the Palestinian city of Hebron.

Sept. 11, 2001 Al Qaeda Islamists kill nearly 3,000 people by flying hijacked planes into the World Trade Center and Pentagon; a third hijacked plane crashes in Pennsylvania.

2002 Sectarian fighting between Hindus and Muslims in Gujarat, India, kills more than 800 people — mostly Muslims.

2006 Palestinians elect Hamas, a radical Islamic party, to lead the government.

2008 Sixty Christians die after outbreak of fundamentalist Hindu violence against Christians in India. . . . Pakistan-based Islamists launch coordinated attacks in Mumbai, India, killing 164 people. . . . Troops from Congo, Uganda and South Sudan launch ongoing joint offensive to crush Uganda's fundamentalist Lord's Resistance Army. . . . Israel launches major attack on Gaza in effort to weaken Hamas, resulting in 1,300 Palestinian deaths.

the coalition became the most prominent voice in the Christian movement, largely by publishing voter guides on how local politicians voted on specific social issues important to Christian fundamentalists. Many credit the coalition with helping the Republican Party, which had embraced their platform on social issues, to take majority control of the U.S. Congress in the 1994 midterm elections.[53]

Some U.S. fundamentalists segregated themselves from mainstream society — which they saw as immoral — and educated their children at home.[54] A strand of race-based fundamentalism also emerged, called the Christian Identity movement, which claimed the Bible was the history of the white race and that Jews were the biological descendants of Satan. A Christian Reconstructionist movement, led by preacher Mark Rushdoony, emerged as well, advocating local theocracies that would impose biblical law.[55] The reconstructionists oppose government schools and demand that civil disputes be settled in church courts and that taxes be limited to 10 percent of income (based on the tithe). Through its books, the movement has had a significant influence on other Christian political organizations.[56]

Meanwhile, a fundamentalist Catholic movement emerged in Europe after French Archbishop Marcel Lefebvre refused to accept changes introduced by the Vatican in the 1960s, notably saying Mass in languages other than Latin.[57] Other conservative Catholic movements include Opus Dei, founded by Spanish priest Josemaria Escriva in 1928. Today it is based in Rome, has 75,000 members in 50 countries and appeals to well-educated lay Catholics.[58] In the United States, a group of Catholic intellectuals — including Michael Novak, Weigel and Richard John Neuhaus — became known as the "theocons" and allied themselves with Protestant evangelicals in opposing abortion and gay rights.[59]

Bush's presidency was a high point for U.S. evangelicals. Bush announced during the 2000 campaign that he was a "born again" Christian whose favorite philosopher was Jesus Christ — "because he changed my heart." He also told a Texas evangelist that he felt God had chosen him to run for president, and he was accused of "creeping Christianization" of the federal government by establishing an Office for Faith-Based Initiatives, which critics claimed was just a vehicle for channeling tax dollars to conservative Christian groups.[60]

Bush liberally used religious rhetoric — declaring, for example, after the 9/11 attacks that his mission was "to rid the world of evil."[61] He named Missouri Sen. John Ashcroft, a fellow evangelist, as attorney general and filled his administration with Christian conservatives, such as Monica Goodling, a young Justice Department official who vetted candidates for executive appointments by checking their views on moral issues like abortion.[62]

Christian missionaries have been evangelizing — spreading their faith — since the 16th century, but fundamentalist strands have grown increasingly prominent in recent decades. Pentecostalism — which began in 1901 when a Kansas Bible studies student, Agnes Ozman, began "speaking in tongues" — is the dominant form of Protestantism in Latin America.[63] In Guatemala, evangelicalism began to overtake the Roman Catholic Church in the 1980s after Catholicism was seen as too European and elitist.[64] Although Pentecostals usually distinguish themselves from run-of-the-mill fundamentalists, both are part of the evangelical family.

In Africa, Christian fundamentalism developed its strongest base in sub-Saharan regions — particularly Nigeria, triggering rising tensions and sporadic violence between the country's Christian and Muslim populations. U.S. Christian fundamentalists have helped to spread an extreme brand of Christianity to Africa, according to Cedric Mayson, director of the African National Congress' Commission for Religious Affairs, in South Africa. "We are extremely concerned about the support given by the U.S. to the proliferation of right-wing Christian fundamentalist groups in Africa," Mayson wrote, as "they are the major threat to peace and stability in Africa."[65]

Uganda became home to the militant Christian fundamentalist Lord's Resistance Army. Its leader Joseph Kony — known as the "altar boy who grew up to be a guerrilla leader" — has transformed an internal Ugandan power struggle into an international conflict by roaming across Sudan and the Democratic Republic of Congo, kidnapping children en route for use as soldiers after slaughtering their parents.[66]

Patrick Makasi, the LRA's former director of operations, called Kony "a religious man" who "all the time . . . is talking about God. Every time he keeps calling many people to teach them about the legends and about God. That is how he leads people."[67]

Officials in the 'Stans' Uneasy About Islamization

Education is a key battleground

"The crowd in the airport parking lot was jubilant despite the cold, with squealing children, busy concession stands and a tangle of idling cars giving the impression of an eager audience before a rock concert," wrote journalist Sabrina Tavernise of a scene in Dushanbe, the capital of Tajikistan.[1]

"But it was religion, not rock 'n roll, that had drawn so many people," she wrote. The families were there to meet relatives returning from the Hajj — the pilgrimage to Mecca that Muslims strive to undertake at least once in their lifetime. Last year, 5,200 Tajiks participated — 10 times more than in 2000.

The refurbished Juma Mosque in Tashkent, Uzbekistan, reflects Islam's resurgence in Central Asia, where 18 years after the breakup of the former Soviet Union neighboring Iran and Saudi Arabia are exerting their influence on the vast region.

Since gaining independence from the anti-religious Soviet Union, Tajikistan has been re-embracing its Islamic roots, and a Westerner in the country — who asked to remain unnamed — worries the nation of 7.2 million people may adopt an extreme form of Islam. "Every day you can see on our streets more women wearing the veil and more men with beards," he says.

But while many women in Central Asia today do cover themselves from head to toe, it is "extremely rare" for them to cover their faces as well, which was not unusual in pre-Soviet Tajikistan and Uzbekistan, says Martha Brill Olcott, a senior associate at the Carnegie Endowment for International Peace in Washington, who has traveled there frequently since 1975.

The region is undergoing a wide mix of outside influences, not all of them Islamic, Olcott notes. For example, some women have begun wearing the hijab (a headscarf pinned tightly around the face so as to cover the hair) worn by modern Islamic women in the West, while others, notably in Uzbekistan, imitate secular Western fashions such as short skirts and visible belly piercing.

The Westerner in Tajikistan fears that the government's efforts to block the growing Islamization may be having the opposite effect. Government policies "are too severe," he says. "They give long prison sentences to young men and shut down unregistered mosques. This just strengthens people's resolution to resist an unfair system."

Further, he suggests, "If they developed local economies more, people would not think about radical Islam." Without economic development, "Tajikistan could become another Afghanistan or Iran."

Tajikistan, one of the poorer countries in the region, is in the midst of reverse urbanization due to economic decline, with

77 percent of the population now living in rural areas compared to 63 percent in the mid-1980s.[2] A million Tajiks work in Russia.

In neighboring Uzbekistan, the picture is similar. Olcott likens the California-sized nation of 27 million people to an "ineffective police state. There are restrictions, but people can get around them and — more important — they are not afraid to get around them." She says the government's response is erratic: "If you do not draw attention to yourself, you can be an Islamist. But if you preach and open schools or wear very Islamic dress, you can get into trouble."

Christian missionaries are also active in Central Asia. Russian-dubbed broadcasts from U.S. televangelist Pat Robertson are aired throughout the region. According to the Tajikistan-based Westerner, after the 1991 fall of the Soviet Union "Jehovah's Witnesses, Baptists and Adventists came from Russia, Western Europe, South Korea and the United States. The locals were friendly to them because they provided humanitarian aid to poor people." However, authorities in the region have recently clamped down — especially on the Jehovah's Witnesses, he says.[3]

In Kazakhstan authorities have cracked down on Protestants and repressed the Hindu-based Hare Krishnas, while in Kyrgyzstan a new law makes it harder to register religious organizations.[4]

In Kyrgyzstan, the authorities are in a quandary about whether to allow a new political movement, the Union of Muslims, to be set up because bringing Islam into politics violates the constitution. Yet union co-founder Tursunbay Bakir Uulu argues that a moderately Islamic party would help stabilize the country. "Currently Hizb ut-Tahrir is conquering the Issyk-Kul region," he warned. "Religious sects are stepping up their activities. We want moderate Islam, which has nothing to do with anti-religious teaching and which respects values of other world religions, to fill this niche."[5]

The Islamization began in the 1980s, when Soviet President Mikhail Gorbachev eased restrictions on religious worship that had been enforced by the communists for decades. After the Soviet Union's collapse, the relaxation accelerated as the Central Asian republics became independent nations. Muslim missionaries flocked to the region, and conservative Islamic schools, universities and mosques quickly sprang up, many financed by foundations in oil-rich Arab states like Saudi Arabia, where the ultra-fundamentalist Wahhabi Muslim sect is the state-sponsored religion.[6]

Many Central Asians see embracing conservative Islam as a way to define themselves and reject their Russian-dominated communist past. Curiously, their increasing exposure to secular culture through Russia-based migrant Tajik workers appears to be having a Westernizing influence on the society even as Islam is growing: "Five years ago, I could not wear shorts on the street," said the Westerner in Tajikistan. "Now in summer you can see a lot of Tajik men and even girls wearing shorts in the cities, although not in the villages."

The rise of Islam is strongest in Uzbekistan, Tajikistan and Kyrgyzstan, while Turkmenistan and Kazakhstan have stronger secular traditions. Uzbek authorities initially encouraged Islamization, believing it would help strengthen national identity. But by the late 1990s, they were afraid of losing control to radical elements and began repressing militant groups like the Islamic Movement of Uzbekistan and Hizb ut-Tahrir.[7] A jail-break by Islamists in Andijan, the Uzbek capital, in May 2005 triggered violent clashes between government forces and anti-corruption protesters — whom the government claimed were Islamic extremists — resulting in 187 deaths.[8]

Meanwhile, the Saudis are sending Islamic textbooks that promote their own conservative brand of Islam to schools in the region.[9] Saudi-Uzbek ties stretch back to the 1920s, when some Uzbeks fled to Saudi Arabia, according to Olcott.

But Saudi-inspired fundamentalism "is not a major factor" in Turkmenistan yet, says Victoria Clement, an assistant professor of Islamic world history at Western Carolina University, who has lived in Turkmenistan. "There are maybe a few individuals, but the government has not allowed madrasas [Islamic religious schools] since 2003." Even so, she notes, "when I went to the mosques, I saw clerics instructing the kids in the Koran, which technically they should not have been doing [under Turkmen law], but I do not think it was harmful."

Nevertheless, the Turkmen education system is growing more Islamic, Clement says, as new schools follow the model devised by Turkish preacher Fethullah Gulen. "They do not have classes in religion, but they teach a conservative moral code — no drinking, smoking, staying out late at night. I think it is a great alternative to the Islamic madrasas," she says.

Olcott says while the quality of education in the Gulen schools may be good, it is "still very Islamic." Gulen himself now lives in the United States, having left Turkey after being accused of undermining secularism.

The Westerner in Tajikistan notes, however, that in their efforts to stem the growth of radical Islam authorities have a bit of a blind spot when it comes to education. "In most Tajik villages, the children's only teacher is the person who can read the Koran in Arabic, and that is dangerous. The government makes demands about how students look — ties and suits for example — but does not care about what they have in their minds."

Islam Booming in the "Stans"

Several of the nations in Central Asia dubbed "the Stans" are rediscovering their Islamic roots, including Tajikistan and Uzbekistan. The Islamization began in the 1980s, when then Soviet President Mikhail Gorbachev eased restrictions on religious worship.

[1] Sabrina Tavernise, "Independent, Tajiks Revel in Their Faith," *The New York Times*, Jan. 3, 2009, www.nytimes.com/2009/01/04/world/asia/04tajik.html?emc=tnt&tntemail0=y.

[2] *Ibid.*

[3] Felix Corley, "Tajikistan: Jehovah's Witnesses Banned," Forum 18 News Service (Oslo, Norway), Oct. 18, 2007, www.forum18.org/Archive.php?article_id=1036; Felix Corley, "Turkmenistan: Fines, beatings, threats of rape and psychiatric incarceration," Forum 18 News Service (Oslo, Norway), Nov. 25, 2008, www.forum18.org/Archive.php?article_id=1221.

[4] Mushfig Bayram, "Kazakhstan: Police Struggle against Extremism, Separatism and Terrorism — and restaurant meals," Forum 18 News Service, Nov. 21, 2008, www.forum18.org/Archive.php?article_id=1220; and Mushfig Bayram, "Kyrgyzstan: Restrictive Religion Law passes Parliament Unanimously," Forum 18 News Service (Oslo, Norway), Nov. 6, 2008, www.forum18.org/Archive.php?article_id=1215.

[5] "Kyrgyz Experts Say Newly Set Up Union of Muslims Aims for Power," *Delo No* (Kyrgyzstan), BBC Monitoring International Reports, Dec. 9, 2008.

[6] See Martha Brill Olcott and Diora Ziyaeva, "Islam in Uzbekistan: Religious Education and State Ideology," Carnegie Endowment for International Peace, July 2008, www.carnegieendowment.org/publications/index.cfm?fa=view&id=21980&prog=zru.

[7] *Ibid.*, p. 2.

[8] For background, see Kenneth Jost, "Russia and the Former Soviet Republics," *CQ Researcher*, June 17, 2005, pp. 541-564.

[9] *Ibid.*, p. 19.

Getty Images/Chip Somodevilla

Anti-abortion demonstrators carry a statue of the Virgin Mary during the March for Life in Washington, D.C., on Jan. 22, 2009. The rally marked the 35th anniversary of the Supreme Court's landmark *Roe v. Wade* decision legalizing abortion in the United States. Fundamentalist Christians continue to exert significant influence on U.S. policies governing abortion, birth control and gay rights.

Islamic Fundamentalism

Originating in the 7th century with the Prophet Mohammad, Islam considers the Koran sacred both in content and form — meaning it should be read in the original language, Arabic. Muslims also follow the Hadith, Mohammad's more specific instructions on how to live, which were written down after he died. Though Islamic scholars have interpreted both texts for centuries, fundamentalists use the original texts.

The concept of a militant Islamic struggle was developed by scholar Taqi ad-Din Ahmad Ibn Taymiyyah (1263-1328), who called for "holy war" against the conquering, non-Muslim Mongols.[68] The Saudi-born Islamic scholar Muhammed Ibn Abd-al-Wahhab (1703-1792) criticized the Ottoman Empire for corrupting the purity of Islam. The descendants of one of Wahhab's followers, Muhammed Ibn Saud, rule Saudi Arabia today.[69]

Responding to the dominating influence of Western powers that were colonizing the Islamic world at the time, Egyptian schoolteacher Hasan Al-Banna set up the Muslim Brotherhood in 1928 to re-Islamize Egypt. The organization later expanded to other Arab countries and to Sudan.[70] "They copied what the Christian missionaries were doing in Africa by doing social work," notes Islamic studies Professor Dallal. "But they had no

vision for 'the state,' and they paid a price for this because the state ultimately suppressed them."

In the 1950s the extremist group Hizb ut-Tahrir, which advocates a single Islamic state encompassing all predominantly Muslim countries, emerged and spread across the Islamic world. In the mid-1950s, while imprisoned in Egypt by the secular government, the U.S.-educated Egyptian scholar and social reformer Qutb (1906-1966) wrote *Milestones*, his diatribe against the permissiveness of the West, which persuaded many Muslims they needed to get more involved in politics in order to get their governments to make their societies more Islamic. In Pakistan, the politician Sayyid Abul A'la Mawdudi (1903-1979) urged Islamists to restore Islamic law by forming political parties and getting elected to political office, according to Dallal.

The 1973 oil crisis helped to spread conservative Islam by further enriching Saudi Arabia, which set up schools, universities and charities around the world advocating ultraconservative wahhabi Islam. And the 1979 Iranian Revolution — in which the pro-Western Shah Mohammad Reza Pahlavi was deposed in a conservative Shia Muslim revolt led by Ayatollah Ruhollah Khomeini — installed the first Islamic theocracy in the modern era.

In 1991 Islamists were voted into power in Algeria, but the military refused to let them govern, triggering a bloody civil war that the secularists eventually won. In Afghanistan, the ultraconservative Pakistan-sponsored Taliban seized power in 1996 and imposed their strict version of Islamic law — outlawing music, forbidding girls from going to school or leaving their homes without a male relative, forcing women to completely cover their bodies — even their eyes — in public, requiring men to grow beards and destroying all books except the Koran.[71] After the al Qaeda terrorist attacks of 9/11, the United States ousted the Taliban, which had been sheltering bin Laden.

Al Qaeda, a Sunni Muslim group that originated in Saudi Arabia, had been based in Afghanistan since the 1980s, when it helped eject Soviet occupiers, with U.S. aid. But in the 1990s bin Laden redirected his energies against the United States after American troops were stationed in his native Saudi Arabia, home to several sacred Muslim shrines.

After the U.S.-led invasion of Iraq in 2003, al Qaeda urged its followers to switch their attentions to Iraq, which became a magnet for Islamist jihadists. In 2007 al Qaeda attacks in Iraq escalated to such a level of violence — including attacking Shia mosques and repressing local Sunnis — that other Islamic groups like the Muslim Brotherhood repudiated them.[72]

In Europe, meanwhile, beginning in the 1980s the growing Muslim immigrant population began to attach greater importance to its religious identity, and some turned to violence. Algerian extremists set off bombs in Paris subways and trains in 1995-1996; Moroccan-born Islamic terrorists killed 191 people in train bombings in Madrid in 2004; and British-based al Qaeda operatives of mainly Pakistani origin killed 52 people in suicide train and bus bombings in London in 2005.[73] And an al Qaeda cell based in Hamburg, Germany, plotted the 9/11 attacks on the World Trade Center towers and the Pentagon.

The estimated 5 million Muslims in the United States — who are a mix of immigrants and African-Americans — are more moderate than their Western European counterparts.[74] Poverty is likely to have played a role in making European Muslims more radical: Whereas the average income of American Muslims is close to the national average, Muslims' average income lags well behind the national average in Spain, France, Britain and Germany.[75]

Meanwhile, the creation of Israel in 1948 — fiercely opposed by all of its Arab neighbors — and its successive expansions in the Gaza Strip and West Bank have helped to spur Islamic fundamentalism in the region. To Israel's north, the Shia-Muslim Hezbollah group emerged in the 1980s in Lebanon with the goal of destroying Israel and making Lebanon an Islamic state. The Sunni-Muslim group Hamas — an offshoot of the Muslim Brotherhood — won elections in the Palestinian territories in 2006. Hamas, which was launched during the Palestinian uprising against Israel of 1987, has forged strong links with Islamic fundamentalists in Iran and Saudi Arabia.[76]

Fundamentalist Jews

Predating both Islam and Christianity, Judaism takes the Torah and Talmud as its two holy texts and believes that the Prophet Moses received the Ten Commandments — inscribed on stone tablets — from God on Mount Sinai.[77] Fundamentalist Jews believe they are God's chosen people and that God gave them modern-day Israel as their homeland. A defining moment in this narrative is

Members of the ultra-Orthodox Chabad-Lubavitch Jewish fundamentalist movement attend the funeral in Israel of two members of the missionary sect killed last fall during Islamist militant attacks in Mumbai, India.

AFP/Getty Images/Jack Guez

the destruction of the second Jewish Temple in Jerusalem in 70 A.D., which triggered the scattering of Jews throughout the world for nearly 2,000 years.

Jews began returning to their spiritual homeland in significant numbers in the early 1900s with the advent of Zionism — a predominantly secular political movement to establish a Jewish homeland, founded by the Austro-Hungarian journalist Theodor Herzl in the late 19th century in response to rising anti-Semitism in Europe. The migration was accelerated after Nazi Germany began persecuting the Jewish people in the 1930s in a racially motivated campaign that resulted in the Holocaust and the murder of 6 million Jews and millions of others.[78] Today, a third the world's 15 million Jews live in Israel; most of the rest live in the United States, with substantial Jewish communities in France, Argentina and Canada.

Fundamentalist Jews regret that Israel was established as a secular democracy rather than a theocracy. While most Israelis support the secular model, there is a growing minority of ultra-Orthodox (Haredi) Jews for whom the Torah and Talmud form the core of their identity. They try to observe 613 commandments and wear distinctive garb: long black caftans, side curls and hats for men and long-sleeve dresses, hats, wigs and scarves for women.[79] The Haredim dream of building a new Jewish temple in Jerusalem where the old ones stood, which also happens to be the site of the Dome on the Rock — one of Islam's most revered shrines. The fundamentalist

Islamic Fundamentalism Limits Women's Rights

But Muslim women disagree on the religion's impact

As a high official in Saudi Arabia, Ahmed Zaki Yamani crafted many of the kingdom's laws, basing them on Wahhabism, the strict form of Islam that is Saudi Arabia's state religion. Under those laws, Muslim judges "have affirmed women's competence in all civil matters," he has written, but "many of them have reservations regarding her political competence." In fact, he added, one of Islam's holiest texts, the Hadith, "considered deficiency a corollary of femaleness."[1]

Since the 1970s, the Saudis have used their vast oil wealth to spread their ultra-conservative form of Islam throughout the Middle East, North Africa and South and Central Asia, including its controversial view of women as unequal to men. Under Saudi Wahhabism, women cannot vote, drive cars or mix freely with men. They also must have a male guardian make many critical decisions on their behalf, which Human Rights Watch called "the most significant impediment to the realization of women's rights in the kingdom."[2]

The advocacy group added that "the religious establishment has consistently paralyzed any efforts to advance women's rights by applying only the most restrictive provisions of Islamic law, while disregarding more progressive interpretations."[3]

In her autobiography, *Infidel*, Somali-born writer and former Dutch politician Ayaan Hirsi Ali writes about how shocked she was as a young girl when her family moved from Somalia's less conservative Islamic society to Saudi Arabia, where females' lives were much more restricted. "Any girl who goes out unaccompanied is up for grabs," she says.

Raised a Muslim but today an outspoken critic of Islam, Hirsi Ali says Saudi Arabia has had a "horrific" influence on the Muslim world — especially on women. In Africa, she says, religious strictures against women going out in public can have dire consequences, because many women must work outside the home for economic reasons.

While Wahhabism is perhaps the most extreme form of Islam, Hirsi Ali doubts any form of Islam is compatible with women's rights. "Islamic feminism is a contradiction in terms," she says. "Islam means 'submission.' This is double for women: She must appeal to God before anyone else. Yet this same God tells your man he can beat you."

In 2004, Dutch filmmaker Theo Van Gogh was murdered by a Muslim man angered by a film he made portraying violence against women in Islamic societies. Hirsi Ali, then a member of the Dutch parliament, had written the script for the movie, and the assassin left a note on Van Gogh's body threatening her.

She believes the entire philosophical underpinnings of Islam are flawed. For example, she says, she had been taught that Muslim women must wear the veil so they will not corrupt men, yet, "when I came to Europe I could not understand how women were not covered, and yet the men were not jumping on them. Then I saw all it took was to educate boys to exercise self-control. They don't do that in Saudi Arabia, Iran and Pakistan."

But forcing women to cover themselves is not the only way conservative Muslim societies infringe on women's rights. Until recently in Pakistan, rape cases could not be prosecuted unless four pious Muslim men were willing to testify that they had witnessed the attack. Without their testimony the victim could be prosecuted for fornication and alleging a false crime, punishable by stoning, lashing or prison.[4]

Ali's views are not shared by Asmaa Abdol-Hamid, a young, Danish Muslim politician of Palestinian parentage who lived in the United Arab Emirates before moving to Denmark at age 6. Covering oneself, she says, "makes women more equal because there is less focus on her body. . . . When you watch an ad on television, it is always women in bikinis selling the car."

A social worker, local council member representing a left-wing party and former television-show host, Abdol-Hamid is a controversial figure in Denmark. She wears a hijab and refuses to shake hands with men. "I prefer to put my hand on my heart," she explains. "That's just my way of greeting them. It's not that shaking hands is un-Islamic."

She has her own view of Islam's emphasis on female submission. "If women want to obey their husbands, it's up to them." However, "I could not live the Arab lifestyle, where the men beat the women. That's not Islam — it's Arab." In a global study of women's rights, Arab states accounted for 10 of the 19 countries with the lowest ranking for women's equality.[5]

Many fundamentalist Muslims say the freedoms advocated by secular women's-rights advocates disrupt the complementary nature of male and female roles that have been the basis of social unity since the rise of Islam. A Palestinian Islamic jihadist, known only as Mujahida, said women should "return to their natural and [Koran-based] functions as child-bearers, home-keepers and educators of the next generation." She rejects women's-rights advocates who urge women to take their abusive husbands to secular courts.

Muslim "family mediators," she said, were best placed to resolve such disputes.[6]

According to the Washington-based Pew Research Center, more than a third of Jordanians and Egyptians oppose allowing women to choose whether or not to veil, although the percentage is falling.[7] Also on the decline: the number of those who support restrictions prohibiting men and women from working in the same workplace.[8] In Saudi Arabia, such restrictions limit women's employment, because employers must provide separate offices for women.[9]

However, Pew found considerable support in Muslim nations for restricting a woman's right to choose her husband. For example, 55 percent of Pakistanis felt the family, not the woman, should decide.[10]

In Nigeria, Islamic fundamentalism has hurt women's rights, according to Nigerian activist Husseini Abdu. "Although it is difficult separating the Hausa [Nigerian tribe] and Islam patriarchal structure, the reintroduction or politicization of sharia [Islamic law] in northern Nigeria has contributed in reinforcing traditional, religious and cultural prejudices against women," Abdu says.[11] This includes, among other things, the absence of women in the judiciary, discrimination in the standards of evidence in court cases (especially involving adultery) and restrictions in the freedom of association.[12]

Christian countries are not immune from criticism for limiting women's rights. Human Rights Watch found that in Argentina the Catholic Church has had a hand in establishing government policies that restrict women's access to modern contraception, sex education and abortion.[13] And fundamentalist Christian groups have played a significant role in restricting sex education and the availability of birth control and abortion services in the United States.

But while Islamic countries are often criticized for their treatment of women, the world's two most populous Muslim nations, Pakistan and Indonesia, have both elected female leaders in the past — the late Benazir Bhutto in Pakistan and Megawati Sukarnoputri in Indonesia. The world's largest Christian country, the United States, has never had a female president.

Ayaan Hirsi Ali (right), a Somali-born former member of the Dutch parliament, has been threatened with death for her outspoken criticism of Islam's treatment of women in Islam. But Danish Muslim politician and social worker Asmaa Abdol-Hamid (left) attributes repressive gender-based policies in Muslim countries to local culture, not the Koran.

In Iran, an Islamic theocracy since 1979, a debate is raging over whether to allow women to inherit real estate, notes Shireen Hunter, an Iranian-born author and visiting scholar at Georgetown University in Washington. "Reformers are also trying to have the age of [marriage] consent raised from 9 to 16 years. This will take time," she says, because "trying to blend Islam and modernity is hard. It is easier to just say, 'Let's go back to fundamentalism.' "

Yet Abdol-Hamid argues that "fundamentalism does not have to be a bad thing. In Islam, going back to the Koran and Hadith would be good."

Does Hirsi Ali see anything positive about a woman's life in Islamic societies? "I have never seen Muslim women doubt their femininity or sensuality," she says. "Western women question this more. They are less secure. They are always thinking, 'Am I really equal?' "

[1] Ahmed Zaki Yamani, "The Political Competence of Women in Islamic Law," pp. 170-177, in John J. Donohue and John L. Esposito, *Islam in Transition: Muslim Perspectives* (2007).

[2] "Perpetual Minors — Human Rights Abuses Stemming from Male Guardianship and Sex Segregation in Saudi Arabia," Human Rights Watch, April 19, 2008, p. 2, www.hrw.org/en/node/62251/section/1.

[3] *Ibid.*

[4] Karen Foerstel, "Women's Rights," *CQ Global Researcher*, May 2008, p. 118.

[5] *Ibid.*

[6] Loren D. Lybarger, *Identity and Religion in Palestine: The Struggle between Islamism and Secularism in the Occupied Territories* (2007), p. 105.

[7] In Jordan, 37 percent of respondents opposed women being allowed to choose whether to veil, compared to 33 percent in Egypt.

[8] The Pew Global Attitudes Project, "World Publics Welcome Global Trade — But Not Immigration," Pew Research Center, Oct. 4, 2007, p. 51, http://pewglobal.org/reports/pdf/258.pdf.

[9] "Perpetual Minors — Human Rights Abuses Stemming from Male Guardianship and Sex Segregation in Saudi Arabia," *op. cit.*, p. 3.

[10] Pew, *op. cit.*, p. 50.

[11] Carina Tertsakian, "Political Shari'a? Human Rights and Islamic Law in Northern Nigeria," Human Rights Watch, Sept. 21, 2004, p. 63, www.hrw.org/en/reports/2004/09/21/political-shari.

[12] *Ibid.*

[13] See Marianne Mollmann, "Decisions Denied: Women's Access to Contraceptives and Abortion in Argentina," Human Rights Watch, June 14, 2005, www.hrw.org/en/node/11694/section/1.

Haredim are represented by several different political parties in Israel — each with a distinct ideology.

A newer strain of Jewish fundamentalism, the Gush Eminum movement, grew out of the 1967 Israeli-Arab War, in which Israel captured large swathes of Syrian, Egyptian and Jordanian territory. Founded by Rabbi Zvi Yehuda Kook, it believes Israel's victory in that war was a sign that God wanted Jews to settle the captured territories. Israeli authorities initially opposed such actions but did a U-turn in 1977, setting up settlements to create a buffer to protect Israel from hostile Arab neighbors. There now are some 500,000 settlers, and they have become a security headache for the Israeli government, which protects them from attacks from Palestinians who believe they have stolen their land.[80]

Meanwhile the Chabad movement — founded in the 18th century in Lubavitch, Russia, by Rabbi Schoeur Zalman — operates outside of Israel.[81] "They are very religious communities that have become missionaries, even though Jews are not supposed to convert non-Jews, and conversion is very difficult and mostly refused," says Anne Eckstein, a Belgian Jewish journalist. "They are especially active in ex-Soviet countries where the Holocaust and Soviet power wiped out the Jewish community or reduced it to a bare minimum."

Fundamentalism in India

Unlike Christianity, Islam and Judaism, which are monotheistic, Hinduism has thousands of deities representing an absolute power. In addition, it is based not on a single text but the belief that the universe is impersonal and dominated by cosmic energy.[82] Hindu fundamentalism emerged in the early 20th century, partly in reaction to proselytizing by Muslim and Christian missionaries. Some Hindus came to believe that their country needed to be made more Hindu, and that only Hindus could be loyal Indians.

Indian politician Vinayak Damodar Savarkar wrote the book *Hindutva*, the philosophical basis for Hindu fundamentalism.[83] Its cultural pillar is an organization called Vishva Hindu Parishad, founded in 1964, which has had a political wing since the 1980 establishment of the Bharatiya Janata Party, whose leader, Atal Bihari Vajpayee, was prime minister from 1998-2004.

The assertion of Hindu religious identity provoked unease among some of India's 20 million Sikhs, who worship one God and revere the *Adi Granth*, their holy book.[84] Indian Prime Minister Indira Gandhi was murdered in 1984 by two of her Sikh bodyguards in revenge for sending troops to storm the Sikhs' holiest shrine, the Golden Temple, which had been occupied by militant Sikh separatists. Hundreds of people were killed in the botched government operation.[85]

CURRENT SITUATION
Political Battles

Christian conservatives remain a potent force in American political life, even though they appear to have lost some of their political clout with the election of a liberal, pro-choice president and a decidedly more liberal Congress.

In the 2008 U.S. presidential election, evangelicals were briefly buoyed by the nomination of a Christian conservative, Alaska Gov. Sarah Palin, as the Republican vice presidential candidate. But their hopes of having another evangelical in high office were dashed when Palin and her running mate, Sen. John McCain, R-Ariz., were comfortably beaten by their Democratic rivals in November.

Palin was raised as a Pentecostal and regularly attended the Assemblies of God church in Wasilla, Alaska. In a Republican National Convention speech, she stressed the need to govern with a "servant's heart" — which in the evangelical world means Christian humility.[86]

But as details of her religious and political views were revealed, secular Americans began to question her candidacy. Video footage surfaced of her being blessed by a Kenyan pastor in 2005 who prayed for her to be protected from "every form of witchcraft" and for God to "bring finances her way" and to "use her to turn this nation the other way around."[87] Palin was also videotaped speaking at the same church in June 2008, calling a $30 billion gas pipeline project in Alaska "God's will" and the war in Iraq "a task that is from God."[88]

While Palin ultimately may have hurt the Republican ticket more than helping, the passage on Election Day of referenda banning gay marriage in several states — including California — shows that Christian conservatism remains a significant force. And across the American South and heartland, religious conservatives have pressured state and local governments to pass a variety of "family" and faith-based measures, ranging from

Is Islamic fundamentalism more dangerous than Christian fundamentalism?

YES Maajid Nawaz
*Director, Quilliam Foundation,
London, England*

Written for *CQ Global Researcher*, February 2009

While not all Muslim fundamentalists are a threat, certain strands of Muslim fundamentalism are more dangerous than Christian fundamentalism. This is simply a truth we must face up to as Muslims. The first stage of healing is to accept and recognize the sickness within. Until such recognition comes, we are lost.

But if Muslim fundamentalism is only a problem in certain contexts, this is not true of political Islam, or Islamism. Often confused with fundamentalism, political Islamism is a modernist project to politicize religion, rooted in the totalitarian political climate of post-World War I Egypt. But this ideology didn't restrict itself to political goals. Instead, its adherents aspired to create a modern, totalitarian state that was illiberal but not necessarily fundamentalist.

In the 1960s, the Muslim Brotherhood — Egypt's largest Islamist group — failed to impose their non-fundamentalist brand of Islam in Egypt. Instead, they fled to religiously ultra-conservative Saudi Arabia. Here they allied with reactionary fundamentalists. It is from this mix of modernist Islamism and fundamentalism that al Qaeda and jihadist terrorism emerged. It was in Saudi Arabia that Osama bin Laden was taught by Muslim Brotherhood exiles. It was from Saudi Arabia that streams of Muslim fundamentalists traveled to Afghanistan and Pakistan where they fell under the spell of the Egyptian Islamist Abdullah Azzam, another inspiration for bin Laden. The root of the present terrorist danger is the alliance between modernist political Islamists and Muslim fundamentalists.

This global jihadist terrorism — modern in its political ideals and tactics yet medieval in both its religious jurisprudence and justification for violence — is more dangerous than Christian fundamentalism. I believe that such terrorism, far from representing the fundamentals of Islam, is actually un-Islamic. However, a Christian may similarly argue that attacking abortion clinics is un-Christian. We both need to acknowledge the role that religion plays in motivating such individuals.

So, having recognized this problem, how can Muslims tackle it? It is not enough for Muslims to merely take a stand against terrorism and the killing of innocent civilians. This is the very least that should be expected of any decent human being. Muslims must also challenge both conservative fundamentalism and the modern Islamist ideology behind jihadist terrorism. Islamism is to blame, alongside Western support for dictatorships, for the situation we face today.

NO Radwan Masmoudi
*President, Center for the Study of Islam
and Democracy, Washington, D.C.*

Written for *CQ Global Researcher*, February 2009

The term "fundamentalism" can be misleading, because the overwhelming majority of Muslims believe the Koran is the literal word of God and a guide for the individual, the family and society to follow on everything social, political and economic. In a recent Gallup Poll, more than 75 percent of Muslims — from Morocco to Indonesia — said they believe Islamic laws should be either the only source or one of the main sources of laws in their countries. Under a U.S. definition of "fundamentalism," these people would all be considered "fundamentalists."

However, the overwhelming majority of Muslims are peaceful and reject violence and extremism. In the same poll, more than 85 percent of Muslims surveyed said they believe democracy is the best form of government. Thus, they are not interested in imposing their views on others but wish to live according to the teachings of their religion while respecting people of other religions or opinions. Democracy and respect for human rights — including minority rights and women's rights — are essential in any society that respects and practices Islamic values.

It would be a terrible mistake to consider all fundamentalist Muslims a threat to the United States or to mankind. Radical and violent Muslim extremist groups such as al Qaeda and the Taliban represent a tiny minority of all Muslims and a fringe minority of religious (or fundamentalist) Muslims. These extremist groups are a threat both to their own societies and to the West. But they do not represent the majority opinion among religious-based groups that are struggling to build more Islamic societies through peaceful means.

Many Christian fundamentalist groups have resorted to violence, specifically attacks against abortion clinics in the United States. In addition, prominent Christian fundamentalist leaders, such as John Hagee, Pat Robertson and others say Islam is the enemy and have called for the United States to invade Muslim countries like Iraq, Afghanistan and even Iran. These wars have cost the lives of more than 1 million innocent people in these countries and could still cause further deaths and destruction around the world. The devout of all faiths should condemn the killing of innocents and the self-serving labeling of any religion as the "enemy" against which war should be waged. Surely, one — whether Muslim or Christian — can be extremely devout and religious without calling for violence or hoping for Armageddon.

Jewish Settlements Stir Outrage and Support

Left-wing Israelis criticize Israel last December for allowing fundamentalist Jews to build settlements in the Palestinian territories (top). Evangelicals from the U.S.-based Christians United for Israel movement (bottom) support the settlements during a rally in Jerusalem last April. Many analysts say pressure from American fundamentalist Christians led former President George W. Bush, a born-again Christian, to offer unqualified support for Israel and to invade Iraq — policies that have exacerbated U.S.-Muslim relations.

restrictions on access to birth control and abortion to requirements that "intelligent design" be taught in place of or alongside evolution in schools. The laws have triggered ire — and a slew of lawsuits — on the part of groups intent on retaining the Constitution's separation of church and state.[89]

Meanwhile, thousands of conservative Episcopalians in the United States have abandoned their church because of the hierarchy's tolerance of homosexuality and are teaming up with Anglican Protestants in Africa who share their conservative views.[90]

In Latin America, evangelical television preachers are using their fame to launch themselves into politics, notes Dennis Smith, a U.S.-born Presbyterian mission worker who has lived in Guatemala since 1977. He says that in Brazil, Pentecostal preacher Edir Macedo cut a deal with President Luiz Inacio Lula de Silva in which Macedo got to hand-pick the country's vice president. In Guatemala Harold Caballeros, a Pentecostal who preaches that the Mayan Indians there have made a pact with the devil by clinging to their traditional beliefs, is trying to become president, Smith adds.

In Africa, the Somali parliament on Jan. 31 elected a moderate Islamist cleric, Sheik Sharif Ahmed, as the country's new president. The election occurred just as the hard-line Islamist al-Shabaab militia took control of the central Somali town of Baidoa and began imposing its harsh brand of Islamic law there.[91]

Rising Violence

Attacks on Christian minorities in Iraq and India — and efforts to forcibly convert them — have escalated in recent months.

In November militants said to be from the Pakistan-based Lashkar-e-Taiba carried out a meticulously planned attack in Mumbai, India, killing 164 people in a shooting spree that targeted hotels frequented by Western tourists.[92] Ex-Islamist Nawaz says of the group: "I know them well. They want to reconquer India. They see it as being under Hindu occupation now because it was once ruled by Muslim emperors of Turko-Mongol descent. They use the territorial dispute between India and Pakistan over the sovereignty of Kashmir as a pretext for pursuing their global jihad agenda."

Lisa Curtis, a research fellow for South Asia at the Heritage Foundation in Washington, believes that Pakistan is playing a sinister role here. "The Pakistan military's years of support for jihadist groups fighting in Afghanistan and India," she says, is "intensifying linkages between Pakistani homegrown terrorists and al Qaeda."

India's suspicion that forces within the Pakistani government have given Lashkar-e-Taiba a free rein is further straining an already tense relationship between the two nations.

The Lashkar attackers also killed two young Jewish missionaries, Rabbi Gavriel Holtzberg and his wife Rivkah, in an assault on the Chabad center in Mumbai, where they had been based since 2003. While some accuse the Chabad of proselytizing, Rabbi Avi Tawil, who studied with U.S.-born Gavriel Holtzberg for two years in Argentina, insists, "He did not force anyone to accept his philosophy. He was doing social work — working with prisoners for example."

But the Mumbai attacks were not the only violence perpetrated by religious extremists in India last year. Between August and December, members of the paramilitary, right-wing Hindu group Bajrang Dal — using the rallying cry "kill Christians and destroy their institutions" — murdered dozens of Christians, including missionaries and priests, burned 3,000 homes and destroyed more than 130 churches in Orissa state.[93] The attackers were angered at proselytizing by Pentecostal missionaries in the region and tried to force Christians to convert back to Hinduism.[94]

Martha Nussbaum, a professor of law and ethics at the University of Chicago and author of the recent book *The Clash Within: Democracy, Religious Violence and India's Future*, writes that no one should be surprised right-wing Hindus "have embraced ethno-religious cleansing." Since the 1930s, "their movement has insisted that India is for Hindus, and that both Muslims and Christians are foreigners who should have second-class status in the nation."[95]

India's bloodiest religiously based violence in recent years was the slaughter of up to 2,000 Muslim civilians by Hindu mobs in Gujarat state in 2002.[96] A Bajrang Dal leader boasted: "There was this pregnant woman, I slit her open. . . . They shouldn't even be allowed to breed. . . . Whoever they are, women, children, whoever . . . thrash them, slash them, burn the bastards. . . . The idea is, don't keep them alive at all; after that, everything is ours."[97]

In Iraq last fall, in the northern city of Mosul, some 400 Christian families were forced to flee their homes after attacks by Sunni Muslim extremists.[98]

In Nigeria, sectarian violence between Christians and Muslims in the city of Jos spiked again in late November, leaving at least 300 dead in the worst clashes since 2004, when 700 people died. Religious violence in Nigeria tends to break out in the "middle belt" between the Muslim north and the predominantly Christian south.[99]

Then in December Israel launched a massive offensive against the Islamist Hamas government in the Gaza Strip, in response to Hamas's continuous rocket attacks into Israel; at least 1,300 Palestinians died during the 22-day assault. An uneasy truce now exists, but Hamas remains defiant, refusing to accept Israel's right to exist and vowing to fight for the creation of an Islamic Palestinian state in its place.[100]

While most commentators focus on the political dimension of the conflict, Belgian Jewish journalist Anne Eckstein is as concerned about Hamas's religious extremism. "I see nothing in them apart from hatred and death to all who are not Muslims. . . . Jews first but then Christians and everybody else. And those who believe that this is not a war of civilization are very mistaken."

Also in December, troops from, Uganda, southern Sudan and the Democratic Republic of Congo launched a joint offensive to catch Lord's Resistance Army (LRA) leader Kony.[101] The LRA retaliated, massacring hundreds. Kenya-based evangelical Professor Nkansah insists the LRA is "not really religious — no one has ever seen them praying. They are just playing to the Christian communities in Uganda. If they were true Christians, they would not be destroying human life like they are."

Even in areas where religious violence has not broken out, a certain fundamentalist-secular tension exists. In the United Kingdom, for example, a debate has broken out over whether Muslim communities should be allowed to handle family matters — such as divorce and domestic violence cases — in Muslim courts that apply Islamic law. These increasingly common tribunals, despite having no standing under British law, have "become magnets for Muslim women seeking to escape loveless marriages."[102] In Africa, the Tanzanian parliament is having a similar debate, with proponents noting that Kenya, Rwanda and Uganda have had such courts for decades.[103]

In Israel, the majority-secular Jewish population has begun to resent ultra-Orthodox Jewish men who subsist on welfare while immersing themselves in perpetual study of the holy texts. "They claim this is what Jews did in the past, but this is nonsense," says Jerusalem-based journalist Gorenberg, who notes that ultra-Orthodox wives often work outside the home in order to support their very large families. The Haredim are trying to restore ancient Judaism by weaving priestly garments in the traditional way, producing a red heifer using genetic engineering and raising boys in a special compound kept ritually pure for 13 years, says Gorenberg, a fierce critic of fundamentalist Jews.[104]

Many secular Israelis also resent the religious Jews that have settled in the Palestinian territories, arguing they make Muslims hate Israel even more and thus threaten Israel's very security.

OUTLOOK

More of the Same?

Al Qaeda's Egyptian-born chief strategist, Ayman Al-Zawihiri, is very clear about his goal. "The victory of Islam will never take place until a Muslim state is established in the heart of the Islamic world, specifically in the Levant [Eastern Mediterranean], Egypt and the neighboring states of the [Arabian] Peninsula and Iraq."[105]

Former-Islamist Nawaz says such a state would not, as fundamentalists claim, be a return to the past but a modernist creation, having more in common with the totalitarian regimes of 20th-century Europe than with the tolerant Islamic caliphates in the Middle Ages. He thinks Islamists have the greatest chance of seizing power in Egypt and Uzbekistan.

Given the Islamization that she has observed on numerous visits to Uzbekistan, Martha Brill Olcott, a senior associate at the Carnegie Endowment for International Peace in Washington, predicts the country will not remain secular. Because the Muslims there are Sunni, she thinks they will follow an Egyptian or Pakistani model of government.

Georgetown Professor Dallal predicts Iran will remain the world's only theocracy. "I do not think the Iranian model will be replicated," he says. "The religious elite is more institutionalized and entrenched there than elsewhere."

And although young Iranians are more secular than their parents and have been disenchanted with the religious rulers, "We should not assume this is a deep-rooted trend," warns Iranian-born author Hunter. "Look at Arab countries: Forty years ago we thought they were going secular, but not now."

As for Islamist militancy, the signs are mixed. While a Pew survey showed a drop in support for global jihad among Muslims overall, it also found that young Muslims in the United States were more likely to support radical

Islam than their parents. Fifteen percent of 18-29-year-olds thought suicide bombing could be justified compared to just 6 percent of those over 30.[106]

And even if, as some analysts suggest, al Qaeda is faltering, other Islamist groups may thrive, such as Hezbollah in Lebanon, Hamas in Gaza and Pakistan's Lashkar-e-Taiba. They attract popular support because they also provide social services, unlike al Qaeda, whose bloody campaigns have alienated most Muslims.[107]

The Israel-Palestine conflict, intractable as ever, will continue to be grist for the Islamist mill. Bin Laden has urged Muslims to "kill the Americans and their allies [and] to liberate the Al-Aqsa Mosque," which is located on the Temple Mount in Jerusalem that Israel has controlled since 1967.[108]

In the Palestinian territories, "Islamist symbols, discourses and practices have become widely disseminated across the factional spectrum," according to Ohio State's Lybarger, but whether it continues depends on the actions of Israel, the United States and other Arab states toward Palestine, he says.[109] Many observers hope President Obama and his newly-appointed Middle East envoy George Mitchell will be able to broker a peace deal, given Obama's aggressive outreach to the Muslim world.

In the United States, the Christian right is likely to remain strong, even as Obama moves to overhaul Bush's faith-based initiatives. Secularists may ask Obama to prohibit groups receiving government funds from discriminating in hiring based on religious beliefs. "Hiring based on religious affiliation is justified," says Stanley Carlson-Thies, director of the Center for Public Justice in Washington, D.C. "Would you ask a senator not to ask about political ideology when selecting staff? A ban would [be] a sweeping change."[110]

Looking farther afield, Baptist minister Land says "by 2025 the majority of Christians . . . will be African, Latin American and Asian. That is where evangelical Christianity is growing fastest." The fastest-growing Christian denominations are in Nigeria, Sudan, Angola, South Africa, India, China and the Philippines, according to the World Christian Database.[111]

But Kenya's Nkansah doubts that Christian-based political parties will emerge in sub-Saharan Africa. "In North Africa almost everyone is Muslim, so it is easier to have Islamic parties. But here, there is more of a mix, and politicians do not want to create unnecessary tensions."

In Guatemala, American Presbyterian missionary Smith says, "Since neither modernity nor democracy has been able to bring security, the rule of law, social tolerance or broad-based economic development" evangelical television preachers will "continue to have great power for the foreseeable future."

Meanwhile, a glimpse of Asia's future might be found in South Korea. "As dusk turns to dark in this capital city," journalist Mosettig wrote, "the skyline glitters with more than the urban lights of office towers and apartment blocks. From the hills that define Seoul's topography and neighborhoods, it is easy to spot lighted electric crosses. They are among the most visible reminders of just how deeply Christianity shapes South Korea."[112]

NOTES

1. Richard A. Oppel Jr. and Pir Zubair Shah, "In Pakistan, Radio Amplifies Terror of Taliban," *The New York Times*, Jan. 24, 2009, www.nytimes.com/2009/01/25/world/asia/25swat.html?_r=1&scp=1&sq=Taliban%20Pakistan&st=cse.

2. "The U.S. Religious Landscape Survey," Pew Forum on Religion and Public Life, Feb. 25, 2008, p. 170, http://religions.pewforum.org.

3. Michelle Goldberg, *Kingdom Coming: The Rise of Christian Nationalism* (2007), p. 7.

4. *Ibid.*, p. 8.

5. Dominionism, Goldberg notes, is derived from a theocratic sect called Christian Reconstructionism, which advocates replacing American civil law with Old Testament biblical law.

6. See World Evangelical Alliance Web site, www.worldevangelicals.org. For background, see David Masci, "Evangelical Christians," *CQ Researcher*, Sept. 14, 2001, pp. 713-736.

7. Quoted in Eliza Griswold, "God's Country," *The Atlantic*, March 2008, www.theatlantic.com/doc/200803/nigeria.

8. Michael Mossetig, "Among Sea of Glittery Crosses, Christianity Makes Its Mark in South Korea," PBS, Nov. 5, 2007, www.pbs.org/newshour/indepth_coverage/asia/koreas/2007/report_11-05.html. For background, see Alan Greenblatt and Tracey Powell,

"Rise of Megachurches," *CQ Researcher*, Sept. 21, 2007, pp. 769-792.

9. Presentation by Wang Zuoan, China's deputy administrator of religious affairs, Sept. 11, 2008, at the Brookings Institution, Washington, D.C.

10. Estimates provided by Samuel Heilman, Sociology Professor and expert on Jewish fundamentalism at City University of New York.

11. "Christians Attacked in Two States of India" World Evangelical Alliance Web site, Dec. 15, 2008, www.worldevangelicals.org/news/view.htm?id=2277.

12. Loren D. Lybarger, *Identity and Religion in Palestine: The Struggle between Islamism and Secularism in the Occupied Territories* (2007), p. 73.

13. See National Counter Terrorism Center's Worldwide Incidents Tracking System, http://wits.nctc.gov.

14. The Shia, who make up 15 percent of the world's 1.4 billion Muslims, believe only the prophet Mohammad's family and descendants should serve as Muslim leaders (imams). Sunnis — who make up the other 85 percent — believe any Muslim can be an imam. Iran is the world's most Shia-dominated country, while there are also significant Shia communities in Iraq, Turkey, Lebanon, Syria, Kuwait, Bahrain, Saudi Arabia, Yemen, Pakistan and Azerbaijan.

15. Lybarger, *op. cit.*

16. "Sharia stoning for Nigeria man," BBC News, May 17, 2007, http://news.bbc.co.uk/2/hi/africa/6666673.stm.

17. For background, see John Felton, "Child Soldiers," *CQ Global Researcher*, July, 2008.

18. Scott Shane, "Global Forecast by American Intelligence Expects Al Qaeda's Appeal to Falter," *The New York Times*, Nov. 20, 2008, www.nytimes.com/2008/11/21/world/21intel.html?_r=1&emc=tnt&tntemail0=y.

19. "Country Reports on Terrorism," Office of the Coordinator for Counterterrorism, U.S. Department of State, April 2008, www.state.gov/documents/organization/105904.pdf.

20. Martin Marty and R. Scott Appleby, eds., *Fundamentalisms Comprehended* (The Fundamentalism Project), 2004, University of Chicago Press.

21. Source: Talk by Egyptian scholar and human rights activist Saad Eddin Ibrahim, at Woodrow Wilson International Center for Scholars, Washington, D.C., Sept. 8, 2008.

22. For background, see Brian Beary, "Future of Turkey," *CQ Global Researcher*, December 2007.

23. Raja Kamal, "Israel's fundamentalist Jews are multiplying," *The Japan Times*, Aug. 21, 2008, http://search.japantimes.co.jp/cgi-bin/eo20080821a1.html.

24. *Ibid.*

25. Mike Madden, "Sundown on Colorado fundamentalists," *Salon.com*, Nov. 2, 2008, www.salon.com/news/feature/2008/11/03/newlifechurch/index.html?source=rss&aim=/news/feature.

26. Susan Jacoby, "Religion remains fundamental to US politics," *The Times* (London), Oct. 31, 2008, www.timesonline.co.uk/tol/comment/columnists/guest_contributors/article5050685.ece.

27. "Human Security Brief 2007," Human Security Report Project, Simon Fraser University, Canada, May 21, 2008, www.humansecuritybrief.info.

28. "Unfavorable views of Jews and Muslims on the Increase in Europe," Pew Research Center, Sept. 17, 2008, p. 4, http://pewglobal.org/reports/pdf/262.pdf.

29. *Ibid.*

30. Andrew MacIntyre and Douglas E. Ramage, "Seeing Indonesia as a normal country: Implications for Australia," Australian Strategic Policy Institute, May 2008, www.aspi.org.au/publications/publication_details.aspx?ContentID=169&pubtype=5.

31. Michael Sullivan, "Megachurch Symbolizes Indonesia's Tolerance," National Public Radio, Oct. 19, 2008, www.npr.org/templates/story/story.php?storyId=95847081.

32. Comments from Pew Forum on Religion and Public Life discussion, "Between Relativism and Fundamentalism: Is There a Middle Ground?" March 4, 2008, Washington, D.C., http://pewforum.org/events/?EventID=172.

33. Sarah Glazer, "Radical Islam in Europe," *CQ Global Researcher*, November 2007.

34. Sayyid Qutb, *Milestones*, SIME (Studies in Islam and the Middle East) *Journal*, 2005, p. 125, http://majalla.org/books/2005/qutb-nilestone.pdf.

35. Lybarger, *op. cit.*

36. See Goldberg, *op. cit.*, p. 8.

37. *Ibid.*, p. 208.

38. "Human Security Brief 2007," *op. cit.*, p. 19.

39. Osama Bin Laden, "Text of Fatwa Urging Jihad Against Americans," Feb. 23, 1998, in John J. Donohue and John L. Esposito, *Islam in Transition: Muslim Perspectives* (2007), pp. 430-432.

40. "Tanzania: Muslim paper says war on terror guise to fight Islam," BBC Worldwide Monitoring, Aug. 24, 2008 (translation from Swahili of article in Tanzanian weekly Islamic newspaper *An-Nuur*, Aug. 15, 2008).

41. Barbara Crossette, "The World: (Mid) East Meets (Far) East; A Challenge to Asia's Own Style of Islam," *The New York Times*, Dec. 30, 2001.

42. Pew Global Attitudes Project, "Islamic Extremism: Common Concern for Muslim and Western Publics," July 14, 2005, p. 25, http://pewglobal.org/reports/pdf/248.pdf.

43. Griswold, *op. cit.*

44. Zaki Chehab, *Inside Hamas — The Untold Story of the Militant Islamic Movement* (2007), p. 104.

45. Gabriel Almond, Scott Appleby and Emmanuel Sivan, *Strong Religion: The Rise of Fundamentalisms Around the World* (The Fundamentalism Project), The University of Chicago Press, 2003, p. 110.

46. Rachid Ghannouchi, "The Participation of Islamists in a Non-Islamic Government," in Donohue and Esposito, *op. cit.*, pp. 271-278.

47. Jason Burke, "Don't believe myths about sharia law," *The Guardian* (United Kingdom), Feb. 10, 2008, www.guardian.co.uk/world/2008/feb/10/religion.law1. For background, see Robert Kiener, "Crisis in Pakistan" *CQ Global Researcher*, December 2008, pp. 321-348.

48. Oppel and Shah, *op. cit.*

49. Brenda E. Brasher, *Encyclopedia of Fundamentalism* (2001), p. 397.

50. *Ibid.*, pp. 202-204.

51. *Ibid.*, pp. 465-467.

52. *Ibid.*, p. 186.

53. For background, see the following *CQ Researchers*: Kenneth Jost, "Religion and Politics," Oct. 14, 1994,

pp. 889-912; and David Masci, "Religion and Politics," July 30, 2004, pp. 637-660.

54. For background, see Rachel S. Cox, "Home Schooling Debate," *CQ Researcher*, Jan. 17, 2003, pp. 25-48.

55. David Holthouse, "Casting Stones: An Army of radical Christian Reconstructionists is preparing a campaign to convert conservative fundamentalist churches," Southern Law Poverty Center, winter 2005, www.splcenter.org/intel/intelreport/article.jsp?aid=591.

56. Brasher, *op. cit.*, pp. 407-409.

57. *Ibid.*, p. 86.

58. *Ibid.*

59. Adrian Wooldridge, "The Theocons: Secular America Under Siege," *International Herald Tribune*, Sept. 26, 2006, www.iht.com/articles/2006/09/25/opinion/booktue.php.

60. See Paul Harris, "Bush says God chose him to lead his nation," *The Guardian*, Nov. 2, 2003, www.guardian.co.uk/world/2003/nov/02/usa.religion; and Melissa Rogers and E. J. Dionne Jr., "Serving People in Need, Safeguarding Religious Freedom: Recommendations for the New Administration on Partnerships with Faith-Based Organizations," The Brookings Institution, December 2008, www.brookings.edu/papers/2008/12_religion_dionne.aspx. For background, see Sarah Glazer, "Faith-based Initiatives," *CQ Researcher*, May 4, 2001, pp. 377-400.

61. James Carroll, "Religious comfort for bin Laden," *The Boston Globe*, Sept. 15, 2008, www.boston.com/news/nation/articles/2008/09/15/religious_comfort_for_bin_laden.

62. For background, see Dan Eggen and Paul Kane, "Goodling Says She 'Crossed the Line'; Ex-Justice Aide Criticizes Gonzales While Admitting to Basing Hires on Politics," *The Washington Post*, May 24, 2007, p. A1.

63. Brasher, *op. cit.*, p. 154.

64. Almond, Appleby and Sivan, *op. cit.*, p. 171.

65. Cedric Mayson, "Religious Fundamentalism in South Africa," African National Congress Commission for Religious Affairs, January 2007, http://

thebrenthurstfoundation.co.za/Files/terror_talks/Religious%20Fundamentalism%20in%20SA.pdf.

66. Rob Crilly, "Lord's Resistance Army uses truce to rearm and spread its gospel of fear," *The Times* (London), Dec. 16, 2008, www.timesonline.co.uk/tol/news/world/africa/article5348890.ece.

67. *Ibid.*

68. Brasher, *op. cit.*, p. 37.

69. For background, see Peter Katel, "Global Jihad," *CQ Researcher*, Oct. 14, 2005, pp. 857-880.

70. Almond, Appleby and Sivan, *op. cit.*, pp. 177-79.

71. Brasher, *op. cit.*, p. 37.

72. "Human Security Brief 2007," *op. cit.*

73. For background, see Glazer, "Radical Islam in Europe," *op. cit.*

74. "World Christian Database," Center for the Study of Global Christianity, Gordon-Conwell Theological Seminary, www.worldchristiandatabase.org/wcd/home.asp.

75. "Muslim Americans: Middle Class and Mostly Mainstream," Pew Forum on Religion and Public Life, May 22, 2007, p. 4, http://pewforum.org/surveys/muslim-american.

76. Chehab, *op. cit.*, pp. 134-150.

77. Brasher, *op. cit.*, p. 255.

78. "World Christian Database," *op. cit.*

79. Brasher, *op. cit.*, p. 255.

80. *Ibid.*, p. 204.

81. See American Friends of Lubavitch Washington, D.C., www.afldc.org.

82. Brasher, *op. cit.*, p. 222.

83. Almond, Appleby and Sivan, *op. cit.*, pp. 136-139.

84. *Ibid.*, pp. 157-159.

85. *Ibid.*

86. John L. Allen Jr., "McCain's choice a nod not only to women, but post-denominationalists," *National Catholic Reporter*, Aug. 30, 2008, http://ncrcafe.org/node/2073.

87. Garance Burke, "Palin once blessed to be free from witchcraft," The Associated Press, Sept. 25, 2008, http://abcnews.go.com/Politics/wireStory?id=5881256. Video footage at www.youtube.com/watch?v=QIOD5X68lIs.

88. Alexander Schwabe, "Sarah Palin's Religion: God and the Vice-Presidential Candidate," *Spiegel* online, Sept. 10, 2008, www.spiegel.de/international/world/0,1518,577440,00.html. Video footage at www.youtube.com/watch?v=QG1vPYbRB7k.

89. For background see the following *CQ Researchers*: Marcia Clemmitt, "Intelligent Design," July 29, 2005, pp. 637-660; Kenneth Jost and Kathy Koch, "Abortion Showdowns," Sept. 22, 2006, pp. 769-792; Kenneth Jost, "Abortion Debates," March 21, 2003, pp. 249-272; and Marcia Clemmitt, "Birth-control Debate," June 24, 2005, pp. 565-588.

90. See Karla Adam, "Gay Bishop Dispute Dominates Conference; Anglican Event Ends With Leader's Plea," *The Washington Post*, Aug. 4, 2008, p. A8.

91. Jeffrey Gettleman and Mohammed Ibrahim, "Somalis cheer the selection of a moderate Islamist cleric as President," *The New York Times*, Feb. 1, 2009, www.nytimes.com/2009/02/01/world/africa/01somalia.html.

92. Ramola Talwar Badam, "Official: India received intel on Mumbai attacks," The Associated Press, *Denver Post*, Dec. 1, 2008, www.denverpost.com/business/ci_11111305.

93. Somini Sengupta, "Hindu Threat to Christians: Convert or Flee," *The New York Times*, Oct. 12, 2008, www.nytimes.com/2008/10/13/world/asia/13india.html?pagewanted=1&_r=1&sq=Christians percent20India&st=cse&scp=1.

94. "Indian Christians Petition PM for Peace in Orissa at Christmas," World Evangelical Alliance Web site, Dec. 14, 2008, www.worldevangelicals.org/news/view.htm?id=2276.

95. Martha Nussbaum, "Terrorism in India has many faces," *Los Angeles Times*, Nov. 30, 2008, p. A35.

96. For background, see David Masci, "Emerging India," *CQ Researcher*, April 19, 2002, pp. 329-360.

97. Quoted in Nussbaum, *op. cit.*

98. "Iraq: Christians trickling back to their homes in Mosul," IRIN (humanitarian news and analysis service of the U.N. Office for the Coordination of Humanitarian Affairs), Nov. 6, 2008, www.irinnews.org/Report.aspx?ReportId=81317.

99. Ahmed Saka, "Death toll over 300 in Nigerian sectarian violence, The Associated Press, Nov. 29, 2008," www.denverpost.com/breakingnews/ci_11101598.

100. Gilad Shalit, "Hamas rejects Israel's Gaza cease-fire conditions," *Haaretz*, Jan. 28, 2009, www.haaretz.com/hasen/spages/1059593.html.

101. Scott Baldauf, "Africans join forces to fight the LRA," *The Christian Science Monitor*, Dec. 16, 2008, www.csmonitor.com/2008/1217/p06s01-woaf.html.

102. Elaine Sciolino, "Britain Grapples With Role for Islamic Justice," *The New York Times*, Nov. 18, 2008, www.nytimes.com/2008/11/19/world/europe/19shariah.html?_r=1&emc=tnt&tntemail0=y.

103. "Tanzania: Islamic Courts Debate Splits Legislators," *The Citizen* (newsletter, source: Africa News), Aug. 14, 2008.

104. Gershom Gorenberg, "The Temple Institute of Doom, or Hegel Unzipped," *South Jerusalem* (Blog), July 8, 2008, http://southjerusalem.com/2008/07/the-temple-institute-of-doom-or-hegel-unzipped.

105. See Katel, *op. cit.*, p. 859.

106. "Muslim Americans: Middle Class and Mostly Mainstream," *op. cit.*

107. Scott Shane, "Global Forecast by American Intelligence Expects Al Qaeda's Appeal to Falter," *The New York Times*, Nov. 20, 2008, www.nytimes.com/2008/11/21/world/21intel.html?_r1&emc=tnt&tntemail0=y.

108. Bin Laden, *op. cit.*

109. Lybarger, *op. cit.*, p. 244.

110. Carlson-Thies was speaking at a discussion on faith-based initiatives organized by the Brookings Institution in Washington, D.C. on Dec. 5, 2008.

111. See 'fastest growing denominations' category in "World Christian Database," *op. cit.*

112. Michael Mosettig, "Among Sea of Glittery Crosses, Christianity Makes its Mark in South Korea," Nov. 5, 2007, Public Broadcasting Service, www.pbs.org/newshour/indepth_coverage/asia/koreas/2007/report_11-05.html.

BIBLIOGRAPHY

Books

Almond, Gabriel A., Scott Appleby and Emmanuel Sivan, *Strong Religion: The Rise of Fundamentalisms Around the World, University of Chicago Press,* **2003.**
Three history professors synthesize the findings of a five-volume project that looks at 75 forms of religious fundamentalism around the world.

Brasher, Brenda E., ed., *Encyclopedia of Fundamentalism, Routledge,* **2001.**
Academics provide an A-Z on Christian fundamentalism — from its origins in the United States to its spread to other countries and religions.

Donohue, John J., and John L. Esposito, *Islam in Transition: Muslim Perspectives, Oxford University Press,* **2007.**
Essays by Muslim thinkers address key questions, such as the role of women in Islam, the relationship between Islam and democracy and the clash between Islam and the West.

Lybarger, Loren D., *Identity and Religion in Palestine: The Struggle between Islamism and Secularism in the Occupied Territories, Princeton University Press,* **2007.**
A U.S. sociologist who spent several years in the Palestinian territories explores how groups promoting fundamentalist Islam have gradually eclipsed secular nationalism as the dominant political force.

Thomas, Pradip Ninan, *Strong Religion, Zealous Media: Christian Fundamentalism and Communication in India, SAGE Publications,* **2008.**
An associate professor of journalism at the University of Queensland, Australia, examines the influence of U.S televangelists in India and the battle for cultural power between Hindu, Muslim and Christian fundamentalists. SAGE is the publisher of *CQ Global Researcher.*

Articles

"The Palestinians: Split by geography and by politics," *The Economist,* **Feb. 23, 2008, www.economist .com/world/mideast-africa/displaystory.cfm?story_ id=10740648.**
The secular organization Fatah controls the West Bank while the Islamist group Hamas is in charge in Gaza.

Crilly, Rob, "Lord's Resistance Army uses truce to rearm and spread its gospel of fear," *The Times* **(London), Dec. 16, 2008, www.timesonline.co.uk/ tol/news/world/africa/article5348890.ece.**
A violent military campaign led by Ugandan Christian fundamentalists threatens to destabilize the neighboring region.

Griswold, Eliza, "God's Country," *The Atlantic,* **March 2008, pp. 40-56, www.theatlantic.com/ doc/200803/nigeria.**
An author recounts her visit to Nigeria, a deeply religious country where Christian and Muslim clerics compete to grow their flocks, and religious tensions often spill over into violence.

Tavernise, Sabrina, "Independent, Tajiks Revel in Their Faith," *The New York Times,* **Jan. 3, 2009, www.nytimes.com/2009/01/04/world/asia/04tajik .html?emc=tnt&tntemail0=y.**
The Central Asian republic has become increasingly Islamic since its independence from the Soviet Union, with strong influence from Saudi Arabia.

Traynor, Ian, "Denmark's political provocateur: Feminist, socialist, Muslim?" *The Guardian,* **May 16, 2008, www .guardian.co.uk/world/2007/may/16/religion.uk.**
The controversial Danish politician Asmaa Abdol-Hamid, a devout Muslim, hopes to become the first person elected to the Danish parliament to wear the Islamic headscarf.

Reports and Studies

"Islamic Extremism: Common Concern for Muslim and Western Publics," *The Pew Global Attitudes Project,* **July 14, 2005, http://pewglobal.org/reports/pdf/248.pdf.**
A U.S.-based research center surveys public opinion in 17 countries on why Islamic extremism is growing.

MacIntyre, Andrew and Douglas E. Ramage, "Seeing Indonesia as a normal country: Implications for Australia," *Australian Strategic Policy Institute,* **May 2008, www.aspi.org.au/publications/publication_ details.aspx?ContentID=169&pubtype=5.**
Two Australian academics argue that claims of rampant Islamic fundamentalism in Indonesia — the world's most populous Muslim country — are exaggerated.

Mayson, Cedric, "Religious Fundamentalism in South Africa," *African National Congress, Commission for Religious Affairs*, January 2007, http://the-brenthurstfoundation.co.za/Files/terror_talks/Religious%20Fundamentalism%20in%20SA.pdf.
A South African activist blames growing fundamentalism in South Africa on U.S. Christian fundamentalists.

Olcott, Martha Brill and Diora Ziyaeva, "Islam in Uzbekistan: Religious Education and State Ideology," *Carnegie Endowment for International Peace*, July 2008, www.carnegieendowment.org/publications/index.cfm?fa=view&id=21980&prog=zru.
Two academics chart the growth of Islam in the Central Asian republic.

For More Information

Association of Evangelicals in Africa, www.aeafrica.org. A continent-wide coalition of 33 national evangelical alliances and 34 mission agencies that aims to "mobilize and unite" evangelicals in Africa for a "total transformation of our communities."

European Jewish Community Centre, 109 Rue Froissart, 1040 Brussels, Belgium; (32) 2-233-1828; www.ejcc.eu. Office of the Chabad Jewish missionary movement's delegation to the European Union.

Evangelical Graduate School of Theology, N.E.G.S.T., P.O. Box 24686, Karen 00502, Nairobi, Kenya; (254) 020-3002415; www.negst.edu. An Evangelical Christian institution devoted to the study of religion in Africa.

Forum 18 News Service, Postboks 6603, Rodeløkka, N-0502 Oslo, Norway; www.forum18.org. News agency reporting on government-sponsored repression of religion in Central Asia.

Organisation of the Islamic Conference, P.O. Box 178, Jeddah 21411, Saudi Arabia; (966) 690-0001; www.oic-oci.org. Intergovernmental organization with 57 member states, which promotes the interests of the Muslim world.

The Oxford Centre for Hindu Studies, 15 Magdalen St., Oxford OX1 3AE, United Kingdom; (44) (0)1865-304-300; www.ochs.org.uk. Experts in Hindu culture, religion, languages, literature, philosophy, history, arts and society.

Pew Forum on Religion and Public Life, 1615 L St., N.W., Suite 700, Washington, DC 20036-5610; (202) 202-419-4550; http://pewforum.org. Publishes surveys on religiosity, including fundamentalist beliefs, conducted around the world.

World Christian Database, BRILL, P.O. Box 9000, 2300 PA Leiden, The Netherlands; (31) (0)71-53-53-566; www.worldchristiandatabase.org. Provides detailed statistical data on numbers of believers, by religious affiliation; linked to U.S.-based Center for the Study of Global Christianity, Gordon-Conwell Theological Seminary.

World Evangelical Alliance, Suite 1153, 13351 Commerce Parkway, Richmond, BC V6V 2X7 Canada; (1) 604-214-8620; www.worldevangelicals.org. Network for evangelical Christian churches around the world.

Worldwide Incidents Tracking System, National Counter Terrorism Center, University of Maryland, College Park, MD 20742; (301) 405-1000; http://wits.nctc.gov. Provides detailed statistics on religiously inspired terrorist attacks across the world from 2004-2008.

Hate Groups

Is Extremism on the Rise in the United States?

Peter Katel

Richard Poplawski, 22, faces murder charges in Pittsburgh after allegedly shooting and killing three police officers on April 4, 2009. Three weeks earlier, Poplawski, who is tattooed on his chest with what he reportedly described as an "Americanized" Nazi eagle, apparently posted an anti-Semitic message on Stormfront, a neo-Nazi Web site. The number of active hate groups in the nation has jumped to 926 groups — a 50 percent increase — since 2000.

From *CQ Global Researcher*,
May 2009.

Two police officers drove up to a brick house in the middle-class Pittsburgh neighborhood of Stanton Heights on April 4, responding to an emergency call from a woman about her 22-year-old son. "I want him gone," Margaret Poplawski told a 911 operator.[1]

She also said that he had weapons, but the operator failed to share that crucial information with the police, who apparently took no special precautions in responding. Seconds after officers Stephen J. Mayhle and Paul J. Sciullo walked into the house, Richard Poplawski opened fire, killing both men. He then shot and killed Eric Kelly, a policeman outside the house. After a four-hour stand-off, Poplawski surrendered.[2] Hours after that, the Anti-Defamation League and a *Pittsburgh Post-Gazette* reporter traced a March 13 Web post by Poplawski to the neo-Nazi Web site Stormfront.

"The federal government, mainstream media and banking system in these United States are strongly under the influence of — if not completely controlled by — Zionist interest," the post said. "An economic collapse of the financial system is inevitable, bringing with it some degree of civil unrest if not outright balkanization of the continental U.S., civil/revolutionary/racial war. . . . This collapse is likely engineered by the elite Jewish powers that be in order to make for a power and asset grab."[3]

Obsessions with Jewish conspiracy, racial conflict and looming collapse of the political and social order have long festered in the extreme outposts of U.S. political culture. While extremists typically become active in times of social and economic stress, Timothy McVeigh, the Oklahoma City bomber, struck in 1995 during a

Hate Groups Active in All But Two States

Hate groups were active in all the states except Hawaii and Alaska in 2008, according to the Southern Poverty Law Center. Iowa, California, Texas and Mississippi had the largest concentrations of groups.

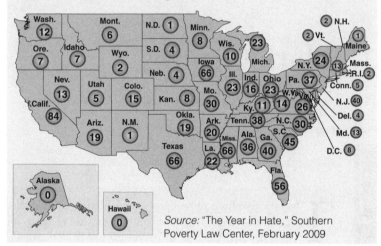

Source: "The Year in Hate," Southern Poverty Law Center, February 2009

relatively tranquil, prosperous time. (*See "Background," p. 90.*)

Now, law enforcement officials warn, dire conditions throughout the country have created a perfect storm of provocations for right-wing extremists. In the midst of fighting two wars, the country is suffering an economic crisis in which more than 5 million people have lost their jobs, while the hypercharged debate over immigration — and the presence of about 12 million illegal immigrants — continues unresolved.[4]

"This is the formula — the formula for hate," says James Cavanaugh, special agent in charge of the Bureau of Alcohol, Tobacco, Firearms and Explosives (ATF) Nashville, Tenn., division and a veteran investigator of far-right extremists. "Everything's aligning for them for hate."

The Department of Homeland Security (DHS) drew a similar conclusion in early April, adding a concern over the apparent rekindling of extremist interest in recruiting disaffected military veterans.

"The consequences of a prolonged economic downturn . . . could create a fertile recruiting environment for right-wing extremists and even result in confrontations

between such groups and government authorities," the DHS said.[5]

The election of Barack Obama as the nation's first African-American president also could prompt an extremist backlash. "Obama is going to be the spark that arouses the white movement," the Detroit-based National Socialist Movement* — considered a leading neo-Nazi organization — announced on its Web site.[6]

But the Obama effect will be negligible among hardcore, violent extremists, says an ex-FBI agent who worked undercover in right-wing terrorist cells in the early 1990s. "They're in an alternative universe," says Mike German, author of the 2007 book *Thinking Like a Terrorist*, and now a policy counselor to the American Civil Liberties Union on national-security issues. "When you believe the American government is the puppet of Israel, whether Obama is the face of the government instead of George W. Bush makes little difference."

Indeed, says Columbia University historian Robert O. Paxton, the Obama victory demonstrated that the country's worrisome conditions haven't sparked widespread rejection of the political system — the classic catalyst for major upsurges of extremism. "Sure, we have a black president, but if the Right were really at the door, we wouldn't have elected him," says Paxton, a leading scholar of European fascism. (*See sidebar, p. 88.*)

Still, Paxton and others caution that the sociopolitical effects of the economic crisis may take a while to hit. The Montgomery, Ala.-based Southern Poverty Law Center (SPLC), which tracks the Ku Klux Klan and other "hate groups," reports activity by 926 such groups in 2008, a 50 percent increase over the number in 2000.[7] "That is a real and a significant rise," says Mark Potok, director of the center's Intelligence Project. Despite the increased activity, the center says there's nothing approaching a mass movement. Moreover, drawing connections between extremist

---

* "Nazi" is the German-language contraction of "National Socialist."

organizations and hate crimes can be complicated.

"Most hate crimes are not committed by members of organized hate groups," says Chip Berlet, senior analyst for Political Research Associates of Somerville, Mass., who has been writing about the far right for a quarter-century. "These groups help promote violence through their aggressive rhetoric. But you're more likely to be victim of hate crime from a neighbor."

For example, three young men from Staten Island, N.Y., charged with beating a 17-year-old Liberian immigrant into a coma on presidential election night last year were not accused of membership in anything more than a neighborhood gang. Their victim, who also lives on Staten Island, said his attackers, one of them Hispanic, yelled "Obama" as they set on him.[8]

Mental health problems also may play a role in such violence, not all of which is inspired by hate rhetoric. In the single deadliest attack on immigrants in memory, Jiverly Wong is charged with killing 13 people (and then himself) at an immigrants' service center in Binghamton, N.Y., one day before Poplawski's alleged killings in Pittsburgh. Eleven of Wong's victims were immigrants, like Wong, a native of Vietnam. Wong left a note in which he complained of his limited English-speaking ability and depicted himself as a victim of police persecution.[9]

But in other recent cases in which immigrants were targeted, the alleged shooters did invoke far-right views. Keith Luke, 22, who lived with his mother in the Boston suburb of Brockton, was charged in January with killing a young woman, shooting and raping her sister and killing a

Dozens of Extremist Events Planned This Summer

More than two dozen gatherings of white extremists will be held around the nation this summer, according to the Anti-Defamation League. Many are being held in traditional Ku Klux Klan (KKK) strongholds in the South and Midwest by groups such as the KKK, National Socialist Movement and Christian Identity organizations.

Upcoming Extremist Events in the United States
(Partial list, May-October)

Location	Event
Russelville, Ala.	Courthouse rally organized by Church of the National Knights of the Ku Klux Klan.
Odessa, Mo.	Paramilitary training organized by the Missouri Militia.
Phoenix, Ariz.	Gathering organized by neo-Nazi Nationalist Coalition Arizona with invitations to members of Stormfront, a hate Web site.
York County, Pa.	Open meeting of the neo-Nazi National Socialist Movement for current and interested members.
Marshall, Texas	KKK cookout on private property organized by the United White Knights.
Las Vegas, Nev.	Workshop organized by Paper Advantage, a sovereign citizen group advocating right-wing anarchy.
Champaign County, Ohio	Paramilitary training with the Unorganized Militia of Champaign County.
Burlington, N.C.	Conference organized by the neo-Confederate North Carolina Chapter of League of the South.
New Albany, Miss.	KKK rally at county courthouse followed by a gathering and cross-burning on private property.
Dawson Springs, Ky.	Annual Nordic Fest white power rally organized by the Imperial Klans of America.
Oceana and Muskegon counties, Mich.	Camping trip organized by the white-supremacist forum White Pride Michigan.
Schell City, Mo.	National youth conference organized by Church of Israel, whose followers practice Christian Identity, a racist and anti-Semitic religion.
Jackson, Miss.	Annual national conference of racist group Council of Conservative Citizens.
Sandpoint, Idaho	Weekend conference organized by America's Promise Ministries, practitioners of Christian Identity.
Pulaski, Tenn.	Weekend gathering commemorating the birthday of Nathan Bedford Forrest — the first KKK leader — including a march, cross-burning and fellowship.

Source: Anti-Defamation League

AP Photo/Bradley C. Bower

Members of the World Order of the Ku Klux Klan, one of scores of Klan groups in the United States, rally on Sept. 2, 2006, at Gettysburg National Military Park, site of a decisive Civil War battle.

72-year-old man — all immigrants from Cape Verde. His planned next stop, police said, was a synagogue. Luke, whom one law enforcement source described as a "recluse," allegedly told police he was "fighting extinction" of white people.[10]

A similar motive was expressed by a 60-year-old Destin, Fla., man charged with killing two Chilean students and wounding three others, all visiting Florida as part of a cultural-exchange program. Shortly before the killings, Dannie Roy Baker had asked a neighbor, "Are you ready for the revolution?" And last summer, he had sent e-mails to Walton County Republican Party officials — who forwarded them to the sheriff's office. One said, in part, "The Washington D.C. Dictators have already confessed to rigging elections in our States for their recruiting dictators to overthrow us with foreign illegals here."[11]

Some immigrant advocates say such comments indicate that extremists are exploiting resentment of immigrants in the hope of stirring up more attacks.

"It is the perfect vehicle, particularly with the decline of the economy," says Eric Ward, national field director of the Chicago-based Center for New Community, which works with immigrants. "With American anxiety building, they hope that they can use immigrants as scapegoats to build their movement."

"Illegals are turning America into a third-world slum," says one of a series of leaflets distributed in the New Haven, Conn., area in early March by North-East White Pride (NEWP). "They come for welfare, or to take our jobs and bring with them drugs, crime and disease."

The NEWP Web site carries the cryptic slogan, "Support your local 1488." In neo-Nazi code, "88" represents "Heil Hitler," words that begin with the eighth letter in the alphabet. And "14" stands for an infamous, 14-word racist dictum: "We must secure the existence of our people and a future for white children." Its author was the late David Lane, a member of the violent neo-Nazi organization, The Order, who died in prison in 2007.[12]

The Order, whose crimes included the murder of a Jewish radio talk-show host in Denver in 1984, sprang from the far-right milieu, as did Oklahoma City bomber McVeigh. And a source of inspiration in both cases was a novel glorifying genocide of Jews and blacks, *The Turner Diaries*, authored by the late William Pierce, founder of the neo-Nazi National Alliance, based in West Virginia.[13]

Pierce's death from cancer in 2002 was one of a series of developments that left a high-level leadership vacuum in the extremist movement. One of those trying to fill it is Billy Roper, 37, chairman of White Revolution, a group based in Russellville, Ark. Roper predicts that racial-ethnic tensions will explode when nonstop immigration from Latin America forces the violent breakup of the United States.

"We're at a pre-revolutionary stage, where it's too late to seek recompense through the political process, and too early to start shooting," Roper says.

As police and scholars monitor extremist groups, here are some of the key questions they are asking:

Could the election of a black president and the nation's economic crisis spark a resurgence of far-right political activity or violence?

The precedent-shattering nature of Obama's presidency could provide enough of a spark for racist reaction, some extremism experts argue. Others question whether that's enough to propel significant numbers of people into outright rejection of the political system, even amid the nation's economic turbulence. They note that organized racist violence against African-Americans was already fading by the late 1960s, after civil rights had become the law of the land.

Nonetheless, at least some members of the far right are reacting. Shortly before the presidential election last year, federal agents charged an 18-year-old from Arkansas and a 20-year-old from Tennessee with plotting to kill Obama after first killing 88 black people, beheading 14 of them — apparent references to the "88" and "14" codes. The father of one of the young men said the alleged plans were no more than "a lot of talk." According to the SPLC, the 20-year-old, Daniel Cowart, had been a probationary member of a new and active skinhead organization, Supreme White Alliance, though the organization said he'd been expelled before the alleged murder plot was conceived.[14]

Michael Barkun, a professor of political science at Syracuse University, says older extremists may see Obama's election as a big favor to their movement. "They tend to think of it as a great recruiting tool," says Barkun, who specializes in political and religious extremism. "My sense is that from their point of view, they would see it as a continuation of what they regard as the marginalization of the white population: 'See, we were right all along.' "

But extremists may be disappointed, Barkun adds, given how the election itself showed the extent to which racism has weakened. Still, the economic crisis offers recruiting possibilities to extremists, because millions of people are suffering its effects. "I would be surprised if the economic crisis did not produce some very nasty side effects," he says, citing the pseudo-constitutional interpretations adopted by the "Posse Comitatus" movement that flourished in the 1980s. "Certainly some of the

fringe legal doctrines on the far right lend themselves to exploitation here."*

Yet for a segment of U.S. society, Obama's election is already stoking the fires of rage, says another veteran observer of the far right. Michael Pitcavage, investigative research director for the Anti-Defamation League, says that immediately after the election, extremists with MySpace pages started including the slogan, "I have no president."

These are anecdotal signs, Pitcavage acknowledges. But he notes that at least one president in the recent past did prompt an extreme reaction on the far right. "The election of Bill Clinton, I would call one of the secondary causes of the resurgence of right-wing extremism in the 1990s," he says. Clinton's Vietnam War draft avoidance and his evasive acknowledgement of past drug use aroused enormous anger among extremists (as among mainstream conservatives), Pitcavage says — sentiments that expanded into conspiracist views after a violent confrontation between federal law enforcement officers and a heavily armed religious group in Waco, Texas.

But at least one right-wing writer on racial issues says that in his circles Obama's presidency has had little effect. "We have always had sophisticated readers whose views of the world are not going to be knocked askew by some unforeseen political event," says Jared Taylor, editor of *American Renaissance*, a magazine based in Oakton, Va., a Washington suburb. "Though I don't wish to detract at all from the symbolic importance of a non-white American president, it's very much part of a predictable sequence. Readers of *American Renaissance* don't necessarily approve of the idea of a black president, but it's not something that wakes them up to something they weren't aware of before." Taylor greeted Obama's election with an article headlined, "Transition to Black Rule?"[15]

Taylor's magazine opposes all anti-discrimination and affirmative-action laws but doesn't espouse violence. However, attendees at the magazine's annual conference in 2006 included well-known extremists, including

---

* Posse Comitatus means "power of the county," a phrase that adherents used to denote the supposed illegitimacy of the federal government. The Posse Comitatus Act of 1878 was passed to remove the U.S. Army from domestic law enforcement activities.

David Duke. When the former Louisiana Klan leader raised the issue of Jewish influence, a Jewish attendee walked out. Taylor later wrote that he would never exclude Jews, adding, "Some people in the [*American Renaissance*] community believe Jewish influence was decisive in destroying the traditional American consensus on race. Others disagree."[16]

As for the ailing economy, Taylor says it hasn't been helping his publication. "We haven't seen any sort of sudden leap in subscribers," he says. "If anything, the economic conditions are bad for us because we're a non-profit organization. We depend on contributions; people have less to contribute."

Still, the sociopolitical consequences of the economic crisis transcend financial problems at individual outposts of right-wing opinion.

Cavanaugh, the longtime ATF official, is one of many who sees the global economic meltdown as an echo of the crisis in Germany's Weimar Republic in the 1920s and early '30s, which enabled Hitler's National Socialist Party to come to power.

"This is how they recruited," says Cavanaugh. "Nazism was founded on blaming the Jewish people for the economic crisis." In today's United States, Cavanaugh hypothesizes, extremists could try to make immigrants the group responsible for the crisis.

But Cavanaugh doubts that Obama's presidency, per se, appeals to extremists. Many of them view the conventional political system as the "Zionist Occupation Government," or ZOG. "The president has done more to unite the country — you can feel it," he says. "That doesn't help hate groups get stronger. They can rail against any president, and they have. Any president to them is the head of ZOG."

Are immigrants in danger from extremist violence?

Black Americans have been far and away the major targets of 20th-century extremist violence.

But organized racist violence, from cross-burning to bombings, lynching and assassinations of black community leaders or white civil rights supporters, has faded from the scene, despite episodic hate crimes that sometimes target Jews as well as blacks.

Obama's election demonstrated the extent to which the black-white divide in American life has narrowed.

Indeed, when it comes to arousing political passion, race has been replaced by illegal immigrants, who number an estimated 12 million in the United States.[17]

"Black people are here, and no one is talking about deporting them," says Taylor of *American Renaissance*. "Immigration is a current and constant flow that is, in my view, only building up problems and conflict for the future, and that's a process that could be stopped. That is why it is much more a subject of political interest."

Bipartisan congressional legislation to provide a "path to citizenship" — restrictionists prefer the term "amnesty" — for illegal immigrants stalled during the George W. Bush administration.

Aside from mainstream political debate over the solution to illegal immigration, immigrant advocates say they're worried that violence against Latinos — or brown-skinned people thought to be immigrants — is on the rise. According to the most recent FBI statistics, there were 830 attacks of various kinds on Hispanics in 2007. By comparison, 1,087 attacks were made on homosexuals, who are also frequent targets of hate speech.[18] In 2000, there were 557 reported attacks on Hispanics compared to 1,075 attacks against homosexuals.[19]

But both conservatives and liberals take a dim view of those FBI statistics. Marcus Epstein, a conservative anti-immigration activist who draws a line between his views and those of extremists, criticizes the FBI categorization scheme for using the ethnic term "Hispanic" only for crime victims. Offenders, by contrast, are listed only by race, so "Hispanic" doesn't appear. The result, he argues, is that statistics are skewed so that any Hispanic hate-crime perpetrators are statistically invisible. (The FBI says that the agency "does not agree" that its categories "render the data invalid for statistical purposes.")

Epstein, executive director of The American Cause, a conservative organization founded by political commentator and immigration restrictionist Pat Buchanan, is particularly concerned about illegal immigrants with criminal records committing further crimes. He cites the case of Manuel Cazares, who turned himself in to police in Hannibal, Mo., in March, saying he'd killed an ex-girlfriend and a male friend of hers. Cazares, a Mexican citizen, was in the United States illegally, but police hadn't checked his status, although federal immigration authorities said his name wasn't in their database.[20] "Illegal immigrants kill American citizens — that greatly outweighs the number of crimes committed by right-wing white Americans against immigrants," Epstein says.

He cites a statistical analysis by Edwin S. Rubinstein, an economic consultant in Indianapolis and former senior fellow at the Hudson Institute, a conservative think tank. Writing on the VDare Web site, which opposes immigration except by white people, Rubinstein, while acknowledging that national data on crime and ethnicity are thin, extrapolated from California and national figures to estimate that in any given year illegal immigrants "could kill 2.6 persons per day across the U.S."[21]

The vast majority of violent crimes fall within city and state jurisdictions, not all of which collect data on ethnicity. Mark Hugo Lopez, associate director of the Pew Hispanic Center, and co-author of a recent report on Hispanics and federal crime, says, "The reason that we used federal statistics is that those are the cleanest data." The Pew study showed that 70 percent of Latino offenders were non-citizens, and that 3.1 percent of all Latino convicts were sentenced for crimes of violence, including murder.[22]

Others warn that hate crime statistics aren't reliable where immigrants are concerned. "One of the difficulties we have is getting certain communities to report hate crime," said Brian Levin, director of the Center for the Study of Hate and Extremism at California State University, San Bernardino. Illegal immigrants are especially reluctant, says Levin, in a widely shared observation.[23]

In any event, supercharged rhetoric from extremists has ratcheted up fear among immigrants and their advocates. Ward of the Center for New Community says that recent episodes of violence targeting immigrants reflect a general hostility toward immigrants that he's sensing on the street. For example, he says, following an organizational meeting in Wilmer, Minn., a town in the meat-processing factory belt of the upper Midwest, "A woman pulls up behind a car of our field people and starts screaming racial epithets."

Though of little significance by itself, Ward says it reflects an atmosphere that reminds him of "things I saw in the 1980s and '90s during the rise of the neo-Nazi movement." He adds, "These kinds of incidents, I would call an early warning of what will be the backlash."

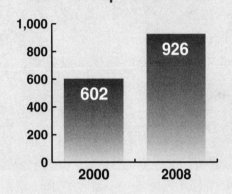

Hate Groups Increased by 50 Percent

The number of hate groups active in the United States — including skinheads, the Ku Klux Klan and neo-Nazis — increased more than a 50 percent from 2000 to 2008.

Hate Groups in the U.S.

Source: "The Year in Hate," Southern Poverty Law Center, February 2009

Immigration restrictionists argue that their political foes are whipping up passions in an effort to create the appearance that Latinos in general and immigrants in particular face growing danger.

"All hate crimes are abominable, and any decent person would oppose them no matter who the target is," says Ira Mehlman, national media director of the Federation for American Immigration Reform (FAIR), which advocates restricting immigration. "But they are hyping the statistics on hate crimes. Hate crimes against Hispanics are much fewer in actual number than attacks against gays or Jews, who represent much smaller percentages of the population."

Hard-core extremists still rank Jews as their No. 1 enemy, says Pitcavage at the Anti-Defamation League, which was formed in 1913 to combat anti-Semitism.

Some of the most horrific hate crimes are committed by "mission offenders," or mentally ill people who hear

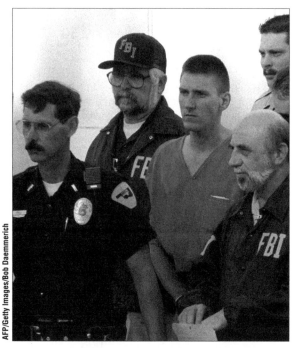

AFP/Getty Images/Bob Daemmerich

Oklahoma City bomber Timothy McVeigh, a neo-Nazi Army veteran, was executed in 2001 for killing 168 people, including 19 children, at the Murrah Federal Building. While extremists typically become active in times of social and economic stress, McVeigh struck in 1995 during a period of relative tranquility.

voices that command them to rid the world of a particular set of evildoers, Pitcavage says.[24] While they may target Jews — and those are often some of the most horrific crimes — "racial/ethnic targets" — including Latinos and immigrants in general — do run a risk from hate crime because they're "more visually identifiable and thus better targets of opportunity," he says.

Is right-wing and extremist speech encouraging hate crimes?

The killings of three Pittsburgh police officers intensified the ongoing debate over free speech and its consequences. Some liberal and left-wing commentators saw Richard Poplawski's horrific crime as an outgrowth, at least in part, of the far-right conspiracy culture that had influenced him, judging by his Web posts. In addition, they say, his rage had been stoked by conservative commentators. Still, the Pittsburgh reporter who helped trace those posts argues in the online magazine *Slate*

that the writings reveal more inner torment than ideology.

Journalist Dennis B. Roddy wrote that Poplawski also posted to a non-racist conspiracist site — Infowars, which describes its politics as libertarian. There, the alleged cop-killer "seemed to find . . . a bridge from the near-mainstream to a level of paranoid obsession in search of an explanation for his life's failures. For that, one does not need an ideology, just an inclination."[25]

Nevertheless, Roddy acknowledges that Poplawski complained on Infowars that the site neglected race. Other commentators insisted that Poplawski's posts follow a clear pattern. "Poplawski's black-helicopter and anti-Semitic ravings put him at the outer edge of the right," wrote Gary Kamiya, executive editor of *Salon*, a liberal online magazine. "But his paranoid fear that Obama was going to take away his AK-47 is mainstream among conservatives . . . fomented by the NRA and echoed by right-wing commentators from Lou Dobbs to Limbaugh."[26]

Kamiya doesn't propose limiting free-speech rights, but he does argue that extreme anti-Obama and gun-rights rhetoric is bound to produce more episodes like the Pittsburgh shootings.

The U.S. Supreme Court has ruled that even hate-filled racist speechmaking is protected by the First Amendment. In 1969, the court overturned the terrorism-advocacy conviction of an Ohio Ku Klux Klan leader who'd given a speech including a call to "send the Jews back to Israel," and to "bury the niggers." The court ruled unanimously that the government may not "forbid or proscribe advocacy of the use of force or of law violation except where such advocacy is directed to inciting or producing imminent lawless action."[27]

Worries about the effects of vicious and hyperbolic speech haven't only come from the left. In 2005, Freedom House, a human-rights advocacy organization then headed by former CIA director James Woolsey, a neo-conservative, issued a report accusing the government of Saudi Arabia of disseminating "hate propaganda" — targeting Christians, Jews and converts from Islam — in religious publications sent to mosques.[28]

In late March, an American writer of Arab descent wrote on a conservative Web site that American Muslims who get their news on satellite TV from the Middle East are, in effect, being brainwashed into a pro-jihadist

CHRONOLOGY

1930s-1960s *Attempts to create U.S. versions of European fascism fail, but far-right activists build smaller organizations after World War II.*

1934 The Rev. Charles Coughlin ("Father Coughlin") gains a nationwide following for denouncing President Franklin D. Roosevelt and Jews.

1941-1942 Coughlin is forced off the air and another far-right leader, William Dudley Pelley, is sent to prison for sedition.

1952 Anti-Semite Gerald L.K. Smith fails to persuade the Republican Party to link communism and Jews.

1958 John Birch Society is founded.

1963 Ku Klux Klan members bomb a black church in Birmingham, Ala., killing four young girls.

1967 American neo-Nazi leader George Lincoln Rockwell is killed by an embittered ex-aide.

1969 U.S. Supreme Court rules that a Ku Klux Klan leader's denunciations of blacks and Jews are constitutionally protected speech.

1970s-1980s *Anti-government and anti-Jewish organizations turn to violence, most often against police officers, who are seen as agents of the "Zionist Occupation Government."*

1971 Anti-Semitic, Christian Identity activist William Potter Gale formulates the doctrine underlying the radically anti-government Posse Comitatus movement, which by 1976 has at least 12,000 members, according to the FBI.

1978 *The Turner Diaries,* a genocide fantasy by neo-Nazi William Pierce (pseudonym: Andrew Macdonald), is published.

1983 Posse Comitatus leader Gordon Kahl kills two federal marshals in North Dakota, later dies in a shootout with federal agents in Arkansas.

1984 The Order, a small extremist group inspired by *The Turner Diaries,* murders a Jewish talk-show host in Denver

who had denounced racism. . . . The group's founder is killed later in a shootout in Washington state.

1988 A federal jury in Arkansas acquits 14 right-wing extremists, including five members of The Order, on sedition and other charges.

1990s *Extremist violence climaxes in armed confrontations with federal officers.*

1992 An attempt to arrest survivalist and Christian Identity proponent Randy Weaver in Ruby Ridge, Idaho, ends with the deaths of a marshal and Weaver's wife and young son.

1993 Extremist leaders gather in Estes Park, Colo., to plan cooperation with less-threatening groups. . . . Federal siege of the Branch Davidian religious-cult compound in Waco, Texas, leads to deaths of more than 80 people. . . . Extremists depict Ruby Ridge and Waco as examples of government ruthlessness. . . . Outrage at government helps build "patriot militia" movement.

1995 Timothy McVeigh, an extremist military veteran inspired by *The Turner Diaries,* detonates truck bomb outside Alfred P. Murrah Federal Building in Oklahoma City, killing 168 people. . . . Militia membership declines.

2000s *Extremist movement erodes further following 9/11 attacks and the removal of major figures by death and imprisonment, but economic crisis ignites fears of a resurgence.*

2001 McVeigh executed by lethal injection.

2004 Richard Butler, influential leader of Idaho-based "Aryan Nations," dies of natural causes.

2005 Up-and-coming extremist leader Matthew Hale, founder of World Church of the Creator, is sentenced to 40 years for conspiracy to commit murder.

2009 Homeland Security Department warns extremists could exploit economic crisis as a recruiting opportunity; critics blast department for focusing on ideology rather than criminal acts.

Concern About Extremism Rising in Europe

Czech Republic expels ex-Klan leader David Duke.

Memories of the horrific consequences of far-right extremism remain strong in Europe. Yet nearly 65 years after the Nazi Holocaust, the extreme right has been gaining ground in parts of the continent, prompting worries that ultranationalism is on the upswing.

"The possibilities for a rise of the far right in the light of the financial and economic crisis are there," Anton Pelinka, a professor of politics at Central European University in Budapest, Hungary, told *The Guardian*, a leading British newspaper.[1]

So far, the European far right is advancing further — at the polls and in the expansion of illegal neo-Nazi organizations — than in the United States. But the gains by European extremists give heart to their U.S. counterparts, who have long maintained ties to Europe, though some European governments do their best to disrupt the relationships. In April, the Czech Republic expelled ex-Ku Klux Klan leader David Duke, a neo-Nazi, who had been invited by an extremist Czech group to lecture in Prague and Brno.

And the British government announced in early May that it had barred — among others — Don Black, founder of the Stormfront Web site, from entering Britain.

Duke's aborted visit notwithstanding, transatlantic ties may have frayed somewhat following the 2002 death of William Pierce. The American neo-Nazi leader had been traveling regularly to Europe for meetings, says Mark Potok, Intelligence Project director at the Southern Poverty Law Center, in Birmingham, Ala. But even if Duke fails to take Pierce's place as emissary to the Old World, American far-right Web sites commonly post links to extremist Web sites and news from Europe.[2]

The news is plentiful. In Austria, the country's two far-right parties together won 29 percent of the vote in national parliamentary elections last year. One of the parties had been founded by Jörg Haider, who died in a car crash shortly after the vote. Haider made his brand of politics a major force by combining salesmanship, xenophobic opposition to immigration and appeals to the Nazi heritage of Adolf Hitler's country of birth.

Haider had been forced to quit as a provincial governor in 1991 (he was reelected in 1999) after praising Hitler's "orderly employment program." And in 1995 he praised Waffen SS veterans as "decent men of character who remained faithful to their ideals."[3]

Indicators of the growing strength of extremism extend into Germany and Britain as well as parts of the former Soviet bloc. In Russia, where ultranationalist groups, including neo-Nazis, are part of the political landscape, there were at least 85 systematic killings of migrant workers from Central Asia, as well as others seen as ethnically non-Slavic, in 2008, according to the Sova Center, a Moscow-based hate crime-monitoring group. The victims included a migrant worker from Tajikistan who was beheaded. Human-rights advocates who denounce these killings have been threatened with death themselves.[4]

Violence isn't limited to Russia. In late 2008, the police chief of Passau, a Bavarian town with a strong neo-Nazi presence, was stabbed following his 2008 order to open the grave of a former Nazi who had been buried with an illegal Swastika flag.[5]

The attack took place against a backdrop of increasing violence by German neo-Nazi organizations. A German newspaper reported that violent crimes originating in the extremist right increased by 15 percent during the first 10 months of 2008. And a government research institute reported that a greater segment of male teenagers — 5

outlook. "We must never underestimate the power of hate propaganda," Nonie Darwish wrote, "because, quite simply, it works. Believe it or not, if you grow up hearing 'holy' cursing day in and day out, it can feel and sound normal, justified and even good." Darwish didn't call for banning the transmissions.[29]

But the more explosive recent disputes over speech arise from the immigration conflict. At the center of the controversy are radio and cable TV commentators like Glenn Beck, of Fox News. In June 2007 (before he had joined Fox), Beck read on his radio program a fake commercial for "Mexinol" — a fuel produced from the bodies of illegal immigrants from Mexico.[30]

"We have a butt load of illegal aliens in our country," said the fake ad, which was ascribed to Evil Conservative Industries. "With Mexinol, your raw materials come to you in a seemingly never-ending stream." Beck tried to put some distance between himself and the ad's authors, percent — were involved in neo-Nazi groups than in mainstream politics in 2007-2008. In formerly communist-ruled eastern Germany, nearly 10 percent of youths participated in far-right groups.[6]

Throughout Western Europe, the enormous growth of immigrant populations, especially from Muslim countries, has provided the biggest boost to right-wing parties — from traditional conservative groups to neo-Nazis — over the past two decades.

However, the European far right's growth isn't uniform. In France, Jean-Marie Le Pen, an apologist for Nazism who was one of the pioneers of the post-World War II extreme right, saw his National Front party win only 4.3 percent of the vote in parliamentary elections in 2007.[7] Analysts said that President Nicolas Sarkozy effectively co-opted Le Pen's anti-immigration politics, though without the ethnic and religious extremism. In 2002, Le Pen had finished second in the first round of the presidential race.[8]

Le Pen's counterparts across the English Channel are showing more success. The British National Party (BNP) is seen by some British politicians as likely to win the most votes in an election in June to choose European Parliament representatives. BNP leaders portray their party as defending the country against non-white immigrants. Pro-immigrant policies "have made white Britons second-class citizens," the party says.[9]

Meanwhile, the BNP is trying to play down its historic anti-Semitism. Party leader Nick Griffin wrote in 2007 that taking an "Islamophobic" stance "is going to produce on average much better media coverage than . . . banging on about 'Jewish power.' "[10]

That purely tactical shift notwithstanding, others in the European political world argue that old-school anti-Semitism is flourishing — on the left as well as the right — often disguised as opposition to Israeli policies.

"The extravagant rhetoric of the demagogic left and right is gaining ground, and the most obvious manifestation is the return of anti-Semitism as an organizing ideology," Dennis

MacShane, a Labor Party member of Parliament, wrote in late 2008. "As jobs are lost and welfare becomes meaner and leaner, the politics of blaming the outsider can only grow."[11]

[1] Quoted in Kate Connolly, "Haider is our Lady Di," *The Guardian*, Oct. 18, 2008, p. A29. For background, see Sarah Glazer, "Anti-Semitism in Europe," *CQ Global Researcher*, June 2008, pp. 149-181.

[2] For example, see "Stormfront forum, international," www.stormfront.org/forum/forumdisplay.php?f=18; Kinism.net — Occidental Christianity, http://kinism.net/; The French Connection, http://iamthewitness.com/; League of American Patriots, http://leagueap.org/wordpress/?page_id=17.

[3] Quoted in Matt Schudel, "Jörg Haider; Politician Made Far-Right Party a Force in Austria," *The Washington Post*, Oct. 12, 2008, p. C8.

[4] Michael Schwirtz, "Migrant Worker Decapitated in Russia," *The New York Times*, Dec. 13, 2008; Luke Harding, "Putin's worst nightmare: Their mission is to cleanse Russia of its ethnic 'occupiers,'" *The Observer* magazine (U.K.), Feb. 8, 2009, p. 32; "Neo-Nazis threaten to murder journalists in Russia," Committee to Protect Journalists, Feb. 11, 2009, http://cpj.org/2009/02/neo-nazis-threaten-to-murder-journalists-in-russia.php.

[5] Nicholas Kulish, "Ancient City's Nazi Past Seeps Out After Stabbing," *The New York Times*, Feb. 12, 2009, p. A18; "Police Chief Long Reviled by NPD Leadership," *Spiegel Online International*, Dec. 19, 2008, www.spiegel.de/international/germany/0,1518,597645,00.html.

[6] *Ibid.*; and "German teens drawn to neo-Nazi groups — study," Reuters, March 17, 2009, http://in.reuters.com/article/worldNews/idINIndia-38554620090317.

[7] In 2008, Le Pen was fined 10,000 Euros for having called the Nazi occupation of France "not especially inhumane, even if there were a number of blunders." Quoted in "Le Pen fined over war comments," *The Irish Times* (Reuters), Feb. 9, 2008, p. A10.

[8] Adam Sage, "Hard-up National Front sells office to immigrants," *The Times* (London), Aug. 13, 2008, p. A37.

[9] "Immigration — time to say ENOUGH!" British National Party, undated, http://bnp.org.uk/policies-2/immigration. Also see Andrew Grice, "The BNP are now a bigger threat than ever," *The Independent* (London), April 10, 2009, p. A12.

[10] Quoted in Matthew Taylor, "BNP seeks to bury antisemitism and gain Jewish votes in Islamophobic campaign," *The Guardian* (London), April 10, 2008, p. A17.

[11] Denis MacShane, "Europe's Jewish Problem," *Newsweek*, International Edition, Dec. 15, 2008, p. 0.

though in a lighthearted tone. "I don't even know if that's conservative," he said, chuckling. "That would be . . . psychotic, perhaps?"[31]

Last year, Janet Murguía, president of the National Council of La Raza, a leading Hispanic organization, cited the segment in calling for cable channels "to clean up the rhetoric of their own commentators or take them out of their chairs." She argued that much of the

commentary by the hosts and some of their guests spurred anti-immigrant violence. "When free speech transforms into hate speech, we've got to draw that line."[32]

Epstein of The American Cause argues that Murguía is trying to "muzzle" free speech. The painful reality of the nation's economic crisis, not anti-immigrant rhetoric — explains more about anti-Hispanic violence, he says.

"People should not hold an individual Hispanic responsible for the fact that wages are being depressed, and they can't get a job, or that schools are overcrowded, that there's an increase in crime in the community," he says. "But that's the reason these people are lashing out. In the few cases of [violence], they're responding to the problems that immigration causes."

Epstein argues that mainstream anti-immigration groups like FAIR provide a legitimate channel for citizens who favor limiting immigration to express their views. "If there was no one actually speaking for Americans, they're going to turn to more radical groups," he says. Epstein posts his writings on the VDare Web site but says he doesn't agree with all the views expressed on the site, some of them virulently racist.

A recent post by one contributor argued that hiring people of South Asian Indian ancestry guaranteed "corruption and ethnocentric discrimination"; another opined that hiring better public school teachers and firing less competent ones means "on net, firing blacks and hiring whites." And another contributor attacked "the cultural pollution of our 'entertainment industry,' which promotes diversity, multiculturalism and white demoralization."[33]

Cavanaugh of the ATF says he's aware that a constellation of legal organizations provide moral backing even for violent actions. In the civil rights days, such groups were known as the "white-collar Klan," he says. "They support people who will go out and do those things."

But, he says, free speech is free speech. "Is it illegal?" he asks rhetorically. "It's awful, but I can't do much about awful, and I shouldn't be able to."

BACKGROUND

Building Movements

Extreme-right political movements reached their peak in the 1930s in the United States and abroad. Adolf Hitler came to power in Germany in 1933. Benito Mussolini, originator of the term "fascism," who began his rule of Italy in 1922, soon forged an alliance with Hitler. Other far-right movements triumphed in Central Europe. The United States, of course, never succumbed to totalitarian rule. But the American extreme right did command a sizable sector of public opinion.[34]

As in Germany and elsewhere (though not to a major extent in Italy), hatred of Jews played a key role in the American right-wing mobilization, with communists and socialists close behind on the enemies list.

Henry Ford, founder of the Ford Motor Co., actively spread anti-Semitism in the 1920s, using a newspaper that he owned, the *Dearborn Independent*, to publish vast amounts of propaganda about a Jewish plot for world domination.[35]

After Ford withdrew from public anti-Semitic activity under pressure from Jewish organizations and the U.S. government, other leaders emerged. Gerald L. K. Smith, a minister and failed political candidate allied with hate-mongers, denounced President Franklin D. Roosevelt (FDR) and African-Americans as well as Jews. William Dudley Pelley led the fascist Silver Legion — the "Silver Shirts" — which dedicated itself mainly to marches and other publicity-seeking events expressing hatred of Jews, blacks and all minorities.

The Rev. Charles Coughlin, a Roman Catholic priest, known as "Father Coughlin," soared to national prominence and influence through radio broadcasts from his church outside Detroit. At first a Roosevelt supporter, the "radio priest" by 1934 was raging against FDR and the Jews, on whom he blamed the Great Depression.

After the United States entered World War II, the Catholic Church and the federal government forced Coughlin off the air. Pelley was convicted in 1942 of sedition and intent to cause insurrection in the military and was sentenced to 15 years in prison.[36]

By war's end, American fascism as a mass movement had ended. But a core of committed activists kept the far right alive, spurred on by the Cold War against the Soviet Union and the first stirrings of the civil rights movement.[37]

As public opposition to communism grew, Smith preached that Jews and communists were one and the same and that the Holocaust never occurred.

The founding of the John Birch Society in 1958 marked the reemergence of conspiratorial, far-right views — minus the anti-Semitism — in respectable society. Birch Society doctrine viewed the United Nations as a communist organization. Founder Robert Welch, an executive in his brother's candy company, went further, calling President Dwight D. Eisenhower "a dedicated, conscious agent of the communist conspiracy."[38]

Welch's wild accusation stoked outrage in the political mainstream. President Harry S. Truman reportedly called the Birch Society "the Ku Klux Klan, without nightshirts."[39]

By the mid-1960s, the Klan — established in 1866 in Pulaski, Tenn. — had become the center of extremist resistance to the civil rights movement. Members and ex-members of the secret organization carried out some of the most notorious crimes of the era, including the 1963 bombing of the 16th Street Baptist Church in Birmingham, Ala., in which four young girls were killed; the assassination of civil rights leader Medgar Evers in Jackson, Miss., that same year; the murder of three civil rights workers in 1964 in Neshoba County, Miss.; and the killing of another civil rights worker in Alabama in 1965.[40]

Anti-civil rights violence ebbed after enactment of the Voting Rights Act in 1965. From then on, the extremist right became steadily more influenced by neo-Nazism. George Lincoln Rockwell, founder of the American Nazi Party, pioneered the white-nationalist trend. The former Navy pilot and World War II veteran was shot and killed by a dismissed follower in 1967.[41]

Rockwell had been a mentor to William Pierce, a former university physics professor who in 1974 founded the National Alliance, which became a major influence in the extremist right. Pierce became nationally notorious in the 1990s as author of *The Turner Diaries*, which laid out a scenario for white genocide of blacks, Jews and "race traitors" — a process led by a secret brotherhood known as The Order, which sets events in motion by blowing up FBI headquarters with a truck bomb.

The first open sign of a Klan-Nazi nexus was the 1979 killing in broad daylight of five Communist Workers Party members who were starting an anti-Klan march in Greensboro, N.C., in 1979.

Fighting and Killing

Less visibly, another trend was under way. An extreme anti-government and anti-Jewish movement founded in 1971 by William Potter Gale began growing, especially in the West and Midwest. Posse Comitatus ("Power of the County") held that the federal government was constitutionally illegitimate. For example, county justices of the peace held legal supremacy over the U.S. Supreme Court, according to Posse ideology, and federal currency was invalid.[42]

Posse alienation went far deeper. An anti-Semitic religious doctrine known as "Christian Identity" exerted deep influence on many Posse leaders and members, including Gale (despite his own definitively proved Jewish descent, which he denied). The doctrine — rejected by all mainstream Christian denominations — holds that white people are the genuine descendants of the Biblical Hebrews. That is, they're God's chosen people, and Jews and blacks are the devil's spawn. By 1976, the FBI estimated Posse membership at 12,000 to 50,000, not including sympathizers.

Posse Comitatus played a major role in raising the level of far-right extremism to a fever pitch in the last two decades of the 20th century. In the early 1980s, economic crisis gripped the Farm Belt, bringing a wave of foreclosures. The Posse launched a major recruiting drive, preaching that Jewish bankers were to blame for the falling grain prices and land values that brought many farmers to ruin.

One Posse tactic was to flood the federal court system with amateur lawsuits to cancel farmers' loan obligations, on the grounds that the loans were illegal. When authorities enforced foreclosure orders, trouble sometimes erupted.

In 1983, Gordon Kahl, a Christian Identity Posse activist who had served a prison term for tax evasion, killed two federal marshals following a meeting to recruit members in North Dakota. Kahl fled and was killed three months later in a gunfight with federal agents in Arkansas. Kahl became a martyr in extremist circles.

An almost identical episode took place the next year near Cairo, Neb., when a Posse sympathizer, Arthur Kirk, was killed in a shootout with state police officers serving foreclosure papers. Before the shooting started, Kirk denounced Jews, bankers and the Israeli intelligence agency, Mossad, to officers trying to get him to surrender.[43]

Ideology aside, some farmers who accepted help from the Posse were trying to survive financial crisis. Another group formed in the 1980s dedicated itself purely to violence.

The Order (its name borrowed from *The Turner Diaries*) vowed to strike the "Zionist Occupation Government" in defense of "White America." Robert Mathews founded the small group with eight other men in the early 1980s. By 1983, The Order had begun committing armed robberies to raise money. In 1984, the group assassinated a Denver radio talk-show host, Alan Berg, who was Jewish, and had argued with racists on the air. Later that same year, the group robbed an armored car of $3.6 million.

Mathews died in a shootout with federal agents on Whidbey Island, near Seattle, in December 1984.

In 1985, 23 surviving members of the group went to trial or pleaded guilty to racketeering charges, with most receiving sentences of 40 to 100 years. David Lane later was sentenced to 150 years in a separate trial for participating in Berg's murder.[44]

Federal prosecutors in Fort Smith, Ark., failed, however to convict Lane and 13 other extremists of sedition in 1988. They'd been charged with plotting to overthrow the government and set up a separate white nation in the Pacific Northwest.[45]

That same year, in that very region, an upsurge of anti-minority violence by skinheads claimed the life of Ethiopian immigrant Mulugeta Seraw, who was bludgeoned to death with a baseball bat by the East Side White Pride gang. Three years later, Tom Metzger, an infamous San Diego extremist, was found responsible for the death, along with others, on the grounds that his White Aryan Resistance group had incited the group who killed Seraw. The verdict, in a civil suit brought by the SPLC, required Metzger and his codefendants to pay $12.5 million to Seraw's family.[46]

Explosion and Aftermath

The violence that marked the 1980s intensified in the '90s, sparked by the botched 1992 arrest of survivalist and Christian Identity adherent Randy Weaver for failing to appear in court on a gun-law charge. (He'd been given the wrong court date.) Weaver had holed up with his family in remote Ruby Ridge, in northern Idaho, which had become a center for the extreme right and was home to Christian Identity leader Richard Butler.[47]

When federal marshals attempted to arrest Weaver, who had not been involved in previous violence, a gunfight broke out in which Weaver's son and a marshal were killed; later, during a siege of the family's cabin, an FBI sniper killed Weaver's wife. Weaver surrendered and was sentenced to 18 months in prison.[48]

FBI handling of the case was widely considered a fiasco, and worse. But on the far right, a more ominous view prevailed: Ruby Ridge seemed to validate conspiracist fears of government violence against gun owners and opponents of the "New World Order" — far-right code for U.N.-controlled global government.

Months after Ruby Ridge, Christian Identity preacher Peter Peters organized a meeting of about 150 extremists

at Estes Park, Colo. In a keynote speech, Louis Beam, a former leader of the Texas Klan and one of those acquitted in the Arkansas sedition case, outlined a strategy of "leaderless resistance" — formation of small cells of committed activists without central direction. A Vietnam veteran, Beam also spoke of the need for "camouflage" — the ability to blend in the public's eye the more committed groups of resistance "with mainstream 'kosher' associations that are generally seen as harmless."[49]

Similarly, others at the meeting advocated uniting with less extreme groups to form a broad anti-government movement.[50]

Meanwhile, a related development had just shocked the mainstream political establishment. David Duke, a former Klan leader who hadn't renounced his anti-black or anti-Jewish views, won the 1991 Republican primary for Louisiana governor. (He went on to lose the general election.)[51]

Following the Estes Park conclave, "militias" sprang up around the country, especially in the rural Midwest and West. Ideas animating the movement included survivalism, gun-rights defense and — among many members, but not all — far-right conspiracy theories. Among those who passed through militia circles was a U.S. Army veteran of the 1990-1991 Persian Gulf War, Timothy McVeigh.

But before McVeigh's name hit the headlines, a series of events near Waco, Texas, would seize national attention and electrify the far right. Members of the Branch Davidian religious cult, led by a fiery preacher named David Koresh, fired on ATF agents attempting to search for guns and ammunition believed to be stored at the Davidians' compound; four agents were killed. On April 19, 1993, after a 51-day siege, FBI agents moved on the compound with tanks. In the conflagration that resulted, Koresh and about 80 other Davidians died, including many children.

A widespread suspicion that FBI teargas canisters started the fire became a certainty on the far right. In those circles, Waco stood as evidence of government ruthlessness. Koresh, who had followed the Weaver case closely, probably wouldn't have been surprised. "Koresh spoke to me frequently on the phone about Ruby Ridge," says Special Agent Cavanaugh of the ATF, who negotiated with the Branch Davidian leader during the siege. Koresh and his top aide "were well-versed in everything that happened there and were spitting out 'New World Order' crackpot conspiracy theories."

In 2000, an outside counsel to the Justice Department concluded that the canisters hadn't started the fire but that Davidians themselves ignited it.[52]

But by then, April 19 had become notorious for another reason. On April 19, 1995, McVeigh detonated a bomb in a rented truck he parked in front of the Alfred P. Murrah Federal Building in Oklahoma City, killing 168 people, including 19 children. Arrested hours later after a traffic stop, McVeigh was later often described as a lone wolf. But, among other activities, he had sold *The Turner Diaries* at gun shows, which were popular with militia members and with extremists in general.

"McVeigh was not a lone extremist; instead, he was trained to make himself look like a lone extremist," wrote former FBI agent German. "It's a right-wing terrorism technique that comes complete with written instruction manuals."[53]

The bombing — for which McVeigh was executed in 2001 — made *Turner Diaries* author Pierce and his National Alliance notorious. But the bombing also saw a steep decline in militia membership, as those without a high level of commitment to extremist politics dropped away.

More blows followed. Pierce died of cancer in 2002. Two years later Butler died; earlier he had lost his Idaho compound after losing a civil lawsuit filed by the Southern Poverty Law Center.[54]

Then, in 2005, Matthew Hale, 33, considered an up-and-coming extremist leader as head of the World Church of the Creator, was sentenced to 40 years in federal prison for conspiring to kill a federal judge. Since his imprisonment, extremist-watchers say, no charismatic leader has emerged from the extremist world.

CURRENT SITUATION

Hate in April

Hitler was born in April, which marks the beginning of the public rally season for right-wing extremists, and for opponents who mount counterdemonstrations.[55]

This year promises to be a busy one for haters. In April alone, 32 conferences, celebrations, militia training sessions and other events were planned by neo-Nazi, Klan, Christian Identity and related organizations in 22 states,

according to the Anti-Defamation League; dozens more events are scheduled into October.[56]

The list includes Hitler birthday commemorations in Illinois and North Carolina and a march by robed Klan members in Pulaski, Tenn., where Confederate veterans founded the Klan.

Counterdemonstrators showed for an NSM rally of about 70 members the day before at the Gateway Arch in St. Louis, Mo. No one was arrested, but the two groups yelled at each other and traded "Heil Hitler" salutes and raised-middle-finger retorts. A second group of counterdemonstrators organized by the ADL held a "rally for respect" at a nearby site.[57]

Commenting on the NSM rally, Lewis Reed, president of the St. Louis Board of Aldermen, said, "It's sad that there are still people today, in 2009, that only want to divide the races and breed hate."[58]

Yet neo-Nazi rallies, at least in major metropolitan areas, typically don't draw big crowds of extremists. In Skokie, Ill., a Chicago suburb with a large Jewish population — including Holocaust survivors — the opening of a state holocaust museum in April drew a neo-Nazi demonstration — of seven people. Twelve thousand people attended the opening ceremony, where former President Bill Clinton spoke.[59]

This year's rally season began with a snag. "East Coast White Unity" and "Volksfront" ("Peoples' Front" in German) had planned to meet in Boston over the April 11 weekend. But after the Boston Anti-Racist Coalition told the Veterans of Foreign Wars (VFW) about the nature of the "Patriot's Day" rally, the VFW withdrew permission to use their hall. Instead, the event was held at an American Legion Hall in Loudon, N.H.[60]

"These racist speakers, bands and their supporters will always have to walk on egg shells and face the very real prospect of their events being exposed to the general public, wherever and whenever they rear their ugly heads," the coalition said in a post on an anarchist Web site.[61]

But Roper of White Revolution replied, "Because a venue, or two, or three, has cancelled on us due to the efforts of anti-white, communist and Jewish activists, the event has not been cancelled and will go on," he said. "We plan for such eventualities in depth."[62]

For its part, One People's Project, an anti-supremacist organization, says it infiltrates neo-Nazi and Klan groups to find out about planned events in time to organize

'Fascism' Label Comes in Handy for Critics

But respected writers say it's a legitimate — if unlikely — concern.

Accompanying today's worries about an extremist resurgence are fears that the United States could, if economic conditions worsen, embrace fascism — the totalitarian ideology that modern hate groups champion.

But the concern focuses on the federal government itself, not fringe, neo-Nazi organizations. Indeed, some of President Barack Obama's foes are calling him a fascist, the same label some had applied to President George W. Bush.

The labeling would seem to show once again that "fascist" is one of the most loosely applied — and handy — terms in the political lexicon. Nevertheless, fascism isn't foreign to the United States, even though the word comes from 1920s Italy. Italian dictator Benito Mussolini coined "fascismo" to name the violence-glorifying, socialist-hating and ultranationalist movement he formed after World War I, appropriating a term then used for militant political groups of all stripes.[1]

Notwithstanding those Italian roots, Robert Paxton, one of the leading historians of the European far right, wrote that the first fascist group in history may have been the Ku Klux Klan. "By adopting a uniform . . . as well as by their techniques of intimidation and their conviction that violence was justified in the cause of their group's destiny," wrote Paxton, a Virginia native, "the first version of the Klan in the defeated American South was arguably a remarkable preview of the way fascist movements were to function in interwar Europe."[2]

But Paxton, an emeritus professor of social science at Columbia University, dismisses the attempt to label Obama fascist as a desperation move. "When there's a popular figure and you can't get a grip on opposing him, you call him a fascist," he says. "As opposed to Hitler and Mussolini in uniform, shrieking into microphones and juicing up the nationalism of crowds, Obama is a calm, reasonable person whose basic drives have all been toward bolstering democracy and the rule of law."

Obama's extreme critics insist otherwise. Obama heads a "Gestapo government," conservative blogger David Limbaugh (brother of radio commentator Rush Limbaugh) told a radio interviewer. And *The American Spectator*, a conservative magazine, likened Obama's economic policies to those of Mussolini.[3]

The author of the *Spectator* piece, senior editor Quinn Hillyer, added that he wouldn't go so far as to compare Obama's administration to that of Adolf Hitler, whose version of fascism turned out far deadlier than the Italian original. Still, he wrote, "The comparison of today's situation to that of Italian fascism is no mere scare tactic but a serious concern."[4]

In calling Obama a fascist, critics may simply be hoping for better results than they got when they tried pinning the "socialist" label on him during and after the 2008 presidential campaign. "We've so overused the word 'socialism' that it no longer has the negative connotation it had 20 years ago, or even 10 years ago," Sal Anuzis, former chairman of the Michigan Republican Party, told *The New York Times*. "Fascism — everybody still thinks that's a bad thing."[5]

To be sure, only a small minority accepts "fascist" as a compliment. But aiming it at a politician after first denouncing him as a leftist seems an odd tactic, given fascists' historic hatred of socialists.[6]

But that seemed to bother Obama's foes as little as the fact that they were borrowing from the vocabulary that some critics of the Bush administration used in 2001-2008.

The liberal group MoveOn.org, for instance, created an ad in 2004 that tried to connect Bush to Hitler, intoning: "A nation warped by lies. Lies fuel fear. Fear fuels aggression. Invasion. Occupation. What were war crimes in 1945 is foreign policy in 2003."[7]

Liberal author Naomi Wolf made a similar case in her book *The End of America*, published toward the end of the Bush administration.[8]

countermobilizations. "We can't keep on allowing groups like the Klan, Aryan Nations, National Alliance, National Vanguard and the National Socialist Movement to hold society at-large hostage," Daryle Lamont Jenkins of One People's Project said.[63]

On April 19, 2008, 30 to 40 members of the National Socialist Movement (NSM) rallied in Washington for an anti-immigration march from the National Mall to the U.S. Capitol. They were greeted by raucous counterdemonstrators, five of whom were arrested for allegedly assaulting police officers with pepper spray and a pole.[64]

White supremacist gatherings don't tend to be large affairs. Roper told a reporter by phone from the New Hampshire event that 200 people were participating,

"The Nazis rose to power in a living, if battered, democracy," Wolf wrote. "Dictators can rise in a weakened democracy even with a minority of popular support."[9]

Drawing in part from Paxton's most recent book on fascism, Wolf argued that erosions of civil liberties under the Bush administration paralleled events in Italy and Germany as Mussolini and Hitler moved toward totalitarian rule.

Followers of the neo-Nazi NPD party stand defiantly near a "Berlin against Nazis" poster during a demonstration in Berlin on May 1, 2009. Anti-immigration neo-Nazis and skinheads often clash with anti-fascists on May Day in Germany.

Hitler upon winning election as chancellor in 1933. "You can draw some parallels — with care," he says. "The focus should be on steps away from the rule of law."

Still, Paxton discourages complacency. "In three years, if we're not out of this mess, we could see something that would call itself the patriotic party or the minutemen, a symbol that has a nice nationalistic resonance," he says. "It would sweep up all the discontented from the left and the right; it would be light

But these arguments leave out the widespread loss of faith in democracy, and the state of near-civil war that served as the backdrop to the rise of fascism in Italy and Germany, Paxton says.

By contrast, Americans opposed to Bush expressed their discontent within the system, by voting in Obama, Paxton notes. And the political climate even before that, when Wolf was writing, didn't begin to approach the Italian and German precedents. "In the collection of preconditions, you need something worse," he says. "A lost war, big-time national humiliation — we might get there, but we're not quite there yet — and a sense that our existing way of doing politics isn't working. And then power moving to the streets, with paramilitary organizations. I don't see any of that."

Paxton does agree that the detention and intelligence-gathering policies adopted after the Sept. 11, 2001, terrorist attacks could be compared with early moves by

on ideology. The immigration issue would be a very plausible gathering point for some sort of movement like this."

[1] Robert O. Paxton, *The Anatomy of Fascism* (2004), pp. 4-5.

[2] *Ibid.*, p. 49.

[3] Quinn Hillyer, "Il Duce, Redux?" *The American Spectator*, April 2, 2009, http://spectator.org/archives/2009/04/02/il-duce-redux. Limbaugh quoted in Carla Marinucci and Joe Garofoli, "Fascist? Socialist? Attacks on Obama take a shrill tone," *San Francisco Chronicle*, April 9, 2009, p. A1.

[4] Hillyer, *op. cit.*

[5] Quoted in John Harwood, "But Can Obama Make the Trains Run on Time?" *The New York Times*, April 20, 2009, www.nytimes.com/2009/04/20/us/politics/20caucus.html?scp=1&sq=fascism&st=cse.

[6] Paxton, *op. cit.*, pp. 60-67.

[7] Marinucci and Garofoli, *op. cit.*

[8] Naomi Wolf, *The End of America: Letters of Warning to a Young Patriot, A Citizen's Call to Action* (2007).

[9] *Ibid.*, pp. 39-40.

making it one of the bigger events of its type. But no independent confirmation was available.

In 2005, Roper organized a protest demonstration outside an event in Boston commemorating the 60th anniversary of the liberation of Nazi death camps. Police and counterprotesters far outnumbered Roper and his dozen or so demonstrators.[65]

However, on occasion, supremacists' crowds have been bigger, and violence has erupted. In 2002, about 60 supporters of the now-imprisoned Matthew Hale's World Church of the Creator gathered in York, Pa., where a former mayor and eight others had been charged in the 1969 death of a black woman during a racially charged riot. Several hundred counterprotesters fought with Hale's supporters in the city streets, as police tried to separate the groups. Twenty-five people were arrested.[66]

However, in April of that year, only about 30 to 40 neo-Nazis showed up in York for a Hitler's birthday celebration.[67]

Free Speech, Hate Speech

Some conservatives are attacking the Department of Homeland Security (DHS) examination of far-right extremism as a barely disguised attack on political foes of the Obama administration.

"One of the most embarrassingly shoddy pieces of propaganda I'd ever read out of DHS," thundered conservative blogger Michelle Malkin. Others in the conservative blogosphere shared her view that the report tried to tie conservatives to extremists.[68] Homeland Security Secretary Janet Napolitano later responded that the agency is on "the lookout for criminal and terrorist activity but we do not — nor will we ever — monitor ideology or political beliefs."[69]

The report noted that extremists are especially interested in recruiting veterans, an observation that triggered angry criticism from some veterans' organizations (see below). In essence the 14-page assessment holds that economic turmoil, the election of a black president and a growing number of veterans — whom right-wing extremists have a documented interest in recruiting — are creating a climate in which far-right extremism could flourish again. Specifically, the report said the DHS "assesses that right-wing extremist groups' frustration over a perceived lack of government action on illegal immigration has the potential to incite individuals or small groups toward violence." But any such violence would likely be "isolated" and "small-scale."[70]

Though critics later said the DHS failed to distinguish between extremists and mainstream political advocates, the report did try to draw that line. Debates on gun rights and other constitutional issues are often intense — but perfectly legal, the report said. "Violent extremists," it added, "may attempt to co-opt the debate and use the controversy as a radicalization tool."[71]

But Berlet of Political Research Associates argues that the report itself crosses into the potentially unconstitutional territory of monitoring ideological trends.

"The government should not be in the business of undermining radical ideas," he says. "As citizens we have

a responsibility to challenge rhetoric that demonizes and scapegoats, but I don't think the First Amendment allows the government to be in that battle."

Despite attacks from the left as well as right, some commentators defended the report against its critics. "This DHS assessment was begun more than a year ago, before Barack Obama was even nominated," blogger Charles Johnson — a political independent who had been popular with conservative critics of Islam — wrote on his influential "Little Green Footballs" site. "It was not done at the behest of the Obama administration. . . . The DHS report is not intended to target anyone but the most extreme elements of the far right, and it's depressing to see so many bloggers jumping to totally unwarranted conclusions."[72]

Reaction to the document may have been especially intense because it followed closely on an uproar that greeted disclosure of a report on the "Modern Militia Movement" in Missouri. It was produced by a "fusion center," one of 70 around the country that were set up by law enforcement agencies after Sept. 11 to ensure that intelligence is shared between federal, state and local officers. The report mostly summarized information on extremist activities in the 1990s and outlined some ideas said to be circulating now on the far right.[73]

But the report lumped together extremists and mainstream political activists with no violent inclinations. "Militia members most commonly associate with third-party political groups," the report said, going on to name supporters of 2008 libertarian presidential candidate Bob Barr, Constitution Party candidate Chuck Baldwin and Rep. Ron Paul, R-Texas, who ran for the Republican Party presidential nomination.[74]

"This smacks of totalitarian regimes of days gone by," said Baldwin, one of many to react furiously to the document.[75]

Within weeks, the Missouri State Highway Patrol had apologized to the three politicians and replaced the head of the fusion center.[76]

Not all critics came from the right. "This is part of a national trend where intelligence reports are turning attention away from people who are actually doing bad things to people who are thinking thoughts that the government, for whatever reason, doesn't like," former FBI agent German told The Associated Press.[77]

The ACLU, where German is now a policy counselor, noted that the North Central Texas Fusion System had produced a report in February that tied former Rep. Cynthia McKinney and former U.S. Attorney General Ramsey Clark to "far left groups" that allegedly sympathize with the Iranian-backed Hezbollah militia of Lebanon and other armed movements in the Middle East.[78]

Fusion centers, German said, are an "equal opportunity infringer" on civil rights of citizens on the right and the left.[79]

Indeed, DHS says that it produced a report earlier this year on left-wing extremists. That report soon leaked out as well. The document forecast a rise in cyber-attacks aimed at businesses, especially those deemed to be violators of animal rights.[80]

Extremism-watchers, for their part, greeted the DHS report as an echo of their own conclusions. "This Homeland Security report reinforces our view that the current political and economic climate in the United States is creating the right conditions for a rise in extremist activity," said Potok of the SPLC.[81]

But one of the center's most ferocious left-wing critics, writer Alexander Cockburn, ridiculed that reasoning, accusing the center of "fingering militiamen in a potato field in Idaho" instead of "attacking the roots of Southern poverty, and the system that sustains that poverty as expressed in the endless prisons and death rows across the South, disproportionately crammed with blacks and Hispanics."[82]

Fights are also continuing over broadcasters' commentaries. In Boston, radio station WTKK-FM suspended right-wing radio talk-show host Jay Severin after he responded to the influenza outbreak with comments including: "So now, in addition to venereal disease and the other leading exports of Mexico — women with mustaches and VD — now we have swine flu." Mexicans, he said, are "the world's lowest of primitives."[83]

Franklin Soults, a spokesman for Massachusetts Immigrant and Refugee Advocacy Coalition, called Severin's language "dehumanizing."

Severin himself referred questions to his lawyer, George Tobia, who told the *Boston Globe* that he expected the broadcaster to be back on the air soon. "But I don't know when."[84]

Recruiting Veterans

Discharged from the U.S. Marine Corps after being arrested for allegedly taking part in armed robberies at two hotels in Jacksonville, N.C., a former lance corporal now faces prosecution for allegedly threatening President Obama's life.

Kody Brittingham, 20, who served in the 2nd Tank Battalion, 2nd Marine Division, was indicted in February for the alleged threat by a federal grand jury in Raleigh, N.C. An unnamed federal law enforcement official told the Jacksonville (N.C.) *Daily News* that the charge followed discovery of a journal in Brittingham's barracks at Camp Lejeune in which he laid out a plan to kill Obama, who at that point hadn't yet been inaugurated. Investigators reportedly also found white-supremacist literature among Brittingham's possessions.[85]

How plausible the alleged assassination plans were is not clear. But the arrest did reawaken concerns about white-supremacist and neo-Nazi recruitment of men with military training, especially those with combat experience (Brittingham, however, had never served overseas).

Those concerns aren't limited to extremist-watchers from advocacy organizations. An FBI report last year counted 203 individuals with "confirmed or claimed" military experience who had been spotted in extremist groups since the Sept. 11 attacks, which effectively marked the beginning of a period in which hundreds of thousands of military personnel began acquiring battlefield experience.[86]

Those 203 individuals represent a minuscule fraction of the country's 23.8 million veterans or 1.4 million active-duty personnel, the report acknowledged.[87]

The recent DHS assessment discussed extremist groups' interest in recruiting veterans, only to prompt outraged reaction from some veterans' organizations and some politicians. "To characterize men and women returning home after defending our country as potential terrorists is offensive and unacceptable," House Republican leader John Boehner of Ohio said in a press release. "The Department of Homeland Security owes our veterans an apology."[88]

In discussing extremists' interest in veterans, the FBI said that neo-Nazis were not discouraged by the small number of vets who might be responsive to recruiting pitches.

"The prestige which the extremist movement bestows upon members with military experience grants them the potential for influence beyond their numbers," said the report, which is marked "unclassified/for official use only/law enforcement sensitive." The report, now available

Is anti-immigration rhetoric provoking hate crimes against Latinos?

YES
Mark Potok
Director, Intelligence Project, Southern Poverty Law Center

NO
Marcus Epstein
Executive Director, The American Cause

Written for *CQ Researcher*, April 2009

Written for *CQ Researcher*, April 2009

Across the board, nativist organizations in America have angrily denounced those who suggest that demonizing rhetoric leads to hate violence. One of them even recently issued a press release criticizing the "outrageous behavior" of groups like the Southern Poverty Law Center that propose such a link and "provide no proof whatsoever."

Nativist organizations take the remarkable position that hate speech directed against Latino immigrants has no relationship at all to hate crime — not even the utterly false allegations that Latinos are secretly planning to hand the American Southwest over to Mexico, are far more criminal than others, are bringing dread diseases to the United States, and so on.

In addition to defying common sense, that head-in-the-sand approach completely ignores the statements that are typically made by hate criminals during their attacks.

Take the case of Marcelo Lucero, who was allegedly murdered by a gang of white teenagers in the Long Island town of Patchogue, N.Y., last November. Prosecutors say the suspects told detectives they regularly went "beaner jumping" — beating up Latinos — and that they used racial epithets during the attack. "Let's go find some Mexicans to [expletive] up," one said beforehand, according to *Newsday*.

Nativist groups use the fact that we don't know precisely where the teens' fury comes from to deny it was related to nativist demonization. But just because it's not possible to pinpoint the exact source of their racial anger — rhetoric from nativist groups, their parents, local anti-immigrant politicians, or pundits — does not mean it magically popped into the assailants' minds.

There is also hard evidence to back up the link between demonization and violence. According to FBI statistics, anti-Latino hate crimes went up 40 percent between 2003 and 2007 — the very same period that saw a remarkable proliferation of nativist rhetoric.

Experts agree that there is a link. "Racist rhetoric and dehumanizing images inspire violence perpetrated against innocent human beings," says Jack Levin, a nationally known hate crime expert at Northeastern University. "It's not just the most recent numbers. It's the trend over a number of years that lends credibility to the notion that we're seeing a very real and possibly dramatic rise in anti-Latino hate incidents."

Ignoring the role that demonization plays in such violence is a surefire way to generate more of it. Marcelo Lucero's murder is only the latest in a sad list of violent incidents inspired by ugly rhetoric that will certainly grow longer.

Last year, Barack Obama accused broadcasters Lou Dobbs and Rush Limbaugh of "feeding a kind of xenophobia." He added that their broadcasts were a "reason why hate crimes against Hispanic people doubled last year."

Obama's facts and logic are plain wrong. The FBI found only 745 anti-Latino hate crimes nationwide in 2007, down from 770 in 2006. In fact anti-Hispanic hate crimes per capita dropped 18 percent over the last decade.

Most of these hate crimes were for minor offenses, such as graffiti or name-calling, with only 145 aggravated assaults, two murders and no rapes in 2007. To put this in perspective, former Hudson Institute economist Ed Rubenstein estimates illegal aliens murder at least 949 people a year.

There is also no evidence that hate crimes are motivated by the immigration-control movement. Those who claim there's a connection cannot point to a single, significant commentator or politician who has advocated violence against Latinos. Nor can they find a single hate crime committed by their followers.

Although whites are the vast majority of listeners of conservative talk radio and television, they committed only 52 percent of hate crimes against Latinos — a percentage well below their proportion of 66 percent of the population. Moreover, Los Angeles County classified 42 percent of black-on-Hispanic hate crimes as "gang related." This is not to suggest that blacks cannot be racist, but that they are unlikely to be influenced by the purveyors of supposed anti-immigrant rhetoric.

The 2008 murder of José Osvaldo Sucuzhanay in Brooklyn by blacks who targeted him because they mistook him as gay was denounced as a significant anti-Hispanic, anti-immigrant hate crime by all New York politicians and by *The New York Times*. Even when they were at large, the race of the killers was rarely mentioned.

Groups like the Southern Poverty Law Center that perpetuate misconceptions about anti-Latino hate crimes make no secret of their goals. They want supporters of immigration control silenced because, in the words of La Raza president Janet Murguía, "We have to draw the line on freedom of speech, when freedom of speech becomes hate speech."

These organizations run relentless smear campaigns accusing virtually all opponents of illegal immigration — no matter how nuanced or tempered — of hate speech that must not be allowed on the airwaves, in print, or in front of Congress.

Before we abandon our core democratic principles of free speech and open debate in the name of stopping hate crimes, we should at least get our facts straight.

online, has circulated among journalists and nongovernmental specialists.[89]

Among a handful of specific cases, the FBI noted that two privates in the elite Army 82nd Airborne Division received six-year prison sentences for attempting to sell body armor and other equipment in 2007 to an undercover agent posing as a white-supremacist movement member. And in 2005, a former Army intelligence analyst who'd been convicted of a firearms violation founded a skinhead group that reportedly advocated training members in firearms, knife-fighting, close-quarters combat and "house sweeps."[90]

The FBI intelligence assessment followed an investigation by the SPLC. In 2006 the center published a detailed report that quoted neo-Nazi vets, a supremacist who had renounced the extremist cause, as well as a Defense Department investigator. Extremists "stretch across all branches of service, they are linking up across the branches once they're inside, and they are hard-core," investigator Scott Barfield told the SPLC. "We've got Aryan Nations graffiti in Baghdad."[91]

Worries about a neo-Nazi presence in the military had surfaced years before U.S. troops were deployed to Iraq and Afghanistan. The trigger was the random murder in 1995 of a black man and woman in Fayetteville, N.C., by two soldiers in the elite Army 82nd Airborne Division, whose home base is nearby Fort Bragg. In the uproar that followed, 22 members of the 82nd — including those arrested for the killing — were found by the Army to have extremist ties.[92]

But far-right efforts to penetrate the Armed Forces apparently continued. The SPLC published excerpts from a 1999 article in the *National Alliance* magazine by an Army Special Forces veteran who urged young supremacists to sign up. "Light infantry is your branch of choice," he wrote, "because the coming race war, and the ethnic cleansing to follow, will be very much an infantryman's war. It will be house-to-house, neighborhood-by-neighborhood, until your town or city is cleared and the alien races are driven into the countryside where they can be hunted down and 'cleansed.' "[93]

Supremacists who enlisted were told to stay undercover: "Do not — I repeat, do not — seek out other skinheads. Do not listen to skinhead 'music.' Do not keep 'racist' or 'White-supremacist tracts' where you live. During your service you will be subjected to a constant barrage of equal opportunity drivel. . . . Keep your mouth shut."[94]

Members of the National Socialist Movement demonstrate on the grounds of the U.S. Capitol on April 19, 2008. Fifteen years earlier, on another April 19, a fire during an FBI siege at the Branch Davidian compound outside Waco, Texas, killed David Koresh and about 80 followers, including many children.

OUTLOOK
Guns in Holsters

The possibility that far-right extremists will emerge from the margins is as uncertain as the course of today's economic crisis, veteran analysts say.

For their part, extremists including Roper of White Revolution harbor no doubt that the medium-term future will see the outbreak of major racial and ethnic violence accompanying the breakup of the United States. "A lot of people might think it's impossible, but if you had gone to those same people in 1980 and told them the Berlin Wall was going to fall and the Soviet Union was going to collapse without a single missile being launched, they would have thought that was impossible too," Roper says.

Others would argue that U.S. society and government have firmer foundations than the Soviet system, which came to power in 1917 and sustained itself first by mass terror and then by mass repression.

In any event, the consensus among monitors of the far right is that extremist intensity hasn't even reached the level of the 1990s — the point at which the extremist movement "goes from red-hot to white-hot," as Pitcavage of the ADL puts it.

A key indicator of the latter stage is the discovery of major conspiracies or actual large-scale attacks, such as the Oklahoma City bombing. "In the 1980s and mid-'90s, a variety of white-supremacist or anti-government extremist groups had huge plots — start a white revolution, break off part of the country, hit military targets," Pitcavage says. "What they shared was an elaborate large-scale conception, often far larger than actual capabilities. If we start seeing some more of these we will know that things are starting to go white-hot again."

The present crisis is too new to suddenly spawn a new wave of high-intensity extremism, Pitcavage adds. "Movements don't start overnight," he says. "It takes a while for people to experience these things and form a reaction to them."

But Barkun at Syracuse University says today's conditions are far more alarming than those of the "white-hot" years. War and global economic crisis alone open the possibility of a new extremism paradigm, he says.

"We're in an economic situation which is so dire and so long-lasting that it will have social and political effects," Barkun says. "Things may develop along entirely novel lines that don't necessarily arise out of pre-existing groups, or that can readily be placed along the right-wing continuum, where the extreme right and the extreme left come together."

He adds that he hasn't seen any evidence of this taking place. However, left-right extremes have met before, at least elsewhere. Mussolini's early fascist movement took in former socialists like him. The "socialist" in Germany's National Socialist (Nazi) Party did express some — short-lived — opposition to capitalism. Attempts by some European far-rightists to co-opt left-wing anarchists represent an attempt to revive that tradition.

Also up in the air, to Barkun and others, is whether America's tradition of racial conflict will reassert itself in a country whose demography has been transformed from the old, white majority-black minority pattern.

One effect of the growing Latino political presence likely will be an accommodation by the Republican Party, where most support for tougher immigration control has centered, says Potok of the Southern Poverty Law Center. The result would be that white, non-Hispanic voters alienated by demographic change fall away from the conventional political system. "When that happens, a lot of these people would just go home, but some percentage of them would go into that extremist world," he speculates. "For them, there's no way out of a multiracial system. So it's 'Let's go off and start our own country.' "

On the organizational side, Potok theorizes, the absence of major, controlling figures, such as Pierce of the National Alliance and Butler of Aryan Nations, may be a danger sign. "I understand that a lot of really scary people, like The Order, came out of the Alliance," he says, adding that some extremist leaders have a history of depicting a need for violence only at some indefinite point in the future. "Leaders ultimately have the effect of holding people back: 'We're going to kill the Jews, but keep your guns in your holsters.' "

NOTES

1. Quoted in Jonathan D. Silver, "911 Operator Failed to Warn About Weapons," *Pittsburgh Post-Gazette*, April 7, 2009, p. A1. Unless otherwise indicated, all details of this event are drawn from *Post-Gazette* articles published April 5-8, 2009.

2. Quoted in Michael A. Fucco, "Deadly Ambush Claims the Lives of 3 City Police Officers," *Pittsburgh Post-Gazette*, April 5, 2009, p. A1.

3. Quoted in Dennis B. Roddy, "On Web: Racism, Anti-Semitism, Warnings," *Pittsburgh Post-Gazette*, April 7, 2009, p. A1.

4. "The Employment Situation: March 2009," U.S. Bureau of Labor Statistics, April 3, 2009, www.bls.gov/news.release/empsit.nr0.htm; Jeffrey Passel and D'Vera Cohn, "Trends in Unauthorized Immigration," Pew Hispanic Center, Oct. 2, 2008, http://pewhispanic.org/reports/report.php?ReportID=94. *CQ Researcher* has published reports on immigration going back to the early 1920s. Three of the most recent are: Reed Karaim, "America's Border Fence," Sept. 19, 2008, pp. 745-768; Alan Greenblatt, "Immigration Debate," Feb. 1, 2008, pp. 97-120; and Peter Katel, "Real ID," May 4, 2007, pp. 385-408.

5. "Rightwing Extremism: Current Economic and Political Climate Fueling Resurgence in Radicalization and Recruitment," Homeland Security Department, April 7, 2009, http://images.logicsix.com/DHS_RWE.pdf.

6. "Why Obama is Good for Our Movement," National Socialist Movement, undated, www.nsm88.org/activities/why obama is good for our movement

.html. See also Alan Greenblatt, "Race in America," *CQ Researcher*, July 11, 2003, pp. 593-624.

7. David Holthouse, "The Year in Hate," Intelligence Report, Southern Poverty Law Center, spring 2009, www.splcenter.org/intel/intelreport/article.jsp?aid=1027. For background, see Kenneth Jost, "Hate Crimes," *CQ Researcher*, Jan. 8, 1993, pp. 1-24.

8. Tom Hays, "Feds charge 3 men in election bias attacks," The Associated Press, Jan. 7, 2009; Christine Hauser and Colin Moynihan, "Three Are Charged in Attacks on Election Night," *The New York Times*, Jan. 8, 2009, p. A25.

9. Manny Fernandez and Javier C. Hernandez, "Binghamton Victims Shared a Dream of Living Better Lives," *The New York Times*, April 5, 2009, www.nytimes.com/2009/04/06/nyregion/06victims.html?scp=7&sq=Jiverly Binghamton&st=cse; Al Baker and Liz Robbins, "Police Had Few Contacts With Killer," *The New York Times*, April 7, 2009.

10. Quoted in Jessica Fargen, "Sicko Kill Plot Emerges," *Boston Herald*, Jan. 23, 2009, p. 5; Milton J. Valencia, "Father of attacked Brockton sisters calls for justice," *Boston Herald*, Jan. 24, 2009, p. B3.

11. Quoted in Melissa Nelson, "FL man acted oddly before Chilean students' deaths," The Associated Press, March 13, 2009.

12. "Hate on Display: A Visual Database of Extremist Symbols, Logos and Tattoos," ADL, undated, www.adl.org/hate_symbols/numbers_14-88.asp. For a Web site filled with praise for Lane see www.freetheorder.org/dlrip.html.

13. Jeffrey Gettleman, "William L. Pierce, 68; Ex-Rocket Scientist Became White Supremacist," *Los Angeles Times*, July 24, 2002, p. B10.

14. Quoted in John Krupa, "Teen in plot lists drinking as his job," *Arkansas Democrat-Gazette*, Oct. 29, 2008; see also Holthouse, *op. cit.*

15. Jared Taylor, "Transition to Black Rule," *American Renaissance*, Nov. 14, 2008, www.amren.com/mtnews/archives/2008/11/transition_to_b.php.

16. Jared Taylor, "Jews and American Renaissance," *American Renaissance*, May 2006, www.amren.com/mtnews/archives/2006/04/jews_and_americ.php.

17. Passel and Cohn, *op. cit.*

18. "Hate Crime Statistics, Victims, 2007," FBI, www.fbi.gov/ucr/hc2007/table_07.htm.

19. *Ibid.*

20. Jim Salter, "Mo. town outraged over killings, illegal immigrant," The Associated Press, March 20, 2009; "Hannibal murder suspect is illegal alien," The Associated Press, March 4, 2009.

21. Edwin S. Rubinstein, "Illegals kill a dozen a day?" *VDare*, Jan. 12, 2007, www.vdare.com/rubenstein/070112_nd.htm.

22. Mark Hugo Lopez and Michael T. Light, "A Rising Share: Hispanics and Federal Crime," Pew Hispanic Center, Feb. 18, 2009, p. 4, http://pewhispanic.org/files/reports/104.pdf.

23. Quoted in Sarah Burge, "Hate Crimes Continue Their Rise in Riverside County," *Press-Enterprise* (Riverside, Calif.), July 20, 2006, p. B1. See also Denes Husty III, "Crime vs. Hispanics up," *The News-Press* (Fort Myers, Fla.) Feb. 11, 2007, p. A1, and Troy Graham, "Hate Crime Statistics Belie Truth," *Daily Press* (Newport News, Va.), Jan. 30, 2000, p. A1.

24. "A Local Prosecutor's Guide For Responding to Hate Crimes," American Prosecutors Research Institute, undated, www.ndaa.org/pdf/hate_crimes.pdf.

25. Dennis B. Roddy, "An Accused Cop Killer's Politics," *Slate*, April 10, 2009, www.slate.com/id/2215826/.

26. Gary Kamiya, "They're coming to take our guns away," *Salon.com*, April 7, 2009, www.salon.com/opinion/kamiya/2009/04/07/richard_poplowski.

27. Quoted in Adam Liptak, "The Nation: Prisons to Mosques; Hate Speech and the American Way," *The New York Times*, Jan. 11, 2004. The Supreme Court decision is *Brandenburg v. Ohio*, 395, U.S. 444 (1969).

28. Quoted in Katherin Clad, "Group cites Saudi 'hate' tracts," *The Washington Times*, Jan. 29, 2005, p. A1.

29. Nonie Darwish, "Muslim Hate," *FrontPageMagazine.com*, March 25, 2009, www.frontpagemag.com/Articles/Read.aspx?GUID=A629F1F3-BBBA-420D-8C31-D340A577A083.

30. "Glen Beck joins Fox News," Reuters, Oct. 16, 2008, www.reuters.com/article/televisionNews/idUSTRE49G0NW20081017.

31. Eric Boehlert and Jamison Foser," On radio show, Beck read 'ad' for refinery that turns Mexicans into fuel," *County Fair blog*, Media Matters for America, June 29, 2007, (audio clip is posted), http://media-matters.org/items/200706290010.

32. Ariel Alexovich, "A Call to End Hate Speech," *The New York Times*, *The Caucus blog*, Feb. 1, 2008, http://thecaucus.blogs.nytimes.com/2008/02/01/a-call-to-end-hate-speech/?scp=1&sq=murguia%20hate%20speech&st=Search; "President and CEO Janet Murguia's Remarks at the Wave of Hope press briefing," National Council of La Raza, Jan. 31, 2008, www.nclr.org/content/viewpoints/detail/50389/.

33. Steve Sailer, "What Obama hasn't figured out yet," *Vdare*, April 27, 2009, http://blog.vdare.com/archives/2009/04/27/what-obama-hasnt-figured-out-yet-better-teachers-means-___/; Patrick Cleburne, "More Indians means more . . .," *Vdare*, April 19, 2009, http://blog.vdare.com/archives/2009/04/19/more-indians-means-morefill-in-blank/; Cooper Sterling, "Tom Tancredo at American University: Maybe It Is About Race," *Vdare*, March 14, 2009, www.vdare.com/sterling/090314_tancredo.htm.

34. Unless otherwise indicated this subsection draws on Robert O. Paxton, *The Anatomy of Fascism* (2004); William E. Leuchtenburg, *Franklin D. Roosevelt and the New Deal* (1963); and Chip Berlet and Matthew N. Lyons, *Right-Wing Populism in America: Too Close for Comfort* (2000); Daniel Levitas, *The Terrorist Next Door: The Militia Movement and the Radical Right* (2002).

35. See Binjamin Segel, *A Lie and a Libel: The History of the Protocols of the Elders of Zion* (1996). For an article in the *Dearborn Independent* that takes the Protocols as fact, see Henry Ford and the editors of the *Dearborn Independent*, " 'Jewish Protocols' Claim Partial Fulfillment," www.churchoftrueisrael.com/Ford/original/ij12.html.

36. Biographical sketch in "William Dudley Pelley Collection," University of North Carolina at Asheville, D. H. Ramsey Library, http://toto.lib.unca.edu/findingaids/mss/pelley/default_pelley_william_dudley.htm.

37. Unless otherwise indicated, this subsection draws on Levitas, *op. cit.*; and Berlet and Lyons, *op. cit.*

38. Quoted in *ibid.*, p. 180.

39. Quoted in Thomas M. Storke, "How Some Birchers Were Birched," *The New York Times*, Dec. 10, 1961.

40. See Shaila Dewan, "Revisiting '64 Civil Rights Deaths, This Time in a Murder Trial," *The New York Times*, June 12, 2005, p. A26; Manuel Roig-Franzia, "Reopened Civil Rights Cases Evoke Painful Past," *The New York Times*, Jan. 10, 2005, p. A1. For background on the KKK, see the following *Editorial Research Reports*, predecessor to *CQ Researcher*: K. Lee, "Ku Klux Klan," July 10, 1946; W.R. McIntyre, "Spread of Terrorism and Hatemongering," Dec. 3, 1958; H.B. Shaffer, "Secret Societies and Political Action," May 10, 1961; R.L. Worsnop, "Extremist Movements in Race and Politics," March 31, 1965; S. Stencel, "The South: Continuity and Change," March 7, 1980, and M.H. Cooper, "The Growing Danger of Hate Groups," May 12, 1989.

41. Fred P. Graham, "Rockwell, U.S. Nazi, Slain," *The New York Times*, Aug. 26, 1967.

42. Except where otherwise indicated, this subsection is drawn from Levitas, *op. cit.*, and James Ridgeway, *Blood in the Face: The Ku Klux Klan, Aryan Nations, Nazi Skinheads, and the Rise of a New White Culture* (1990).

43. Wayne King, "Right-Wing Extremists Seek to Recruit Farmers," *The New York Times*, Sept. 20, 1985, p. A13. See also "Arthur Kirk: Kirk & Radical Farm Groups," nebraskastudies.org, undated, www.nebraskastudies.org/1000/frameset_reset.html?www.nebraskastudies.org/1000/stories/1001_0112.html.

44. "Supremacists Sentenced," *The Washington Post*, Dec. 4, 1987; "Five White Supremacists Get Long Prison Terms," *Los Angeles Times*, Feb. 7, 1986, p. A41; "40-Year Sentences Given to 5 in White-Supremacist Group," *The New York Times* (The Associated Press), Feb. 8, 1986, p. A17.

45. "13 Supremacists Are Not Guilty of Conspiracies," *The New York Times*, April 8, 1988, p. A14.

46. Richard A. Serrano, "Metzger Must Pay $5 Million in Rights Death," *Los Angeles Times*, Oct. 23, 1990, p. A1.

47. Elaine Woo, "Richard Butler, 86; Supremacist Founded the Aryan Nations," *Los Angeles Times*, Sept. 9, 2004, p. B8.

48. David Johnston with Stephen Labaton, "F.B.I. Shaken by Inquiry Into Idaho Siege," *The New York Times*, Nov. 25, 1993, p. A1.

49. Louis Beam, "Leaderless Resistance," February 1992, www.louisbeam.com/leaderless.htm. See also "Militias," in Peter Knight, ed., *Conspiracy Theories in American History: An Encyclopedia* (2003), pp. 467-476.

50. Leonard Zeskind, "Armed and Dangerous," *Rolling Stone*, Nov. 2, 1995.

51. Megan K. Stack, "Duke Admits Bilking Backers," *Los Angeles Times*, Dec. 19, 200, p. A22.

52. Susan Schmidt, "Investigation Clears Agents at Waco," *The Washington Post*, July 22, 2000, p. A1. See also "Final Report to the Deputy Attorney General Concerning the 1993 Confrontation at the Mt. Carmel Complex," John C. Danforth, Special Counsel, Nov. 8, 2000, www.apologeticsindex.org/pdf/finalreport.pdf.

53. Mike German, *Thinking Like a Terrorist: Insights of a Former FBI Undercover Agent* (2007), p. 71.

54. Woo, *op. cit.*; "William Pierce, 69, Neo-Nazi Leader, Dies," *The New York Times*, July 24, 2002, p. A16.

55. "Hitler's birthday was April 20, 1889. Unwelcome distinction as Hitler's birthday burdens Austrian town," *The Globe and Mail* (Toronto), (Reuters), April 20, 1989.

56. "Schedule of Upcoming Extremist Events: 2009," regularly updated, www.adl.org/learn/Events_2001/events_2003_flashmap.asp.

57. Steve Giegerich, "Angry words fill air at neo-Nazi rally," *St. Louis Post-Dispatch*, April 19, 2009, p. A4.

58. Quoted in *ibid.*

59. Lisa Black, "Holocaust museum opens to 'fight capacity for evil,' " *Chicago Tribune*, April 20, 2009, p. A8.

60. Padraig Shea," Spurned by Hub hall, supremacist group holds rally in N.H.," *The Boston Globe*, April 12, 2009, p. B3; "White supremacists' event shifted to N.H.," UPI, April 12, 2009.

61. "We shut down the fascists!" Boston Anti-Racist Coalition, April 8, 2009, www.anarkismo.net/article/12633.

62. Billy Roper, "One If By Land, Two If By Sea," *White Revolution*, April 8, 2009, http://whiterevolution.com.

63. "Ku Klux Klan Coming to Your Town?" *The Tennessee Tribune* (Nashville), July 6, 2006, p. C8.

64. "Arrests, fights break out at neo-Nazi march," wtop.com, April 19, 2009, www.wtop.com/?sid=1389944&nid=25. Video available at Albert Xavier Barnes, "The Arrests, Counter-Demo," undated, www.truveo.com/The-Arrests-Counter-Demo-NSM-March-on-DC-19/id/3760920024.

65. Brooke Donald, "Two arrested outside Boston Holocaust gathering," The Associated Press, May 9, 2005.

66. R. Scott Rappold, "Mobs clash in York," *York Sunday News*, Jan. 13, 2002 , p. A1.

67. Marc Levy, "White supremacist rally sparsely attended," The Associated Press, April 22, 2002.

68. Michelle Malkin, "Confirmed: The Obama DHS hit job on conservatives is real," michellemalkin.com, April 14, 2009, http://michellemalkin.com/2009/04/14/confirme-the-obama-dhs-hit-job-on-conservatives-is-real/. See also Stephen Gordon, "Homeland Security document targets most conservatives and libertarians in the country," *The Liberty Papers* (blog), April 12, 2009, www.thelibertypapers.org/2009/04/12/homeland-security-document-targets-most-conservatives-and-libertarians-in-the-country.

69. Quoted in "Napolitano defends report on right-wing extremist groups," CNN, April 15, 2009, www.cnn.com/2009/POLITICS/04/15/extremism.report/.

70. "Rightwing Extremism. . . .," *op. cit.*, p. 5.

71. *Ibid.*, p. 6.

72. "About That DHS Report on Right-Wing Extremism," *Little Green Footballs*, April 14, 2009, http://littlegreenfootballs.com/article/33364_About_That_DHS_Report_on_Right-Wing_Extremism.

73. "The Modern Militia Movement," MIAC [Missouri Information Analysis Center] Strategic Report, Feb. 20, 2009, pp. 3-4, www.scribd.com/doc/13290698/The-Modern-Militia-MovementMissouri-MIAC-Strategic-Report-20Feb09-; David A. Lieb, "Analysis: Militia report unites ACLU, Republicans," The Associated Press, April 6, 2009.

74. "Modern Militia Movement," *op. cit.*

75. Chad Livengood, "Agency apologizes for militia report on candidates," *Springfield* (Mo.) *News-Leader*, p. A1.

76. Chris Blank, "Mo. Patrol names new leader for information center," The Associated Press, April 6, 2009.

77. Quoted in Lieb, *op. cit.*

78. Quoted in "Prevention Bulletin," North Central Texas Fusion System, Feb. 19, 2009, p. 4, www.privacylives.com/wp-content/uploads/2009/03/texasfusion_021909.pdf.

79. Quoted in Lieb, *op. cit.*

80. "Leftwing Extremists Likely to Increase Use of Cyber Attacks over the Coming Decade," Department of Homeland Security, Jan. 26, 2009, www.fas.org/irp/eprint/leftwing.pdf.

81. Quoted in "Homeland Security: Economic, Political Climate Fueling Extremism," Southern Poverty Law Center, April 15, 2009.

82. Quoted in *ibid.* Alexander Cockburn, "King of the Hate Business," *The Nation*, May 18, 2009, www.thenation.com/doc/20090518/cockburn.

83. Quoted in David Abel, "WTKK-FM suspends Severin for derogatory comments about Mexicans," *The Boston Globe*, April 30, 2009, www.boston.com/news/local/breaking_news/2009/04/_jay_severin.html.

84. Quoted in *ibid.*

85. Lindell Kay, "U.S. charges former Marine with making a threat against Obama," *Jacksonville Daily News*, Feb. 27, 2009, www2.journalnow.com/content/2009/feb/27/us-charges-former-marine-with-making-a-threat-agai.

86. "White Supremacist Recruitment of Military Personnel since 9/11," FBI, Counterterrorism Division, July 7, 2008, http://wikileaks.org/wiki/FBI:_White_Supremacist_Recruitment_of_Military_Personnel_2008.

87. *Ibid.*

88. "Boehner: Homeland Security Report Characterizing Veterans as Potential Terrorists is 'Offensive and Unacceptable,' " press release, April 15, 2009, http://republicanleader.house.gov/News/DocumentSingle.aspx?DocumentID=122567.

89. "White Supremacist Recruitment . . . ," *op. cit.* See also Jim Popkin, "White-power groups recruiting from military," "Deep Background — NBC News Investigates," July 16, 2008, http://deepbackground.msnbc.msn.com/archive/2008/07/16/1202484.aspx.

90. "White Supremacist Recruitment," *op. cit.*

91. David Holthouse, "A Few Bad Men," *Intelligence Report*, Southern Poverty Law Center, July 7, 2006, www.splcenter.org/intel/news/item.jsp?pid=79.

92. Art Pine, "Ft. Bragg Troops Restricted After Swastikas Are Painted," *Los Angeles Times*, July 17, 1996, p. A9; William Branigin and Dana Priest, "3 White Soldiers Held in Slaying of Black Couple," *The Washington Post*, Dec. 9, 1995, p. A1.

93. "Planning a Skinhead Infantry," sidebar to "A Few Bad Men," *op. cit.*, www.splcenter.org/intel/news/item.jsp?sid=21.

94. *Ibid.*

BIBLIOGRAPHY

Books

Berlet, Chip, and Matthew N. Lyons, *Right-Wing Populism in America: Too Close For Comfort*, Guilford Press, 2000.
Longtime analysts of the far right chronicle the long history of a movement that's larger than right-wing extremism.

German, Mike, *Thinking Like a Terrorist*, Potomac Books, 2007.
A former FBI agent recounts his undercover assignments in violent, far-right cells while arguing for government focus on law-breaking, not ideology.

Levitas, Daniel, *The Terrorist Next Door: The Militia Movement and the Radical Right,* **St. Martin's Press, 2002.**

The life of Posse Comitatus founder William Potter Gale provides the framework for an independent scholar's detailed history of domestic militias.

Paxton, Robert O., *The Anatomy of Fascism,* **Alfred A. Knopf, 2004.**

A leading scholar of the European extreme right distinguishes between its historic relics and the elements that survive.

Raspail, Jean, *The Camp of the Saints,* **Charles Scribner's Sons, 1975.**

Popular on the far right, this novel by a well-known French writer anticipates the fervent opposition to immigration from developing countries by depicting it as an invasion that will topple Western democratic societies.

Ridgeway, James, *Blood in the Face: Ku Klux Klan, Aryan Nations, Nazi Skinheads, and the Rise of a New White Culture,* **Thunder's Mouth Press, 1990.**

Journalist Ridgeway's prescient book includes documentary extremist material.

Articles

Blow, Charles M., "Pitchforks and Pistols," *The New York Times,* **April 3, 2009, www.nytimes .com/2009/04/04/opinion/04blow.html.**

A columnist argues that apocalyptic talk from conservative commentators preaching revolution and warning of gun-grabbing plans by the Obama administration may set off unstable minds.

Hedgecock, Roger, "Disagree with Obama? Gov't has eyes on you," WorldNetDaily, April 13, 2009, http:// wnd.com/index.php?fa=PAGE.view&page Id=94799.

The conservative columnist who obtained the first leaked copy of the Department of Homeland Security's recent assessment of the far right attacks it as a justification for political surveillance of Obama administration critics.

Jenkins, Philip, "Home-grown terrorism," *Los Angeles Times,* **March 10, 2008, p. A17.**

During the presidential campaign, a prominent Penn State historian of religion forecast a new wave of right-wing extremism — and of repressive Democratic response.

Roddy, Dennis B., "An Accused Cop Killer's Politics," *Slate,* **April 10, 2009, www.slate.com/id/2215826/.**

A reporter who investigated the man charged in the recent Pittsburgh police killings finds his political ideas jumbled.

Serrano, Richard A., " '90s-style extremism withers," *Los Angeles Times,* **March 11, 2008, p. A1.**

Writing before the latest wave of concern about extremism, a veteran correspondent reported that the far right hadn't recovered from the blows it suffered early in the decade.

Shapiro, Walter, "Long Shadow," *The New Republic,* **April 1, 2009, www.tnr.com/politics/story.html? id=9b2152b7-07fc-4503-9f33-4e2d222161d8.**

A veteran political writer sees a likely surge in populist rage with violent undertones.

Reports and Studies

"The Modern Militia Movement," Missouri Information Analysis Center, Feb. 20, 2009, www.scribd.com/ doc/13290698/The-Modern-Militia-Movement Missouri-MIAC-Strategic-Report-20Feb09.

The report, later repudiated by Missouri officials, triggered a nationwide controversy over government intrusion in political debate.

"Rightwing Extremism: Current Economic and Political Climate Fueling Resurgence in Radicalization and Recruitment," Department of Homeland Security, April 7, 2009, www.fas.org/irp/eprint/right-wing.pdf.

The controversial evaluation of the potential for a resurgence of the far right prompted a backlash against governmental monitoring of ideological trends.

"White Supremacist Recruitment of Military Personnel since 9/11," Federal Bureau of Investigation, July 7, 2008, http://wikileaks.org/wiki/FBI:_White_Supremacist_ Recruitment_of_Military_Personnel _2008.

This recent and more focused FBI report on extremists' interest in recruiting veterans received little attention, except among specialists.

For More Information

The American Cause, 501 Church St., Suite 315, Vienna, VA 22180; (703) 255-2632. Educational organization founded in 1993 by conservative commentator Pat Buchanan that supports "conservative principles of national sovereignty, economic patriotism, limited government and individual freedom."

Anti-Defamation League, Law Enforcement Agency Research Network; http://adl.org. A monitoring and research program aimed mainly at keeping law enforcement agencies up to date on extremism.

Federal Bureau of Investigation, J. Edgar Hoover Building, 935 Pennsylvania Ave., N.W., Washington, DC 20535; www.fbi.gov/hq/cid/civilrights/hate.htm. Provides statistics, information on the agency's anti-hate crime program and links to other sites.

Political Research Associates, 1310 Broadway, Suite 201, Somerville, MA 02144; (617) 666-5300; www.publiceye .org. A left-oriented think tank that investigates the far right.

Southern Poverty Law Center, 400 Washington Ave., Montgomery, AL 36104; www.splcenter.org/. Specializes in suing extremist organizations; maintains a research arm that monitors the extreme right.

Stormfront, P.O. Box 6637, West Palm Beach, FL 33405; (561) 833-0030; www.stormfront.org/forum. A heavily trafficked far-right site.

White Aryan Resistance, Tom Metzger P.O. Box 401, Warsaw, IN 46581; www.resist.com. A Web site maintained by a longtime extremist leader.

Nuclear Proliferation and Terrorism

Can "Rogue" States and Terrorists Acquire Nuclear Weapons?

Mary H. Cooper

5

AFP Photo/Philippe Lopez

Terrorist leader Osama bin Laden, left, with his deputy, Ayman al-Zawahiri, has said he wants to use a nuclear bomb against the West. The recent sale of black-market nuclear-weapons technology to North Korea and Iran and the terrorist bombing of passenger trains in Madrid, killing more than 190 people, have intensified concerns about nuclear weapons falling into the hands of "rogue" states or terrorists.

From *CQ Researcher*, April 2, 2004.

oncern about nuclear terrorism rose to new levels when A.Q. Khan, the revered father of Pakistan's nuclear bomb, confessed recently to peddling nuclear weapons technology to Libya and other rogue states.

Khan's dramatic confession punctured any remaining illusions that 60 years of nonproliferation efforts had kept the world's most dangerous weapons out of the hands of countries hostile to the United States and its allies. Moreover, he enhanced fears that terrorist groups bent on destroying the United States — like Osama bin Laden's al Qaeda network — may be closer than anyone had realized to acquiring nuclear weapons.

"A nuclear 9/11 in Washington or New York would change American history in ways that [the original] 9/11 didn't," says Graham Allison, director of Harvard University's Belfer Center for Science and International Affairs. "It would be as big a leap beyond 9/11 as 9/11 itself was beyond the pre-attack illusion that we were invulnerable."

Khan's January confession followed the revelation that he had operated a busy black-market trade in centrifuges, blueprints for nuclear-weapons equipment to enrich uranium into weapons-grade fuel and missiles capable of delivering nuclear warheads. Khan's vast network involved manufacturers in Malaysia, middlemen in the United Arab Emirates and the governments of Libya, North Korea and Iran.[1]

Several countries in Khan's network were known to have violated the 1968 Nuclear Non-Proliferation Treaty (NPT) and hidden their weapons programs from inspectors for the U.N.'s

107

Russia Has Most Nuclear Warheads

Russia and the United States have most of the more than 28,000 nuclear warheads stockpiled today. India, Israel and Pakistan — which have not signed the Nuclear Non-Proliferation Treaty (NPT) — have enough nuclear materials to produce more than 300 warheads. North Korea and Iran are both thought to be developing nuclear bombs. It is unknown whether terrorist groups have or are developing nuclear weapons.

Worldwide Nuclear Stockpiles

Country	Nuclear Weapons (estimated)
NPT Signatories	
China	410
France	350
Russia	18,000
United Kingdom	185
United States	9,000
Non-NPT Signatories*	
India	95 (max.)
Israel	200 (max.)
Pakistan	52 (max.)
Maximum total	**28,292**

* The number of warheads that could be produced with the amount of weapons-grade nuclear material these countries are thought to possess. The total number of assembled weapons is not known.

Source: Carnegie Endowment for International Peace, 2004

International Atomic Energy Agency (IAEA).[2] NPT signatories promise to forgo nuclear weapons in exchange for help from the world's five official nuclear powers — the United States, Russia, China, France and Britain — in building civilian nuclear power plants.

In fact, North Korea has bragged that it is developing nuclear weapons, Iraq tried for years to produce weapons-grade fuel, and Iran recently barred IAEA inspections from its nuclear facilities amid allegations that it was developing a bomb. Libya's admission in December that it, too, had tried to build the bomb blew the cover on Khan's network. (*See sidebar, p. 118.*)

But the extent of Khan's black-market activities stunned even the most seasoned observers. "I was surprised by the level of commerce in the supporting supply network," says Charles B. Curtis, president of the Nuclear Threat Initiative, an advocacy group that calls for stronger measures to stop the spread of nuclear weapons. "While there had been suggestions that the Pakistanis were nefariously engaged in both Iran and North Korea, the extent of the engagement in Libya and indications that there was an attempt to market proliferation technology in Syria exceeded the darkest suspicions of the intelligence community."

Given the grim realities of the post-9/11 world, fear of nuclear terrorism has dominated the international response to Khan's revelations. President Bush has proposed several measures to strengthen international anti-proliferation efforts. "In the hands of terrorists, weapons of mass destruction would be a first resort," Bush said. "[T]hese terrible weapons are becoming easier to acquire, build, hide and transport. . . . Our message to proliferators must be consistent and must be clear: We will find you, and we're not going to rest until you're stopped."[3]

But many experts say the president's proposals will not provide adequate safeguards against these lethal weapons. Wade Boese, research director of the Arms Control Association, a Washington think tank, commends the administration for emphasizing proliferation and pointing out that it is the most serious threat facing the United States today. However, he notes, since 9/11, the Bush administration has only "maintained the status quo" on funding for programs that deal with the threat of nuclear proliferation.

"The Khan network underscores the fact that we're in a race to tighten down security around [nuclear-weapons technology] so the terrorists can't get it," Boese says. "If this is such an urgent priority, which it is, why not fund it like it is and recognize that we're in a race with the terrorists?"

During the Cold War, both the United States and the Soviet Union understood that using nuclear weapons would amount to mass suicide. The doctrine of mutual assured destruction — MAD — ensured that a nuclear attack by one superpower would unleash a full-scale response by the other, resulting in annihilation on a national, if not global, scale. Consequently, the theory went, rational leaders would avoid using nuclear weapons at all costs.

But al Qaeda and other radical Islamist organizations don't appear to operate under such constraints. Their suicide bombers embrace death as martyrdom in their quest to destroy the "Great Satan."[4] And because they operate in a number of countries and have no permanent, identifiable headquarters, terrorist groups also have no "return address" to target for a counterattack.

As a result, keeping weapons-grade plutonium and highly enriched uranium out of the hands of terrorists is the only sure way to block terrorists from building nuclear bombs, many experts say.

"The essential ingredients of nuclear weapons are very hard to make and don't occur in nature," notes Matthew Bunn, a nuclear-terrorism expert at the Belfer Center. "But once a well-organized terrorist group gets hold of them, it could make at least a crude nuclear explosive."

Instructions for making a nuclear bomb are not secret; they are even on the Internet. "The secret is in making the nuclear material," Bunn points out, "and that, unfortunately, is the secret that A.Q. Khan was peddling."

While the ability of terrorists to stage a full-scale nuclear attack is of paramount concern, experts say the use of a conventional explosive device containing radioactive waste — a so-called dirty bomb — is far more likely. A dirty bomb in an urban area could contaminate dozens of city blocks, fomenting panic and costing tens of billions of dollars in lost revenues and devalued real estate, even if it claimed no human lives.[5]

"A dirty bomb is pretty likely to happen," says Leonard S. Spector, director of the Center for Nonproliferation Studies' Washington office, a part of the Monterey Institute of International Studies. A dirty bomb can be made easily with radioactive materials, such as cesium, used in X-ray machines and other commonplace diagnostic equipment. Moreover, he points out, civilian nuclear-waste facilities are much easier to penetrate than weapons facilities.

Getty Images

Protesters in Seoul, South Korea, burn a North Korean flag and an effigy of Kim Jong Il on Dec. 28, 2003, calling on North Korea's leader to end the country's efforts to build a nuclear bomb.

"We have to do our best to control as much of the radioactive material as possible," he says, "but it's already the subject of criminal activities. So we're recommending that people get ready for this one."

As policymakers examine the impact of Khan's nuclear black marketeering on U.S. counterproliferation policy, these are some of the questions being considered:

Is the Non-Proliferation Treaty still an effective shield against the spread of nuclear weapons?

The United States launched the atomic age when it detonated the first atomic bomb in 1945. But after Britain, China, France and the Soviet Union developed their own nuclear weapons, the great powers sought to put the nuclear genie back in the bottle. The landmark 1968 Non-Proliferation Treaty embodied a "grand bargain," by which the five countries with nuclear arsenals agreed to help the rest of the world develop nuclear power for peaceful uses in exchange for the non-nuclear states' promise to forgo nuclear weapons. The IAEA was to oversee compliance with the treaty, which enjoyed near universal support.

However, India, Israel and Pakistan — all of which have since developed nuclear weapons — never signed the treaty. And North Korea, which signed but later renounced the treaty, recently boasted that it is on the threshold of developing nuclear weapons.

The absence of universal adherence to the NPT reveals the treaty's basic weakness. "The fact that a very

A Chronology of Nuclear Close Calls

The superpowers came close to using nuclear weapons several times during the Cold War, sometimes due to tensions that might have escalated, and sometimes due to simple accidents or mistakes. The end of the Cold War in 1991, however, did not end the threat of nuclear conflict.

First year of Korean War, 1950-51 — President Harry S. Truman sends atomic weapons to Guam for possible use against North Korea; Strategic Air Command makes plans to coordinate an atomic strike. Gen. Douglas MacArthur pushes for attacks on China, possibly using atomic weapons.[1]

The Offshore Islands Crises, 1954-55, 1958 — Testing America's resolve, China bombs Quemoy and Matzu, two Nationalist-held islands near the mainland. U.S. officials warn they will use atomic weapons to defend the islands.[2]

Mistake in Greenland, October 1960 — The American early-warning radar system in Thule, Greenland, mistakenly reports a "massive" Soviet missile launch against the United States. A reflection on the moon 250,000 miles away is thought to be a missile launch 2,500 miles away.[3]

Flashpoint Berlin, 1961 — Soviet threats regarding West Berlin prompt President John F. Kennedy to consider a nuclear first-strike against the U.S.S.R. if it attacks the city.[4]

Cuban Missile Crisis, October 1962 — President Kennedy considers invading Cuba to remove Soviet nuclear missiles, unaware the Soviets plan to respond with nuclear weapons. The Strategic Air Command goes to Defense Condition 2 (DEFCON 2), the second-highest state of readiness, for the only time in U.S. history. After an American naval quarantine of the island, Soviet Premier Nikita Khrushchev withdraws the missiles.[5]

B-52 Crash in Greenland, January 1968 — A B-52 carrying four thermonuclear bombs crashes near the U.S. early-warning base in Greenland. If the bombs' safety features had failed, the detonation could have been viewed as a surprise attack on America's early-warning system, prompting nuclear retaliation.[6]

Sino-Soviet Conflict, 1969 — Soviet Defense Minister Andrei Grechko advocates a nuclear strike against China to deal with what is perceived as an inevitable future war. Fearing the U.S. reaction, the Soviets refrain.[7]

Yom Kippur War, October 1973 — Egypt and Syria attack Israel, and after initial successes face military disaster. The Soviet Union indicates it might intervene to rescue its client states if Israel continues to refuse a cease-fire; Soviet airborne forces are put on alert, and U.S. military forces also go on alert. Israel agrees to a cease-fire and the superpower crisis ends.[8]

War Game Turns 'Real' at NORAD, 1979-80 — In November 1979, a technician at the North American Air Defense (NORAD) facility in Cheyenne Mountain, Colo., accidentally places a training tape simulating a

small number of individuals — nobody believes that A.Q. Khan was acting alone — can create a network that provides some of the most worrisome states on the planet with the technology needed to produce nuclear weapons is very troubling," Bunn says. "It shows that the NPT regime is only as strong as its weakest links. We can secure 90 percent of the nuclear material to very high levels, but if the other 10 percent is vulnerable to theft, we still won't have solved the problem because we're dealing with intelligent adversaries who will be able to find and exploit the weak points."

In fact, some experts say that weaknesses doom the NPT to failure. "Arms-control regimes are not capable of dealing with the hard cases," says John Pike, a defense policy expert and founding director of GlobalSecurity .org, a nonprofit organization that studies emerging security threats.

"The logic of the NPT just doesn't get you very far in Tehran [Iran] or Pyongyang [North Korea]," Pike says. "It's not going to matter to India or Pakistan, which have their own fish to fry. And the Israelis are not going to let go of their arsenal until there is a just and lasting peace in the Middle East," Pike says. "I'm afraid we're rapidly approaching a situation in which there are more nuclear-weapons states outside the NPT than inside, and the treaty itself provides no way whatsoever of addressing that problem."

The nonproliferation regime also lacks adequate verification and enforcement provisions, critics say. "The NPT was a confidence-building measure, not a true

nuclear attack on the United States into the base computer system. The mistake is corrected in six minutes —
but after the president's airborne command post is
launched. Twice in June 1980, false attack warnings
caused by faulty computer chips send bomber crews rac-
ing for their planes.[9]

Tension in Europe, Early 1980s — After the Soviet
Union deploys new nuclear missiles in Europe, the United
States follows suit. Soviet leader Yuri Andropov fears NATO
is planning a nuclear first-strike and orders Soviet intelligence to find the non-existent evidence. Tension in Europe
decreases when Mikhail Gorbachev replaces Andropov.[10]

Soviet Pacific Fleet, August 1984 — A rogue officer at
the Soviet Pacific Fleet in Vladivostok broadcasts an unauthorized war alert to Soviet naval forces, which, like
American vessels, are armed with nuclear weapons. Soviet,
U.S. and Japanese forces all prepare for battle. After 30
minutes, the alert is determined to be false.[11]

Norwegian Sea, January 1995 — Russian radar detects
an inbound missile over the Norwegian Sea, and President
Boris N. Yeltsin opens his nuclear command briefcase and
confers with his military commanders. The missile turns
out to be a Norwegian weather rocket.[12]

Kargil, Kashmir, May-July 1999 — A year after
nuclear tests by India and Pakistan, Pakistan invades Kargil,
in Indian-controlled Kashmir, and battles Indian forces
from May until July. The crisis between the two rival
nuclear powers is described as "warlike." Pakistan withdraws in July under heavy international pressure.[13]

**Attack on the Indian Parliament, December 2001-
January 2002** — Islamic militants probably connected to
Pakistan's intelligence service attack India's Parliament. India
demands that Pakistan cease supporting Islamic fighters.
Hundreds of thousands of troops face off at the Indo-Pakistani
border; both sides discuss a possible nuclear exchange. Tensions
ease after Pakistan cracks down on Islamist groups.[14]

— *Kenneth Lukas*

[1] Burton Kaufman, *The Korean Conflict* (1999).

[2] John W. Garver, *Foreign Relations of the People's Republic of China* (1993), pp. 50-60.

[3] Center for Defense Information (CDI), www.cdi.org/Issues/NukeAccidents/accidents.htm.

[4] Fred Kaplan, "JFK's First Strike Plan," *The Atlantic Monthly*, October 2001, pp. 81-86.

[5] Graham Allison and Philip Zelikow, *Essence of Decision* (1999).

[6] Scott D. Sagan, *The Limits of Safety* (1993), pp. 180-193.

[7] Garver, *op. cit.*, pp. 305-310.

[8] P. R. Kumaraswamy (ed.), *Revisiting the Yom Kippur War* (2000).

[9] Sagan, *op. cit.*, pp. 228-233.

[10] Christopher Andrew and Vasili Mitrokhin, *The Sword and the Shield* (1999).

[11] CNN, www.cnn.com/SPECIALS/cold.war/episodes/12/spotlight/.

[12] CNN, *op. cit.*

[13] Yossef Bodansky, "The Kargil Crisis in Kashmir Threatens to Move into a New Indo-Pak War, With PRC Involvement," *Defense & Foreign Affairs Strategic Policy*, May/June 1999, p. 20.

[14] Seymour M. Hersh, "The Getaway," *The New Yorker*, Jan. 28, 2002, p. 36.

arms-control treaty," says C. Paul Robinson, director of
Sandia National Laboratories, a division of the Energy
Department's National Nuclear Security Administration.
Robinson also was chief U.S. negotiator of the U.S.-
Soviet Threshold Test Ban and Peaceful Nuclear
Explosions Treaties, both ratified in 1990. None of the
requirements normally found in arms-control treaties to
verify compliance were included in the NPT, he says. "So
there's nothing in the original NPT designed to catch
cheaters."

After the 1991 Persian Gulf War, the nuclear nonproliferation community was surprised to learn that Iraq
had been secretly developing nuclear weapons. So an
"Additional Protocol" was added to the NPT allowing
for more thorough inspections of suspected weapons
facilities, but only 38 countries have ratified it. In any
case, Robinson dismisses the protocol as little more than
a "Band-Aid."

Even IAEA Director Mohamed ElBaradei said the
NPT regime does not prevent nuclear proliferation. "You
need a complete overhaul of the export-control system,"
he said. "It is not working right now."[6]

But the Bush administration says if the NPT and the
IAEA oversight powers are strengthened, nonproliferation can remain a credible goal. On Feb. 11, Bush outlined seven steps designed to make the regime more
effective in dealing with the threat of what the State
Department calls "rogue" states and nuclear terrorism,
including U.S. Senate approval of the Additional
Protocol (*see p. 122*).

Other analysts say world dynamics have changed so dramatically since the NPT took effect that the nonproliferation regime needs a revolutionary overhaul. "The treaty was about controlling states and governments, not rogue individuals or terrorists who get their hands on these weapons," says Boese of the Arms Control Association. "The nonproliferation regime needs to be modified to better address this gap."

"The system has been pretty remarkable and successful, but is now in sufficient need of radical repair that we need a big jump forward," says Allison of the Belfer Center, who as assistant Defense secretary oversaw the Clinton administration's efforts to reduce the former Soviet nuclear arsenal. "We should now build a global alliance against nuclear terrorism, and the core of its strategy should be the doctrine of what I call the three 'Nos:' "[7]

- "No loose nukes" — Allison coined the phrase a decade ago to describe weapons and weapons-grade materials inadequately secured against theft. "These weapons and materials must be protected to a new security standard adequate to prevent nuclear terrorists from attacking us," he says. Under Allison's proposal, all nuclear states would have to be certified by another member of the nuclear club that all their nuclear materials had been adequately secured. The NPT has no such requirement.
- "No new nascent nukes" — New production of highly enriched uranium and plutonium would be barred. "If you don't have either one of them, you don't have a nuclear weapon," Allison says.
- "No new nuclear weapons" — Noting North Korea's nuclear ambitions, Allison acknowledges that this is the most difficult but potentially most important goal. "To accept North Korea as a new member of the nuclear club would be catastrophic," Allison says, "because North Korea historically has been the most promiscuous proliferator on Earth."

North Korea has sold nuclear-capable missiles to Iraq, Pakistan and other would-be nuclear powers. If Pyongyang develops a nuclear arsenal, most experts agree, other countries in the region, including South Korea, Japan and Taiwan, would be tempted to jettison the NPT and develop their own arsenals in defense, setting off a potentially disastrous regional arms race.

"A nuclear North Korea," Allison says, "would blow the lid off the previous arms control and nuclear proliferation regime."

Is the United States doing enough to halt nuclear proliferation?

Since the fall of the Soviet Union in 1991, the United States has concentrated its nonproliferation efforts on preventing the theft or sale of nuclear weapons and materials left in Russia, Ukraine and other former Soviet republics. The 1991 Soviet Nuclear Threat Reduction Act — renamed the Cooperative Threat Reduction (CTR) program in 1993 — was designed to help former Soviet satellite countries destroy nuclear, chemical and biological weapons and associated infrastructure. Nicknamed Nunn-Lugar after the law's original sponsors (Sens. Sam Nunn, D-Ga., and Richard G. Lugar, R-Ind.), it also established verifiable safeguards against the proliferation of such weapons.

Recent U.S. efforts to control the worldwide supply of nuclear weapons and materials have focused almost solely on the CTR program: More than 50 former Soviet nuclear-storage sites have been secured and new security systems installed. Besides locking up nuclear materials and establishing security perimeters around the storage sites, says Robinson of Sandia Labs, the CTR program installs detection equipment to warn of any movement of the guarded material. "This material is being locked up and safeguarded," Robinson says. Sandia designs and installs the nuclear-security systems and trains foreign technicians on their use.

But critics say the agreement is woefully inadequate. "Very, very little progress has taken place," says Curtis of the Nuclear Threat Initiative, which Nunn co-founded. "There is an inertia that simply must be overcome with presidential leadership in all the participant countries."

The Bush administration recognizes the importance of securing Russia's nuclear stockpiles. In 2002, the United States, along with Britain, France, Canada, Japan, Germany and Italy, agreed to spend $20 billion over 10 years to support CTR programs — with half of it, or $1 billion a year, to come from the United States.

But that amounts to only about a quarter of 1 percent of the current Defense Department budget of about $401 billion, Bunn points out. "Amazingly," he adds, despite the new terrorist threats throughout the world,

U.S. funding for the CTR programs "hasn't increased noticeably since Sept. 11."

Bunn is not alone. A task force led by former Sen. Howard H. Baker Jr., R-Tenn., and former White House Counsel Lloyd Cutler in January 2001 called for a tripling in annual CTR spending — to $3 billion a year.[8]

Inadequate funding has slowed the pace of securing Russia's nuclear sites, critics say. "We're not doing all that we know how to do and all that we must to keep these weapons and materials safe," Curtis says. After more than a decade of Nunn-Lugar efforts, only half of Russia's nuclear weapons have been adequately secured, Curtis points out.

Critics of the war against Iraq suggest that the campaign to topple Saddam Hussein expended precious resources that could have gone toward halting the spread of nuclear materials. The first order of business in combating nuclear terrorism, Allison says, is to list potential sources of nuclear weapons, in order of priority. "Saddam clearly had nuclear ambitions, and the CIA said that over the course of a decade he might realize them," Allison says. "So he deserved to be on the list somewhere down there, but he wasn't in the top dozen for me."

The nuclear weapons and materials that remain vulnerable to theft in Russia are at the top of Allison's list, primarily because of the magnitude of the problem. "We've still got 120 metric tons of highly enriched uranium and plutonium in Russia alone that we haven't even begun security upgrades on," Curtis points out.

Second on Allison's list is North Korea. By repudiating the Clinton administration's "Agreed Framework" with North Korea and refusing to engage in negotiations with the regime until it renounces its nuclear program, Allison says the Bush administration has allowed "North Korea to just about declare itself a nuclear-weapons state. For the past three years, they have been given a pass. And what have they been doing while they got a pass? They've been creating more plutonium every day, as they are today." Recent six-party talks in Beijing aimed at halting North Korea's nuclear-weapons program ended without significant progress.[9]

Third on Allison's priority list is Pakistan. Because it is not a party to the NPT, Pakistan's nuclear-weapons inventory is unknown. But according to a recent CIA analysis, Pakistan's Khan Research Laboratories has been providing North Korea with nuclear fuel, centrifuges and warhead designs since the early 1990s.[10] No one

knows how many other customers Khan supplied over the past decade.

"A coherent strategy has got to deal with the most urgent potential sources of supply to terrorists first," Allison says. "When all this other stuff has been happening, why was Iraq the focus of attention for two years?"

Although no evidence that Iraq had recently pursued nuclear weapons has been found since the United States invaded the country over a year ago, Bush continues to defend his decision to overthrow Hussein's regime in the name of counterproliferation.

"The former dictator of Iraq possessed and used weapons of mass destruction against his own people," Bush said on Feb. 11. "For 12 years, he defied the will of the international community. He refused to disarm or account for his illegal weapons and programs. He doubted our resolve to enforce our word — and now he sits in a prison cell, while his country moves toward a democratic future."

Although Russia and Pakistan are widely regarded as the biggest potential sources of nuclear proliferation, the United States has a mixed record on safeguarding its own nuclear materials. The United States exported highly enriched uranium to 43 countries for nearly four decades as part of the Atoms for Peace program, sanctioned by the NPT, to help other countries acquire nuclear technology for peaceful purposes. The uranium was supposed to be returned to the United States in its original form or as spent fuel. But according to a recent report by the Energy Department's inspector general, the United States has made little headway in recovering the uranium, which is enough to make about 1,000 nuclear weapons.[11]

"While we should be locking up materials at risk wherever we can and recovering them when needed, the Department of Energy has been leisurely pursuing its program to recover highly enriched uranium at risk in research facilities around the world," Curtis says. "This is a leisure that we can ill afford."

Should nonproliferation policy aim to eliminate all nuclear weapons?

Article VI of the NPT requires countries with nuclear weapons to take "effective measures" to end the arms race and work toward nuclear disarmament. This was an essential component of the "grand bargain" used to lure the rest of the world to forgo nuclear arms.

Defusing North Korea and Iran

The good news: Only two so-called rogue nations are suspected of trying to build nuclear weapons. (Libya recently promised to end its bomb-making efforts, and Iraq never was close to having a bomb, U.N. inspectors say.) The bad news: The two rogue nations are North Korea and Iran.

North Korea is considered the more immediate threat. The shaky truce that ended the bloody Korean War (1950-53) has not removed the threat of hostilities between the reclusive, authoritarian regime and U.S.-supported South Korea, which relies on a large U.S. military presence for much of its defense.

Under the 1994 Agreed Framework brokered by President Bill Clinton, North Korea agreed to freeze production of plutonium — needed in the production of some nuclear weapons — in exchange for U.S. energy assistance and improved diplomatic relations. That agreement fell apart in October 2002, when the Bush administration accused North Korean leader Kim Jong Il of trying to enrich uranium in violation of the Non-Proliferation Treaty (NPT).

In January 2003, North Korea withdrew from the NPT and kicked out U.N. International Atomic Energy Agency (IAEA) inspectors. North Korea has continued to deny it has a uranium-enrichment program but openly acknowledges its plutonium program, which may already have produced one or two nuclear weapons.

The most recent talks aimed at ending North Korea's nuclear-weapons ambitions, held in late February 2004 in Beijing, also involved China, Russia, Japan and South Korea. The talks failed to overcome the impasse between the Bush administration, which insists on the "complete, verifiable and irreversible dismantlement" of North Korea's nuclear programs before the United States will agree to improve bilateral relations, provide economic and energy assistance and offer "security guarantees" that it will not invade North Korea.

Prospects for the success of follow-up talks soured further on March 20, when North Korea warned it would expand its nuclear-weapons program if the yearly U.S.-led military exercises in South Korea proceed as scheduled in late March.[1]

Iran's nuclear ambitions raised concern two years ago with the discovery of a large uranium-enrichment plant south of Tehran, the capital. Iran, a signatory to the NPT, claims its nuclear program is used purely to generate electricity. In mid-March, after the IAEA censured Tehran for not fully disclosing its nuclear program, Iran

As the sole remaining superpower, the United States plays a key role in leading the world toward disarmament. "Nonproliferation strategies have always been linked to U.S. efforts to reduce reliance on its nuclear forces, so there's always been an arms control link to the NPT as part of the essential bargain," says Curtis of NTI. "The world community also considers it a prerequisite for the United States to exercise its moral leadership on nonproliferation, that it be seen to be living up to its side of that bargain."

During the Cold War, the United States and the Soviet Union, which had amassed vast nuclear arsenals, signed a series of treaties that first limited, and then began to reduce, the number of nuclear weapons on each side.[12] On May 24, 2002, President Bush and Russian President Vladimir V. Putin signed the latest of these, the Strategic Offensive Reductions Treaty (SORT). It called on the two countries to reduce their current number of strategic nuclear warheads by nearly two-thirds by Dec. 31, 2012 — to 1,700-2,200 warheads.

"President Putin and I have signed a treaty that will substantially reduce our strategic nuclear warhead arsenals to . . . the lowest level in decades," Bush declared at the Moscow signing ceremony. "This treaty liquidates the Cold War legacy of nuclear hostility between our countries."

But critics say the so-called Moscow Treaty will be far less effective in ridding the world of nuclear weapons than the president's comments suggest. "The agreement doesn't require the destruction of a single warhead or a single delivery vehicle," says Boese of the Arms Control Association. Warheads that are removed from deployment could be disassembled or stored rather than destroyed. "Also, the agreement's limit is actually in effect temporarily barred the agency from the country. Inspections were set to resume on March 27.

Meanwhile, IAEA Director Mohamed ElBaradei has appealed to President Bush to launch talks with Iran aimed at improving bilateral relations, which have remained hostile since Islamic clerics wrested control of Iran from the U.S.-supported regime of Shah Mohammed Reza Pahlavi in 1979.

Ending Iran's and North Korea's nuclear ambitions will require convincing both countries that they don't need nuclear weapons to defend themselves, experts say. "To strengthen the international nonproliferation regime, we're going have to provide security assurances as well as economic aid," says Matthew Bunn, a nuclear-weapons expert at Harvard University's Belfer Center for Science and International Affairs. "There's going to have to be some kind of security assurance that the United States isn't going to invade Iran and overthrow its government. That's the center of the discussion with North Korea as well."

Failure to do so may lead to regional arms races that could quickly get out of control. If North Korea produces a nuclear arsenal, predicts John Pike of GlobalSecurity.org, Japan may feel sufficiently threatened to transform some of its civilian power-plant nuclear materials to build nuclear weapons in self-defense. "Then South Korea is going to need them, and Taiwan's going to need them," he says. "That will make China want to have more, which will prompt India to need more, and then Pakistan will, too."

North Korean leader Kim Jong Il

AFP Photo

[1] United Press International, "N. Korea Warns U.S. over War Exercises," March 20, 2004.

for just one day — Dec. 31, 2012," Boese says. "Because neither side has to destroy anything after that day, presumably they could then rebuild their arsenals."

After the Sept. 11 terrorist attacks, the Bush administration toughened U.S. policy on nuclear weapons and other weapons of mass destruction (WMD). The new national strategy to combat nuclear, biological and chemical weapons, issued in December 2002, called for strengthening "traditional measures — diplomacy, arms control, multilateral agreements, threat-reduction assistance and export controls." But for the first time, the United States openly warned that it would pre-emptively attack adversaries thought to be preparing to use weapons of mass destruction against the United States.

"U.S. military forces . . . must have the capability to defend against WMD-armed adversaries, including, in appropriate cases, through pre-emptive measures," the administration declared. "This requires capabilities to detect and destroy an adversary's WMD assets before these weapons are used."[13]

Meanwhile, the administration's latest Nuclear Posture Review, sent to Congress on Dec. 31, 2001, called for research into new types of nuclear weapons and outlined new uses for them.[14] As part of that policy, the administration has initiated research into the "bunker buster," a missile armed with a low-yield (less than five kilotons) nuclear warhead designed to penetrate and destroy enemy arsenals or other targets buried deep underground. To enable research to proceed, Congress last year overturned a Clinton-era ban on research and development of low-yield nuclear weapons.[15]

"The reason it was important to reduce or get rid of the prohibition on low-yield nuclear weapons was not because we're trying to develop or are developing low-yield nuclear weapons," said National Nuclear Security Administrator Linton Brooks. "That's a misconception. . . . What we said was that the amendment was poorly drawn and it prohibited research that could lead to a low-yield nuclear weapon."[16] In fact, research on high-powered "bunker buster" bombs commenced in 2003, after Congress overturned the ban.[17]

Since taking office, the administration has rejected arms control as an essential tool for reducing the nuclear threat. Shortly after being sworn into office, Bush said he would not resubmit the 1996 Comprehensive Test Ban Treaty to the Senate for ratification. He also abrogated the 1972 U.S.-Soviet Anti-Ballistic Missile Treaty, which barred signatories from building national defense systems to protect against ballistic-missile attack — a move designed to discourage the superpowers from building more nuclear weapons to overcome such defenses.

Bush instead announced he would pursue earlier plans to build a National Missile Defense System while seeking a "new strategic framework" for dealing with Russia that would focus on reductions in nuclear weapons.[18] The first U.S. anti-missile defense facility, scheduled for deployment in Alaska this summer, has faced criticism for its technical flaws and for undermining the United States' credibility as a strong advocate of nuclear disarmament.[19]

"The current U.S. approach to proliferation emphasizes non-treaty methods and military means, including the effort to deploy a national missile defense system," said John Cirincione, director for nonproliferation at the Carnegie Endowment for International Peace. "The system faces formidable technical challenges and is unlikely to be militarily effective anytime in this decade. Every system within the missile-defense program is behind schedule, over budget and underperforming."[20]

While supporters of the administration's nuclear policy say the changes were needed to protect the United States in a new era of uncertainty, critics say they undermine the administration's credibility in its calls to strengthen global anti-proliferation measures.

"If you're trying to build a consensus [on halting proliferation] while at the same time saying we need a few more different nuclear weapons, I would say those are inconsistent arguments," Allison says. "I've negotiated on behalf of the U.S. government many times when I felt I had a weak hand, but I couldn't imagine keeping a straight face in trying to argue these two goals at the same time."

BACKGROUND

Manhattan Project

The nuclear age traces its origins to 1938, when scientists in Nazi Germany split the nucleus of a uranium atom, releasing heat and radiation. The potential of nuclear fission, as the process was called, to produce weapons of unparalleled power prompted a recent refugee from Germany — Albert Einstein — to alert President Franklin D. Roosevelt. "[T]he element uranium may be turned into a new and important source of energy in the immediate future," the already-legendary physicist wrote. ["T]his new phenomenon," he added, could lead "to the construction of bombs . . ., extremely powerful bombs of a new type."[21]

In 1939, even before the United States entered World War II or realized the full implications of Einstein's warning, Roosevelt established the first federal uranium-research program. Fission research led to further advances, including the 1940 discovery of the element plutonium by physicists at the University of California, Berkeley. After the United States entered the war against Japan, Germany and Italy in December, the race to beat Germany in developing an atomic bomb accelerated under a secret Army Corps of Engineers program known as the Manhattan Project.*

By September 1944, after less than two years of work, Manhattan Project researchers had begun producing plutonium for weapons. On July 16, 1945, they detonated an experimental atomic bomb known as "the Gadget" from a tower in the New Mexico desert. Less than three weeks later, on Aug. 6, U.S. airmen dropped an atom bomb nicknamed "Little Boy" on Hiroshima, followed on Aug. 9 by the detonation of "Fat Man" over Nagasaki. Two days later, Japan surrendered. World War II was over

---

* Atomic weapons get their energy from the fission, or breaking apart, of the nucleus of an atom of uranium or plutonium. Hydrogen — or thermonuclear — weapons get their energy largely from fusion, the formation of a heavier nucleus from two lighter ones. Both types of weapons are known collectively as nuclear weapons.

C H R O N O L O G Y

1930s-1980s *Atomic Age begins and evolves into the Cold War.*

1938 Scientists in Nazi Germany split the nucleus of a uranium atom. A year later, the U.S. Manhattan Project enters the race to create an atomic bomb.

Aug. 6, 1945 U.S. drops an atomic bomb on Hiroshima, Japan, followed on Aug. 9 by another on Nagasaki, killing a total of more than 250,000 people. Two days later, Japan surrenders, ending World War II.

1949 The Soviet Union tests its first atomic weapon.

Dec. 8, 1953 President Dwight D. Eisenhower's "Atoms for Peace" proposal calls for using fissionable material "to serve the peaceful pursuits of mankind."

1957 International Atomic Energy Agency (IAEA) is created to promote peaceful use of nuclear energy.

May 26, 1958 Eisenhower opens first U.S. nuclear power plant, at Shippingport, Pa.

1964 China joins the United States, Soviet Union, Britain and France in the "nuclear club" of officially recognized nuclear-weapons states.

July 1, 1968 Nuclear Non-Proliferation Treaty (NPT) is signed by 98 countries after a decade of talks.

1969 Treaty of Tlatelolco bars nuclear weapons from Latin America. Brazil and Argentina are the last nations to sign, in the 1990s.

1981 Israel destroys an Iraqi nuclear reactor, claiming it was being used to produce fuel for weapons.

1990s *Cold War ends, posing new proliferation threats.*

1991 Soviet Union collapses. . . . Persian Gulf War against Iraq, an NPT signatory, reveals that Saddam Hussein had been trying to develop nuclear weapons. . . . Soviet Nuclear Threat Reduction Act sponsored by Sens. Sam Nunn, D-Ga., and Richard G. Lugar, R-Ind., authorizes the United States to help former

Soviet-bloc countries destroy nuclear, chemical and biological weapons and establishes verifiable safeguards against their proliferation.

1993 Nunn-Lugar program is broadened and renamed the Cooperative Threat Reduction (CTR) program. . . . South Africa becomes first country with nuclear weapons to renounce its nuclear program and join the NPT.

October 1994 North Korea agrees to freeze its plutonium production in exchange for U.S. assistance in producing energy.

1996 President Bill Clinton signs the Comprehensive Test Ban Treaty.

1998 India and Pakistan join Israel on the list of non-NPT signatories with nuclear weapons.

2000s *Massive terrorist attacks raise the specter of nuclear terrorism.*

Sept. 11, 2001 Suicide airline hijackers linked to Osama bin Laden's al Qaeda terrorist group kill nearly 3,000 people in the worst terrorist attacks in U.S. history.

2002 President Bush disavows the U.S. pact with North Korea and calls on Kim Jong Il to renounce his nuclear ambitions as a condition of the resumption of U.S. aid.

March 19, 2003 U.S. troops invade Iraq but find no weapons of mass destruction.

Dec. 19, 2003 Libya agrees to terminate its nuclear-weapons program, revealing evidence of a Pakistan-based black market in nuclear technology.

Feb. 6, 2004 Pakistani President Pervez Musharraf pardons Abdul Qadeer Khan, founder of Pakistan's nuclear-weapons program, for selling nuclear technology to Iran, North Korea, Libya and possibly others.

Feb. 11, 2004 President Bush responds to the revelations about Khan's network with a seven-point plan to strengthen the NPT and IAEA's enforcement powers.

Fall of a Nuclear Black Marketeer

As A.Q. Khan tells it, the horrors of religious intolerance he witnessed as a 10-year-old Muslim in India turned him into the world's leading black-market merchant of nuclear-bomb materials.[1]

"I can remember trains coming into the station full of dead Muslims," Khan recalled recently, describing the sectarian violence that broke out in Bhopal following Indian independence from Britain. "The [Hindu] Indian authorities were treating the Muslims horribly."[2]

Six years later, Khan fled north to the newly independent Islamic nation of Pakistan. But the slaughter he had seen as a youngster left Khan with an enduring enmity toward India and shaped his life's work, spurring him to develop Pakistan's nuclear bomb.

In the 1960s, Khan pursued postgraduate studies in metallurgy in Western Europe and later worked in the Netherlands at a uranium-enrichment plant run by Urenco, a Dutch-British-German consortium. There he learned about uranium enrichment and the design of sophisticated centrifuges needed to produce weapons-grade nuclear fuel.

Khan reportedly smuggled Urenco's centrifuge designs into Pakistan in the mid-1970s after Prime Minister Zulfikar Ali Bhutto invited him to establish the country's nuclear-weapons program. A Dutch court in 1983 convicted him in absentia of attempted espionage for stealing the designs, but the conviction was overturned.

As the director of Pakistan's nuclear program, Khan became adept at procuring equipment and technology —

both legally and on the black market — and did little to conceal his activities. He even published a brochure with a photo of himself and a list of nuclear materials available for sale or barter, including intermediate-range ballistic missiles. Investigators say Khan's network stretched from Europe to Turkey, Russia and Malaysia. Khan himself traveled to North Korea at least 13 times to swap his nuclear technology for Korean missile technology, and U.N. inspectors have discovered documents in Iraq suggesting that he offered to help Saddam Hussein build a nuclear weapon in 1990, just before the first Gulf War.[3]

By 1998, when India first tested nuclear devices, Khan was quick to follow suit. Now the bitter adversaries were both in the "nuclear club."

Khan became an instant hero to Pakistanis, whose hatred of India permeates the national culture. Schools, streets and children were named after him. Indeed, most Pakistanis appeared forgiving when Khan confessed in February following revelations he had illegally supplied nuclear technology to North Korea, Libya and Iran.

But Khan's admissions — and the fact that he was not punished for selling nuclear secrets to rogue states — infuriated many Americans and others in the West. "It sends a horrible signal," said David Albright, president of the Institute for Science and International Security, a nonpartisan think tank dedicated to educating the public on scientific issues affecting international security. "It basically says,

and the "Atomic Age" had begun. Within weeks of the bombings, the death toll had climbed to more than 100,000 people — mainly civilians.

The enormous loss of civilian lives sparked intense debate over the future of atomic weapons. The Manhattan Project cost the U.S. government almost $20 billion (in today's dollars), including the construction of reactors and lab facilities at more than 30 sites, such as Los Alamos, N.M., Oak Ridge, Tenn., and Hanford, Wash. In 1946, the American representative to the newly created United Nations Atomic Energy Commission, Bernard M. Baruch, proposed the elimination of atomic weapons, but the Soviet Union rejected the proposal. In 1947, Congress replaced the Manhattan Project with the civilian

Atomic Energy Commission, which assumed control over atomic research and weapons facilities around the country.

The postwar deterioration of relations with the Soviet Union effectively ended the nuclear debate in the United States and prompted the administration of President Harry S. Truman to intensify production of nuclear weapons, especially the next generation of more powerful, thermonuclear weapons. The first Soviet atomic bomb test and the rise of communism in China in 1949, followed the next year by the outbreak of the Korean War, fueled U.S. policymakers' support of the weapons program. By the early 1950s, both sides in the rapidly escalating Cold War had developed hydrogen bombs.

'Yeah, your wrists will be slapped, but, boy, you're going to make millions of dollars.' "[4]

Khan professes bewilderment at the outrage his proliferation activities have engendered. "They dislike me and accuse me of all kinds of unsubstantiated and fabricated lies because I disturbed all their strategic plans, the balance of power and blackmailing potential in this part of the world," he said. "I am not a madman or a nut. . . . I consider myself a humble, patriotic Pakistani who gave his best for his country."

Indeed, while Islamic extremism is rising in Pakistan, the moderate Khan is married to a Dutch national, and neither she nor their daughters wear the veil typically worn by conservative Muslims.

Kahn's enduring popularity helps explain why Pakistani President Pervez Musharraf pardoned him — and why the Bush administration accepted Musharraf's claim that he knew nothing of Khan's illicit activities. Others say the United States did not push Musharraf to punish Khan because of a deal in which Pakistan would help U.S. troops find terrorist leader Osama bin Laden, thought to be hiding in Pakistan's northwest territories (*see p. 122*).

"They correctly judged that the United States would blow hot and cold on the question of nuclear proliferation, depending on the temper of the times," says defense-policy analyst John Pike, director of GlobalSecurity.org, a non-profit organization studying emerging security threats. "Blaming the black market all on A.Q. Khan and letting Musharraf say he had no idea what was going on is just a way for everybody to have their cake and eat it, too."

Pakistani nuclear scientist Abdul Qadeer Khan

[1] Unless otherwise noted, information in this section is based on Peter Grier, Faye Bowers and Owais Tohid, "Pakistan's Nuclear Hero, World's No. 1 Nuclear Suspect," *The Christian Science Monitor*, Feb. 2, 2004.

[2] Khan was interviewed by the Human Development Foundation, an expatriate Pakistani group in Shaumburg, Ill., www.yespakistan.com.

[3] "The Black Marketeer," "Nightline," ABC News, March 8, 2004.

[4] *Ibid.*

With momentum building for still more nuclear research, calls to abandon the new technology ran into resistance from those promoting nuclear power as a cheap, virtually inexhaustible source of energy. Fission releases large amounts of heat, which can be harnessed to power a steam turbine to generate electricity.

On Dec. 8, 1953, President Dwight D. Eisenhower presented his "Atoms for Peace" proposal to the United Nations, calling for creation of an international atomic energy agency "to devise methods whereby this fissionable material would be allocated to serve the peaceful pursuits of mankind."

The Soviet Union beat the United States in the race to introduce nuclear power, starting up the world's first plant in 1954. With federal support and AEC oversight, General Electric, Westinghouse Electric and other U.S. companies invested heavily in the new technology. On May 26, 1958, Eisenhower opened the first U.S. nuclear power plant, at Shippingport, Pa.

For the next 20 years — until the partial meltdown at Pennsylvania's Three Mile Island nuclear plant in 1979 and the catastrophic accident at the Soviet plant at Chernobyl in 1986 — nuclear power accounted for a growing percentage of the world's electricity.

Today nuclear power accounts for 16 percent of global electricity generated at some 440 plants in 30 countries.[22] A handful of countries depend on nuclear power for more than half of their electricity, but only about 20 percent

Components from Libya's nuclear weapons program are displayed by Secretary of Energy Spencer Abraham at the Y-12 National Security Complex in Oak Ridge, Tenn., on March 15, 2004. Libyan leader Muammar el-Qaddafi ended the country's isolation by renouncing weapons of mass destruction and joining the world nonproliferation regime.

of the power generated in the United States comes from nuclear reactors.

Nonproliferation Efforts

Eisenhower's Atoms for Peace proposal bore fruit in 1957, when the IAEA was established as an independent U.N. body charged with promoting the peaceful use of nuclear energy. The agency was responsible for inspecting nuclear research facilities and power plants to ensure that they were not being used to build nuclear weapons.[23]

It already was becoming clear, however, that stronger measures were needed to prevent nuclear proliferation. Britain, which had participated in the U.S. nuclear development program, tested its first nuclear device in 1952 and quickly built several hundred warheads. France developed its nuclear capability independently and began building a nuclear arsenal in 1960. In 1964, China tested its first nuclear weapon, becoming the fifth and last nuclear-weapon state recognized under the NPT.

Faced with the prospect of dozens more countries acquiring the bomb within a few decades, the United States and 17 other countries began talks in 1958 aimed at halting the further spread of nuclear weapons. A proposal by Ireland envisioned a commitment by all nuclear-weapons states not to provide the technology to other countries. In theory, non-nuclear countries would benefit from such an arrangement because it would ensure that

their neighbors would also remain nuclear-free. But non-nuclear states called for more incentives to accept this permanent state of military inferiority.

In 1968, after a decade of negotiations, 98 countries signed the Nuclear Non-Proliferation Treaty (NPT). The agreement recognized the original five nuclear-weapons states — the United States, the Soviet Union, France, the United Kingdom and China — defined as countries that had "manufactured and exploded a nuclear weapon or other nuclear explosive device prior to 1 January 1967." The IAEA was charged with monitoring compliance with the treaty. Countries that signed the treaty agreed to refrain from producing, obtaining or stockpiling nuclear weapons.

The treaty expanded on the Irish resolution by offering more incentives to refrain from building nuclear weapons. The nuclear states agreed to help other countries develop civilian nuclear power plants and also, under Article X, to take "effective measures" to end the arms race and work toward nuclear disarmament.

But the treaty set no timetables for disarmament, enabling the nuclear powers to keep their arsenals virtually indefinitely. The NPT's Article X contains another important loophole — it allows signatories to withdraw from the treaty without penalty for unspecified "supreme interests."

With 188 parties, the NPT has the broadest support of any arms control treaty. Only three countries — India, Israel and Pakistan — have not signed the pact and are believed to possess finished nuclear weapons or components that could be rapidly assembled. Israel began developing its nuclear capability in the 1950s with French assistance. The United States has refrained from pressing its chief Middle Eastern ally on its nuclear program, and Israel has never acknowledged its arsenal, thought to number 98-172 warheads. In 1998, India and Pakistan — engaged in a longstanding border dispute — acknowledged their nuclear status. Both India (50-90 warheads) and Pakistan (30-50 warheads) are believed to store their nuclear weapons in the form of separate components that can be assembled at short notice.[24]

Over the past decade, the international nonproliferation regime has scored some important successes. In the 1990s, Argentina and Brazil agreed to abandon their nuclear-weapons ambitions, signed the NPT and became the last two Latin American countries to sign the 1969 Treaty of Tlatelolco, which barred nuclear weapons from the

33-nation region. After the Soviet Union's collapse, the former Soviet republics of Belarus, Kazakhstan and Ukraine voluntarily relinquished to Russia all the nuclear weapons Moscow had deployed on their territory during the Cold War. And, in 1993, after the fall of apartheid, South Africa became the first nuclear-armed country to voluntarily dismantle its entire nuclear-weapons program.

Mushrooming Nukes

For all the NPT's success in containing nuclear weapons, it has failed to keep non-signatories, and even some "renegade states" that signed the treaty, from pursuing nuclear capabilities. Almost as soon as it signed the NPT in 1968, Iraq began developing nuclear weapons with help from France and Italy, presumably to counter Israel's arsenal. Israel destroyed an Iraqi reactor in 1981, claiming it was being used to produce fuel for weapons. Nevertheless, Iraq continued its clandestine program, as weapons inspectors discovered upon entering Iraq after its defeat in the 1991 Gulf War.

After the war, U.S.-led condemnation of Iraq's nuclear-weapons program resulted in U.N. sanctions that prohibited trade with Iraq. The sanctions were later eased to allow Iraq to sell a limited amount of oil to buy food and medical supplies, but by the end of the 1990s, Iraq was in the throes of an economic crisis.

Although the Bush administration cited evidence that Iraq had continued its nuclear-weapons program to justify last year's invasion and toppling of Hussein, recent inspections have turned up no signs Hussein was pursuing nuclear weapons. "It turns out we were all wrong," said former weapons inspector David Kay of U.S. suspicions that Iraq possessed weapons of mass destruction. "And that is most disturbing."[25]

Another NPT "renegade," North Korea is considered to pose a far greater risk. A party to the NPT since 1985, North Korea launched a clandestine nuclear program centered on production of plutonium, which could be used to make nuclear weapons. Although North Korea insisted that its program was intended only to generate electricity, in 1993 it barred IAEA inspectors from viewing its facilities, precipitating a crisis in the nonproliferation regime. In October 1994, the Clinton administration brokered an "Agreed Framework," whereby North Korea agreed to freeze plutonium production in exchange for U.S. assistance to compensate for any energy lost due to

the reactor shutdown. President Bush disavowed the pact in 2002 as bowing to nuclear blackmail and called on North Korea's Kim Jong Il to renounce his nuclear ambitions as a condition of resuming aid to the impoverished country.

Concerned that nuclear weapons or weapons-grade materials might fall into the hands of renegade states or terrorist groups, the United States, the Soviet Union and 38 other countries with nuclear technology established the Nuclear Suppliers Group in 1985, agreeing to control exports of civilian nuclear material and related technology to non-nuclear-weapon states. And to restrict the proliferation of nuclear-capable missiles, the United States and six other countries in 1987 set up the Missile Technology Control Regime, a voluntary agreement that has since been expanded to more than 30 countries.

The collapse of the Soviet Union signaled the end of both the Cold War and the nuclear standoff dominated by the military doctrine of mutual assured destruction But the post-Cold War peace, welcome as it was, ushered in a new era of uncertainty in which concern over nuclear proliferation took the place of superpower nuclear brinkmanship. The resulting economic and political upheavals left Russia — the Soviet successor state — poorly equipped to maintain security over the vast nuclear arsenal it inherited.

Recognizing the proliferation risk posed by Russia's arsenal, Congress passed the so-called Nunn-Lugar measure. Since it became law in 1991, the United States has helped Russia deactivate some 6,000 nuclear warheads, retrain 22,000 nuclear-weapons scientists and remove all the nuclear weapons deployed in the former Soviet republics of Belarus, Kazakhstan and Ukraine. Nunn-Lugar also has helped destroy hundreds of Soviet missiles, seal nuclear test facilities and dismantle submarine-based nuclear warheads.

CURRENT SITUATION
Black Market Revealed

A.Q. Khan's black market in nuclear weapons and materials began to unravel on Dec. 19, 2003, when Libya told the United States and Britain it would terminate its nuclear-weapons program. Although the North African country had not developed warheads, it was found to have imported numerous key components, including sophisticated centrifuges needed to enrich uranium into fuel for bombs.

The Bush administration claims much of the credit for this unexpected victory in the fight against nuclear proliferation. "The success of our mission in Libya underscores the success of this administration's broader nonproliferation efforts around the world," said Energy Secretary Spencer Abraham at a special press tour of seized Libyan nuclear materials and equipment on display at the department's Oak Ridge labs on March 15. "What you have witnessed represents a big, big victory in the administration's efforts to combat weapons of mass destruction."

Administration critics dispute this claim, citing reports that Libyan leader Muammar el-Qaddafi had been convinced by his son and presumptive heir, 31-year-old Saif al-Islam Qaddafi, to end the country's isolation by renouncing weapons of mass destruction and joining the world nonproliferation regime.[26] Libya has suffered severe economic privation since coming under U.N.-sponsored economic sanctions for its involvement in the 1988 bombing of a Pan-Am flight over Lockerbie, Scotland, which killed 270 people.

U.N. sanctions, imposed in 1992, were lifted in September 2003, after Libya accepted responsibility for the bombing and agreed to pay $2.7 billion in compensation to families of the Pan Am victims. Although the Bush administration lifted a ban on travel to Libya after it renounced its nuclear program, other U.S. economic sanctions remain in place.[27]

"Muammar's son thought his dad had run the country into a ditch," says Pike of GlobalSecurity.Org. "But when the dynastic handoff of a country from father to son becomes the primary determinant of our disarmament success, then we're running on a pretty thin reed."

When they entered Libyan facilities in January, IAEA inspectors said they discovered crates of nuclear equipment that only could have come from sources with advanced nuclear programs of their own. Subsequent investigations uncovered a complex web of international transactions that led to a factory in Malaysia, transshipment facilities in Dubai, an intercepted cargo ship in Italy, shipments to Iran and ultimately to Khan himself. In January, after acknowledging his role in establishing the nuclear black market, Khan was pardoned by Pakistani President Pervez Musharraf, who claimed he knew nothing of Khan's undercover business.

Nuclear experts dismiss Musharraf's disavowal as ludicrous. Khan's prominent role as the father of Pakistan's nuclear arsenal made him a highly visible national hero who made no attempt to conceal his lavish lifestyle in his impoverished country and who actually had published brochures describing nuclear materials and equipment that were for sale from his lab for more than a decade.

"The pattern of activity was at such a large scale that it's inconceivable that the Pakistani government didn't know about this all along," Pike says. "It's like asking me to believe that [U.S. nuclear pioneer] Ed Teller was secretly selling hydrogen bombs out of the back of a pickup truck."

But the Bush administration did not question Musharraf's disavowal of knowledge about Khan's activities. Since the Pakistani leader emerged as an outspoken ally of the United States in its war on terrorism after Sept. 11, the administration clearly has been loath to undermine his standing in an Islamic country where anti-American feelings and support for al Qaeda run high. Musharraf has narrowly escaped two assassination attempts, attributed to al Qaeda, in recent months.[28]

Moreover, the Bush administration needs Musharraf's cooperation in order to find al Qaeda leader Osama bin Laden — considered by some to be the mastermind of the 9/11 attacks — and his top lieutenants. Some observers suggest that the Bush administration decided to accept Musharraf's denial of knowledge about Khan's network in exchange for permission for U.S. forces to enter the rugged area on the Pakistani side of the border with Afghanistan, believed to be a key stronghold of al Qaeda militants and possibly bin Laden himself.[29] Up to now, U.S. forces have had to limit their searches to the Afghan side of the border.

Although administration spokesmen deny the existence of such a deal, American military officials have announced plans for a "spring initiative" on the Afghan side of the border.[30] Already, signs are emerging that an offensive is under way. On March 16, on the eve of a visit to Pakistan by Secretary of State Colin L. Powell, Pakistani troops suffered numerous casualties in gun battles in the border region.[31]

Bush's Response

President Bush responded to the revelations about Khan's network with a seven-point plan to strengthen the NPT and IAEA's enforcement powers. On Feb. 11, the president called for the expansion of his Proliferation Security Initiative, a year-old international effort to seize nuclear materials on the high seas while in transit to or from rogue states. In 1999 and 2000, years before Bush's initiative, Indian and British authorities seized two North Korean shipments of missile components and related equipment en route to Libya.[32]

Bush also called on the U.N. Security Council to adopt a resolution requiring all states to criminalize proliferation of components that could be used to make weapons of mass destruction and to strengthen export controls on them. And he proposed expanding U.S. efforts to secure Russia's nuclear weapons and materials under the Nunn-Lugar program.

In addition, Bush called for closing the loophole in the NPT that allows aspirants to the nuclear club to enrich and reprocess fuel used in civilian nuclear reactors and proposed that only signatories of the Additional Protocol be allowed to import equipment for civilian reactors. To strengthen the IAEA, Bush proposed a new measure to beef up the agency's safeguards and verification powers. Finally, he recommended barring countries being investigated for alleged NPT violations from holding positions of influence in the IAEA.

"We've shown that proliferators can be discovered and can be stopped," Bush said. "Terrorists and terror states are in a race for weapons of mass murder, a race they must lose."

Weapons analysts praised Bush's recommendations. "It was a very important speech," says Curtis of the Nuclear Threat Initiative. "It addressed a number of areas that require U.S. leadership and international cooperation."

But Curtis also says the United States needs to do more to dispel the perception that it holds itself to a different standard than the rest of the world regarding proliferation. "Missing from the speech was some meaningful initiative on addressing the strategic nuclear weapons that the United States and Russia still maintain in very large numbers and, under the Treaty of Moscow, may retain into the indefinite future," Curtis says.

To others, Bush's speech exemplified the administration's unilateral approach to pursuing U.S. interests. "President Bush's speech was a series of measures that would constrain everybody else," says Bunn of Harvard's Belfer Center. "There was no mention of anything that would constrain the United States."

Vehicles entering the United States from Canada pass through radiation detectors at the Blaine, Wash., border crossing. Experts say terrorists are far more likely to deploy a small, easily transported conventional explosive device containing radioactive waste — a so-called dirty bomb — than to explode a nuclear bomb.

In Pike's view, the Bush administration's nuclear policies have left the United States with few viable options. "Right now, our declaratory policy is one of attacks to disarm our enemies' weapons infrastructure, followed up by military invasion and regime change," he says. That's the policy that led to the war in Iraq, which did not yet possess nuclear weapons. But the same policy cannot be applied to a state like North Korea, which may harbor nuclear weapons, for fear of igniting a global holocaust. "So we have an extraordinarily alarming declaratory policy that's basically frightened the living daylights out of the rest of humanity, [but which] we're not prepared to implement. That puts us in the worst of all possible worlds."

OUTLOOK

Crumbling Coalition?

The March 11 bombing of commuter trains in Madrid has lent further urgency to the international war on terrorism. Ten separate explosions at the rush hour ripped through the trains, killing more than 190 commuters and wounding some 1,400.[33] After initially blaming Basque separatists for the attacks, the government announced two days later that it had arrested five people with suspected links to al Qaeda.

Will U.S. policies keep nuclear weapons away from terrorists?

YES   President George W. Bush

From a speech at the National Defense University, Feb. 11, 2004

On Sept. 11, 2001, America and the world witnessed a new kind of war. We saw the great harm that a stateless network could inflict upon our country, killers armed with box cutters, mace and 19 airline tickets. Those attacks also raised the prospect of even worse dangers — of other weapons in the hands of other men. The greatest threat before humanity today is the possibility of secret and sudden attack with chemical or biological or radiological or nuclear weapons. . . .

America, and the entire civilized world, will face this threat for decades to come. We must confront the danger with open eyes, and unbending purpose. I have made clear to all the policy of this nation: America will not permit terrorists and dangerous regimes to threaten us with the world's most deadly weapons. . . .

We're determined to confront those threats at the source. We will stop these weapons from being acquired or built. We'll block them from being transferred. We'll prevent them from ever being used. One source of these weapons is dangerous and secretive regimes that build weapons of mass destruction to intimidate their neighbors and force their influence upon the world. These nations pose different challenges; they require different strategies. . . .

I propose to expand our efforts to keep weapons from the Cold War and other dangerous materials out of the wrong hands. In 1991, Congress passed the Nunn-Lugar legislation. Sen. [Richard] Lugar had a clear vision, along with Sen. [Sam] Nunn, about what to do with the old Soviet Union. Under this program, we're helping former Soviet states find productive employment for former weapons scientists. We're dismantling, destroying and securing weapons and materials left over from the Soviet . . . arsenal. . . .

Over the last two years, a great coalition has come together to defeat terrorism and to oppose the spread of weapons of mass destruction — the inseparable commitments of the war on terror. We've shown that proliferators can be discovered and can be stopped. We've shown that for regimes that choose defiance, there are serious consequences. The way ahead is not easy, but it is clear. We will proceed as if the lives of our citizens depend on our vigilance, because they do.

Terrorists and terror states are in a race for weapons of mass murder, a race they must lose. Terrorists are resourceful; we're more resourceful. They're determined; we must be more determined. We will never lose focus or resolve. We'll be unrelenting in the defense of free nations, and rise to the hard demands of dangerous times.

NO   Natural Resources Defense Council

From a statement, Feb. 12, 2004, www.nrdc.org.

Nunn-Lugar funds are not being used to "dismantle and destroy" Russian nuclear weapons (as opposed to missile silos and obsolete strategic bombers and submarines). In fact, the recently signed Moscow Treaty between the United States and Russia allows Russia to keep SS-18 "heavy" strategic ballistic missile systems that would otherwise have been destroyed under the START II and START III treaties.

Despite years of cooperation, the United States still has no firm idea of how many and which types of Russian nuclear warheads and bombs have been dismantled. As former Sen. Sam Nunn has indicated, the Nunn-Lugar program suffers from inadequate funding. President Bush cites the 2002 G-8 Summit agreement to provide $20 billion over 10 years, but even here the participating countries used accounting tricks to avoid increasing previous commitments. Moreover, some of this money is earmarked to build a plutonium fuel-fabrication plant in Russia that many observers believe will increase the potential that plutonium will be diverted and used for illicit purposes.

President Bush so far has refused to commit to destroying more than a few hundred of the more than 10,000 nuclear weapons still in the United States' nuclear weapons stockpile. The Strategic Offensive Reduction Treaty (SORT) negotiated with Russia in 2002 — the Moscow Treaty — does not require the elimination of a single nuclear missile silo, submarine, missile warhead, bomber or bomb. . .

President Bush failed to address the longer-term problem, and long-term proliferation pressures, arising from a world permanently and inequitably divided into declared nuclear weapons states under the Non-Proliferation Treaty (NPT), de-facto nuclear weapon states outside the treaty (India, Pakistan and Israel), nonweapon states that have abandoned the treaty (North Korea) and states with varying degrees of nuclear expertise (Iran) that are presently bound by their treaty commitment not to acquire nuclear weapons but could elect to withdraw from the NPT at any time.

Nor did President Bush discuss how and when the United States and other nuclear weapon states would take further steps to fulfill their Non-Proliferation Treaty commitments to eliminate their nuclear arsenals. On the contrary, the Bush administration is spending record amounts revitalizing the U.S. nuclear weapons complex. . . .

There are two distinct kinds of threats facing the United States, one having to do with the proliferation of [weapons of mass destruction] by nation states and the second with threats posed by terrorists. The president's proposals focused on threats posed by the spread of nuclear weapons, materials and technologies to nation states rather than those by terrorists.

The next day, March 14, Spaniards went to the polls and removed Prime Minister José Maria Aznar, a staunch U.S. ally in the war against terrorism, from office. Spain's new leader, Socialist José Luis Rodríguez Zapatero, renewed Spain's commitment to fight terrorism. But he promised to fulfill a campaign pledge to withdraw Spain's 1,300-man contingent of peacekeepers in Iraq by June 30. He is one of Europe's most outspoken critics of the war.

Calling the occupation of Iraq "a fiasco," Zapatero has outlined an approach to fighting terrorism that relies on international cooperation, which he says differs sharply from the administration's tactic. "Fighting terrorism with Tomahawk missiles isn't the way to defeat terrorism," he said. "I will listen to Mr. Bush, but my position is very clear and very firm. . . . Terrorism is combated by the [rule] of law."[34]

Zapatero may be expressing the views of more than a demoralized Spanish electorate. According to a new international survey, opposition to the war in Iraq and U.S. international policies has intensified in Europe. A growing percentage of Europeans polled said they want to distance their fate from the United States by adopting independent foreign and security policies through the European Union. More than half support a European foreign policy independent from that of the United States. Even in Britain, the administration's strongest war on terrorism ally, support for an independent European foreign policy has risen from 47 percent in April 2002 to 56 percent in the current poll.[35]

The Bush administration has downplayed any notion of a rift between the United States and its European allies. "We don't think countries face a choice — being European or being trans-Atlantic," said an administration official following Secretary of State Powell's March 24 trip to Spain to attend a memorial service for victims of the Madrid bombing. "All of us, especially in the NATO alliance, are almost by definition both. . . . European nations don't have to choose between good relations with Europe and good relations with the United States."

Foiling Nuclear Terror

The Madrid bombing — the worst incident of terrorist violence in Europe since the Pan Am bombing — coming as it did on the heels of the exposure of Khan's nuclear-smuggling network, will likely intensify debate over how to deal with the threat of nuclear terrorism. Bin Laden

has made no secret of his desire to use a nuclear bomb as the ultimate weapon against the West, and weapons experts say events are fast outpacing policies deigned to avert such a catastrophe.

"The Bush administration and the president himself have rightly said that the ultimate specter is al Qaeda with a nuclear weapon," says Harvard's Allison. "But this administration has no coherent strategy for preventing nuclear terrorism. That's a pretty serious charge, but I think it's correct."

Administration supporters reject that view. "President Bush has transported the fight the terrorists began back to their land," wrote former Sen. Alfonse M. D'Amato, R-N.Y. "He refuses to allow them to contaminate our soil with their hatred. He has stood firm in the face of the terrorist threat, despite constant harping from critics who would second-guess his leadership."[36]

Still, IAEA Director General ElBaradei paints a grim picture of nuclear proliferation's future and calls for a revolutionary overhaul of international systems and policies to prevent nuclear terrorism. "Eventually, inevitably, terrorists will gain access to such materials and technology, if not actual weapons," he wrote. "If the world does not change course, we risk self destruction."

ElBaradei calls for globalization of worldwide security. "We must abandon the traditional approach of defining security in terms of boundaries — city walls, border patrols, racial and religious groupings," he wrote recently in *The New York Times*. "The global community has become irreversibly interdependent, with the constant movement of people, ideas, goods and resources.

"In such a world, we must combat terrorism with an infectious security culture that crosses borders — an inclusive approach to security based on solidarity and the value of human life. In such a world, weapons of mass destruction will have no place."[37]

NOTES

1. See Ellen Nakashima and Alan Sipress, "Insider Tells of Nuclear Deals, Cash," *The Washington Post*, Feb. 21, 2004, p. A1.

2. For background, see Mary H. Cooper, "Non-Proliferation Treaty at 25," *The CQ Researcher*, Jan. 27, 1995, pp. 73-96.

3. From a speech at the National Defense University in Washington, D.C., Feb. 11, 2004.

4. For background, see Mary H. Cooper, "Hating America," *The CQ Researcher*, Nov. 23, 2001, pp. 969-992, and David Masci and Kenneth Jost, "War on Terrorism," *The CQ Researcher*, Oct. 12, 2001, pp. 817-840.

5. See Michael A. Levi and Henry C. Kelly, "Weapons of Mass Disruption," *Scientific American*, November 2002, pp. 76-81.

6. ElBaradei spoke at IAEA headquarter in Vienna, Feb. 5, 2004. See Peter Slevin, "U.N. Nuclear Chief Warns of Global Black Market," *The Washington Post*, Feb. 6, 2004, p. A18.

7. For a detailed description, see Graham Allison, "How to Stop Nuclear Terrorism," *Foreign Affairs*, January/February 2004, pp. 64-74.

8. Howard Baker and Lloyd Cutler, "A Report Card on the Department Of Energy's Nonproliferation Programs with Russia," Jan. 10, 2001.

9. See Steven R. Weisman, "Lasting Discord Clouds Talks on North Korean Nuclear Arms," *The New York Times*, March 14, 2004. For background, see Mary H. Cooper, "North Korean Crisis," *The CQ Researcher*, April 11, 2003, pp. 321-344.

10. See David E. Sanger, "U.S. Sees More Arms Ties between Pakistan and Korea," *The New York Times*, March 14, 2004, p. A1.

11. See Joel Brinkley and William J. Broad, "U.S. Lags in Recovering Fuel Suitable for Nuclear Arms," *The New York Times*, March 7, 2004, p. A8.

12. For a list of nuclear arms-control treaties and their provisions, see "Treaties and Agreements," U.S. State Department, www.state.gov, and Nuclear Threat Initiative, "WMD411," www.nti.org. For background, see Mary H. Cooper, "Weapons of Mass Destruction," *The CQ Researcher*, March 8, 2002, pp. 193-116.

13. "National Strategy to Combat Weapons of Mass Destruction," The White House, December 2002, p. 3.

14. "Findings of the Nuclear Posture Review," U.S. Department of Defense, released Jan. 9, 2002; www.defenselink.mil.

15. The measure was included in the 1994 Defense Authorization Act.

16. From an interview with *Arms Control Today*, January/February 2004; www.armscontrol.org.

17. See Joseph C. Anselmo, "Opponents See New Arms Race in Push for Nuclear Research," *CQ Weekly*, Feb. 21, 2004, pp. 498-500.

18. For background, see Mary H. Cooper, "Bush's Defense Policy," *The CQ Researcher*, Sept. 7, 2001, pp. 689-712.

19. See Bradley Graham, "Missile Defense Still Uncertain," *The Washington Post*, March 12, 2004.

20. Cirincione testified before a special meeting of the Danish Parliament, April 24, 2003.

21. For the text of Einstein's letter, see Robert C. Williams and Philip L. Cantelon, eds., *The American Atom* (1984), cited in Stephen I. Schwartz, ed., *Atomic Audit* (1998). Unless otherwise noted, information in this section is based on Schwartz.

22. Data from www.iaea.org and the Nuclear Energy Institute, www.nei.org.

23. For background, see David Masci, "The United Nations and Global Security," *The CQ Researcher*, Feb. 27, 2004, pp. 173-196.

24. For background, see David Masci, "Emerging India," *The CQ Researcher*, April 19, 2002, pp. 329-360.

25. Kay testified before the Senate Armed Services Committee, Jan. 28, 2004.

26. See Michael Evans, "Libya Knew Game Was Up Before Iraq War," *The Times* (London), March 23, 2004, p. 8.

27. See "Top U.S. Official Visits Libyan Leader," The Associated Press, March 23, 2004.

28. See Salman Masood, "Link to Qaeda Cited in Effort to Assassinate Pakistan Chief," *The New York Times*, March 17, 2004.

29. See Seymour M. Hersh, "The Deal," *The New Yorker*, March 8, 2004, pp. 32-37.

30. See David Rohde, "U.S. Announces New Offensive Against Taliban and al Qaeda," *The New York Times*, March 14, 2004, p. 4.

31. See Sulfiqar Ali, "Firefight in Pakistan Claims 32 Lives; Troops Hunting for Militants Clash with

Tribesmen in a Region Bordering Afghanistan," *Los Angeles Times*, March 17, 2004, p. A13.

32. See J. Peter Scoblic, "Indefensible," *The New Republic*, March 8, 2004, p. 14.

33. See Aparisim Ghosh and James Graff, "Terror on the Tracks," *Time*, March 22, 2004, p. 32.

34. From an interview on radio Onda Cero quoted in "New Spain PM Firm on Troop Withdrawal," The Associated Press, March 17, 2004.

35. Pew Research Center for the People & the Press, "A Year After Iraq War, Mistrust of America in Europe Ever Higher, Muslim Anger Persists," March 16, 2004; people-press.org.

36. Alfonse D'Amato, "Bush Will Win War on Terrorism," *Newsday*, March 22, 2004.

37. Mohamed ElBaradei, "Saving Ourselves from Self-Destruction," *The New York Times*, Feb. 12, 2004, p. A37.

BIBLIOGRAPHY

Books

Allison, Graham, *Nuclear Terrorism: The Ultimate Preventable Catastrophe* (*Henry Holt*), **forthcoming.**
A former Defense Department official outlines his strategy for strengthening the nuclear nonproliferation regime to prevent the spread of nuclear weapons to terrorists.

Blix, Hans, *Disarming Iraq, Pantheon*, **2004.**
The head of the U.N. weapons inspection team in Iraq asserts that the inspectors would have proved conclusively that Iraq no longer possessed weapons of mass destruction had the Bush administration given them more time before invading.

Frum, David, and Richard Perle, *An End to Evil: How to Win the War on Terror, Random House*, **2003.**
A former Bush speechwriter (Frum) and a former administration Defense official call current policies in the war on terrorism a choice between "victory or holocaust."

Weissman, Steve, and Herbert Krosney, *The Islamic Bomb, Times Books*, **1981.**
Two authors describe how Pakistan and Iraq launched programs to develop nuclear weapons more than two decades ago.

Articles

Cirincione, Joseph, and Jon B. Wolfsthal, "North Korea and Iran: Test Cases for an Improved Nonproliferation Regime?" *Arms Control Today*, **December 2003.**
Innovative measures to strengthen anti-proliferation measures may be needed to keep North Korea and Iran from developing nuclear weapons.

Hersh, Seymour, "The Deal," *The New Yorker*, **March 8, 2004, pp. 32-37.**
President Bush may have accepted Pakistani President Pervez Musharraf's pardon of his top nuclear scientist's black marketing activities in exchange for letting U.S. troops pursue al Qaeda inside Pakistan.

Kagan, Robert, and William Kristol, "The Right War for the Right Reasons," *The Weekly Standard*, **Feb. 23, 2004.**
Although weapons of mass destruction have not been uncovered, two conservative commentators say that ridding the world of Saddam Hussein more than justifies the war against Iraq.

Pollack, Kenneth M., "Spies, Lies, and Weapons: What Went Wrong," *The Atlantic Monthly*, **January/February 2004, pp. 78-92.**
A former CIA analyst examines how U.S. intelligence wrongfully concluded that Saddam Hussein's regime was actively pursuing nuclear, biological and chemical weapons.

Sokolski, Henry, "Taking Proliferation Seriously," *Policy Review*, **October/November 2003.**
A conservative analyst argues the United States should call for strong measures to close loopholes in the Nuclear Non-Proliferation Treaty.

Weisman, Steven R., "Lasting Discord Clouds Talks on North Korea Nuclear Arms," *The New York Times*, **March 14, 2004, p. 10.**
A proposal to overcome an impasse in six-party talks to end North Korea's nuclear-weapons program has failed to gain acceptance, forcing a postponement of future talks.

Reports and Studies

Baker, Howard, and Lloyd Cutler, "A Report Card on the Department of Energy's Nonproliferation

Programs with Russia," *Russia Task Force, Secretary of Energy Advisory Board*, Jan. 10, 2001.
The panel calls for greater efforts to keep nuclear weapons and materials in the former Soviet Union out of the hands of terrorists.

Cochran, Thomas B., and Christopher E. Paine, "The Amount of Plutonium and Highly-Enriched Uranium Needed for Pure Fission Nuclear Weapons," *Natural Resources Defense Council*, April 15, 1995.
The environmental-protection advocacy organization questions the standards the International Atomic Energy Agency (IAEA) uses to determine the amount of weapons-grade material needed to build a nuclear weapon.

Federation of American Scientists, Natural Resources Defense Council and Union of Concerned Scientists, "Toward True Security: A U.S. Nuclear Posture for the Next Decade," June 2001.
Three organizations that support arms control say drastically reducing the U.S. nuclear arsenal is essential to countering nuclear proliferation.

Ferguson, Charles D., *et al.*, "Commercial Radioactive Sources: Surveying the Security Risks," Center for Nonproliferation Studies, *Monterey Institute of International Studies*, January 2003.
Numerous sources of commercial radioactive material are vulnerable to terrorist theft. The authors call for an education campaign to prepare the public for a "dirty-bomb" attack.

The White House, "National Strategy to Combat Weapons of Mass Destruction," December 2002.
The Bush administration's post-Sept. 11 strategy contemplates preemptively attacking adversaries armed with nuclear, chemical or biological weapons before they can attack the United States.

For More Information

Arms Control Association, 1726 M St., N.W., Washington, DC 20036; (202) 463-8270; www.armscontrol.org. A nonpartisan membership organization dedicated to promoting support for effective arms-control policies.

Belfer Center for Science and International Affairs, John F. Kennedy School of Government, Harvard University, 79 JFK St., Cambridge, MA 02138; (617) 495-1400; http://bcsia.ksg.harvard.edu. Provides information on technical and political aspects of nonproliferation policy.

Bureau of Nonproliferation, U.S. Department of State, 2201 C St., N.W., Washington, DC 20520; (202) 647-4000; www.state.gov. Administers policies to prevent the spread of weapons of mass destruction.

Center for Nonproliferation Studies, Monterey Institute of International Studies, 460 Pierce St., Monterey, CA 93940; (831) 647-4154; http://cns.miis.edu. A nongovernmental organization devoted to research and training on nonproliferation issues.

GlobalSecurity.org, 300 N. Washington St., Suite B-100, Alexandria, VA 22314; (703) 548-2700; www.globalsecurity.

org. A Web site maintained by veteran defense-policy analyst John Pike containing exhaustive information on U.S. defense policies, including nonproliferation strategy.

Nonproliferation Policy Education Center, 1718 M St., N.W., Suite 244, Washington, DC 20036; (202) 466-4406; www.npec-web.org. A project of the Institute for International Studies that promotes understanding of proliferation issues.

Nuclear Cities Initiative, U.S. Department of Energy, NA-24, 1000 Independence Ave., S.W., Washington, DC 20585; www.nnsa.doe.gov. Helps the Russian Federation downsize its nuclear weapons complex by establishing private business opportunities for nuclear scientists living in three of the former Soviet Union's closed cities.

Nuclear Threat Initiative, 1747 Pennsylvania Ave., N.W., 7th Floor, Washington DC 20006; (202) 296-4810; www.nti.org. Seeks to increase global security by reducing the risk from nuclear, biological and chemical weapons. The Web site contains a wealth of information.

Terrorism and the Internet

Should Web Sites That Promote Terrorism Be Shut Down?

Barbara Mantel

AP Photo/Ellis County Sheriff's Department

Hosam Maher Husein Smadi, a Jordanian teenager in the United States illegally, pleaded not guilty on Oct. 26 of trying to blow up a 60-story Dallas skyscraper. Smadi reportedly parked a vehicle in the building's garage on Sept. 24 hoping to detonate explosives with a cellphone. FBI agents, posing as al-Qaeda operatives, had been keeping tabs on Smadi after discovering him on an extremist Web site earlier this year where he stood out for "his vehement intention to actually conduct terror attacks in the United States."

From *CQ Researcher*, November 2009.

In March 2008 a participant on the pro al-Qaeda online forum ek-Is.org posted six training sessions for aspiring terrorists. The first was entitled: "Do you want to form a terror cell?" Using the name Shamil al-Baghdadi, the instructor described how to choose a leader, recruit members and select initial assassination targets. The second lesson outlined assassination techniques.[1]

"Although the first two training lessons often contain very basic instructions that may be less significant for experienced jihadis, they provide essential training for novices," said Abdul Hameed Bakier, a Jordanian terrorism expert who translated and summarized the training manual.[2]

The sessions then progressed to more sophisticated topics. Lesson three explained in more detail how to carry out assassinations, including: suicide attacks using booby-trapped vehicles or explosive belts; sniper attacks using Russian, Austrian and American rifles and direct attacks through strangling, poison and booby-trapped cellular phones.[3] Lesson four explained how to steal funds, and the final two lessons gave detailed instructions on how to conduct "quality terror attacks," including strikes against U.S. embassies.[4]

While this particular forum can no longer be accessed under its original domain name, Web sites controlled or operated by terrorist groups have multiplied dramatically over the past decade.

"We started 11 years ago and were monitoring 12 terrorist Web sites," says Gabriel Weimann, a professor of communication at Haifa University in Israel and a terrorism researcher. "Today we are monitoring more than 7,000."

Analysts say nearly every group designated as a foreign terrorist organization by the U.S. State Department now has an online presence, including Spain's Basque ETA movement, Peru's Shining Path, al Qaeda, the Real Irish Republican Army and others.[5] (*See list, p. 131.*)

The Internet appeals to terrorists for the same reasons it attracts everyone else: It's inexpensive, easily accessible, has little or no regulation, is interactive, allows for multimedia content and the potential audience is huge.[6] And it's anonymous.

"You can walk into an Internet café, enter a chat room or Web site, download instructions to make a bomb, and no one can find you," says Weimann. "They can trace you all the way down to the computer terminal, but by then you'll already be gone."

Terrorism on the Internet extends far beyond Web sites directly operated or controlled by terrorist organizations. Their supporters and sympathizers are increasingly taking advantage of all the tools available on the Web. "The proliferation of blogs has been exponential," says Sulastri Bte Osman, an analyst with the Civil and Internal Conflict Programme at Nanyang Technological University in Singapore. Just two years ago, Osman could find no extremist blogs in the two predominant languages of Indonesia and Malaysia; today she is monitoring 150.

The University of Arizona's "Dark Web" project, which tracks terrorist and extremist content in cyberspace, estimates there are roughly 50,000 such Web sites, discussion forums, chat rooms, blogs, Yahoo user groups, video-sharing sites, social networking sites and virtual worlds.[7] They help to distribute content — such as videos of beheadings and suicide attacks, speeches by terrorist leaders and training manuals — that may originate on just a few hundred sites.

Security experts say terrorist groups use the Internet for five general purposes:

- **Research and communication:** The Sept. 11, 2001, terrorists who attacked the World Trade Center and the Pentagon used the Internet to research flight schools, coordinate their actions through e-mail and gather flight information.[8]
- **Training:** Global Islamic Media Front, a propaganda arm of al Qaeda, issued a series of 19 training lessons in 2003 covering topics like security, physical training, weapons and explosives. The document was later found on a computer belonging to the terrorist cell responsible for the 2004 train bombings

in Madrid, Spain, that killed 191 people. But most material is posted by individuals who use the Internet as a training library.[9]
- **Fundraising:** In 1997 the rebel Tamil Tigers in Sri Lanka stole user IDs and passwords from faculty at Britain's Sheffield University and used the e-mail accounts to send out messages asking for donations.[10]
- **Media operations:** Before his death in 2006, Abu Musab al Zarqawi, the mastermind behind hundreds of bombings, kidnappings and killings in Iraq, posted gruesome videos of terrorist operations, tributes immortalizing suicide bombers and an Internet magazine offering religious justifications for his actions.[11]
- **Radicalization and recruitment:** In 2006, Illinois resident Derrick Shareef pleaded guilty to attempting to acquire explosives to blow up a mall in Rockford, Ill. Although not part of a terrorist organization, he was inspired in part by violent videos downloaded from a Web site linked to al Qaeda.[12]

The use of the Internet for recruitment and radicalization particularly worries some authorities. But experts disagree over the extent to which cyber content can radicalize and convert young men and women into homegrown supporters of — or participants in — terrorism.

The Internet is where "the gas meets the flame," says Evan F. Kohlmann, a senior investigator with the NEFA Foundation, a New York-based terrorism research organization.* "It provides the medium where would-be megalomaniacs can try and recruit deluded and angry young men . . . and magnify that anger to convince them to carry out acts of violence." The Internet replaces and broadens the traditional social networks of mosques and Arabic community centers, which have come under intense government scrutiny since 9/11, says Kohlmann.

A frequent expert witness in terrorism cases, Kohlmann says the Internet comes up in nearly every prosecution. For instance, Hamaad Munshi — a British national convicted in 2008 of possessing materials likely to be used for terrorism — participated in an online British extremist group that shared terrorist videos and used chat rooms to discuss its plans to fight overseas.[13] He was arrested at age 16.

The group's ringleader, then 22-year-old Aabid Khan, another Briton, used the chat rooms to incite Munshi to fight, Kohlmann says; the youth's grandfather also

* NEFA stands for "Nine Eleven Finding Answers."

Internet Offers Vast Potential for Spreading Terror

The Internet has opened global communication channels to anyone with computer access, creating a simple and cheap venue for spreading terrorist ideology. Interestingly, the regions with the largest concentrations of terrorist groups — the Middle East and Asia — have some of the lowest Internet usage rates. The highest rates are in developed countries, such as the United States, Canada, Australia and New Zealand.

World Internet Usage Rates, by Region

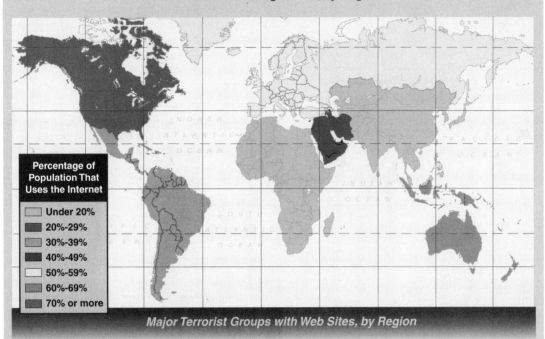

Percentage of Population That Uses the Internet

- Under 20%
- 20%-29%
- 30%-39%
- 40%-49%
- 50%-59%
- 60%-69%
- 70% or more

Major Terrorist Groups with Web Sites, by Region

Middle East: Hamas, Lebanese Hezbollah, al-Aqsa Martyrs Brigades, Fatah Tanzim, Popular Front for the Liberation of Palestine, Palestinian Islamic Jihad, Kahane Lives Movement, People's Mujahidin of Iran, Kurdish Workers' Party, Popular Democratic Liberation Front Party, Great East Islamic Raiders Front

Europe: Basque Euskadi Ta Askatasuna, Armata Corsa, Real Irish Republican Army

Latin America: Tupac-Amaru, Shining Path, Colombian National Liberation Army, Armed Revolutionary Forces of Colombia, Zapatista National Liberation Army

Asia: Al Qaeda, Japanese Supreme Truth, Ansar al Islam, Japanese Red Army, Hizb-ul Mujahidin, Liberation Tigers of Tamil Eelam, Islamic Movement of Uzbekistan, Moro Islamic Liberation Front, Lashkar-e-Taiba, Chechnyan Rebel Movement

Sources: "World Internet Penetration Rates by Geographic Region," Internet World Stats, June 30, 2009, www.internetworldststs.com/stats.htm; Gabriel Weimann, "Terror on the Internet," 2006

Terrorist Web Sites Have Proliferated

The number of Web sites run by terrorists or their supporters has grown since 1998 from a dozen to more than 7,000, with pro-jihad sites predominating, according to researcher Gabriel Weimann of Israel's Haifa University.

No. of Terrorist Web Sites

Source: Gabriel Weimann, Haifa University, Oct. 20, 2009

International Centre for the Study of Radicalisation and Political Violence at King's College in London. "In most cases, radicalization requires would-be terrorists to come in contact with social groups of people in the real world."

For instance, he pointed out, while much of Munshi's extremist activism took place online, "his radicalisation had been initiated in the 'real world.' " Through a friend at a local mosque, Munshi had met Khan, who spotted Munshi's computer expertise and groomed him to become a part of his online network. "It was the early meetings with Khan and some of his friends that helped turn a boy interested in religion into a young man dedicated to killing 'non-believers,' " according to Neumann.[15]

"There is anecdotal evidence out there, but no one has done a systematic study to show that radicalization via the Internet is a reality," says Maura Conway, a terrorism expert at Dublin City University in Ireland. Nevertheless, she adds, "governments are certainly acting as if radicalization through the Internet is possible, putting in place legislation that curbs how people can interact online."

As terrorists' presence on the Internet continues to grow, here are some of the questions being asked:

Should governments block terrorist Web sites?

Many of those who think the Internet is a major terrorist recruiting tool say authorities should simply shut down terrorists' sites.

Often the call comes from politicians. "It is shocking the government has failed to shut down a single Web site, even though Parliament gave them that power," Britain's opposition security minister, Baroness Pauline Neville-Jones, said last March. "This smacks of dangerous complacency and incompetence."[16]

In France, a minister for security said she wanted to stop terrorist propaganda on the Internet.[17] And a European Commission official called for a Europe-wide prohibition on Web sites that post bomb-making instructions.[18]

Although governments have shut down terrorist Web sites when they felt the information posted was too great a threat, some critics say such a move is legally complicated, logistically difficult and unwise.

Last year, three of the most important discussion forums used by Islamist terrorist groups disappeared from the Internet, including ek-Is.org, which had posted the six-part training manual. Jordanian terrorism expert

blamed the Internet. "This case demonstrates how a young, impressionable teenager can be groomed so easily through the Internet to associate with those whose views run contrary to true Muslim beliefs and values," Yakub Munshi said after the teen's conviction.[14]

But other researchers say online terrorism sites are largely about preaching to the choir and have limited influence on non-terrorists. "There has been very little evidence that the Internet has been the main or sole driver in radicalization," says Peter Neumann, director of the

Bakier says counterterrorism officials were so worried about the site that he "used to get requests from concerned agencies to translate the exact texts posted on ek-Is.org that were referenced in my articles. It was that serious."

"It is widely assumed that Western intelligence agencies were responsible for removing the three sites," and probably without the cooperation of the Internet service providers (ISPs) that host the sites, says Neumann, of King's College. "It would have required the cooperation of all the ISPs in the world," because those Web sites were not accessible at all, he explains. Instead, he thinks intelligence agencies may have launched so-called denial-of-service attacks against the sites, bombarding them with so many requests that they crashed. This September, one of the sites resurfaced; however, many experts believe it is a hoax.[19]

But government takedowns of terrorist sites — by whatever method — are not common, say many researchers. First, there are concerns about free speech.

"Who is going to decide who is a terrorist, who should be silenced and why?" asks Haifa University's Weimann. "Who is going to decide what kind of Web site should be removed? It can lead to political censorship."

Concern about free speech may be more acute in the United States than elsewhere. Current U.S. statutes make it a crime to provide "material support" — including expert advice or assistance — to organizations designated as terrorist groups by the State Department.[20] However, the First Amendment guarantee of free speech may trump the material support provisions.

"Exceptions to the First Amendment are fairly narrow" says Ian Ballon, an expert on Internet law practicing in California. "Child pornography is one, libelous or defamatory content another. There is no terrorism exception per se." Words that would incite violence are clearly an exception to the First Amendment, he says, "but there is a concept of immediacy, and most terrorism sites would not necessarily meet that requirement." A 1969 Supreme Court case, *Brandenburg v. Ohio*, held that the government cannot punish inflammatory speech unless it is inciting or likely to incite imminent lawless action.[21]

In Europe, where free-speech rights are more circumscribed than in the United States, the legal landscape varies. Spain, for instance, outlaws as incitement "the act of performing public ennoblement, praise and/or justification of a terrorist group, operative or act," explains

Tunisian Moez Garsallaoui, right, and his wife Malika El Aroud, the widow of an al-Qaeda suicide bomber, were convicted in Switzerland's first Internet terrorism trial of running pro-al-Qaeda Web sites that showed executions. Garsallaoui served three weeks in prison; El Aroud received no jail time. They are continuing their online work from Belgium, where El Aroud is described by Belgian State Security chief Alain Winants as a "leading" Internet jihadist.

British officials, including Prime Minister Gordon Brown, center right, visit a London cyber security firm on June 25 during the launch of a new government campaign to counter cyber criminals and terrorists.

Raphael Perl, head of the Action Against Terrorism Unit at the Organization for Security and Co-operation in Europe, a regional security organization with 56 member nations, based in Vienna, Austria. And the U.K. passed the Terrorism Acts of 2000 and 2006, which make it an

Southeast Asian Sites Now Espouse Violence

Extremist Web sites using the two main languages in Indonesia and Malaysia have evolved since 2006 from mostly propagandizing to providing firearm and bomb-making manuals and encouraging armed violence.

How the Sites Evolved

2006-July 2007	Posted al-Qaeda and Jemaah Islamiyah propaganda (videos, photographs, statements, etc.); articles about how Muslims are victimized and the necessity to fight back; celebrations of mujahidin victories; conspiracy theories; anger directed at the West; local grievances linked to global jihad; endorsements of highly selective Islamic doctrines
August 2007	First posting of manual on how to hack Web sites
February 2008	First posting of bomb-making manual and bomb-making video compilation in Arabic; emergence of a password-protected forum
April 2008	First posting of a firearm manual
Present	All of the above posted/available

Source: "Contents of Bahasa and Malay Language Radical and Extremist Web Sites, 2006 to 2009," in "Countering Internet Radicalisation in Southeast Asia," S. Rajaratnam School of International Studies, Singapore, and Australian Strategic Policy Institute, 2009

offense to collect, make or possess material that could be used in a terrorist act, such as bomb-making manuals and information about potential targets. The 2006 act also outlaws the encouragement or glorification of terrorism.[22] Human Rights Watch says the measure is unnecessary, overly broad and potentially chilling of free speech.[23]

Yet, it does not appear that governments are using their legal powers to shut down Web sites. "I haven't heard from any ISP in Europe so far that they have been asked by the police to take down terrorist pages," says Michael Rotert, vice president of the European Internet Service Providers Association (EuroISPA).

For one thing, says Rotert, there is no common, legal, Europe-wide definition of terrorism. "We are requesting a common definition," he says, "and then I think notice and takedown procedures could be discussed. But right now, such procedures only exist for child pornography."

But even if a European consensus existed on what constitutes terrorism, the Internet has no borders. If an ISP shuts down a site, it can migrate to another hosting service and even register under a new domain name.

Instead of shutting down sites, some governments are considering filtering them. Germany recently passed a filtering law aimed at blocking child pornography, which it says could be expanded to block sites that promote terrorist acts. And Australia is testing a filtering system for both child pornography and material that advocates terrorism.

The outcry in both countries, however, has been tremendous, both on technical grounds — filtering can slow down Internet speed — and civil liberties grounds. "Other countries using similar systems to monitor Internet traffic have blacklisted political critics," wrote an Australian newspaper columnist. "Is this really the direction we want our country to be heading? Communist China anyone? Burma? How about North Korea?"[24]

Ultimately, filtering just may not be that effective. Determined Internet users can easily circumvent a national filter and access banned material that is legal elsewhere. And filtering cannot capture the dynamic parts of the Internet: the chat rooms, video sharing sites and blogs, for instance.

Even some governments with established filtering laws seem reluctant to remove terrorist sites. The government owns Singapore's Internet providers and screens all Web sites for content viewed as " 'objectionable' or a potential threat to national security."[25] Yet Osman, of the Nanyang Technological University, says the government is not blocking Web sites that support terrorism. "I can still get access to many of them," she says, "so a lot of other people can, too."

In fact, counterterrorism officials around the world often prefer to monitor and infiltrate blogs, chat rooms, discussion forums and other Web sites where terrorists and sympathizers converse. If the sites remain active, they can be mined for intelligence.

"One reason [for not shutting down sites] is to take the temperature, to see whether the level of conversation is going up or down in terms of triggering an alert among security agencies," says Anthony Bergin, director of research at the Australian Strategic Policy Institute.

Another purpose is to disrupt terrorist attacks, says Bergin. Just recently, the violent postings of Texas resident Hosan Maher Husein Smadi to an extremist chat room attracted the attention of the FBI, which was monitoring the site. Agents set up a sting operation and arrested the 19-year-old Jordanian in late September after he allegedly tried to detonate what he thought was a bomb, provided by an undercover agent, in the parking garage beneath a Dallas skyscraper.[26]

Should Internet companies do more to stop terrorists' use of the Web?

Between 100 and 200 Web sites are the core "fountains of venom," says Yigal Carmon, president of the Middle East Media Research Institute, headquartered in Washington, D.C., with branch offices in Europe, Asia and the Middle East. "All the rest, are replication and duplication. You need to fight a few hundred sites, not thousands."

And many of these sites, he says, are hosted in the West. American hosting services, for instance, are often cheaper, have sufficient bandwidth to accommodate large video files and enjoy free-speech protection. But the companies often don't know they are hosting a site that, if not illegal, is perhaps violating their terms-of-service agreements.

Most Internet Service Providers, Web hosting companies, file-sharing sites and social networking sites have terms-of-service agreements that prohibit certain content. For instance, the Yahoo! Small Business Web hosting service states that users will not knowingly upload, post, e-mail, transmit or otherwise distribute any content that is "unlawful, harmful, threatening, abusive, harassing, tortious, defamatory, vulgar, obscene, libelous, invasive of another's privacy, hateful or racially, ethnically or otherwise objectionable."

It also specifically forbids users from utilizing the service to "provide material support or resources . . . to any organization(s) designated by the United States government as a foreign terrorist organization."

But Yahoo! also makes clear that it does not pre-screen content and that "You, and not Yahoo!, are entirely responsible for all Content that you upload, post, transmit, or otherwise make available."[27]

Some policy makers want Internet companies to begin screening the sites they host. Last year in the U.K., for instance, the House of Commons's Culture, Media and Sport Select Committee recommended that the "proactive review of content should be standard practice for sites hosting user-generated content."[28]

Internet companies, as well as civil libertarians and privacy advocates, disagree. "We do not think that ISPs should monitor anything since they are just in the business of transferring bits and bytes," says Rotert of EuroISPA. "We still believe in privacy laws."

David McClure, president and CEO of the U.S. Internet Industry Association, concurs. "If I'm a Web hoster, it is not my job to go snooping through the files and pages that people put on those Web sites," says McClure. "It's my job to keep the servers and the hosting service running." And, according to McClure, no U.S. law compels them to do more. Under the Telecommunications Act of 1996, McClure says, companies that host Web sites are not legally responsible for their content.

Still, ISPs and Web hosting companies do remove sites that violate their terms-of-service agreements, once they are aware of them. Since 9/11 a variety of private watchdog groups — like the SITE Intelligence Group and Internet Haganah — have made it their business to track jihadi Web sites.

Some anti-jihadist activists, like Aaron Weisburd — who created and runs Internet Haganah — have even contacted ISPs in an effort to shame them into taking down sites. Perhaps hundreds of sites have been removed with his help. "It is rare to find an Internet company that does not care or that actively supports the terrorist cause," he says.

Weisburd says some sites should be left online because they are good sources of intelligence, "while many other sites can — and arguably should — be taken down." He says the main reason to remove them is not to get them off the Internet permanently — which is extremely difficult to do — but to track individuals as they open new accounts in order to gather evidence and prosecute them.

AP Photo/Sankei Shimbum/Kiyohiro Oku

Members of the Peruvian revolutionary movement Tupac Amaru flash victory signs after seizing the Japanese ambassador's residence in Lima in December 1996, along with hundreds of hostages. The morning after the seizure, the rebels launched a new era in terrorist media operations by posting a 100-page Web site, based in Germany. As the four-month siege dragged on, the group updated the site periodically, using a laptop and a satellite telephone. The hostages were eventually rescued in a raid by the Peruvian military.

But ISPs don't always follow through. "Even when you get a complaint about a Web site that may be violating the terms of service, many Web hosting services may be unlikely to pursue it," says McClure. Investigating complaints is time-consuming and expensive, he says, and "once you start pursuing each complaint, you are actively involved in monitoring, and the complaints will skyrocket."

To monitor how the big Internet platforms respond to user complaints, Neumann, of King's College, suggests forming an Internet Users Panel, which could name and shame companies that don't take users' complaints seriously. "We don't want the panel to be a government body," says Neumann. "We are proposing a body that consists of Internet users, Internet companies and experts." It could publicize best practices, he says, and act as an ombudsman of last resort. ISPs would fund the panel.

But Neumann's proposal does not sit well with the ISPs. "A lot of people propose that ISPs do a lot of things," says McClure, "and what they want is for ISPs to do a lot of work for nothing."

Carmon also objects to relying on ISPs and Web hosting companies to respond to user complaints. "It's a totally untrustworthy system because you don't know who is making the complaint and why," Carmon says. "I issue a complaint against your Web site, but I may be settling an account against you, I may be your competitor in business." So ISPs must be very careful in evaluating complaints, which takes time, he says; ISPs don't want to be sued.

Instead, Carmon proposes creating what he calls a Civic Action Committee, based at an accredited research organization, which would monitor the Web and recommend sites that ISPs should consider closing. The committee would be made up of "intellectuals, writers, authors, people known for their moral standing, activists and legislators from different political parties," says Carmon.

Rotert is doubtful. "The ISPs in Europe would follow only government requests for notice and takedown procedures," he says, "because the ISPs know they cannot be held liable for destroying a business by taking down a site if the order came from the police."

Conway, of Dublin City University, has another objection to private policing of the Internet. "The capacity of private, political and economic actors to bypass the democratic process and to have materials they find politically objectionable erased from the Internet is a matter of concern," she said. Governments might want to consider legislation not just to regulate the Internet — "perhaps, for example, outlawing the posting and dissemination of beheading videos — but also writing into law more robust protections for radical political speech."[29]

Does cyberterrorism pose a serious threat?

Last year Pakistani President Asif Ali Zardari issued the following decree: "Whoever commits the offence of cyberterrorism and causes death of any person shall be punishable with death or imprisonment for life."[30]

In March India's cabinet secretary warned an international conference that cyber attacks and cyberterrorism are looming threats. "There could be attacks on critical infrastructure such as telecommunications, power distribution, transportation, financial services, essential public utility services and others," said K. M. Chandrasekhar. "The damage can range from a simple shutdown of a computer system to a complete paralysis of a significant portion of critical infrastructure in a specific region or even the control nerve centre of the entire infrastructure."[31]

Politicians, counterterrorism officials and security experts have made similarly gloomy predictions about cyberterrorism since 9/11 — and even before. But to date there have been no such attacks, although an ex-employee of a wastewater treatment plant in Australia used a computer and a radio transmitter to release sewage into parks and resort grounds in 2000.

Cyberterrorism is generally defined as highly damaging computer attacks by private individuals designed to generate terror and fear to achieve political or social goals. Thus, criminal hacking — no matter how damaging — conducted to extort money or for bragging rights is not considered cyberterrorism. (Criminal hacking is common. A year ago, for instance, criminals stole personal credit-card information from the computers of RBS WorldPay and then used the data to steal $9 million from 130 ATMs in 49 cities around the world.[32]) Likewise, the relatively minor denial-of-service attacks and Web defacements typically conducted by hackers aligned with terrorist groups also are not considered cyberterrorism.[33]

Skeptics say cyberterrorism poses only a slim threat, in part because it would lack the drama of a suicide attack or an airplane crash. "Let's say terrorists cause the lights to go out in New York City or Los Angeles, something that has already happened from weather conditions or human error," says Conway, of Dublin City University. "That is not going to create terror," she says, because those systems have been shown they can rapidly recover. Besides, she adds, terrorist groups tend to stick with what they know, which are physical attacks. "There is evolution but not sea changes in their tactics."

Even if terrorists wanted to launch a truly destructive and frightening cyber attack, their capabilities are very limited, says Irving Lachow, a senior research professor at the National Defense University in Washington, D.C. "They would need a multidisciplinary team of people to pull off a cyberterrorism attack," he says.

"A lot of these critical facilities are very complicated, and they have hundreds of systems," he continues. To blow up a power plant, for instance, a terrorist group would need an insider who knows which key computer systems are vulnerable, a team of experienced hackers to break into these systems, engineers who understand how the plant works so real damage can be done, a computer simulation lab to practice and lots of time, money and secrecy.

"At the end of the day, it's a lot easier just to blow something up," Lachow says.

But others fear that as governments continue to foil physical attacks, terrorists will expand their tactics to include cyberterrorism. Some analysts warn that terrorists could purchase the necessary expertise from cyber criminals. That, said Steven Bucci, IBM's lead researcher for cyber security, would be "a marriage made in Hell."[34]

According to Bucci, cybercrime is "a huge (and still expanding) industry that steals, cheats and extorts the equivalent of many billions of dollars every year." The most insidious threat, he said, comes from criminal syndicates that control huge botnets: worldwide networks of unwitting personal computers used for denial-of-service attacks, e-mail scams and distributing malicious software.[35]

The syndicates often rent their botnets to other criminals. Some analysts fear it's only a matter of time before a cash-rich terrorist group hires a botnet for its own use. "The cyber capabilities that the criminals could provide would in short order make any terrorist organization infinitely more dangerous and effective," said Bucci, and the permutations are "as endless as one's imagination." For example, terrorists could "open the valves at a chemical plant near a population center," replicating the deadly 1984 chemical accident in Bhopal, India.[36]

And a full-fledged cyberterrorism attack is not the only disturbing possibility, say Bucci and others. Perl at the Organization for Security and Co-operation believes terrorists are much more likely to use a cyber attack to amplify the destructive power of a physical attack. "One of the goals of terrorism is to create fear and panic," says Perl, "and not having full access to the Internet could greatly hamper governments' response to a series of massive, coordinated terrorist incidents." For example, terrorists might try to disable the emergency 911 system while blowing up embassies.

Some experts are particularly concerned that al Qaeda could launch a coordinated attack on key ports while simultaneously disabling their emergency-response systems, in order to immobilize the trade-dependant global economy. Al-Qaeda leaders have made it clear that destroying the industrialized world's economy is one of the group's goals.

But Dorothy Denning, a professor of conflict and cyberspace at the Naval Postgraduate School in Monterey, Calif., said, "Terrorists do not normally integrate

Governments Now Prosecute Suspected Online Terrorists

New laws apply to online activities.

Governments around the world have prosecuted suspected terrorists before they carry out acts of violence, but not many have been prosecuted solely for their alleged online activities in support of terrorism.

Those cases have been hampered by concerns about restricting free speech, the desire to monitor terrorist-linked sites for intelligence and the difficulty of identifying individuals online. Here are some examples of such cases:

Sami Al-Hussayen — A 34-year-old graduate student in computer science at the University of Idaho, Al-Hussayen was arrested in February 2003 and accused of designing, creating and maintaining Web sites that provided material support for terrorism. It was the U.S. government's first attempt at using statutes prohibiting material support for terrorism to prosecute activity that occurred exclusively online. The definition of "material support" used by the prosecutors had been expanded under the Patriot Act of 2001 to include "expert advice or assistance."

Al-Hussayen had volunteered to run Web sites for two Muslim charities and two Muslim clerics. But prosecutors alleged that messages and religious fatwas on the sites encouraged jihad, recruited terrorists and raised money for foreign terrorist groups. It didn't matter that Al-Hussayen had never committed a terrorist act or that he hadn't written the material. Prosecutors said it was enough to prove that he ran the Web sites and knew the messages existed.

Jurors were not convinced, however. They acquitted Al-Hussayen in June 2004. "There was no direct connection in the evidence they gave us — and we had boxes and boxes to go through — between Sami and terrorism," said one juror.[1]

The case attracted national attention, and according to University of Idaho law professor Alan Williams, "triggered a heated debate focused mainly on a key question: Were Al-Hussayen's Internet activities constitutionally protected free speech or did they cross the line into criminal and material support to terrorism?"[2]

The U.S. Supreme Court is scheduled to hear challenges to the material support statute — which critics complain is too vague — in two related cases this session.[3]

Younis Tsouli — In late 2005, British police arrested 22-year-old Tsouli, a Moroccan immigrant and student who prosecutors alleged was known online as "Irhaby 007" — or Terrorist 007. The government linked Tsouli and his accomplices Waseem Mughal and Tariq al-Daour to "the purchase, construction and maintenance of a large number of Web sites and Internet chat forums on which material was published which incited acts of terrorist murder, primarily in Iraq."[4]

Tsouli had been in active contact with al Qaeda in Iraq and was part of an online network that extended to Canada, the United States and Eastern Europe. In July 2007, Tsouli, Mughal and Al-Daour "became the first men to plead guilty to inciting murder for terrorist purposes" under the U.K.'s Terrorism Act of 2000.[5]

Samina Malik — In November 2007 the 23-year-old shop assistant became the first woman convicted of terrorism in the United Kingdom when she was found guilty of "possessing information of a kind likely to be useful to a person committing or preparing an act of terrorism."[6]

Malik had downloaded and saved on her hard drive *The Terrorist's Handbook*, *The Mujahideen Poisons Handbook* and other documents that appeared to support violent jihad.

multiple modes of attack." If coordinating cyber and physical attacks did become their goal, Denning would expect to see evidence of failed attempts, training, discussions and planning. "Given terrorists' capabilities today in the cyber domain, this seems no more imminent than other acts of cyberterror," she said. "At least in the near future, bombs remain a much larger threat than bytes."[37]

But that doesn't mean critical infrastructure is secure from cyber criminal syndicates or nation-states, which do have the technical know-how, funds and personnel to launch a damaging attack, Denning said. "Even if our critical infrastructures are not under imminent threat by terrorists seeking political and social objectives," she said, "they must be protected from harmful attacks conducted for other reasons, such as money, revenge, youthful curiosity and war."[38]

She had also written violent poems about killing nonbelievers. Her defense portrayed her as a confused young woman assuming a persona she thought was "cool."

Her conviction sparked public outrage. Muhammed Abdul Bari, secretary general of the Muslim Council of Britain, said, "Many young people download objectionable material from the Internet, but it seems if you are Muslim then this could lead to criminal charges, even if you have absolutely no intention to do harm to anyone else." An appeals court later overturned her conviction and clarified a new requirement that suspects must have a clear intent to engage in terrorism.[7]

Ibrahim Rashid — In 2007 German prosecutors charged the Iraqi Kurdish immigrant with waging a "virtual jihad" on the Internet. They argued that by posting al-Qaeda propaganda on chat rooms, Rashid was trying to recruit individuals to join al Qaeda and participate in jihad. It was Germany's first prosecution of an Islamic militant for circulating propaganda online.[8]

"This case underscores how thin the line is that Germany is walking in its efforts to aggressively target Islamic radicals," wrote Shawn Marie Boyne, a professor at Indiana University's law school. "While active membership in a terrorist organization is a crime . . . it is no longer a crime to merely sympathize with terrorist groups or to distribute propaganda."[9] Thus, the prosecution had to prove that Rashid's postings went beyond expressing sympathy and extended to recruiting. The court found him guilty in June 2008.

Saïd Namouh — On Oct. 1, the 36-year-old Moroccan resident of Quebec was convicted under Canada's Anti-Terrorism Act of four charges largely related to his online activities. In March 2007 he had helped publicize a video warning Germany and Austria that they would suffer a bomb attack if they didn't withdraw their troops from Afghanistan. He also distributed violent videos on behalf of Global Islamic Media Front, a propaganda arm of al Qaeda. Intercepted Internet chats revealed Namouh's plans to explode a truck bomb and die a martyr. "Terrorism is in

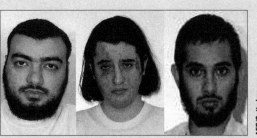

Tariq al-Daour, Younis Tsouli and Waseem Mughal (left to right), in 2007 became the first to plead guilty to inciting murder for terrorist purposes online under the U.K.'s Terrorism Act of 2000.

our blood, and with it we will drown the unjust," Namouh said online.[10]

— Barbara Mantel

---

[1] Maureen O'Hagan, "A terrorism case that went awry," seattletimes.com, Nov. 22, 2004, http://seattletimes.nwsource.com/html/local-news/2002097570_sami22m.html.

[2] Alan Williams, "Prosecuting Website Development Under the Material Support in Terrorism Statutes: Time to Fix What's Broken," *NYU Journal of Legislation & Public Policy*, 2008, p. 366.

[3] The cases are *Holder v. Humanitarian Law Project*; *Humanitarian Law Project v. Holder*, 08-1498; 09-89. See http://onthedocket.org/cases/2009.

[4] Elizabeth Renieris, "Combating Incitement to Terrorism on the Internet: Comparative Approaches in the United States and United Kingdom and the Need for an International Solution," *Vanderbilt Journal of Entertainment and Technology Law*, vol. 11:3:673, p. 698, 2009.

[5] *Ibid.*

[6] *Ibid.*

[7] *Ibid.*, pp. 699-700.

[8] Shawn Marie Boyne, "The Criminalization of Speech in an Age of Terror," working paper, June 12, 2009, p. 7, http://ssrn.com/abstract=1418496.

[9] *Ibid.*

[10] Graeme Hamilton, "Quebec terror plotter undone by online activities," *National Post*, Oct. 1, 2009, www.nationalpost.com/news/story.html?id=2054720.

BACKGROUND

Growth and Evolution

After seizing the Japanese embassy in Lima, Peru, on Dec. 17, 1996, the Tupac Amaru communist rebels "launched a new era in terrorist media operations," wrote Denning. The next morning the group had a Web site with more than 100 pages up and running out of

Germany, which it updated using a laptop and a satellite telephone.[39]

"For the first time, terrorists could bring their message to a world audience without mediation by the established press or interference by the government," Denning said. They could offer the first news accounts to the media, and they could use the Web site to communicate directly with their members and supporters. "The advantage the

CHRONOLOGY

1990s *Terrorist groups discover the Internet's usefulness for fundraising and publicity.*

1996 After seizing the Japanese embassy in Lima, Peruvian revolutionary movement Tupac Amaru creates a Web site to publicize its actions.

1997 Sri Lanka's Tamil Tigers use stolen Sheffield University faculty members' computer IDs and passwords to solicit donations.

1998 Researchers looking for online terrorism sites discover al Qaeda's Web site, www.alneda.com.

1999 Nearly all 30 U.S.-designated foreign terrorist organizations have an Internet presence.

2000-2005 *Extremist Web sites and discussion forums multiply; first prosecution of man accused of providing material online in support of terrorists fails.*

July 20, 2000 Terrorism Act of 2000 makes it illegal in the U.K. to collect, make or possess information likely to be used in terrorism.

2001 The 9/11 attackers use the Internet to research flight schools and flights and to coordinate their actions. On Oct. 26, 2001, President George W. Bush signs the USA Patriot Act, which prohibits "material support" for terrorists.

2003 Abdelaziz al-Muqrin, leader of al Qaeda in Saudi Arabia, pioneers several digital magazines, including *Sawt al-Jihad* (*The Voice of Jihad*).

2004 Video of the decapitation of kidnapped U.S. businessman Nicholas Berg is released on a Malaysian Web site. . . . University of Idaho graduate student Sami Omar al-Hussayen is acquitted of fostering terrorism online after his lawyers raise freedom of expression issues. Autobiography of Imam Samudra, mastermind of the 2002 Bali nightclub bombings that killed 202, promotes online credit-card fraud to raise funds. . . . Saudi Arabia launches the Sakinah Campaign, in which Islamic scholars steer religious questioners away from online extremists.

2005 YouTube, launched in February, quickly becomes repository for jihadist video content and commentary.

More than 4,000 Web sites connected to terrorist groups are on the Internet.

2006-Present *Governments reauthorize and expand antiterrorism laws; U.K. begins prosecuting those who use the Internet to "incite" others to commit terrorist acts.*

2006 President Bush reauthorizes Patriot Act. . . . U.K. passes Terrorism Act of 2006, outlawing encouragement or glorification of terrorism; civil libertarians raise concerns about free speech. . . . U.S. State Department creates Digital Outreach Team with two Arabic-speaking employees who converse online with critics of U.S. policies.

2007 EU police agency Europol begins "Check the Web" program, in which member states share in monitoring and evaluating terrorists' Web sites. . . . In July, U.K. resident Younis Tsouli pleads guilty to inciting terrorism after he and two associates used stolen credit cards to register Web site domains that promote terrorisim. . . . Samina Malik becomes the first woman convicted of terrorism in the U.K. for having documents that support violent jihad on her computer. A court of appeals later overturns her conviction, questioning her intent to engage in terrorism.

2008 Three important Islamist terrorist discussion forums disappear from the Internet; analysts assume counterterrorism agencies bombarded the sites with denial-of-service attacks. . . . On Nov. 6, Pakistan's president makes cyberterrorism punishable with death or life imprisonment. . . . In its first prosecution for promoting terrorism online, a German court finds Iraqi Kurdish immigrant Ibrahim Rashid guilty of waging a "virtual jihad" for attempting to recruit individuals online to join al Qaeda and participate in jihad.

2009 Canadian resident Saïd Namouh is convicted on Oct. 1 of planning terrorist acts and distributing jihadist propaganda via the Internet. . . . On Oct. 26 Jordanian teenager Hosam Maher Husein Smadi pleads not guilty of plotting to blow up a Dallas skyscraper on Sept. 24. FBI agents had been keeping tabs on Smadi after discovering him on an extremist Web site earlier this year. . . . Researchers are tracking more than 7,000 Web sites connected to terrorist groups and their supporters.

Web offered was immeasurable and recognized by terrorist groups worldwide."[40]

By the end of 1999, nearly all of the 30 organizations designated by the U.S. State Department as foreign terrorist organizations had a presence on the Internet. By 2005, there were more than 40 designated terrorist groups and more than 4,300 Web sites serving them and their supporters. Today, the number of such Web sites exceeds 7,000, according to Weimann, of Haifa University.[41]

Of these groups, Islamic terrorists have perhaps made the most use of the Internet. When al Qaeda suffered defeat in Afghanistan directly after 9/11, its recruiters in Europe "who had previously encouraged others to travel to mujahidin training camps in Afghanistan, Bosnia-Herzegovina and Chechnya began radically changing their message," wrote Kohlmann, of the NEFA Foundation. "Their new philosophy emphasized the individual nature and responsibility of jihad."[42] Recruits did not necessarily have to travel abroad; they could learn what they needed online.

Thus the Internet became a vital means for communication amid a global law enforcement clampdown on suspected terrorists.

Al Qaeda's first official Web site was the brainchild of a senior Saudi operative — and one-time Osama bin Laden bodyguard — Shaykh Youssef al-Ayyiri. The site contained audio and video clips of the al-Qaeda leader, justification for the 9/11 attacks and poetry glorifying the attackers and — on its English version — a message to the American people.[43]

After al-Ayyiri's 2003 death during a clash with Saudi security forces, his top lieutenant, Abdelaziz al-Muqrin, took control. He was a "firm believer in using the Web to disseminate everything from firsthand accounts of terrorist operations to detailed instructions on how to capture or kill Western tourists and diplomats," according to Kohlmann. Before he was killed by Saudi forces in 2004, al-Muqrin created several digital magazines, including *Sawt al-Jihad*, or *The Voice of Jihad*. The author of an article in its inaugural issue told readers, "The blood [of the infidels] is like the blood of a dog and nothing more."[44]

While al Qaeda's Saudi Arabian network pioneered the use of online publications, Kohlmann said, "The modern revolution in the terrorist video market has occurred in the context of the war in Iraq and under the watchful eye of Jordanian national Abu Musab al-Zarqawi." Until his death in 2006, Zarqawi led al Qaeda in Iraq and was known for "his penchant for and glorification of extreme violence

— particularly hostage beheadings and suicide bombings," many of them captured on video, including the murder of American civilian contractor Nicholas Berg.[45]

"Images of orange-clad hostages became a headline-news staple around the world — and the full, raw videos of their murders spread rapidly around the Web."[46]

Content on militant Islamist Web sites in Southeast Asia tends to "mimic the contents and features of their Arabic and Middle Eastern online counterparts," according to a study from the Australian Strategic Policy Institute. "Although they aren't yet on par in operational coordination and tradecraft, they are catching up."[47]

Between 2006 and July 2007, extremist content on radical Bahasa Indonesia (the official language of Indonesia) and Malay language Web sites consisted of propaganda from al Qaeda and the Indonesian jihadist group Jemaah Islamiyah. The sites celebrated mujahidin victories, aired local grievances linked to the global jihad and posted highly selective Koranic verses used to justify acts of terror. In August 2007, one of the first postings of instructions on computer hacking appeared, and in the first four months of 2008 the first bomb-making manual, bomb-making video and a password-protected forum emerged.[48] (*See box, p. 134.*)

Not all terrorist organizations use the Internet to showcase violence. Many, such as FARC (Revolutionary Armed Forces of Colombia), focus on human rights and peace. "In contrast to al Qaeda's shadowy, dynamic, versatile and often vicious Web sites," wrote Weimann, "the FARC sites are more 'transparent,' stable and mainly focused on information and publicity."

Established in 1964 as the military wing of the Colombian Communist Party, FARC has been responsible for kidnappings, bombings and hijackings and funds its operations through narcotics trafficking.[49] Yet there are no violent videos of these attacks. Instead, FARC Web sites offer information on the organization's history and laws, its reasons for resistance, offenses perpetrated by the Colombian and U.S. governments, life as a FARC member and women and culture. Weimann called the sophisticated FARC Web sites "an impressive example of media-savvy Internet use by a terrorist group."[50]

From Web 1.0 to 2.0

Terrorist content can now be found on all parts of the Internet, not just on official sites of groups like FARC and al Qaeda and their proxies. Chat rooms, blogs, social

'Terrorists Are Trying to Attract Young Recruits'

An interview with the director of the Dark Web project.

The University of Arizona's Dark Web project, funded by the National Science Foundation, studies international terrorism using automated computer programs. The project has amassed one of the world's largest databases on extremist/terrorist-generated Internet content. Author Barbara Mantel recently interviewed Hsinchun Chen, the project's director.

CQ: What is the purpose of Dark Web?

HC: We examine who terrorists talk to, what kind of information they disseminate, what kind of new violent ideas they have, what kind of illegal activities they plan to conduct. We're looking at Web sites, forums, chat rooms, blogs, social networking sites, videos and virtual worlds.

CQ: How difficult is it to find terrorist content on the Web?

HC: From Google you can find some, but you won't be able to get into the sites that are more relevant, more intense and more violent.

CQ: So how do sympathizers find these sites?

HC: Typically people are introduced by word of mouth, offline. And there are different degrees of openness on these sites.

CQ: For example?

HC: There are many sites that require an introduction; they may require a password; moderators may also ask a series of questions to see if you are from the region, if you are real and if you are in their targeted audience.

CQ: How does the Dark Web project find these sites?

HC: We have been collaborating for six or seven years with many terrorism study centers all around the world, and they have been monitoring these sites for some time. So they know how to access these Web sites and whether they are legitimate forums. But most of them do not have the ability to collect all the content; they can do manual review and analysis.

So these researchers will give us the URLs of these sites, and they'll give us the user names and passwords they've been using to gain access. Once we get this information, we load it into our computer program, and the computers will spit out every single page of that site and download that into our database.

CQ: How much material are we talking about?

HC: The researchers we work with can analyze maybe hundreds or thousands of pages or messages, but we collect and analyze maybe half a million to 10 million pages easily.

CQ: How do you know that a site is actually linked to a terrorist group or supporter?

HC: Remember we start off with the URLs that terrorism researchers think are important. We also do "crawling" to find new sites. Any Web site will have links to other sites, and by triangulating those links from legitimate sites, we can locate other legitimate sites.

CQ: After finding the content, do you analyze it?

HC: Our claim to fame is analysis. We have techniques that look at social network linkages, that categorize the content into propaganda, training, recruiting, etc., and techniques that determine the sophistication of Web sites. We have a technique that looks at the extent of the violent sentiment in these sites and techniques that can determine authorship.

networking sites and user groups allow conversation and debate among a wide variety of participants.

"Yahoo! has become one of al Qaeda's most significant ideological bases of operations," wrote researchers Rita Katz and Josh Devon in 2003. "Creating a Yahoo! Group is free, quick and extremely easy. . . . Very often, the groups contain the latest links to jihadist Web sites, serving as a jihadist directory."[51] A Yahoo! user group is a hybrid between an electronic mailing list and a discussion forum. Members can receive posted messages and photos through e-mail or view the posts at the group's Web site.

While much of the original content on the terrorist-linked sites was text-based, videos began to play a much larger role after 2003, especially for militant Islamist organizations and their supporters. "Nevertheless, much of this video content remained quite difficult to access for Westerners and others, as it was located on Arabic-only Web sites" that were often frequently changing domain names and were therefore used "only by those who were strongly committed to gaining access," according to a study co-authored by Conway, of Dublin City University.[52]

CQ: None of this is done manually?

HC: Everything I talk about — almost 90 percent — is entirely automated.

CQ: What trends you are noticing?

HC: I'm not a terrorism researcher, but there are trends that we observe on the technology end. Terrorists are trying to attract young recruits, so they like to use discussion forums and YouTube, where the content is more multimedia and more of a two-way conversation. We also see many home-grown groups cropping up all over the world.

CQ: Do you share this information with government agencies?

HC: Many agencies — I cannot name them — and researchers from many countries are using the Dark Web forum portal.

CQ: How does the portal work?

HC: There is a consensus among terrorism researchers that discussion forums are the richest source of content, especially the forums that attract sometimes 50,000 members to 100,000 members. So we have created this portal that contains the contents from close to 20 different, important forums. And these are in English, Arabic and French. The French ones are found in North Africa.

We also embedded a lot of search, translation and analysis mechanisms in the portal. So now any analyst can use the content to see trends. For example, they can see what are the discussions about improvised explosive devices in Afghanistan, or they can look at who are the members that are interested in weapons of mass destruction.

CQ: Are these forums mostly extremist jihadi forums?

HC: Yes, they are. That's what analysts are primarily interested in. We are also creating another portal for multimedia content that will be available in another month or two. That would contain material from YouTube, for instance.

Hsinchun Chen oversees the University of Arizona's Dark Web project, which analyzes terrorists' online activities.

CQ: Do you collect information from U.S. extremist sites?

HC: We collect from animal-liberation groups, Aryan Nation and militia groups, but that is just for our research purposes. We don't make it available to outsiders. Government lawyers advise us against giving that kind of information out to them or to the outside world. It's a civil liberty issue.

CQ: Even if that material is open source material, available to anyone who finds their Web site?

HC: Even if it is open source.

But the advent of YouTube in 2005 changed the situation dramatically, Conway wrote, playing an increasing role in distributing terrorist content. Not only did YouTube become an immediate repository for large amounts of jihadist video content, but the social-networking aspects of the site allowed a dialogue between posters and viewers of videos.[53]

Terrorists-linked groups also have used mass e-mailings to reach broad audiences, according to Denning. "The Jihadist Cyber-Attack Brigade, for example, announced in May 2008 they had successfully sent 26,000 e-mails

to 'citizens of the Gulf and Arab countries explaining the words of our leader Usama Bin Ladin.'"[54]

Terrorists and Cybercrime

Terrorists increasingly have turned to the Internet to raise funds, often through cybercrime. "We should be extremely concerned about the scope of the credit-card fraud problem involving terrorists," according to Dennis Lormel, a retired special agent in the FBI. Although there is "limited or no empirical data to gauge the extent

Political Change Is Main Attack Motivation

Four out of six types of cyber attacks or threats are politically motivated. Attackers typically use "malware," or malicious software that spreads viruses, or denial-of-service attacks to disrupt Web sites of individuals, companies, governments and other targets.

Cyber Threat	Motivation	Target	Method
Cyberterror	Political or social change	Innocent victims	Computer-based violence or destruction
Hacktivism*	Political or social change	Decision-makers or innocent victims	Web page defacements or denial of service
Black Hat Hacking**	Ego, personal enmity	Individuals, companies, governments	Malware, viruses, worms or hacking
Cybercrime	Economic gain	Individuals, companies	Malware for fraud or identity theft; denial of service for blackmail
Cyber Espionage	Economic or political gain	Individuals, companies, governments	Range of techniques
Information War	Political or military gain	Infrastructures, information-technology systems and data (private or public)	Range of techniques

Hacking to promote an activist's political ideology.

** *Hacking just for the challenge, bragging rights or due to a personal vendetta.*

Source: Franklin D. Kramer, Stuart H. Starr and Larry Wentz, eds., "Cyber Threats: Defining Terms," Cyberpower and National Security *(2009)*

of the problem . . . there are compelling signs that an epidemic permeates," he wrote.[55]

In his jailhouse autobiography, Imam Samudra — convicted of masterminding the 2002 nightclub bombings in Bali, Indonesia, that killed 202 people — includes a rudimentary outline of how to commit online credit-card fraud, or "carding."

"If you succeed at hacking and get into carding, be ready to make more money within three to six hours than the income of a policeman in six months," Samudra writes. "But don't do it just for the sake of money." Their main duty, he tells readers, is to raise arms against infidels, "especially now the United States and its allies."[56] Although Samudra's laptop revealed an attempt at carding, it's not clear he ever succeeded.

But others have. Younis Tsouli, a young Moroccan immigrant in London who made contact with al Qaeda online, and two associates used computer viruses and stolen credit-card accounts to set up a network of communication forums and Web sites that hosted "everything from tutorials on computer hacking and bomb making to videos of beheadings and suicide bombing attacks in Iraq," said Lormel.[57]

The three hackers ran up $3.5 million in charges to register more than 180 Web site domains at 95 different Web hosting companies and purchased hundreds of prepaid cellphones and more than 250 airline tickets. They also laundered money through online gaming sites.[58]

Even though both Samudra and Tsouli are in jail, "they left their successful tradecraft on Web pages and in chat rooms for aspiring terrorists to learn and grow from," noted Lormel.[59]

CURRENT SITUATION
Alternative Voices

Western governments and terrorism experts are concerned that the United States and other nations are not providing a counter message to online militant Islamists.

"The militant Islamist message on the Internet cannot be censored, but it can be challenged," says Johnny Ryan, a senior researcher at the Institute of International and European Affairs in Dublin, Ireland. But governments and societies, he says, for the most part, have ceded the dialogue in cyberspace to extremists, who are highly skilled at crafting their message.

That message "is mostly emotional," according to Frank Cilluffo, director of the Homeland Security Policy Institute at The George Washington University in Washington, D.C. It "uses images, visuals and music to tell a powerful story with clear-cut heroes and villains."

Societies interested in countering that message should not shy away from emotion either, he argues. "Who are the victims of al Qaeda?" Cilluffo asks, "and why don't we know their stories?" Western and Arab-Muslim media rarely reveal victims' names unless they are famous or foreign, he points out. Personal stories about victims "from the World Trade Center to the weddings, funerals, schools, mosques and hotels where suicide bombers have brought untold grief to thousands of families, tribes and communities throughout the Muslim world" could be told in online social networks, he suggested, "creating a Facebook of the bereaved that crosses borders and cultures."[60]

Raising doubts is "another powerful rhetorical weapon," says Ryan, who suggests exploiting the chat rooms and discussion forums frequented by prospective militants and sympathizers. Moderate Islamic voices should question the legitimacy of al Qaeda's offensive jihad, disseminate the arguments of Muslim scholars who renounce violence and challenge militant Islamists' version of historical relations between the West and Islam, according to Ryan.[61]

The U.S. Department of State has begun its own modest online effort. In November 2006 it created a Digital Outreach Team with two Arabic-speaking employees. The team now has 10 members who actively engage in conversations on Arabic-, Persian- and Urdu-language Internet sites, including blogs, news sites and discussion forums. Team members identify themselves as State Department employees, but instead of posting dry,

The Top 10 Jihadi Web Forums

The most influential jihadi online forums serve as virtual community centers for al Qaeda and other Islamic extremists, according to Internet Haganah — an online network dedicated to combating global jihad. Jihadi Web addresses, which are often blocked, change frequently.

1 ***al-Faloja***
Highly respected among terrorists; focuses on the Iraq War and the Salafi-jihadi struggle.

2 ***al-Medad***
Was associated with Abu Jihad al-Masri, the al-Qaeda propaganda chief killed in a U.S. missile strike in Pakistan on Oct. 30, 2008; disseminates Salafi-jihadi ideology.

3 ***al-Shouaraa***
Originally named el-Shouraa, it was blocked, but later reemerged with a new name; has North African influences; no longer active.

4 ***Ana al-Muslm***
Very active; was used by al Qaeda to communicate with Abu Musab al-Zarqawi (Osama bin Laden's deputy in Iraq) until he was killed by U.S. forces in 2006.

5 ***al-Ma'ark***
Has been slowly and steadily building an online following in recent years.

6 ***al-Shamukh***
Successor to al-Mohajrun, a militant Islamic organization that was banned in the U.K. in 2005; provides radio broadcasts.

7 ***as-Ansar***
Features English and German invitation-only spin-off sites; a favorite among Western jihadists.

8 ***al-Mujahideen***
Attracts a strong contingent of Hamas supporters, with an overall global jihad perspective; especially focused on electronic jihad.

9 ***al-Hanein***
Has a significant amount of jihadi content tinged by Iraqi, Egyptian and Moroccan nationalism.

10 ***at-Tahaddi***
Sunni jihadist; recruits from Somali, Taliban and other terrorist groups.

Source: "Top Ten List of Jihadi Forums," Internet Haganah, a project of The Society for Internet Research, Aug. 3, 2009, http://internethaganah.com/harchives/006545. html; Jamestown Foundation

AP Photo/West Yorkshire Police/PA Wire

Hamaad Munshi — a British national convicted in 2008 of possessing materials likely to be used for terrorism — was 16 when he was arrested after participating in an online British extremist group. The trial revealed that Munshi had downloaded details on how to make napalm and grenades and wished to become a martyr by fighting abroad.

policy pronouncements they create "engaging, informal personas for [their] online discussions." The team's mission is "to explain U.S. foreign policy and to counter misinformation," according to the State Department.[62]

No one knows the full impact of the team's efforts, but the project has come in for criticism. "They should be larger," says Matt Armstrong, an analyst and government advisor who writes a blog on public diplomacy at mountainrunner.us, "and they should be coordinated to a much greater degree with the production side of the State Department." The team's Internet conversations should directly shape a post on the State Department Web site or on its radio program, he says.

But Duncan MacInnes, principal deputy coordinator at the State Department's Bureau of International

Information Programs, says the scale of the Digital Outreach Team is about right, although it could use one or two more Persian speakers and possibly expand into more languages. "Having too many people blogging in a fairly small blogosphere would raise our profile, and we felt [it] would create a reaction against us. You don't want to overdo it." Also, he says, the team does not work in isolation. It writes a biweekly report about the issues, concerns and misunderstandings members encounter online, which goes to hundreds of people inside the State Department.

Others question whether the government should be the one to hold this dialogue. "The state is not in a position to be the primary actor here because it lacks credibility in online forums," says Ryan.

"The best approach is to provide young people with the information and the intellectual tools to challenge this material themselves on various Web forums," says Bergin, of the Australian Strategic Policy Institute. "It's got to be provided by stakeholders in the Muslim community themselves, from community workers, religious figures and parents."

The Sakinah Campaign

Many terrorism analysts cite Saudi Arabia's Sakinah Campaign as a model program. Internet use in the kingdom has grown rapidly since access first became available there 10 years ago. Since 2000, the kingdom's total number of Internet users has risen from roughly 200,000 to more than 7 million today, out of an overall population of nearly 29 million.[63]

Meanwhile, extremist Web sites in the kingdom have multiplied from 15 sites in 1998 to several thousand today, even though the Saudi government controls Internet access and blocks sites featuring gambling, pornography and drug and alcohol use, according to Christopher Boucek, a researcher at the Carnegie Endowment for International Peace. Extremist sites "often appear faster than they can be identified and blocked," said Boucek.[64]

Responding to that trend, the Sakinah Campaign since 2004 has used volunteer Islamic scholars "to interact online with individuals looking for religious knowledge, with the aim of steering them away from extremist sources." These scholars have "highly developed understandings of extremist ideologies, including the religious interpretations used

Is cyberterrorism a significant global threat?

YES
Mohd Noor Amin
Chairman, International Multilateral Partnership Against Cyber Threats Selangor, Malaysia

Written for *CQ Global Researcher*, November 2009

Alarm bells on cyberterrorism have been sounding for more than a decade, and yet, hacktivism aside, the world still has not witnessed a devastating cyber attack on critical infrastructure. Nothing has occurred that caused massive damage, injuries and fatalities resulting in widespread chaos, fear and panic. Does that mean the warnings were exaggerated?

On the contrary, the convergence of impassioned politics, hacktivism trends and extremists' growing technological sophistication suggests that the threat of cyberterrorism remains significant — if not more urgent — today. Although hacktivists and terrorists have not yet successfully collaborated to bring a country to its knees, there is already significant overlap between them. Computer-savvy extremists have been sharpening their skills by defacing and hacking into Web sites and training others to do so online. Given the public ambitions of groups like al Qaeda to launch cyber attacks, it would be folly to ignore the threat of a major cyber assault if highly skilled hackers and terrorists did conspire to brew a perfect storm.

Experts are particularly concerned that terrorists could learn how to deliver a simultaneous one-two blow: executing a mass, physical attack while incapacitating the emergency services or electricity grids to neutralize rescue efforts. The scenario may not be so far-fetched, judging from past cyber attacks or attempts, although a certain level of technical skill and access would be needed to paralyze part of a nation's critical infrastructure. However, as shown by an oft-cited 2000 incident in Australia, a single, disgruntled former employee hacked into a wastewater management facility's computer system and released hundreds of thousands of gallons of raw sewage onto Sunshine Coast resort grounds and a canal.

Vital industrial facilities are not impenetrable to cyber attacks and, if left inadequately secured, terrorists and hackers could wreak havoc. Similarly, the 2008 cyber attacks that caused multicity power outages around the world underscore the vulnerabilities of public utilities, particularly as these systems become connected to open networks to boost economies of scale.

If this past decade of terrorist attacks has demonstrated the high literacy level, technological capability and zeal of terrorists, the next generation of terrorists growing up in an increasingly digitized and connected world may hold even greater potential for cyberterrorism. After all, if it is possible to effect visibly spectacular, catastrophic destruction from afar and still remain anonymous, why not carry it out?

NO
Tim Stevens
Associate, Centre for Science and Security Studies, King's College London

Written for *CQ Global Researcher*, November 2009

Cyberterrorism is the threat and reality of unlawful attacks against computer networks and data by an individual or a nongovernmental group to further a political agenda. Such attacks can cause casualties and deaths through spectacular incidents, such as plane crashes or industrial explosions, or secondary consequences, such as crippled economies or disrupted emergency services.

We have seen many attempts to disrupt the online assets of governments, industry and individuals, but these have mercifully not yet caused the mass casualties predicted by the term "cyberterrorism." The assumption that terrorists might use cyberspace in such attacks is not in question, but the potential threat that cyberterrorism poses is accorded disproportionate weight in some circles.

Cyberterrorism resulting in civilian deaths is certainly one possible outcome of the convergence of technology and political aggression. That it has not happened yet is a function of two factors. First, the ongoing vigilance and operational sophistication of national security agencies have ensured that critical infrastructure systems have remained largely unbreached and secure. And second, like all self-styled revolutionaries, terrorists talk a good talk.

Although a terrorist group might possess both the intent and the skill-sets — either in-house, or "rented" — there is little evidence yet that any group has harnessed both to serious effect. Most attacks characterized as "cyberterrorism" so far have amounted to mere annoyances, such as Web site defacements, service disruptions and low-level cyber "skirmishing" — nonviolent responses to political situations, rather than actions aimed at reaping notoriety in flesh and blood.

It would be foolish, however, to dismiss the threat of cyberterrorism. It would also be disingenuous to overstate it. Western governments are making strides towards comprehensive cyber security strategies that encompass a wide range of possible scenarios, while trying to overcome agency jurisdictional issues, private-sector wariness and the fact that civilian computer systems are now seen as "strategic national assets."

As it becomes harder to understand the complexities of network traffic, identify attack vectors, attribute responsibility and react accordingly, we must pursue integrated national and international strategies that criminalize the sorts of offensive attacks that might constitute cyberterrorism. But designating the attacks as terrorism is a taxonomic firewall we should avoid.

to justify violence and terrorism," according to Boucek.[65] The campaign is officially an independent, nongovernmental project, even though several government ministries encourage and support it.

According to Abdullah Ansary, a lawyer and former lecturer at King Abdul-Aziz University in Saudi Arabia, al Qaeda has issued several statements over the Internet cautioning their followers not to engage in dialogues with members of the Sakinah Campaign, a sign that the campaign is having an impact on al Qaeda's membership.[66] The campaign itself periodically releases the number of people it says it has turned away from extremism. In January 2008, it announced it had "convinced some 877 individuals (722 male and 155 female) to reject their radical ideology across more than 1,500 extremists Web sites."[67]

But in 2007, after the government arrested members of seven terrorist cells operating in the kingdom, several columnists complained that the Sakinah Campaign and other government supported programs trying to reform extremists were ineffective and not getting to the root of the problem. According to translations from the Middle East Media Research Institute, columnist Abdallah bin Bajad Al-'Utaibi wrote in the Saudi daily *Al-Riyadh*: "There are schoolteachers, imams in the mosques, preachers and jurisprudents who do nothing but spread hatred and *takfir** in our society. They should be prosecuted for their actions, which lay down the foundations for terrorism."[68]

Ansary said the government must make wider reforms if it wants to prevent young people from turning to extremism. The government must "speed up the process of political reform in the country, widening popular participation in the political process, improving communication channels of both the government and the public, creating effective communication among branches of government, continuing the efforts in overhauling the Saudi educational system and boosting the role of women in the society."[69]

In late 2006, the Sakinah Campaign expanded its role and created its own Web site designed to "serve as a central location for people to turn to online with questions about Islam."[70]

Government-funded Sites

Similar Web sites have been set up in other countries to offer alternative messages to terrorist propaganda.

The Islamic Religious Council of Singapore — the country's supreme Islamic authority, whose members are appointed by the country's president — has several interactive Web sites to counter extremist strands of Islam. The sites feature articles, blogs and documentary videos targeted at young people and host an online forum where religious scholars answer questions about Islam. One site specifically challenges the ideology of Jemaah Islamiyah, the jihadist group responsible for the deadly 2002 nightclub bombing in Bali and the July 2009 bombings of the Marriott and Ritz Carlton hotels in Jakarta. The organization wants to establish a pan-Islamic theocratic state across much of Southeast Asia.[71]

But the effectiveness of such sites is difficult to gauge. "To a certain extent it is helping to drown out extremist voices online," says Osman, of Nanyang Technological University in Singapore, "but for those who are actively seeking extremist ideology, these kinds of Web sites don't appeal to them."

A similar project in the United Kingdom also meets with skepticism. On its Web site, the Radical Middle Way calls itself "a revolutionary grassroots initiative aimed at articulating a relevant mainstream understanding of Islam that is dynamic, proactive and relevant to young British Muslims."[72] It rejects all forms of terrorism, and its site has blogs, discussions, videos, news and a schedule of its events in the U.K. Its two dozen supporters and partners are mostly Muslim organizations as well as the British Home Office, which oversees immigration, passports, drug policy and counterterrorism, among other things.

"We are arguing that this is not money well spent," says Neumann of King's College. "The kind of money the government is putting into the Web site is enormous, and the site doesn't attract that much traffic."

The government money has also caused at least some young people to question the group's credibility. One blogger called the group "the radical wrong way" and wrote that "because the funding source is so well known, large segments of alienated British Muslims will not have anything to do with this group. . . . If anything, such tactics will lead to even further alienation of young British Muslims — who will rightly point out that this kind of U.S./U.K.-funded version of Islam is just another strategy in the ongoing war on Islam."[73]

Neumann and Bergin recommend instead that governments give out many small grants to different Muslim

---

* *Takfir* is the act of identifying someone as an unbeliever.

organizations with ideas for Web sites and see if any can grow to significance without dependence on government funds.

In the end, individual governments' direct role in providing an online alternative narrative to terrorist ideology may, out of necessity, be quite small because of the credibility issue, say analysts. Instead, they say, governments could fund Internet literacy programs that discuss hate propaganda, adjust school curriculums to include greater discussion of Islam and the West and encourage moderate Muslim voices to take to the Web. Cilluffo, of the Homeland Security Policy Institute, said the United Nations could lead the way, sponsoring a network of Web sites, publications and television programming.

"The United Nations can and should play a significant role," Cilluffo said, "bringing together victims to help meet their material needs and raising awareness by providing platforms through which to share their stories."[74]

OUTLOOK

Pooling Resources

Web sites that promote terrorism are here to stay, although governments and Internet companies will occasionally shut one down if it violates the law or a terms-of-service agreement. Such decisions can only be reached after prolonged monitoring and "must weigh the intelligence value against the security risk posed by the Web site," says Jordanian terrorism expert Bakier.

But monitoring the thousands of Web sites, discussion forums, chat rooms, blogs and other open sources of the Web requires trained personnel with expertise in the languages, cultures, belief systems, political grievances and organizational structures of the terrorist groups online. Because such personnel are scarce, most experts agree that nations should pool their resources. "It is hardly possible for one individual member state to cover all suspicious terrorism-related activities on the Internet," according to a European Union (EU) report.[75]

Good intentions aren't enough. "There are lots of conferences, lots of declarations, lots of papers, but in reality, you have different counterterrorism agencies not sharing information, competing, afraid of each other, sometimes in the same state and also across borders," says Haifa University's Weimann.

Above, an Internet café in Sydney. Many Australians oppose government plans to build what critics call the Great Aussie Firewall — a mandatory Internet filter that would block at least 1,300 Web sites prohibited by the government.

Europol, the EU police agency, began a program in 2007 called Check the Web, which encourages member nations to share in monitoring and evaluating open sources on the Web that promote or support terrorism. The online portal allows member nations to post contact information for monitoring experts; links to Web sites they are monitoring; announcements by the terrorist organizations they are tracking; evaluations of the sites being monitored and additional information like the possibility of legal action against a Web site.

Weimann, who calls the program a "very good idea and very important," says he cannot directly evaluate its progress, since access is restricted to a handful of counterterrorism officials in each member nation. But he does speak to counterterrorism experts at workshops and conferences, where he hears that "international cooperation — especially in Europe — is more theoretical than practical."

When asked if barriers exist to such cooperation, Dublin City University's Conway says, "Emphatically, yes! These range from protection-of-institutional-turf issues — on both a national and EU-wide basis — to potential legal constraints." For instance, she says, some member states' police are unsure whether or not they need a court order to monitor and participate in a Web forum without identifying themselves. Others disagree about the definition of a terrorist and what kinds of sites should be watched.

These barriers may not be the program's only problem. "It might be a disadvantage that so far just EU countries participate," according to Katharina von Knop, a professor of international politics at the University of the Armed Forces, in Munich, Germany, thus limiting the expertise available.[76]

NOTES

1. Abdul Hameed Bakier, "An Online Terrorist Training Manual — Part One: Creating a Terrorist Cell," *Terrorism Focus*, vol. 5, no. 13, The Jamestown Foundation, April 1, 2008. The ek-Is.org Web site has also gone under various other names, including ekhlass.org.

2. *Ibid.*

3. Bakier, *op. cit.*, "Part Two: Assassinations and Robberies," vol. 5, no. 14, April 9, 2008.

4. Bakier, *op. cit.*, "Part Three: Striking U.S. Embassies," vol. 5, no. 15, April 16, 2008.

5. Gabriel Weimann, *Terror on the Internet*, United States Institute of Peace Press (2006), p. 51.

6. *Ibid.*, p. 30.

7. University of Arizona, "Artificial Intelligence Lab Dark Web Project," www.icadl.org/research/terror/.

8. "The 9/11 Commission Report," www.9-11commission.gov/report/index.htm.

9. Anne Stenersen, "The Internet: A virtual training camp?" Norwegian Defense Research Establishment, Oct. 26, 2007, p. 3, www.mil.no/multimedia/archive/00101/Anne_Stenersen_Manu_101280a.pdf.

10. Dorothy Denning, "Terror's Web: How the Internet Is Transforming Terrorism," Handbook on Internet Crime, 2009, p. 19, http://faculty.nps.edu/dedennin/publications/Denning-TerrorsWeb.pdf.

11. *Ibid.*, p. 4.

12. "Violent Islamic Extremism, the Internet, and the Homegrown Terrorist Threat," U.S. Senate Committee on Homeland Security and Governmental Affairs, May 8, 2008, pp. 2, 13, http://hsgac.senate.gov/public/_files/IslamistReport.pdf.

13. "Safeguarding Online: Explaining the Risk Posed by Violent Extremism," Office of Security and Counter Terrorism, Home Office, Aug. 10, 2009, p. 2, http://

security.homeoffice.gov.uk/news-publications/publication-search/general/Officers-esafety-leaflet-v5.pdf?view=Binary.

14. *Ibid.*

15. Peter Neumann and Tim Stevens, "Countering Online Radicalisation: A Strategy for Action," The International Centre for the Study of Radicalisation and Political Violence, Kings College London, 2009, p. 14, www.icsr.info/news/attachments/1236768445ICSROnlineRadicalisationReport.pdf.

16. Clodagh Hartley, "Govt Can't Stop 'Web of Terror,'" *The Sun* (England), March 20, 2009, p. 2.

17. "Interview given by Mme. Michèle Alliot-Marie, French Minister of the Interior, to Le Figaro," French Embassy, Feb 1, 2008, www.ambafrance-uk.org/Michele-Alliot-Marie-on-combating.html.

18. Greg Goth, "Terror on the Internet: A Complex Issue, and Getting Harder," IEEE Computer Society, March 2008, www2.computer.org/portal/web/csdl/doi/10.1109/MDSO.2008.11.

19. Howard Altman, "Al Qaeda's Web Revival," *The Daily Beast*, Oct. 2, 2009, www.thedailybeast.com/blogs-and-stories/2009-10-02/is-this-al-qaedas-website.

20. Gregory McNeal, "Cyber Embargo: Countering the Internet Jihad," *Case Western Reserve Journal of International Law*, vol. 39, no. 3, 2007-08, p. 792.

21. *Brandenburg v. Ohio*, www.oyez.org/cases/1960-1969/1968/1968_492/.

22. "Safeguarding Online: Explaining the Risk Posed by Violent Extremism," *op. cit.*, p. 3.

23. Elizabeth Renieris, "Combating Incitement to Terrorism on the Internet: Comparative Approaches in the United States and the United Kingdom and the Need for an International Solution," *Vanderbilt Journal of Entertainment and Technology Law*, vol. 11:3:673, 2009, pp. 687-688.

24. Fergus Watts, "Caught out by net plan," *Herald Sun* (Australia), Dec. 29, 2008, p. 20, www.heraldsun.com.au/opinion/caught-out-by-net-plan/story-6frfifo-1111118423939.

25. Weimann, *op. cit.*, p. 180.

26. "Jordanian accused in Dallas bomb plot goes to court," CNN, Sept. 25, 2009, www.cnn.com/2009/CRIME/09/25/texas.terror.arrest/index.html.

27. http://smallbusiness.yahoo.com/tos/tos.php.

28. Neumann and Stevens, *op. cit.*, p. 32.

29. Maura Conway, "Terrorism & Internet Governance: Core Issues," U.N. Institute for Disarmament Research, 2007, p.11. www.unidir.org/pdf/articles/pdf-art2644.pdf.

30. Isambard Wilkinson, "Pakistan sets death penalty for 'cyber terrorism,' " *Telegraph.co.uk*, Nov 7, 2008, www.telegraph.co.uk/news/worldnews/asia/pakistan/3392216/Pakistan-sets-death-penalty-for-cyber-terrorism.html.

31. "Cyber attacks and cyber terrorism are the new threats," *India eNews*, March 26, 2009, www.indiaenews.com/print/?id=187451.

32. Linda McGlasson, "ATM Fraud Linked in RBS WorldPay Card Breach," Bank info Security, Feb. 5, 2009, www.bankinfosecurity.com/articles.php?art_id=1197.

33. Dorothy Denning, "A View of Cyberterrorism Five Years Later," 2007, pp. 2–3, http://faculty.nps.edu/dedennin/publications/Denning-TerrorsWeb.pdf.

34. Steven Bucci, "The Confluence of Cyber-Crime and Terrorism," Heritage Foundation, June 15, 2009, p. 6, www.heritage.org/Research/NationalSecurity/upload/hl_1123.pdf.

35. *Ibid.*, p. 5.

36. *Ibid.*, p. 6.

37. Dorothy Denning, *op. cit.*, p. 15.

38. *Ibid.*

39. Denning, "Terror's Web: How the Internet is Transforming Terrorism," *op. cit.*, p. 2.

40. *Ibid.*

41. Weimann, *op. cit.*, p. 15.

42. Evan Kohlmann, " 'Homegrown' Terrorists: Theory and Cases in the War on Terror's Newest Front," *The Annals of the American Academy of Political and Social Science*, July 2008; 618; 95. p. 95.

43. Denning, "Terror's Web: How the Internet is Transforming Terrorism," *op. cit.*, p. 3.

44. Kohlmann, *op. cit.*, p. 101.

45. *Ibid.*

46. David Talbot, "Terror's Server," *Technology Review.com*, Jan. 27, 2005, www.militantislammonitor.org/article/id/404.

47. Anthony Bergin, *et al.*, "Countering Internet Radicalisation in Southeast Asia," The Australian Strategic Policy Institute Special Report, March 2009, p. 5.

48. *Ibid.*, p. 6.

49. Weimann, *op. cit.*, pp. 75-76.

50. Weimann, *op. cit.*, p. 75.

51. Rita Katz and Josh Devon, "WWW.Jihad.com," *National Review Online*, July 14, 2003, http://nationalreview.com/comment/comment-katz-devon071403.asp.

52. Maura Conway and Lisa McInerney, "Jihadi Video & Auto-Radicalisation: Evidence from an Exploratory YouTube Study," 2008, p. 1, http://doras.dcu.ie/2253/2/youtube_2008.pdf.

53. *Ibid.*, p. 2.

54. Denning, "Terror's Web: How the Internet is Transforming Terrorism," *op. cit.*, p. 5.

55. Dennis Lormel, "Terrorists and Credit Card Fraud . . . A Quiet Epidemic," Counterterrorism Blog, Feb. 28, 2008, http://counterterrorismblog.org/2008/02/terrorists_and_credit_card_fra.php.

56. Alan Sipress, "An Indonesian's Prison Memoir Takes Holy War Into Cyberspace," *The Washington Post*, Dec. 14, 2004, p. A19, www.washingtonpost.com/wp-dyn/articles/A62095-2004Dec13.html.

57. Lormel, *op. cit.*

58. Dennis Lormel, "Credit Cards and Terrorists," Counterterrorism Blog, Jan. 16, 2008, http://counterterrorismblog.org/2008/01/credit_cards_and_terrorists.php.

59. Dennis Lormel, "Terrorists and Credit Card Fraud . . . ," *op. cit.*

60. Frank Cilluffo and Daniel Kimmage, "How to Beat al Qaeda at Its Own Game," *Foreign Policy*, April

2009, www.foreignpolicy.com/story/cms.php?story_id=4820.

61. Johnny Ryan, "EU must take its anti-terrorism fight to the Internet," *Europe's World*, Summer 2007, www.europesworld.org/EWSettings/Article/tabid/191/ArticleType/ArticleView/ArticleID/21068/Default.aspx.

62. Digital Outreach Team, U.S. Department of State, www.state.gov/documents/organization/116709.pdf.

63. "Middle East Internet Usage and Population Statistics," *Internet World Stats*, www.internetworldstats.com/stats5.htm.

64. Christopher Boucek, "The Sakinah Campaign and Internet Counter-Radicalization in Saudi Arabia," *CTC Sentinel*, August 2008, p. 2, www.carnegieendowment.org/files/CTCSentinel_Vol1Iss9.pdf.

65. *Ibid.*, p. 1.

66. Abdullah Ansary, "Combating Extremism: A brief overview of Saudi Arabia's approach," *Middle East Policy*, Summer 2008, vol. 15, no. 2, p. 111.

67. *Ibid.*

68. Y. Admon and M. Feki, "Saudi Press Reactions to the Arrest of Seven Terrorist Cells in Saudi Arabia," Inquiry and Analysis, no. 354, MEMRI, May 18, 2007.

69. Ansary, *op. cit.*, p. 111.

70. Boucek, *op. cit.*, p. 3.

71. Bergin, *op. cit.*, p. 19.

72. www.radicalmiddleway.co.uk.

73. "A radical wrong way," Progressive Muslims: Friends of Imperialism and Neocolonialism, Oct. 31, 2006, http://pmunadebate.blogspot.com/2006/10/radical-wrong-way.html.

74. Cilluffo and Kimmage, *op. cit.*

75. "Council Conclusions on Cooperation to Combat Terrorist Use of the Internet ("Check the Web")," Council of the European Union, May 16, 2007, p. 3, http://register.consilium.europa.eu/pdf/en/07/st08/st08457-re03.en07.pdf.

76. Katharina von Knop, "Institutionalization of a Web-Focused, Multinational Counter-Terrorism Campaign," *Responses to Cyber Terrorism* (2008), p. 14.

BIBLIOGRAPHY

Books

Jewkes, Yvonne, and Majid Yar, eds., *The Handbook on Internet Crime, Willan Publishing*, 2009.
British criminology professors have compiled essays by leading scholars on issues and debates surrounding Internet-related crime, deviance, policing, law and regulation in the 21st century.

Kramer, Franklin D., Stuart H. Starr and Larry K. Wentz, eds., *Cyberpower and National Security, Potomac Books*, 2009.
Experts write about cyber power and its strategic implications for national security, including an assessment of the likelihood of cyberterrorism.

Sageman, Marc, *Leaderless Jihad: Terror Networks in the Twenty-First Century, University of Pennsylvania Press*, 2008.
A senior fellow at the Center on Terrorism, Counter-Terrorism, and Homeland Security in Philadelphia examines the impact of the Internet on global terrorism, including its role in radicalization, and strategies to combat terrorism in the Internet age.

Weimann, Gabriel, *Terror on the Internet, United States Institute of Peace Press*, 2006.
A professor of communication at Haifa University in Israel explores how terrorist organizations exploit the Internet to raise funds, recruit members, plan attacks and spread their message.

Articles

Boucek, Christopher, "The Sakinah Campaign and Internet Counter-Radicalization in Saudi Arabia," *CTC Sentinel*, August 2008.
Saudi Arabia enlists religious scholars to engage in dialogue on the Internet with individuals seeking out religious knowledge in order to steer them away from extremist beliefs.

Cilluffo, Frank, and Daniel Kimmage, "How to Beat al Qaeda at Its Own Game," *Foreign Policy*, April 2009, www.foreignpolicy.com.

Two American terrorism experts recommend using Web sites, chat rooms, social networking sites, broadcasting and print to tell the stories of Muslim victims of militant Islamist terror attacks.

Goth, Greg, "Terror on the Internet: A Complex Issue, and Getting Harder," *IEEE Distributed Systems Online*, vol. 9, no. 3, 2008.
Counterterrorism agencies cringe when posturing by politicians leads to the dismantling of terrorist Web sites they've been monitoring.

Labi, Nadya, "Jihad 2.0," *The Atlantic Monthly*, July/August, 2006.
With the loss of training camps in Afghanistan, terrorists turned to the Internet to find and train recruits.

Talbot, David, "Terror's Server — How radical Islamists use Internet fraud to finance terrorism and exploit the Internet for Jihad propaganda and recruitment," *Technology Review.com*, Jan. 27, 2008.
Terrorists use the Internet for fundraising, propaganda and recruitment, but government and the Internet industry responses are limited by law and technology.

Reports and Studies

Bergin, Anthony, *et al.*, "Countering Internet Radicalisation in Southeast Asia," Australian Strategic Policy Institute, March 2009.
The director of research at the institute traces the evolution of extremist and terrorist-linked content from static Web sites to the more dynamic and interactive parts of the Internet.

Boyne, Shawn Marie, "The Criminalization of Speech in an Age of Terror," Indiana University School of Law-Indianapolis, working paper, June 12, 2009.
A law professor compares prosecution of incitement to terror in Germany, the U.K. and the United States.

Conway, Maura, "Terrorism & Internet Governance: Core Issues," *Disarmament Forum*, 2007.
A terrorism expert at Dublin City University in Ireland explores the difficulties of Internet governance in light of terrorists' growing use of the medium.

Denning, Dorothy, "Terror's Web: How the Internet is Transforming Terrorism," *Naval Postgraduate School*, 2009.
A professor of conflict and cyberspace discusses the implications of shutting sites down versus continuing to monitor sites or encouraging moderate voices to engage in dialogue online with terrorist sympathizers.

Neumann, Peter R., and Tim Stevens, "Countering Online Radicalisation: A Strategy for Action," *The International Centre for the Study of Radicalisation and Political Violence*, 2009.
Shutting down terrorist sites on the Internet is expensive and counterproductive, according to the authors.

Renieris, Elizabeth, "Combating Incitement to Terrorism on the Internet," *Vanderbilt Journal of Entertainment and Technology Law*, vol. 11:3:673, 2009.
The author compares U.S. and U.K. laws used to prosecute incitement to terrorism on the Internet.

For More Information

Australian Strategic Policy Institute, 40 Macquarie St., Barton ACT 2600, Australia; (61) 2 6270 5100; www.aspi .org.au. Nonpartisan policy institute set up by the Australian government to study the country's defense and strategic policy choices.

EuroISPA, 39, Rue Montoyer, B-1000 Brussels, Belgium; (32) 2 503 2265; www.euroispa.org. World's largest association of Internet service providers.

Homeland Security Policy Institute, George Washington University, 2300 I St., N.W., Suite 721, Washington, DC 20037; (202) 994-2437; www.gwumc.edu/hspi. A think tank that analyzes homeland security issues.

Institute for International and European Affairs, 8 North Great Georges St., Dublin 1, Ireland; (353) 1 8746756; www.iiea.com. A think tank that analyzes how global and European Union policies affect Ireland.

International Centre for Political Violence and Terrorism Research, Nanyang Technological University, South Spine S4, Level B4, Nanyang Ave., Singapore 639798; (65) 6790 6982; www.pvtr.org. Studies threats and develops countermeasures for politically motivated violence and terrorism.

International Centre for the Study of Radicalisation and Political Violence, King's College London, 138-142 Strand, London, WC2R 1HH, United Kingdom; (44) 207 848 2098; http://icsr.info/index.php. A think tank set up by King's College London, the University of Pennsylvania, the Interdisciplinary Center Herzliya (Israel) and the Jordan Institute of Diplomacy.

Internet Haganah, http://internet-haganah.com/haganah/index.html. Tracks, translates and analyzes extremist Islamic sites on the Web.

The Jamestown Foundation, 1111 16th St., N.W., Suite #320, Washington, DC 20036; (202) 483-8888; www .jamestown.org. Informs policy makers about trends in societies where access to information is restricted.

Middle East Media Research Institute, P.O. Box 27837, Washington, DC 20038-7837; (202) 955-9070; www.memri .org. Provides translations of Arabic, Persian, Turkish and Urdu-Pashtu media and analyses political, ideological, intellectual, social, cultural and religious trends in the Middle East.

NEFA Foundation, (212) 986-4949; www1.nefafoundation .org. Exposes those responsible for planning, funding and executing terrorist activities, with a particular emphasis on Islamic militant organizations.

Norwegian Defense Research Establishment, FFI, P.O. Box 25, NO-2027 Kjeller, Norway; (47) 63 80 70 00; www .mil.no/felles/ffi/english. The primary institution responsible for defense-related research in Norway.

Organization for Security and Co-operation in Europe, Action Against Terrorism Unit, Wallnerstrasse 6, 1010 Vienna, Austria; (43) 1 514 36 6702; www.osce.org/atu. Coordinates anti-terrorism initiatives among European nations.

7

Understanding Islam

Is Islam Compatible With Western Values?

Kenneth Jost

A Muslim woman in Blackburn, England, protests in October 2006 against criticism of face veils by House of Commons leader Jack Straw. Disputes over veils have erupted in several European countries, as well as the United States, reflecting the increasingly strained relations between Islam and the West.

From *CQ Researcher*, November 3, 2006.

Aishah Azmi was dressed all in black, her face veiled by a *niqab* that revealed only her brown eyes through a narrow slit.

"Muslim women who wear the veil are not aliens," the 24-year-old suspended bilingual teaching assistant told reporters in Leeds, England, on Oct. 19. "Integration [of Muslims into British society] requires people like me to be in the workplace so that people can see that we are not to be feared or mistrusted."

But school officials defended their decision to suspend Azmi for refusing to remove her veil in class with a male teacher, saying it interfered with her ability to communicate with her students — most of them Muslims and, like Azmi, British Asians.

"The school and the local authority had to balance the rights of the children to receive the best quality education possible and Mrs. Azmi's desire to express her cultural beliefs," said local Education Minister Jim Dodds.[1]

Although an employment tribunal rejected Azmi's discrimination and harassment claims, it said the school council had handled her complaint poorly and awarded her 1,100 British pounds — about $2,300.

Azmi's widely discussed case has become part of a wrenching debate in predominantly Christian England over relations with the country's growing Muslim population.

In September, a little more than a year after subway and bus bombings in London claimed 55 lives, a government minister called on Muslim parents to do more to steer their children away from violence and terrorism. Then, in October, a leaked report

The Muslim World

Islam is the world's second-largest religion (after Christianity), with an estimated 1.2 billion adherents. Some 40 nations from Senegal in West Africa to Indonesia in Southeast Asia either are virtually all Muslim or have Islamic majorities. Another 14 nations have substantial Muslim minorities. Indonesia has the world's largest Muslim population — 215 million people — followed by India, with approximately 150 million. In addition, several million Muslims live in nations of the Islamic diaspora (insert). From 1997 to 2002, Islam grew by nearly 7 percent; Christianity grew slightly less than 6 percent.

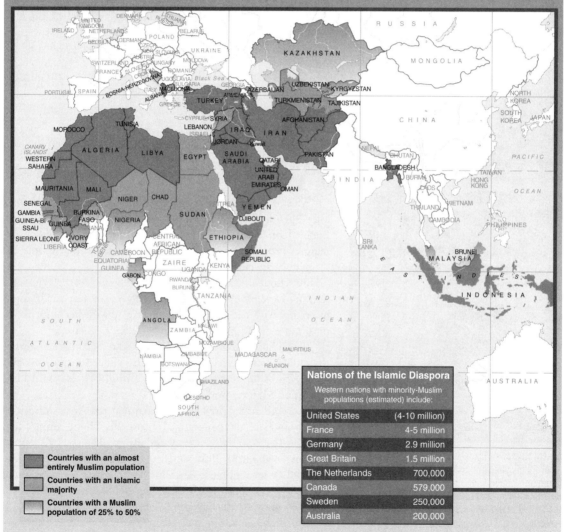

Nations of the Islamic Diaspora

Western nations with minority-Muslim populations (estimated) include:

United States	(4-10 million)
France	4-5 million
Germany	2.9 million
Great Britain	1.5 million
The Netherlands	700,000
Canada	579,000
Sweden	250,000
Australia	200,000

Countries with an almost entirely Muslim population

Countries with an Islamic majority

Countries with a Muslim population of 25% to 50%

Sources: Paul Grieve, *Islam: History, Faith and Politics: The Complete Introduction,* 2006; Central Intelligence Agency, *The World Factbook,* 2006.

being prepared by the interfaith adviser of the Church of England complained that what he called the government's policy of "privileged attention" toward Muslims had backfired and was creating increased "disaffection and separation."[2]

The simmering controversy grew even hotter after Jack Straw, leader of the House of Commons and former foreign secretary under Prime Minister Tony Blair, called full-face veils "a visible statement of separation and difference" that promotes separatism between Muslims and non-Muslims. Straw, whose constituency in northwestern England includes an estimated 25 percent Muslim population, aired the comments in a local newspaper column.

Hamid Qureshi, chairman of the Lancashire Council of Mosques, called Straw's remarks "blatant Muslim-bashing."[3]

"Muslims feel they are on center stage, and everybody is Muslim-bashing," says Anjum Anwar, the council's director of education. "They feel very sensitive."

Britain's estimated 1.5 million Muslims — comprising mostly Pakistani or Indian immigrants and their British-born children — are only a tiny fraction of Islam's estimated 1.2 billion adherents worldwide. But the tensions surfacing in the face-veil debate exemplify the increasingly strained relations between the predominantly Christian West and the Muslim world.

The world's two largest religions — Christianity has some 2 billion adherents — have had a difficult relationship at least since the time of the European Crusades against Muslim rulers, or caliphs, almost 1,000 years ago. Mutual suspicion and hostility have intensified since recent terrorist attacks around the world by militant Islamic groups and President George W. Bush proclaimed a worldwide "war on terror" in response to the Sept. 11, 2001, attacks in the United States.[4]

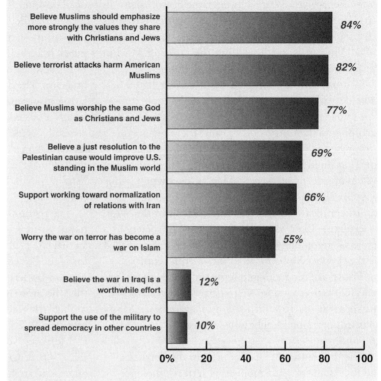

How American Muslims View the Issues

Most Muslim voters in America oppose terrorist attacks and say they harm U.S. Muslims. More than half worry President Bush's "war on terror" has become a war on Islam.

Believe Muslims should emphasize more strongly the values they share with Christians and Jews	84%
Believe terrorist attacks harm American Muslims	82%
Believe Muslims worship the same God as Christians and Jews	77%
Believe a just resolution to the Palestinian cause would improve U.S. standing in the Muslim world	69%
Support working toward normalization of relations with Iran	66%
Worry the war on terror has become a war on Islam	55%
Believe the war in Iraq is a worthwhile effort	12%
Support the use of the military to spread democracy in other countries	10%

Source: Council on American-Islamic Relations, October 2006

Bush, who stumbled early on by referring to a "crusade" against terrorism, has tried many times since then to dispel perceptions of any official hostility toward Islam or Muslims generally. In Britain, Blair's government has carried on a 40-year-old policy of "multiculturalism" aimed at promoting cohesion among the country's various communities, Muslims in particular.

Despite those efforts, widespread distrust of Islam and Muslims prevails on both sides of the Atlantic. In a recent poll in the United States, 45 percent of those surveyed said they had an unfavorable view of Islam — a higher percentage than registered in a similar poll four years earlier. (*See chart, p. 161.*)

British Muslim leaders also say they feel increasingly hostile anti-Muslim sentiments from the general public and government officials. "Muslims are very fearful, frustrated, upset, angry," says Asghar Bukhari, a spokesman for the Muslim Public Affairs Committee in London. "It's been almost like a mental assault on the Muslim psyche here."

As the face-veil debate illustrates, the distrust stems in part from an array of differences between today's Christianity and Islam as variously practiced in the so-called Muslim world, including the growing Muslim diaspora in Europe and North America. (*See map, p. 156.*)

In broad terms, Islam generally regards religion as a more pervasive presence in daily life and a more important source for civil law than contemporary Christianity, according to the British author Paul Grieve, who wrote a comprehensive guide to Islam after studying Islamic history and thought for more than three years.[5] "Islam is a system of rules for all aspects of life," Grieve writes, while Western liberalism limits regulation of personal behavior. In contrast to the secular nation-states of the West, he explains, Islam views the ideal Muslim society as a universal community — such as the *ummah* established by the Prophet Muhammad in the seventh century.

Those theological and cultural differences are reflected, Grieve says, in Westerners' widespread view of Muslims as narrow-minded and extremist. Many Muslims correspondingly view Westerners as decadent and immoral.

The differences also can be seen in the debates over the role Islam plays in motivating terrorist violence by Islamic extremist groups such as al Qaeda and the objections raised by Muslims to what they consider unflattering and unfair descriptions of Islam in the West.

Muslim leaders generally deny responsibility for the violence committed by Islamic terrorists, including the 9/11 terrorist attacks in the United States and subsequent attacks in Indonesia, Spain and England. "Muslim organizations have done more than ever before in trying to advance community cohesion," Anwar says. They also deny any intention to deny freedom of expression, even though Muslims worldwide denounced a Danish cartoonist's satirical portrayal of Muhammad and Pope Benedict XVI's citation of a medieval Christian emperor's description of Islam as a violent religion.

For many Westerners, however, Islam is associated with radical Muslims — known as Islamists — who either advocate or appear to condone violence and who

take to the streets to protest unfavorable depictions of Islam. "A lot of traditional or moderate Islam is inert," says Paul Marshall, a senior fellow at Freedom House's Center for Religious Freedom in Washington. "Many of the people who disagree with radicals don't have a developed position. They keep their heads down."

Meanwhile, many Muslims and non-Muslims alike despair at Islam's sometimes fratricidal intrafaith disputes. Islam split within the first decades of its founding in the seventh century into the Sunni and Shiite (Shia) branches. The Sunni-Shiite conflict helps drive the escalating insurgency in Iraq three years after the U.S.-led invasion ousted Saddam Hussein, a Sunni who pursued generally secularist policies.[6] "A real geopolitical fracturing has taken place in the Muslim world since the end of the colonial era," says Reza Aslan, an Iranian-born Shiite Muslim now a U.S. citizen and author of the book *No god but God*.

The tensions between Islam and the West are on the rise as Islam is surging around the world, growing at an annual rate of about 7 percent. John Voll, associate director of the Prince Alwaleed bin Talal Center for Christian-Muslim Understanding at Georgetown University, notes that the growth is due largely to conversions, not the high birth rates that are driving Hinduism's faster growth.

Moreover, Voll says, Muslims are growing more assertive. "There has been an increase in intensity and an increase in strength in the way Muslims view their place in the world and their place in society," he says.

Teaching assistant Azmi's insistence on wearing the *niqab* exemplifies the new face of Islam in parts of the West. But her choice is not shared by all, or even, most of her fellow Muslim women. "I don't see why she needs to wear it," says Anwar. "She's teaching young children under 11." (Azmi says she wears it because she works with a male classroom teacher.)

Muslim experts generally agree the Koran does not require veils, only modest dress. Observant Muslim women generally comply with the admonition with a head scarf and loose-fitting attire. In particularly conservative cultures, such as Afghanistan under Taliban rule, women cover their entire bodies, including their eyes.

Still, despite the varying practices, many Muslim groups see a disconnect between the West's self-proclaimed tolerance and its pressure on Muslims to conform. "It's a Muslim woman's right to dress as she feels appropriate, given her religious views," says Ibrahim Hooper, director of communications for the Council on American-Islamic Relations in Washington. "But then when somebody actually makes a choice, they're asked not to do that."

Indeed, in Hamtramck, Mich., a judge recently came under fire for throwing out a small-claims case because the Muslim plaintiff refused to remove her full-face veil. (*See sidebar, p. 166.*)

As the debates continue, here are some of the questions being considered:

Is Islam a religion that promotes violence?

Within hours of the London subway and bus bombings on July 7, 2005, the head of the Muslim World League condemned the attacks as un-Islamic. "The heavenly religions, notably Islam, advocate peace and security," said Abdallah al-Turki, secretary-general of the Saudi-funded organization based in Mecca.[7]

The league's statement echoed any number of similar denunciations of Islamist-motivated terrorist attacks issued since 9/11 by Muslims in the United States and around the world. Yet many non-Muslim public officials, commentators, experts and others say Muslims have not done enough to speak out against terrorism committed in the name of their religion.

"Mainstream Muslims have not stepped up to the plate, by and large," says Angel Rabasa, a senior fellow at the RAND Corp., a California think tank, and lead author of a U.S. Air Force-sponsored study, *The Muslim World after 9/11*.[8]

Muslim organizations voice indignant frustration in disputing the accusation. "We can always do more," says Hooper. "The problem is that it never seems to be enough. But that doesn't keep us from trying."

Many Americans, in fact, believe Islam actually encourages violence among its adherents. A CBS poll in April 2006 found that 46 percent of those surveyed believe Islam encourages violence more than other religions. A comparable poll four years earlier registered a lower figure: 32 percent.[9]

Those perceptions are sometimes inflamed by U.S. evangelical leaders. Harsh comments about Islam have come from religious leaders like Franklin Graham, Jerry Falwell, Pat Robertson and Jerry Vines, the former president of the Southern Baptist Convention. Graham called

Pakistani Muslims torch a Danish flag during a February 2006 protest in Karachi to denounce a Danish cartoonist's satirical depictions of the Prophet Muhammad. First published in September 2005, the cartoons provoked protests from Muslims throughout the world.

Islam "a very evil and wicked religion," and Vines called Muhammad, Islam's founder and prophet, a "demon-possessed pedophile." Falwell, on the CBS news magazine "60 Minutes" in October 2002, declared, "I think Muhammad was a terrorist."[10]

Mainstream Muslims insist Islam is a peaceful religion and that terrorist organizations distort its tenets and teachings in justifying attacks against the West or other Muslims. But Islamic doctrine and history sometimes seem to justify the use of violence in propagating or defending the faith. The dispute revolves around the meaning of *jihad*, an Arabic word used in the Koran and derived from a root meaning "to strive" or "to make an effort for."[11] Muslim scholars can point to verses in the Koran that depict *jihad* merely as a personal, spiritual struggle and to others that describe *jihad* as encompassing either self-defense or conquest against non-believers.

Georgetown historian Voll notes that, in contrast to Christianity, Islam achieved military success during Muhammad's life and expanded into a major world empire within decades afterward. That history "reinforces the idea that militancy and violence can, in fact, be part of the theologically legitimate plan of the Muslim believer," says Voll.

"Islam, like all religions, has its historical share of violence," acknowledges Stephen Schwartz, an adult convert to Islam and executive director of the Center for

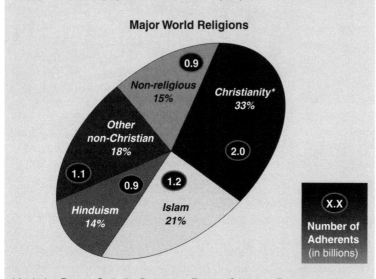

Islam Is Second-Largest Religion

Twenty-one percent of the world's 6 billion population, or 1.2 billion people, are Muslims. Christianity is the largest denomination, with 33 percent of the population, or 2 billion people.

Major World Religions

Non-religious 15% — 0.9
Christianity* 33% — 2.0
Other non-Christian 18% — 1.1
Hinduism 14% — 0.9
Islam 21% — 1.2

X.X
Number of Adherents (in billions)

* Includes Roman Catholic, Protestant, Eastern Orthodox, Pentecostal, Anglican, Evangelical and other sects.

Totals do not add to 100 percent due to rounding.

Sources: www.adherents.com; Angel M. Rabasa, et. al., "The Muslim World After 9/11"; Encyclopedia Britannica online

Islamic Pluralism in Washington. "But there's no reason to single out Islam."

Modern-day jihadists pack their public manifestos with Koranic citations and writings of Islamic theologians to portray themselves as warriors for Allah and defenders of true Islam. But Voll and others stress that the vast majority of Muslims do not subscribe to their views. "You have a highly visible minority that represents a theologically extreme position in the Muslim world," Voll says.

In particular, writes Seyyed Hossein Nasr, a professor of Islamic studies at George Washington University, Islamic law prohibits the use of force against women, children or civilians — even during war. "Inflicting injuries outside of this context," he writes, "is completely forbidden by Islamic law."[12]

Rabasa says, however, that Muslims who disapprove of terrorism have not said enough or done enough to

mobilize opposition to terrorist attacks. "Muslims see themselves as part of a community and are reluctant to criticize radical Muslims," he says.

In addition, many Muslims are simply intimidated from speaking out, he explains. "Radicals are not reluctant to use violence and the threat of violence," he says. Liberal and moderate Muslims are known to receive death threats on their cell phones, even in relatively peaceful Muslim countries such as Indonesia.

Voll also notes that Islamic radicals have simply outorganized the moderates. "There is no moderate organization that even begins to resemble some of the radical organizations that have developed," he says.

In Britain, Bukhari of the Muslim Public Affairs Committee criticizes Muslim leaders themselves for failing to channel young people opposed to Britain's pro-U.S. foreign policy into non-violent political action. "Children who could have been peaceful react to that foreign policy in a way that they themselves become criminals," he says.

The Council on American-Islamic Relations' Hooper details several anti-terrorism pronouncements and drives issued following the London bombings by various Muslim groups and leaders in Britain and in the United States, including *fatwas*, or legal opinions, rejecting terrorism and extremism.[13]

For his part, Omid Safi, an associate professor of Islamic studies at the University of North Carolina in Chapel Hill, points out that virtually every Muslim organization in the United States issued condemnations of violence almost immediately after the 9/11 terrorist attacks.[14]

"How long must we keep answering this question?" Safi asks in exasperation. But he concedes a few moments later that the issue is more than perception. "Muslims must come to terms with our demons," he says, "and one of those demons is violence."

Is Islam compatible with secular, pluralistic societies?

In 2003, Germany's famed Deutsche Oper staged an avant-garde remake of Mozart's opera "Idomeneo," which dramatizes the composer's criticism of organized religion, with a scene depicting the severed heads of Muhammad, Jesus, Buddha and Poseidon. That production was mounted without incident, but the company dropped plans to restage it in November 2006 after police warned of a possible violent backlash from Muslim fundamentalists.

The cancellation prompted protests from German officials and artistic-freedom advocates in Europe and in the United States, who saw the move as appeasement toward terrorists. Wolfgang Bornsen, a spokesman for conservative Chancellor Angela Merkel, said the cancellation was "a signal" to other artistic companies to avoid any works critical of Islam.[15]

The debate continued even after plans were discussed to mount the production after all — with enhanced security and the blessing of German Muslim leaders. "We live in Europe, where democracy was based on criticizing religion," remarked Philippe Val, editor of the French satirical magazine *Charlie Hebdo.* "If we lose the right to criticize or attack religions in our free countries . . . we are doomed."[16]

As with the issue of violence, Islam's doctrines and history can be viewed as pointing both ways on questions of pluralism and tolerance. "There are a great many passages [in the Koran] that support a pluralistic interpretation of Islam," says the RAND Corp.'s Rabasa. "But you also

Negative Impressions of Islam Have Increased

The percentage of Americans with a favorable view of Islam dropped from 30 percent in 2002 to 19 percent in April 2006. There was a similar increase in the percentage who believe Islam encourages violence more than other religions.

What is your impression of Islam?

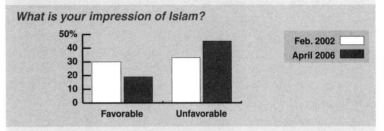

Compared with other religions, Islam encourages violence . . .

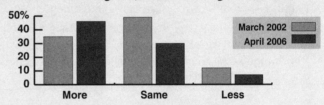

What is your impression of . . . ?

	Favorable	Unfavorable	Don't Know
Protestantism/other Christians	58%	12%	30%
The Catholic religion	48	37	15
The Jewish religion	47	16	37
Christian fundamentalist religions	31	31	38
The Mormon religion	20	39	41
Islam	19	45	36
Scientology	8	52	40

Do you know more or less about Islam now than you did five years ago?

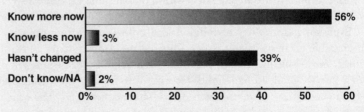

Sources: CBS News Poll, April 2006; Gallup Poll, 2002

Basic Tenets of Islam

Islam is the youngest of the world's three major monotheistic religions. Like the other two, Judaism and Christianity, Islam (the word means both "peace" and "submission") holds there is but one God (Allah). Muslims believe God sent a number of prophets to teach mankind how to live according to His law. Muslims consider Jesus, Moses and Abraham as prophets of God and hold the Prophet Muhammad as his final and most sacred messenger. Many accounts found in Islam's sacred book, the Koran (Qur'an), are also found in sacred writings of Jews and Christians.

There are five basic pillars of Islam:

- **Creed** — Belief in God and Muhammad as his Prophet.
- **Almsgiving** — Giving money to charity is considered a sacred duty.
- **Fasting** — From dawn to dusk during the month of Ramadan.
- **Prayer** — Five daily prayers must be given facing Mecca, Islam's holiest city.
- **Pilgrimage** — All Muslims must make a *hajj* to Mecca at least once during their lifetime, if they are physically able.

find a great many that would support an intolerant interpretation."

"Intellectual pluralism is traditional Islam," says Schwartz at the Center for Islamic Pluralism. An oft-quoted verse from the Koran specifically prohibits compulsion in religion, he says. Voll and other historians agree that Muslim countries generally tolerated Christians and Jews, though they were often subject to special taxes or other restrictions.

"Islam is the only major religious system that has built-in protections for minorities," says Hooper at the Council on American-Islamic Relations. "You don't see the kind of persecutions of minorities that we often saw in Europe for hundreds of years. Many members of the Jewish community fled to find safety within the Muslim world."

Even so, Islam's view of religion and politics as inseparable creates difficult issues. Outside the Arab world, most Muslims live in practicing democracies with fair to good human-rights records. But some Muslim countries — Arab and non-Arab — have either adopted or been urged to adopt provisions of Islamic law — *sharia* — that are antithetical to modern ideas of human rights, such as limiting women's rights and

prescribing stoning or amputations as criminal penalties.

Muslims participating in a society as a minority population face different issues, according to author Grieve. "Islam is difficult to accommodate in a determinedly secular Western society where almost all views are equally respected, and none is seen as either right or wrong," he writes.[17]

The tensions played out in a number of controversies in recent years were provoked by unflattering depictions of Islam in Europe. A Danish cartoonist's satirical view of Muhammad provoked worldwide protests from Muslim leaders and groups after they were publicized in early 2006. Scattered violence resulted in property damage and more than 30 deaths.

Somewhat similarly, Pope Benedict XVI drew sharp criticism after a Sept. 12, 2006, lecture quoting a medieval Christian emperor's description of Islam as "evil and inhuman." Along with verbal denunciations, protesters in Basra, Iraq, burned an effigy of the pope. Within a week, he disclaimed the remarks and apologized.

Freedom House's Marshall says such controversies, as well as the cancellation of the opera in Berlin, strengthen radical Muslim elements. "Bending to more radical demands marginalizes the voices of moderate Muslims and hands over leadership to the radicals," he says.

Many Muslims in European countries, however, view the controversies — including the current debate over the veil in England — as evidence of pervasive hostility from the non-Muslim majorities. "There is a growing hatred of Muslims in Britain, and anybody who bashes Muslims can only get brownie points," says Bukhari of the Muslim Public Affairs Committee.

"These are not friendly times for Western Muslims," says Safi, at the University of North Carolina. "Whenever people find themselves under assault, opening their arms and opening their hearts is difficult."

Does Islam need a "reformation"?

If Pakistan's Punjab University expected a chorus of approval when it decided to launch a master's program in musicology in fall 2006, it was in for a surprise. At the Lahore campus, the conservative Islamic Assembly of Students, known as I.J.T., rose up in protest.

Handbills accused school authorities of forsaking Islamic ideological teachings in favor of "the so-called enlightened moderation" dictated by "foreign masters." Undeterred, administrators opened the program for enrollment in September. When fewer students applied than expected, they blamed the poor response in part on the I.J.T. campaign.[18]

The episode reflects how Islam today is evolving differently in the West and in some parts of the Muslim world. Many Muslim writers and scholars in the United States and Europe are calling for Islam to adapt to modern times by, for example, embracing pluralism and gender equality. Introducing a collection of essays by "progressive" Muslims, the University of North Carolina's Safi says the movement seeks to "start swimming through the rising waters of Islam and modernity, to strive for justice in the midst of society."[19]

In much of the Muslim world, however, Islam is growing — in numbers and intensity — on the strength of literal interpretations of the Koran and exclusivist attitudes toward the non-Muslim world. "In the Muslim world in general, more extreme or reactionary forms of Islam are getting stronger — in Africa, Asia and the Middle East," says Freedom House's Marshall, who has previously worked on issues pertaining to persecution of Christians around the world.

Islamist groups such as I.J.T. talk about "reforming" or "purifying" Islam and adopting Islamic law as the primary or exclusive source of civil law. In fact, one version of reformed Islam — Wahhabism* or the currently preferred term Salafism — espouses a literalistic reading of the Koran and a puritanical stance toward such modern practices as listening to music or watching television. It has been instituted in Saudi Arabia and has advanced worldwide because of financial backing from the oil-rich kingdom and its appeal to new generations of Muslims.

---

* Wahhabism originated in the Arabian peninsula in the late 1700s from the teachings of Arabian theologian Muhammad ibn Abd al Wahhab (1703-1792).

"The Salafi movement is a fringe," says the RAND Corp.'s Rabasa. "But it's growing because it's dynamic and revolutionary, whereas traditional Islam tends to be conservative. It has this appeal to young people looking for identity."

But the Center for Islamic Pluralism's Schwartz, an outspoken critic of Salafism, says many Muslims are rejecting it because of its tendency to view other branches of Islam as apostasy. "People are getting sick of this," he says. "They're tired of the social conflict and upheaval."

Voll at the Center for Christian-Muslim Understanding also says some Muslim legal scholars are disputing literalistic readings of *sharia* by contending that the Islamic law cited as divinely ordained is actually "a human construct subject to revision."

Some Western commentators refer to a "reformation" in calling for a more liberal form of Islam. Nicholas D. Kristof, a *New York Times* columnist who focuses on global human-rights issues, sees "hopeful rumblings . . . of steps toward a Muslim Reformation," especially on issues of gender equality. He notes that feminist Muslim scholars are reinterpreting passages in the Koran that other Muslims cite in justifying restrictions on women, such as the Saudi ban on women driving.[20]

Safi says he avoids the term reformation because it has been adopted by Salafists and also because it suggests a need to break from traditional Islam. He says "progressive" Muslims return to the Prophet's vision of the common humanity of all human beings and seek "to hold Muslim societies accountable for justice and pluralism."

Rabasa also says reformation is historically inappropriate as a goal for liberal or progressive Muslims. "What is needed is not an Islamic reformation but an Islamic enlightenment," says Rabasa. The West's liberal tradition, he notes, was produced not by the Reformation but by the Enlightenment — the 18th-century movement that used reason to search for objective truth.

Whatever terms are used, the clash between different visions of Islam will be less susceptible to resolution than analogous disputes within most branches of Christianity because Islam lacks any recognized hierarchical structure. Islam has no pope or governing council. Instead, each believer is regarded as having a direct relationship with God, or Allah, with no ecclesiastical intermediary.

"In the face of contemporary Islam, there is absolutely the sense of an authority vacuum," says Safi. Islam's future, he adds, "is a question that can only be answered by Muslims."

BACKGROUND

Two Faces of Islam

Islam began as the faith of a small community of believers in Arabia in the seventh century and grew within a matter of decades to be the dominant religion of a powerful empire. The Muslim world expanded over the next 1,000 years, eventually stretching from Spain and western Africa east to China, the Indian subcontinent and Indonesia, but most of that world came under European domination in the 1700s and 1800s. The 20th century opened with roiling debates within Islam between secular nationalists and Islamic fundamentalists over how best to regain a measure of the glories of times past.[21]

Muhammad (c. 570-632) was a respected businessman in the commercial and religious center of Mecca when, according to Islamic belief, he received the divine revelation now preserved in the Koran. The central monotheistic message — "there is no god but Allah" — incorporated beliefs of Judaism and Christianity and challenged the prevailing polytheism as well as the wealth and status of Mecca's power structure.

Facing possible assassination, Muhammad accepted an invitation in 622 to serve as a judge in Medina, 400 kilometers to the north. There, the Prophet became — as historian Voll describes it — the leader of the *ummah*, or community, "in all matters of life," both religious and temporal. By the time of his death in 632, the new Muslim community was successfully established. Mecca had been defeated and incorporated into the *ummah* in important ways. Today, observant Muslims are called to undertake a pilgrimage, or *hajj*, to Mecca at least once in their lives.

Within barely three decades, the Muslim community became a major global empire by conquering the Persian Empire to the east and the Syrian territories of the Byzantine Empire to the west. But the rapid expansion ended with a civil war (656-661) that split Islam into two traditions that, as Voll relates, live on to this day. The mainstream or Sunni tradition — sunna refers to the life and sayings of the Prophet — traces its origins to the first four "rightly guided" *khalifahs* (caliphs), successors to Muhammad. Sunni Muslims combine an emphasis on consensus and piety with a pragmatic focus on governmental stability.

The Shia tradition — shi'ah is Arabic for faction or party — begins with Ali, a cousin of Muhammad who became the leader of a breakaway group of mutinous troops and others in Medina in 656. Ali — viewed by his supporters as Muhammad's rightful successor — prevailed militarily, only to be murdered five years later. Shi'a Islam reflects a belief in a divinely guided imam, or leader, with authority unbound by human consensus or pragmatic reasons of state.

The Muslim world expanded initially through military conquest and later through global trade. During the golden age of Islam (750-1300), Islamic civilization dominated in art, architecture, mathematics and other fields as Christian Europe languished during the so-called Dark Ages before 1000. Over the next 500 years, the rising states of Europe waged war against Muslim rule — most famously in the seven Christian Crusades fought between 1095 and 1291 — in an unsuccessful effort to free the Holy Land from rule by Muslim "infidels."

To more tangible effect, the Mongols began their conquest of the Islamic states early in the 13th century. Later, the Christian reconquest of Spain ended Muslim rule on the Iberian Peninsula in 1492, while Christian forces stopped the Muslim Ottoman Empire's advance from the Balkans at the gates of Vienna in the 16th and 17th centuries. Even as Muslim military might receded, however, Muslim merchants were gaining converts for Islam in Africa, central Asia and India.

Most of the Muslim world came under European control in the 1700s and 1800s, but Islam remained the dominant religion and most important source of resistance to European expansion. The decline of Muslim power provoked self-examination and calls for reform. One of the Islamic "reformers" was Muhammad ibn Abd al-Wahhab (1703-1792), an Arabian theologian who preached a strict interpretation of the Koran. Wahhab allied himself with a prince, Muhammad Ibn Saud, whose family would unite the Arabian Peninsula two centuries later. In contrast to Wahhab, reformers in the late 19th century such as Muhammad Abduh in Egypt and Sayyid Ahmad Khan in India sought to integrate Islam with modernity by showing that faith and reason were compatible and that Islam and the West were not necessarily in conflict.

World War I marked the end of one era in the history of Islam and the beginning of another. The Ottoman Empire, allied with Germany, was defeated, occupied and dismembered. At the heart of the former empire, the Turkish nationalist Mustafa Kemal Ataturk established a

CHRONOLOGY

Before 1900 *Islam grows from origins in 7th-century Arabia to become dominant religion of a global empire but recedes as European nations become colonial powers in 18th, 19th centuries.*

1900-1970 *Muslim world throws off European rule.*

1932 Kingdom of Saudi Arabia formed, adopts radical Islamist branch of Wahhabism as state religion.

1947-48 Pakistan becomes world's first avowedly Islamist state following Indian independence, partition. . . . Indonesia gains independence to become world's most populous Muslim nation. . . . Israel established, displacing Palestinians and creating lasting conflict with Arabs, Muslims.

1952 Col. Gamal Abdel Nasser gains power in Egypt, adopts secular Arab socialism as platform.

1965 Immigration and Naturalization Services Act of 1965 abolishes national-origins quota system in U.S., opening door for more Muslim immigrants.

1970s-1980s *Radical Islam advances in Muslim world despite resistance, reluctance by conservative regimes.*

1979 Iranian Revolution ousts U.S.-backed Reza Shah Pahlavi, brings Ayatollah Ruholla Khomeini to power as head of Islamist regime.

1987 Osama bin Laden, a wealthy Saudi expatriate, forms al Qaeda terrorist network as "base" for Islamic crusade.

1989 Islamic National Front gains power in Sudan, triggering long civil war against Christian south.

1990s *Islamist movements have gains, setbacks.*

1990-91 U.S.-led invasion drives Saddam Hussein's Iraq out of Kuwait; U.S. forces use Saudi Arabia as staging area, angering bin Laden.

1991 Algerian military cancels scheduled parliamentary run-off to thwart possible victory by Islamic Salvation Front.

1996 Islamist Taliban movement gains power in Afghanistan.

2000-Present *Islamist movement advances; U.S. declares "war on terror" after 9/11 attacks.*

Sept. 11, 2001 Terrorist attacks on the World Trade Center and the Pentagon kill nearly 3,000. President George W. Bush declares war on "global terrorism," wins international support for invasion of Afghanistan over its role in harboring bin Laden, al Qaeda; Arabs, Muslims targeted in domestic crackdown.

2002 Islamic Justice and Development Party wins parliamentary majority in secular Turkey.

2003 U.S.-led invasion ousts Iraq's Hussein but fails to bring order as insurgency grows into civil war between majority Shiites and long-dominant Sunnis.

2004 France bans wearing of religious garb, including Muslim head scarves, by public school pupils. . . . Terrorist bombing of Madrid subway kills 190 people. . . . Dutch filmmaker Theo Van Gogh slain, apparently over film critical of Islam's treatment of women.

2005 Shiites gain upper hand in Iraqi parliamentary elections; banned Muslim Brotherhood makes gains in Egyptian assembly. . . . More than 50 people killed in terrorist subway, bus bombings in London. . . . Taliban resurgent in Afghanistan. . . . Muslims riot in France.

2006 Danish cartoonist's satirical depictions of Prophet Muhammad provoke protests, violence in much of Muslim world. . . . Militant Hamas wins majority in Palestinian elections, displacing more moderate Palestine Liberation Organization. . . Pope Benedict XVI draws fire for quoting medieval emperor's criticism of Islam. . . . German opera company cancels production of opera with satirical depiction of Islam, other faiths. . . . British officials criticize Muslim veil (*niqab*) as separatist.

U.S. Muslims Feel 'Under a Spotlight'

A taxicab board in Minneapolis vetoes a plan to make it easier for Muslim drivers to refuse on religious grounds to transport passengers carrying alcoholic beverages.

A local school board member in Ohio objects when a high-school principal allows two Muslim students to be excused during lunchtime as they fasted during Ramadan.

A judge in Michigan dismisses a Muslim woman's complaint against a car rental company because she refuses to remove her veil while testifying.[1]

The United States' rapidly growing Muslim population is presenting American society with a host of new issues. At the same time, many Americans anxious about terrorism are distrustful or fearful of Muslims around the world and here at home.

Government officials from President George W. Bush on down have tried to dispel Americans' concerns about U.S. Muslims generally. But government action against alleged Islamist terrorist cells or Muslim charities suspected of funding terrorists has created widespread feelings of official harassment or persecution among American Muslims.

"They really feel they're completely under a spotlight," says author Geneive Abdo, author of the new book *Mecca and Main Street*. Muslims "went from being a virtually invisible minority [before 9/11] to being completely the focus of attention" ever since.[2]

In fact, Muslims are barely mentioned in most accounts of the building of America, even though Arab explorers may have reached the New World seven centuries before Columbus. Many of the African slaves transported to the English Colonies brought their Muslim faith with them, as did some of the Arab immigrants who came to the United States from the Ottoman Empire in the late 19th and early 20th centuries.[3]

Muslims did not begin immigrating in substantial numbers, however, until after the 1965 Immigration Act, which abolished national quotas favoring northern European countries. Today, a survey by Georgetown University's Center for Muslim-Christian Understanding and the polling firm Zogby International indicates that about two-thirds of the country's more than 4 million Muslims immigrated to this country.[4] But Islam is the country's fastest-growing religion also in part because of an increasing number of conversions by Americans of other faiths.

In contrast to Europe — where Muslim immigrants have been predominantly lower-income — the United States has been receiving a larger proportion of well-educated, higher-income professionals and managers. Overall, about 62 percent of American Muslims have a college degree, according to a survey by the Council on American-Islamic Relations (CAIR), while 43 percent have household incomes above $50,000.[5]

The demographics make American Muslim communities a generally inhospitable environment for radical Islamists, observers say. "What we have here among Muslim-Americans is a very conservative success ethic," says John Zogby, president of Zogby International in Utica, N.Y., whose polling firm surveys the Muslim-American community.[6]

American Muslims have been becoming more observant for several years. Abdo cites a survey indicating that mosque attendance doubled from 1994 to 2000. From her own reporting, Abdo says Muslims generally and younger Muslims in particular have become more pious since 9/11 and more assertive in speaking up for Islam in the face of public criticism or ignorance. Still, the CAIR survey found that only 31 percent of those questioned — slightly less than one-third — attend mosque weekly, while 27 percent said they attend seldom or never.

With their growing numbers and the growing sense of being under siege, Muslims have been increasingly active

new, avowedly secular state while the Muslim lands to the east were divided into French and British protectorates. Nationalism helped drive opposition to European colonial rule among Muslims in India, Indonesia and elsewhere.

As Voll recounts, other emerging movements advocated a more all-encompassing adoption of Islam in modern society, including the Muslim Brotherhood, established in Egypt by Hasan al-Banna (1906-1949), and the Jama'at-I Islami (Islamic Society), founded in India in 1941 under the leadership of Mawlana Abu al-Ala Mawdudi (1903-1979). These movements criticized the secularism of Western life and called for applying Islam to economics and politics as well as to individual religious life.

politically in the years since 9/11. Muslim and Arab political action committees have been increasing campaign contributions, and a growing number of Arab-Americans have been seeking elective office: 49 in 2004, 52 in 2006, according to the Arab-American Institute. Keith Ellison, a black attorney who converted to Islam as a college student, is highly favored to be elected on Nov. 7 as a Democrat in Minnesota's 5th Congressional District, becoming the country's first Muslim member of Congress.[7]

President Bush's role in the war on terror and the Iraq conflict appears to have cost him heavily among Muslim-Americans. A plurality of Muslims supported Bush over Al Gore in the 2000 presidential election, but Muslims heavily favored Democrat John Kerry over Bush in 2004, according to the Georgetown-Zogby survey. In its more recent poll, CAIR found that 42 percent of those surveyed identified as Democrats compared to 17 percent as Republicans.

Muslims' growing visibility and assertiveness produces a reflexive defensiveness among many public officials, commentators and private citizens. "We are a Christian nation, not a Muslim nation," school board member Jennifer Miller in Mason, Ohio, said when complaining about the Mason High School principal's decision to accommodate the two Muslim students' wishes to be excused from the lunchroom during Ramadan.

Muslim and Arab-American groups also continue to report increases in anti-Muslim incidents. But Reza Aslan, an Iranian-American author, plays down their importance. "They're obviously a problem," says Aslan, "but they're not representative of the larger perception of Muslim or Islam among Americans."

"There's always going to be a sector of American society that is unaccepting not only of Muslims but of any group that is 'the other,' " Aslan continues. "It's going to take a while for Americans to recognize Islam not as a religion of the other but as part of the country's rich, pluralistic religious experience."

Muslim friends dine at an Afghan restaurant in Alexandria, Va., in October 2006 after daytime fasting during the Islamic holy month of Ramadan.

[1] See Oren Dorell, "Cabbies, culture clash at Minn. airport," *USA Today*, Oct. 11, 2006, p. 3A; Michael D. Clark, "Room for Fasting Muslims Raises Furor at School Board," *Cincinnati Enquirer*, Oct. 26, 2006, p. 1A; Zachary Gorchow, "Veil Costs Her Claim in Court," *Detroit Free Press*, Oct. 22, 2006, p. 1.

[2] Interview with Madeleine Brand, "Day to Day," National Public Radio, Sept. 11, 2006.

[3] Some historical background drawn from Geneive Abdo, *Mecca and Main Street: Muslim Life in America After 9/11* (2006). See also Mary H. Cooper, "Muslims in America," *CQ Researcher*, April 30, 1993, pp. 361-384.

[4] Project MAPS/Zogby International, "Muslims in the American Public Square: Shifting Political Winds and Fallout from 9/11, Afghanistan, and Iraq," October 2004 (www.projectmaps.com/AMP2004report.pdf). Project MAPS — "Muslims in the American Public Square" — was a project of the Center for Muslim-Christian Understanding, Georgetown University, funded by the Pew Charitable Trusts.

[5] Council on American-Islamic Relations, "American Muslim Voters: A Demographic Profile and Survey of Attitudes," Oct. 24, 2006; www.cair.com/pdf/American_Muslim_Voter_Survey_2006.pdf.

[6] Quoted in Alexandra Marks, "Radical Islam finds US to be 'sterile ground,'" *The Christian Science Monitor*, Oct. 23, 2006, p. 1.

[7] See Claude R. Marx, "American Arabs and Muslims Begin to Flex Political Muscles," Jewish Telegraphic Agency, Oct. 25, 2006.

Islamist Movements

The Muslim world threw off European rule after World War II and gained control of its own destiny for the first time in several centuries. Many majority-Muslim countries followed a secular path, several under leaders who combined socialist programs with authoritarian practices. Oil-rich Saudi Arabia, however, adopted Wahhabism as the state religion and followed its dictates by imposing a pervasive web of social controls. Strict Islamist movements contended with secular regimes elsewhere but gained power in only two: Iran (1979) and Sudan (1989). Meanwhile, the establishment of Israel in 1948 — with the strong support of the United States and its European allies — created a deep estrangement between the Muslim world and the West.

Two of the most populous Muslim-majority countries gained their independence shortly after World War II. Muslims joined in the resistance to British rule in India that brought independence in 1947 along with the partition of the subcontinent into a secular, predominantly Hindu India and a separate, majority-Muslim Pakistan. A year later, an Indonesian independence movement led by the nationalist leader Sukarno threw off Dutch colonial rule, but he elevated nationalism and socialism over Islamism during his nearly two decades in power. Islam played a larger role in Pakistan as the source of national identity, but the government defined its policies in largely secular terms through the 1950s and '60s.

Egypt, partially independent since 1922, won full independence from Britain after World War II. Col. Gamal Abdel Nasser came to power in a military coup in 1952 and disappointed Islamist supporters by espousing a largely secularized Arab socialism. Nasser banned the Muslim Brotherhood in 1954 after an attempted assassination and imprisoned many of its members. Among those jailed was Sayyed Qutb, a U.S.-educated author whose anti-Western Islamic manifestos continued to inspire radical Islamist movements even after his execution in 1966 for attempting to overthrow the state.

Iran provided a different model of a secular, majority-Muslim country through the 1970s. The United States and Britain helped install Reza Shah Pahlavi on the Peacock Throne in 1941 and used him in 1953 to engineer the ousting of Prime Minister Mohammed Mossadegh, who had called for nationalizing the Anglo-Iranian Oil Co. Combined with U.S. and British aid, Pahlavi's Westernizing policies helped spur economic growth. But his support for women's rights and his good relations with Israel angered Islamic fundamentalists — along with his harsh, autocratic practices — led to his downfall in the 1979 Iranian Revolution that propelled the Ayatollah Ruholla Khomeini to power as head of an Islamist regime.

The Iranian Revolution marked the beginning of a new era that, as historian Voll explains, saw political Islam move from militant, often-underground opposition into the mainstream of political life in many majority-Muslim countries. Many Muslims — significantly including well-educated professionals — came to view such Islamization of state and society as a more promising path for the Muslim world than the leftist ideologies and nationalist state policies that had held sway in the postwar era. As Islamist parties formed, however, they met resistance from conservative monarchies and regimes that had relied on traditional Islam for support but viewed more radical Islam as a challenge.

Islamization, including the adoption of *sharia*, advanced in many parts of the Muslim world from the 1970s on, despite the resistance or reluctance of conservative regimes.[22] Egyptian President Anwar Sadat promised to adopt *sharia* but angered fundamentalists by signing a peace treaty with Israel in 1979. Two years later, he was assassinated by members of the Muslim Brotherhood. His successor, Hosni Mubarak, has tried alternately to co-opt the organization with partial Islamization or to suppress it with mass arrests. In Pakistan, President Muhammad Zia al-uh-Haq instituted strict enforcement of Islamic law during his 11-year dictatorship before his death in 1988 in a still unexplained plane crash. The government has been largely secular since, but — as author Grieve writes — has "trotted out" *sharia* as "a diversion" from recurrent crises.[23]

A military coup brought the Islamic National Front to power in Sudan in 1989, ushering in pervasive Islamization despite opposition from most Muslims and a bloody civil war aimed at the Christian minority in the country's south. The fundamentalist Taliban movement pursued a similar policy of thorough Islamization during the five years it effectively controlled Afghanistan (1996-2001), but only three countries formally recognized the regime: Pakistan, Saudi Arabia and United Arab Emirates.

In the most important setback for Islamist movements, the Islamic Salvation Front in Algeria appeared on the verge of winning a majority in a second round of balloting for the national parliament in 1992, but the military suspended the election after the front's strong showing in the first round in December 1991. The move touched off a civil war that claimed an estimated 200,000 lives before the front's military wing surrendered in 2002.

Iran instituted *sharia* to some extent but also left elements of the old civil-justice system in place. Electoral victories by secularizing reformers in the 1990s further slowed Islamization. Despite setbacks, however, the advance of Islamization could be seen across the Muslim world, even in such traditionalist countries as Indonesia and Malaysia.

'War on Terror'

The 9/11 terrorist attacks on the United States came after a decade of growing militancy by Islamic extremist groups and ushered in a period of increased tensions between Muslims worldwide and the United States and its allies in Europe and in the Middle East. Muslims in the United States complained of harassment and discrimination in the immediate aftermath of the attacks, despite efforts by President Bush to dispel anti-Muslim attitudes. Increased Muslim immigration in Europe fueled conflicts in several countries, including England, France and the Netherlands. The United States, meanwhile, initially found support within the Muslim world for its invasion of Afghanistan but encountered widespread opposition from Muslim populations and leaders after the invasion of Iraq in 2003.

The Sept. 11 attacks were readily traced to the terrorist organization al Qaeda, led by the wealthy Saudi expatriate Osama bin Laden. Bin Laden had fought with other Islamic militants to drive the Soviet Union from Afghanistan and then turned his attention to the United States and his former homeland after the Saudi government agreed to allow "infidel" U.S. troops to use the country — home to Islam's holiest sites — as a staging area for the 1991 Persian Gulf War. With backing from the United Nations and quiet support from some Muslim countries, the United States responded to the 9/11 attacks by launching an invasion to oust Afghanistan's Islamist Taliban regime for its role in harboring al Qaeda.[24]

Within the United States, meanwhile, Muslims bore the brunt of a crackdown aimed at ferreting out terrorists, potential terrorists or terrorist sympathizers. Government investigators asked hundreds of foreign Muslims legally in the United States to submit to voluntary questioning about terrorists in or outside the United States. Later, immigration officials moved to track down Muslim immigrants who had failed to comply with deportation orders issued before the attacks. The Council of American-Islamic Relations accused the government of "sacrificing the civil rights of Arabs and Muslims in the name of fighting terrorism." At the same time, the group blamed "anti-Muslim agitation on television and radio" for what it described as "the worst" wave of anti-Muslim hate crimes in U.S. history.[25]

Islamic-inspired head coverings are displayed at a shop near Paris. France banned the wearing of "conspicuous" religious symbols — such as Muslim head scarves, Jewish skullcaps and large Christian crosses — in public schools, but the measure is seen as aimed primarily at creeping fundamentalism among France's 5 million Muslims.

Getty Images/Joel Robine

The U.S.-led invasion of Iraq in 2003 ousted the dictatorial Saddam Hussein but left the United States in the middle of a sectarian dispute between the country's long dominant Sunni minority and the Shiite majority, which had suffered under Hussein's rule. The Sunni-Shiite conflict provided the backdrop for difficult political negotiations in the writing of a new constitution and contentious campaigning in the run-up to the January 2005 parliamentary elections, where Shiites emerged with a near majority. Armed Sunni and Shiite militias continued battling for control after the election even after the leading Shiite cleric, Grand Ayatollah Ali al-Sistani, called in July 2006 for all Iraqis "to exert maximum effort to stop the bloodletting."

In Europe, meanwhile, ethnic and religious tensions were surfacing as increased immigration from Muslim countries and high birthrates combined to make Islam the fastest-growing religion on the continent.[26] Increased religiosity in Europe's 15-million-strong Muslim community — as measured by construction of mosques or attendance at prayers — coincided with widespread feelings of alienation, especially among young, native-born Muslims. In France — with more than 5 million Muslims — riots erupted in the mostly Muslim suburbs of Paris and other French cities in October 2005 amid complaints of high unemployment and frequent discrimination. The burgeoning new minority is also challenging European concepts of national and

A police officer removes a computer from a house in London on Aug. 11, 2006, following the arrest of 24 men, mostly Muslim fundamentalists, believed to be involved in a plot to blow up planes flying from Britain to the United States. Police said the men had ties to the al Qaeda terrorist network.

personal identity, as when France banned Muslim girls from wearing head scarves in schools in 2004.

In addition to generalized grievances, Europe also fell victim to terrorist attacks by Islamists. The bombing of three Madrid train stations at rush hour in March 2004 left 190 people dead and more than 1,200 injured; a year and three months later coordinated bombings of three subway trains and a bus in London killed 52 people plus the four bombers. In the Netherlands, meanwhile, the Dutch filmmaker Theo Van Gogh was slain in November 2004 by a 26-year-old Moroccan after he had directed a film critical of Islam's treatment of women. And in August 2006 police in England arrested 24 people, nearly all of them Muslims, on charges of plotting to detonate explosives aboard aircraft destined for the United States.

Within the Muslim world, Islamic groups were making significant gains in several countries, according to historian Voll.[27] In Turkey, the Islamic Justice and Development Party won an outright majority in the parliament in 2002. In Egypt, the still-illegal Muslim Brotherhood won almost a quarter of the seats in 2005. In Iran, Mahmoud Ahmadinejad, a non-cleric who emphasized populist issues of poverty and economic justice, was elected president in 2005 with the support of the country's more conservative clergy. The United States found itself facing a resurgent Taliban in Afghanistan along with the escalating conflicts between Sunni and Shiite groups in Iraq. And in January 2006 the militant Palestinian group Hamas won an unexpected and resounding victory in elections for the Palestinian Legislative Council, defeating the more moderate Palestine Liberation Organization.

Many Muslims in the United States and elsewhere viewed the trends as a backlash against the widespread perception that the U.S.-proclaimed war on terror amounted to a war against Islam. "More and more you're seeing moderate Muslims being pushed away from the movement toward progressivism and moving toward the other camp," says author Aslan.

CURRENT SITUATION

Muslim Identities

Muslims around the world are returning to their normal routines following Ramadan, the Islamic calendar's holiest month, traditionally marked by dawn-to-dusk fasting, daily prayers and self-examination. The apparent worldwide increase in observances of Ramadan corresponds with Islam's increasing visibility and importance in the Muslim world and elsewhere — and the increasingly cacophonous debate over the role and meaning of Islam in the modern world.

"There is a very open and public debate in many cases about who speaks for Islam throughout the [Muslim world]," says Dale Eickelman, a professor of anthropology and human relations at Dartmouth College, in Hanover, N.H. "Even in areas where there are repressive regimes, this debate has become increasingly public."

"Within the greater Middle East there is now a much greater emphasis on Islam as the primary source of

Should Islam liberalize its view of women's rights?

YES
Omid Safi
Associate Professor, Islamic Studies,
University of North Carolina Co-chair, Study of
Islam Section, American Academy of Religion

Written for *CQ Researcher*, October 2006

This loaded and misguided question suggests that Islam must change fundamentally to recognize the rights of women. Instead, I would suggest that a profound reading of the Koran leads one to conclude that God has formed both men and women already in full possession of humanity at every layer: physically, emotionally, intellectually and spiritually. Humanity's God-given capacity to bear the divine covenant is shared by men and women, Muslim and non-Muslim.

The Islamic tradition historically has cultivated such a beautiful understanding. But local and cultural gender roles have shaped Islamic thought and practice in some domains — particularly in Islamic law — and the patriarchal prejudices of pre-modern societies have crept into historical interpretations of Islam. So when we encounter statements suggesting women are deficient in reason and intellect — statements that we also find in the pre-modern Jewish, Christian and Greek traditions — we must ask whether these understandings reflect God's call for humanity and the example of the Prophet Muhammad or whether they reflect the patriarchies of human societies.

The Koran and Islamic law in many ways were centuries ahead of developments elsewhere regarding women's rights. Muslim women had the right to own and inherit property, manage their own finances and pray to God directly without using male intermediaries. Yet today much work remains to be done in Muslim communities with respect to gender issues. In Iran and Saudi Arabia women are told they must cover their hair this way or that way, and in Turkey, France and Great Britain they are told not to cover themselves this way or that way. Where is the recognition that women must come to God on their own terms? That seems to be the challenge of our day with respect to Islam and women's rights.

The emerging women's rights movement in Islam insists that a proper understanding of Islam will recognize men and women as spiritual and social equals. To be successful, it must insist on its own religious legitimacy and tap into the rich reservoirs of Islamic sources. In other words, it is not a matter of "restoring" or "giving back" women's rights, it is a matter of recognizing that women are divine creations intended to fully possess rights and privileges. The manifestations of patriarchy — both inside and outside of religious traditions — that have robbed humans of their vitality and moral agency must be dismantled.

NO
Stephen Schwartz
Executive Director,
Center for Islamic Pluralism

Written for *CQ Researcher*, October 2006

Islam need not liberalize its view of women because problems of women's rights are not inherent to Islam. While Islam unfortunately is perceived in the West as a bastion of female oppression, this results from the conjunction of differing perspectives on the religion.

There are many ways to be Muslim, just as there are many ways to be Christian, Buddhist or Jewish. Although Islamic prayer is performed in Arabic and the Koran was delivered in Arabic, Islamic practice and culture are not restricted to an Arab paradigm. While the worst anti-female practices are maintained in the Arabian peninsula and its near neighbors, so-called honor killings have been exported to the non-Muslim world by uneducated people. But honor killings are also known to occur among non-Muslims.

Moreover, Arab customs are subject to change. A women's protest movement centered in Jiddah — near the holy cities of Mecca and Medina — opposes mandatory face covering and other forms of intimidation by the Saudi-Wahhabi religious militia or *mutawwa*. The women point out that they never covered their faces in the past, do not wish to do so now and say the *mutawwa* should return to their place of origin in eastern Arabia.

If women in the region of Mecca and Medina reject oppressive practices, how can such practices be considered Islamic? Similarly, the vast majority of young Bosnian Muslim women — who served as soldiers or mobilized civilians in the war of the 1990s in which 250,000 Muslims died — refuse to cover their hair, much less their faces.

Islam settled in the Eastern world, where progress has always been slow. But Islam also contrasts with other traditions in its early empowerment of women. Islam allowed women to divorce from the beginning, while divorce is still obstructed for Catholic and Orthodox Jewish women. Islam also abolished female infanticide — one of the first Islamic "reforms" among peninsular Arabs.

Muslim women never suffered bound feet or the common Indian habit of sari death. Capitalist democracies in Korea, Japan and East Asia do not encourage women to have political or media careers, while Muslim countries — even some of the most extreme — have female political leaders such as Tansu Ciller in Turkey. Israeli Arabs have *sharia* courts with women judges.

Social problems in Islamic countries reflect local culture and history, not the Islamic faith.

identity," says Freedom House's Marshall. From his travels, Marshall says he sees the change not only in avowedly Islamist countries such as Saudi Arabia, Sudan and Iran but also in more secular Egypt, the most populous Arab nation and the historic seat of Islamic learning. "Each time I go there, the number of women who are completely covered up is increasing," he says.

Egypt's authoritarian President Mubarak continues to have a difficult relationship with the Muslim Brotherhood, which won 88 seats in the national parliament in 2005 despite being officially banned since 1954. In October, Mohammed Mahdi Akef, the leader of the Brotherhood, said the government barred him from traveling to Saudi Arabia for Islamic rituals. "They promised to let me travel but then banned me," Akef told The Associated Press. "It's nonsense."[28]

Meanwhile, religious officials and Egyptians generally appear to be less tolerant of opposing religious views. As noted in *The New York Times*, religious officials moved in three recent cases either to condemn or seek criminal prosecutions of people or publications for promoting unpopular religious views. "The people, of course, oppose anybody who talks about things that violate religion," remarked Sheik Omar el-Deeb, deputy in charge of Al Azhar, the famed Islamic seminary and university founded in the 10th century.[29]

The religious resurgence among Muslims coincides with increased religiosity elsewhere in the world — including in the United States, according to historian Voll. Eickelman also notes historical parallels to the role that religion played in the Solidarity movement in Poland and in the liberation-theology movements in Latin America in the 1980s.

As in those historical examples, Islam's present-day appeal in majority-Muslim countries stems in large part from the failures of established governments, Eickelman says. Secular authorities "have not been seen to be concerned" with improving the standard of living or reducing economic inequality, he says. "It's not clear that religious authorities can do better," Eickelman adds, but Muslim publics are increasingly willing to give them a chance.

Other experts stress that Islamist movements are — in contrast to their negative image in the West — neither monolithic nor necessarily anti-democratic. Established regimes, not Islamists, are the major impediments to democratic reform, according to Amr Hanzawy, an Egyptian and a senior fellow at the Carnegie Endowment for International Peace. Islamist groups are eager to participate in politics, he says, both to capitalize on their popular appeal and to gain protection from repression.[30]

As in Egypt, secular governments elsewhere are resisting the Islamist advance. In Syria, the government of President Bashar al-Assad bans the Muslim Brotherhood, which is allied with the secular opposition in calling for political reforms. In Tunisia, the government of President Zine Al-Abidine Ben Ali is conducting a campaign against Islamic head scarves, calling them "sectarian."

Any efforts to contain the religious impulse — whether by existing regimes or from Western governments or groups — appear unlikely to succeed, according to many experts. "Anybody trying to secure an audience in the Muslim-majority world would want to indicate a respect for Islam," says Eickelman. "You have to have answers on how to make society better — and better for religious reasons."

Religious Clashes

Suspended Muslim teaching assistant Aishah Azmi is still fighting for the right to wear a veil in her classroom but with little public support in England. Meanwhile, the veil controversy is sparking debate in other Western countries, including the United States — adding to tensions created by other clashes between Islam and the non-Muslim world.

The Muslim Member of Parliament (MP) from Azmi's constituency is among those urging her not to appeal an unfavorable ruling by an employment tribunal on her suspension. The tribunal rejected Azmi's claim that the local school council in northern England discriminated against her by suspending her for refusing to take off the veil in class, although it awarded her about $2,300 because the council had "victimized" her.

MP Shahid Malik said that local Muslim parents have told him they would not send their children to schools where women teachers wore the veil. "I would appeal to Mrs. Azmi just to let this thing go," Malik said the day after the ruling. "There is no real support for it."[31]

Reefat Drabu, the chair of social and family affairs at the Muslim Council of Britain, declared that Azmi's position was making things harder for Muslim communities in Britain. He said publicity about the case since September has led to "more attacks on Muslim women" and mosques and "a continuous hammering of Muslims throughout the country."

Azmi herself was avoiding additional comment after talking with reporters on the day of her decision. Nick

Whittingham, her lawyer, said she was tired and feeling pressure after the verdict. "I expect she wishes it would all go away," he said. Still, Whittingham said he was exploring grounds for an appeal and considering seeking additional legal aid to take the case further, even possibly to the European Court of Human Rights.

Muslim leaders noted that wearing the veil is generally not considered obligatory and that only about 5 percent of Muslim women in Britain do. But an encouraging sign for women who choose to wear the veil emerged in a poll that showed a generation gap on the issue: 65 percent of Britons over age 65 expressed discomfort with the veil but only 31 percent of 18- to 24-year-olds.[32]

Meanwhile, the controversy in Britain focused attention on similar episodes elsewhere in Europe. Jan Creemers, mayor of the small Belgian town of Maaseik, banned the *niqab* earlier in 2006 — and reportedly won the backing of most of the town's Moroccan Muslim population. Other Belgian towns followed suit. Italy's anti-terrorist laws have the effect of a ban by prohibiting hiding one's face.[33]

In addition, France effectively bars Muslim public school pupils from wearing even the less obtrusive head scarf under a law that bans religious accessories. Several states in Germany bar schoolteachers from wearing head scarves.

The issue flared in the United States when a state district judge in Michigan threw out a Muslim woman's court case because she refused to remove her veil when she testified. Judge Paul Paruk told Ginnah Muhammad that he needed to see her face in order to judge her veracity.

Meanwhile, the Vatican appears to be making progress toward healing the rift that Pope Benedict XVI created on Sept. 12 with a lecture that included a medieval Christian emperor's critical comment about Islam.[34] The quotation was part of what amounted to a contemporary interfaith dialogue between the Byzantine emperor Manuel II Paleologus and a Persian Muslim.

As Benedict recounted, the emperor described Islam in blunt terms: "Show me just what Muhammad brought that was new, and there you will find things only evil and inhuman, such as his command to spread by the sword the faith he preached." News accounts of the speech provoked outrage in much of the Muslim world and forced Benedict to dissociate himself from the criticism. The views, he said, "were a quotation from a medieval text which does not in any way express my personal thought."

Iraqi youngsters inspect the remnants of a car bomb that killed nine people and wounded 27 in a largely Shiite area of Baghdad on Oct. 9, 2006. Fighting between Sunni and Shiite Muslims is helping to drive the escalating insurgency in Iraq three years after the U.S.-led invasion ousted Saddam Hussein.

The pope also met in the Vatican with representatives of all Muslim nations that had diplomatic representation. By late October, the efforts at rapprochement appeared to be bearing fruit. In a letter to the pope, 38 Muslim leaders accepted his explanation and welcomed his call for dialogue between Christians and Muslims.

OUTLOOK

Misunderstandings?

When France moved to ban head scarves from public schools in 2004, Britain's Labor government pointedly dissociated itself from any limits on religious attire. "In Britain we are comfortable with the expression of religion," Foreign Office Minister Mike O'Brien said. "Integration does not require assimilation."[35]

Two years later, however, Prime Minister Tony Blair joined in criticizing the wearing of the Muslim veil as a "sign of separation." And Blair's government — concerned about the homegrown Islamist extremists blamed for the London subway and bus bombings in 2004 and a foiled airplane sabotage plot last August — is quietly funding an Islamic Web site appealing for moderation and distributing CDs promoting moderation to Muslim students at universities.[36]

Among Muslims and non-Muslims alike, many Britons view the recent pronouncements from government officials on the veil issue as divisive. "If we go and demonize a substantial section of our own population, my advice would be to watch out," says Roger Ballard, an anthropologist affiliated with the University of Manchester who has studied the Pakistani Muslim community in Pakistan and England.

Bukhari of the London-based Muslim Public Affairs Committee says the criticisms amount to a "vilification" of Muslims from some quarters — due in part to the separation between Britain's Muslim and non-Muslim communities. "If you don't know a Muslim, you don't hang around with Muslims, then you have no one to rely on for your perceptions of Muslims besides the media," he says.

"Both the Muslim community and the non-Muslim community need to communicate with each other about each other," says Anwar with the Lancashire Council of Mosques. "I'm not very keen on this word 'tolerate.' I prefer understanding."

A combination of historical and contemporary circumstances, however, makes understanding Islam difficult both for the non-Muslim West and for Muslims themselves.

Historically, the three "religions of the book" — Judaism, Christianity and Islam — may share a common heritage, but they have engaged in theological, cultural and political disagreements and conflicts through much of the past 14 centuries. Islam and Christianity came to hold sway over different parts of the globe — the Muslim world and the Christian West — while Islam and Judaism have been drawn into a deadly conflict in their common homeland because of the Israeli-Palestinian dispute.

Mutual fears and recriminations have intensified since the 9/11 attacks and the proclaimed war on terror, according to British author Grieve. "To rise up with this nationalist fury was to completely misunderstand the event," he says.

Muslims reacted with understandable defensiveness, Grieve continues. "Islam in the current world situation has taken on this combative stance," he says. "It explains to them why their life is not just right."

Foreign-policy issues appear certain to be a continuing source of division, at least for the short term. Most notably, the Israeli-Palestinian dispute is "an open wound, a symbol for Muslims of the fundamental injustice of the region," according to progressive Muslim scholar Safi at the University of North Carolina. The Iraq insurgency may pit Sunnis against Shiites, but the vast majority of Muslims

in the region appear united in wanting the United States to withdraw.

In Britain — as in many other parts of Europe — many Muslims expect divisions to increase. "Nothing's going to change," says Bukhari. "It's only going to get worse."

Prospects for successful integration may be better in the United States. "Attitudes toward Muslims in America are more accepting than in Europe," says author Aslan.

But Anwar says Muslims must also engage in self-examination. "As a Muslim community, we need to look at extremism internally," she says. "Are we really living our faith to the high standards we impose, or have we separated the religion from the faith?

"If Muslims started to live the faith as it is, then we can make a difference," Anwar continues. "The United Kingdom is a very fertile land, and it can take on new philosophies. But it has to be give-and-take. It will take time, but it will happen."

NOTES

1. Coverage from these London newspapers, all on Oct. 20, 2006: Andrew Norfolk, " 'I won't be treated as an outcast,' says Muslim teacher in veil row," *The Times*; Ian Herbert, "Teaching assistant 'victimised' for wearing veil, tribunal rules," *The Independent*; Martin Wainwright, "Tribunal dismisses case of Muslim woman ordered not to teach in veil," *The Guardian*. See also Jake Morris, "The Great Veil Debate," *The Mirror*, Oct. 14, 2006, p. 9.

2. Jonathan Wynne-Jones, "Drive for multi-faith Britain deepens rifts, says Church," *Daily Telegraph*, Oct. 8, 2006.

3. See David Harrison, "Government policy on multiculturalism has been left in tatters," *The* [London] *Daily Telegraph*, Oct. 8, 2006. Other accounts of controversy taken from various English newspapers in October 2006. For coverage in a U.S. newspaper, see Alan Cowell, "British Leader Stirs Debate With His Call to Raise Veils," *The New York Times*, Oct. 7, 2006, p. A8.

4. For background, see these *CQ Researcher* reports: Peter Katel, "Global Jihad," Oct. 14, 2005, pp. 857-880; David Masci and Kenneth Jost, "War on Terrorism," Oct. 12, 2001, pp. 817-848.

5. Paul Grieve, *Islam: History, Faith and Politics: The Complete Introduction* (2006), pp. 21-22.

6. For background, see Pamela M. Prah, "War in Iraq," *CQ Researcher*, Oct. 21, 2005, pp. 881-908; and David Masci, "Rebuilding Iraq," *CQ Researcher*, July 25, 2003, pp. 625-648.

7. For the full text of his remarks, see www.aljazeera .com/me.asp?service_ID=8831.

8. Angel M. Rabasa, *et al.*, *The Muslim World after 9/11* (2004).

9. CBS News, "Poll: Sinking Perceptions of Islam," April 12, 2006 (www.cbsnews.com). The telephone survey of 899 adults was conducted April 9-12; the sampling error was plus or minus three percentage points. The February 2002 survey was by Gallup.

10. Laurie Goodstein, "Seeing Islam as 'Evil' Faith, Evangelicals Seek Converts," *The New York Times*, May 27, 2003, p. A1; The Associated Press, "Threats and Responses; Muhammad a Terrorist to Falwell," *The New York Times*, Oct. 4, 2002, p. A17.

11. See Sohail H. Hashmi, "Jihad," in *Encyclopedia of Religion and Politics* (2nd ed.), 2006 [forthcoming].

12. Seyyed Hossein Nasr, "Islam and the Question of Violence," *Al-Serat: A Journal of Islamic Studies*, Vol. XIII, No. 2, available at www.al-islam.org/ al-serat/IslamAndViolence.htm.

13. See Noreen S. Ahmed-Ullah, "Muslim Decree to Oppose Terrorism," *Chicago Tribune*, July 28, 2005, p. C12; Laurie Goodstein, "From Muslims in America, a New Fatwa on Terrorism," *The New York Times*, July 28, 2005, p. A14.

14. Safi has collected some of the post-9/11 statements at http://groups.colgate.edu/aarislam/response .htm.

15. Account drawn from Judy Dempsey and Mark Landler, "Opera Canceled Over a Depiction of Muhammad," *The New York Times*, Sept. 27, 2006, p. A1; Craig Whitlock, "Fear of Muslim Backlash Cancels Opera," *The Washington Post*, Sept. 27, 2006, p. A24.

16. Quoted in Jeffrey Fleishman, "Europe Raising Its Voice Over Radical Islam," *Los Angeles Times*, Oct. 16, 2006, p. A4.

17. Grieve, *op. cit.*, p. 318.

18. See "Punjab University to Start Masters in Musicology Despite Protests," *Financial Times Global News Wire*, Sept. 17, 2006; "Pakistani students campaign against dance, music, theatre," Indo-Asian News Service, June 3, 2006. See also Aryn Baker, "No Dates, No Dancing," *Time*, Oct. 8, 2006.

19. Safi, *op. cit.*, p. 2.

20. Nicholas D. Kristof, "Looking for Islam's Luthers," *The New York Times*, Oct. 15, 2006, sec. 4, p. 13.

21. Background drawn from John O. Voll, "Islam," in Robert Wuthnow (ed.), *Encyclopedia of Politics and Religion* (2nd ed.) (forthcoming December 2006).

22. Some background drawn from Paul Marshall (ed.), *Radical Islam's Rules: The Worldwide Spread of Extreme Shari'a Law* (2005); Grieve, *op. cit.*

23. *Ibid.*, p. 170.

24. For background see David Masci and Kenneth Jost, "War on Terrorism," *CQ Researcher*, Oct. 12, 2001, pp. 817-848.

25. Council on American-Islamic Relations, "American Muslims: One Year After 9-11," 2002, pp. 1-2.

26. Some background drawn from David Masci, "An Uncertain Road: Muslims and the Future of Europe," Pew Forum on Religion and Public Life, October 2005 (www.pewforum.org).

27. Voll, *op. cit.*

28. "Muslin Brotherhood head says Egypt bars him from travel to Saudi Arabia," The Associated Press, Oct. 11, 2006.

29. See Michael Slackman, "A Liberal Brother at Odds With the Muslim Brotherhood," *The New York Times*, Oct. 21, 2006, p. A4.

30. See "Engagement or Quarantine: How to Deal with the Islamist Advance," Carnegie Endowment for International Peace, June 28, 2006 (synopsis at www .carnegieendowment.org).

31. Quoted in Paul Stokes, "Muslim MP tells veiled class assistant to give up fight," *The Daily Telegraph* [London], Oct. 21, 2006, p. 8. Other background and quotes drawn from Paul Malley, "Top MPs in warning to Muslim," *Daily Star*, Oct. 21, 2006, p. 2; Huw Thomas, "Veil hang-ups

may pass," *The Times Educational Supplement*, Oct. 27, 2006, p. 21.

32. Cited in *ibid.*

33. "Muslim Veils Spark Debate in Europe," Voice of America English Service, Oct. 21, 2006.

34. See "Visit to Turkey a stern test for Vatican after Muslim outrage," *Irish Times*, Oct. 23, 2006.

35. Shola Adenekan, "British criticism of headscarf ban," BBC News, Feb. 10, 2004.

36. See Patrick Hennessy and Melissa Kite, "Al-Qaeda is winning the war of ideas, says Reid," *The Sunday Telegraph* [London], Oct. 22, 2006, p. 1.

BIBLIOGRAPHY

Books

Abdo, Geneive, *Mecca and Main Street: Muslim Life in America After 9/11*, Oxford University Press, 2006.
Author-journalist Abdo combines first-hand reporting in Muslim communities in the United States with broad background knowledge of Islam to produce an insightful portrait of American Muslims five years after the 9/11 terrorist attacks. Includes five-page bibliography.

Aslan, Reza, *No god but God: The Origins, Evolution, and Future of Islam*, Random House, 2005.
An Iranian-American Muslim recounts the history of Islam from the pre-Islamic era in Arabia to what he describes as the current "Islamic Reformation" under way in much of the Muslim world. Aslan is a fellow at the University of Southern California and Middle East expert for CBS News. Includes glossary, notes and six-page list of works consulted.

Grieve, Paul, *A Brief Guide to Islam: History, Faith and Politics: The Complete Introduction*, Carroll and Graf Publishers, 2006.
Grieve, a British author, studied Islam for three years while researching his second novel and turned his research into a comprehensive guide to the history of Islam, its doctrines and practices, and Islam's relations with the non-Muslim world. Includes 14-page glossary and other reference materials.

Lippman, Thomas W., *Understanding Islam: An Introduction to the Muslim World* (3rd rev. ed.), 2002.
Lippman, a longtime newspaper correspondent in the Middle East, provides a well-organized primer on Islam's beliefs and practices, Muhammad's life and teachings, the Koran, law and government under Islam and Islam's history to present times. Includes compact glossary, bibliography.

Marshall, Paul (ed.), *Radical Islam's Rules: The Worldwide Spread of Extreme Shari'a Law*, Freedom House's Center for Religious Freedom, 2005.
Eight contributors examine the adoption or advance of "extreme" shari'a law in Saudi Arabia, Iran, Pakistan, Sudan, Nigeria, Malaysia, Indonesia and Afghanistan. Includes chapter notes. Marshall, a senior fellow at the Center for Religious Freedom, is also co-author with Roberta Green and Lela Gilbert of *Islam at the Crossroads: Understanding Its Beliefs, History, and Conflict* (Baker Books), 2002.

Rabasa, Angel M., *et al.*, *The Muslim World After 9/11*, RAND, 2004.
Eight contributors examine the political role and impact of Islam in the Muslim world, region by region. Includes glossary, 11-page bibliography and other reference material.

Safi, Omid (ed.), *Progressive Muslim: On Justice, Gender, and Pluralism*, Oneworld, 2003.
Fourteen contributors articulate the views of progressive Muslims on contemporary Islam, gender justice and pluralism. Safi is associate professor of Islamic studies at the University of North Carolina-Chapel Hill. Includes chapter notes, eight-page list of recommended readings.

Schwartz, Stephen, *The Two Faces of Islam: Saudi Fundamentalism and Its Role in Terrorism* (2nd ed.), Doubleday, 2003.
Schwartz, a former journalist and now executive director of the Center for Islamic Pluralism, writes a strongly critical account of the origins of the radical form of Islam called Wahhabism and Saudi Arabia's role in its advance in the United States and around the world. Includes notes, bibliography.

Schulze, Reinhard, *A Modern History of the Islamic World,* **New York University Press, 2002.**
Schulze, a professor of Islamic studies at the University of Berne, provides a comprehensive account of the history of the Islamic world from the rise of nationalism and independence movements in the early 20th century through the reassertion of Islamic ideologies beginning in the 1970s. Includes notes, chronology, glossary, 26-page bibliography.

Articles

Voll, John O., "Islam," in Robert Wuthnow (ed.), *Encyclopedia of Politics and Religion* **(2d ed.),** *CQ Press,* **2006 [forthcoming].**
The director of the Center for Muslim-Christian Understanding at Georgetown University provides an overview of the history and beliefs of Islam from its seventh-century origins to the present.

Reports and Studies

Council on American-Islamic Relations, **"The Status of Muslim Civil Rights in the United States 2006: The Struggle for Equality," 2006.**
The report by the Washington-based council notes a 30 percent increase in reported anti-Muslim incidents in 2005 over the previous year along with poll results indicating widespread negative perceptions of Muslims among Americans.

On the Web

"Islam and Islamic Studies Resources," a Web site maintained by Prof. Alan Godlas of the University of Georgia's Department of Religion (www.uga.edu/islam), provides a comprehensive and well-organized compendium of information and material on Islam.

For More Information

Center for Islamic Pluralism, (202) 232-1750; www.islamicpluralism.org. A think tank that opposes the radicalization of Islam in America.

Center for Muslim-Christian Understanding, Georgetown University, 37th & O Sts., N.W., Washington, DC 20057; (202) 687-8375; http://cmcu.georgetown.edu/. Dedicated to achieving a better understanding between Islam and Christianity and between the Muslim world and the West.

Center for Religious Freedom, 1319 18th St., N.W., Washington, DC 20036; (202) 296-5101; http://crf.hudson.org/. Defends against religious persecution of all groups throughout the world.

Center for the Study of Islam and Democracy, 1050 Connecticut Ave., N.W., Suite 1000, Washington, DC 20036; (202) 772-2022; www.islam-democracy.org. Studies Islamic and democratic political thought and merges them into a modern Islamic democratic discourse.

Council on American-Islamic Relations, 453 New Jersey Ave., S.E., Washington, DC 20003; (202) 488-8787; www.cair.com. Works to enhance understanding of Islam and empower American Muslims.

Pew Forum on Religion & Public Life, 1615 L St., N.W., Suite 700, Washington, DC 20036-5610; (202) 419-4550; www.pewforum.org. The nonpartisan forum "seeks to promote a deeper understanding of how religion shapes the ideas and institutions of American society."

8

Crisis in Pakistan

Can the Fragile Democracy Survive?

Robert Kiener

Asif Ali Zardari became Pakistan's new president in September after the resignation of Pervez Musharraf in August. The widower of slain former Prime Minister Benazir Bhutto (in portrait), Zardari faces a multitude of challenges, including a spike in terrorist bombings, rising Islamic fundamentalism, a weakened democracy, a faltering economy and growing anger over U.S. anti-terrorist strikes into Pakistani tribal territories.

From *CQ Global Researcher*, December 2008.

Just after 8 p.m. on September 20 a large truck crashed into the security gates in front of the heavily guarded Marriott Hotel in Islamabad. Seconds later, suicide bombers in the truck detonated its tarpaulin-covered cargo — more than 1,200 pounds of TNT and RDX explosives — killing at least 54 people, injuring hundreds and destroying much of the luxurious landmark.[1]

For visitors and residents alike, the Marriott had been more than a hotel. It was the meeting place for Westerners as well as Pakistan's elite, attracting businessmen, government officials and journalists. Located in the heart of Pakistan's capital — just a few hundred yards from Parliament and the homes of the president and prime minister — the well-guarded Marriott had been a secure and quiet oasis in a boisterous city. Indeed, newly elected President Asif Ali Zardari and other top leaders had reportedly been scheduled to dine there on the night of the attack, changing their plans only at the last minute.[2]

The blast — quickly dubbed Pakistan's 9/11 — came on the very day of President Zardari's maiden address to Parliament, in which he promised to banish terrorists from Pakistan: "We must root out terrorism and extremism wherever and whenever they may rear their ugly heads."[3]

Shortly after the bombing, Interior Minister Rehmam Mali echoed other Pakistani officials and Western diplomats when he claimed the attack had been organized by Taliban militants associated with al Qaeda based in Pakistan's vast, mountainous region known as the Federally Administered Tribal Areas (FATA), which borders Afghanistan.[4]

AFP/Getty Images/Aamir Qureshi

179

Between a Rock and a Hard Place

Sandwiched between Afghanistan and India, Pakistan has been battered by growing terrorism and Islamic fundamentalism, a weakening democracy and a faltering economy. Some observers question whether the fledgling democracy — the size of Texas and Tennessee combined and the world's second-largest Muslim nation — could become a failed state. Taliban militants linked to the al Qaeda terrorist organization are based in the lawless mountain region of Pakistan bordering Afghanistan known as the Federally Administered Tribal Areas, where terrorist leader Osama bin Laden is thought to be hiding. Conflict with India over Kashmir adds to Pakistan's growing instability.

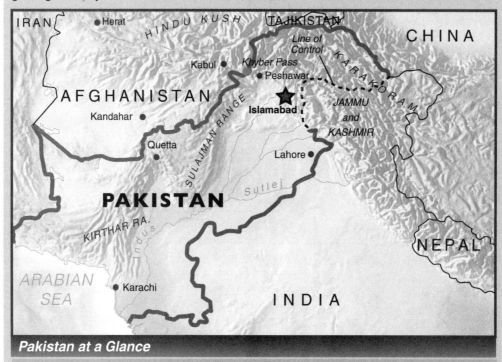

Pakistan at a Glance

Area: 310,402 sq. miles, or about the size of Texas and Tennessee combined; excludes disputed areas of Jammu and Kashmir.

Population: 156.9 million (2006), excluding Jammu and Kashmir; growing at 2% (2008 estimate)

Unemployment rate: 5.6% (2007)

Religion: Muslim — 95%, other (Christian and Hindu) — 5%

Government: The president is elected for a five-year term by the provincial assemblies and the Parliament, which consists of the Senate and the National Assembly. The prime minister — elected by the National Assembly — is head of the ruling party or coalition and is considered the head of government. The president — who is the head of state — oversees the military and can dissolve the National Assembly, effectively dismissing the prime minister and triggering new elections.

Economy: Decades of internal political disputes and an ongoing confrontation with India, primarily over Jammu and Kashmir, have discouraged foreign investment. Since 2001, economic recovery has been bolstered by significant foreign assistance, renewed access to global markets and reforms recommended by the International Monetary Fund — notably, privatization of the banking sector. Gross domestic product grew by 6-8 percent from 2004 to 2007, and poverty levels decreased by 10 percent since 2001.

Sources: Political Handbook of the World 2008, CQ Press, 2008; The World Factbook, Central Intelligence Agency

"All roads lead to FATA," said Mali, referring to the remote, lawless area where many believe Osama bin Laden — mastermind of the 9/11 terrorist attacks in the United States — is hiding.[5]

Ever since Pakistani troops stormed Islamabad's Red Mosque in mid-2007 to root out militants who had occupied it, killing an estimated 100 people during the takeover, a coalition of Taliban groups known as Tereek Taliban-e-Pakistan has declared war on the Pakistani government. Many experts see Pakistan's handling of the Red Mosque incident as a turning point that eventually led to the September attack on the Marriott.

The horrific blast left nearly 60 people dead and a smoldering 40-foot-wide by 25-foot-deep crater in front of the burned-out hotel. It also delivered a chilling message. "The bombing sent a signal to the fragile government and authorities that militants had muscle and could extend that muscle into the very heart of the capital," explains Farzana Shaikh, the Pakistani author of the forthcoming *Making Sense of Pakistan* and an associate fellow at London's Royal Institute of International Affairs. "They were telling the government they are a force to be reckoned with."

Since the Sept. 11, 2001, terrorist attacks on the United States, more and more militants have sought safe haven in FATA and in the equally rugged North-West Frontier Province (NWFP), the smallest of the country's four provinces. (*See map, p. 183.*) "Militants are launching attacks on Afghanistan and Pakistan itself from these regions," says Hassan Abbas, a former Pakistani government official and now a fellow at Harvard University's John F. Kennedy School of Government. "Years of neglect, incompetent governance and failure to effectively fight religious extremism have allowed the Taliban and other extremist groups to expand their influence there."

As many observers have confirmed, Taliban warlords have taken near-total control inside the tribal areas, effectively replacing Pakistani government control with their own strict form of Islam.[6] In addition, say American officials, al Qaeda has hundreds of terrorist training camps throughout FATA.[7] Many believe that former Prime Minister Benazir Bhutto's December 2007 assassination was ordered by Taliban leader Baitullah Mehsud, who is based in the region. (*See sidebar, p. 188.*) In a recent Council on Foreign Relations report, former State Department official Dan Markey wrote, "Should another 9/11-type attack take place in the United States, it will likely have its origins in this area."[8]

Almost overnight, the growth and influence of the terrorists has put Pakistan on the radar screens of leaders around the world. Many point to the world's second-most-populous Muslim nation as a "safe haven" for terrorists and home to a growing militant movement that threatens its stability. The late November terrorist attacks in Mumbai that killed more than 173 people underscored that point. India has blamed the deadly assaults on a Pakistani militant group, Lashkar-e-Taiba, dedicated to ending Indian rule in Kashmir. (*See story, p. 194.*) The attacks are expected to harm Indo-Pakistan relations, since India has complained bitterly in the past that Islamabad allows militants to strike India from within Pakistan's borders.

As tensions between the two countries rise, the security of Pakistan's nuclear weapons also is being questioned. With a weakening economy and social unrest spreading within its borders, many are asking whether Pakistan could soon become a "failed state" with a deadly arsenal at risk.

"Pakistan may be the single, greatest challenge facing the next American president," contends Pakistan expert Stephen Philip Cohen, a fellow at the Brookings Institution think tank in Washington, D.C.[9]

Along with the Taliban, other extremist movements are on the rise across the nation. For example, Balochistan Province, which covers 44 percent of Pakistan, is home to burgeoning nationalistic insurgencies. And a secular separatist movement has taken root in Sindh Province, the backbone of Pakistan's economy.

As a result, terrorism-related violence has racked up grim statistics. During the first eight months of 2008, 324 blasts, including 28 suicide attacks, killed more than 619 people throughout the country.[10] In fact, more people were killed in suicide bombings in Pakistan during the first eight months of 2008 than in Iraq or Afghanistan, according to Pakistan's Inter Services Intelligence agency, the ISI. But last year was even bloodier: Some 2,100 citizens, soldiers and police died in terrorism-related violence, plus nearly 1,500 terrorists, according to the South Asia Terrorism Portal, run by the Institute for Conflict Management in Delhi, India.[11] The U.S. government's National Counterterrorism Center puts the non-terrorist toll at 1,335. (*See graph, p. 182.*)

Terror Attack Fatalities Jump Five-Fold

Attacks by al Qaeda and other terrorist groups killed more than 1,300 security personnel and civilians in Pakistan in 2007 — a fivefold increase from just three years earlier. Most of the victims, by far, have been civilians — with nearly 1,000 killed in 2007.

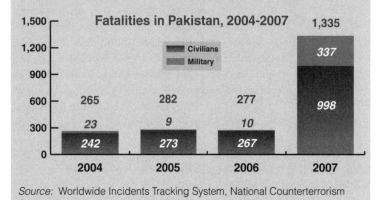

Fatalities in Pakistan, 2004-2007

Source: Worldwide Incidents Tracking System, National Counterterrorism Center

The brutality of the attacks has been staggering. For instance, this past summer:

- In Waziristan, a mountainous region in the FATA, Mehsud's followers slaughtered 22 government negotiators who had come to discuss a cease-fire pact.[12]
- In July a terrorist killed 19 people when he blew himself up near the Red Mosque, marking the one-year anniversary of the July 2007 siege there.[13]
- Two suicide bombers in August killed more than 60 people outside Pakistan's largest weapons factory in Wah, some 20 miles north of Islamabad.[14]

As the many al Qaeda and Taliban-inspired attacks show, Pakistan has become ground zero in global terrorism. But militants' attacks are only part of Pakistan's troubles. "Terrorism, militancy and separatism are symptoms of Pakistan's bigger problem," explains Akbar Ahmed, Pakistan's former high commissioner to Great Britain and the holder of the Ibn Khaldun chair in Islamic Studies at American University in Washington, D.C. "The nation is in crisis. Many are beginning to call it a 'failed state.' "

Amid the turmoil, President Zardari, Bhutto's widower, is scrambling to unify his splintered nation. But he faces

massive challenges. He must balance relations with the United States — which is urging him to step up attacks on militants in FATA — with the concerns of many Pakistanis who believe the war on terror has nothing to do with Pakistan. According to a recent Pew survey, nearly two-thirds of Pakistanis feel the United States is one of the countries posing the greatest threat to Pakistan.[15]

Zardari cannot be seen as being "Washington's puppet," but that increasingly is the perception, especially since the U.S. military recently has been crossing into Pakistan to attack terrorist strongholds. And on Nov. 18 American troops in Afghanistan fired an artillery barrage at insurgents in Pakistan's tribal region.[16] Meanwhile, the new president must appease opposition parties — especially the powerful wing of the Pakistan Muslim League headed by former Prime Minister Nawaz Sharif that dropped out of the coalition government this year — and the military, which fell from power when unpopular Gen. Pervez Musharraf resigned the presidency on Aug. 18, 2008.

"Political stability is a key to Pakistan's survival," explains Shaikh at the Royal Institute of International Affairs. "But the present leaders are at a disadvantage. Years of military rule have stunted the development of political rule."

And with the recent weakening of Pakistan's formerly robust economy — gross domestic product grew on average nearly 7 percent annually under Musharraf — the outlook appears even more forbidding. The rupee has hit an all-time low against the dollar, and inflation — about 30 percent — is the highest in 30 years. In October Standard & Poor's cut Pakistan's credit rating for the second time this year; foreign investors are pulling out of the stock market; and foreign-exchange reserves are running out.[17]

According to *The Economist* magazine's Intelligence Unit, the economy is in a "state of crisis."[18] With economic woes come higher taxes and higher costs on staples like food and power. Electricity shortages are soaring, along with food prices, which jumped more than 20 percent last March.[19] In October protesters in Lahore, the country's second-largest city, ransacked a power company's offices and burned their electric bills. Phasing out government subsidies on imported fuel has led to skyrocketing prices for everything from gasoline to cooking oil.

"Every day that passes, things get worse. . . . The economy is in a downspin," said Zubair Iqbal, a Pakistani economist retired from the International Monetary Fund and now an adjunct scholar at the Middle East Institute in Washington.[20]

Relations with India, recently on the mend after years of conflict over Kashmir and other issues, received a huge setback after the recent terrorist attacks in Mumbai. Although Zardari has labeled Kashmiri guerrillas as "terrorists" and says Pakistan will not continue its "nuclear first-strike option," the Mumbai attacks have damaged that progress.

Pakistan's myriad woes threaten to further fragment an already splintered nation. The weak economy and a notoriously anemic education system make young, dissatisfied Pakistanis more susceptible to recruitment by insurgents. "The more people become socially and economically marginalized, the greater the risk for instability," explains Harvard's Abbas. "Chaos — with the streets full of angry, violent protesters — is a real possibility unless these problems are addressed."

Since its founding in 1947, Pakistan has survived despite constantly lurching between democracy and military dictatorships, but some wonder if the oncoming "perfect storm" of insurrection, political fragility, a weakening economy and an increasingly disenfranchised populace may finally topple

A Diverse Linguistic Landscape

Pakistan's numerous tongues reflect the country's ethnic and religious diversity (top). Although Urdu is the official language, only 8 percent of the population uses it as their primary language, while 48 percent speak Punjabi. Balochistan is the largest of Pakistan's four provinces (bottom).

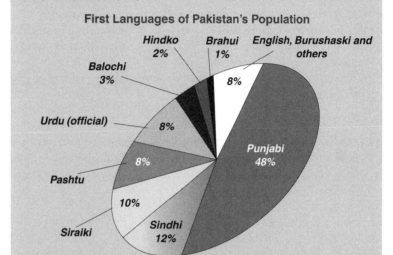

First Languages of Pakistan's Population

Hindko 2%, Brahui 1%, English, Burushaski and others 8%, Balochi 3%, Urdu (official) 8%, Pashtu 8%, Siraiki 10%, Sindhi 12%, Punjabi 48%

Pakistan's Four Provinces

Source: The World Factbook, Central Intelligence Agency

the nation. The situation in Pakistan is "very bad," with the country itself "on the edge," according to U.S. officials who recently drafted a top secret National Intelligence Estimate. One official portrayed the situation in Pakistan as: "No money, no energy, no government."[21]

"Pakistan is in even scarier shape than most of the so-called experts are willing to admit," wrote Sumit Ganguly, a longtime Pakistan watcher and director of research at the Center on American and Global Security at Indiana University. "Pakistan is facing an existential crisis — on its streets and in its courts, barracks and Parliament."[22]

As Pakistan fights for its survival, here are some of the questions being asked:

Can Pakistan control its radical militants?

When Adm. Mike Mullen, chairman of the U.S. Joint Chiefs of Staff, addressed the powerful House Armed Services Committee in September, he sent a clear message to both Pakistan and the militants that operate within its borders. He called for "a new, more comprehensive military strategy for the region that covers both sides of that border," adding that the United States must work with Pakistan to "eliminate safe havens." Until then, he continued, "the enemy will only keep coming."[23]

In marked contrast to previous U.S. comments, analysts say, Mullen was expressing America's impatience with Pakistan's lack of control over its border regions and the resulting effect on the U.S. war in Afghanistan. "In the past, Washington has listened to Pakistan's explanations of [its] inability to control the militants in these areas and subsequently refrained from pushing the Pakistani leadership harder for fear of disrupting bilateral relations," noted Lisa Curtis, senior research fellow on South Asia at the conservative Heritage Foundation.[24]

But times have changed. The United States has lost confidence in Pakistan's ability to control the militancy within its borders. And with U.S. forces in Afghanistan coming under attack from al Qaeda and Taliban militants operating from safe havens in Pakistan, the United States is pushing Zardari to step up Pakistan's anti-insurgent campaign. Many experts say the United States has a right to be frustrated, having sent more than $11 billion to Pakistan since 9/11, primarily in military aid intended to help combat the militants.[25]

Is the "gloves off" approach working? Pakistan's Army Chief of Staff, Gen. Ashfaq Parvez Kayani, claims his campaign against the Taliban and al Qaeda in the tribal area of Bajaur has killed 1,500 insurgents over the last year. But he strongly criticized a cross-border raid by U.S. troops on Sept. 4, vowing to defend Pakistan's "sovereignty and territorial integrity" at all costs.[26] Meanwhile, analysts say it is still too early to tell whether Pakistan's military is fully behind the battle against Islamic extremists.

It's also unclear whether Pakistan has the political will to clean out the terrorists. According to Husain Haqqani, Pakistan's ambassador to the United States, "The great majority of Pakistan's elected leaders believe firmly that fighting terrorism is Pakistan's own war."[27]

But experts disagree on this point. Recent parliamentary proceedings showed little evidence that Pakistani politicians have the will to battle the terrorists.[28] This potential impasse highlights a recurring problem with what President Zardari has called "Pakistan's war."

"If Pakistan ever wants to control the militants, it needs to have the political will and the [military] capacity to succeed," says former State Department official Markey. "Right now, it has problems with both."

Convincing Pakistan's people and politicians that going to war against the militants is in the nation's best interest is proving to be a tough sell.

"Many members of Parliament are reluctant to come out in support of a war on militants," explains Shuja Nawaz, a Pakistani political analyst and author of *Crossed Swords: Pakistan, Its Army and the Wars Within.* "Some are concerned that the present government may not be stable, and they are also reluctant to advocate violence against fellow Muslims. But the government has to convince all interested parties that a new, much broader, insurgency is affecting the man on the street, and that it is penetrating to the very heart of the country."

Some believe Pakistan needs a "national consensus" to curb the militants. "The recent program to curb militancy that the Parliament has drawn up is a first step," says the Royal Institute of International Affairs' Shaikh. "But Pakistan is a divided Muslim state, and many will never agree to fight what is seen as war against other Muslims."

For example, the Jamiat Ulema-e-Islam-Fazl, a religious party that is part of the ruling coalition with the Pakistan Peoples Party, recently proposed that the army immediately stop fighting the militants in FATA. "This is not a war we want to be part of," said Jehangir Tareen, a Pakistan Muslim

League politician, expressing the feeling of many in his party. "There is a sentiment that we are being pushed to do this by the United States. We want this war to end."[29]

Clearly, the government has a long way to go to convince more Pakistanis that the war against terrorists operating in Pakistan is their war, not just America's.

The political will to back such a fight is important, but having the military capacity to carry out that battle is even more important. Although Pakistan's military has lost more than 2,000 soldiers in battles against the militants, some wonder if the military is firmly convinced of the need for the conflict.

"The army has to come out and support Zardari's strong statements in deed and word," pointed out Pakistan expert Cohen at the Brookings Institution. So far, however, it has been silent, he noted.[30]

The military's silence may have more to do with politics than strategy. "The army wants the government to lead and take the political responsibility for going after the extremists so that the army's present unpopularity does not get worse," noted Lahore-based journalist and author Ahmed Rashid.[31]

The military has also been criticized for not having a credible approach to the fight against extremists, particularly since the military oversaw the buildup of lawless militancy during Musharraf's rule. "The army lacks strategy or coherence — one day bombing villages in FATA, the next day announcing ceasefires and offering compensation to the militants," noted Rashid. "It has failed to protect the people of FATA — some 800,000 of a population of just 3.5 million have fled the region since 2006 — terrified of both the army and the Taliban."[32]

The military also needs fundamental operational and structural changes, including — first — retooling itself for counterinsurgency. "The army has long been fixated on war with India," notes Markey. "It needs to change its culture and retrain its members in counterinsurgency methods."

Harvard's Abbas believes Pakistan needs a new "central command" to wage war on the militants. "Presently, there is no coordination, no planning with the civilian outfits. No agency is in complete control of this war," he says. Law enforcement also needs to be modernized and brought into the war, he contends. "Historically, where terrorism was defeated it was by law enforcement. Police have had successes in Pakistan at this, why not empower them?"

Getty Images

AP Photo/David Guttenfelder

Terrorists Target Luxury Hotels

Two hotels popular with foreigners — Islamabad's luxurious Marriott (top) in Pakistan and the Taj Mahal in Mumbai, India (bottom) — were attacked recently by Pakistani terrorists, according to intelligence officials. Pakistan officials say the Sept. 20 Marriott attack, which killed nearly 60 people and has been dubbed "Pakistan's 9/11," was organized by al Qaeda-linked Taliban militants based in Pakistan's Federally Administered Tribal Areas. Indian officials say the three days of savage assaults in late November at several locations in Mumbai, which killed 173 and have been called "India's 9/11," were carried out by Islamic extremists from Pakistani-controlled Kashmir. The same group has attacked India on several previous occasions, aggravating tensions between the two nuclear-armed neighbors.

In the end, though, guns alone are not enough to defeat militancy. Economic, educational and social infrastructure improvements in the region will help win hearts and minds, say many experts. "A closer look into Pakistan's counterinsurgency strategy since the launch of

Lawless Tribal Areas Harbor Terrorists

Pakistan's Federally Administered Tribal Areas, stretching along the Pakistan-Afghanistan border, consist of seven Pashtun-dominated "agencies": Khyber, Kurram, Orakzai, Mohmand, Bajaur, North Waziristan and South Waziristan. The British created the enclave to give maximum autonomy to the fiercely independent Pashtuns and to serve as a buffer between then-undivided India and Afghanistan. Smuggling, drug trafficking and gun-running flourish in the region, which has become a safe haven for Taliban and al Qaeda insurgents.

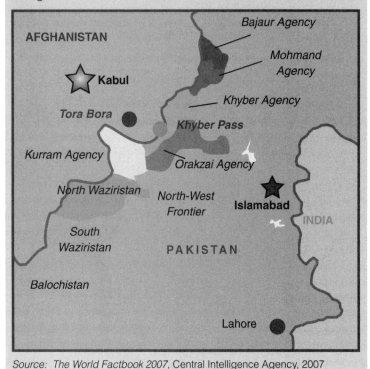

Source: The World Factbook 2007, Central Intelligence Agency, 2007

operations in 2003 reveals a policy focused entirely on a military approach, wholly ignoring the prospect of winning hearts and minds of local Pashtun tribesmen," wrote Pakistani journalist Imtiaz Ali. "For that reason more than any other, the seven-year-long counterinsurgency strategy pushed single-handedly by former President Musharraf has proved ineffective, if not downright disastrous."[33]

In the end, it is likely that only a modernized, coordinated and multilateral approach to combating militancy will work. As Gen. Kayani has noted, "There are no quick fixes in this war. Falling for short-term gains while ignoring our long-term interest is not the right way forward."[34]

Can democracy survive in Pakistan?

How important is democracy to some Pakistanis? If last February's election — after nearly 10 years of rule by military dictatorship — was anything to go by, it can be a matter of life and death.

On Feb. 9, 2008, a suicide bomber killed 27 and injured more than 30 attending a political rally near Charsadda in the NWFP. A week later another suicide bomber killed 47 and injured 109 outside a candidate's residence in the FATA town of Parachinar. In March alone, 37 workers from different political parties were killed.[35]

But committed voters were not deterred. Waiting her turn to vote in Rawalpindi on Feb. 18, 57-year-old Sakina Bibi spoke for many when she said, "I am not worried. It is up to God. If I am meant to die, I will die here."[36]

Such courage speaks to the point made by American University's Ahmed: "Pakistanis know the nation was founded on democracy. If democracy fails, Pakistan fails. Remember how we returned to democracy this time. It wasn't thanks to the Americans who preached democratic ideals while supporting a dictator. Lawyers, activists and people marching peacefully in the streets fought for it. Democracy is the lifeblood of Pakistan."

But democracy is more than just free elections. In order to work, elections must be supported by a free press, an unfettered judiciary and a viable opposition, say experts. Before being toppled, President Musharraf attacked some in the West for its "obsession" with democracy. Give Pakistan time, was his message.

But Pakistan's front pages loudly disagreed. "No, not an obsession!" blared a typical headline.[37] When asked recently how important it was to live in a democratic country, 8.4 out of 10 Pakistani respondents ranked it very high.[38]

Nonetheless, the country has been plagued by a "revolving-door democracy," with civilian governments regularly being replaced by military dictatorships. In fact, no elected government has ever completed its term in office. The military has ruled Pakistan for more years than civilians have, severely stunting democratic institutions. "History shows that dictatorships destroy the social fabric of societies and diminish the capacity of state institutions to function effectively," says Abbas of Harvard.

How, then, can democracy survive? For starters, Pakistan's political parties must become more representative of the nation's diversity, says former State Department official Markey. "Pakistan has elections and aspirations to democracy, but it needs effective, representative political parties for it to grow and prosper," he contends.

For too long Pakistan's major political parties have been dynastic, feudal, family-run and representative of the small ruling elite, say Pakistan analysts. Many are merely "affinity groups of the rich and famous," according to Brookings's Cohen. Real political parties, unlike interest groups or nongovernmental organizations, "will aggregate diverse and even conflicting interests."[39]

Most democracy experts also say a democracy needs an informed, educated populace, newspapers that are free to report what they want and an independent judiciary. No Pakistani politician denies that the country needs a better education system in order for democracy to grow and survive. But those same politicians seem to have done little to help the Pakistanis who cannot read or write — nearly half of the adult population — or the 40 percent of children who don't attend school.

Furthermore, the military inhibits democracy's survival in Pakistan. As an old Pakistani joke goes, "All countries have armies, but here, an army has a country." Although the army is no longer in power, it still has a strong influence on political matters. Experts say Pakistan's government must establish ways it can work with the military without being dominated by it. To foster democracy, "Pakistan needs a policy process that integrates civilian activities with military activities," says Markey.

Although Gen. Kayani assures the government he has no desire to return the military to the "governing business," history makes many Pakistanis skeptical. "To ensure that, the military needs to be contained," says Shaikh, of

Militants from the Tereek Taliban-e-Pakistan group in South Waziristan guard some of the 38 police and security personnel they kidnapped in September. The group has declared war on the Pakistani government. Since then 25 of the hostages have been released.

the Royal Institute of International Affairs. Many experts agree that the military needs to take a back seat while Pakistan finds a workable model of democracy.

"Pakistan has been ruled by military regimes for over half its existence," wrote the Heritage Foundation's Curtis. "The military's pervasive involvement in civilian affairs has stifled the development of civil society and democratic institutions. The time has come to reverse this trend. Pakistan's future stability depends on it."[40]

With few exceptions — such as Pakistan's founder Mohammad Ali Jinnah — the nation's democratic leaders have been less than stellar. Civilian leaders who followed in the wake of military dictator Gen. Mohammad Zia ul-Haq have been especially criticized. "Most Pakistanis believe that post-Zia politicians have been self-seeking, corrupt and unprincipled," wrote Owen Bennett Jones, a BBC journalist and author of *Pakistan: Eye of the Storm*.[41] *The Economist* was even blunter: "In truth, both Miss Bhutto and Mr. [Nawaz] Sharif were lousy prime ministers."[42]

Some of the blame for weak democratic leadership can be laid at the doorstep of autocratic and dictatorial military governments. "Civilian successor governments acquire and retain these powers from the military regime," explains Pakistani political analyst Nawaz. "These mitigate against free-flowing democracy." President Zardari, for example, has retained many

AFP/Getty Images/Chand Kahn

Deadly Taliban Commander Stays in the Shadows

Baitullah Mehsud is linked to scores of suicide attacks in Pakistan.

For someone who has been called "The Newest Enemy No. 1 in the War on Terror," and "al Qaeda's newest triggerman," remarkably little is known about Baitullah Mehsud, the powerful commander of Taliban forces in South Waziristan, part of Pakistan's mountainous and lawless Federally Administered Tribal Areas.[1]

He is said to have planned scores of suicide attacks on government and military targets in Pakistan, and many believe he ordered the Dec. 27 assassination of former Prime Minister Benazir Bhutto. But, according to *Jane's Terrorism and Insurgency News*, although he has become "the most powerful militant commander in Pakistan, he remains a shadowy figure with perhaps a larger-than-life reputation."[2]

After fighting for the Taliban in Afghanistan in the 1990s, the black-bearded jihadist leader first popped up on anti-terrorist radar screens after being promoted to a Taliban command position following the death of militant leader Nek Mohammad, who was killed in a missile attack in June 2004.[3]

Since then, Mehsud's rise to power reflects the transformation of Pakistan into al Qaeda's main battleground and safe haven. In December 2007 he was appointed to head the Pakistan Taliban movement, known as Tereek Taliban-e-Pakistan. Operating under Afghan Taliban commander Jalaluddin Haqqani, Mehsud is believed to command some 20,000 fighters.[4]

Mehsud shuns publicity and refuses to have his photograph taken. During those rare occasions when he gives interviews, he covers his face with a black cloth.[5] He reportedly rarely sleeps in the same bed two nights in a row and travels in a convoy surrounded by armed guards. A Pashtun tribesman, Mehsud was born in the South Waziristan village of Landidog and is said to be in his mid-30s. According to one analyst, Mehsud is "not well educated" but is famous for his political acumen and military skills. His colleagues say he's "a natural leader who has great ability to infuse vitality among his followers."[6]

Mehsud once admitted to an interviewer that he has crossed into Afghanistan to fight foreign troops. It is, he claims, the duty of Muslims to wage jihad against "the infidel forces of America and Britain." As he told the BBC last year, "Only jihad can bring peace to the world."[7]

Last year Mehsud said his aim was to target London and New York City.

powers more associated with a dictator than a democratic leader, such as immunity from prosecution and the power to dissolve Parliament and to select Supreme Court judges.

Zardari also must live down his reputation as "Mr. Ten Percent" — a reference to his alleged involvement in kickback schemes while serving as investment minister during his wife's second term. Another hurdle: Because the president is appointed by the Parliament instead of having to face a popular vote, Zardari, like Musharraf before him, has absolute power without a mandate from the electorate.

He does have determination, however. Referring to the 11 years he spent in jail on various charges (he was never convicted of anything), he has written: "Those years made me a stronger person and hardened my resolve to fight for democracy. I wish I could do it at my wife's side. Now I must do it in my wife's place."[43] Only time will tell if he can nurture democracy in such harsh surroundings.

There may be some within the military as well as militants who do not see democracy as a necessity for Pakistan, but most analysts agree it is a prerequisite for the nation's survival. "Democracy must survive," says American University's Ahmed, "It is crucial to Pakistan's existence."

Ambassador Haqqani is optimistic. "Like all transitions, the transition from one-man rule to a pluralist system will be tough," he said. "But Pakistanis have proven their commitment to the democratic idea after four failed military dictatorships in 60 years."[44]

Perhaps the last words on the importance of democracy's survival in Pakistan should go to the dynamic Bhutto, who gave her life for it. As she reportedly told her son Bilawal, who may one day inherit her mission,

Intelligence sources cite reports of a Mehsud-dispatched terrorist cell recently arrested in Spain as proof of his global ambitions. He and his troops are skilled fighters. In August 2007 they captured more than 250 Pakistani soldiers, who reportedly surrendered without a fight. Mehsud then demanded that the military pull out of the tribal area and the government release 30 imprisoned militants. To emphasize his demands he had three of the soldiers beheaded. President Pervez Musharraf soon released 25 of the jailed militants.

Given Mehsud's penchant for secrecy, it's not surprising that Pakistani papers and television news reports have been full of reports that he was gravely ill, dying or already dead from illnesses ranging from diabetes to typhoid or attacks by the Pakistani military. In October 2008, however, a Taliban spokesman in Pakistan said he was "fit and well."[8]

Apparently Mehsud knows it is only a matter of time before he falls victim to a Pakistan army bullet or a U.S. drone missile. As he reportedly told a Taliban leader, "The Angel of Death is flying over our heads all the time."[9]

Pakistan's top Taliban leader Baitullah Mehsud, center, with back to camera, talks to reporters in South Waziristan. Mehsud reportedly masterminded recent suicide attacks on government and military targets in Pakistan and may have ordered the assassination of former Prime Minister Benazir Bhutto last year.

[1] Sami Yousafzai and Ron Moreau, "Al Qaeda's newest triggerman," *Newsweek*, Jan. 14, 2008.

[2] "Pakistan's Most Wanted," *Jane's Terrorism and Insurgency News*, Feb. 12, 2008.

[3] See David Rohde and Mohammed Khan, "Ex-Fighter for Taliban Dies in Strike in Pakistan," *The New York Times*, June 19, 2004, p. A6.

[4] Syed Shoaib Hasan, "Profile: Baitullah Mehsud," BBC News, Dec. 28, 2007.

[5] "Where is Baitullah Mehsud," *The Nation*, Sept. 28, 2008, www.nation.com.pk/pakistan-news-newspaper-daily-english-online/Regional/Karachi/29-Sep-2008/Where-is-Baitullah-Mehsud.

[6] Sohail Abdul Nasir, "Terrorism Focus: Baitullah Mehsud: South Waziristan Unofficial Amir," Jamestown Foundation, www.jamestown.org, July 5, 2006.

[7] Hasan, *op. cit.*

[8] "Top Pakistan militant not dead," BBC News, Oct. 1, 2008.

[9] Yousafzai and Moreau, *op. cit.*

"Democracy is the best revenge." And just before returning to Pakistan last year, she said, "This is the beginning of a long journey for Pakistan back to democracy, and I hope my going back is a catalyst for change. We must believe that miracles can happen."[45]

Are Pakistan's nuclear weapons secure?

Pakistanis could not believe their eyes. On Feb. 4, 2004, a national hero broke down in tears as he confessed his crime, broadcast on millions of television screens across the nation. But this was no mere politician begging for forgiveness. It was Abdul Qadeer Khan, the Pakistani nuclear scientist who had achieved cult status for his role in creating the nation's first nuclear bomb. "A.Q. Kahn," as he is known, confessed to masterminding and running a global, black-market operation trading in nuclear weapon-making materials.

For 15 years, Kahn had sold designs and technology necessary to manufacture the fuel for nuclear weapons to Iran, North Korea and Libya. He was arrested after the United States discovered a shipment of parts for centrifuges that were believed to have been manufactured in Malaysia to his design and were being shipped from Dubai to Libya.[46] An official of the International Atomic Energy Agency dubbed Khan's operation the "Wal-Mart of private-sector proliferation."[47]

How did Khan carry out his illicit operation for so long? Although he claimed to have received no help from Pakistan's military, few believe he could have acted without its assistance. The day after his tearful confession, President Musharraf pardoned him and put him under house arrest, where he remains to this day.

Khan's global operation caused many to question the safety of Pakistan's nuclear arsenal. With militancy and political and religious unrest threatening the world's only nuclear-armed Islamic nation, one question has special relevance today: Could al Qaeda or another terrorist group gain control of one of Pakistan's nuclear weapons?

"The Pakistanis have an enormous national interest in making their nuclear weapons secure, because they see them as a guarantee against Indian aggression or destruction," says former State Department official Markey. "So they have devoted a lot of resources to safeguard them."

Intelligence sources estimate that Pakistan, which tested its first nuclear weapon in 1998, has an estimated 50-120 nuclear warheads, held in secret locations. Various nuclear components reportedly are stored in heavily guarded underground bunkers at military bases around the country. After the 9/11 terrorist attacks, at the urging of the United States, Pakistan agreed to upgrade the security of its nuclear weapons. The United States has spent almost $100 million on a secret program to help Pakistan secure the weapons, according to *The New York Times*.[48]

"I don't see any indication right now that security of those weapons is in jeopardy, but clearly we are very watchful, as we should be," said Joint Chiefs Chairman Mullen last November.[49]

Harvard's Abbas, who has studied the system, notes, "Experts say the command-and-control system is very advanced. The army has taken the best from the U.S. and the UK." The personnel guarding the facilities reportedly were trained in the United States. In addition, a multilayered system of safeguards surrounds the weapons, and officials in charge are screened for everything from mental instability to having sympathies for al Qaeda or the Taliban.

Pakistan also protects the weapons' integrity by isolating the triggers (the fissile core) from the rest of the weapons. Thus, thieves would have to take over several bunkers to get a complete bomb. "Although the U.S. experts may not have visited the bunkers, because the Pakistanis jealously guard their exact location, the U.S. has offered its most advanced safeguards," says political analyst Nawaz.

However, "There is a concern that pro-Islamist military officers could gain access to the weapons in the future," says Shaikh, at London's Royal Institute of International Affairs. And some experts worry about renegade or rogue scientists helping militants acquire or design a bomb.

There is reason for such concern. In 2001 two Pakistani nuclear scientists were detained on suspicion of passing secrets to the Taliban. One of them, Sultan Bashiruddin Mahmood, had met several times with bin Laden in 2000 and 2001. Bin Laden reportedly asked the deeply conservative Muslim two chilling questions: "How can a nuclear bomb be made? Can you help us make one?" Both meetings occurred before 9/11. Mahmood claims he turned bin Laden down.[50]

Another scenario keeps analysts up at night: Workers inside a nuclear facility smuggle out and sell "fissile" material — the enriched uranium or plutonium needed to build a nuclear bomb. As former U.N. weapons inspector David Albright told *The Washington Post*, "They may look for an opportunity to make a quick buck. You may not be able to get the whole weapon, but maybe you can get the core."[51]

Retired Brig. Gen. Shaukat Qadir, a Pakistani nuclear expert, disagrees. "Both the weapons and the fissile material are accorded the same level of security," he told the BBC. "The material therefore has the same chance of being stolen as the weapons."[52]

Despite all the recent concerns — Khan, the Marriott and World Trade Center bombings, domestic political turmoil and recent militant uprisings — Pakistan claims its weapons are secure.

"I am confident of two things," said former Deputy Director of the CIA John E. McLaughlin, who helped expose Khan's nuclear perfidy. "That the Pakistanis are very serious about securing this material, but also that someone in Pakistan is very intent on getting their hands on it."[53]

BACKGROUND

Early Beginnings

Pakistan's history can be traced back 8,000 years to the Mehgarh settlement in what is now Balochistan. But its roots are more easily followed from the flourishing Indus civilization, which peaked around 2500-1500 B.C. on the banks of the Indus River in what is now Pakistan and India.

Ruins of the civilization's two major cities — Harappa and Mohenjo Daro — can still be seen in Pakistan. This advanced society, which boasted a sophisticated bureaucracy, collapsed around 1500 B.C. — possibly due to catastrophic floods or because the river changed its course — and was replaced by a series of foreign invaders.[54]

The Aryans, whose Vedic beliefs would evolve into Hinduism, came into the region from Central Asia about that time, followed by the Persians, who conquered the Punjab in around 500 BC. Alexander the Great came over the Hindu Kush mountains and took over most of what is now Pakistan in 326 BC. The region changed hands frequently, becoming part of the Mauryan Empire, then falling to Greeks from Bactria, Scythians from Afghanistan, Parthians, the Kushans, Guptas and the Huns, who invaded the region from their base in central Asia in the 5th century.[55]

Islam arrived via Muslim traders in the early 8th century. By the 11th century Muslims invaded Pakistan from Persia, and eventually a Muslim kingdom was established along the Indus Valley. The Mughals — under fabled rulers Babur, Akbar, Shah Jahan and Aurangzeb — dominated the subcontinent during the 16th and 17th centuries. Remnants of their artistic legacy can be seen today in the Taj Mahal in India and numerous examples in Pakistan.

Eventually, the Mughal Empire weakened, and local rulers replaced its rulers. Persians, Afghans, Sikhs and others controlled the region that is modern Pakistan. Officially, the Mughals were finally toppled in 1857, when the British ousted their last ruler, Bahdur Shah II, who had been controlled by the British East India Company. By the early 20th century the British, thanks to inroads first made by the company, controlled all of what is now Pakistan and India or, as they dubbed it, "British India."

British educational reforms exacerbated already strained relations between the Hindus and Muslims in the region. While Hindus saw school attendance as a way to advance within the colonial system, most Muslims favored their own schools. Then, as more and more Hindus earned jobs in business and government, the Muslims — many of whom were working as farmers and laborers — began to feel disenfranchised.

Not wanting to be left out in a growing bid for autonomy from the British and wanting to make sure their rights were secured, Muslims in 1906 formed the All India Muslim League to balance the Hindu-dominated India National Congress Party. Eventually, inspired by poet and philosopher Allama Mohammed Iqbal, a movement for a Muslim state took hold. By 1940 the Muslim League, headed by Muhammad Ali Jinnah, was demanding a separate state for Muslims in the Muslim-majority areas of northwestern and northeastern India. The name, "Pakistan" was chosen because it means "land of the pure" in Urdu, and its letters stand for the states it would include: Punjab, the Afghan States (NWFP), Kashmir, Sind and Tan (for Balochistan).

But when the British and Indians rejected the plan for Pakistan's independence (both were reluctant to divide the subcontinent), violence broke out between Hindus and Muslims. Britain finally agreed to partition the sub-continent in 1947, and a mass migration involving nearly 20 million people ensued — with Hindus and Sikhs heading east and Muslims heading west to their new homelands. More than half a million were killed in religious-based violence in the process. On Aug. 14, 1947, Pakistan declared independence, as did India a day later.

As the etymology of its name suggests, Pakistan is a complex mix of ethnic groups. The Punjabis comprise the largest ethnic group followed by the Pashtuns, Sindhis, Saraikis, Muhajirs (Muslim migrants from India) and the Balochs. The Punjabis are considered the most powerful, with Punjab being the richest and most populous province. While the country is ethnically diverse, it is religiously homogeneous: 95 percent Muslim.

Quest for Democracy

Shortly after independence, India and Pakistan went to war over the ownership of the states of Jammu and Kashmir — on Pakistan's northeastern border with India — which was 85 percent Muslim, but whose former Hindu ruler had decided to join India during the partition. The United Nations interceded and brokered a cease-fire in 1948, but both India and Pakistan retained control over portions of Kashmir. The two nations have been battling over control ever since, a feud that has blocked closer relations and even led in part to both countries obtaining nuclear arsenals. (*See map and story, p. 194.*)

The Kashmir dispute remains highly sensitive. "Obtaining justice for Muslim Kashmiris living in the India-administered parts of the state has been a central goal of Pakistan's foreign and security policy for five decades," wrote Cohen of Brookings. "Pakistan has tried diplomatic, military and low-level military pressure on

India to hold a plebiscite (as recommended in several U.N. resolutions) or to negotiate a change in the status quo, all to no avail."[56]

With independence, the question of whether Pakistan should become a democracy or an Islamic theocracy was hotly debated. Instead of choosing a strictly secular democratic or purely Islamic model, early leaders tried to blend the two, leaving many to wonder: "Was Pakistan a Muslim state or a state in which Muslims live?" Like the Kashmir problem, the uncertainty has caused repercussions throughout Pakistan's short history.[57]

Jinnah seemed to contradict his earlier democratic yearnings in 1948, when he summarily dismissed the Congress-led government of North-West Frontier Province and dictated to the Bengali-speaking residents of East Pakistan that Urdu would be the nation's official language. Both decisions would have serious consequences.

In 1953, after Jinnah's death, Governor-General Ghulam Muhammad dismissed the country's first civilian government. It was the first of many such upheavals and set in motion Pakistan's destructive cycle of democratic civilian governments replaced by military dictatorships. In 1954 the Supreme Court justified Muhammad's actions with the "theory of necessity" — which has been used by the judiciary to justify "nearly every dismissal of a civilian government and every military takeover" since then, wrote BBC correspondent M Ilyas Khan.[58]

In 1956 Pakistan became the Islamic Republic of Pakistan. But after two years of civilian rule, Gen. Mohammed Ayub Khan ousted the civilian government. Khan would be the first in a long line of military leaders to command the country. The military would seize power again in 1969 under Gen. Agha Muhammad Yahya Khan and in 1977, when Gen. Muhammad Zia ul-Haq ousted Zulfikar Ali Bhutto. In 1999 Gen. Musharraf overthrew Muhammad Nawaz Sharif, who had been elected for the second time in 1997.

The army's fondness for governing follows a recurring pattern. First, the army warns the citizenry, which it regards as incompetent or foolish, that the government is not functioning properly, wrote the Brookings Institution's Cohen. "Second, a crisis leads to army intervention, which is followed by the third step: attempts to 'straighten out' Pakistan, often by introducing major constitutional changes. Fourth, the army, faced with growing civilian discontent, 'allows' civilians back into

office; and fifth, the army reasserts itself behind a façade of civilian government, and the cycle repeats itself."[59]

Although the army held power throughout the 1960s, a military failure eventually ushered in a civilian government. For years Bengali speakers in East Pakistan had been feeling disenfranchised by what they saw as Islamabad's lack of recognition. After the December 1970 election, disgruntled East Pakistanis won a majority of seats in Parliament and sought full autonomy. When negotiations on a new political arrangement failed, the Pakistani army cracked down in March 1971. A harsh martial law was imposed, and many East Pakistanis were killed; millions fled to India. A bitter insurgency began, and ultimately in December 1971 India intervened militarily. Outgunned and outmanned, 90,000 Pakistani soldiers surrendered after two weeks of fighting, and East Pakistan became independent Bangladesh.

India's actions left deep wounds. "India's decision to invade East Pakistan in support of the Bengali independence movement inflicted on Pakistan a humiliation from which it has still not recovered," wrote the BBC's Jones. "India's victory left a wound that festers to this day."[60]

The loss also propelled a civilian government, led by President Zulfikar Bhutto, into power. But six years later the military ousted Bhutto; he was convicted of ordering the murder of a political opponent (a charge many say was untrue) and was executed in 1979. The next civilian government came to power in 1988, and two parties shared rule for the next 10 years — a rare, 10-year democratic interregnum led by Benazir Bhutto, the daughter of the late president, and Pakistan Muslim League-N leader Sharif. Each served two terms. Pakistan would not see its next civilian government until 2008, after Benazir Bhutto's assassination.

But even though the military was officially out of power for a decade, from 1988-1998, it did not relinquish control of the government. Pakistan's civilian rule is usually the result of "a masterful manipulation of the political stage," with the military and intelligence agencies playing a major role in "rigging polls, underwriting political parties and dismissing prime ministers," according to political analyst Seth Kaplan, author of *Fixing Fragile States*.[61]

During the 1980s, the U.S. Central Intelligence Agency worked closely with the Pakistan intelligence services, funneling up to $3 billion worth of weapons to Afghan fighters, called mujahedin, to help them oust the Soviets.

CHRONOLOGY

1940-1950s *Pakistan becomes independent; constitution adopted. The first of many military dictatorships declares martial law.*

1947 Pakistan gains independence, with Muhammad Ali Jinnah — leader of the All India Muslim League — as governor-general. First Indo-Pakistan war over Kashmir begins.

1948 Jinnah dies.

1951 The nation's first prime minister, Liaquat Ali Khan, is assassinated; Governor-General Khawaja Nazimuddin succeeds him.

1956 The first constitution is adopted, declaring Pakistan the world's first Islamic republic; Governor-General Iskander Mirza becomes Pakistan's first president.

1958 Mirza is sent into exile and Gen. Mohammed Ayub Khan assumes presidency after a military coup.

1960s *Pakistan goes to war with India over Kashmir for second time; martial law is declared.*

1965 Second Indo-Pakistan war over Kashmir lasts for six weeks.

1969 Gen. Agha Muhammad Yahya Khan becomes president.

1970s *Pakistan goes to war with India again; East Pakistan secedes; martial law is declared again.*

1971 Civil war erupts after East Pakistan tries to secede; Pakistan goes to war with India; East Pakistan becomes Bangladesh. . . . President Khan resigns; former Foreign Minister Zulfiqar Ali Bhutto becomes president.

1973 A new constitution is adopted; Bhutto resigns presidency to become prime minister.

1977 Gen. Muhammad Zia ul-Haq overthrows Bhutto, proclaims martial law.

1979 Bhutto is hanged for ordering the assassination of a political rival.

1980s *With U.S. aid, Pakistan supports the Northern Alliance's eight-year struggle to expel Soviets from Afghanistan.*

1988 Zia dies in plane crash. . . . Bhutto, 37, daughter of Zulfiqar Ali, becomes Pakistan's first female prime minister.

1990s *Nawaz Sharif becomes prime minister. Gen. Pervez Musharraf takes power after military coup.*

1990 Bhutto's government is dismissed; Sharif, leader of the Pakistan Muslim League, becomes prime minister.

1993 Bhutto becomes prime minister again. She is dismissed three years later.

1997 Sharif becomes prime minister again.

1998 Pakistan tests its first nuclear weapon.

1999 Musharraf overthrows Sharif in a military coup. Bhutto and her husband are sentenced to five years in prison for alleged money laundering; the convictions are set aside in 2001.

2000-Present *Military returns to power. U.S. invades Afghanistan after 9/11 terror attacks; fleeing terrorists settle in Pakistan's tribal areas. Musharraf resigns; Bhutto is assassinated; elections held.*

2004 Nuclear scientist A.Q. Khan confesses to international nuclear weapons trading; Musharraf pardons him.

2005 Earthquake kills up to 80,000 people in northern Pakistan.

2007 Musharraf removes chief justice, sparking huge demonstrations by lawyers; Musharraf declares state of emergency. . . . 100 people die when army attacks Red Mosque in Islamabad; Bhutto returns from exile and is assassinated.

2008 Musharraf resigns; Bhutto's widower Asif Ali Zardari becomes president. Islamabad Marriott Hotel is attacked by terrorists. Terrorists, allegedly from Pakistan, kill 173 people in Mumbai, India.

Truck Convoy Sparks Hope in Kashmir

Reopening trade route links Pakistani and Indian sectors.

A convoy of 16 trucks — each piled high with apples, walnuts, spices, honey and other items — recently rumbled west across the "Peace Bridge" from the India-controlled sector of Kashmir into the Pakistani sector. Onlookers waved banners and cheered the smiling drivers. After six decades of hostility in Kashmir, the two nations had finally re-opened trade links.

"Today marks the beginning of the dismantling of the border," said Mubeen Shah, president of the Kashmir Chamber of Commerce and Industries, reflecting the hopes of many. "I am sure this trade will grow and help bring peace in the region."[1]

India and Pakistan have been fighting for control of the mountainous, rugged Himalayan region of Kashmir ever since Pakistan was partitioned from India in 1947. Muslim Pakistanis saw the mostly Muslim state as logically theirs; India claimed it for its Hindu populace because it had been ruled by a Hindu maharaja who chose to join India after partition. On April 21, 1948, the United Nations Security Council, via Resolution 47, called for a national referendum on Kashmir's future. Pakistan was willing, but India has continued to object.[2]

The 60-year-long battle for Kashmir — punctuated by two additional wars — has impeded political and economic relations between India and Pakistan and made life for Kashmiris intolerable. Pakistan occupies about one-third of the region, and India occupies most of the rest, with China holding a small area. The so-called 463-mile long Line of Control (LOC) running through the Himalayas separates the Pakistani and Indian sectors.

While the 1948 war between India and Pakistan initially divided Kashmir, they again fought over the region in 1965. A U.N.-negotiated cease-fire ended that war. But rugged Kashmir has rarely been peaceful for long, and the two went to war again in 1971.

Pakistan wants control of Kashmir not just because of its Muslim population. The region also contains the headwaters of several key rivers that flow through Pakistan's farming regions. India doesn't want to lose face and fears that if Kashmir is allowed to secede, other Indian states could follow suit.

Since 1989 a growing Islamist separatist movement against Indian rule in Kashmir has added fuel to the

AP Photo/Mukhtar Khan

For the first time in six decades, trade between India and Pakistan resumes in the Himalayan region of Kashmir on Oct. 21. A convoy of trucks festooned with flags and decorations and laden with fruit, honey, garments and spices crosses the fortified frontier.

long-simmering conflict. While some of the separatists seek independence, others want Kashmir united with Pakistan. Tens of thousands of lives have been lost as Kashmiri Muslims — joined by Islamic militants with backing from Pakistan and others — have tried to force the Indians out of Kashmir. India claims Pakistan supports the insurgents, calling its aid "cross-border terrorism."

Kashmiri militants have attacked India on numerous occasions. In December 1999, a group hijacked an Indian airliner and a year later attacked Indian citizens inside New Delhi's Red Fort. In December 2001 terrorists said to be sympathetic to Kashmiri separatists attacked the Indian Parliament.[3]

Although it was unclear who was responsible for the horrific terrorist attacks in Mumbai last week, many claimed it was organized by Lashkar-e-Taiba, the largest Islamic separatist group in Kashmir, also said to be responsible for the 2001 assault on India's Parliament.[4]

In 1999 Gen. Pervez Musharraf of Pakistan sent troops into Indian-occupied Kashmir and took control of several hundred square miles, including the mountainous, mostly Muslim region of Kargil. Occupying the high, fortress-like region would give Pakistan an offensive advantage over the Indian army. In response, India flooded Kargil with troops. Suddenly, what had been a regional, traditional border spat looked like it might escalate into a terrifying nuclear confrontation as the two nuclear powers battled one another.

When the United States learned Pakistan was preparing covertly to deploy nuclear weapons against India, President Bill Clinton insisted that its ally retreat from the region and cancel all plans to use the weapons against India. In early July, after Pakistani Prime Minister Nawaz Sharif asked Clinton to intervene on Pakistan's behalf against India, Clinton told him he would but sternly warned Sharif that he was "messing with nuclear war." Sharif agreed to remove Pakistan's forces from the disputed region.[5]

Despite the pullback, Clinton famously described Kashmir as "the most dangerous place on earth." That was borne out in May 2002 when India accused Pakistan of backing Islamic militant incursions into the Indian section of Kashmir. The two powers amassed nearly a million troops on their borders, and Pakistan again rattled its nuclear sword by test firing nuclear-capable missiles. Indian Defense Minister George Fernandes responded by declaring, "India can survive a nuclear attack but Pakistan cannot." Both sides eventually backed down.[6]

In 2004, Pakistan and India entered into ongoing peace negotiations. Among the sticking points: India wants the Line of Control to become the official border, but Pakistan lays claim to additional Muslim-majority areas. Many insurgents reject both claims and want independence.

The cross-border truck convoys grew out of an agreement by Pakistan's newly elected President Asif Ali Zardari and Indian Prime Minister Manmohan Singh during a recent U.N. meeting.[7]

Does the reopened trade route signal a thaw? "The roots of the Kashmir conflict remain; Kashmiris seek self-determination; India and Pakistan each claim to be the rightful owners," writes Rajon Manon, professor of International relations at Lehigh University and author of *The End of Alliances*. "But commerce that continues and expands can create mutual gains that widen benefits and build trust. And trust is what's needed for any advances — however incremental — on the Kashmir dispute. That's why those trucks are so important."[8]

Disputed Kashmir

Pakistan and India have fought three wars over Kashmir, a beautiful, mountainous region the size of Kansas located between the two nuclear-armed countries, and Muslim militants from Kashmir have made repeated terrorist attacks inside India. Many regard Kashmir as the globe's most likely nuclear flashpoint.

Source: Indo American Kashmir Forum

[1] Sudip Mazumdar, "Some Thawing of Relations in Kashmir," *Newsweek,* Oct. 23, 2008, http://blog.newsweek.com/blogs/ov/archive/2008/10/23/some-thawing-of-relations-in-kashmir.aspx.

[2] Owen Bennett Jones, *Pakistan: The Eye of the Storm* (2003), pp. 56-70.

[3] See Neil MacFarquhar, "3rd Attempt to Free Pakistani Militant," *The New York Times,* Dec. 29, 1999, p. A14; Barry Bearak, "Gunmen Kill 3 at Garrison in New Delhi's Center," *The New York Times,* Dec. 23, 2000, p. A5; and Rama Lakshmi, "Indians Blame Attacks On Pakistan-Based Group," *The Washington Post,* Dec. 15, 2001, p. A23.

[4] "Mumbai probe focuses on Pakistan-based militants" Agence France-Presse, Dec. 1, 2008, www.google.com/hostednews/afp/article/ALeqM5hSh98EQFTH33W9oGoMskBm0x2ZeA.

[5] "Pakistan 'prepared nuclear strike,'" BBC News, May 16, 2002, http://news.bbc.co.uk/2/hi/south_asia/1989886.stm.

[6] Michael Richardson, "India and Pakistan are not 'imprudent' on nuclear option; Q&A/George Fernandes," *The International Herald Tribune,* June 3, 2002.

[7] Somini Sengupta, "India and Pakistan open Kashmir trade route," *The New York Times,* Oct. 22, 2008, www.nytimes.com/2008/10/22/world/asia/22kashmir.html.

[8] Rajan Menon, "Progress in Kashmir," *Los Angeles Times,* Oct. 25, 2008, www.latimes.com/news/opinion/commentary/la-oe-menon25-2008oct25,0,809573.story.

One of the militant anti-Soviet leaders to receive U.S. funds was bin Laden. While up to 1 million Afghans died during the struggle, nearly 3 million — including many Taliban and al Qaeda fighters — fled to neighboring Pakistan's border areas, where many have remained. The Soviets, who had invaded Afghanistan on Christmas Eve in 1979, were finally expelled in late 1989.[62]

After that, the Afghan communists held onto power for three more years, and were finally ousted in 1992. Then a series of warlords — many corrupt and oppressive — seized power until challenged and overthrown by the next one, paving the way for a strong, religiously conservative military force to come in and take over the country.

Taliban Gathers Strength

It is some of the most inhospitable terrain in the world. Known officially as the Federally Administered Tribal Areas (FATA), the mountainous, mostly lawless stretch of land between Afghanistan and Pakistan's North-West Frontier Province is home to some of the world's most fiercely independent fighters, including the tough, much-feared Pashtun warriors who have resisted rule by outsiders — and their own government — for centuries. Today, it is now home for a newer, equally notorious fighter: the Taliban.

The Taliban (which means "religious students") were Pashtun students educated in Pakistani madrassas, or Muslim religious schools, who first rose to prominence in 1994 after being assigned by Pakistan security forces to protect truck convoys in Afghanistan. They proved to be capable fighters. Within two years, with the help of the Pakistanis, they had kicked out the Kabul government and controlled much of Afghanistan.

The Taliban set up a repressive Islamic government headed by Mullah Mohammed Omar, the group's spiritual and military leader, which enforced strict Islamic law, or sharia, and banned music and television, which they considered "non-Islamic" and "frivolous."

Following the Afghan war against the Soviets, bin Laden resettled in Sudan. But in 1996 — under pressure from Egypt, Saudi Arabia and the United States — Sudan expelled him, and he returned to Afghanistan. The Taliban offered him and his al Qaeda fighters a refuge, and allowed him to set up training camps. He seemed to have found a safe haven in Afghanistan.

However, all this changed after 9/11, when the United States demanded that the Taliban turn over bin Laden and his followers. When the Taliban refused, the United States began bombing Afghanistan and supporting the Northern Alliance resistance movement. By December 2001 the Taliban, bin Laden and his followers all had fled to the mountainous border region between Afghanistan and Pakistan.[63]

Since then, the Taliban has regrouped, operating training camps in the Pakistan regions of North and South Waziristan and Balochistan. Beginning in 2003 they began counter-attacking against Afghan, U.S. and NATO forces in Afghanistan. Their presence also influenced the build-up of a home-grown "Pakistani Taliban" movement, comprised mainly of local Pashtuns sympathetic to Taliban causes, leading to the area being nicknamed Talibanistan.[64]

Although the government has consistently denied that it aids the Taliban, a recent RAND Corporation report accused Pakistani intelligence agents and paramilitary forces of helping train the insurgents and informing them about U.S. troop movements in Afghanistan. The think tank identified several insurgent groups that, along with the Taliban, "regularly ship weapons, ammunition and supplies into Afghanistan from Pakistan, and a number of suicide bombers have come from Afghan refugee camps based in Pakistan."[65]

The Taliban continued to launch attacks into Afghanistan. Indeed, 2006 was the deadliest year of fighting since the 2001 war. In 2005 there were 25 suicide bombings in Afghanistan; in 2006 there were 139.[66] Throughout the spring, Taliban militants swept into southern Afghanistan, launching attacks on Afghan and U.S. troops. That September, Musharraf brokered a peace agreement with the Pakistani Taliban, which critics claimed offered the militants a safe haven.

But once Musharraf held up his end of the deal by scaling back military operations in the tribal areas, suicide bombings and cross-border raids into Afghanistan picked up. "The state has withdrawn and ceded this territory," said Samina Ahmed of the Brussels-based International Crisis Group. "[The Taliban] have been given their own little piece of real estate."[67]

With the Taliban and al Qaeda fighters safely ensconced in Pakistan's tribal areas, terrorism now threatens to infiltrate Pakistan proper. Recently, "Militants began moving out of the FATA and into the rest of Pakistan, taking control of the towns and villages in North-West Frontier Province. Militants began attacking Pakistani police and soldiers," wrote *New York Times* correspondent Dexter Filkins. "Inside the FATA, Mehsud was forming the Tehreek Taliban-e-Pakistan, an umbrella party of some 40 Taliban groups that claimed as its goal the domination of Pakistan. Suddenly, the Taliban was not merely a group of militants who were useful in extending Pakistan's influence into Afghanistan. They were a threat to Pakistan itself."[68]

Within a relatively short time, homegrown terrorists would be blamed for both the assassination of Bhutto, the Marriott Hotel suicide bombing and the attacks in Mumbai, India. The war being waged by the Taliban, bin Laden, al Qaeda and others was getting deadlier and deadlier. As Pakistan's Interior Minister Mali would say shortly after the Marriott tragedy, "All roads lead to FATA."

CURRENT SITUATION

Fighting Intensifies

Since August, remotely operated U.S. Predator "drone" missiles have been striking inside Pakistan. At least 20 attacks have occurred, sometimes in conjunction with raids by American commandos on the ground.[69]

For instance, on Sept. 3 helicopter-borne Special Forces soldiers killed 20 people in a raid on a suspected militant hideout in South Waziristan.[70] Soon afterwards, a U.S. drone launched five missiles at a compound thought to belong to Afghan Taliban commander Jalaluddin Haqqani. Although it missed Haqqani, it allegedly killed several al Qaeda operatives, along with women and children.

Meanwhile, the United States continues to pressure the Pakistani army to confront the militants more aggressively. The Pakistanis have been battling the insurgents in remote places like Bajaur, Dera Adam Khel and Swat.[71] In late October the army claimed to have captured Loi Sam in the Bajaur tribal region, killing 1,500 militants after a two-month battle. The town had been described as a "mega-sanctuary" for militants.[72]

When confronted, the militants fight back with intimidation, weapons and suicide bombers. Since July 2007 more than 90 suicide attacks on civilian, military and Western targets have killed nearly 1,200 people.[73]

With battles raging around them, many residents have fled. In Bajaur alone, more than 200,000 people have abandoned their homes, cattle and crops for makeshift camps near Peshawar or in Afghanistan.[74] "Every day, their lives are threatened by the pounding [Pakistani] jets that sweep into the valleys on bombing runs and by the clattering helicopter gunships that the Pakistan military is using to spearhead its assaults," reported London's *Independent*. "The people sitting in the dust are the so-called 'collateral damage' of Pakistan's own war on terror."[75]

In other efforts to appease Washington, the Pakistan government recently banned the umbrella militant group Tehreek Taliban-e-Pakistan based in South Waziristan and headed by Taliban warlord Mehsud, who is blamed for planning numerous suicide attacks. (*See sidebar, p. 188.*)[76]

However, a recent move to encourage tribal militias — lashkars — to fight the Taliban and al Qaeda has been "far from promising," according to *The New York Times*.[77] The lashkars are lightly armed and are vulnerable to suicide bombers. In early November, a suicide bomber killed 23 lashkars as they prepared to attack Taliban hideouts near Bajaur. Several weeks earlier, more than 50 Bajaur tribesmen were killed while discussing plans to attack the Taliban.[78]

Without military backing the lashkars have little hope of effectively combating the militants. A case in point: After being promised military backing, some men in Hilal Kel, a village in a Taliban-dominated region of Bajaur, formed a lashkar. The Taliban responded by bringing in 600 reinforcements from Afghanistan, a resident told *The New York Times*.[79]

"The Taliban sowed terror by kidnapping and executing four tribal leaders of the lashkar, leaving their bodies on the roadside, their throats slit," wrote *Times* reporters Jane Perlez and Pir Zubair Shah. Villagers then fled or surrendered.[80]

Opposing the U.S.

Some U.S. experts remain unconvinced that Pakistan is committed to confronting the militants. Many, for example, have accused Pakistan's Inter Services Intelligence (ISI) agency of supporting al Qaeda and Taliban operatives. Last summer, for instance, CIA Deputy Director Stephen Kappes reportedly handed Islamabad evidence that ISI officials were involved in the Taliban's suicide bombing of the Indian embassy in the Afghan capital of Kabul on July 7, 2008, in which 54 people were killed.[81]

Pakistan has begun recruiting tribal militias — lashkars — to fight Islamic extremists, but the militias are lightly armed and vulnerable to suicide bombers, so the results have been disappointing. The Taliban have responded by bringing in reinforcements from Afghanistan and executing four tribal leaders as a warning to others.

Meanwhile, some experts are pushing the United States to step up its cross-border incursions into Pakistan, despite protests from Pakistan over the forays. "Decisions to take decisive action will be Pakistani, but the U.S. should make it openly clear that the U.S. cannot wait for Pakistan to make such decisions and will have to treat Pakistani territory as a combat zone if Pakistan does not act," wrote Anthony Cordesman, a defense expert at the Center for Strategic and International Studies in Washington. "Pakistan cannot both claim sovereignty and allow hostile non-state actors to attack Afghanistan, U.S., and NATO . . . forces from its soil. Pakistan must understand that use of [unpiloted aircraft], limited Special Forces and hot-pursuit/defense operations in Pakistani territory will continue until Pakistan takes action to secure its own territory and borders."[82]

Such sentiments help to wedge President Zardari's infant government even more firmly between a rock and a hard place. "America has to realize its actions and rhetoric are increasing anti-American sentiment among the Pakistanis," explains Harvard's Abbas. Indeed, in a stern signal to Washington, Pakistan's Parliament in October passed a resolution calling for dialog with militants and ending military action against them.

Raza Rabbani, a member of the ruling Pakistan Peoples Party, said, "We need to prioritize our own national-security interests. As far as the U.S. is concerned, the message that has gone with this resolution will definitely ring alarm bells, *vis-à-vis* their policy of bulldozing Pakistan."[83]

Another member of Parliament was even blunter. "Our country is burning," he told *The Guardian*. "We don't want Bush to put oil on the fire. We want to extinguish this fire."[84]

The next week Pakistan protested to U.S. Ambassador Anne W. Patterson about U.S. missile strikes in the border region. "It was emphasized that such attacks were a violation of Pakistan's sovereignty and should be stopped immediately," said a Foreign Ministry spokesman.[85] And when Gen. David Petraeus, new head of the U.S. Central Command, recently met Pakistani officials, he heard widespread criticism of the U.S. missile strikes.

"Continuing drone attacks on our territory, which result in loss of precious lives and property, are counterproductive and difficult to explain by a democratically elected government," President Zardari said after meeting with Petraeus. "It is creating a credibility gap."[86]

As the gap widens, pressure mounts on Zardari to distance himself and his government from the United States. Meanwhile, Sharif, a former prime minister and head of the second-biggest party in Pakistan's coalition, pulled out of the coalition and stepped up verbal attacks on the United States. Thus, Zardari's fragile, new democracy must now fend off the United States, the opposition, an enraged populace and militants.

Ahmed, the former high commissioner to Great Britain now at American University, echoes many in Pakistan when he says the United States must change its military policy. "Bombing tribal people has not solved anything. If the United States carries on as it has, it risks losing Pakistan. And if you lose Pakistan, you lose Afghanistan, and your war on terror collapses!"

Obama Optimism

After Barack Obama's inauguration on Jan. 20, his administration should reassess Pakistan's strategic importance, says Seth Jones, a terrorism expert at the RAND Corporation think tank. "Pakistan should be No. 1," Jones contends. "The most serious homeland threat to the United Sates from abroad comes from militant groups operating in Pakistan."[87]

Moreover, having sent at least $11.2 billion in overt aid to Pakistan since 9/11, most of which was for military spending, experts agree the United States should provide more help for Pakistan's people and infrastructure.[88] Many see a pending proposal — co-sponsored by newly elected

Should the United States pursue militants inside Pakistan?

YES

Malou Innocent
Foreign Policy Analyst,
Cato Institute

Written for *CQ Global Researcher,* November 2008

Militants use Pakistan's lawless, highly porous western frontier with Afghanistan, known as the Federally Administered Tribal Areas (FATA), to slip into and out of Afghanistan and attack U.S. and NATO troops. To complicate matters, FATA lies within the territorial confines of Pakistan but remains formally outside of its constitution. Thus, U.S. policy makers must carefully consider how to approach this unpoliced region without further destabilizing a nuclear-armed, Muslim-majority, front-line state in America's "war on terror."

Ideally, the United States, NATO and Pakistan should work together to meet shared challenges in the region. But over the past several years, Pakistan's army has proven unable — and at times unwilling — to uproot militant havens and has lost thousands of soldiers in confrontations with insurgents. In FATA, many soldiers lack proper training, equipment and communication gear, rendering vulnerable villages even more susceptible to militant attacks.

Even worse, Islamabad and Washington are on different pages strategically. Elements of the Inter Services Intelligence Directorate (ISI), Pakistan's national intelligence agency, still support the Afghan Taliban. The ISI supported pro-Taliban insurgents allegedly responsible for the July 7, 2008, bombing of the Indian Embassy in Kabul, according to U.S. intelligence. And many Pakistani defense planners admit their country has turned a blind eye to the Taliban's depredations in order to use them as a proxy force against the Afghan government, which they say is pro-India.

Thus, the United States has no choice but to attack militants inside Pakistan. A judicious approach would be to employ low-level, clear-and-hold operations along the Afghan-Pakistan frontier to limit cross-border movement and respond aggressively to attacks against troops and civilians.

It might even be necessary to deploy up to a few hundred U.S. Special Forces personnel within Pakistan as part of a larger operation in support of local Pakistani security forces — but nothing more. Large-scale military action would further radicalize FATA's indigenous population and push wavering tribes further into the Taliban camp.

Meanwhile, on a strategic level, America should engage in vigorous regional diplomacy with all countries surrounding land-locked Afghanistan. Overall, U.S. policy toward Pakistan is complicated and imperfect. But achieving success in Afghanistan requires a judicious campaign against militant sanctuaries inside Pakistan.

NO

Shuja Nawaz
Political analyst, author, Crossed Swords:
Pakistan, Its Army, and the Wars Within

Written for *CQ Global Researcher,* November 2008

Pakistan is in the midst of a series of crises. A fledgling civilian government is trying to gain control of the country and its army after eight years of military rule. Its economy is in free fall, with depleted reserves, roaring inflation and shortages of power and food. Increasing militancy threatens security, especially in the tribal areas along the Afghan border, which has become a base for attacks on U.S. forces in Afghanistan.

The continuation of unilateral U.S. drone attacks on militant targets inside the Pakistani tribal belt has already angered the local population and embarrassed the government and army. It exposes Pakistan's inability to protect its own borders or to rein in the United States, a country with whom Pakistan has chosen to ally itself in the so-called war on terror. If anything could help coalesce opposition to the shaky civilian regime and perhaps upend it, it would be yet another incursion by U.S. forces against militant targets inside Pakistan.

By trying to draw Pakistan into fighting the war on U.S. terms, the United States has undermined Pakistan's effectiveness. Rather than giving Pakistani forces the intelligence and capacity to undertake military operations, the United States has been tardy in giving Pakistan the wherewithal to fight the insurgents. And it has taken it upon itself to execute a policy of hot pursuit into Pakistan to defend its own troops in Afghanistan. While this policy may have achieved some results, the process has alienated a non-NATO ally and its population.

The United States could help control militancy inside Pakistan by speeding up the supply of modern, night-vision goggles and helicopters to Pakistani forces on the border so they can better track and interdict militants hiding or traveling in or out of Afghanistan. And it could collaborate more closely on intelligence, allowing Pakistanis themselves to fight militancy inside their own country.

To underpin these military relationships, the United States needs to accelerate the flow of economic assistance to Pakistan, to allow it to recover from the effects of global inflation. These funds could help provide employment, health care and better education to the Pakistanis, especially the impoverished 3.5 million in the border region that the militants call home. Attacking the roots of militancy in a fragile democracy is better than bombing it at will.

Vice President Joseph Biden and Sen. Richard Lugar — to commit $1.5 billion per year in non-military spending as an excellent first step.

During his campaign for president, Sen. Obama expressed support for the Biden-Lugar aid bill, which he co-sponsored, and most analysts think there is enough bipartisan support for it to pass during the next Congress. If there is one stumbling block, it may be financial: Will the United States be willing to spend the funds the bill has earmarked for aid?

"We need to redefine the terms of engagement between Pakistan and the United States," said former Pakistani Ambassador to the United States Tariq Fatmi. "Our importance should not be confined merely to the war on terror." Fatmi said many believe Obama will move the United States away from policies pursued by the Bush administration.[89]

Brookings's Cohen agrees. "Washington needs to rethink its approach to Pakistan," he said.[90] In fact, the new administration is expected to reexamine U.S. policy toward both Afghanistan and Pakistan. After deciding on the size of the U.S. military buildup in Afghanistan and how to strengthen that government, the Obama administration also must decide how to deal with militant sanctuaries inside Pakistan and whether or not it can reconcile with the Taliban and help to stabilize Pakistan.

As former Assistant Secretary of State Richard C. Holbrooke recently wrote in *Foreign Affairs*, "Getting policy toward Islamabad right will be absolutely critical for the next administration — and very difficult. . . . The continued deterioration of the tribal areas poses a threat not only to Afghanistan but also to Pakistan's new secular democracy, and it presents the next president with an extraordinary challenge."[91]

The Center for American Progress recently published a report that summarizes the need for a revamped U.S. policy toward Pakistan: "A fundamental strategic shift in U.S. policy on Pakistan should occur away from a narrow focus on military and intelligence cooperation. Pakistan's problems will not be solved by military means alone. Long-term stability in Pakistan depends not only on curtailing extremism and militancy in Pakistan but on strengthening Pakistan's economy and democracy and on reducing tensions between Pakistan and its neighbors."[92]

"Pakistanis now eagerly await change in Washington's policy towards their country," wrote Nasim Zehra, a fellow at Harvard's Asia Center and a former special envoy from Pakistan on U.N. reforms. "With Barack Obama in the White House and a democratic government in Pakistan, they look forward to greater cooperation within the framework of genuine dialogue, greater trust and mutual respect."

Especially among Pakistanis in North-West Frontier Province, there is hope for a lessening of conflict and, in turn, fewer drone missile attacks. As Zehra noted, "Perhaps as a sign of this region's clamor for peace, last month a group of young students in Peshawar collected $200 to contribute to Obama's election campaign. Their message, broadcast throughout Pakistan, was: 'We are sending Obama this money for his campaign so that when he becomes president he will not attack our homeland.' "[93]

OUTLOOK

Doomsday Scenarios

Pakistan is often described as "fragile." But these days that may be too optimistic. Buffeted by Islamic uprisings, a weakened government, a faltering economy and pressure from abroad, Pakistan faces an uncertain future.

"There are few other countries where you could say things could so totally implode or turn out OK, because we are not seeing any pattern yet," says former U.S. State Department official Markey. "There's so much uncertainty."

The "Whither Pakistan?" question has been vexing experts for decades as the nation has veered between "emerging democracy" and "failed state." Analysts sketch out three possible scenarios for Pakistan's future.

In the first, democracy survives with an improved balance between the military and civilian sectors. More capable civilian leaders emerge and Pakistan, helped by the international community, becomes more integrated with the global economy, especially with neighboring India and Afghanistan. "The situation in Afghanistan may change and lead to discussions with the militants; a strong center could emerge in Pakistani politics; and the government and the military could achieve a balanced relationship," says Pakistani political analyst Nawaz.

In the second scenario, Pakistan continues to alternate between civilian and military rule, which has played out since independence in 1947. "I don't see anything that suggests this pattern is going to shift in any fundamental way," says Shaikh, at London's Royal Institute of International Affairs. Some believe that if control of the country continues to flip-flop between ineffective civilian governments and dictatorial military rulers, the populace will become even more alienated than in the past. "That's one way you could envision an Iran-style revolution or a civilian strongman coming to power," says Markey. "It could lead to Pakistan becoming an extremist or an authoritarian state."

In the most chilling scenario, Pakistan gradually falls apart. Institutions weaken and disappear. Militants, extremists and even criminals take over. Eventually, the country spirals down into a failed state that threatens the region and the world.

Indeed, the term "failed state" is heard more and more regarding Pakistan. According to *Foreign Policy* magazine's "Failed States Index," Pakistan moved to ninth from the top this year, from 12th last year.[94]

To prevent a further descent into chaos, Pakistan must first curb militancy within its borders and then address social, economic and political shortcomings, experts say. Cease-fire negotiations reportedly are already underway with some militants. It is the rare Pakistan expert who doesn't stress that the United States must stop attacks on Pakistani soil while the government enters into talks with militants.

"The U.S., meanwhile, should end direct military strikes in the area, even if these are conducted with the knowledge and cooperation of Pakistan's military," writes Harvard's Abbas. "Force has never worked with the Pashtun tribes, and there is no evidence that this has changed. There are real signs that the new government is considered a credible partner in the tribal areas. It needs to be given time to find a way out of the endless cycle of violence."[95]

Establishing better relations with India, especially in light of the recent Mumbai terrorist attacks, is also seen as crucial. If this year's reopening of the Kashmir border to trade is any indication, the region will breathe easier.

As Benazir Bhutto once wrote, "It is time for new ideas. It is time for creativity. It is time for bold commitment. And it is time for honesty, both among people and between people."

She also believed deeply in Pakistan and its future, predicting shortly before she was assassinated, "Time, justice and the forces of history are on our side."[96]

Getty Images/Jeff J. Mitchell

More than 200,000 people were forced to abandon their homes — and at least 800 were killed — during a major Pakistani military assault in August on militants in the troubled Bajaur district. Many took refuge in makeshift camps near Peshawar (above). "The people sitting in the dust are the so-called 'collateral damage' of Pakistan's own war on terror," wrote reporters for London's Independent.

But not everyone is optimistic. In his much-admired analysis of Pakistan's future, the Brookings Institution's Cohen wrote, "In summary, the human material is there to turn Pakistan into a modern state, but it has been systematically squandered for three generations by an elite persuaded that Pakistan's critical strategic location would be enough to get it through critical times. Now, the distant future has arrived, with Pakistan unequipped to face a fast-changing world while coping with new and mounting domestic problems."[97]

NOTES

1. "How to beat the terrorists?" *The Economist*, Sept. 23, 2008, www.economist.com/research/articlesBy Subject/displaystory.cfm?subjectid=1604388&story_id=12284547.

2. Carlotta Gall, "Bombing at hotel in Pakistan kills at least 40," *The New York Times*, Sept. 21, 2008, www.nytimes.com/2008/09/21/world/asia/21islamabad.html.

3. "Address of President of Pakistan Asif Ali Zardari to the Parliament," Sept. 20, 2008, www.satp.org/satporgtp/countries/pakistan/document/papers/speechpresident.htm.

4. Jane Perlez, "Pakistan's faith in its new leader is shaken," *The New York Times*, Sept. 27, 2008, www.nytimes .com/2008/09/27/world/asia/27pstan.html?em. Also see Roland Flamini, "Afghanistan on the Brink," *CQ Global Researcher*, June 2007, pp. 125-150.

5. The Associated Press, "Change of Plans saved Pakistani leaders from blast," *USA Today*, Sept. 22, 2008, www.usatoday.com/news/world/2008-09-22-pakistan-change-of-plans_ N.htm.

6. Dexter Filkins, "Right at the edge," *The New York Times Magazine*, Sept. 7, 2008, www.nytimes .com/2008/09/07/magazine/07pakistan-t.html.

7. Quoted in Paul Wiseman and Zafar Sheikh, "Militants flourish in Pakistan's tribal areas," *USA Today*, Oct. 1, 2008, www.usatoday.com/news/world/2008-10-01-tribes_N.htm.

8. See Daniel Markey, "Hotbed of Terrorism," Council on Foreign Relations, Aug. 11, 2008, www.cfr.org/publication/16929/hotbed_of_terror.html?breadcrumb=%2Fbios%2F13611%2Fjayshree_bajoria%3Fpage%3D2.

9. Stephen P. Cohen, "The Next Chapter," Brookings Institution, Oct. 10, 2008, www.brookings .edu/reports/2008/09_pakistan_cohen.aspx?rssid= cohens.

10. "Pakistan Assessment 2008," *South Asian Terrorism Portal*, www.satp.org/satporgtp/countries/pakistan/.

11. *Ibid.*

12. Aryn Baker, "Dangerous Ground," *Time*, July 10, 2008, www.time.com/time/magazine/article/0,9171,1821495,00.html?iid=digg_share.

13. *Ibid.*

14. Jane Perlez, "64 in Pakistan die in bombing at arms plant," *The New York Times*, Aug. 21, 2008, www .nytimes.com/2008/08/22/world/asia/22pstan .html?_r=1&hp&oref=slogin.

15. "Musharraf's Support Shrinks, Even As More Pakistanis Reject Terrorism . . . and the U.S.," http://pewresearch.org/pubs/561/pakistan-terrorism.

16. The Associated Press, "Afghanistan: Attack in Pakistan," *The New York Times*, Nov. 18, 2008, www.nytimes.com/2008/11/19/world/asia/19briefs-ATTACKINPAKI_BRF.html?partner=rss&emc=rss.

17. "The Last Resort," *The Economist*, Oct. 23, 2008, www.economist.com/world/asia/displaystory.cfm? story_id=12480386.

18. "China to Pakistan's rescue?" *The Economist*, Oct. 16, 2008, www.economist.com/agenda/displaystory .cfm?story_id=12445315.

19. Baker, *op. cit.*

20. David Lynch, "Global financial crisis may hit hardest outside U.S.," *USA Today*, Sept. 30, 2008, www .usatoday.com/money/economy/2008-10-29-global-financial-crisis_N.htm.

21. Jonathan Landay, "New intelligence report says Pakistan is 'on Edge,' " McClatchy Newspapers, Oct. 14, 2008, www.mcclatchydc.com/world/story/53926.html.

22. Sumit Gangult, "Danger ahead for the most dangerous place in the world," *The Washington Post*, Oct. 12, 2008, www.washingtonpost.com/wp-dyn/content/article/2008/10/09/AR2008100901206.html.

23. "Secretary Gates and Admiral Mullen testify," Institute for the Study of War, Sept. 11, 2008, www .understandingwar.org/print/315.

24. Lisa Curtis, "Combating terrorism in Pakistan: going on the offensive," Heritage Foundation, July 15, 2008, www.heritage.org/research/AsiaandthePacific/wm1991.cfm.

25. See Caroline Wadhams, *et al.*, "Partnership for Progress: Advancing a new strategy for prosperity and stability in Pakistan and the region," Center for American Progress, November 2008, p. 63, www.americanprogress.org/issues/2008/11/pdf/pakistan.pdf.

26. "US to focus on Pakistani border," BBC, Sept. 10, 2008, http://news.bbc.co.uk/2/hi/south_asia/7609073.stm.

27. Husain Haqqani, "The Capital Interview: Fighting terrorism is Pakistan's own war," Council on Foreign Relations, Oct. 21, 2008, www.cfr.org/publication/17567/.

28. Jane Perlez, "Pakistani legislators show little appetite for a fight," *The New York Times*, Oct. 21, 2008, www.nytimes.com/2008/10/21/world/asia/21pstan .html.

29. *Ibid.*

30. Stephen Philip Cohen, "A Pakistani response to the Marriott Attack," Brookings Institution, Sept. 22, 2008, www.brookings.edu/opinions/2008/0922_pakistan_cohen.aspx?rssid=LatestFromBrookings.

31. Ahmed Rashid, "Pakistan's New Stage of Struggle," BBC News, Aug. 20, 2008, http://news.bbc.co.uk/2/hi/south_asia/7571085.stm.

32. Ahmed Rashid, "Pakistan on the Brink," *Yale Global Online*, Sept. 19, 2008, http://yaleglobal.yale.edu/display.article?id=11350.

33. Imtiaz Ali, "Foreign policy challenges for new US president," *Yale Global Online*, Oct. 31, 2008, http://yaleglobal.yale.edu/display.article?id=11538.

34. B. Raman, "PAK-US SNAFU," *International Terrorism Monitor: Paper No. 442*, South Asia Analysis Group, Sept. 13, 2008, www.southasiaanalysis.org/papers29/paper2843.html.

35. Faraz Khan, "10 months, 10 parties, 100 killed," *Daily Times*, Oct. 31, 2008, www.dailytimes.com.pk/default.asp?page=2008%5C10%5C31%5Cstory_31-10-2008_pg12_1.

36. Aryn Baker, "Pakistan votes amid tension," *Time*, Feb. 18, 2008, www.time.com/time/world/article/0,8599,1714206,00.html.

37. Lyce Doucet, "Pakistan ponders meaning of democracy," BBC News, Feb. 17, 2008, http://news.bbc.co.uk/2/hi/programmes/from_our_own_correspondent/7247096.stm.

38. "Pakistanis want larger role for both Islam and democracy," USIP.org, Jan. 7, 2008, www.usip.org/newsmedia/releases/2008/0107_pakistan_opinion.html.

39. Stephen Philip Cohen, *The Idea of Pakistan* (2004), p. 278.

40. Lisa Curtis, "Pakistan: Stumbling Towards Democracy," Heritage Foundation, Aug. 10, 2007, www.heritage.org/press/commentary/ed081007b.cfm.

41. Owen Bennett Jones, *Pakistan: The Eye of the Storm* (2003), p. 230.

42. "The World's Most Dangerous Place," *The Economist*, Jan. 5, 2008, www.economist.com/opinion/displaystory.cfm?story_id=10430237.

43. Asif Ali Zardari, "Democracy within our reach," *The Washington Post*, Sept. 4, 2008, www.washingtonpost.com/wp-dyn/content/article/2008/09/03/AR2008090303131.html.

44. Husain Haqqani, "America is better off without Musharraf," *The Wall Street Journal*, Aug. 21, 2008, http://online.wsj.com/article/SB121927727332058621.html?mod=googlenews_wsj.

45. Benazir Bhutto, *Reconciliation: Islam, Democracy, and the West* (2008), p. 2.

46. Paul Reynolds, "On the trail of the black market bombs," BBC News, Feb. 12, 2004, http://news.bbc.co.uk/2/low/americas/3481499.stm.

47. Jonathan Manthorpe, "Pakistani scientist ran a nuclear Wal-Mart," *Vancouver Sun*, Aug. 26, 2006, www.canada.com/vancouversun/columnists/story.html?id=328861ae-88b1-46f7-b14c-89 f7fbd78239.

48. David E. Sanger and William J. Broad, "US secretly aids Pakistan in guarding nuclear arms," *The New York Times*, Nov. 18, 2007, www.nytimes.com/2007/11/18/washington/18nuke.html.

49. *Ibid.*

50. "Osama Wanted Nuke Help," The Associated Press, Dec. 30, 2002, http://uttm.com/stories/2002/12/30/world/main534727.shtml.

51. Joby Warrick, "Lack of knowledge about arsenal may limit US options," *The Washington Post*, Nov. 11, 2007, www.washingtonpost.com/wp-dyn/content/article/2007/11/10/AR2007111001684_pf.html. Also see Roland Flamini, "Nuclear Proliferation," *CQ Global Researcher*, January 2007, pp. 1-26.

52. Syed Shoaib Hasan, "Are Pakistan's nuclear weapons safe?" BBC News, Jan. 23, 2008, http://news.bbc.co.uk/2/hi/south_asia/7190033.stm.

53. Sanger and Broad, *op. cit.*

54. Ahmad Hasan Dani, "Pakistan: History through the centuries," www.geocities.com/pak_history/pak.html.

55. "History of Pakistan," www.geocities.com/pak_history/.

56. Cohen, *op. cit.*, p. 6.

57. Jones, *op. cit*, p. 11.

58. M. Ilyas Khan, "Pakistan's circular history," BBC News, Aug. 11, 2007, http://news.bbc.co.uk/2/hi/south_asia/6940148.stm.

59. Cohen, *op. cit.*, p. 124.

60. Jones, *op. cit.*, p. xiii.

61. Seth Kaplan, *Fixing Fragile States* (2008), p. 151.

62. For background, see Flamini, "Afghanistan on the Brink," *op. cit.*

63. For background, see David Masci and Kenneth Jost, "War on Terrorism," *CQ Researcher*, Oct. 12, 2001, pp. 817-848; and Kenneth Jost, "Rebuilding Afghanistan," *CQ Researcher*, Dec. 21, 2001, pp. 1041-1064.

64. Hassan Abbas, "A profile of Tehrik-I-Taliban Pakistan," *CTC Sentinel*, January 2008.

65. "US Think tank: Pakistan helped train Taliban, gave info on US troops," The Associated Press, June 9, 2008, www.iht.com/articles/ap/2008/06/09/asia/AS-GEN-Afghan-Pakistan.php.

66. Brian Glyn Williams and Cathy Young, "Cheney attack reveals suicide bombing patterns," Jamestown Foundation, Nov. 21, 2008, www.jamestown.org/news_details.php?news_id=222.

67. Aryn Baker, "The truth about Talibanistan," *Time*, April 2, 2007, www.time.com/time/magazine/article/0,9171,1601850,00.html.

68. Dexter Filkins, "Right at the edge," *The New York Times*, Sept. 7, 2008, pp. 52-61, 114-116, www.nytimes.com/2008/09/07/magazine/07pakistan-t.html.

69. Candace Rondeaux, "Suspected US airstrike kills 6 fighters in Pakistan," *The Washington Post*, Nov. 19, 2008, www.washingtonpost.com/wp-dyn/content/article/2008/11/19/AR2008111903714.html?hpid=sec-world.

70. Aryn Baker, "US stepping up operations in Pakistan," *Time*, Sept. 10, 2008 www.time.com/time/world/article/0,8599,1840383,00.html.

71. Jane Perlez, "Confronting Taliban, US finds itself at war," *The New York Times*, Oct. 3, 2008, www.nytimes.com/2008/10/03/world/asia/03pstan.html.

72. "Pakistan captures militant stronghold," The Associated Press, Oct. 26, 2008, http://news.yahoo.com/s/ap/20081025/ap_on_re_as/as_pakistan.

73. "Missile attacks, apparently by US, kill 27 in Pakistan, including Qaeda operative," The Associated Press, Oct. 31, 2008, www.nytimes.com/2008/11/01/world/asia/01drone.html?ref=world.

74. Jane Perlez, "As Taliban overwhelm police, Pakistanis hit back," *The New York Times*, Nov. 2, 2008, www.nytimes.com/2008/11/02/world/asia/02pstan.html; "Pakistanis flee into Afghanistan," BBC News, Sept. 29, 2008, http://news.bbc.co.uk/2/hi/south_asia/7642015.stm.

75. Andrew Buncombe and Omar Waraich, "Exclusive dispatch: Pakistan's Hidden War," *The Independent*, Oct. 23, 2008, www.independent.co.uk/news/world/asia/exclusive-dispatch-pakistans-hidden-war-969784.html.

76. Huma Yusuf, "Pakistan bans Taliban outfit amidst military campaign," *The Christian Science Monitor*, Aug. 26, 2008, www.csmonitor.com/2008/0825/p99s01-duts.html.

77. Jane Perlez and Pir Zubair Shah, "Pakistan uses tribal militias in Taliban war," *The New York Times*, Oct. 23, 2008, www.nytimes.com/2008/10/24/world/asia/24militia.html?hp.

78. Jane Perlez and Pir Zubair Shah, "Pakistan's tribal militias walk a tightrope in fight against Taliban," *The New York Times*, Oct. 24, 2008, www.nytimes.com/2008/10/24/world/asia/24militia.html?hp.

79. Zahid Hussain and Matthew Rosenberg, "Bombing targets Pakistan militia," *The Wall Street Journal*, Nov. 6, 2008.

80. Perlez and Shah, *op. cit.*

81. Mark Mazzetti and Eric Schmitt, "Pakistanis aided attack in Kabul," *The New York Times*, Aug. 1, 2008, www.nytimes.com/2008/08/01/world/asia/01pstan.html?_r=1&hp&oref=slogin.

82. Anthony Cordesman, "US Security interests after Musharraf," Center for Strategic and International Studies, Aug. 21, 2008, www.csis.org/component/option,com_csis_pubs/task,view/id,4810/.

83. Saeed Shah, "US risks overplaying hand with Pakistan strikes," *The Guardian*, Oct. 24, 2008.

84. *Ibid.*

85. Jane Perlez, "Pakistan tells US to stop strikes in tribal zones," *The New York Times*, Oct. 29, 2008, www .nytimes.com/2008/10/30/world/asia/30pstan.html.

86. Jane Perlez, "Petraeus in Pakistan, hears complaints about missile strikes," *The New York Times*, Nov. 4, 2008, www.nytimes.com/2008/11/04/world/asia/04pstan.html?partner=rssnyt&emc=rss.

87. Aryn Baker, "Pakistan: Negligent on terror?" *Time*, June 30, 2008, www.time.com/time/world/article/0,8599,1819125,00.html.

88. Wadhams, *et al.*, *op. cit.*

89. Nick Schifrin and Habibullah Khan, "Will Obama change US Pakistan policy?" ABC News, Nov. 5, 2008, http://abcnews.go.com/International/story?id=6189479&page=1.

90. Cohen, *op. cit.*

91. "An expanding war in Afghanistan awaits next US president," Agence France-Presse, Nov. 1, 2008, http://afp.google.com/article/ALeqM5iwbu3ED jze-Li-CDAI-yx8VzqBrw.

92. Wadhams, *et al.*, *op. cit.*

93. Nasim Zehra, "Obama and Pakistan: Mutual Trust, Respect and Understanding," Asia Society, Nov. 5, 2008, http://asiasociety.org/resources/081105_obama_pakistan.html.

94. "The Failed States Index 2008," *Foreign Policy*, 2008, www.foreignpolicy.com/story/cms.php?page=1&story_id=4350.

95. Hassan Abbas, "Exorcising General's Ghost," *Khaleed Times*, July 13, 2008, www.khaleejtimes.com/DisplayArticleNew.asp?section=opinion&xfile=data/opinion/2008/july/opinion_july54.xml.

96. Bhutto, *op. cit.*

97. Cohen, *op. cit*, p. 299.

BIBLIOGRAPHY

Books

Abbas, Hasaan, *Pakistan's Drift into Extremism: Allah, the Army and America's War on Terror*, 2004.
A Harvard fellow and former member of Pakistan's anti-corruption police force explores how radicalism has shaped and influenced the nation's development.

Ahmed, Akbar, *Journey Into Islam: The Crisis of Globalization, Brookings Institution Press*, 2007.
A noted Islamic studies professor, joined by several non-Muslim students, sets out on an international trip to numerous Muslim countries to explore the importance of improved dialog between the Muslim and non-Muslim worlds.

Bhutto, Benazir, *Reconciliation: Islam, Democracy, and the West, Harper Collins*, 2008.
The former prime minister finished writing this gripping account of her return to Pakistan just days before her assassination. She explores the complex relationship between the Middle East and the West and shows how democracy and Islam can coexist.

Cohen, Stephen Philip, *The Idea of Pakistan, The Brookings Institution*, 2004.
A respected historian examines the military, religious, political and other factors that make Pakistan one of the world's least understood countries.

Haqqani, Husain, *Pakistan: Between Mosque and Military, Carnegie Endowment for International Peace*, 2005.
Pakistan's ambassador to the United States (former journalist and academic) examines the relationships between Pakistan's military and religious sectors.

Jones, Owen Bennett, *Pakistan: Eye of the Storm, Yale University Press*, 2002.
A BBC correspondent formerly based in Pakistan offers an excellent examination of the complex relationships between the country's society, military and political sectors.

Kaplan, Seth D., *Fixing Fragile States: A New Paradigm for Development, Praeger Security International*, 2008.
In this wide-ranging study, the author examines Pakistan and six other countries that appear to be teetering on the brink of "failed state" status.

Kux, Dennis, *The United States and Pakistan 1947-2000: Disenchanted Allies, Woodrow Wilson Center Press*, 2001.
A retired State Department South Asia specialist and career diplomat offers a detailed, informative survey of post-independence U.S.-Pakistan relations.

Nawaz, Shuja, *Crossed Swords: Pakistan, Its Army and the Wars Within, Oxford University Press,* **2008.**
A Pakistani journalist with impeccable contacts inside Pakistan's military provides a landmark study of the military's role in aiding — and hampering — Pakistan's development.

Rashid, Ahmed, *Descent into Chaos: The United States and the Failure of Nation Building in Pakistan, Afghanistan and Central Asia, Viking,* **2008.**
The Pakistani author of *Taliban* examines domestic and foreign forces that have helped turn Pakistan into a volatile flashpoint.

Talbot, Ian, *Pakistan: A Modern History, Palgrave Macmillan,* **2005.**
A British academic provides a thorough, well-researched account of the founding of Pakistan and its political history.

Articles

Filkins, Dexter, "Right at the Edge," *The New York Times,* Sept. 7, 2008, pp. 52-61, 114-116, www.nytimes .com/2008/ 09/07/magazine/07pakistan-t.html.
A seasoned foreign correspondent interviews militants, security forces and civilians in Pakistan's tribal areas.

Moreau, Ron, and Mark Hosenball, "Pakistan's Dangerous Double Game," *Newsweek,* Sept. 22, 2008.
A first-hand exploration of the U.S. military's recent, more aggressive approach to attacking militants inside Pakistan.

Reports and Studies

"The Next Chapter: The United States and Pakistan," *Pakistan Policy Working Group, Brookings Institution,* **September 2008.**
A group of experts on U.S.-Pakistan relations offers suggestions on how Washington can rethink its approach to Pakistan.

Grare, Frederic, "Rethinking Western Strategies Toward Pakistan: An action agenda for the United States and Europe," *Carnegie Endowment for International Peace,* **2007.**
A leading expert on South Asia calls for a new strategy to encourage the Pakistan military to promote civilian rule.

Markey, Dan, "Securing Pakistan's Tribal Belt," *Council on Foreign Relations,* **July/August 2008.**
A noted South Asia expert and former State Department officer examines issues shaping modern-day Pakistan.

Reidel, Bruce, "Pakistan and Terror: The Eye of the Storm," *The Annals of the American Academy,* **July 2008.**
A former CIA official and NATO adviser provides an overview of the present security situation in Pakistan.

For More Information

Carnegie Council, 170 E. 64th St., New York, NY 10021; (212) 838-4120; www.cceia.org. Think tank that advocates ethical decision-making in international policy.

Council on Foreign Relations, 58 E. 68th St., New York, NY 10021; (212) 434-9400; www.cfr.org. Promotes a better understanding of the foreign-policy choices facing the United States and other governments.

Human Rights Commission of Pakistan (HRCP), Secretariat/Punjab Chapter, Aiwan-I-Jamjoor, 107-Tipu Block, New Garden Town, Lahore 54600, Pakistan; (92) (042) 5838341; www.hrcp-web.org. Nongovernmental organization that acts as a clearinghouse for information on human rights abuses throughout Pakistan.

International Crisis Group, 149 Ave. Louise, Level 24, B-1050 Brussels, Belgium; +32-(0)-2-502-90-38; www.crisisgroup.org. Nongovernmental organization that uses field-based analysis and high-level advocacy to prevent violent conflict worldwide.

International Institute for Strategic Studies, 13-15 Arundel St., Temple Place, London WC2R 3DX, United Kingdom; +44-(0)-20-7379-7676; www.iiss.org. Think tank focusing on international security with emphasis on political-military conflict.

Islamabad Policy Research Institute, House No. 2, Street No. 15, Margella Rd., Sector F-7/12, Islamabad, Pakistan; +92-51-921-3680-2; www.ipripak.org. Evaluates national and international political-strategic issues and developments affecting Pakistan and surrounding countries.

Pakistan Institute of Legislative Development and Transparency, # 7, 9th Ave., F-8/1 Islamabad — 44000, Pakistan; +92-51-111 123 345; www.pildat.org. An independent, nonpartisan, nonprofit research and training institution that aims to strengthen democracy and democratic institutions in Pakistan.

Radical Islam in Europe

Are Terrorists Expanding Their Recruiting Efforts?

Sarah Glazer

9

Pakistani Muslims burn the Danish flag in Karachi on Feb. 14, 2006, to protest Danish newspaper cartoons they said blasphemed the Prophet Mohammed. Worldwide protests sparked by the cartoons reflected many young Muslims' feeling that the Muslim world is under attack by the West

AP Photo/Shakil Adil

From *CQ Global Researcher*, April 17, 2009.

A recent spate of attempted terrorist plots by Muslims in Europe has revived questions about how much of the threat is homegrown — the outgrowth of disaffection among European Muslims — and how much is orchestrated abroad.

On Sept. 4 German authorities announced they had foiled a plan to blow up an American military base in Frankfurt. Their arrest of a member of Germany's large Turkish community — long considered one of Europe's most peaceful Muslim immigrant groups — along with two German-born converts to Islam raised new questions about Germany as a locus of radicalization and its success at integrating Muslim residents.

Police said the planned explosion could have been more deadly than the 2004 train bombings in Madrid, which killed 191 people, and the 2005 London transit attack that killed 52 commuters.[1]

On the same day as the announcement of the German arrests, Muslims in Copenhagen were charged with planning a bombing attack in Denmark, suggesting that domestic discontent in the country — where Muslim immigrants complain of job discrimination and a newspaper triggered worldwide protests among Muslims two years ago by publishing cartoons seen as ridiculing Mohammed — may have provided fertile ground for Islamic terrorism.[2]

This past summer, Britons were shocked to learn that Muslims suspected of trying to blow up the Glasgow, Scotland, airport on June 30 included middle-class Indian and Middle Eastern doctors working for the National Health Service — not alienated youths without jobs. The news came the day after the same suspects had allegedly tried to set off a car bomb outside a London nightclub

More European Muslims Favor Suicide Bombings

Muslims in France, Spain and Great Britain are twice as likely as American Muslims to condone suicide bombings of civilians. About one in six Muslims in the three countries say bombing civilians to defend Islam is justifiable.

Can the suicide bombing of civilians to defend Islam be justified?

Muslims who said yes in ...

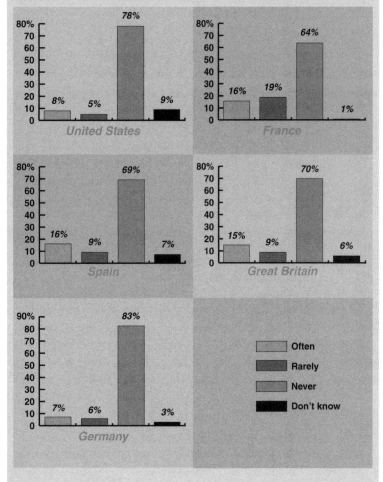

* Percentages may not total 100 due to rounding.

Source: "Muslim Americans: Middle Class and Mostly Mainstream," Pew Research Center, May 2007

and just before the anniversary of the July 7, 2005, London transit bombings. One of the suicide bombers from that attack had left a video in a strong Yorkshire accent — a startling reminder that "a British lad" had been radicalized at home even if he also had links to militants abroad.[3]

All three events spurred soul-searching in Britain, Germany, Denmark, Scotland and elsewhere. Experts often blame Western foreign policies, including the war in Iraq, for the young Muslims' outrage and their feeling that the Muslim world is under attack by the West. But the long-held belief by some European leaders that opposing the Iraq War would immunize their countries from Muslim terrorist attacks appeared dashed by the plot in Germany, which opposed the war. Authorities said the bombing scheme was linked to Germany's military presence in Afghanistan.[4]

To what extent does the violence that Europe is experiencing reflect a failure to integrate immigrants and their children into Western society?

"There is a sense in our societies that the radicalism was not created by the United States [foreign policy] but caused by the lack of integration," Christoph Bertram, the former director of the Institute of Security Affairs in Berlin, told *The New York Times* the week after the German and Danish arrests."[5]

Reflecting that concern, British Prime Minister Gordon Brown in July announced that in addition to beefing up border police he was proposing a fourfold increase in "hearts and minds" programs like citizenship classes in Britain's 1,000 *madrasas* (Islamic religious schools, usually attached to a mosque), and English-language training for imams.

"A tough security response is vital, but to be safe in the longer term we need to reach people before they are drawn into violent extremism," said Hazel Blears, Britain's Secretary of State for Communities and Local Government.[6]

Other analysts argue that radical fundamentalism originates from increasingly well-organized international networks seeking out and finding the few estranged individuals ready to commit violence. The German and Danish plotters were said to have received training and instructions in Pakistan. And in September, European authorities warned that a newly strengthened al Qaeda, operating from the lawless, tribal border region between Pakistan and Afghanistan, was stepping up plans to target Europe and the United States.[7]

Meanwhile, a recent New York City Police Department (NYPD) intelligence report concluded that the terrorists involved in the 2004 Madrid bombings, the London transit attack and the group in Hamburg, Germany, that planned the Sept. 11, 2001, terrorist attacks in the United States were "unremarkable" local residents, some with advanced degrees from European universities. Moreover, the report said, the process of radicalization seems to be accelerating, and terrorists are getting younger. "We now believe it is critical to identify the al Qaeda-inspired threat at the point where radicalization begins," the report said, a conclusion shared by a 2006 British intelligence report.[8]

Jytte Klausen, a professor of comparative politics at Brandeis University who has studied the profiles of 550 alleged terrorists arrested since the 9/11 attacks, disputes the idea that terrorism is primarily the fruit of "home-grown" radicals who have not been integrated into society. "This is not primarily about integration, though better integration might be preventative," she says. "It has a lot to do with transnational networks and ethnic origins: Political developments in Pakistan are getting

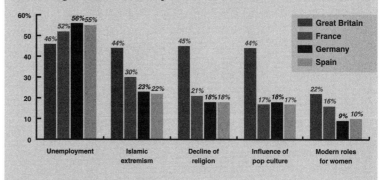

Jobs Are Top Muslim Concern

Most Muslims in Europe worry more about unemployment than about religious and cultural issues, such as the rise of extremism and the decline of religion. They are least concerned about the role of women in modern society.

Percentage of Muslims very worried about . . .

Legend: Great Britain, France, Germany, Spain

	Great Britain	France	Germany	Spain
Unemployment	46%	52%	56%	55%
Islamic extremism	44%	30%	23%	22%
Decline of religion	45%	21%	18%	18%
Influence of pop culture	44%	17%	18%	17%
Modern roles for women	22%	16%	9%	10%

Source: "Muslims in Europe: Economic Worries Top Concerns About Religious and Cultural Identity," Pew Global Attitudes Project, July 2006

filtered through Britain's back door; the radical groups piggyback on the migrant stream."

British writer Ed Husain describes his recruitment in the 1990s in London by Islamists — Muslims who advocate an Islamic state, in some cases by violent means — in his 2007 memoir *The Islamist.* Husain argues that two factors prompt those drawn to political Islamic ideology to contemplate violence: the scorn heaped on non-Muslims by radical fundamentalists and the growing conviction that the world's Muslims need their own transnational state — or caliphate — governed by strict religious law, called sharia.

But others, like sociologist Tahir Abbas of England's University of Birmingham, say the notion of a Muslim caliphate is still an abstract one — an aspiration that isn't much different from European nations joining together in the European Union. And some of the London organizations where Husain says he was radicalized, such as Hizb ut-Tahrir and the controversial East London Mosque, claim they do not advocate violence to achieve the goal of a global Islamic state. Some groups say they only advocate the return of an Islamic state in Muslim countries. For example, Hizb ut-Tahrir says it works to bring "the Muslim world" under the caliphate but that in

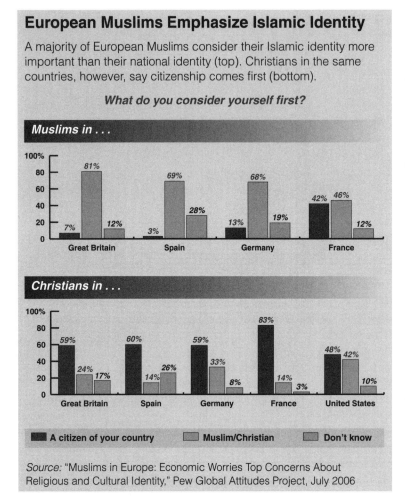

European Muslims Emphasize Islamic Identity

A majority of European Muslims consider their Islamic identity more important than their national identity (top). Christians in the same countries, however, say citizenship comes first (bottom).

What do you consider yourself first?

Muslims in . . .

Great Britain: 7%, 81%, 12%
Spain: 3%, 69%, 28%
Germany: 13%, 68%, 19%
France: 42%, 46%, 12%

Christians in . . .

Great Britain: 59%, 24%, 17%
Spain: 60%, 14%, 26%
Germany: 59%, 33%, 8%
France: 83%, 14%, 3%
United States: 48%, 42%, 10%

■ A citizen of your country   ■ Muslim/Christian   ■ Don't know

Source: "Muslims in Europe: Economic Worries Top Concerns About Religious and Cultural Identity," Pew Global Attitudes Project, July 2006

Meanwhile, most experts agree that Muslims in Europe have not been as easily incorporated into society as they have in the United States, which might explain their openness to radical ideas. Polls show Muslims in France, Spain and Britain are twice as likely as U.S. Muslims to say suicide bombs can be justified. (*See graph, p. 210.*) Notably, support in Europe for suicide bombings is highest among Muslim adults under age 30 — supporters make up 35 percent of young Muslims in Great Britain and 42 percent in France. There were an estimated 15 million Muslims in the European Union in 2006, not counting the 70 million Muslims in Turkey.[12]

One measure of European Muslims' alienation from Western governments and news sources is the surprisingly large majorities who don't accept that recent terrorist acts were carried out by Muslims. An astonishing 56 percent of British Muslims don't believe Arabs carried out the 9/11 attacks, according to a poll by the Pew Research Center, a result commonly explained as acceptance of one of the conspiracy theories blaming Jews, Israel's secret police or the Bush administration.[13] But Abbas, who is Muslim himself, suggests another explanation for the widespread skepticism: Most Muslims are in denial because they are so shocked at the thought that fellow Muslims could carry out such a violent act.

Experts on Islam also hasten to point out that sympathizing with suicide bombers or sharing fundamentalist beliefs doesn't mean one will become a terrorist. Some of the fear about the call for an Islamic state by groups like Hizb ut-Tahrir — a group that calls for the end of Israel and which Britain has considered banning — is misplaced, Abbas believes. "People look at the surface, see dogma and . . . see it as a menacing threat. Yes, lots of people are hotheaded and mad, but they dip in and out

the West it does "not work to change the system of government."[9] (*See sidebar, p. 214.*)

Some Muslim leaders in Britain, including Syed Aziz Pasha, secretary general of the Union of Muslim Organizations of the UK and Ireland, have pushed for sharia law in Britain — but only as it pertains to family matters like marriage, and only for Muslims. One poll shows about a third of British Muslims would rather live under sharia.[10]

Husain, a former member of Hizb ut-Tahrir, remains skeptical of the group's nonviolent stance: "The only difference between Islamists from Hizb ut-Tahrir and jihadists is that the former are waiting for their state and caliph before they commence jihad, while the latter believes the time for jihad is now."[11]

of these organizations just as often as they're sprouting up. Young people need to find themselves, need to search for meaning to their lives," he says.

Yet, even if a group doesn't advocate terrorism to achieve an Islamic state, parties advocating Islamic rule through peaceful means should also be resisted because they aim to establish a "totalitarian" theocracy, argues Martin Bright, a journalist who has investigated radical links to Muslim groups in Britain. "We make a mistake if we think that just because people are engaged in the electoral process that's necessarily a good thing; Mussolini and Hitler were also engaged in the electoral process," says Bright, political editor at the *New Statesman*, a left-leaning political weekly published in London. Radical asylum seekers are often careful not to commit violence in Britain and other European countries that accept them for fear of deportation, he says, but still support jihad abroad.

When Muhammad Abdul Bari — secretary general of the British Muslim Council, an umbrella group representing Muslims — suggested last year that British non-Muslims adopt more Islamic ways, including arranged marriages, one critic interpreted it as a call for adopting sharia law.[14] A recent BBC documentary reported that sharia courts in Nigeria, operating strictly according to Koranic prescriptions, have ordered limbs amputated as a punishment for thievery, public flogging and stoning of women accused of adultery.[15] Critics like Bright say that given the potential for such brutal punishments, accompanying repressive attitudes towards women and frequently virulent anti-Semitism, the real struggle facing the West is about ideology, not terrorism.

The recent foiled bombing attempts have prompted calls in England and France to allow police to detain terrorist suspects for longer periods to give police more time to investigate. But groups like Human Rights Watch say Muslims are already bearing the brunt of law enforcement and immigration policies that violate their human rights.[16] In the long run, terrorist crackdowns can be counter-productive if they merely alienate mainstream Muslims, say civil liberties advocates.

By failing to heed moderate Muslims' warnings in the 1990s that clerics were preaching violence, law-enforcement services in Britain alienated the very communities they need to help them, says Hisham A. Hellyer,

AP Photo/Peter MacDiarmid

A mangled bus is a grim reminder of the four rush-hour suicide bombings by Muslim terrorists that killed 52 London commuters and injured hundreds in July 2005. The attacks added to Europeans' concerns about how well they were integrating Muslim immigrants and their children.

Senior Research Fellow at the University of Warwick and author of a forthcoming report from the Brookings Institution in Washington on counterterrorism lessons from Britain for the West. An important lesson for the West, he says, is to not cut off contact with Muslim groups who may be conservatively religious but not violent.

Some experts, including Director of National Intelligence Mike McConnell, fear the United States could be the next target of European terrorists. McConnell told the Senate Judiciary Committee in September that al Qaeda is recruiting Europeans for explosives training in Pakistan because they can more easily enter the United States without a visa.[17]

Peter Skerry, a professor of political science at Boston College who is writing a book about Muslims

Foreign Domination Sparked Radical Islamic Thought

Muslim writers protested British, U.S. interventions.

The radicalization of Islam has historic roots reaching back to the 1930s, '40s and '50s, when Muslim writers were also protesting colonialism and what they saw as imperialistic British and U.S. interventions in the Middle East.

The Muslim Brotherhood, founded in Egypt in 1928, sought to couple resistance to foreign domination with establishment of an Islamic state run by sharia law, which imposes strict interpretations of the *Koran*. The Brotherhood at first worked closely with the secret Free Officers revolutionary movement led by Gamal Abdel Nasser and Anwar al-Sadat, which aimed at overthrowing the British regime and the Egyptian royal family.

But after the group's military coup toppled the Egyptian monarchy in 1952, Nasser's regime sorely disappointed the Brotherhood as insufficiently Islamic. A failed assassination attempt on Nasser by an embittered Brotherhood member in 1954 prompted the secular government to brutally suppress the movement and imprison its leaders.

One of those imprisoned leaders was Sayyid Qutb, known by his followers as "The Martyr," whose anti-Western writings would become extremely influential in the jihadist movement. In 1948, while on a study mission to the United States, he wrote with distaste of the sexual permissiveness and consumerism he saw, comparing the typical American to a primitive "caveman."[1] Alienated by America's hedonism, he argued the only way to protect the Islamic world from such influences would be to return to strict Islamic teachings.

Qutb spent most of the last decade of his life imprisoned in Egypt, where he was tortured. While in prison he wrote *Milestones*, his famous work espousing his vision of Islam as inseparable from the political state, and concluded the regime was a legitimate target of jihad.[2] He was convicted of sedition in 1966 and hanged.

The ideas of writers like Qutb have been adopted by radical Islamic groups (Islamists) today, generating concern in the West. An updated version of *Milestones*, published in Birmingham, England, in 2006 and prominently displayed at the bookstore next to the controversial East London Mosque contains a 1940s-era instruction manual by another member of the Muslim Brotherhood with chapter headings like "The Virtues of Killing a Non-Believer for the Sake of Allah" and "The Virtues of Martyrdom."[3]

The Muslim Brotherhood was "really the first organization to develop the idea that you could have an Islamic state within the modern world," according to *New Statesman* political editor Martin Bright.[4]

Although the Brotherhood is sometimes represented as moderate in comparison to jihadist groups like al Qaeda, Bright notes its motto remains to this day: "Allah is our objective. The Prophet is our Leader. The *Qu'uran* [*Koran*] is our constitution. Jihad is our way. Dying in the way of Allah is our highest hope." In 1981, Sadat, who had become Egypt's president, was assassinated by four members of a Brotherhood splinter group.[5]

Robert S. Leiken, director of the Immigration and National Security Program at the Nixon Center in Washington, D.C., recently interviewed leaders of the Brotherhood in Europe and the Middle East. He concluded the organization "depends on winning hearts through gradual and peaceful Islamization" and is committed to the electoral process. However, the group does authorize jihad in countries it considers occupied by a foreign power.[6]

For instance, Yusuf al-Qaradawi, the Brotherhood's spiritual leader, has supported suicide bombing in the Palestinian occupied territories and called it a duty of every Muslim to resist American and British forces in Iraq.[7]

Jamaat-e-Islami, the radical Asian offshoot of the Muslim Brotherhood, originated in British India first as a religious

in America, says homegrown terrorists are less likely in the United States because there is more ethnic diversity among American Muslims, and they are more educated and wealthier than European Muslims. They are also less of a presence. Muslims constitute less than 1 percent of the U.S. population, compared movement in 1941 and then as a political party committed to an Islamic state in 1947. It is the oldest religious party in Pakistan and also has wings in Bangladesh and Kashmir.

The party was founded by Abdul A'la Maududi, a Pakistani journalist who promoted a highly politicized, anti-Western brand of Islam. In his writings, Maududi asserts that Islamic democracy is the antithesis of secular Western democracy because the latter is based on the sovereignty of the people, rather than God.

Maududi was the first Muslim to reject Islam as a religion and re-brand it as an ideology — political Islam. His writing strongly influenced Qutb during his years in prison. British former radical Ed Husain writes that the organizations in London where he first heard Islam described as a political ideology in the 1990s — the Young Muslim Organization and the East London Mosque — both venerated Maududi.[8]

But while Maududi urged gradual change through a takeover of political institutions, Qutb argued for "religious war," seizing political authority "wherever an Islamic community exists," and jihad "to make this system of life dominant in the world."[9]

In support, Qutb cited the Prophet Mohammed's declaration of war on the infidels of Mecca. Qutb tarred all Christian, Jewish and Muslim societies of his time as *jahili* — disregarding divine precepts — because their leaders usurped Allah's legislative authority. "When I read *Milestones*, I felt growing animosity toward the *kuffar* (non-Muslims)," Husain writes.[10]

Husain would eventually move on to an even more radical group, Hizb ut-Tahrir (Party of Liberation), founded in Jerusalem in 1953 by Palestinian theologian and political activist Taqiuddin an-Nabhani. While Qutb and Maududi argued that Muslims had a religious duty to establish an Islamic state, Nabhani "provided the details of how to achieve it," writes Husain — through military coups or assassinations of political leaders.[11]

Today, Hizb ut-Tahrir says it seeks to establish a caliphate, or Islamic state governing all Muslims, through an "exclusively political" rather than violent method.[12] However, the group was recently denounced by a former senior member, Maajid Nawaz, who told the BBC that according to the group's own literature, the caliphate is "a

state that they are prepared to kill millions of people to expand."[13]

Today, reverence for the writings of Qutb or Maududi should be a litmus test for any Islamist group's level of radicalism, according to Husain. But University of Birmingham sociologist Tahir Abbas cautions that Maududi's writing "is about trying to fight off the yoke of colonialism as much as developing a pan-Islamic identity. When it comes to Maududi, he's writing for his time — and people take it out of context."

Indeed, to the uninitiated, the writings of both Qutb and Maududi come across as rather dry, if fiercely loyal, interpretations of the *Koran* as the supreme word.

Still, Maududi's party, Jamaat-e-Islami, has spawned its share of leaders preaching violent hatred against the West. Hossain Sayeedi, a Jamaat-e-Islami member of the Bangladesh Parliament, has compared Hindus to excrement. In public rallies in Bangladesh, he has urged that unless they convert to Islam, "let all the American soldiers be buried in the soil of Iraq and let them never return to their homes."[14]

---

[1] Sayyid Qutb, *Milestones* (2006), p. 8.

[2] For background, see Peter Katel, "Global Jihad," *CQ Researcher*, Oct. 14, 2005, pp. 857-880.

[3] Qutb, *op. cit.*, p. 266.

[4] Martin Bright, "When Progressives Treat with Reactionaries: The British State's Flirtation with Radical Islamism," *Policy Exchange*, 2006, p. 21.

[5] *Ibid.*, p. 14.

[6] Robert S. Leiken and Steven Brooke, "The Moderate Muslim Brotherhood," *Foreign Affairs*, March/April 2007, pp. 107-119.

[7] Bright, *op. cit.*, p. 20.

[8] Ed Husain, *The Islamist* (2007), p. 24. In this book, Maududi is spelled Mawdudi.

[9] Qutb, *op. cit.*, p. 86.

[10] *Ibid.*

[11] *Ibid.*, pp. 91, 96.

[12] "Radicalisation, Extremism & 'Islamism,' " *Hizb ut-Tahrir Britain*, July 2007, www.hizb.org.uk/hizb/images/PDFs/htb_radicalisation_report.pdf.

[13] Richard Watson, "Why Newsnight's Interview with Former HT Member is Essential Viewing," BBC, Sept. 13, 2007, www.bbc.co.uk/blogs/newsnight/2007/09/why_newsnights_interview_with_former_ht_member_is.html.

[14] Quoted in Bright, *op. cit.*, p. 22.

---

to an estimated 8-9 percent in France, 5.6 percent in the Netherlands, 3.6 percent in Germany and 3 percent in Britain.[18]

But the European experience has American law enforcers casting a worried glance eastward, and some are redoubling efforts to forge links with American Muslims.[19] As they do, here are some of the debates taking place in academic, political and citizen arenas in Europe and the United States:

Has Europe's terrorism been caused by a failure to integrate Muslims into society?

In the early 1990s, the isolation of the Bangladeshi neighborhood in East London where writer Husain grew up made it relatively easy for radical Islamist groups to recruit him to their vision of a transnational Islamic state, he writes in his memoir.

The lack of contact with mainstream British culture and society helps explain why many young Muslims insist that the recent attack on the Glasgow airport and 9/11 itself must be the creation of the government and the media, Husain believes. "When you're in that world, what others say [has] no meaning," he says. "You see them as non-believers headed for hell anyway."

But integration is a two-way street, and Husain says the traditional coldness of the English toward outsiders makes it difficult for anyone to easily enter their society.

Supporting that view is a *Financial Times* poll conducted last August that found Britons are more suspicious of Muslims than are other Europeans or Americans. Only 59 percent of Britons thought it possible to be both a Muslim and a citizen of their country, a smaller proportion than in France, Germany, Spain, Italy or the United States. British citizens also were the most likely to think a major terrorist attack was likely in their country in the next 12 months, to consider Muslims a threat to national security and to believe Muslims had too much political power in their country.[20]

French immigration historian Patrick Weil, a senior research fellow at the University of Paris's National Center for Scientific Research, says France accepts Muslims as fellow citizens and friends more easily than the British.

"The English have fought [work and educational] discrimination among the elite, and they've been quite successful, but they've been bad at cultural integration," he says. In France, it's the opposite: "We're very bad at ending discrimination but much better at integration."

Among the Europeans polled, the French are the most likely to have Muslim friends, accept a son or daughter marrying a Muslim and think Muslims are unjustly the subject of prejudice.[21] In the same vein, more French Muslims think of themselves as French first

and Muslim second than in the other three countries polled, according to a Pew survey.[22] (*See graph, p. 212.*)

That may help explain why France has been spared a major Muslim terrorist attack since the mid-1990s. The 2005 riots in Paris's poorer, heavily Muslim suburbs were protests against racial and economic discrimination driven by a desire to be part of France, rather than a separatist Muslim movement, Weil and other experts believe. Even when Muslims were protesting France's 2004 head-scarf ban in public schools, their chant was decidedly Francophile: "First, Second, Third Generation: We don't give a damn: Our home is Here!"[23]

Weil, a member of a commission appointed in 2003 by former French President Jacques Chirac that recommended banning "conspicuous religious symbols" in schools, claims the headscarf ban has helped to integrate Muslims into France's secular system and has given Muslim girls a better chance at educational equality. As evidence, he points out the ban was implemented without the need for police enforcement. The *Koran* became a bestseller during the head-scarf debate, a sign that non-Muslims wanted to learn more about Islam, he says. The head-scarf rule "includes you in the system" of basic French values, he says.

But John R. Bowen, an anthropologist at Washington University in St. Louis and author of *Why the French Don't Like Headscarves*, thinks the ban incurred resentment in the Muslim community. Nevertheless, he argues in a recent article, Muslims and non-Muslims in France "are far more willing to get on with the task of building a multireligious society than are the Dutch, British or Spanish — or even Americans."[24]

French Muslims, for instance, are not calling for sharia law, as do many British Muslims, he notes. Partly that's historical: Many North Africans arrive speaking fluent French and have a sense of affiliation to their former colonial power. Most French Muslims also tend to live in more ethnically mixed areas, while in England entire Bangladeshi villages seem to have been plopped down in single neighborhoods.

Most experts also give credit to the French police and domestic intelligence service. "The French really monitor their Muslims closely, so if someone is preaching a radical sermon they'll know right away and have much less compunction than the British to say, 'You can't do that,' or find a way to get rid of the guy" by deporting him, says Bowen.

Surprisingly, a French government adviser on religious affairs, Bernard Godard, who specialized in Muslim neighborhoods while serving with the French police and domestic intelligence service, ascribes France's lack of Muslim terrorism not to the country's policing efforts but to its policy of non-engagement in Iraq. "France is a little country that is not considered dangerous," he says. And it is harder to recruit North African Muslims for terrorism than Middle Easterners, he suggests. "They have no reason to do something against France."

The French also are much more inclusive toward newcomers than their neighbors. The French government gives newly arrived immigrants hundreds of hours of free French-language lessons to help qualify them for employment. In contrast, observes Bowen, the Netherlands recently required would-be immigrants — even the spouses of Dutch residents — to prove that they already speak good Dutch before they arrive, but provide no help in learning the language. "The Dutch are using language to exclude Muslims, the French to integrate them," he says.[25]

Similarly, Germany recently proposed requiring that immigrants show on their naturalization applications that they agree with German public opinion — a tactic some have called the policing of "un-German" thought. Turks and other Muslims see the plan as discriminatory, according to a study by the International Crisis Group (ICG). Nevertheless, the report concluded that Germany's approach to its mainly Turkish Muslim population was "paying off" — judging from the lack of terrorist incidents or riots in Germany compared to the experiences of Britain and France.[26] (The ICG report was issued before the recent foiled German plot.)

But Boston College political scientist Jonathan Laurence, the author of the ICG report on Germany and a book published last year on integration in France, says the recent German plot involving a Turkish resident doesn't change his "cautious optimism."[27]

Since Germany has traditionally treated Turkish immigrants as "guestworkers" rather than citizens, most of today's Turkish population still holds only Turkish citizenship even though half were born in Germany. A 2000 law opened the door to citizenship but under very restrictive rules. Laurence says German Turks have less "political frustration" than Muslims in other European countries because they have lower expectations as a result of German citizenship laws. "They don't feel as entitled

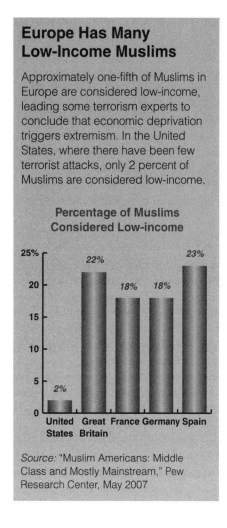

Europe Has Many Low-Income Muslims

Approximately one-fifth of Muslims in Europe are considered low-income, leading some terrorism experts to conclude that economic deprivation triggers extremism. In the United States, where there have been few terrorist attacks, only 2 percent of Muslims are considered low-income.

Percentage of Muslims Considered Low-income

Source: "Muslim Americans: Middle Class and Mostly Mainstream," Pew Research Center, May 2007

to success or mobility because they have not been included in the German dream," he says.

But he doubts that there are "any direct causal links" between a lack of integration and recent terrorist attempts in Europe. "There are too many other poorly integrated groups that don't turn to terror," he says.

If failure to integrate were the cause, "We'd have masses of people joining the jihad, which is not happening," says Jocelyne Cesari, director of Harvard University's Paris-based Islam in the West study group and author of the 2004 book *When Islam and Democracy Meet: Muslims in Europe and the United States.*

In fact, she continues, "All national ideologies in Europe are in crisis," as indicated by France's failure to ratify the EU constitution.[28] And for some young people, Islamic ideologies fill the vacuum left by national identity, she says.

That's what has happened in Britain, argues British *Daily Mail* journalist Melanie Phillips in her book *Londonistan*. England has become the epicenter of Islamic terrorism, she argues, in part because of shame about British national identity. "British society presented a moral and philosophical vacuum that was ripe for colonization by predatory Islamism," she writes.[29] "Driven by postcolonial guilt . . . Britain's elites have come to believe that the country's identity and values are by definition racist, nationalist and discriminatory."[30]

Ironically, points out Brandeis political scientist Klausen, England has the most terrorism in Europe even though it is one of Europe's most integrated countries by measures like education. The young Islamist radicals described in Husain's memoir are all middle class and well integrated, she points out, including Husain, who worked in a bank. "We have a movement of radical groups recruiting among middle-class, upwardly mobile young Muslims," she says.

Klausen blames England's terrorism on international political networks and a generational counterculture that has found violence-prone individuals. In her study of four Danish-born Muslim teenagers convicted in connection with an October 2005 plot to blow up the U.S. embassy in Sarajevo, she found many similarities to the shooters at Colorado's Columbine High School in 1999. In her ongoing study of 550 people arrested for terrorism since 9/11, she was surprised to find a high degree of petty-criminal histories, suggesting these are not mainstream Muslims. And a highly traditional, religious background does not seem to be a predictor either. "The argument that democracy is illegitimate is what turns them on," she says.

Although unemployment is high among young Muslim men in Britain, it isn't among terrorists arrested there, according to Klausen, suggesting only a tenuous link between inequality or discrimination and political anger.[31]

So is terrorism the result of a lack of integration or the influence of external terrorist networks? "It's both," according to Robert S. Leiken, director of the Immigration and National Security Program at the Nixon Center, a think tank in Washington, D.C. Europe, he says, currently has two kinds of jihadists: "outsiders" — typically radical imams, asylum seekers or students fleeing from

crackdowns against Islamist agitators in the Middle East — and "insiders"— second- or third-generation children of immigrants.[32]

"That's why Britain is the most dangerous country," according to Leiken. "It has the confluence of these two sources of jihad."

Has Britain's multiculturalism fostered social isolation and extremism?

Various books, columns and think-tank reports recently have blamed Britain's multicultural ethos for creating segregation along religious lines and, in some eyes, providing fertile ground for extremist Islamic ideas. Last year Prime Minister Tony Blair's Communities Secretary Ruth Kelly launched a study commission to examine whether multiculturalism* was causing greater ethnic-minority separateness.[33]

By the time the commission reported back in June, the term "multiculturalism" had disappeared from the report in favor of a new buzzword, "community cohesion," which some columnists took as a reflection of the government's growing anxiety about its earlier approach.[34]

Some critics say multiculturalism encourages Britons to elevate Islamic values over British values. Schools have ceased to transmit "either the values or the story of the nation" because in a multicultural classroom, the "majoritarian culture is viewed as illegitimate and a source of shame," writes Phillips in *Londonistan*.[35]

In that vacuum, it's easy for Islamic radicalism to step in, some argue. For instance, in the state school Husain attended in Britain, Muslim children attended separate assemblies managed by a front organization for the revolutionary Islamic movement Jamaat-e-Islami. It then administered tests promoting Islam as an ideology that sought political power.[36]

The debate over British schools' abdication of responsibility for teaching about Islam is strikingly different from the debate in the United States, where the struggle has usually been over whether officially authorized textbooks or curricula should give more prominence to the nation's traditionally ignored ethnic groups. Compared to Canada, where multiculturalism is a curriculum taught from kindergarten, the term in Britain is "a bit

---

* Multiculturalism is often described as the idea that all races, religions and ethnicities should be equally valued and respected.

murky," creating a "confused debate," says Canadian-born Abdul-Rehman Malik, a contributing editor at *Q-News*, an edgy magazine aimed at young British Muslim professionals.

To some critics, multiculturalism means the funding of local religious groups, which the critics blame for increasing tensions between Muslims and people of other faiths. A report issued this year by Policy Exchange, a conservative London think tank, concludes that the growth of radical Muslim politics has been "strongly nurtured by multicultural policies at the local and national level since the 1980s."[37]

Muslims' focus on religious identity and their sense that they are victims of discrimination "feeds into the broader narrative of victimhood that radical Islam in Britain is all about," says lead author Munira Mirza. "A lot of radical Islam in Britain is about saying, 'We Muslims are under attack; the West is against us.' "

Yet aside from legislation outlawing discrimination, which has been broadened to include religious discrimination, it's hard to point to any one government policy that's explicitly multicultural, says Sarah Spencer, associate director at the University of Oxford's Centre on Migration, Policy and Society and former deputy chairwoman of the government's Commission for Racial Equality.

Rather than multiculturalism causing the separation, "the factors that promote separation are socioeconomic ones," she maintains, such as housing clustered in poor neighborhoods.

Nevertheless, some critics argue that multiculturalism pervades both the public and private sectors in myriad ways, sometimes by just leaving Muslim communities alone.

The London-based Centre for Social Cohesion recently reported that the Islamic sections in public libraries in Tower Hamlets, London's most heavily Muslim borough, were dominated by fundamentalist literature — preaching terrorism and violence against women and non-Muslims.[38] This is a prime example of taxpayer-funded multicultural policy promoting radical Islam, according to center director Douglas Murray. A Muslim seeking to learn more about his faith from the library "couldn't help but be pushed toward the more extreme interpretation," he says.

The "most horrifying example" of let-them-alone multiculturalism, says Murray, is the estimated dozen Muslim women who are murdered in Britain each year

in "honor killings" by fathers and brothers. An independent commission is investigating how police handled the case of a 20-year-old Kurdish woman killed by her father after she repeatedly sought help from authorities.

Police "may be worried that they will be seen as racist if they interfere in another culture," said Diana Sammi, director of the Iranian and Kurdish Women's Rights Organization.[39]

Women's advocates have sought legislation to protect women from forced marriages — already outlawed in Norway and Denmark — which they see as strongly linked to honor killings (*see p. 233*). But University of Chicago anthropologist Richard Schweder cautions it's not clear that honor killings in the Muslim community occur with more frequency than passion killings of adulterous partners by Western husbands. Other experts suggest that police may have failed to follow through on these cases for other reasons, perhaps having more to do with their own racism or their attitudes towards domestic violence.

Leiken of the Nixon Center says Britain's "separatist form of multiculturalism" offered radical Islamists from Algeria and other Muslim countries refuge and the opportunity to preach openly during the 1990s at a time when the French government was denying asylum to radical Muslims.[40] Britain's multicultural ideology "meant the legal system was lenient, and police often found themselves in a situation where they couldn't do anything" when moderate Muslims complained about radical clerics taking over their mosques, Leiken says.

Outspoken multiculturalism critic Kenan Malik, an Indian-born writer and lecturer living in London, complains government leaders were "subcontracting out" their relationship with Muslim citizens by dealing almost exclusively with clerics or official groups like the British Muslim Council, which has been accused of having radical links. And in a report published last year, journalist Bright criticized government officials for championing a group that promotes "a highly politicised version of Islam."[41]

"Why should British citizens who happen to be Muslim rely on clerics?" Malik asks. "It encourages Muslims to see themselves as semi-detached Britons."

Many French experts tend to agree the British laissez faire approach to multiculturalism failed because the government "created a higher identification with the [religious] group and left all authority with the religious leaders," in the words of Riva Kastoryano, a senior

AP Photo/Bangalore Mirror

Kafeel Ahmed died of severe burns a month after his attempted car bombing of Glasgow International Airport on June 30, 2007. Iraqi doctor Bilal Abdullah was also in the car and was charged with attempting a bombing. Ahmed, an engineer from India, was among eight Muslims — including three physicians working for Britain's National Health Service — charged in connection with attempted car bombings in Glasgow and London.

research fellow at the University of Paris's National Center for Scientific Research, who has written a book on multiculturalism in Europe.

Indeed, when it comes to local government funding, Malik said, "multiculturalism has helped to segregate communities far more effectively than racism."[42]

For example, during the 2005 Birmingham riots in Britain, blacks and Asians turned against one another. But 20 years earlier, black and Asian youths had joined together in riots there to protest police harassment and poverty. What changed, according to Malik, was the local government's "multicultural response" — setting up consultation groups and allocating funding along faith lines. "Different groups started fighting one another

for funding, and the friction led to the riots between the two communities" in 2005, he says.

But the University of Birmingham's Abbas claims the 2005 riots were triggered by economic issues, ignited by a bogus radio story about a 14-year-old Caribbean girl who supposedly had been raped repeatedly by several Asian men. Abbas says that urban legend fed existing resentments over Asian takeovers of traditionally Caribbean businesses, like hair salons, in an area already suffering from declining jobs and ethnic rivalry over the drug market.

"It had nothing to do with multiculturalism," says Abbas.

Multiculturalism is more of an ideal about how to approach diversity and rid the country of its historic colonial baggage rather than a specific policy, in Abbas's view. To the extent it's been tried it varies greatly from one city to another, he stresses. "Multiculturalism hasn't been given its full testing period yet," he says. "We cannot easily say that because of multiculturalism we have the problems we have."

Would cracking down on terrorism violate civil liberties?

After the most recent foiled bombing plots in Britain, the Labor government proposed extending from 28 days to up to 56 days the period police can hold terrorist suspects without charge — a proposal opposed by both the Conservative and the Liberal Democratic parties.

The government says plots have become so complicated that police need more time to investigate. According to British police, big terrorism cases against one or two suspects can involve the investigation of 200 phones, 400 computers, 8,000 CDs, 6,000 gigabytes of data and 70 premises across three continents.[43]

In unveiling his anti-terror measures, Prime Minister Gordon Brown anticipated resistance from Parliament, which two years earlier had ratcheted down Blair's 90-day detention proposal to 28 days — a doubling of the then-14-day detention period.

"Liberty is the first and founding value of our country," Brown said. "Security is the first duty of our government."[44]

But Human Rights Watch says the extension would violate human rights law. The proposed 28 days is still more than twice as much as any other European country, and the government now releases more than half those accused in terrorism cases without charge, the group points out.[45]

CHRONOLOGY

19th Century *European nations colonize much of Muslim world. British colonization of India sparks mass Muslim immigration to Europe by end of century.*

1900-1960s *European rule in Islamic world ends. Muslims establish their own states. . . . Fundamentalist (Islamist) political groups emerge, some espousing a pan-Muslim caliphate. Muslim workers begin emigrating to Europe.*

1928 Radical Muslim Brotherhood is founded in Egypt.

1941 Islamist Jamaat-e-Islami party is founded in Pakistan.

1947-48 Pakistan becomes world's first avowedly Islamist state. . . . Israel is established, displacing Palestinians and creating lasting conflict with Arabs, Muslims.

1952 Col. Gamal Abdel Nasser topples Egyptian monarchy.

1953 Radical Islamic party Hizb ut-Tahrir is founded in Jerusalem.

1954 Brotherhood member tries to assassinate Nasser, who then imprisons leaders, including Sayyid Qutb. Qutb writes *Milestones* — manifesto of political Islam.

1964 *Milestones* is published.

1970s *Movement for Islamic state advances; Europe limits immigration to families, causing more Muslim emigration.*

1979 Iranian Revolution ousts U.S.-backed Reza Shah Pahlavi, brings Ayatollah Ruholla Khomeini to power.

1980s *Saudi Arabia, India, Pakistan and Iran seek to dominate Muslim world, send missionaries to Europe.*

1981 Scarman Report blames racial discrimination for South London Brixton riots, calls for multicultural approach toward Muslims.

1986 French pass strong terrorist-detention laws after spate of bombings.

1987 Saudi millionaire Osama bin Laden forms al Qaeda terrorist network.

1989 Iran's Khomeini calls for murder of Salmon Rushdie for his allegedly blasphemous depiction of Mohammed in *The Satanic Verses.*

1990s *Al Qaeda, other Islamist groups shift from national liberation to terrorism.*

1995 Algerian terrorists bomb Paris Metro.

1998 Al Qaeda calls on Muslims to kill Americans and their allies.

2000s *Islamist terrorists target Europe.*

Sept. 11, 2001 Terrorists attack World Trade Center and Pentagon.

December 2001 British Muslim Richard Reid tries to ignite "shoe bomb" aboard Paris-Miami flight.

2004 France bans Muslim head scarves in public schools. . . . Muslim terrorists kill 191 people in Madrid subway bombing. . . . Radical Islamist kills Dutch filmmaker Theo Van Gogh.

2005 London transit bombings kill 52. . . . Riots erupt in Muslim suburbs of Paris, other French cities.

2006 Danish cartoonist's depictions of Mohammed provoke protests worldwide. . . . Group of 23 mostly British Muslims are arrested on Aug. 10 on suspicion of planning to blow up transatlantic planes. . . . On Sept. 1 Muslims are arrested for running a terrorist camp in Sussex, Britain. . . . Britain expands detention powers against suspected terrorists.

2007 Europe and U.S. reported to be targets of revived al Qaeda. . . . Eight Muslims charged in failed car bombings in London, Glasgow; Bombing plots foiled in Germany, Denmark. British Prime Minister Gordon Brown proposes longer detention for terror suspects; British government encourages expansion of Muslim schools. . . . Spanish court convicts 21 in connection with 2004 Madrid train bombing; clears 3 alleged leaders.

What Makes a Person 'British'?

Stereotypical views are challenged.

At a North London pub, young professionals with pints in hand were engaged in a favorite national pastime — the Pub Quiz, a competition usually focused on trivia or sports.

But this quiz was different: It came from the test immigrants must take when applying for citizenship — popularly known as the "Britishness test." The 24-question exam was introduced in 2005 after former Home Secretary David Blunkett insisted that new immigrants should have a command of the English language and understand the nature of British life, customs and culture.

Not one of the 100 (mostly British) volunteers passed, an announcement greeted with applause, hilarity and shouts of "Deported!"

Teams with ad hoc names — like "As British as a pint of Guinness" — competed to answer such questions as, How many members are in Northern Ireland's Assembly? Who is the monarch not allowed to marry? and, curiously, What proportion of the United Kingdom population has used illegal drugs?

The highest score was 17, by Rohan Thanotheran, a Sri Lanka-born accountant who has lived in England since 1962.[1]

"Who would bother to learn those facts?" he asked later, suggesting the quiz was a desperate attempt by the government to reclaim nationalism at a time when symbols like the English flag are being hijacked by the far right.

Pub-goers are not the only British citizens who have failed. Member of Parliament Mike Gapes — who has supported the test, saying, "Nationalism is something that should be earned and not just given away" — flunked when 10 of the questions were posed to him during an interview.[2]

The test has been criticized for lengthening the application process and promoting a "siege mentality" among Britons towards foreigners.[3]

Many young people in the pub clearly found the questions comical, and several questioned the very idea of testing someone's "Britishness."

"The meaning of citizenship is not about knowing what percent of Christians in the U.K. are Catholics. Those are things most British citizens don't know. It doesn't make us any less British," said Munira Mirza, a writer, graduate student and founding member of The Manifesto Club, which organized the event to challenge stereotypical views of identity and Britishness.

A slim 29-year-old with shoulder-length black hair, Mirza was born in England of Pakistani Muslim parents. She describes herself as British-Asian but is quick to add that such ethnic and religious labels are "increasingly irrelevant to people, especially of my age, who grow up here and don't think of ourselves as ethnic categories." For example, she resists requests from TV producers to present the Muslim point of view. "You know what they're thinking: 'Only Muslims can connect with other Muslims.' It's quite a close-minded view," she says.

Two other quiz-takers from Muslim backgrounds in this distinctly secular crowd said they sometimes felt forced to

Longer detentions would "clearly discriminate" against Muslim communities and be "counterproductive in making Muslims willing to cooperate with police" because they arouse such resentment, says Ben Ward, associate director for Europe and Central Asia at Human Rights Watch in London. Polls show that more than half of British Muslims already lack confidence in the police, he says. Muslim groups like the Muslim Council of Britain oppose the extension on similar grounds.

Allowing telephone wiretap evidence in court — another change being considered by the government — would be more effective in pursuing terrorist cases, says Ward. Britain is the only Western country that bans wiretap evidence in

criminal prosecutions, he says, because its security services oppose revealing their methods.

Of all the counterterrorism measures being proposed in Europe, Human Rights Watch is "most concerned" about the United Kingdom, says Ward. But when it comes to existing practice, many experts consider France the most draconian.

From September 2001 to September 2006, France deported more than 70 people it considers "Islamic fundamentalists," including 15 Muslim imams, according to a recent Human Rights Watch report.[46]

The advocacy group argues that deportations require a much lower standard of evidence than identify with their parents' foreign heritage because English peers persisted in seeing them as foreigners.

Lani Homeri, 26, a fashionably dressed law student with striking dark eyes and long raven hair, was born in Britain of Iraqi Kurdish parents who emigrated in the 1970s. She finds it odd how frequently she is asked whether she is Muslim, especially, she says, since she wears Western clothing and is "not a practicing Muslim."

A 28-year-old male pub-goer born in Sweden of Iranian parents who had fled the Islamic revolution said hostile questions about Islam from native-born Britons often made him defensive. "I'm agnostic, but when people attack Islam, I start defending it, even though it messed up my country," he said. "People like me, who want a secular government, start to protect their government because it's attacked on stupid grounds."

Misperceptions about Islam could help explain a recent poll conducted by Harris Interactive for the *Financial Times*, which found the British are more suspicious of Muslims than other Europeans or Americans. Only 59 percent of Britons thought it possible to be both a Muslim and a citizen of their country, a smaller proportion than in France, Germany, Spain, Italy or the United States.[4]

Although the poll was taken before the foiled attacks in London and Glasgow in June, the memory of previous attacks, like the 7/7 transit bombings of July 7, 2005, may have hardened British attitudes. British citizens were also the most likely to predict a major terrorist attack in their country in the next 12 months, to consider Muslims a threat to national security and to believe Muslims had too much political power in their country.[5]

Mirza says those polls didn't reflect her own experience living in Britain. But she blames a "multicultural ethos" for forcing people to increasingly identify themselves with a particular ethnic or religious community, whether it is students taught to identify with people of their own race in history class or community leaders jockeying with ethnic groups for government funding.

A report Mirza coauthored for the London think tank Policy Exchange blames the methods Britain uses to encourage multiculturalism — such as providing local funding that can only be claimed by groups defined by ethnic or religious identity — for nurturing "a culture of victimhood" among Muslims, laying the groundwork for young people to turn to Muslim political groups.[6]

The rise of extremist groups is somewhat understandable "at a time when other political identities like 'left' and 'right' are not very appealing," Mirza observes, noting that young people are also gravitating to other forms of extremism, such as violence in the name of animal rights.

"We should be winning these young people over to other ideas," she says. "Unless you deal with that major problem, you will always find people will turn to something else that's offering a vision."

---

[1] Justin Gest, "How Many of 100 Britons Passed the Citizenship Exam? Not One," Sept. 29, 2007, *The Times* (London), www.timesonline .co.uk/tol/news/uk/article2554235.ece.

[2] Daniel Adam, "Redbridge Fails Britishness Test," *Rising East*, May 2006, www.uel.ac.uk/risingeast/archive04/journalism/adam.htm.

[3] *Ibid.*

[4] Daniel Dombey and Simon Kuper, "Britons 'More Suspicious' of Muslims," *Financial Times*, Aug. 19, 2007, www.FT.com.

[5] *Ibid.*

[6] Munira Mirza, *et al.*, "Living Apart Together: British Muslims and the Paradox of Multiculturalism," *Policy Exchange*, 2007, p. 18.

---

judicial prosecutions and violate human rights because they often expose deportees to torture in their home countries. "Our point is not that all these guys are completely innocent, but even if someone is guilty of involvement in terrorism, France has a duty to make sure they're not sending them back to a place where they're facing threat of torture" — a serious risk even for an innocent person returned home once he's slapped with a terrorist label, says Judith Sunderland, author of the Human Rights Watch report on France's deportations.

"When we talk to people in Muslim communities, there's a lot of fear; they know they're being watched, and they're concerned about what they can say," says Sunderland. "We spoke to imams who said anytime they say anything in defense of someone accused of terrorism, they know they will be on someone's watch list." This fear erodes Muslims' trust in law enforcement and makes them less willing to cooperate in terrorism cases, she says.

But Godard, the adviser to the French Interior Ministry who has served as a specialist on Arab communities in both the national police and security services, dismisses her concerns. "Fifteen imams [removed] in 10 years — it's nothing," he says with a shrug.

Human Rights Watch is also concerned about France's use of its "criminal conspiracy" charge, which it says requires a low standard of evidence. "People are being detained for up to two years on very flimsy evidence," says Ward.

Godard shares this concern, complaining that the prosecutorial judges in France's special terrorism courts have "too much power" and that the source of evidence is not made public.

But many French citizens are happy with the system because they think it has kept them safe from terrorism, concedes Sunderland. France's surveillance system may curtail civil liberties, agrees Kastoryano, at the National Center for Scientific Research, but she adds, "This debate is in America, not here; no one here will talk about civil liberties."

As for the government's contention that its spying, secret files, deportations and special courts have been effective against terrorism, Sunderland says, "We don't have the information the French intelligence services have and have no way of verifying if they dismantled terrorist networks and prevented specific attacks, which is what the French government repeatedly claims."

When someone appeals a deportation in France, the only thing the government provides is an unsigned and undated "white paper" summarizing intelligence information, Sunderland says, "but not the sources or methodology, and the defendant can't go behind the information and figure out where it's coming from."

Proponents of expanded powers for the state argue that an exaggerated concern for human rights in England has inhibited authorities from pursuing terrorist suspects compared to France.

After France's experience with terrorists in the mid-1980s, new legislation extended the detention period for suspects. Using the 1986 law, the French "cleaned out outsiders, and the [radicals] went to Britain if they didn't go to jail," claims the Nixon Center's Leiken. By 1994, "that was a big problem in Britain."

By contrast, Britain's 30 years of experience with the Irish Republican Army (IRA) left British police unprepared for today's brand of Islamic terrorism, with no foreign-intelligence capacity and insufficient time to investigate the computer technology used by Islamic plotters, according to Peter Clarke, head of the Metropolitan Police Counter Terrorism Command. That inexperience was evident in the police shooting in the London underground of Brazilian electrician Jean Charles de Menezes on July 22, 2005, mistaken for one

of the terrorists who had tried to detonate bombs on London's transit system the day before. The London Metropolitan police force was found guilty Nov. 1 of putting the public at risk during the bungled operation.

Unlike the IRA, Clarke says, today's terrorism threat is global, with players willing to die who are quickly replaced. Networks re-form quickly, no warnings are given and weaponry (like fertilizer bombs) is unconventional, he says.[47]

He cites the case of Dhiren Barot, an al Qaeda plotter who left plans on his laptop computer for killing thousands of people in Britain (and the United States) by detonating underground bombs.

After Barot's arrest in 2004, British police had to "race against time" to retrieve enough evidence from the seized computers and other equipment to justify charges at the end of the permitted period of detention.[48] After that experience, the Terrorism Act of 2006 criminalized "acts preparatory to terrorism," and police proposed extending the period terrorist suspects can be held without charge.[49]

In addition, since 2001 British anti-terror laws have given the government — with public support — more leeway to mine databases for information about individuals. "There was an assumption that if it was necessary to hand over our privacy to the state to provide protection, that it was a price worth paying," says Gareth Crossman, policy director at Liberty, a London-based civil liberties advocacy group. Now, the country has so many cameras trained on citizens "the government's privacy watchdog describes England as 'the surveillance society.' "[50]

A recent Liberty report warns privacy could be invaded in the future because of the government's ability to mine data and watch people on the street. Surveillance cameras, more prevalent in Britain than any other country, are credited with tracing autos involved in past terrorist attempts. But Liberty wants the government to regulate where they're placed and how they're operated (many are installed by private companies) to protect ordinary citizens' privacy.[51]

Legislation passed in Britain would authorize a national ID card, though it hasn't been implemented and may never be because of the cost. But Crossman warns the government could use it to trawl through databases for personal information by profiling "the sort of person that might be involved in terrorist activity — purely on the basis of demographic information. It's a real minefield. A young, Muslim male is basically where it will end up. That's hugely sensitive."

BACKGROUND

Muslim Migration

Modern Muslim immigration to Europe began in the late 19th century as a result of Europe's colonial and trading activity, which largely explains the different ethnic groups in each country and to some extent their degree of acceptance by those societies.

The French conquest of Algiers in 1830 eventually led to French control of Algeria, Morocco and Tunisia. Together, British colonization of India (which included modern-day Pakistan and Bangladesh) and Dutch domination of trade in Asia gave the three European countries control over most of the world's Muslims.

At the end of the 19th century, immigration began on a large scale, as France imported low-paid workers from Algeria and other African territories and other countries recruited workers from their colonies and territories.

Following World War II, countries like England sought workers, including many Muslims, to help with reconstruction. By the 1960s, entire Muslim families had begun to settle in Europe.

By 1974, however, a global economic recession had led many countries to limit migration, allowing entry only for family reunification or political asylum. Paradoxically, the policy led to further immigration by families, the only means of entry. The recession also increased Europeans' resentment of immigrants and their children, who were viewed as competing for jobs.

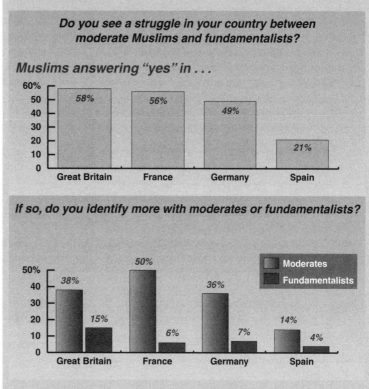

More Muslims Identify With Moderates

More than half of the Muslims in France and Great Britain believe a struggle is going on in their countries between moderate and fundamentalist Islamic ideologies (top). Those who see such a struggle identify overwhelmingly with the moderates (bottom). Britain has the largest percentage of Muslims identifying with the fundamentalists.

Do you see a struggle in your country between moderate Muslims and fundamentalists?

Muslims answering "yes" in . . .

Great Britain 58%, France 56%, Germany 49%, Spain 21%

If so, do you identify more with moderates or fundamentalists?

Moderates / Fundamentalists

Great Britain 38% / 15%, France 50% / 6%, Germany 36% / 7%, Spain 14% / 4%

Source: "Muslims in Europe: Economic Worries Top Concerns About Religious and Cultural Identity," Pew Global Attitudes Project, July 2006

During the 1980s, Muslims' religious identity became more pronounced as young Muslims — frustrated by job discrimination — turned to their religion as a source of identity. Islamic political movements in Iran, North Africa and South Asia also influenced this trend.

The rise of political Islam encouraged Muslims in Europe to form associations based on religion, which heightened Europeans' fears of Islam as growing numbers of Muslim refugees were arriving from wars in Iran, Iraq, Lebanon, Palestine and Bosnia. At this time, as rivalry broke out between different groups in Saudi Arabia, India, Pakistan and Iran for domination of Muslim ideology,

Radical Mosque Says It Has Changed

But skeptics say its hard-core views are hidden.

The atmosphere at the East London Mosque during a dinner held recently with non-Muslim neighbors could not have been more congenial or ecumenical.

Ministers from a local interfaith group and executives in suits from a local hospital philanthropy joined bearded Muslims in skullcaps over plates of Indian food as they broke the Ramadan fast. They had just listened to a mosque lecturer declare, "We're all children of Adam" and "The meaning of Islam isn't terrorism, destruction or violence."

But these reassurances seem at odds with the reputation the mosque developed in the 1990s as a center for radical, young Muslims. And some observers of the London Muslim scene say that beneath its smooth public relations efforts the mosque remains a major center for radical Islam.

"The East London Mosque is at the center of a very sophisticated Jamaat-e-Islami network in Britain," says Martin Bright, political editor for the left-leaning *New Statesman* magazine, referring to the extremist Islamic political party based in Pakistan. "It is essentially the dominant force in the formation of Islamist ideology in Britain — and Europe." Jamaat-e-Islami and other Islamists espouse an Islamic state governed by sharia law.

But on two recent visits to the mosque, including the imam's weekly Friday sermon, talk of radicalism was absent. Instead the imam admonished the congregation for giving too little to charity. ("You give rice, but it's probably not even Basmati.")

Sumaia Begum, 19, a Londoner of Bangladeshi parentage dressed in black from head scarf to figure-concealing skirt, had just listened to the sermon in the secluded second-floor women's section, crowded with Bangladeshis and Somalis in somber black head-coverings. She seemed unaware of the mosque's reputation. "I'd love to live in an Islamic state, but bombing innocent people here — that's

not right," she said. "Bearing and raising children — for us, that is our jihad."

Critics of Islamist ideology say mosques like East London often have two faces — a moderate one for the public and a hard-core ideology they might only reveal at summer indoctrination camps for young people.

"At the Friday sermon, which is open to the public, they would not preach hatred," says Irfan Al Alawi, international director of the Center for Islamic Pluralism, a London think tank that promotes religious tolerance. "They would have before 7/7" (the July 7, 2005, London transit bombings). "But when it became obvious they were being investigated because of links with jihadists in Pakistan, they became somewhat cautious."

Throughout the late 1980s, the mosque, located at the heart of London's densest Bangladeshi neighborhood, was home to rival Jamaat-e-Islami factions in Britain, according to British author Ed Husain, a former radical who says he first encountered extremist rhetoric at the mosque in the 1990s, when most of its committee members were affiliated with the movement.[1]

Today, he writes, the Saudi-trained imam of the big mosque continues to lead a faction opposed to modernizing elements and prohibits gatherings of opponents of Islamism and of the strict Saudi version of Islam — Wahhabism.[2]

But Dilowar Khan, the director of the mosque and the gleaming London Muslim Center next door (built with government, private and Saudi funding), says he and his fellow Muslims at the mosque, like Husain, have moved away from the separatist views espoused in the 1990s, with their single-minded focus on replacing secular regimes in the Muslim world with religious states.

Back then, people were interested in Bangladeshi politics, in which Jamaat-e-Islami was very active, he explains. "Now we're more interested in how to improve

Europe became a target of missionary and proselytizing efforts, helped along by the distribution of petrodollars — mainly from Saudi Arabia — to create mosques, Islamic schools and even university chairs.[52]

Saudi money supported the spread and teaching of the Wahhabi strand of Islam, the official religion of Saudi

Arabia and the guiding spiritual doctrine of al Qaeda. Wahhabism is a fundamentalist form of Islam that preaches strict adherence to Islam's injunctions, including abiding by sharia law.

As Harvard's Cesari explains, since Sept. 11 the apolitical nature of fundamentalist groups has been our life and image here." For instance, he says, the mosque invites local political candidates as speakers and offers various services, ranging from job counseling to computer education.

While the mosque still may have members who are Wahhabis or followers of Jamaat, it does not define itself by any of those sects, according to Khan. He denies any "formal links" to those groups or to the Tablighi-Jamaat, a hard-line Islamic missionary movement that Al Alawi says has also captured much of the mosque's leadership.

As for Jamaat-e-Islami's central mission — to establish a Muslim state — Khan says, "We believe Islam is a complete code of life. . . . What's wrong with a Muslim country establishing an Islamic state by majority rule?"

What about the party's call for establishing sharia rule? "We're not interested in implementing sharia law in this country," he claims. "If the majority of people in Muslim countries want to implement certain laws in their own country, who am I to tell them, 'Don't do that'?" Later, he emphasized that sharia is the very essence of the religion, adding, "People who are against sharia law are enemies of Islam."

Does he advocate sharia courts like those in Nigeria, which order the amputation of limbs and stoning of women as punishments straight from the *Koran*? "That's only about 1 percent of sharia law," he says, which refers to the vast body of religious observance in Islam, including fasting at Ramadan.

Hisham A. Hellyer, an expert on counterterrorism at the University of Warwick and a former visiting fellow at the Washington-based Brookings Institution think tank, says that while Jamaat-e-Islami did have a presence in Britain's activist groups in the 1980s because of members' involvement in their home countries, "It's a bit of a stretch to say they were the direct wings of these organizations in the U.K." He points out, "It's not unusual for politicians in Britain to have been communists as students, but they mature and grow up. That's what happened to leaders in the Muslim community."

A recent TV documentary dramatized the perception that Muslim mosques are not always what they

Muslim religious attire is common in the Bangladeshi East London neighborhood of Whitechapel, home to the East London Mosque, one of Britain's largest.

seem, reporting that Muslim clerics engaged in far more radical language — justifying terrorist bombings, for instance — in private meetings than in public sermons. Since the broadcast, however, some clerics have charged their words were taken out of context. The complaints are being investigated by Britain's broadcasting watchdog.[3]

Such charges and countercharges reflect a problem that Jason Burke, a veteran reporter on the Muslim world for the *British Observer* (of London), says "confronts me daily as a journalist working in the field. Who are our interlocutors? Whose voices best represent the complex, diverse and dynamic societies that are bundled together in that terrible generalization, the 'Muslim world'?"[4]

---

[1] Ed Husain, *The Islamist* (2007), p. 24.

[2] *Ibid.*, p. 280.

[3] BBC, "C4 Distorted Mosque Programme," Aug. 8, 2007, http://news.bbc.co.uk/1/hi/englan.

[4] Preface by Jason Burke in Martin Bright, "When Progressives Treat with Reactionaries," *Policy Exchange*, 2006, p. 7.

---

increasingly questioned as these groups have radicalized their rhetoric against non-Muslims and the West. These movements preach "a theology of intolerance" — referring to all non-Muslims as *kaffir* (or infidel) and aspects of modern life as *haram* (forbidden) — "which can easily become . . . a theology of hate," she writes. Since the

1967 Israeli victory over the Arabs, a feeling of humiliation has combined with a warlike insistence on Islam's superiority over everything Western, democratic and secular.[53]

Individual acts of political terrorism in the 1990s and early 2000s fueled fears of radical Islam in Europe. Between

1995 and 1996, a radical Algerian group seeking an Islamic state in Algeria set off bombs on Paris subways and trains. And, prior to the 1998 World Cup soccer tournament in France, the French arrested 100 members of the group in a preventive action. Radical preachers in Paris and London began to attract young Muslims from the poorer suburbs and cities. Some went to fight in Afghanistan or Iraq, while a few committed terrorist acts at home.

Increased immigration from Muslim countries and high birthrates combined to make Islam the fastest-growing religion on the continent, even as ethnic and religious tensions grew. In October 2005 riots erupted in the Muslim suburbs of Paris and other French cities, with the participants complaining of joblessness and discrimination. Muslims also demonstrated against the proposed ban on Muslim girls wearing head scarves at school, which took effect in 2004.

The Madrid train bombings, the 2004 assassination of Dutch filmmaker Theo Van Gogh by a Dutch-Moroccan and the 2005 London subway explosions — all committed by radical Muslims — led European countries to question how well they were integrating Muslim immigrants and their children.

Anthropologist Bowen attributes the differences in how Muslim communities have been absorbed and the types of politics they've adopted in various European countries to the different ways each country treated its colonies and immigrants from those colonies.

In France, Muslim immigrants are clustered in poor, outer suburbs that include a mix of North Africans — such as Algerians, Moroccans and Tunisians — all of whom speak French and grew up under French rule. North Africans often arrived feeling that they were quasi-French citizens, even if they were second-class citizens, says Bowen.

But in Britain many Muslims live in ethnic enclaves in Bangladeshi or Pakistani neighborhoods where Bengali is spoken in stores and banks, and parents of London-born children often speak no English. As schools in these neighborhoods become 100 percent Asian, some educators are concerned the teaching of English as a first language is being thwarted.[54]

"The French [immigration] story goes back to the beginning of the 20th century," Bowen adds, "whereas in Britain the immigration is much more recent, and the communities are much more closed off."

In addition, he notes, "The French kids from North Africa are more tied into the Muslim Brotherhood, which

says, 'Obey the laws of the country you're in, and try to create conditions to live as a Muslim.' There's none of this talk about creating a separate Islamic state that [the radical group] Hizb-ut-Tahrir runs on."

'Londonistan'

The shift to religiously oriented politics in Britain took place in the 1980s and '90s with the increasing embrace of identity politics and the arrival of Islamist political refugees.

After the 1981 rioting in the impoverished Brixton neighborhood of south London, the Scarman Report called for a multiracial, multicultural approach that would recognize the uniquely different needs of ethnic groups. National and local governments awarded funds to groups identifying themselves as ethnic or racial minorities, including ethnic housing associations, arts centers, radio channels and voluntary organizations. Local governments helped set up representative bodies to consult with Muslims over local issues. The funding of conservative religious organizations like the East London Mosque sometimes came at the expense of secular groups, say critics.[55]

The Rushdie affair led to a seminal moment in Muslim identity politics. In 1988 author Salman Rushdie's novel *The Satanic Verses* infuriated Muslims who felt it ridiculed the Prophet Mohammed. British Muslims formed the U.K. Action Committee on Islamic Affairs to protest the perceived blasphemy. Eventually Iran's supreme religious leader, the late Ayatollah Khomeini, issued a religious edict known as a *fatwa* condemning Rushdie to death. But the anti-Rushdie campaign was led primarily from Pakistan by disciples of the deceased Islamist ideologue Abul A'la Maududi, who founded the Jamaat-e-Islami party in India in 1941.

Book burnings in Bradford, England, widely covered by the media, also raised the profile of radical Islamism among young Muslims. The first Gulf War, the Palestinian intifadas of the late 1980s and early '90s and the slaughter of Muslims in Bosnia also discomfited Muslims about their loyalties.

Radical Islam in Britain has evolved under the influence of Islamist groups operating from Pakistan, Bangladesh and the Middle East. According to Policy Exchange, the conservative think tank in London, money poured in from Saudi Arabia and Pakistan for new religious, publishing and education facilities in Britain, shifting the balance "from more traditional and apolitical Muslim organisations toward more internationalist and politically radical groups," especially those leaning toward Wahhabism.[56]

Indeed, as France and other nations forced Islamists to leave in the 1990s, members of the French secret service dubbed the British capital "Londonistan" for its role as a refuge for Islamist groups.[57]

In the weeks following the attacks on the World Trade Center and the Pentagon, many mainstream British news organizations — including the *Guardian* — accepted that the attacks were a response to suffering in the Palestinian territories and to American support of Israel. In interviews, young British Muslims said 9/11 and later the London bombings of 2005 made them identify as Muslims more than they had before. After the Iraq War started in 2003, Islamists joined with left-wing groups and created the Respect Party on an anti-war platform. "Radical Islam's narrative of the victimised *ummah* [Muslim community] has drawn sustenance from broader public anger at U.S. and U.K. foreign policy," says Policy Exchange.[58]

Terrorist Attacks

The current wave of terrorism can be traced to Feb. 23, 1998, when al Qaeda issued a *fatwa* stating that all Muslims had a duty to kill Americans and their allies — civilian or military. Islamic liberation movements began to shift their emphasis to localized, violent jihad.[59]

The Sept. 11, 2001, attacks were directly tied to al Qaeda, as was the attempt three months later by British-born Muslim Richard Reid to blow up an American Airlines flight from Paris to Miami by lighting explosives in his shoes.

Twenty-nine Muslims living in Spain — including first-generation North Africans from Algeria, Tunisia and Morocco — were charged in connection with the March 2004 bombing of four Madrid trains at rush hour, which killed 191 people and injured more than 1,800.[60] The group included petty drug traffickers as well as university students. Jamal Ahmidan, the plot's Moroccan mastermind, was said to be happily integrated into Spanish society. In October, a Spanish court found 21 people guilty of involvement in the bombing, but three alleged leaders were cleared.[61]

That November, Dutch filmmaker Van Gogh, who had made a film critical of Islam's treatment of women, was stabbed to death on an Amsterdam street by

Railway workers and police in Madrid examine a train destroyed in a terrorist bombing in March 2004 that killed 191 and injured thousands. In late October, 21 of the 29 people charged were found guilty, including North African men from Algeria, Tunisia and Morocco.

Mohammed Bouyeri, 26, the Amsterdam-born son of Moroccans. Bouyeri, whose radicalism began during a seven-month period in prison, belonged to the Hofsted Group, which had considered bombing the Dutch parliament.[62]

Until the most recent plots, post-2001 terrorist attempts in Europe had been seen as independently planned, even if the organizers took their inspiration from al Qaeda. That appears to have been the case in the 2005 London bus and subway suicide-bomb attacks. The first attack, on July 7, involved four British Muslims — three Pakistanis from West Yorkshire and an Afro-Caribbean Muslim convert. All four had Westernized, unremarkable backgrounds, according to the NYPD. A second attack, intended for three underground trains and a bus on July 21, failed because the bombs did not detonate.

On Aug. 10, 2006, 23 individuals — most British citizens and nearly all Muslim — were arrested on suspicion of plotting to blow up transatlantic airliners using liquid explosives. Three weeks later a group of Muslims was arrested for running a terrorist training camp at a former convent school in Sussex. A total of 68 people were arrested, and al Qaeda is suspected of being centrally involved in the bomb plot.[63]

Several doctors in England were arrested in two incidents — trying to blow up cars near a London nightclub on June 29 and driving a burning jeep into the Glasgow airport the next day.

Although the Sept. 11, 2001, attacks were directed by al Qaeda, they were planned by a group of English-speaking Muslims at a mosque in Hamburg, where they had been radicalized.

"Without a group of radicalized jihadists who had been homegrown in the West to lead this plot, the chances of 9/11 being a success would have been reduced considerably," concluded the NYPD intelligence report. "The Hamburg group underwent a process of homegrown radicalization that matched almost exactly those of Madrid, London, Amsterdam."

But unlike the 7/7 bombers who attacked London, the NYPD observes, when members of the Hamburg group went to Afghanistan to fight, they were re-directed to another target in the West, not to their place of residence.[64]

The North London Central Mosque, better known as the Finsbury Park Mosque, became infamous in the early 2000s for its support of radical Islam under the leadership of its fiery imam, Abu Hamza al-Masri. The mosque's attendees included shoe bomber Reid and 9/11 conspirator Zacarias Moussaoui. After British police raided the mosque on Jan. 20, 2003, it eventually was reclaimed by mainstream Muslims.

However, the London-based think tank Policy Exchange found extremist anti-Western, anti-Semitic literature at the mosque and claims a mosque trustee has said he is prepared to be a suicide bomber against Israel, according to a report released Oct. 30.[65]

Since the 2003 raid, law enforcement and security forces have tried to work with other mosque leaders to prevent the incitement to violence that emanated from Finsbury Park and other Salafi mosques in London in the 1990s.* Among the most notorious clerics were:

- Al-Masri, who was sentenced to seven years for incitement to murder in February 2006;
- Abdullah el-Faisal, a Jamaican-born convert sentenced to nine years in 2003 for soliciting the murder of Jews, Americans and Hindus and inciting racial hatred.[66]

---

* Salafi is a term applied broadly to sects that adhere to a supposedly pure form of Islam that they believe was practiced by Islam's ancestors; it often refers to Wahhabis and sometimes to Deobandis, the Muslim Brotherhood and Jamaat-e-Islami.

- Syrian-born self-styled cleric Omar Bakri Mohammed, who helped establish the radical group Al Muhajiroun and called the 9/11 hijackers the "Magnificent 19," has been banned from Britain and currently lives abroad.[67]

Action against radical clerics was authorized by amendments to Britain's Terrorism Act adopted in 2001, 2005 and 2006, which expanded the definition of terrorist offenses. The most recent changes criminalized "incitement to terrorism," providing assistance to terrorists and providing instruction in the use of firearms and explosives. The British government also has been given greater ability to ban political groups. Last year it considered banning both Hizb ut-Tahrir and Al Muhajiroun, which are both active on college campuses.[68]

CURRENT SITUATION

Worsening Threat

The recent string of disrupted plots in Europe signals a "continuing and worsening" radicalization within Europe's Islamic diaspora and a renewed leadership role for al Qaeda, according to a recent report from the International Institute for Strategic Studies (IISS), a leading security think tank in London. Al Qaeda has regrouped as an organization and now has the capacity to carry out another 9/11-magnitude attack, according to the IISS.[69]

Britain is considered the main target, with up to 30 terrorist plots discovered there — some that would have involved mass-casualty suicide attacks, said British intelligence officials last November.[70] Al Qaeda's Pakistan-based leadership was directing its British followers "on an extensive and growing scale," the officials said, and British authorities said they have their eye on 2,000 individuals involved in such plots. In fact, said Britain's domestic intelligence chief Jonathan Evans on Nov. 5, terrorist recruitment is accelerating so quickly that there could now be twice that many — up to 4,000 — potential terrorists living in Britain. Terrorists are grooming British youths as young as 15 to aid in terrorism and have expanded their training bases beyond Pakistan, specifically to Somalia and other areas in East Africa.[71]

Meanwhile, U.S. officials fear Europe's terrorist problems could be exported to the United States because of the ease with which Europeans travel to America. "When you talk to intelligence officials, that's their nightmare," says the Nixon Center's Leiken.

Intelligence officials in Denmark and Washington said at least one suspect in the abortive Copenhagen bombing had direct ties to leading al Qaeda figures. Jakob Scharf, head of Danish intelligence, said Muslim extremists typically are young men, ages 16-25, courted by mentors who identify those predisposed toward a jihadi mindset, radicalize them and put them in touch with others who could help them plan violent action. Denmark became the target of terrorist groups after a conservative Danish newspaper published cartoons two years ago widely seen as mocking Islam.[72]

Fertile Ground

In the past two decades, Europe and the United States have become "crucial battlegrounds" in the rapidly intensifying competition between groups in Saudi Arabia, India, Pakistan and Iran for control of Muslim ideology, according to Harvard's Cesari.[73]

The Saudis spent an estimated $85 billion between 1975 and 2005 to spread fundamentalist Islam by distributing Wahhabi prayer books, dispatching missionaries and imams and building grand mosques in Madrid, Rome, Copenhagen and Great Britain.[74]

The report released last week by Policy Exchange found extremist literature — preaching stoning of adulterers, jihad and hatred for non-Muslims — at a quarter of 100 leading mosques and educational institutions visited in England, including the East London Mosque. (*See sidebar, p. 226.*) Much of the material was distributed by Saudi organizations, found in Saudi-funded institutions or written by members of the Wahhabi religious establishment, the report said.

Historically, there have been two paths to violent extremism, notes Brandeis University's Klausen. A political movement seeking Islamic sovereignty includes the Muslim Brotherhood, the Pakistani party Jamaat-e-Islami, Hizb ut-Tahrir, Hamas and Al Muhajiroun.

Competing with them are puritanical groups like the Deobandi sect and the ultra-conservative Tablighi-Jamaat movement, which consider "recent" innovations, such as the mystically oriented practices of the Sufi Muslims and the worship of saints, as impermissible. Like the political groups, these groups glorify suicide but tend to stress theological and moral, rather than political, arguments.

Courtesy Ed Husain

British writer Ed Husain describes his recruitment in the 1990s in London by radical Islamists in his 2007 memoir. Today Husain, a former member of the group Hizb ut-Rahrir, remains skeptical of its nonviolent stance.

Europe may have proven fertile ground for strict interpretations of Islam, according to Cesari, because some Muslims react to the bewildering range of moral choices in today's globalized Western society with a certain "rigidity of thought and total rejections of cultural pluralism."[75]

But the variety of those arrested for terrorism in recent years suggests there are many reasons young Muslims are drawn to radicalism. For example, about 9 percent are converts, who might have been drawn to other kinds of radical political groups in another era.[76]

For author Husain, one of the few ex-radicals to publicly describe his journey into that world, "it was the serious lack of a sense of belonging here in Britain. We're all left alone like atoms to do our own thing. There's no collective entity. In that vacuum, extremists point to other coherent forms of identity, which are very easy to sign up to."

Questioning Integration

As concern about radical extremism grows, some European governments are rethinking their approach to integrating Muslims and are demanding more from immigrants who want citizenship, including acceptance of their national values.

"It's clear the Dutch and British laissez faire models have outlived their usefulness," says Laurence of Boston College. "No longer will a blank check be given to religious

AT ISSUE

Should the British government fund Muslim faith schools?

YES
Ibrahim Hewitt
Vice Chairman, Association of Muslim Schools, U.K.

Written for *CQ Global Researcher,* October 2007

The right of any group to establish a school and have it paid for by the state is enshrined in the 1944 Education Act. This is not limited to people of any particular religious or political background. Section 76 of the act goes on to say that "pupils are to be educated in accordance with the wishes of their parents." These provisions grew out of a compromise between church and state concerning the church-run schools then in operation. The state took over control of some of the schools while leaving others more or less in the control of the church. That is the context in which the state funding of Muslim schools exists.

Critics of faith schools — read "Muslim schools" — claim state funding is a historical anomaly that should be abolished. Proponents believe that parental choice has a firm basis in history, as made clear by Section 76. Choice has long been exercised by Anglican, Roman Catholic and Jewish parents, to little or no criticism. Now, many of the criticisms of faith schools are surfacing with the existence of Muslim schools, which were established by parents not unreasonably asking for the same choice in return for paying the same taxes toward education as everyone else.

Faith plays a hugely important part in the life of most Muslims — the notion of a "secular Muslim" is actually a contradiction in terms — and we are enjoined by the *Qu'ran* to "enter into Islam wholeheartedly" and not make any differentiation between religious and secular. It follows, therefore, that the education of our children should be within a framework that recognizes the existence and importance of their faith background.

As parents, we have a legal, moral and religious duty to raise and educate our children to become upright and honest citizens. The fact that the law of the land encourages the existence of faith schools as a core education provision in Britain means that parents from all faiths and none have a choice about their children's schools. Those who would have all schools as religion-free zones offer no such choice while overlooking conveniently that a secular approach is not a neutral approach; it is a conscious desire to remove religion from public life — hardly tolerant in a society where many faiths are represented across different communities.

Human-rights legislation makes clear that people should have freedom of religion; to insist on schools in which faith is the only forbidden f-word is both unreasonable and undemocratic. Muslims' taxes pay for schools of all faiths and none, so why shouldn't some of those taxes be used to fund Muslim schools as well?

NO
Terry Sanderson
President, National Secular Society

Written for *CQ Global Researcher,* October 2007

In a country increasingly divided by religion, the prospect of a hundred or more Muslim schools being brought into the state sector is truly terrifying. The British government, by some upside-down logic, has convinced itself that separating children in schools along religious lines will somehow help create "community cohesion."

The government clings to this opinion in the face of all the evidence. Its own advisers have said Muslim communities are "leading parallel lives," that we as a nation are "sleepwalking into segregation" and that segregated schools are a "ticking time bomb."

At present, there are seven Muslim schools paid for by the state. The rest are operating privately. There is little control over what goes on in the fee-paying schools, and the government argues that by bringing them under state control it would be easier to oversee them and ensure that they teach the national curriculum to an acceptable standard.

But the Muslim parents who took their children out of the state system in the first place did so because they felt that what the state offered was not what they wanted. If the state is not going to provide the strictly Islamic education they desire for their children, then they will simply opt out again and set up more private schools. The state will have to compromise if it wants these people on board.

So, rather than the national curriculum changing Muslim schools, it will be Muslim schools that force the national curriculum to change. Before long we will have schools where girls are forced to wear veils. (This has already been advocated by a leading Muslim educator, even for non-Muslim pupils who might seek a place in the school.) We will have state schools where swimming lessons are not permitted, where male teachers cannot teach girls, where there is no music, no representative art and no sporting activities for females unless they are "modestly dressed" in flowing garments.

Because the Church of England and the Catholic Church have traditionally operated about one-third of Britain's state school system, it is now difficult to argue that other religions should not be permitted to have their own "faith schools." But by permitting Islamic schools into the state system, the government is colluding in the very thing it insists it is against — the further separation of an already-isolated community.

The only way out of this unholy mess is to dismantle the whole system of state-operated religious schools and return them to community control.

communities to govern themselves. It led to isolation in which a certain extremism thrived."

In the Netherlands the 90-year-old policy of "pillarization," which permits each faith to set up its own faith schools and organizations, is falling out of favor among the Dutch as they see their own socially progressive mores conflicting with Muslim values.

Increasingly, politicians on both the left and right in the Netherlands are saying about Muslims: "We have to be intolerant of the intolerant," says Jan Duyvendak, a professor of sociology at the University of Amsterdam. Applicants for citizenship are shown a film of topless women and two men kissing. The message it's supposed to send: "If you want to come to the Netherlands, you should be tolerant of this," he says.

Scandinavian countries also feel that their culture and values, including gender equality, are increasingly threatened by Muslim communities that "we have quite failed to integrate," Unni Wikan, a professor of social anthropology at the University of Oslo, told a panel recently in London.[77]

Several Scandinavian governments, for example, have outlawed forced marriages of minors, often imported from a Muslim man's native village or clan. In Norway participation in a forced marriage brings up to 60 years in prison. Denmark requires that spouses brought into the country be at least 24 years old. Other European countries are considering similar laws, says Wikan, because "we're afraid we're leading toward a society that's breaking up into ethnic tribes."

Scandinavians and the Dutch also have become concerned about honor killings of young Muslim women thought to have dishonored the clan. "That kind of honor code sacrifices women on the altar of culture," Wikan said. "We don't want such values to become part of Europe."

In France, President Nicolas Sarkozy, who campaigned on a law-and-order immigration platform, proposed DNA testing of immigrants' children seeking to enter the country to prove they're relatives. He has vowed to expel 25,000 illegal immigrants a year. Sarkozy would also set quotas by geographic regions of the world, an approach immigration historian Weil calls "xenophobic" and which he suspects would be focused on disliked minorities. Sarkozy's proposed immigration package will produce a "backlash from Arabs and blacks," Weil warns.

A Belgian proposal to take a tougher stance on immigration, pushed by parties of the right but increasingly adopted by mainstream parties, has been widely interpreted as targeting Muslims.[78]

Changing Course

A British government report earlier this year moved away from the language of multiculturalism, saying friendships with people from other ethnic groups are the best way to prevent prejudice. Prime Minister Brown has also said a sense of Britishness should be the "glue" tying different ethnic groups together. But some teachers are uncomfortable with new requirements that schools teach patriotism, because they are unsure what it is.[79]

After the foiled June plots in Britain and Glasgow, Brown proposed a three-year, $114-million program to win the hearts and minds of Muslims by conducting citizenship classes in Britain's 1,000 *madrasas* and English-language training for imams.

But Faiz Siddiqui, convenor of the Muslim Action Committee representing more than 700 mosques and imams in Britain, pointed out that "excessive sums of money" — by one estimate $14 billion over the last 25 years — were already coming into the country from Saudi Arabia and other countries to support "radical ideology." He also noted that some imams accused of inciting people to murder, like Abu Hamza, already spoke English.[80]

In an investigative report published last year, the *New Statesman's* Bright found that the British government's main partner in the Muslim community — the Muslim Council of Britain — had links to the religious right both at home and abroad. Leaked memos revealed that the government's decision to make the group its main link to the Muslim community had been heavily influenced by the British Foreign Office, which wanted to maintain connections with opposition movements abroad.[81]

After the report was published, then-Communities Secretary Kelly focused on reaching out to other groups in the community and halted communication altogether with the council, says Bright. One reason for the switch, she said, was the council's boycott of Britain's Holocaust Memorial Day. How Brown will eventually re-connect with the nation's Muslim community remains uncertain.

However, in a speech delivered Oct. 31, Brown's Communities Secretary Blears said the current government "remains absolutely committed" to Blair's shift in priority away from reliance on a few national organizations and toward Muslim groups "actively working to tackle violent extremism."[82]

Muslim Schools

Britain's education department in September recommended that the more than 100 private Muslim schools enter the state-supported system and that faith schools generally should be expanded. The proposal received a deeply divided response.[83] *(See "At Issue," p. 232.)*

The nation's teachers' union expressed concern that the proposal could further divide children ethnically. Moreover, there's no requirement that Muslim schools cover other religions in depth, "which we consider appropriate," said Alison Ryan, policy adviser to the Association of Teachers and Lecturers.

Some moderate Muslims worry the faith schools could become breeding grounds for extremism. Earlier this year, the principal of King Fahd Academy in London confirmed its textbooks described Jews as "apes" and Christians as "pigs" and refused to withdraw them.[84]

Almost half of Britain's mosques are under the control of the conservative Deobandis, who gave rise to the Taliban in Afghanistan, according to a police report cited by the *London Times* in September.[85] And many of them run after-school *madrasas* that could be expanded into state-funded faith schools, some moderate Muslims fear.

But even groups concerned about ethnic separateness acknowledge that a country that supports nearly 7,000 faith schools — mostly Church of England and Catholic — cannot discriminate against Muslims, who currently have only seven state-supported schools.[86] And some hope that with greater government oversight of the curriculum, any tendency toward extremism would be limited.

OUTLOOK

Encouraging Moderation

Concerned that its terrorism problem is largely homegrown, the British government is now trying to curb radicalism. Among other things, the government is trying to encourage moderation by creating a program to educate imams in communicating with young people to reject extremist views and minimum standards for Muslim clerics in

prisons and other public institutions to give them the skills to confront and isolate extremists. It is also supporting local governments that are developing their own accreditation programs for imams employed in their city to help them deliver sermons in English, reach out to young people and resist extremist ideology. All these steps are part of a $114 million program announced by Communities Secretary Blears Oct. 31 to build resilience to violent extremism, including citizenship classes in mosque schools.[87]

The government is also using community-policing techniques to get to know Muslims in the neighborhoods where they think terrorists may be living. Dutch, Spanish and Danish authorities are closely watching Britain's approach to see if it stems the tide of radical recruitment.

Next year, a year-old government-backed group aimed at encouraging moderation in mosques, the Mosques and Imams Advisory Board, plans to issue a code of standards to allow its member mosques and imams to be supervised and regulated. The draft code, the *Observer* reported, would require members to offer programs "that actively combat all forms of violent extremism." Imams would also be expected to make clear to their followers that forced marriages are completely "unIslamic" — as is violence in domestic disputes.[88]

As Oxford University Professor of European Studies Timothy Garton Ash recently observed: "So much now depends on whether the 10 percent" who sympathize with suicide bombers "veer toward the barbaric 1 percent" who thought the London subway bombers were justified or "rejoin the civilized majority."[89]

But Klausen of Brandeis University says that while Britain's new approach has succeeded in establishing links to Muslim leaders, so far it "has failed to build trust among the general Muslim public."[90]

British author Husain says government officials mistakenly think they can deal with radical Islamists' demands rationally. Secular Western leaders have trouble connecting with the annihilation of the West as a religious duty, he says, because they "don't do God."

"Which Islamist demand do you want to do business with?" he asks. "The destruction of Israel? The overthrow of secular government? The establishment of the caliphate? I don't see any of those being up for negotiation," Husain says.

At the same time, it's important not to confuse all conservative religious groups with those committed to terrorism, warns counterterrorism expert Hellyer.

"In a lot of public discourse we have accusations," he says, such as, "This Salafi mosque or this Salafi preacher is 100 percent guilty of all the radical ideologies in the U.K." In fact, he notes, most Salafi Muslims are zealously conservative but not necessarily violent. Those at the Brixton London mosque first attended by shoe bomber Reid tried to dissuade him from radical theologies that preached violence, and as he became increasingly radical he left the mosque.[91]

"I would hate for us to waste resources going after people we don't like rather than people who are a dangerous threat," Hellyer says.

Following the 2005 bombings, the British government launched an Islamic "Scholars' Roadshow" aimed at winning the minds of under-30 Muslims on issues like jihad and extremism. The Muslim magazine *Q-News*, which came out early against suicide bombing, helped organize the event because it agreed with the government that "there needs to be a theological response to violent Islam-inspired radicalism," says contributing editor Malik.

More than 30,000 young Muslims attended — a sign of success. "But we also fought a significant segment of the Muslim community who said: 'Are you promoting Blair's Islam?' " Malik adds.

The British government's tactic of using 'good' Islam to fight 'bad' Islam is likely to be of limited success because it assumes that religious interpretation — not politics — drives radical movements, Brandeis University's Klausen suggests. Terrorists today meet at jihadist video stores, at Internet cafes and in prison — not in mosques, she says. Communities Secretary Blears recently acknowledged this reality, saying the government's new program to counter violent extremism would reach out to young people on the Internet, in cafes, bookshops and gyms. Yet it's hard for outsiders to know which theology to back. The roadshow, for instance, aroused bitter criticism in the press for supporting conservative interpretations of Islam.[92]

The German government, by contrast, has resisted efforts to create a "tame" Islam, saying the state shouldn't influence the theological development of Islam.[93]

Yet the need for Islam-based opposition to extremism is why political moderates like Malik think it was significant when a former senior member of Hizb ut-Tahrir recently

denounced the radical group on the BBC. "Here's a guy who in very measured language is saying, 'I reject on theological and philosophical grounds the ideology of an Islamic state,' " while remaining a Muslim, says Malik. He's opening a debate that "needs to happen on Muslim terms."

Winning that debate will be the real challenge, says journalist Bright, and not just because the West is frightened of terrorism. "If people are prepared to blow up individual innocents in atrocities, then we all know what we think about that," he observes. "More difficult is what we do about separatist, totalitarian ideologies and their effects on our young people. That to me is a more serious problem, because far more people are susceptible to that than to becoming terrorists."

NOTES

1. Jane Perlez, "Seeking Terror's Causes, Europe Looks Within," *The New York Times*, Sept. 11, 2007.

2. Nicholas Kulish, "New terrorism case confirms that Denmark is a target," *International Herald Tribune*, Sept. 16, 2007, p. 3, www.iht.com/articles/2007/09/17/europe/17denmark.php.

3. Paul Reynolds, "Bomber Video 'Points to al-Qaeda,' " BBC, Sept. 2, 2005, http://news.bbc.co.uk/1/hi/uk/4208250.stm.

4. See Perlez, *op. cit.*, and Souad Mekhennet and Nicholas Kulish, "Terrorist mastermind, or victim of mistaken identity?" *International Herald Tribune*, Oct. 12, 2007, p. 3.

5. Perlez, *op. cit.*

6. Karen McVeigh, "70 million [pounds] Promised for Citizenship Lessons in Schools and English-speaking Imams," *The Guardian*, July 26, 2007, p. 5.

7. Declan Walsh, "Resurgent Al-Qaida Plotting Attacks on West from Tribal Sanctuary, Officials Fear," *The Guardian*, Sept. 27, 2007. Also see, Jason Burke, "Target Europe," *The Observer*, Sept. 9, 2007, www.guardian.co.uk. For background, see Roland Flamini, "Afghanistan on the Brink," *CQ Global Researcher*, June 2007, www.cqpress.com.

8. "Radicalization in the West: The Homegrown Threat," NYPD Intelligence Division, 2007, p. 5. Preventing terrorism by tackling the radicalization of

individuals is one part of British intelligence service's four-point strategy: Prevent, Pursue, Protect and Prepare. See also "Countering International Terrorism: The United Kingdom's Strategy," *HM Government*, July 2006, presented to Parliament by the prime minister and secretary of state for the Home Department, www.intelligence.gov.uk.

9. Hizb ut-Tahrir, "Radicalisation, Extremism & 'Islamism,'" July 2007, p. 3, www.hizb.org.uk/hizb/images/PDFs/htb_radicalisation_report.pdf.

10. James Chapman, "Muslims Call for Special Bank Holidays," *Daily Mail*, Aug. 15, 2006.

11. Jane Perlez, "London Gathering Defends Vision of Radical Islam," *The New York Times*, Aug. 7, 2007.

12. Pew Research Center, "Muslim Americans: Middle Class and Mostly Mainstream," May 22, 2007, www.pewresearch.org, pp. 53-54. "Special Report: Islam, America and Europe: Look out, Europe, They Say," *The Economist*, June 22, 2006.

13. *Ibid.*, p. 51. A survey conducted by British Channel 4 in the summer of 2006 found half of Muslims 18-24 believed that 9/11 was a conspiracy by America and Israel. Cited in Munira Mirza, *et al.*, "Living Apart Together: British Muslims and the Paradox of Multiculturalism," *Policy Exchange*, 2007, p. 58.

14. Cited in Melanie Phillips, *Londonistan: How Britain is Creating a Terror State Within* (2007), p. 302. Also see, "British Should Try Arranged Marriages," *Daily Telegraph*, July 10, 2006, www.telegraph.co.uk/news/main.jhtml?xml=/news/2006/06/10/nterr110.xml.

15. "Inside a Sharia Court," "This World," BBC 2, Oct. 1, 2007, http://news.bbc.co.uk/1/hi/programmes/this_world/7021676.stm.

16. "UK: Extended Pre-charge Detention Violates Rights," Human Rights Watch press release, July 26, 2007, and "In the Name of Prevention: Insufficient Safeguards in National Security Removals," Human Rights Watch, June 2007, http://hrw.org/reports/2007/france0607/1.htm#_Toc167263185.

17. The Associated Press, "Quaeda Using Europeans to Hit U.S., Official Says," *International Herald Tribune*, Sept. 26, 2007, p. 8. McConnell's testimony is at www.dni.gov/testimonies/20070925_testimony.pdf.

18. Peter Skerry, "The Muslim Exception: Why Muslims in the U.S. Aren't as Attracted to Jihad as Those in Europe," *Time*, Aug. 21, 2006.

19. Neil MacFarquhar, "Abandon Stereotype, Muslims in America Say," *The New York Times*, Sept. 4, 2007, p. A12.

20. Daniel Dombey and Simon Kuper, "Britons 'More Suspicious' of Muslims," *Financial Times*, Aug. 19, 2007.

21. *Ibid.*

22. Pew Global Attitudes Project, "Muslims in Europe: Economic Worries Top Concerns about Religious and Cultural Identity," July 6, 2006, http://pewglobal.org/reports/display.php?ReportID=254.

23. Presentation by John R. Bowen, University of Chicago International Forum, London, Sept. 29, 2007, as part of "Engaging Cultural Differences in Western Europe" panel.

24. John R. Bowen, "On Building a Multireligious Society," *San Francisco Chronicle*, Feb. 5, 2007.

25. *Ibid.*

26. International Crisis Group, "Islam and Identity in Germany," March 14, 2007, p. 19.

27. Jonathan Laurence and Justin Vaisse, *Integrating Islam: Political and Religious Challenges in Contemporary France* (2006).

28. For background, see Kenneth Jost, "Future of the European Union," *CQ Researcher*, Oct. 28, 2005, pp. 909-932.

29. Phillips, *op. cit.*, p. 22.

30. *Ibid.*, p. 24.

31. Jytte Klausen, "British Counter-Terrorism After 7/7: Adapting Community Policing to the Fight against Domestic Terrorism," *Journal of Ethnic and Migration Studies*, forthcoming, pp. 17-18.

32. See Robert S. Leiken, "Europe's Angry Muslims," *Foreign Affairs*, July/August 2005.

33. Will Woodward, "Kelly vows that new debate on immigration will engage critically with multiculturalism," *The Guardian*, Aug. 25, 2006.

34. Madeleine Bunting, "United Stand," *The Guardian*, June 13, 2007.

35. Phillips, *op. cit.*, p. 25.

36. Ed Husain, *The Islamist* (2007), p. 22.

37. Mirza, *et al.*, *op. cit.*, pp. 6, 18.

38. James Brandon and Douglas Murray, "How British Libraries Encourage Islamic Extremism," Centre for Social Cohesion, August 2007, www.socialcohesion .co.uk/pdf/HateOnTheState.pdf.

39. Emine Saner, "Dishonorable Acts," *The Guardian*, June 13, 2007, p. 18.

40. Leiken, *op. cit.*

41. Martin Bright, "When Progressives Treat with Reactionaries: The British State's Flirtation with Radical Islamism," *Policy Exchange*, 2006, p. 12, www .policyexchange.org.uk/images/libimages/176.pdf.

42. From "Connections," winter 2001, quoted in Tariq Modood, *Multiculturalism: A Civic Idea* (2007), pp. 10-11.

43. Patrick Wintour and Alan Travis, "Brown Sets out Sweeping but Risky 'Terror and Security Reforms,'" *The Guardian*, July 26, 2007, p. 1.

44. *Ibid.*

45. Since 2001, government figures show more than half of those arrested under the 2000 Terrorism Act have been released without charge. Human Rights Watch press release, "UK: Extended Pre-charge Detention Violates Rights," July 26, 2007.

46. Human Rights Watch, "In the Name of Prevention: Insufficient Safeguards in National Security Removals," June 2007, http://hrw.org/reports/2007/france0607/1.htm#_Toc167263185.

47. Peter Clarke, "Learning from Experience: Counter-terrorism in the UK Since 9/11," *Policy Exchange*, 2007, www.policyexchange.org.uk/images/libimages/252.pdf, pp. 19-20.

48. *Ibid.*, p. 27.

49. *Ibid.*

50. See www.liberty-human-rights.org.uk/publications/3-articles-and-speeched/index.shtml.

51. Liberty, "Overlooked: Surveillance and Personal Privacy in Britain," September 2007, www.liberty-human-rights.org.uk.

52. Jocelyne Cesari, *When Islam and Democracy Meet* (2004), pp. 15-16.

53. *Ibid.*, pp. 99-100.

54. Mirza, *op. cit.*, p. 24.

55. *Ibid.*

56. *Ibid.*, pp. 27-28.

57. *Ibid.*

58. *Ibid.*, p. 29.

59. Klausen, *op. cit.*, pp. 14-15. For background, see Peter Katel, "Global Jihad," *CQ Researcher*, Oct. 14, 2005, pp. 857-880.

60. See "Timeline: Madrid investigation," BBC News, April 28, 2004, http://news.bbc.co.uk/2/hi/europe/3597885.stm.

61. NYPD Intelligence Division, *op. cit.*

62. *Ibid.*

63. *Ibid.*, p. 15.

64. *Ibid.*

65. Denis MacEoin, "The Hijacking of Islam: How Extremist Literature is Subverting Mosques in the United Kingdom," Policy Exchange, 2007, www .policyexchange.org.uk.

66. See "Hate preaching cleric jailed," BBC News, March 7, 2003, http://news.bbc.co.uk/2/hi/uk_news/england/2829059.stm.

67. See "Cleric Bakri barred from Britain," BBC News, Aug. 12, 2005, http://news.bbc.co.uk/2/hi/uk_news/4144792.stm.

68. Klausen, *op. cit.*

69. Richard Norton-Taylor, "Al-Quaida has Revived, Spread and is Capable of a Spectacular," *The Guardian*, Sept. 13, 2007, www.guardian.co.uk/alqaida/story/0,,2167923,00.html. Also see "Strategic Survey 2007," International Institute for Strategic Studies, www.iiss.org/publications/strategic-survey-2007.

70. Peter Bergen, "How Osama Bin Laden Beat George W. Bush," *New Republic*, Oct. 15, 2007.

71. Norton-Taylor, *op. cit.* Jonathan Evans, "Address to the Society of Editors," Nov. 5, 2007, www.mi5.gov.uk.

72. Kulish, Sept. 17, 2007, *op. cit.*

73. Cesari, *op. cit.*, p. 96.

74. Jonathan Laurence, "Managing Transnational Islam: Muslims and the State in Western Europe," March 11, 2006, www.jonathanlaurence.net.

75. *Ibid.*, p. 92.

76. Robert S. Leiken and Steven Brooke, "The Quantitative Analysis of Terrorism and Immigration," *Terrorism and Political Violence* (2006), pp. 503-521.

77. University of Chicago International Forum, London, Sept. 29, 2007.

78. Dan Bilefsky, "Belgians Agree on One Issue: Foreigners," *International Herald Tribune*, Oct. 10, 2007.

79. Jessica Shepherd, "What does Britain Expect?" *The Guardian*, July 17, 2007, p. E1.

80. McVeigh, *op. cit.*

81. Bright, *op. cit.*, p. 28.

82. Hazel Blears, "Preventing Extremism: Strengthening Communities," Oct. 31, 2007, www.communities .gov.uk.

83. "Faith in the System," Department of Children, Schools and Families, Sept. 10, 2007.

84. "We Do Use Books that Call Jews 'Apes' Admits Head of Islamic School," *Evening Standard*, Feb. 7, 2007.

85. Andrew Norfolk, "Hardline Takeover of British Mosques," *The Times* (London), Sept. 7, 2007, www.timesonline.co.uk/tol/comment/faith/article 2402973.ece.

86. BBC, "Faith Schools Set for Expansion," Sept. 10, 2007, www.bbc.co.uk.

87. "Major Increase in Work to Tackle Violent Extremism," Department of Communities and Local Government, U.K., Oct. 31, 2007, www.communities.gov.uk/news/ corporate/529021.

88. Jo Revill, "Mosques Told to Obey New Code of Conduct," *The Observer*, Nov. 4, 2007, p. 24.

89. Timothy Garton Ash, "Battleground Europe," *Los Angeles Times*, Sept. 13, 2007, www.latimes.com/ news/opinion/la-oe-garton13sep13,0,979657.story. Also see Klausen, *op. cit.*: One percent of UK Muslims felt the July 2005 London transit bombers were "right," according to a 2006 poll. Ten percent of Germans sympathized with suicide bombers.

90. Klausen, *op. cit.*

91. See "Who is Richard Reid?" BBC, Dec. 24, 2001, www.bbc.co.uk.

92. Klausen, *op. cit.*

93. International Crisis Group, *op. cit.*, p. 31.

BIBLIOGRAPHY

Books

Bowen, John R., *Why the French Don't Like Headscarves: Islam, the State, and Public Space*, Princeton University Press, 2007.
A Washington University anthropologist looks at the furor that led to the 2004 ban on head scarves in French schools.

Cesari, Jocelyne, *When Islam and Democracy Meet: Muslims in Europe and in the United States*, Palgrave, 2004.
The director of Harvard University's Islam in the West program compares the experiences of European and U.S. Muslims.

Husain, Ed, *The Islamist*, Penguin Books, 2007.
A former Muslim radical in London describes his recruitment by extremist Islamist groups in the 1990s.

Modood, Tariq, *Multiculturalism: A Civic Idea*, Polity, 2007.
A University of Bristol sociologist advocates "multicultural citizenship" to integrate Muslims in Britain.

Phillips, Melanie, *Londonistan: How Britain is Creating a Terror State Within*, Gibson Square, 2006.
A journalist blames the rise of Muslim radicalism in London on persistent denial by the British government and a craven form of multiculturalism among leftists.

Qutb, Sayyid, *Milestones*, Maktabah Booksellers and Publishers, 2006.
A leader of the Muslim Brotherhood wrote this inspirational text for radical Islamist groups while in an Egyptian prison.

Articles

Bowen, John R., "On Building a Multireligious Society," *San Francisco Chronicle*, Feb. 5, 2007.
France is doing a better job of absorbing Muslims than other European countries.

Leiken, Robert S., and Steven Brook, "The Moderate Muslim Brotherhood," *Foreign Affairs*, March/April 2007.

The Muslim Brotherhood has moved away from violence in favor of using the electoral process to obtain its goal of an Islamic state in Egypt, France, Jordan, Spain, Syria, Tunisia and the United Kingdom, say leaders.

Perlez, Jane, "From Finding Radical Islam to Losing an Ideology," Sept. 12, 2007, *The New York Times*, www .nytimes.com/2007/09/12/world/europe/12britain .html?_r=1&oref=slogin.
A former senior member of the radical group Hizb ut-Tahrir says he left the group because it preached violence.

Ruthven, Malise, "How to Understand Islam," *The New York Review of Books*, Nov. 8, 2007, pp. 62-66.
Influential jihadist thinkers Maududi and Qutb held more rigid views of sharia than many scholars.

Reports and Studies

"In the Name of Prevention: Insufficient Safeguards in National Security Removals," Human Rights Watch, June 6, 2007, http://hrw.org/reports/2007/ france0607/.
The group argues that France's policy of deporting imams and others it considers Islamic fundamentalists violates human rights.

"Islam and Identity in Germany," International Crisis Group, March 14, 2007, www.crisisgroup.org.
Issued before the latest foiled plot in Germany, this report downplayed the threat of homegrown terrorism in Germany's Turkish community.

"Radicalisation, Extremism & 'Islamism': Realities and Myths in the 'War on Terror,' " Hizb ut-Tahrir Britain, July 2007, www.hizb.org.uk.
The separatist British group lays out its argument for a caliphate in the Muslim world and denies it espouses violence.

"Radicalization in the West: The Homegrown Threat," New York City Police Department Intelligence Division, 2007, http://sethgodin.typepad.com/seths_ blog/files/NYPD_Report-radicalization_in_the_West .pdf.
Muslim terrorists in Europe were generally "well-integrated" into their home countries, according to this study.

Bright, Martin, "When Progressives Treat with Reactionaries: The British State's Flirtation with Radical Islamism," *Policy Exchange*, 2006, www .policyexchange.org.uk.
The *New Statesman's* political editor says the government was pressured to maintain a relationship with radical Muslim groups.

MacEoin, Denis, "The Hijacking of Islam: How Extremist Literature is Subverting Mosques in the United Kingdom," *Policy Exchange*, 2007, www .policyexchange.org.uk/Publications.aspx?id=430.
The group visited leading mosques and schools in Britain and found extremist literature preaching hatred against non-Muslims, anti-Semitism and stoning of adulterers.

Mirza, Munira, *et al.*, "Living Apart Together: British Muslims and the Paradox of Multiculturalism," *Policy Exchange*, 2007, www.policyexchange.org.uk.
A conservative think tank in London blames British multiculturalism policies for dividing people along ethnic lines.

For More Information

Association of Muslim Schools UK, P.O. Box 14109, Birmingham B6 9BN, United Kingdom; +44-844-482-0407; www.ams-uk.org. A Birmingham-based group that "supports and develops excellence in full-time Muslim schools" in the United Kingdom.

Center for Islamic Pluralism, (202) 232-1750; www.islamicpluralism.eu. A Washington-based think tank that is critical of radical Muslim groups.

Centre for Social Cohesion, 77 Great Peter St., Westminster, London SW1P 2EZ, United Kingdom; +44-20-7799-6677; www.socialcohesion.co.uk. A British group critical of Britain's multicultural policy.

Hizb ut-Tahrir, www.hizb.org.uk. Considered one of the more radical Islamic organizations in Britain.

Human Rights Watch, 350 Fifth Ave., 34th Floor, New York, NY 10118-3299; (212) 290-4700; www.hrw.org. An international human rights organization.

Islam in the West Program, Harvard University, 59-61, Rue Pouchet, F-75849 Paris Cedex 17, France; +33-1-40-25-11-22; www.euro-islam.info. A network of scholars who conduct comparative research on Muslims in Europe.

Liberty, 21 Tabard St., London SE1 4LA, United Kingdom; +20-7403-3888; www.liberty-human-rights.org.uk. London-based group, also known as the National Council for Civil Liberties, that advocates for civil liberties.

Muslim Council of Britain, P.O. Box 57330, London E1 2WJ, United Kingdom; +44-845-26-26-786; www.mcb.org.uk. Represents more than 500 Muslim groups, mosques and schools in Britain.

National Secular Society, 25 Red Lion Square, London WC1R 4RL, United Kingdom; +44-20-7404-3126; www.secularism.org.uk. A London-based group that opposes faith schools in Britain.

Policy Exchange, Clutha House, 10 Storey's Gate, London SW1P 3AY, United Kingdom; +20-7340-2650; www.policyexchange.org.uk. A London-based think tank that opposes the British government's multicultural policy and choice of Muslim groups to support.

Saban Center for Middle East Policy, Brookings Institution, 1775 Massachusetts Ave., N.W., Washington, DC 20036; (202) 797-6000; www.brookings.edu/saban.aspx. A Washington-based think tank that studies terrorism.

Stop Islamisation of Europe, +44-122-854-7317; sioe.wordpress.com. A Danish group that has been coordinating street protests in Europe against Islamist stances on issues like sharia.

10

Global Jihad

Does a Terrorist Movement Threaten the West?

Peter Katel

Forensics investigators seek clues in the bombing of four commuter trains in Madrid on March 11, 2004, killing 190 people and injuring more than 1,000. Moroccan jihadists carried out the attack in an apparent effort to force the withdrawal of Spanish troops from Iraq. Since the Sept. 11, 2001, terrorist attacks on the United States, jihadists have carried out at least 107 attacks worldwide.

From *CQ Researcher*,
October 14, 2005.

The images picked up by security cameras at London's Kings Cross subway station showed four seemingly typical commuters — young men carrying backpacks.

Only in retrospect do the video shots seem ominous. They turned up after the men were identified as the suicide bombers who killed themselves and 52 people on three London subways and a bus last July 7.

One of the four was schoolteacher Mohammed Sidique Khan, who was born in England and raised there by his Pakistani Muslim immigrant parents. In early September, the Qatar-based Arabic-language station Al Jazeera ran a chilling, posthumous tape of Khan. In a distinctive Yorkshire accent, he cited "atrocities against my people" and declared: "We are at war, and I am a soldier . . . Our words are dead until we give them life with our blood."[1]

The terrorists cloak their acts in the mantle of jihad — holy struggle — but their precise goals, and the nature of their organization or organizations, are murky. "Unlike the Cold War, here you don't know who the enemy is," says Magnus Ranstorp, director of the Center for Asymmetric Threat Studies at the Swedish National Defense College. "The enemy can be entire societies or sympathizers; and weapons can be low-tech and inexpensive."

On Oct. 1, three suicide bombers killed 26 people on the Indonesian island of Bali — two years after a similar but far more lethal attack there. Anti-terrorism authorities around the world are studying the possible relationship between two Malaysian suspects and Osama bin Laden's al Qaeda terrorist network, considered the world's first jihadist group dedicated to killing Americans and other Westerners. The two suspected bomb makers once may have

Inside the Global Jihadist Network

Osama bin Laden's al Qaeda organization and 12 other mostly regional terrorist groups are currently active, according to a Century Foundation study. They seek to establish Muslim theocracies and view Western powers as enemies of Islam. Anti-Soviet mujahedeen who fought in Afghanistan founded most, and many retain links to al Qaeda. Jihadists' ranks have grown significantly since 9/11, the study says.

Group	Region	Goal	Details
Al Qaeda (the Base)	Northwest Pakistan	Muslim rule in Muslim lands and all non-Muslims evicted; has declared war on the U.S., other Western countries.	Founded in late 1980s; led by Osama bin Laden, Ayman al-Zawahiri. Finances and trains jihadist movements. Conducted 1998 attacks on U.S. embassies in Kenya and Tanzania, 2000 attack on the U.S.S. Cole and the 9/11/01 U.S. attacks.
Abu Sayyaf Group (Bearer of the Sword)	Malaysia, southern Philippines	An Islamic state in Southeast Asia.	Founded in 1991, split off from Moro National Liberation Front; led by Khadaffy Janjalani. Responsible for more than 100 kidnappings, bombings and grenade attacks on Christian targets and foreigners in its first four years. Recently has been taken over by criminals. Beheaded several Christians.
Jemaah Islamiya (JI)	Malaysia, Indonesia	An Islamic state in Southeast Asia by 2025, encompassing Brunei, Indonesia, Malaysia, Singapore, southern Philippines and southern Thailand.	Founded in 1993; led by Azahari Husin, Noordin Mohammad Top. Has several thousand members, links to other jihadists; runs terrorist training camps and Muslim boarding schools throughout region; receives support from al Qaeda and may be part of al Qaeda. JI and al Qaeda planners were apparently preparing a 9/11 "second strike" on U.S. West Coast with planes hijacked in Southeast Asia. New JI leaders appear even more committed to jihad than their predecessors.
Al-Ittihad Al-Islami (AIAI)	Somalia, Ethiopia, Kenya	An Islamic state in Horn of Africa.	Founded in early 1990s in Somalia; led by Hassan Abdullah Hersi al-Turki. Received weapons, funding from bin Laden in late 1990s. Attacks military forces in eastern Ethiopia. May have helped al Qaeda bomb a Kenyan hotel, attempt to shoot down an airliner carrying Israeli tourists in 2002 and attack an Ethio-Kenyan hotel in 2003. May be preparing to attack ships near Horn of Africa.
Islamic Army of Aden-Abyan (IAA)	Southern Yemen	Overthrow Yemen government; establish shari'a law; eject infidels.	Founded in 1998 by Sunni militants; led by Khalid Abdulnabi. Supports al Qaeda activities, including the 2000 attack on U.S.S. Cole. Has hit numerous Western targets, including Yemen Intercontinental Hotel and French oil tanker.
Salafist Group for Preaching and Combat (GSPC)	Algeria, Mali, Libya, Niger Mauritania, and Chad	Topple Algerian government, attack Western targets.	Founded with bin Laden's help in early 1990s; led by Yahya Jawadi, Abu-Ammar and Haydar Abu "The Doctor" Doha. Has 300-700 members in Algeria and Europe; participated in killing 100,000 Algerians in the 1990s. Recruits heavily among Algerian teens, particularly in France, and facilitates al Qaeda funding and recruiting; suspected of helping al Qaeda establish a ricin network in Europe.
Salifiya Jihadiya	Morocco	Establish a Wahhabi government in Morocco.	Founded in 1990s by former Afghan mujahedeen; led by Abdelkrim Mejati, an explosives expert and al Qaeda operative. Recruits in poor Moroccan suburbs; receives direction and funding from al Qaeda. In May 2003, launched suicide bombing attacks in Casablanca — including the Belgian consulate, a Jewish-owned restaurant and a Spanish social club — killing 43.

Source: The Century Foundation, "Defeating the Jihadists: A Blueprint for Action," Nov. 16, 2004

Group	Region	Goal	Details
Ansar al-Islam (AI) (Supporters of Islam)	Northeastern Iraq	Before Iraq war: create a fundamentalist Islamic state in the autonomous Kurdish region. After the war: disrupt Iraqi unification.	Founded in late 2001; led by Abu 'Abdallah al-Shafi'i. Has 500-1,000 Iraqi Kurdish fighters. AI camps used by al Qaeda and Zarqawi to develop toxic weapons in 2002 in exchange for al Qaeda funding. Has lost some prestige and membership to Zarqawi's JTJ and has conducted fewer attacks in past year.
Asbat al-Ansar (League of the Followers)	Lebanon	Advocates Salafism — a return to the ancient caliphate system of government and prevention of peace between Arabs and Israel.	Founded in 1985, by radical Sunnis during Lebanese civil war; led by Abu Muhjin. Has 300 members, mostly Palestinians; bombs non-Islamic targets such as casinos, fast-food restaurants and secular Palestinian groups. In 2003 helped try to assassinate U.S. ambassador to Lebanon Vincent Battle.
Islamic International Brigade (IIB), Riyadus-Salikhin Reconnaissance and Sabotage Battalion of Chechen Martyrs (RAS); Special Purpose Islamic Regiment (SPIR)	Chechnya	Initially, national independence. Now, anti-Western holy war and creation of Islamic theocracy in the Caucasus.	Were founded in late 1990s; led by Shamil Basayev. These are the three main al Qaeda-linked Chechen extremist groups; in 1995 Chechen rebels planted a radiological bomb in a Moscow park but notified reporters and never detonated it. Suspected of conducting chemical weapons experiments. Are increasingly willing to attack commuter trains and airplanes. Took 800 hostages in Moscow's Dubroyka Theater in 2002, which ended in some 120 deaths. In 2004 stormed a school in southern Russia, taking 1,200 hostages; 339 died, half of them children.
Lashkar-e-Tayyba (LeT) (Army of the Pure)	Pakistan	Return Indian Kashmir to Muslim control, incorporating it into Pakistan; overthrow non-Muslim governments worldwide.	Founded in 1989; led by Hafiz Mohammad Saeed. An extreme Sunni group of 1,000 to 3,000 members; fought Soviet Union in Afghanistan in 1980s, forming links with al Qaeda. Attacked Indian Parliament and Indian civilians in markets, police stations, airports and border posts. Funded by real estate in Pakistan, Pakistani sympathizers, Middle Eastern donors and al Qaeda. In 2003 federal grand jury charged 11 men with conspiring with LeT to engage in terrorism. Four pleaded guilty to conspiracy and gun charges; the rest were re-indicted for conspiracy to support al Qaeda and Taliban.
Lashkar-e-Jhangvi (LeJ)	Pakistan	Replace Pakistani government with a radical Sunni Islamic government.	Founded in late 1996; led by Muhammed Ajmal. Has 100 virulently anti-Western Sunni extremists; Pakistani government crackdowns have reduced the group's strength. Once sent operatives to fight with the Taliban regime against the Northern Alliance. Likely funded by Saudi Wahhabi donors and al Qaeda. LeJ operatives provided safe houses and logistics for fleeing al Qaeda and Taliban members in late 2001. Collaborated with al Qaeda in killing reporter Daniel Pearl. Attacks Westerners, Christians and Shiites.

belonged to Jemaah Islamiyah, a Southeast Asian Muslim separatist group.[2]

The recent Bali bombings were only the latest in a steady stream of attacks and attempted attacks — mostly suicide bombings — both before and following the Sept. 11, 2001, attacks on the United States, which killed 2,936 people.

(*See chart, p. 246.*) The attacks reflect the unshaken determination of Muslim terrorists around the world to kill Americans and their allies — with the stated aim of establishing theocracies in the name of Islam in Muslim lands.

"Covert and open Islamic groups have been trying for decades to establish the Islamic state, and so far they have made no progress. . . . Yesterday, we did not dream of a state; today we established states and they fall. Tomorrow, Allah willing, a state will arise and will not fall," an al Qaeda online magazine said last year.[3]

Al Qaeda's top strategist, Ayman al-Zawahiri, has apparently developed that vision into a military strategy. On Oct. 11, U.S. intelligence authorities released what they said was a letter from al-Zawahiri to Abu Musab al-Zarqawi, the top jihadist leader in Iraq. "The victory of Islam will never take place until a Muslim state is established . . . in the heart of the Islamic world, specifically in the Levant, Egypt and the neighboring states of the Peninsula and Iraq," he wrote. With his eye on that prize, al-Zawahiri added that regional conflicts in Chechnya, Afghanistan and elsewhere are "just the groundwork" for the full-scale confrontation in the Arab heartland.[4]

In addition to the hundreds of assaults on Americans and civilians in war-torn Iraq and Afghanistan as well as in Israel and the Palestinian territories, more than 100 major post-9/11 terrorist incidents have occurred in Pakistan, Turkey, Indonesia, Spain, Great Britain, Morocco, Kenya, Chechnya and Russia.

Terrorism experts disagree on whether the world's far-flung jihadists belong to a single global organization, such as al Qaeda, or represent independent or loosely connected cells. Experts also debate the level of support for jihadism among the world's 1.3 billion Muslims.

Yet another unanswered question revolves around the role of U.S. ally Saudi Arabia in spreading Wahhabism, the religiously intolerant branch of Islam that is the Saudis' state religion.

"As of July 2005, U.S. agency officials did not know if the government of Saudi Arabia had taken steps to ensure that Saudi-funded curricula or religious activities in other countries do not propagate extremism," the Government Accountability Office (GAO) reported in September.[5]

Many experts are unwilling to dismiss ties between al Qaeda and other terrorists. One reason for that stance is al-Zawahiri's newly disclosed letter to al-Zarqawi. In words that could be seen either as advice or directive, the al Qaeda leader tells the jihad commander in Iraq to keep targeting Americans rather than Iraqi Shiites. "The majority of Muslims don't comprehend" the slaughter of Shiites, al-Zawahiri writes. Another apparent al Qaeda connection showed up in suicide bomber Khan's posthumous message tape, which bore the al Qaeda logo. The same tape contained a message — apparently added to Khan's original tape — from al-Zawahiri.[6] Experts disagree on whether the evidence indicates al Qaeda commanded the bombings or simply served as a communications link.[7]

A deeper dispute centers on how to fight jihadism. "What I usually hear is a very, very simplistic interpretation — 'If we would just eradicate poverty, [terrorism] would go away.' No it won't," says Michael Taarnby, an expert on terrorism at the Danish Institute for International Studies. " 'And if we create peace in Palestine, that would end the incentive for jihad.' No it won't. If you think you can appease them, think twice."

But some students of terrorism say that while Islamic fundamentalism may provide much of the philosophical impetus for suicide bombings, poverty in the Arab world and U.S. foreign policy (and troops) in the Mideast exacerbate anti-U.S. sentiment that creates willing jihadist recruits.

"If al Qaeda were no longer able to recruit based on the presence of Western combat forces on the Arabian Peninsula," says University of Chicago political scientist Robert Pape, "the remaining transnational network would pose a far smaller threat and simply collapse."

Pape argues that from 1980 to 2004, suicide terrorists everywhere acted to force democratic governments to end military occupations. The Madrid train bombings of 2004 would seem to support his argument, given messages from the bombers and from bin Laden himself warning Spain and European nations in general to pull their forces out of Iraq.[8] In Sri Lanka, Pape notes, the secular Tamil Tiger guerrillas are fighting for a separate state. Palestinian terrorists in Israeli-occupied territories claim the same goal (though at least some of them really want to destroy Israel, Israelis say), and Iraqi insurgents say they want to end foreign occupation.

But Tamils' and Palestinians' territorial demands have nothing to do with global jihadism, argues Richard A. Clarke, former national counterterrorism coordinator in the Bill Clinton and George W. Bush administrations. Hence, the statistical evidence that Pape has assembled isn't helpful in analyzing al Qaeda and its ideological affiliates. "If we could wave a magic wand and solve the Israel-Palestinian problem . . . it wouldn't affect the jihadist movement one iota," says Clarke, who is now a consultant on security issues.

Clarke is among those who argue that the Iraq war is spurring jihadism. But President Bush argued on Oct. 6: "We were not in Iraq on Sept. the 11th, 2001, and al Qaeda attacked us anyway. The hatred of the radicals existed before Iraq was an issue, and it will exist after Iraq is no longer an excuse."

What, then, explains the hatred? Poverty doesn't seem plausible. For example, bin Laden was born into riches; his second-in-command, al-Zawahiri, is a physician; the four 9/11 pilots were university graduates or students; and London bomber Khan had a steady job in an elementary school.

"In the world's poorest countries there is little or no terrorism," writes historian Walter Laqueur, a longtime scholar of extremism. "Imponderable factors might be involved: indoctrination, but also psychological motives. Neither economic nor political analysis will be of much help in gaining an understanding."[9]

Recent history does provide some clues. The jihadist movement largely grew out of the U.S.-supported war against the Soviet occupation of Afghanistan in the 1980s, which drew religiously oriented fighters from various countries, including Egypt, which already had a tradition of Islamist opposition to secular rulers. The shift to an international fight for militant Islam grew out of the defeat of religious nationalists on their home fronts, argues Fawaz A. Gerges, a Lebanese-born political scientist at Sarah Lawrence College. "Jihadis' attacks on America were a desperate attempt to reinvigorate their declining movement," he argues.[10]

Meanwhile, Western nations have had limited success in eliminating terrorists before they kill. To be sure, U.S. and other security agencies say they have stopped many attacks — in his speech, Bush said that 10 "serious" al Qaeda plots, including three aimed at targets in the United States, had been disrupted over the past four years. But specialists say the jihadist world so far has been largely impenetrable to Western security agencies.

Even culturally attuned Arabic-speakers can go astray. Gerges writes in a newly published book that while interviewing jihadists and others in the Middle East in 1999-2000, he missed the key angle. "We underestimated bin Laden's mobilizational skills and charisma as well as his determination to exact revenge on 'the enemies of God.'"[11]

Spouses can miss all the signs as well. In late September, the widow of one of the London suicide bombers told a British newspaper that she had no idea how her "innocent, naive and simple" husband, Jamaican-born Germaine Lindsay, had been transformed into a suicide bomber. "He was so angry when he saw Muslim civilians being killed on the streets of Iraq, Bosnia, Palestine and Israel. . . . Then he is responsible for doing the same thing, but to his fellow British people."[12]

As experts seek to understand what motivates the jihadists and stop their lethal attacks, here are some of the questions they are debating.

Is there a global jihadist organization?

The jihadist terrorists who have bombed and assassinated around the world over the past seven years shared similar targets, techniques and ideology. Yet they didn't all report to the same boss, and didn't even all speak the same languages. "Al Qaeda-linked" has become the common way of describing connections that aren't always clear. Or, as two analysts described non-Iraqi suicide bombers in Iraq: "insurgents who are connected by conviction, if not organization, to a global jihad symbolized by al Qaeda."[13]

Al-Zawahiri's letter to his ally in Iraq does seem to show an effort to enforce ideological unity. "The mujahedeen must not have their mission end with the expulsion of the Americans from Iraq, and then lay down their weapons," al-Zawahiri wrote, going on to lay out a strategy for establishing jihadist rule in Iraq, then expanding the battlefield to Syria, Lebanon and Egypt, before finally confronting Israel.[14]

Al-Zawahiri's organization in Iraq is only one of a host of regional jihadist groups believed to be allied to al Qaeda, at least ideologically. Among them: Abu Sayaf, Philippines; Jemaah Islamiyah, Indonesia, Malaysia; the Salafist Group for Preaching and Combat, Algeria; Salifiya Jihadiya, Morocco; the Islamic International Battalion and other extremist separatists fighting the Russian government in Chechnya; Hizb-I Islami Gulbuddin, Afghanistan; Lashkar-e-Tayibba and Lashkar-e-Jhangvi, Pakistan; and Ansar Al-Islam, Iraq. In many cases, the level of commitment to global jihad, as opposed to regional or nationalist conflicts, is unclear.[15]

A commission headed by former anti-terrorism czar Clarke and formed by The Century Foundation, a New York policy research organization, noted that some

Major Terrorist Attacks Since 9/11

In the three years since the Sept. 11, 2001, attacks, jihadist groups linked to al Qaeda have carried out twice as many major attacks as they and al Qaeda had launched in the three years before 9/11 (see p. 242). According to a new study, 107 jihadist attacks worldwide killed at least 3,007 people between Sept. 11, 2001, and November 2004; authorities disrupted another 18 terrorist plots.

Significant Attacks Since 9/11

Date	Location	Target	Deaths	Group	Method
July 7, 2005	London	3 subways, 1 bus	56	Unknown	Suicide bombs
Sept.1-3, 2004	Beslan, Russia	Parents and children in school building	350	Chechen extremists linked to al Qaeda	Gunfire and explosives
August 2003-September 2004	Iraq	Westerners, soldiers, civilians, hotels and government facilities.	818	Abu Mus'ab al-Zarqawi	Executions, suicide bombs
May 29, 2004	Khobar, Saudi Arabia	Housing for Western oil workers	22	Al Qaeda	Gunfire
March 2, 2004	Quetta, Pakistan	Shiite worshipers	51	Lashkar-e-Jhangvi	Gunfire and grenades
Dec. 25, 2003	Rawalpindi, Pakistan	President Pervez Musharraf	14	Pakistani Islamic extremists linked to al Qaeda	Truck bombs
Nov. 15-20, 2003	Istanbul, Turkey	2 synagogues, British consulate and bank	25	Al Qaeda	Suicide bombs
Nov. 8, 2003	Riyadh, Saudi Arabia	Residential compound	17	Al Qaeda	Suicide bomb
Aug. 5, 2003	Jakarta, Indonesia	Marriott hotel	13	Jemaah Islamiya	Suicide bomb
Aug. 1, 2003	Mozdok, Russia	Military hospital	50	Al Qaeda	Suicide bomb
May 16, 2003	Casablanca, Morocco	Western restaurant, Jewish sites, Belgian consulate	44	Salafi Jihad group affiliated with al Qaeda	Suicide bombs
May 12, 2003	Riyadh, Saudi Arabia	Western housing compounds	35	Al Qaeda	Suicide bombs
May 12, 2003	Znamenskoye, Chechnya	Government building	59	Chechen extremists linked to al Qaeda	Suicide bomb
Dec. 27, 2002	Grozny, Chechnya	Headquarters of Russian-backed Chechen government	80	Chechen extremists linked to al Qaeda	Suicide bomb
Nov. 28, 2002	Mombassa, Kenya	Hotel with Israeli tourists, Israeli plane	16	Al Qaeda	Suicide bomb, missiles
Oct. 23-26, 2002	Moscow	Theater	170	Chechen extremists linked to al Qaeda	Hostage taking
Oct. 12, 2002	Bali, Indonesia	Nightclubs frequented by Westerners	202	Jemaah Islamiya	Car bombs
Sept. 5, 2002	Kabul, Afghanistan	Afghan market	30	Al Qaeda or Gulbuddin Hekmatyar	Car bomb
April 22, 2002	General Santos City, Philippines	Shopping mall	15	Abu Sayyaf Group	Bombs
April 11, 2002	Djerba, Tunisia	Synagogue	20	Al Qaeda	Suicide bomb
Jan. 31, 2002	Karachi, Pakistan	American reporter Daniel Pearl	1	Al Qaeda	Execution
Jan. 22, 2002	Calcutta	U.S. consulate offices	5	Lashkar-e-Tayyiba	Drive-by shooting

Source: The Century Foundation, "Defeating the Jihadists: A Blueprint for Action," Nov. 16, 2004

experts who had thought al Qaeda was severely weakened in 2003-2004 after the U.S. security-agency response to 9/11 have begun revising those views. Those experts believe "that the core al Qaeda organization does still exist as an organization, with a communications network of some sort linking its leaders with cells in Europe and elsewhere." In short, they said, al Qaeda "is clearly still vibrant and dangerous."[16]

Ranstorp at the Swedish National Defense College agrees, arguing that al Qaeda remains very much on the scene. Bin Laden and his closest associates "are still at large," he says. "They are extraordinarily patient."

But Ranstorp, who is leading a research project on jihadist radicalization and recruitment throughout Europe, acknowledges that the picture is complicated. "Disconnected cells" also exist. And he suggests that "professional recruiters" are maintaining a flow of new members, but security agencies don't know who the recruiters are.

However, some specialists say al Qaeda's power has waned. "For all practical purposes that organization is not relevant," says Marc Sageman, a Maryland psychiatrist and former CIA officer. The global jihad "is too decentralized to be anything like an organization. It is basically made up of spontaneously home-grown gangs, competing with each other for headlines."

"You can't call it an organization," says Juan Cole, a University of Michigan historian of the Middle East whose Iraq War-centered blog is frequently cited by Bush administration critics. "It's a loosely affiliated set of networks, often not affiliated at all."

But Michael Scheuer, a CIA veteran of the Afghanistan jihad who later created a unit dedicated to hunting bin Laden, says he is still a serious threat. Al Qaeda remains the source of ideological, strategic and tactical doctrine in the jihad against the West, Scheuer says. Hence, he says of bin Laden, "I think he'd be delighted every morning when he wakes up with the way the war is going."

Indeed, Scheuer argues, bin Laden planned things just the way they have turned out. "Very early on, he decided that the al Qaeda role would be three things. The third in importance would be to conduct military actions against the United States. The second — in his mind more important — was to train insurgent fighters from around the world so they could go back and fight their home governments. And from the very beginning, he has declared that he and al Qaeda are the vanguard and that their mission was to instigate and incite."

Nevertheless, Gerges of Sarah Lawrence argues that bin Laden envisioned himself in a larger role than instigator-in-chief. Bin Laden, Gerges writes, ordered the 9/11 attacks confident they would mobilize a vast army of jihadists to fight the Americans, who then would surely invade Afghanistan in response. The U.S. invasion did come, but not the large number of jihadists that bin Laden expected. Consequently, Gerges writes, some

jihadists have been attacking bin Laden as a disastrous strategist.[17]

Today, Gerges says, "The centralized leadership that used to direct and organize and plan is hibernating deeper and deeper underground and is no longer capable of organizing spectacular attacks along 9/11 lines."

Perhaps the most provocative view comes from military analyst David Ronfeldt. Now on leave from the RAND Corp., a think tank in Palo Alto, Calif., Ronfeldt argues that jihadists should be seen as a global tribe. "It is held together not by command-and-control structures but by a gripping sense of shared belonging, principles of fusion against an outside enemy and a jihadist narrative so compelling that it amounts to both an ideology and a doctrine."[18]

But defining the jihadist movement as a tribe doesn't necessarily mean it lacks structure, he adds in an interview. "There is an organization there. We just don't quite know how to detect it any more."

Are the jihadists motivated by religion?

Jihadists invariably portray themselves as warriors for God. Their public statements are steeped in Quranic citations and the writings of Islamic theologians, suggesting strongly that jihadism is all about religion.

But specialists who reject that conclusion point out that throughout history religious war makers always claim to be fighting for their faith — even when most of their co-religionists disagree. They cite the Hindu fanatic who, in 1948, assassinated the leader of India's independence movement, Mohandas K. Gandhi, who was revered by his fellow Hindus, for allegedly making too many concessions to Muslims.[19] And today, jihadists make up only a tiny fraction of the world's Muslims.

Nonetheless, the jihadists do spring from well-established religious traditions. Bin Laden (and 15 of the 19 attackers on 9/11) were natives of Saudi Arabia, where Wahhabism, the fundamentalist state religion, considers other branches of Islam as outside the faith and has a history of violence toward Shiites and other non-Wahhabi Muslims.[20]

Michigan's Cole suggests that jihadist recruits see Islam more as a national identity than a religion. He theorizes that London subway bomber Khan responded to a recruiting pitch along the following lines: "Islam is in danger of being destroyed. Your people are being oppressed. Islam is the only pillar of truth and proper human behavior. Within 25 years it could be gone. When it's gone, all that's left is hell on earth. There is something you can do — take dramatic action. Demonstrate to the imperial West that Islam is not going to go quietly. When other Muslims see you do this dramatic thing, they will take heart from it and may take dramatic actions of their own."

But ex-CIA officer Scheuer argues that religious faith makes up an inseparable part of the jihadist mindset. "I would have thought Christian evangelicals [like President Bush] would understand this," Scheuer says, referring to the jihadist assertion that foreign presence on the Arabian Peninsula profanes the Muslim holy cities of Mecca and Medina, much as they object to Israel's possession of all of Jerusalem. A Western taboo against seeing another religion as a threat prevents frank discussion of jihadism, Scheuer insists.

Scheuer says he's simplifying but not distorting. "When people take me to task for generalizing and referring to 'Muslims' as if they are a single, monolithic group, they're right. It's a diverse Islamic world, but bin Laden recognized that early on. He has created a movement that looks to the United States as the key oppressor of the Muslim world. He is a national-security threat because he has encouraged and strengthened the perception of us as attacking Islam."

Daniel Byman, who directs Georgetown University's Security Studies Program and served on the staff of the National Commission on Terrorist Attacks Upon the United States (the "9/11 Commission"), argues that jihadists' religious rhetoric amounts to a delivery system for a nationalistic message. "There is a strong sense that Muslims are under attack; to me, that dynamic is more comparable to nationalism than religion per se."

Nevertheless, Byman acknowledges that attacks on Shiite Muslims in Iraq (and Pakistan) by Sunni jihadists do reveal the influence of a sectarian reading of the Quran and of Islamic history. "The jihadist agenda is vast," he explains. "Some elements enjoy broad sympathy, others none. This is like many broad ideologies, where parts appeal to different constituents — some parts only to the core, and other parts to a wider range of followers."

Most Westerners, coming from a political culture that remains largely secular, may not recognize the realities of a movement rooted in religion. But Husain Haqqani, a Pakistani scholar and former diplomat who teaches

international relations at Boston University, notes that jihadists are exceeding the norms of Muslim societies. Only jihadists, he says, "think of Islam as an ideology rather than as a religion." The vast majority of Muslims don't look on their religion that way, he says.

Jihadists, "all think they have a religious obligation to create an Islamic state," says Haqqani, who is also a visiting scholar at the Carnegie Endowment for International Peace. "They all think that Islam's political aspect is an integral part of the religion. They have a lot of anger against the West. A lot of their ideology is not well thought out, but for them it's enough."

Taarnby of Denmark's Institute for International Studies argues that religious devotion can't be separated from other factors that drive a tiny minority of Muslims into jihadist ranks. "Economic stagnation, massive unemployment, the question of identity — all this combined with a newfound religious identity" — are among the ingredients, he says.

Non-Muslims who view jihadists as upholders of traditional religious faith are missing the fact that the jihadists are actually wedded to the culture of today's world, Taarnby argues. "The entire project of dissecting the Quran, looking for passages that justify the killing of infidels and crusaders — that is modern literary criticism, not traditional belief," he says.

For all that, jihadist ideology does have roots in a form of Muslim thought that dates back hundreds of years, says Ali Al-Ahmed, a native of Saudi Arabia who directs a Washington-based research and advocacy group, the Institute for Gulf Affairs. Al-Ahmed is a member of Saudi Arabia's Shiite minority, which has a long history of discrimination and mistreatment at the hands of the Wahhabi Sunni monarchy.[21]

"Part of Sunni Arab Islam is their eternal belief that they should exert control over the world, that, 'We as Muslims are responsible for this world and this universe, and all non-Muslims should be under us and all Muslims, because we are the true group of Islam.' That is why in Saudi Arabia, [Shiites] are not allowed to be head of anything."

Are Western governments dealing effectively with the global jihadists?

After the 9/11 attacks, President Bush launched a "war on terror," but the terrorists continue to attack around the world, even as the United States claims it has prevented many attacks. The latest terrorist strikes in Europe have provoked widespread concern about the alienation of European-born children of Muslim immigrants. Bin Laden apparently remains on the loose, along with his top associate, al-Zawahiri. A U.S. intelligence community think tank, the National Intelligence Council, says some experts think the war in Iraq is training a new generation of jihadist terrorists.[22]

In this climate Western governments' response to jihadist terrorism has been challenged by critics who say the West doesn't understand the nature of the jihadist threat, or what is required to defeat it.

To a great extent the argument centers on the war in Iraq — even though its objective was to destroy the regime of Saddam Hussein, whose Baath Party was essentially a secular organization. "Everybody has used 9/11 for their own purposes, including Bush, and one of his purposes was to get Saddam," says Robert Leiken, immigration and national security director at the Nixon Center. The Washington think tank is a haven for foreign-policy "realists," who distrust the notion of fighting wars in the name of spreading democracy. "Iraq has, on the whole, been a mistake from the point of view of fighting the global jihad and al Qaeda. One way to start back-pedaling would be to stop talking about the 'war on terror' and start talking about the fight against terrorism. The Europeans point out that it's a fight — police, prosecutors, intelligence" — rather than a military operation.

But what the jihadists declared was *war*. And — at the jihadists' insistence — it's global, the Washington-based British columnist Christopher Hitchens argues. "The peaceniks love to ask: 'When and where will it all end?' " Hitchens writes. "The answer is easy: It will end with the surrender or defeat of one of the contending parties." He adds: "It is out of the question — plainly and absolutely out of the question — that we should surrender the keystone state of the Middle East to a rotten, murderous alliance between Baathists and bin Ladenists."[23]

But not all opponents of the Iraq war are "peaceniks." Former anti-terrorism czar Clarke, who had been a major advocate in the Clinton and Bush administrations for aggressive action against bin Laden and al Qaeda, argues that the Iraq war diverted resources from the anti-jihadist

campaign.[24] Even worse, says Clarke, a fierce critic of Bush's anti-terrorism strategy, "It's the judgment of every Western intelligence service — including the CIA — that Iraq has created many more jihadists and motivated ones that previously existed. No expert in or out of government argues with that."

Ranstorp of the Swedish National Defense College, however, maintains the outlook isn't that bleak. "To some extent, we can pat ourselves on the back. We have had some successes, we understand the adversary better," he says, citing successes like the 2003 arrest of Khalid Shaikh Mohammed of Pakistan, who introduced bin Laden to the idea of using hijacked airliners as weapons.[25]

Nonetheless, says Ranstorp, the war in Iraq has created a gulf between the United States and Europeans. Referring to Michael Moore, the savagely anti-Bush filmmaker and writer, Ranstorp says that in Europe, "More people believe in [him] than President Bush. When you have that, something is seriously wrong."

Outside government, criticism of Bush administration anti-terrorism policy is pervasive. "But I don't see a great wellspring of ideas from people who say they're doing everything wrong," says Georgetown's Byman.

Non-American critics often suggest that the U.S. military response is overblown. "These [jihadists] are very small groups," says Rohan Gunaratna, director of the International Center for Political Violence and Terrorism Research in Singapore and a senior fellow at the Combating Terrorism Center at the U.S. Military Academy at West Point. "They do not have enough strength to radicalize large amounts of people. If issues like Iraq are resolved, there is no real rationale for these extremist groups to exist."

BACKGROUND

Origins of Jihad

Jihadists' fundamental claim is that they're fighting the ungodly in the name of God. But the origin of jihad actually lies in conflicts among Muslims — not between Muslims and non-Muslims.[26]

The jihadists argue that they base themselves on the Quran — the holy book Muslims consider to be the word of God. But on Earth, their spiritual forefather is Ibn Taymiyyah, a religious scholar born in the mid-13th

CHRONOLOGY

1300s-1700s *Religious scholars lay the foundations of modern jihadism; Turks take over the Arab empire, which is then invaded by Western countries.*

1300s Religious scholar Ibn Taymiyyah justifies revolt against Muslim rulers.

1400s Turkish Muslims supplant the Baghdad-based Caliphate and found the Ottoman Empire.

1700s Muhammed ibn Abd al-Wahhab condemns Shiites and other schools of Islam as heretics.

1800s-1960s *Ottoman Empire falls. Independent countries eventually are established in Middle East.*

1916 Britain and France divvy up Ottoman Empire.

1928 Egyptian activists establish the Muslim Brotherhood.

1948 U.N. approves founding of Israel.

1952 Col. Gamel Abdel Nasser overthrows British-puppet monarchy in Egypt.

1966 Nasser's government executes Sayyid Qutb, a jihadist activist.

1967 Israel crushes Arab armies in Six-Day War, empowering jihadists.

1970s-1980s *Iranian revolution electrifies radicals in the Muslim world, and Soviet invasion of Afghanistan gives them a cause.*

1973 Arab oil embargo triggers record oil prices, helping to finance a major Saudi missionary campaign throughout the Muslim world.

Feb. 1, 1979 Shah Reza Pahlavi flees Iran; exiled Ayatollah Khomeini returns to form a militantly Muslim government.

Dec. 24, 1979 Soviet Union invades Afghanistan.

1981 Egyptian jihadist soldiers assassinate President Anwar Sadat, retaliating for a 1979 peace accord with Israel.

1985 Saudi exile Osama bin Laden lays the groundwork for al Qaeda, a new global jihad organization.

1990s-2005 *Bin Laden identifies United States as main target to attack.*

1993 Non-al Qaeda cell in New York and New Jersey bombs World Trade Center, killing six people.

Feb. 23, 1998 Bin Laden and Ayman al-Zawahiri call for followers to kill Americans "and their allies" worldwide.

Aug. 7, 1998 Al Qaeda bombers destroy U.S. embassies in Kenya and Tanzania, killing 226, including 12 Americans.

Oct. 12, 2000 Al Qaeda suicide attack on the *U.S.S. Cole* in Yemen kills 17 sailors.

Sept. 11, 2001 Al Qaeda hijackers commit deadliest terrorist attacks in history, killing nearly 3,000 in New York City, rural Pennsylvania and at the Pentagon.

April 15, 2002 Bin Laden and al-Zawahiri praise the Sept. 11 attacks in a videotape on Al Jazeera network.

Oct. 12, 2002 Car bombs hit two tourist-filled nightclubs in Bali, Indonesia, killing 202. Jemaah Islamiya jihadists take responsibility for the incident.

2003 Khalid Shaikh Mohammed, mastermind of the 9/11 plot, is arrested in Pakistan (March 1) . . . On Aug. 5 Jemaah Islamiya bombs Marriott Hotel in Jakarta, killing 13 . . . . In November four car bombs in Istanbul, Turkey, kill 52 at two synagogues, the British consulate and a British bank.

March 11, 2004 Al Qaeda-linked jihadists blow up four commuter trains in Madrid, killing 191 and wounding 1,900.

2005 On July 7, four suicide bombers in London transit system kill themselves and 52 commuters . . . . On Sept. 1, a British-born suicide bomber — on a posthumous videotape — claims "atrocities against my people" spurred him to kill. . . . On Oct. 11 U.S. intelligence officials release letter from al-Zawahiri to al-Zarqawi calling for an Islamic state in the Arab heartland and continued targeting of Americans.

century in what is now Iraq, who advocated rebelling against the invading Mongols — even though they had converted to Islam — on the grounds that they were not true Muslims. For many scholars, the notion that some Muslims are not truly Muslims is the key to the jihadist worldview.

"I have not met a former jihadi — or a potential one — who has not memorized Ibn Taymiyyah's fatwas [religious rulings]," writes Sarah Lawrence College's Gerges.[27]

Taymiyyah was writing at a time when Islam was already some 600 years old and a major religious and political power. Islam had spread rapidly throughout the Middle East after the Prophet Muhammed was born in about 570 in the Arabian Peninsula city of Mecca. He began preaching after claiming a visit from the angel Gabriel, and subsequent revelations were compiled into the Quran.

The Muslim faith springs from its predecessor monotheistic religions, Judaism and Christianity. Muslims believe these religions were also divinely inspired, but that only Islam embodies God's final revelations.

Muhammed eventually overcame opposition from tribal leaders to establish the new religion — which means "submission to God" — in much of Arabia, among its previously polytheistic inhabitants. Islam then began to expand beyond the peninsula after Muhammed died. As it spread, a succession crisis developed between members of the powerful ruling caste — the Umayyad tribe — and partisans of Muhammed's cousin and son-in-law, Ali ibn Abi Talib. In 656 Ali finally became Caliph — leader of both state and religion — after his Umayyad predecessor was assassinated. The two events intensified the conflict, leading to civil war.

At that point the Umayyads were in the majority, and Ali's followers — or his "shiah" (the ancestors of today's Shiites) — were in the minority. Then when Ali was assassinated in 661, the Umayyads returned to power with Damascus as their capital.

The Shiites' status as an aggrieved minority dates from these 7th-century events.

Although the Quran calls Jews and Christians by the respectful title "people of the Book," Muslim and Christian rulers clashed repeatedly through the ages, the echoes of which can be heard in jihadists' epithet "crusaders" when referring to Western military forces.[28]

In 1096, the soldiers of the first Christian Crusade arrived in what is today's Lebanon and Syria to reconquer Jerusalem and nearby biblical lands from the Muslims. But the principalities they set up — in modern-day Libya, Turkey and Jerusalem — did not last. By 1193, Muslim forces had retaken Jerusalem and nearly all Christian-held territory.

Eventually, the Ottoman Empire arose — an Islamic Caliphate, centered in Turkey and stretching from North Africa on the west to the Middle East on the south and east. The empire was a major world power by the end of the 16th century, having advanced into the Balkans and Central Europe and spread Islam as far east as modern-day Indonesia. Culturally and politically, Ottoman civilization stood out for its system of rights and privileges for Christian and Jewish minorities, as well as for its vast intellectual accomplishments, especially in mathematics, science and architecture — following in the footsteps of the earlier Arab Caliphate, based in Baghdad. But Europe surged ahead, especially with the conquest of the Americas and parts of Asia. The beginning of the Ottoman decline was first seen on the battlefield, where a second attempt to conquer Vienna failed in 1683.

In the late 19th century, the Russian, British and French empires seized chunks of Ottoman territory in Central Asia and North Africa. World War I saw the Ottoman Empire's final collapse, speeded along by a British-supported "Arab revolt." Indeed, even before the war ended, its ultimate victors had divvied up the empire, with Britain and France taking most of it.

Britain's territory included Palestine. In 1917, a year before the war's end, British Foreign Secretary Lord Arthur Balfour promised a "homeland for the Jewish people" in Palestine, where the rights of non-Jews would not be prejudiced. The declaration helped set the stage for the later creation of Israel, which followed the extermination of 6 million European Jews — a genocide unleashed in Christian Europe, not in Islamic lands.

Modern Islamism

While Ibn Taymiyyah is the intellectual forerunner of jihadism, Muhammed ibn Abd al-Wahhab is its founding warrior. In the early 18th century, Wahhab led a revolt against the Ottoman Empire, which he accused of corrupting the purity of Islam, in part by allowing veneration of others — including Muhammed — besides God.

Using Modern Technology to Sell Jihadism

The anchorman is masked and his delivery is shaky. At his right hand is a rifle on a tripod; at his left, a Quran. As for the news, most Westerners probably would call it propaganda: Hurricane Katrina is God's punishment on the United States. Mahmoud Abbas, the Palestinian president, is an Israeli "puppet" because he is trying to disarm Hamas; terrorist commander Abu Musa al-Zarqawi explains why he's proud of organizing the killings of Iraqi Shiites.

Welcome to Sout Al-Khaliffa (Voice of the Caliphate), a new Internet video news program. The anchorman's Egyptian accent is the only hint of where the 16-minute Web cast is based. Its ideological home is much clearer. "This is al Qaeda," says Ali Al-Ahmed, the Saudi Arabian founder of the Washington-based Institute of Gulf Affairs, a research and advocacy organization that promotes political reform in Saudi Arabia and neighboring countries.

While no one knows if the new show will last, Web-based Jihad seems here to stay. One of the 9/11 attack planners researched flight schools on the Web, and some of the attackers had kept in touch through e-mail and instant messaging.[1] But the Web now offers jihadists far more: a way to keep their ranks unified and to recruit new members.

Young people no longer need guidance from more experienced jihadists, because today "everything is on the Internet," says Marc Sageman, a psychiatrist who served as a CIA officer assigned to the war in Afghanistan.

For example, a 1,600-page history of jihad, *The International Islamic Resistance Call*, was posted to a Web site in December 2004. The memoir of al Qaeda's second in command, Ayman al-Zawahiri — "Knights Under the Prophet's Banner" — is also available via just a few keystrokes.[2] Last year, two online magazines were posted to the Web: *Sout al-Jihad* (Voice of Jihad) and *Muaskar al-Battar* (Camp al-Battar), whose articles included instructions on how to kidnap and murder hostages.[3] And videotapes were posted to the Internet showing the murders of jihadist hostages Daniel Pearl, a *Wall Street Journal* reporter, in Pakistan in 2002 and of American contractor David Berg in Iraq in 2004.[4]

Jihadism on the Internet has mushroomed in the past decade. When he started monitoring terrorist Web sites seven years ago, Gabriel Weimann — a senior fellow at the United States Institute of Peace — found only 12 such sites. By last year, there were more than 4,000.[5] Among other things, jihadists are using the Web to announce job openings. One al Qaeda-affiliated site has been seeking applications for people to compile news reports from Iraq and other battlefronts. Jihadists bilingual in Arabic and English are also in demand.[6]

The job hunt seems to indicate that the jihadists are planning to beef up their Internet presence. In fact, they have recently begun using English-language videotapes, apparently in an attempt to garner more publicity in the West. Since August, three tapes featuring English-speaking jihadists surfaced on TV networks. One was the posthumous

---

Wahhab and his followers also hated Shiites, and their reverence for their holy men, or imams. In 1801, Wahhabis sacked the holy Shiite city of Karbala (in today's Iraq), and killed thousands.

Wahhab's disciples included a tribal leader named Muhammed Ibn Saud. His descendants founded the nation that bears their family's name — and venerates the Wahhabi sect of Islam. Saudi Arabia was created in 1932, after the House of Saud conquered the area, including the territory surrounding Islam's two holiest places, Mecca and Medina.

The doctrinal marriage between Wahhabism and the Saudi monarchy was a purely local matter until 1973. Until then, the Islamic world included a variety of national

and religious traditions. But when oil prices skyrocketed, making the Saudi government wealthy, it revved up religious proselytizing in the Muslim world. "The objective was to . . . refine the multitude of voices within the religion down to the single creed of the masters of Mecca," writes the French scholar Gilles Kepel.[29]

Earlier, in the 1960s and early '70s, the idea of a newly militant form of Islam had already begun resonating among Muslims, particularly in Egypt. One of the major figures behind this "Islamist" intellectual fervor was an Egyptian writer and activist, Sayyid Qutb, who was active in a large, influential, but illegal movement — the Muslim Brotherhood — founded in 1928. The Brotherhood saw Islam as a political and moral force superior both to British recording by one of the London suicide bombers (*see p. 241*). Another featured a hooded jihadist with an Australian accent threatening attacks, and the third showed a masked jihadist speaking in an American accent, also threatening attacks to come. Jihadist leaders apparently concluded they'd get "more air time and column inches by using English-speakers," said a U.S. counterterrorism official.[7]

Experts say that without the Internet and Arabic-language 24-hour TV news, the jihadist movement might be only a shadow of itself.

Michael Scheuer, a former top CIA agent, has watched the jihad movement embrace the digital revolution. Between 1985 and 1992 he helped the agency support the Mujahedeen warriors who were fighting Soviet occupation troops in Afghanistan. At the time, "They were almost unaware of the rest of the Muslim world," Scheuer says. "I don't think you could have found one in 80 who knew what Palestine was, or Israel."

But last March, he points out, when the Israelis killed Hamas spiritual leader Sheikh Ahmed Yassin, spontaneous demonstrations broke out in the Afghan cities of Jalalabad, Kandahar and Herat.[8] "A decade earlier, that would have been unimaginable," he says. "Bin Laden has the extraordinary good fortune to have arisen and declared war on the United States simultaneously with the advent of Arabic satellite TV and the Internet," he says.

As jihadists become increasingly reliant on the Web, however, intelligence agencies can use it to keep better tabs on them. The New York Police Department's intelligence division, for instance, constantly trolls through Web sites

and chatrooms. "You know you passed the test when suddenly somebody gives you a password to a chat room you didn't know existed," an Egyptian-born New York detective told *The New Yorker's* William Finnegan.

An Iranian-born cop said, "You'll see an offer of a video-clip download. It might be a beheading, or training materials, or proof that someone actually did something." A second Egyptian-born officer shook his head. "This is not Islam," he said.[9]

---

[1] "The 9/11 Commission Report: Final Report of the National Commission on Terrorist Attacks Against the United States," July 22, 2004, pp. 157, 247.

[2] Peter Bergen, "The jihadists export their rage to book pages and Web pages," *The Washington Post, Book World*, Sept. 11, 2005, p. T4. (English-language excerpts of Zawahiri's work are available at: www .liberalsagainstterrorism.com/wiki/index.php/Knights_Under_the_ Prophet's_Banner.)

[3] Lawrence Wright, "The Terror Web," *The New Yorker*, Aug. 4, 2004, p. 40.

[4] "Web Sites Remove Video of Pearl's Death," *The New York Times*, May 25, 2002, p. A4; Steve Fainaru, "Militants in Iraq Release Video of U.S. Captive's Beheading," *The Washington Post*, Sept. 21, 2004, p. A1.

[5] *Ibid.*

[6] Mohammed Al Shafey, "Al Qaeda Website Openly Hiring New Recruits," Asharq Al-Awsat, Oct. 3, 2005; www.asharqalawsat.com/ english/news.asp?section=1&id=1987.

[7] Mark Hosenball, "Bloodcurdling Qaeda Threats — In English," *Newsweek*, Sept. 26, 2005, p. 6.

[8] James Bennet, "Palestinians Swear Vengeance for Killing of Cleric by Israelis," *The New York Times*, March 23, 2004, p. A1.

[9] William Finnegan, "The Terrorism Beat: How is the N.Y.P.D. Defending the City?" *The New Yorker*, July 25, 2005, p. 58.

---

colonial domination and to the secular anti-colonialist movement that overthrew the British-puppet monarchy in 1952, led by Gamel Abdel Nasser.

"The Quran is our constitution," the Brothers declared.[30]

The Brotherhood and later Islamist and jihadist groups were influenced by a religious doctrine known as *salafiyya*, which refers to the Prophet Muhammed's companions. The term is often used interchangeably with "Wahhabi," though some scholars argue that some Salafis are more open to the modern world and democratic politics.

In the ensuing decades, the Brotherhood slowly moderated its message and methods, but Qutb went in the opposite direction. Seeing the threat, Nasser cracked down,

and Qutb and others were arrested. In 1966, Nasser ordered Qutb executed for subversion.

The following year, Nasser led Egypt and two neighboring Arab countries into the Six-Day War with Israel. Israel crushed Egypt, Syria and Jordan. That outcome seemed to prove the Islamists' point: that secular Arab nationalist regimes had grown weak and decadent.

Revolution

By the early 1970s, a population boom, urbanization and the slow decay of nationalist systems in the Middle East provided a perfect setting for the message that failed secular rulers should be overthrown. In Shiite Iran, for instance, Shah (Emperor) Mohammed Reza Pahlavi had alienated

The Rise of Ayman al-Zawahiri

Osama bin Laden may be the world's best-known jihadist, but professional terrorism-watchers believe his chief strategist, Ayman al-Zawahiri, is now the man to study. An Egyptian physician who has spent most of his life in the jihadist movement, he's had a longer and more complicated career than the gaunt Saudi millionaire.

Zawahiri has been taking a bigger place on the world stage of late, making four video or audio statements during the past 13 months. They included a warning to Americans that their choice in the 2004 presidential election would not protect them from future jihadist attacks, a denunciation of U.S. calls for reform in the Middle East and a promise of more attacks like the July 7 mass-transit bombings in London.[1]

Bin Laden made only one appearance during that period, on a video that aired shortly before the U.S. presidential election.[2] "Now the face of al Qaeda is Zawahiri," says Fawaz A. Gerges, a Middle East specialist at Sarah Lawrence College.

For students of jihadism such as Gerges, Zawahiri's rise is something of a scholarly advantage, because he has left a much more detailed paper trail than bin Laden. And Zawahiri's life story is virtually the definitive chronicle of the strategic shift from trying to overthrow Middle Eastern rulers to attacking the United States and former imperial powers.

Born in 1951 to a Cairo family of physicians and religious scholars, the teenage Zawahiri entered the underground Islamist movement aiming to install what the movement viewed as a devout Muslim government. Some Islamists favored revolution, but Zawahiri and others wanted a coup d'état. Though Zawahiri viewed himself as a full-time warrior, he also completed medical studies and became a surgeon.[3]

After moving to Pakistan to help with the Afghan jihad against the Soviet occupation, Zawahiri decided to concentrate on the United States and other Western powers, largely due to bin Laden's influence. The wealthy Saudi had been raised in Wahhabism, the branch of Islam that insists it is the only true form of the faith. "One would have expected Zawahiri . . . a fervent believer in attacking ruling Muslim 'renegades,' to sway the attitudes of . . . bin Laden and slow down the jihadist march against the United States," Gerges writes. But rather than slowing bin Laden's "speeding jihadist caravan, Zawahiri wholeheartedly joined it." [4]

Perhaps the Egyptian played a greater role than the relatively inexperienced bin Laden in building al Qaeda. "The people with Zawahiri had extraordinary capabilities — doctors, engineers, soldiers," said Essam Deraz, an Egyptian who made documentaries about the anti-Soviet war. "They had experience in secret work. They knew how to organize themselves and create cells. And they became the leaders."[5]

Zawahiri and other Egyptian jihadists had been battle-hardened by spending time in prison — and in Zawahiri's case, undergoing torture. "Ayman was beaten all the time — every day," said Montasser al-Zayat, who was imprisoned with Zawahiri following the 1981 assassination of Egyptian President Anwar Sadat and wrote a critical biography of his former prison mate. The torturers finally forced Zawahiri to betray a comrade.

the country's youth and religious leaders by repressing dissent, channeling economic benefits to wealthy friends and allowing large numbers of American military personnel and defense contractors to maintain and operate U.S.-supplied military hardware in Iran.

In 1979, Iran exploded. The shah fled, and power gravitated toward Ayatollah Ruholla Khomeini, a Shiite religious scholar who had been in exile for 15 years in Iraq and France. Khomeini returned to adoring crowds in Tehran on Feb. 1, 1979, and soon assumed total power. Despite the Shiites' minority position in the Muslim world, the Iranian revolution showed that religion could be harnessed to overthrow an oppressive ruler.

On Oct. 6, 1981, a group of soldiers taking part in a military parade in Cairo turned their guns on Nasser's successor, President Anwar Al-Sadat, who had signed a peace treaty with Israel and repressed militant Islamists. The leader of the assassination belonged to a jihadist organization inspired by Qutb's writings.[31]

The soldiers directly involved in the assassination were executed. But almost all other members of the Egyptian

By the time Zawahiri left prison, Gerges writes, "a thirst for vengeance took hold of his soul."[6] Although his target at the time was the Egyptian government, Zawahiri seems to have transferred his spirit of vengefulness to the United States. In 1998, following a CIA takedown of an al Qaeda cell that Zawahiri had formed in Albania, Zawahiri told an Arabic newspaper in London: "We are interested in briefly telling the Americans that their message has been received and that the response, which we hope they will read carefully, is being prepared, because, with God's help, we will write it in the language that they understand."[7] The next day, suicide bombers attacked the U.S. embassies in Tanzania and Kenya, killing 224 people.

For Stephen Schwartz, director of the Center for Islamic Pluralism, who authored an early study of Wahhabism, the level of hatred reflected in that statement and others may also represent Zawahiri's contribution to the Qaeda ideology. "The Egyptians adopted the Wahhabi claims to represent the only genuine Sunni Muslims in the world, and their program for imposition of a strict Islamic state," Schwartz writes, "but they also expressed a deeper hatred and contempt for Westerners based on their experience with British colonial rule."[8]

Zawahiri's own life has given him plenty of opportunity to cultivate those emotions.

Ayman al-Zawahiri

CNN/AFP Photos/Getty Images

---

[1] Alan Cowell, "Al Jazeera Video Links London Bombings to Al Qaeda," *The New York Times*, Sept. 2, 2005, p. A3; Kevin Sullivan, "No. 2 Leader for Al Qaeda Warns," *The Washington Post*, Aug. 7, 2005, p. A3; Kevin Sullivan, "Al Qaeda's No. 2 Blames Blair, Issues Warnings," *The Washington Post*, Aug. 5, 2005, p. A1; "Purported Zawarhi Tape Condemns U.S. 'Reforms,'" The Associated Press, Feb. 21, 2005; Craig Whitlock, "Bin Laden Aide Warns U.S. to Alter Policies," *The Washington Post*, Nov. 30, 2004, p. A14.

[2] Whitlock, *ibid.*

[3] Lawrence Wright, "The Man Behind Bin Laden," *The New Yorker*, Sept. 16, 2002, p. 56.

[4] Fawaz A. Gerges, *The Far Enemy: How Jihad Went Global* (2005), p. 120.

[5] Wright, *op. cit.*

[6] Gerges, *op. cit.*, p. 94.

[7] Wright, *op. cit.*

[8] Stephen Schwartz, "Zawahiri's Threats," *The Daily Standard*, Aug. 4, 2005, http://weeklystandard.com/Content/Public/Articles/000/000/005/922ycjmq.asp.w2w1w.

---

jihadist movement were given three-year prison sentences, including al-Zawahiri, who had taken up the jihadist cause as a teenager. A year before the assassination, he had traveled to Pakistan to support the mujahedeen in Afghanistan, who were fighting to expel Soviet forces that had invaded in 1979.[32]

After his release in 1985, al-Zawahiri returned to Afghanistan, where he forged close ties to a young Saudi millionaire who was playing a key role in organizing the non-Afghan volunteers. His name was Osama bin Laden.

U.S.-Jihadist Alliance

The United States backed the anti-Soviet resistance in Afghanistan, aiming to inflict a Vietnam-sized defeat on the Soviets. Both the Carter and Reagan administrations worked closely with the Saudi government, which was anxious to provide an escape valve for Saudi youth who might otherwise have focused their anger on the monarchy's ties to the United States. For decades, the Saudis had been selling oil to the Americans, who provided military protection — a relationship that deepened in the 1990s, after bin Laden returned home following the 1988 Soviet pullout from Afghanistan.

In 1990, Saudi Arabia felt threatened by Iraq's invasion of neighboring Kuwait. Iraqi dictator Saddam Hussein was then considered a secular nationalist. Bin Laden told the Saudi monarchy that he could assemble an army of Afghanistan veterans to push the Iraqis out of Kuwait. But the Saudi government, already lining up U.S. military support, rebuffed him.

But by then bin Laden already saw the United States as a foe. And he and his comrades considered the world's remaining superpower weaker than most people believed. In the jihadists' eyes, the overthrow of the shah had proved they wouldn't fight to keep a key ally in power.

More signs of apparent U.S. vulnerability followed: In 1983, Reagan withdrew U.S. troops from Lebanon after Iranian-supported Hezbollah guerrillas in Beirut carried out suicide attacks on the U.S. Embassy, killing 63, and the U.S. Marine barracks, killing 241. In neither case did the United States strike back. Ten years later, President Clinton pulled U.S. peacekeeping troops out of Somalia after 18 U.S. soldiers were killed during failed efforts to arrest a local warlord. Bin Laden said the fact that the United States did not retaliate showed "how weak, impotent and cowardly the American soldier is."[33] Later, some al Qaeda members boasted they had trained the Somalis in how to shoot down the U.S. helicopters that were involved in the operation.[34]

Anti-West Jihad

Bin Laden's view of a weak United States led him to argue that jihadists should shift their energies from attacks on Middle Eastern governments. "In his eyes, the center of political gravity and power lies in Washington and New York, not in Cairo, Riyadh, Baghdad, Amman, Algiers or elsewhere," writes Gerges.[35]

The first strike under the new strategy was a 1993 attempt to blow up the World Trade Center. A Kuwaiti-born jihadist of Pakistani ancestry, Ramzi Yousef, master-minded the plot, in which a truck bomb was exploded in the complex's underground garage. But only six people were killed — not 250,000 as he had hoped.[36]

Although bin Laden never claimed responsibility for that attack, Yousef had trained in Afghan jihadist camps and was the nephew of another terrorist, Khalid Sheikh Mohammed, who was later to convince bin Laden to destroy American targets with hijacked aircraft.[37]

Mohammed took the idea to bin Laden in 1996, the same year bin Laden called for the expulsion of Western military forces from Saudi Arabia. Two years later, he took to the world stage again to issue a "Jihad Against Jews and Crusaders." Bin Laden's 1998 fatwah declared that killing "Americans and their allies — civilians and military — is an individual duty for every Muslim who can do it in any country in which it is possible to do it."[38] Al-Zawahiri was a co-signer.

Some six months later, on Aug. 7, 1998, suicide truck-bombers unmistakably tied to al Qaeda simultaneously struck the U.S. embassies in Kenya and Tanzania, killing 226, including 12 Americans.[39] In October 2000, al Qaeda operatives maneuvered an explosives-filled small boat alongside the *U.S.S. Cole*, a Navy destroyer in port in Yemen, blasting a hole in the hull and killing 17 sailors.

Bin Laden became a bigger American target than ever. The attack intensified efforts in the Clinton administration to track down bin Laden and kidnap or kill him.[40]

CURRENT SITUATION

Goodbye 'Londonistan'

For decades, London had been a world center for Muslim political dissidents and radicals of all stripes, including jihadists. Part of a much larger immigrant Muslim population, the activists operated so freely that many British security officials, politicians and journalists came up with the sardonic nickname "Londonistan." It was meant to convey the notion that a virtual separate state had arisen on British soil.

The recent terrorist bombings in London have led British authorities to rethink the asylum and free speech policies that made London a magnet for jihadist preachers and organizers, who used the United Kingdom as a base of operations and recruiting center. Some had enjoyed years of notoriety, including: Abu Hamza (Mustafa Kamel Mustafa), a one-handed, one-eyed Egyptian-born jihad supporter who had been a prayer leader at London's Finsbury Park mosque; Omar Mohammed bin Bakri, a Syrian-born minister who also preached at Finsbury Park; and Yasser Sirri, an Egyptian-born activist whose Islamic Observation Center monitored the "holy struggle" against Western-allied Arab regimes.[41]

Do jihadists hate America because of its freedoms?

YES
Stephen Schwartz
Executive Director, Center for
Islamic Pluralism and Author,
The Two Faces of Islam

Written for the *CQ Researcher*, October 2005

Sunni jihadists do not hate the West; rather, they are contemptuous of the West. This contempt is often aimed less at our freedoms per se than at the triumph of secularism and irreligion, which we in the West tend to equate with freedom. Further, Sunni jihadists, being fundamentalists, are — above all — enemies of pluralism within Islam and in the world at large.

They do not accept the pluralistic shari'a of traditional, conservative and classical Islam; do not accept Islamic spirituality (Sufism); do not recognize that Sunnis and Shiites are both Muslim; and do not maintain the respect for the "People of the Book" (Jews, Christians, Zoroastrians and Hindus) commanded by traditional Islam.

Some Western analysts persistently argue that our policies in the Middle East and elsewhere — rather than these issues — have caused us to be targeted. But Turkey, which opposed the U.S. intervention in Iraq, has been targeted; Morocco and Indonesia have been targeted, and even Saudi Arabia is now experiencing jihadist terror. U.S. policies have little to do with Turkish or Moroccan or Indonesian policies. These countries are targeted because their Islam is pluralistic and non-fundamentalist. Sunni jihadism is motivated by a totalitarian view of the world that hates individual responsibility, public accountability, popular sovereignty and pluralism in general. In this sense, they are fighting a war against the freedoms we cherish. All the rest is incidental.

Unfortunately, this religious totalitarianism originates with a movement that claimed to reform Islam: Wahhabism, emerging 250 years ago in the dank backwaters of the most remote and undeveloped area of the Arabian Peninsula, which, at Riyadh, is the heart of today's Saudi Arabia. Wahhabism set out to purge Islam of its civilizational achievements: art, architecture, philosophy, spirituality and compassion in the administration of law. In addition, it exemplified an Islam that had little or no contact with the great non-Muslim civilizations.

Unlike the Ottoman empire, which it fought, it did not govern millions of Christians; in contrast with the Persians, it did not draw on the immense wisdom of the East; and as distinct from the colossally rich Muslim states of India, it did not contend with the immense task of maintaining Muslim rule, by a minority, over millions of Hindus and other non-Muslims. It came from, and embodied, a void and had no incentive to accept anything about the rest of the world. That spirit is the same that inhabits Islamist terrorism today.

NO
Michael Scheuer
Former CIA Bin Laden specialist;
Author, Imperial Hubris: Why the
West Is Losing the War on Terror

Written for the *CQ Researcher*, October 2005

Clearly, Jihadists hate and attack America because of U.S. foreign policy in the Muslim world. But long after 9/11, America's late and tepid response is prolonged by politically correct and cowardly bipartisan leaders who insist the war is about the freedoms we enjoy. The enemy's core motivations are not mentioned: Unqualified U.S. support for Israel and presence on the Arabian Peninsula, the coddling of Muslim tyrannies, the occupation of Afghanistan and Iraq and the perception that America is attacking Islam.

This assures U.S. defeat, and the leaders hawking it will be judged traitors for knowingly minimizing the size, power and resilience of Osama bin Laden's forces in order to sidestep radioactive domestic issues, such as ties to Israel and Saudi Arabia, energy policy, borders, immigration and other topics. They also will be judged as killers who sent U.S. military overseas as targets, neutered by rules of engagement meant to curry world opinion and avoid the truth that war is about killing until the enemy surrenders or perishes.

Some Islamist leaders do hate us more than our policies. They consider U.S. society evil because it is not ruled by God. But they know Muslims in general do not yet hate Americans, so their dream of a Caliphate requires that Muslims believe Islam is under U.S. attack.

Thus, our policies give the Islamists a war-winning opportunity: Myriad young Muslims would die to attack U.S. policies — U.S. forces in Iraq or absolute support for Israel — but large numbers would not die to eliminate elections, R-rated movies or after-work Miller drafts. So, protecting the foreign policy status quo and repeating the "It's our society and values, stupid!" mantra is treasonous: It gives our foes aid, comfort and unlimited manpower.

The Founders taught us to see the world as it is, not as we want it to be. Today's leaders see the world clearly, but they lie to Americans to protect sacred political cows. George Washington would have said: "They hate us for what we do, because of our policy. Let us fight but also debate a future policy course." Bush, Kerry and Clinton say: "They hate freedom, are a lunatic fringe, we can arrest them all, cling fast to the past."

Time will tell how much blood and treasure is spent before Americans see past the traitors to the mortal threat their nation faces — and if they see it before it is too late.

Although the July 7 bombings recharged the long-running debate over British asylum and free-speech policies, British authorities actually had started pulling up the red carpet following the 9/11 attacks against the United States. The government lifted a ban on extradition, which allowed the United States to press for delivery of Saudi Arabia-born Khalid al-Fawwaz, who ran a London office for bin Laden and is accused in an American indictment of participating in the 1998 embassy bombings in Africa.[42]

But after July 7, Prime Minister Tony Blair called for further measures. A Blair bill now before Parliament would define "encouragement" and "glorification" of terrorism as crimes, along with distribution of terrorist publications. It would also allow police to detain a suspect up to 90 days before filing charges.[43]

"Someone who comes into our country, and maybe seeks refuge here . . . we say if, when you are here, you want to stay here, play by the rules, play fair, don't start inciting people to go and kill other innocent people in Britain," Blair said in defense of his proposal.[44]

A member of Britain's House of Lords, Baron Desmond Ackner, a former judge, was one of several critics of the measure from within the political establishment. "I get the impression we are taking this too far, that there is a great risk that freedom of speech is going to be curtailed," he said in Parliament.[45]

However, some experts on terrorism sided with Blair. "Thank God" for Blair's proposal, says Yosri Fouda, a London-based producer and anchor for "Top Secret," an investigative program on the Al Jazeera network. "I've been calling for a long time to prosecute anyone who would call for hate. These are the kinds of people who hijacked Islam."

Britain is considered the most tolerant country in Europe when it comes to Islamist preachers and activists, but terrorists have found havens elsewhere in Europe as well. Key members of the 9/11 attack squad came together as students in Hamburg, Germany. In Spain, authorities arrested 24 people after 9/11 on charges of working with al Qaeda, in some cases allegedly helping organize the attacks. On Sept. 26, 2005, one of the men was sentenced to 27 years in prison for conspiring with the 9/11 terrorists. Six of the accused were acquitted on all charges.[46] A month earlier, a German court convicted a Moroccan,

Mounir el-Motassadeq, of belonging to the "Hamburg cell" of al Qaeda from which the 9/11 plotters emerged. He was acquitted, however, of helping organize the attacks.[47]

Sleeper Cells?

The jihadist trail through Europe doesn't seem, so far, to continue in the United States. Despite administration assertions after the 9/11 attacks that "sleeper cells" embedded in America were awaiting the moment to strike again, evidence of such cells has been sparse. In Europe, however, there is widespread fear that segregated, sometimes impoverished immigrant communities have been breeding alienation and resentment in their youth — some of whom have been turning to jihadism.

"He was an average, second-generation immigrant," a member of Parliament in the Netherlands said of Dutch-born Mohammed Bouyeri, a 27-year-old of Moroccan origin who slit the throat of a filmmaker, Theo Van Gogh — apparently trying to behead him — for making a movie that portrayed Islam as oppressive to women. In July Bouyeri received a life sentence for the murder. "I should cut everyone's head off who insults Allah or his prophet," Bouyeri said.[48]

With few known exceptions, the United States seems less prone to generating homegrown jihadists. "The American dream is part of the reason," says former CIA officer Sageman, referring to the greater opportunities for economic and social mobility for immigrants in the United States. "Europe needs to be a little more accepting of foreigners."

But the Nixon Center's Leiken warns that Europe's problem could draw closer to American shores. "Like a thief in the night who tries each door, we must assume al Qaeda will probe all our borders," he writes. "But when the front door is ajar, the thief will walk right in. With the VWP [visa waiver program] that door is wide open for European Muslim citizens."[49] Under the program, reciprocal agreements among the United States and Western European and Scandinavian countries allow Europeans to travel to the States without visas, and vice versa.

In fact, at least one terrorist already had tried the visa waiver route. Zacarias Moussaoui, the Frenchman of Algerian origin who pleaded guilty in April to being part of the 9/11 plot, entered the United States without a visa, thanks to his French passport.*[50] Visitors still face screening by immigration inspectors. But a well-trained terrorist who hasn't appeared on any blacklists could enter the United States simply by buying an airline ticket. As of January 2005, citizens from "visa-waiver" countries must have computer-readable passports.[51]

Some immigration specialists say the waivers endanger national security and call for their abolition. "I do not believe that requiring visitors who seek entry into our country to first obtain a visa is an unreasonable burden," Michael Cutler, a retired senior special agent with the former Immigration and Naturalization Service, wrote on the "Counterterrorism Blog" Web site maintained by several terrorism specialists. "It is time to eliminate the visa waiver program and do what any sensible homeowner would do before opening the door to a visitor — make certain that he or she knows who they are letting in."[52]

A trio of experts from the Migration Policy Institute, a Washington-based nonpartisan think tank, argues instead that participation in the waiver program should be conditioned on sharing terrorism intelligence.[53]

For his part, Leiken favors measures short of abolishing the waivers. He proposes that European travelers submit their passport information when buying tickets, which would give U.S. authorities time to run their names through terrorist databases. Abolishing the waivers, he writes, "would exact steep bureaucratic and diplomatic costs and rile the United States' remaining European friends."[54]

Saudi Succession

Saudi Arabia has been in the anti-terrorism spotlight since Sept. 11, 2001. Fifteen of the 19 hijackers were Saudis, and a steady stream of investigations has concluded that the kingdom's missionary campaign for Wahhabi Islam had helped create the religious/political ideology that gave rise to modern jihadism.

In fact, the impetus from Saudi Arabia may have been more than ideological. A task force of the New York-based Council on Foreign Relations, a think tank heavy with former United States officials, reported in 2002 that "for years, individuals and charities based in Saudi Arabia have been the most important source of funds for al Qaeda;

---

* Moussaoui is awaiting sentencing, which is tentatively scheduled for early in 2006. Federal prosecutors are seeking the death penalty.

and, for years, Saudi officials have turned a blind eye to this problem."[55]

But Saudi Arabia is now in the hands of a new leader generally viewed as a moderate and a reformer. King Abdullah bin Abdul Aziz took the throne in August, following the death of his brother, King Fahd bin Abdel Aziz, on Aug. 1. For some of the monarchy's critics, the succession makes possible a loosening of the centuries-old ties between Wahhabism and the Saudi state.

The effect on the jihadist movement could be important. A Saudi lawyer who follows the movement said its doctrine is a product of Wahhabi teachings. Abdel Rahem al-Lahem told an interviewer that Wahhabis believe in striking the first blow against an enemy, whereas other schools of Islam hold that Muslims should fight only after being attacked. A wave of jihadist attacks in Saudi Arabia in which foreigners were targeted but Saudis and other Muslims died has weakened allegiance to the Wahhabi concept of jihad.[56]

To be sure, the Saudi government has always rejected the idea that al Qaeda doctrine is a product of Wahhabism. In 2004, Saudi Foreign Minister Saud Al Faisal said bin Laden's ideology "was ingrained in him by this radicalized cult of the Muslim Brotherhood" — a reference to the Egyptian jihadist movement. "It is not the teaching of the Wahhabi reform movement or any other school indigenous to Saudi Arabia that [caused] his metamorphosis."[57]

Still, observers hope a reformist monarchy could weaken any ties between Wahhabism and jihadism. Stephen Schwartz, an American journalist and executive director of the Center for Islamic Pluralism, which opposes radical Islam, wrote the first English-language book to describe links between Wahhabism and jihadist terror.[58] He saw a sign of hope in statements by a Saudi state cleric, Sheikh Abd Al-Muhsin Al-Abika, condemning al Qaeda terror and calling on bin Laden to surrender and repent. Schwartz, a Sufi Muslim, argued that King Abdullah could propel a Saudi shift along the lines of post-dictatorship transitions in central and Eastern Europe, Asia and Latin America.

"Abdullah may have just the necessary window to being a transition to normality for his country," Schwartz wrote, "from its present standing as the richest but most backward ideological state in the world, a kind of Middle Eastern North Korea or Cuba."[59]

Other Saudi-watchers are less optimistic. Saudi political-reform advocate Al-Ahmed, of the Institute for Gulf

Getty Images/Courtney Kealy

Chanting "death to America," citizens demonstrate in support of terrorist Osama bin Laden outside a mosque in Tripoli, Lebanon, a month after the Sept. 11, 2001, attack on the United States. Support for anti-Western jihadists appears to be slipping among the world's 1.3 billion Muslims.

Affairs, has said that Abdullah's reform credentials have been overstated. "Now that he is king," he wrote, "it is time to test the much-touted 'reformer.' "[60]

Another Saudi-born analyst, Mai Yamani, a research fellow at the Royal Institute of International Affairs in London, described the reformers led by Abdullah as "the acceptable face of the Saudi dictatorship internationally." But in reality, the "hard-line Wahhabi camp . . . controls the security forces, the judiciary system and the real levers of domestic power."[61]

OUTLOOK

Limited Support

Terrorism experts say another strike in the United States is inevitable. Al Qaeda leaders are planning "to undertake in the future a large strategic strike against the United States," says Ranstorp, of Sweden's Center for Asymmetric Threat Studies. "This is a long-term project. What they set in motion on 9/11 was a movement that relies as much on violence as on psychological warfare."

On the other hand, virtually no one sees the jihadists as having gained great support in the worldwide Muslim community. A recent Pew Research Center survey in Muslim countries found varying degrees of support. In Jordan, 57 percent of the respondents considered suicide

bombings and other violent actions to be justifiable in defending Islam. But in Pakistan, upholders of that view declined from 41 percent to 25 percent over the past three years. In Turkey and Morocco, no more than 15 percent of respondents supported violence against civilians.[62]

The attitudes of Muslim youth born and raised in Europe have been attracting the most concern, given Europe's importance as a recruiting ground and a theater of jihadist operations.

"The conflict in Iraq fuels feelings of hatred toward the West among radical and radicalizing Muslims," the Dutch General Intelligence and Security Service (AIVD) concluded in a 2002 report whose conclusions are still widely accepted in Europe. "It is possible that, as the conflict continues and more radicalized Muslims join the jihad in Iraq, they will eventually return as trained and experienced fighters. . . It is also possible that they will become active recruiters of new jihadists in Europe."[63]

In the United States, meanwhile, a federal indictment in August charged four Los Angeles men with planning attacks on military and Jewish targets in the name of jihad. One allegedly founded a jihadist cell in 1997 while incarcerated at California's Folsom prison. "This summer, Americans watched so-called homegrown terrorists unleash multiple bombings in the city of London," U.S. Attorney General Alberto R. Gonzales said in announcing the indictments. "Some in this country may have mistakenly believed that it could not happen here. Today we have chilling evidence that it is possible."[64]

Steve J. Martin, an Austin, Texas-based consultant on prison litigation and court-appointed supervisor for deficient jails across the country, says he has heard no prison officials in any state express concern over radical Islamist organizing. "That doesn't mean it's not there, but if it was very much on the radar screen of corrections people I would be picking something up," Martin says. "I'm in and around these large facilities all the time."

In any event, terrorists don't need many comrades — or a rational cause — to mount major attacks. "For the first time in human history very small groups have, or will have, the potential to cause immense destruction," writes historian Laqueur. "Today's terrorists, in their majority, are not diplomats eager to negotiate or to find compromises. And even if some of them would be satisfied with less than total victory and the annihilation of the enemy, there will always be a more radical group eager to continue the struggle."[65]

NOTES

1. Cited in Ben Russell, "Videotapes Reveal Al-Qa'ida's Link to July 7 London Bombings," *The* [London] *Independent*, Sept. 2, 2005.

2. Marianne Kearney, " 'Demolition Man' touted as most likely suspect," *The* [London] *Daily Telegraph*, Oct. 3, 2005, p. 19; Raymond Bonner, "Bali Suicide Bombers Said to Have Belonged to Small Gang," *The New York Times*, Oct. 7, 2005, p. A3. For background, see "Group Profile: Jemaah Islamiyyah, Terrorism Knowledge Base, www.tkb.org.

3. The Century Foundation, "Defeating the Jihadists: A Blueprint for Action," Nov. 16, 2004, pp. 148-163, http://tcf.org/list.asp?type=PB&pubid=498. See also *Voice of Jihad* magazine, No. 9, posted Jan. 27, 2004, by Middle East Media Research Institute, http://memri.org.

4. For full text of reported letter, see, "Letter in English," Office of the Director of National Intelligence, www.dni.gov/letter_in_english.pdf. See also, Douglas Jehl and Thom Shanker, "Al Qaeda Tells Ally in Iraq to Strive for Global Goals," *The New York Times*, Oct. 7, 2005, p. A10; Douglas Jehl, "Full Qaeda Letter to Iraq Ally Speaks of Group's Global Goal," *The New York Times*, Oct. 12, 2005, p. A6.

5. Government Accountability Office, "International Affairs: U.S. Information Agencies' Efforts to Address Islamic Extremism," September 2005, p. 17.

6. Kim Sengupta, "Bomber's Video: Analysis: Video Shows Bombers Were Not 'Duped;'" *The* [London] *Independent*, Sept. 3, 2005.

7. Kim Sengupta, "Bomber's Video: The Videotape: Defiant Message From Bomber Was Filmed on British Soil, Claim Security Services," *The* [London] *Independent*, Sept. 3, 2005.

8. John Burgess, "Europeans Reject Bin Laden 'Truce,'" *The Washington Post*, April 16, 2001, p. A1. See also James Graff, *et al.*, "Terror's Tracks," *Time*, April 19, 2004, p. 36.

9. Walter Laqueur, "The Terrorism to Come," *Policy Review*, August 2004; www.policyreview.org/aug04/laqueur.

10. Fawaz A. Gerges, *The Far Enemy: Why Jihad Went Global* (2005), p. 273.

11. *Ibid.*, pp. 175-178.

12. "Wife: 7/7 bomber's mind 'poisoned,' " CNN.com, Sept. 23, 2005.

13. Husain Haqqani and Daniel Kimmage, "The Online Bios of Iraq's Suicidology," *The New Republic*, Sept. 22, 2005, p. 14.

14. Jehl and Shanker, *op. cit.*

15. The Century Foundation, *op. cit.*, pp. 21-61.

16. *Ibid.*

17. Gerges, *op. cit.*, pp. 186-188.

18. David Ronfeldt, "Al Qaeda and its Affiliates: A Global Tribe Waging Segmental Warfare?" First Monday (University of Illinois at Chicago Library), Feb. 25, 2005; www.firstmonday.org/issues/issue10_3/ronfeldt/.

19. "Assassination of Gandhi — The Facts Behind," Gandhian Institute, www.mkgandhi.org/index.

20. Febe Armanios, "The Islamic Traditions of Wahhabism and Salafiyya," Congressional Research Service, Dec. 22, 2003.

21. Neil MacFarquhar, "Saudi Shiites, Long Kept Down, Look to Iraq and Assert Rights," *The New York Times*, March 2, 2005, p. A1.

22. National Intelligence Council, "Mapping the Global Future," December 2004, p. 98; www.foia.cia.gov/2020/2020.pdf.

23. Christopher Hitchens, "A War to be Proud Of," *The Weekly Standard*, Sept. 5, 2005; www.hitchensweb.com.

24. See "9/11 Commission Report," 2004, pp. 212-214.

25. *Ibid.*, pp. 145-149.

26. Unless otherwise specified, information in this section is from *The Middle East*, 10th ed., CQ Press, 2005; Bernard Lewis, *The Middle East: A Brief History of the Last 2,000 Years* (1995), and Gilles Kepel, *Jihad: The Trail of Political Islam* (2002).

27. Gerges, *op. cit.*, p. 290n.

28. Lewis, *op. cit.*, p. 211.

29. Kepel, *op. cit.*, p. 70.

30. *Ibid.*, pp. 27-28.

31. Marc Sageman, *Understanding Terror Networks* (2004), pp. 15-16, 32-35.

32. *Ibid.*

33. Gerges, *op. cit.*, p. 53.

34. "The 9/11 Commission Report," *op. cit.*, p. 60.

35. Gerges, *op. cit.*, p. 144.

36. Steve Coll, *Ghost Wars: The Secret History of the CIA, Afghanistan, and Bin Laden, From the Soviet Invasion to September 10, 2001* (2004), pp. 247-251.

37. "The 9/11 Commission Report," *op. cit.*, pp. 153-156.

38. Sageman, *op. cit.*, p. 19.

39. Coll, *op. cit.*, pp. 405-407.

40. *Ibid.*, pp. 407-409, 466-468, 534-537.

41. Brian Brady, *et al.*, "Spotlight is on Most Radical Clerics Allowed to Shelter in 'Londonistan,'" *Scotland on Sunday*, July 24, 2005, p. 16.

42. Sean O'Neill, "Bin Laden's London man may finally be sent to US after 7 years," *The* [London] *Times*, Aug. 31, 2005, p. 9.

43. The text of the terrorism bill can be found at www.statewatch.org/news/2005/sep/terror-bill.pdf.

44. Nigel Morris and Robert Verkaik, "Terror Laws: Backlash will Scupper Anti-Terrorism Bill in the Lords, Say Critics," *The* [London] *Independent*, Sept. 17, 2005.

45. *Ibid.*

46. Elisabeth O'Leary, "Spanish court jails al Qaeda leader for 27 years," Reuters, Sept. 26, 2005.

47. Richard Bernstein, "German Court Convicts Man of Qaeda Ties," *The New York Times*, Aug. 20, 2005, p. A6.

48. Gregory Crouch, "Life term for killer of filmmaker," *International Herald Tribune*, July 27, 2005, p. 1.

49. Robert S. Leiken, "Europe's Mujahideen: Where Mass Immigration Meets Global Terrorism," Center for Immigration Studies Backgrounder, April 2005, p. 11; www.cis.org/articles/2005/back405.html.

50. General Accounting Office, "Border Security: Implications of Eliminating the Visa Waiver Program," November 2002, p. 21.

51. Stephen Yale-Loehr, *et al.*, "Secure Borders, Open Doors: Visa Procedures in the Post-September 11 Era," Migration Policy Institute, August 2005, pp. 159-163.

52. Michael Cutler, "U.S. Visa Waiver Program Should End," Counterterrorism Blog, July 10, 2005; http://counterterror.typepad.com/the_counterterrorism_blog/2005/07/michael_cutler__1.html.

53. Yale-Loehr, *op. cit.*, p. 78.

54. Robert S. Leiken, "Europe's Angry Muslims," *Foreign Affairs*, July-August 2005, p. 120.

55. "Terrorist Financing: Report of an Independent Task Force Sponsored by the Council on Foreign Relations," 2002, p. 8.

56. Neil MacFarquhar, "Saudis Support a Jihad in Iraq, Not Back Home," *The New York Times*, April 23, 2004, p. A1.

57. "The United States and Saudi Arabia: A Relationship Threatened by Misconceptions," Prince Saud al-Faisal, April 27, 2004; transcript at www.cfr.org/publication/6982/united_states_and_saudi_arabia.html.

58. Stephen Schwartz, *The Two Faces of Islam: the House of Sa'ud from Tradition to Terror* (2002).

59. Stephen Schwartz, "The King Who Would be Reformer," *The Weekly Standard*, Aug. 29, 2005.

60. Ali Al-Ahmed, "Time to Test King Abdullah," Sept. 6, 2005, Institute for Gulf Affairs; www.gulfinstitute.org/index.shtml.

61. Mai Yamani, "Old family divisions hit Saudi prospects for a new democratic era," *The Australian*, Aug. 8, 2005, p. 11.

62. "Support for Terror Wanes Among Muslim Publics," Pew Research Center, July 14, 2005, p. 1; http://pewglobal.org/reports/display.php?ReportID=248.

63. "Recruitment for the jihad in the Netherlands: from incident to trend," Dec. 9, 2002, www.aivd.nl/contents/pages/2285/recruitmentbw.pdf.

64. Greg Krikorian and Solomon Moore, "4 Men Indicted in Alleged Plot to Spread Terror in Southland," *Los Angeles Times*, Sept. 1, 2005, p. A1.

65. Laqueur, *op. cit.*

BIBLIOGRAPHY

Books

Coll, Steve, *Ghost Wars: The Secret History of the CIA, Afghanistan, and Bin Laden, From the Soviet Invasion to September 10, 2001, Penguin Press,* **2004.**
Coll offers a meticulous account of the American transition from jihad partner in Afghanistan to enemy of the jihadist movement.

Farah, Douglas, *Blood From Stones: The Secret Financial Network of Terror, Broadway Books,* **2004.**
A former *Washington Post* reporter investigates an al Qaeda financing network in West Africa's diamond and gold trade.

Fouda, Yosri, and Nick Fielding, *Masterminds of Terror: The Truth Behind the Most Devastating Attack the World Has Ever Seen, Mainstream Publishing,* **2003.**
A top investigative reporter for Al-Jazeera gleaned a detailed account of the 9/11 plot from two al Qaeda masterminds before they were arrested.

Gerges, Fawaz A., *The Far Enemy: Why Jihad Went Global, Cambridge University Press,* **2005.**
Gerges chronicles and analyzes a debate held outside the view of most non-speakers of Arabic — jihadists' disagreement over whether to keep waging war at home or to target the West.

Kepel, Gilles, *Jihad: The Trail of Political Islam, Belknap Press of Harvard University Press,* **2002.**
A French scholar who specializes in Muslim societies details how some followers of "political Islam" turned to violence.

Sageman, Marc, *Understanding Terror Networks, University of Pennsylvania Press,* **2004.**
The author's credentials are well suited for analyzing how jihadist cells connect to a larger movement. Sageman, now a psychiatrist, was assigned as a CIA officer to the U.S. support mission to the anti-Soviet Afghanistan jihad.

Scheuer, Michael, *Imperial Hubris: Why the West is Losing the War on Terrorism, Potomac Books,* **2004.**
Also a CIA veteran of the Afghanistan jihad, Scheuer founded the agency's anti-bin Laden unit. He rips into the official American response to the modern jihadist.

Schwartz, Stephen, *The Two Faces of Islam: Saudi Fundamentalism and its Role in Terrorism, Anchor Books,* **2003.**
Schwartz wrote the first English-language book to make a full-scale case for a connection between the Saudi school of religion and jihadism.

Articles

Bergen, Peter, "Reading Al Qaeda: The jihadists export their rage to book pages and Web pages," *The Washington Post Book World,* **Sept. 11, 2005, p. T4.**
One of the tiny handful of pre-9/11 Al Qaeda-watchers offers a guide to primary sources on jihadism available in English.

Caryl, Christian, "Why They Do It," *The New York Review of Books,* **Sept. 22, 2005, p. 28.**
A review-essay by a journalist with Iraq experience analyzes a half-dozen recent books on suicide terrorism.

Hayes, Stephen, and Thomas Joscelyn, "The Mother of All Connections; A special report on the new evidence of collaboration between Saddam Hussein's Iraq and Al Qaeda," *The Weekly Standard,* **July 18, 2005.**
Writers for the neoconservative publication lay out a case that Saddam Hussein and Al Qaeda were linked.

Mayer, Jane, "The Search for Osama: Did the government let bin Laden's trail go cold?" *The New Yorker,* **Aug. 4, 2003, p. 26.**
A Washington-based journalist investigates whether the U.S. government dropped the ball in pursuing bin Laden.

Reports and Studies

"Defeating the Jihadists: A Blueprint for Action," *The Century Foundation,* **Nov. 16, 2004.**
A commission headed by former national counterterrorism czar Richard A. Clarke concludes that beefing up intelligence and law enforcement capabilities and other measures is more effective than conventional warfare in fighting jihadists. Includes compendium of post-9/11 terrorist incidents worldwide.

Blanchard, Christopher M., "Al Qaeda: Statements and Evolving Ideology," *Congressional Research Service,* **Feb. 4, 2005, www.fas.org/irp/crs/RL32759 .pdf.**

A writer for Congress's nonpartisan research arm examines the course of al Qaeda doctrine as reflected in public statements.

Hamzawy, Amr, "The Key to Arab Reform: Moderate Islamists," *Carnegie Endowment for International Peace, Policy Brief,* **August, 2005, http://carnegieendowment.org/files/pb40.hamzawy.FINAL.pdf.**

Islamists who reject jihadist doctrine offer the best hope for democracy in the Arab world, writes an Egyptian political scientist.

Wiktorowicz, Quintan, "The New Global Threat: Transnational Salafis and Jihad," Oct. 5, 2001, http://groups.colgate.edu/aarislam/wiktorow.htm. A longtime scholar of jihadist thought traces its historical and religious roots.

For More Information

Counterterrorism Blog; http://counterterrorismblog.org/. A Web log featuring frequent posts by regular contributors, mostly former law enforcement officials and congressional staffers; also links to news stories and research reports.

Heritage Foundation, 214 Massachusetts Ave., N.E., Washington, DC 20002; (202) 546-4400; www.heritage.org. A leading conservative think tank that has published studies on various aspects of international terrorism and anti-terrorism measures.

Institute for Counter-Terrorism, The Interdisciplinary Center, P.O. Box 167, Herzlia, 46150, Israel; www.ict.org.il. A think tank that offers detailed profiles of terrorist organizations and brief reports on a variety of terrorist-related issues.

International Crisis Group, 1629 K Street, N.W., Suite 450, Washington, DC 20006; (202) 785-1601; www.crisisgroup.org. A Brussels-based conflict resolution organization that monitors such issues as international terrorism and Islamism, with a series of on-the-ground reports on both topics.

Middle East Media Research Institute, P.O. Box 27837, Washington, DC 20038; (202) 955-9070; www.memri.org.

An organization that provides translations from Arabic, Farsi and Hebrew publications and runs the Jihad and Terrorism Studies Project, with translations of al Qaeda communiqués and similar material.

RAND Corporation, Terrorism and Homeland Security Research Area, 1200 South Hayes St., Arlington, VA 22202-5050; (703) 413-1100; www.rand.org. A long-established think tank that runs an active terrorism study project (not limited to jihadist-related topics), with numerous publications available online.

Royal Institute of International Affairs, Chatham House, 10 St. James Square, London SW1Y 4LE; +44-207 957 5700; www.riia.org. Offers a limited but worthwhile series of publications on terrorism-related topics.

Terrorism Knowledge Base, P.O. Box 889, Oklahoma City, OK 73101; (405) 232-5121; www.mipt.org. Organized by the National Memorial Institute for the Prevention of Terrorism — created by survivors of the Oklahoma City bombing of 1995 — the database is a compendium of terrorist attacks (not limited to jihadist attacks) dating back to 1968.

Human Rights Issues

*Are They a Low Priority Under
President Obama?*

Kenneth Jost

The Dalai Lama says he is not upset about not meeting with President Obama during his visit to Washington in early October. Obama postponed meeting with the Tibetan leader to avoid offending the Chinese government over its treatment of Tibetan dissidents; the meeting will occur after Obama visits China in November. Human rights advocates see the postponement as a sign of weakness in the administration's support for human rights and democratization.

Getty Images/Ralph Orlowski

From *CQ Researcher*,
October 30, 2009.

As a young boy, Tenzin Gyatso, the 14th Dalai Lama, received a gift in his Tibetan homeland from President Franklin D. Roosevelt: a gold watch showing the phases of the moon and the days of the week.

Nearly seven decades later, the leader of the Tibetan government in exile as well as the spiritual leader of Tibetan Buddhists had the watch with him in 2007 as another U.S. president, George W. Bush, bestowed on him the Congressional Medal of Freedom.

When he visited Washington in early October, however, the 74-year-old Buddhist monk was less warmly received by the current president, Barack Obama. To avoid offending the Chinese government over its political and cultural struggles with Tibetan dissidents, Obama decided to postpone a personal meeting with the Dalai Lama until after the president's visit to China in November.

Administration officials insisted that deferring what has been since 1991 a regular drop-in at the White House was no slight. They noted that the postponement had been agreed to in meetings between the Dalai Lama's advisers and one of Obama's closest aides, Valerie Jarrett, in advance of the monk's weeklong visit to Washington in early October.

The Dalai Lama himself brushed off any hint of hurt feelings from the postponement. In an Oct. 7 interview, he told CNN's Wolf Blitzer that he considered Obama "sympathetic" to the Tibetan cause and expected the president to raise the issue with Chinese leaders during his mid-November visit. "More serious discussion is better than just a picture, so I have no disappointment," he said.[1]

Global Freedom Declines for Third Year

Global freedom suffered its third consecutive year of decline in 2008, according to the annual survey by Freedom House. Overall, the human rights monitoring and advocacy organization rated 89 countries with a total population of 3.1 billion as free, 62 countries with 1.4 billion people as partly free and 42 countries with 2.3 billion people as not free.

Notable developments during the year, according to the report, included declines in Russia and in the non-Baltic countries of the former Soviet Union; stagnation in the Middle East and North Africa and substantial reversals for democracy in sub-Saharan Africa. The group also voiced disappointment with China's failure to improve its human rights situation during the year it hosted the Summer Olympic Games.

Among countries of particular importance to the United States, Iraq was credited with registering a small gain because of ebbing violence and reduced political terror, while Afghanistan was moved from partly free to not free because of "rising insecurity and increasing corruption and inefficiency in government institutions."

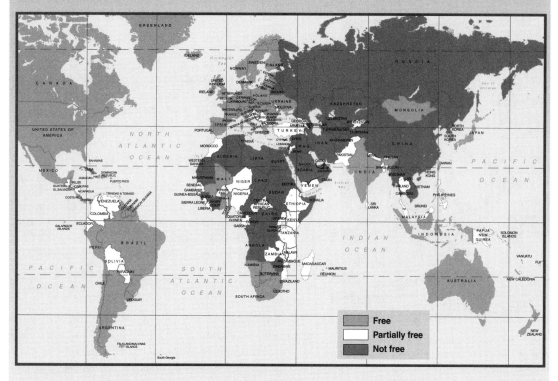

Source: "Freedom in the World 2009," Freedom House, www.freedomhouse.org/template.cfm?page=363&year=2009

Human rights advocates, however, see the postponement as a mistake in itself and a troubling sign of weakness in the Obama administration's approach in promoting human rights and democratization in other countries. "It plays into the narrative that the administration will defer to power rather than principle," says Tom Malinowski, Washington director for Human Rights Watch.

"That obviously sends a message," says Elisa Massimino, chief executive officer of Human Rights First. "Decisions like that can be very powerfully damaging to the solidarity with the people who we claim to be standing with."

Obama cheered human rights advocates with the steps he took in his first days in office to scrap some of the controversial detention and interrogation policies that his predecessor, Bush, had adopted to deal with suspected terrorists following al Qaeda's Sept. 11, 2001, attacks on the United States. "You can't overstate the importance of that in terms of sending a signal to our own people and to the rest of the world that the United States is going to return to taking those commitments to fundamental human rights seriously," says Massimino.

In the months since then, however, human rights advocates on the political left and political right have been finding more to fault than to praise in Obama's dealings with countries viewed as human rights violators.

"They haven't yet come up with a consistent approach to human rights as to what they're trying to get in human rights as opposed to what they're trying to get country by country," says Jennifer Windsor, executive director of Freedom House, an older group generally seen as more conservative than such newer organizations as Human Rights First and Human Rights Watch. "I sort of wonder why it's taking them so long," Windsor says. "They keep on apologizing."

"So far, his administration has been characterized by a marked turning away from interest in human rights and democracy that has been a feature of United States foreign policy since the presidency of Jimmy Carter," says Joshua Muravchik, a fellow at the Foreign Policy Institute at Johns Hopkins University's School of Advanced and International Studies in Washington and a leading neoconservative expert on human rights.

Grumbling about the president's human rights record was already widespread before Obama became the unanticipated recipient on Oct. 9 of this year's Nobel Peace Prize. In selecting Obama, the Norwegian Nobel Committee said he had created "a new atmosphere of international politics," adding, "Democracy and human rights are to be strengthened."[2]

A few hours later, Obama said he was "surprised" and "humbled" by the award. "I do not feel that I deserve to be in the company of so many transformative figures that have been honored by this prize," he said. But Obama said he would accept the award as "a call to action to confront the common challenges of the 21st century."

The reaction to the award in the United States and around the world was decidedly mixed. "Too early," said Lech Walesa, the Polish labor leader and later prime minister who was the 1983 Nobel laureate. But other previous winners applauded the selection. In a congratulatory letter, the Dalai Lama, the 1989 laureate, told Obama that the Nobel committee "has rightly noted your efforts towards a world without nuclear weapons and your constructive role in environmental protection."

Within the United States, Democrats and some Republicans voiced approval of the selection, but many GOP politicians were unenthusiastic to negative. Much of the reaction among mainstream media commentators and bloggers was skeptical, even from some liberals. (*See "At Issue," p. 282.*)

The divisions over the peace prize mirror experts' evaluations of Obama's contributions on human rights issues after nine months in office. "The jury is still out, but I think the Obama administration is headed in the right direction," says David Kaye, head of the International Human Rights Clinic at UCLA Law School and a former State Department official under Presidents Bill Clinton and George W. Bush.

But Michael Mandelbaum, director of the foreign policy program at Johns Hopkins, says the administration has downplayed human rights. "They very conspicuously backed away from the strong advocacy of rights, from putting that at the center of their policies and putting that at the center of their rhetoric," he says.

The United States took the lead after World War II in the adoption of international human rights agreements, but human rights took a back seat to global power politics during the tensest years of the Cold War. In the late 1970s, however, President Jimmy Carter made human rights an explicit centerpiece of U.S. foreign policy. Every president since then has continued the stated commitment to human rights, though in markedly different ways.[3]

President George W. Bush continued to voice support for human rights and used his second inaugural address in 2005 to put promoting democracy at the center of his foreign policy goals. The results of Bush's policies — in Iraq, the Mideast and the rest of the world — are disputed. Whatever Bush's final legacy may be, many experts and advocates say Obama is shaping his approach to the issues in conscious distinction with Bush's more aggressive

Obama: Democracy Is a Human Right

President Obama has stressed the importance of democracy and human rights in four recent speeches to international audiences, beginning with a widely hailed address at Cairo University in June. Human rights groups say they are encouraged by Obama's remarks but are looking for more concrete actions from the administration to support democratization and civil society movements.

"America does not presume to know what is best for everyone, just as we would not presume to pick the outcome of a peaceful election. But I do have an unyielding belief that all people yearn for certain things: the ability to speak your mind and have a say in how you are governed; confidence in the rule of law and the equal administration of justice; government that is transparent and doesn't steal from the people; the freedom to live as you choose. These are not just American ideas; they are human rights. And that is why we will support them everywhere."

— remarks at Cairo University, Cairo, Egypt, June 4, 2009

"The arc of history shows us that governments which serve their own people survive and thrive; governments which serve only their own power do not. Governments that represent the will of their people are far less likely to descend into failed states, to terrorize their citizens, or to wage war on others. Governments that promote the rule of law, subject their actions to oversight, and allow for independent institutions are more dependable trading partners. And in our own history, democracies have been America's most enduring allies, including those we once waged war with in Europe and Asia — nations that today live with great security and prosperity."

— remarks at the New Economic School graduation, Moscow, July 7, 2009

"America will not seek to impose any system of government on any other nation — the essential truth of democracy is that each nation determines its own destiny. What we will do is increase assistance for responsible individuals and institutions, with a focus on supporting good governance — on parliaments, which check abuses of power and ensure that opposition voices are heard; on the rule of law, which ensures the equal administration of justice; on civic participation, so that young people get involved; and on concrete solutions to corruption like forensic accounting, automating services, strengthening hotlines, and protecting whistle-blowers to advance transparency and accountability."

— remarks to the Ghanaian Parliament, Accra, July 11, 2009

"Democracy cannot be imposed on any nation from the outside. Each society must search for its own path, and no path is perfect. Each country will pursue a path rooted in the culture of its people and in its past traditions. And I admit that in the past America has too often been selective in its promotion of democracy. But that does not weaken our commitment, it only reinforces it. There are basic principles that are universal; there are certain truths which are self-evident — and the United States of America will never waver in our efforts to stand up for the right of people everywhere to determine their own destiny."

— remarks to United Nations General Assembly, New York, Sept. 23, 2009

Source: The White House, www.whitehouse.gov/the_ press_office

Admirers note that Obama has given four major foreign policy speeches reaffirming U.S. support for human rights, most recently at the United Nations General Assembly. (*See box at left.*) They also point out that Obama appointed two longtime human rights advocates to pivotal posts at the State Department. Harold Hongju Koh, a former Yale Law School dean, is serving as the department's legal adviser; Michael Posner, the longtime head of Human Rights First, was confirmed in late September as assistant secretary of state for human rights, democracy and labor. "These two guys are really, really committed to a value-driven, human rights-oriented U.S. foreign policy," UCLA's Kaye says.

The admirers acknowledge, however, and critics emphasize that Obama has also sought to "engage" with several countries with deplorable human rights records, including Egypt, Syria, Iran and Myanmar (formerly Burma). Muravchik accuses Obama of "a rush to have new and friendly relations with a whole series of the most cruel and dictatorial regimes."

The debate over Obama's policies takes place against what Freedom House describes in its most recent annual report as the third consecutive year of decline in global freedom. The report credits Bush — and his two predecessors, Clinton and his father George H. W. Bush — with helping promote positive developments for democracy since the end of the Cold War. But it also points to "a turnaround in democracy's fortunes" in Bush's second term and points to "the

approach. "They are almost afraid to speak out against human rights abuses in any country because it's going to be like Bush," says Freedom House's Windsor.

lack of . . . durable gains" in the Middle East and North Africa as "a major disappointment for American policy."[4] (*See map, p. 266.*)

Apart from the changes in the post-9/11 interrogation and detention policies, Obama's most concrete action to date is the decision to join the United Nations Human Rights Council, a U.N. forum reconstituted in 2006 that the Bush administration pointedly boycotted. As with Obama's moves on anti-terrorism policies, reactions to the decision divide along ideological lines: Liberals support the move; conservatives do not. (*See sidebar, p. 916.*)

Obama's trip to China will be closely watched for new clues on how human rights fits in with other U.S. interests — economic, diplomatic, strategic — in dealing with countries with less than exemplary human rights records.

As the president prepares for the trip, here are some of the major questions that human rights watchers are debating:

Is the Obama administration deemphasizing human rights in U.S. foreign policy?

In a visit to China and other Asian countries in February, Secretary of State Hillary Rodham Clinton raised eyebrows among human rights advocates by appearing to put rights issues below other U.S. concerns. In comments to the traveling press corps, Clinton said the United States would continue pressing China on Tibet, Taiwan and free-speech issues, but added, "Our pressing on those issues can't interfere with the global economic crisis, the global climate change crisis and the security crisis."

Human rights groups complained in advance about signals that human rights issues were to be downgraded on the trip. "Extremely disappointed," said Amnesty International USA. Today, many human rights advocates continue to question Clinton's statement. "We're not going to talk about human rights until we solve global warming and the economic crisis?" asks Muravchik, the Johns Hopkins fellow. "That gives them a pretty large margin of impunity."[5]

Beyond U.S.-China relations, the administration appears to be basing its human rights policies on a view that private diplomacy is more effective than public rhetoric in encouraging authoritarian governments to turn away from repressive policies. Human rights advocates on the left and right disagree.

"They're saying they want to achieve real gains and to engage in order to get something accomplished," says

Secretary of State Hillary Rodham Clinton visits with South African soldiers assigned to U.N. peacekeeping duties in the Democratic Republic of the Congo during her weeklong visit to war-torn Africa in August. Earlier in the year she was criticized for saying human rights should not "interfere" with U.S.-China relations.

Freedom House's Windsor. "In the past, we have not seen quiet diplomacy work."

"It's not enough to say we're going to talk with people," says Massimino of Human Rights First. "It's not an end in itself."

A former Bush administration official goes further. "It seems clear to me that the Obama administration has no human rights policy," Elliott Abrams, deputy national security director for democracy in Bush's second term and now a senior fellow with the Council on Foreign Relations, tells the conservative *FrontPageMagazine.com*. "That is, while in some inchoate sense they would like respect for human rights to grow around the world, as all Americans would, they have no actual policy to achieve that goal — and they subordinate it to all their other policy goals."[6]

Other human rights advocates, however, say the criticism is overblown. "The administration understandably wanted to distinguish itself from what it saw as the [Bush administration's] overly messianic and at times aggressive and hectoring approach toward these issues," says Human Rights Watch's Malinowski. "The narrative of Bush cared and Obama doesn't," he adds, "is extraordinarily simplistic and misguided."

Thomas Carothers, vice president for studies at the Carnegie Endowment for International Peace in Washington, also says the criticism of Obama's policies is exaggerated.

Report on Abuses in Gaza Sparks Concern

Critics see anti-Israel tilt by U.N. Human Rights Council.

Israel launched a three-week air and ground assault on Gaza in December 2008 aimed at stopping Palestinian militants from firing missiles at civilian targets across the border. During and after the invasion, the ruling Hamas government in Gaza charged that Israeli forces had committed war crimes by wantonly attacking Palestinian civilians.[1]

Now, a respected South African jurist has found both sides responsible for endangering civilians during the conflict. In a report commissioned by the United Nations Human Rights Council, Judge Richard Goldstone recommends that Israel and Gaza conduct their own investigations of human rights abuses by their side during the fighting. If no investigations are forthcoming within six months, Goldstone wants the U.N. Security Council to turn the dispute over to the International Criminal Court.[2]

Goldstone's report has drawn critical reactions from both sides. Israel has condemned Goldstone, who is Jewish, for furthering what they perceive to be the council's constant berating of the Jewish state.[3] Many Israelis complain that complying with the investigation would be fruitless because the council is already biased against them.

While Hamas has lauded Goldstone for denouncing Israeli military tactics and agreed to investigate some portions of the report, the rival Palestinian Authority originally decided to defer action, citing an inadequate number of people needed to support an investigation. However, after facing criticism for their decision, the authority requested that the U.N. conduct a special session on the conflict.

Several prominent human rights organizations, specifically Amnesty International and Human Rights Watch, have defended the report for calling attention to rights abuses. The U.N.'s top human rights official, Navi Pillay, has offered her endorsement, as well.

The report has focused worldwide attention on the Human Rights Council, a 47-nation body created in 2006 to replace a larger U.N. human rights forum widely denounced as ineffective. Critics said the earlier U.N. Commission on Human Rights was unsuccessful at prosecuting nations that violated human rights and showed poor judgment in allowing countries with questionable human rights records, including China and Russia, to be members. Under President George W. Bush, the United States criticized the commission and refused to join the council.

President Obama changed the policy, however, and the United States joined the council in May 2009. Critics say the council is still fundamentally flawed and inordinately critical of Israel. But human rights groups are applauding the shift. They say that U.S. involvement and an altered structure will help bring human rights abusers to justice.

The council has enacted a new, periodic review of all 192 U.N. member states in order to monitor human rights conditions in every state. Council members are chosen by the U.N. General Assembly instead of by the Economic and Social Council, which was previously in charge of elections. Additionally, a complaints procedure allows individuals and organizations to bring potential violations to the attention of the council.[4]

Proponents of the council say the changes signal a vast improvement over the commission, but many claim that a disproportionate amount of time continues to be spent on Israel's alleged human rights violations while others, such as Sudan, face little investigation. The council has appointed an independent expert to monitor Sudan and asked the country to remedy human rights violations but has taken no disciplinary action against the government.[5]

"The idea that we've suddenly gone soft on Russia, on China and so forth tends to be a bit of an overstatement," he says.

Still, Malinowski says human right advocates have cause for concern. Obama's apparent approach, he says, "can easily be interpreted and to some extent is being interpreted by the permanent foreign policy bureaucracy at the State Department as an argument for engaging

[repressive] governments without pressure, without sanctions, without a significant emphasis on what [bureaucrats] dismiss as moral issues."

Muravchik, the Johns Hopkins fellow, says the administration's approach reflects a wrongheaded effort to differentiate Obama's policies from Bush's. "There was an obvious opening in keeping with his desire to be critical

During its three-year existence, the council has passed a resolution on freedom of expression that prohibits limiting expression in order to protect religion. It has examined the continuing conflict in Gaza and passed resolutions aimed at remedying rights violations in Myanmar (formerly Burma) and the Democratic Republic of the Congo (DRC), particularly those involving women and children.

Many cite the ability of the United States to broker the freedom of expression resolution with Egypt as a sign that the council is enacting positive change. However, critics still claim that the council shows favoritism towards some countries, with bloc voting by region significantly furthering that bias. Specifically, the Arab countries and many of the African countries vote together on resolutions, making it difficult to pass those that allow the examination of rights violations in places like the DRC.

The Goldstone report has again brought these criticisms to the surface. In the special session requested by the Palestinian Authority, the council endorsed the report, a move that allows the investigation to be taken before the U.N. Security Council. This is the seventh of 12 sessions in the past year involving Israel — another indication many say, of the rights council's bias against Israel. The United States voted against the report and has veto power over the Security Council's agenda, making it unlikely the investigation will travel that far. China and Russia voted for the report but have since indicated their opposition to involving the Security Council.[6]

Last month, speaking in Geneva, U.S. Assistant Secretary for Democracy, Human Rights and Labor Michael Posner and State Department legal adviser Harold Hongju Koh expressed hope that U.S. involvement in the council would help to create a non-political U.N. body able to support victims and prosecute rights violators.[7] But the United States and Israel have expressed concern that the Goldstone report and proceedings within the rights council demonstrate a political bias against Israel and do not focus enough on human rights violations by the Palestinians.

In a 24-page assessment, Freedom House gives the council mixed ratings, with a passing grade only on the use of so-called special rapporteurs and failing grades on adoption of resolutions on urgent human rights crises. The organization specifically criticizes the council for a "disproportionate" number of resolutions critical of Israel. More broadly, the report concludes that democratic countries on the council have failed to counter the "considerable resources" devoted by a "small but active group" of non-democratic countries to limiting the council's effectiveness in protecting human rights.[8]

— *Emily DeRuy*

[1] For background, see Irwin Arieff, "Middle East Peace Prospects," *CQ Global Researcher*, May 2009, pp. 119-148.

[2] See "Human Rights in Palestine and Other Occupied Arab Territories: Report of the United Nations Fact-Finding Mission on the Gaza Conflict," Sept. 25, 2009, www2.ohchr.org/english/bodies/hrcouncil/docs/12session/A-HRC-12-48.pdf. See Christiane Amanpour, "A Look at the Allegations of Israeli and Hamas War Crimes," CNN International, Sept. 30, 2009, for interviews with Judge Goldstone and former U.S. Secretary of State Madeleine Albright.

[3] See Amir Mizroch, "Grappling with Goldstone," *The Jerusalem Post*, Sept. 18, 2009, p. 9.

[4] See "The Human Rights Council," The U.N. Human Rights Council, www2.ohchr.org/english/bodies/hrcouncil/ for full description of council structure.

[5] "Human Rights Council Establishes Mandate of Independent Expert on Sudan for One Year," U.N. Human Rights Council, June 18, 2009, www.unhchr.ch/huricane/huricane.nsf/view01/91B0E40B4256A0C3C12575D900712245?opendocument. For background, see Karen Foerstel, "Crisis in Darfur," *CQ Global Researcher*, September 2008, pp. 248-270.

[6] See Neil MacFarquhar, "U.N. Council Endorses Gaza Report," *The New York Times*, Oct. 16, 2009, www.nytimes.com/2009/10/17/world/middleeast/17nations.html?_r=1&scp=1&sq=Goldstone%20report%20&st=cse.

[7] "Geneva Press Briefing by Harold Hongju Koh and Michael Posner," United States Mission, Sept. 28, 2009, http://geneva.usmission.gov/2009/09/28/koh-posner/.

[8] See "The U.N. Human Rights Council Report Card: 2007-2009," Freedom House, Sept. 27, 2009, www.freedomhouse.org/uploads/special_report/84.pdf.

of Bush's legacy to say that in this area Bush pronounced good ideas but didn't deliver," Muravchik says. "Instead, he's said that Bush was on the wrong track in essence by telling other governments how to behave."

Obama's engagement strategy, Muravchik concludes, "necessarily involves a downgrading if not betrayal of human rights." Other human rights watchers, however, are prepared to suspend judgment to see what results are achieved by the approach reflected, for example, in Clinton's comments on China.

"A charitable reading of that is that we need to find new tactics; we're not going to engage in a Kabuki dance; that's not getting results," says Massimino of Human Rights First.

"There's a lot to be said for the idea that in pushing a human rights agenda, sometimes and in some places and with some countries it's better to push it quietly," says UCLA professor Kaye. "Over time, it may be that the Obama administration will either see that working or will see it not working. In those situations where they see it not working, they may move the disagreements from the private channels to the more public ones.

"It's too early to conclude that they are sacrificing the human rights agenda for some Kissingerian realpolitik," he concludes, referring to Henry Kissinger, who served as secretary of state under Presidents Richard M. Nixon and Gerald R. Ford. "I don't think that's what's happening."

Is the Obama administration reducing U.S. support for democratization in other countries?

President Obama used one of his first major foreign policy speeches abroad to reaffirm to his Egyptian audience and the broader Muslim world the United States' support for promoting democracy. Democratic principles such as freedom, equality and rule of law "are not just American ideas," Obama said in the June 4 address in Cairo. "They are human rights. And that is why we will support them everywhere."

Obama made no reference in the speech, however, to the repressive policies of his host, Egyptian President Hosni Mubarak. In advance, he even rejected a reporter's suggestion to describe Mubarak as "authoritarian." And when Obama hosted the Egyptian leader at the White House on Aug. 18, the subject of democracy was unmentioned in public comments.[7]

The on-again, off-again invocation of the democracy message leaves human rights advocates less than satisfied. "President Obama could have been more explicit," says Malinowski, the Human Rights Watch director in Washington. "It's important that the president's private messages to leaders like Mubarak be emphasized with public messages. I agree that was a missed opportunity."

Former Bush administration official Abrams bluntly criticized Obama for selecting Cairo as the site of the earlier address and then omitting any mention of human rights in the joint press availability with Mubarak at the White House. "Democracy activists in Egypt have been abandoned," he said in the *FrontPageMagazine.com* interview.

Muravchik, the Johns Hopkins fellow, is similarly critical of Obama's delayed response to evidence of irregularities in the Iranian presidential election in June. "Obama was so devoted to this course of making friends with the dictators that he refused for the first week to say or do anything to encourage the Iranian people," Muravchik says. "After a week went by, it was clear that his stand was untenable in terms of the views of the Iranian people, the American people and the stands of some other Western leaders. So he spoke out, which was all to the good but quite belated."

To democratization expert Carothers, Obama's speech represents a recasting of the Bush administration's approach to promoting democracy. "He set out an alternative rhetorical framework that emphasizes that we will not impose democracy on others, that we recognize that different kinds of democracy exist and that we will be sure not to equate elections with democracy," Carothers says.

Carothers says Obama's approach will be "more appealing to people in many parts of the world." But he adds, "It is clear that this administration is not going to make democracy promotion a major emphasis of its policy."

In Egypt, the administration seems to be trying to heal the rift in U.S.-Egyptian relations, which were seen to have suffered in the Bush years because of his administration's criticisms of Egypt's record on human rights. The Bush policies were widely credited, however, with encouraging some liberalization by the Mubarak government.

Today, human rights advocates say repressive policies are returning in Egypt just as U.S. support for democratization efforts is lagging. "Despite the president's speech, there's been little indication that the Egyptian government's human rights record is at all a concern to this administration or that they're willing to put any material support or diplomatic heft in order to get a reversal of the deteriorating situation in Egypt," says Freedom House's Windsor.

U.S. aid to democratization programs in Egypt, including funding for civil society groups, fell from $55 million in fiscal 2008 to $20 million in the current fiscal year. The Obama administration is proposing a modest increase to $25 million for the current year.

Overall, the administration is requesting $2.81 billion for democratization programs for fiscal 2010, an

CHRONOLOGY

1945-1990s *U.S. takes lead in establishing United Nations, writing international human rights law; U.S. support for democracy tempered by Cold War rivalry with communist bloc.*

1945 United Nations established.

1948 Universal Declaration of Human Rights adopted by the U.N.

1950s U.S. supports coups to oust leftist regimes in Guatemala, Iran; blocks unified election in Vietnam; sends no aid to anti-communist revolt in Hungary.

1960s U.S. role in Vietnam War escalates; U.S. takes no action as Soviet Union crushes reform movement in Czechoslovakia.

1975 Vietnam War ends with fall of Saigon government, reunification under communist regime. . . . Helsinki Accords signed; Soviet bloc agrees to respect human rights.

1977-1981 President Jimmy Carter puts human rights at center of U.S. foreign policy.

1980s U.S. support for right-wing regimes in Central America, contras in Nicaragua widely criticized in U.S., elsewhere; U.S. aid helps oust authoritarian leaders in Philippines, Haiti.

1989 Berlin Wall falls; Eastern European countries throw off communist governments; Cold War ends.

1990s Human rights machinery institutionalized at United Nations: U.N. high commissioner for human rights created; war crimes tribunals established in former Yugoslavia, Rwanda.

2001-Present *Bush administration war on terror policies criticized, democracy promotion legacy questioned; Obama administration criticized for downplaying human rights.*

2001 President George W. Bush launches invasion of Afghanistan for harboring al Qaeda after Sept. 11, 2001, attacks on U.S.; prepares aggressive policies to detain, interrogate "enemy combatants."

2002 U.S. opens prison camp for suspected terrorists at Guantánamo Bay Naval Base in Cuba; move widely criticized in Muslim world and by some European allies. . . .

International Criminal Court established; U.S. declines to participate.

2003 U.S.-led invasion of Iraq topples Saddam Hussein; with U.S. support, parliamentary elections, referendum on new constitution held in 2005.

2004 U.S. labels killings of civilians in Sudan's Darfur province "genocide." . . . With U.S. backing, Hamid Karzai elected president of Afghanistan; parliamentary elections follow in 2005.

2005 Bush, in second inaugural address, promises U.S. support for democracy "in every nation and culture."

2006 U.S. declines to participate in newly created United Nations Human Rights Council.

2008 Bush prepares to leave office with democracy, human rights legacy sharply debated.

January-March 2009 Barack Obama inaugurated; repudiates Bush policies on detention and interrogation; promises to close Guantánamo within year (January). . . . Secretary of State Hillary Rodham Clinton draws fire for saying human rights should not "interfere" with U.S.-China relations (February). . . . U.S. signs U.N. petition favoring decriminalization of homosexual conduct (March). . . .

April-June 2009 U.S. wins election to U.N. Human Rights Council; administration signals support for U.N. convention to eliminate discrimination against women (May). . . . Obama says U.S. will support human rights "everywhere"; U.N. Ambassador Susan Rice indicates administration support for U.N. pact on children's rights (June).

July-September 2009 Clinton visits war-torn Congo during Africa visit (August). . . . Obama tells U.N. General Assembly U.S. has "too often been selective" in promoting democracy (September).

October 2009 Human Rights Council adopts freedom of expression resolution; endorses report opposed by U.S. that accuses Israel of targeting civilians in Gaza; U.S. critics say stance shows need to pull out of council. . . . Clinton, others unveil new policy on Sudan/Darfur; "carrots and sticks" approach criticized by some.

Clinton Vows Opposition to Violence Against Gays

'Killing campaign' in Iraq goes unpunished, rights group says.

The victim was taken from his parents' Baghdad home late one evening in April by four armed, masked men, who shouted insults as they dragged him away. His body was found in a garbage dump in the neighborhood the next day, his genitals cut off and a piece of his throat ripped out.

The victim's offense: He was gay. Three weeks later, when Human Rights Watch investigators spoke with the victim's 35-year-old partner, he struggled to speak. "In Iraq, murderers and thieves are respected more than gay people," he said.[1]

The incident was part of the group's report, published in August, which describes a "killing campaign" by "death squads" that swept through Iraq in the early months of 2009. The campaign was concentrated in Baghdad's Sadr City, the stronghold of supporters of the anti-American Shiite cleric Moktada al-Sadr, but killings also were reported in other cities.

The killings were done "with impunity," according to the report, based on three weeks of on-site interviews by Scott Long, director of Human Rights Watch's LGBT Rights Project, and a second investigator. Iraqi police and security forces did little to investigate or try to halt the killings, the report said. No arrests or prosecutions had been announced when the report was published.

Iraq is one of many countries where violence against lesbian, gay, bisexual or transgender persons occurs and goes unpunished or is even abetted by authorities. In many others, LGBT persons are subject to harassment, intimidation and even prosecution because of their sexual orientation or gender identity. In Senegal, nine people, including the head of an AIDS service organization, were arrested in December 2008 and given long prison sentences the next month, purportedly for engaging in homosexual conduct.[2]

Now, Secretary of State Hillary Rodham Clinton is promising that the United States will do more to track and oppose violence in other countries against LGBT persons. "Where it happens anywhere in the world, the United States must speak out against it and work for its end," Clinton said in a Sept. 11 speech to the Roosevelt Institute in New York City, where she was receiving the institute's Four Freedoms Medal.[3]

Despite widespread criticism of President Obama for allegedly downplaying human rights, LGBT rights advocates are giving the administration positive marks for increased attention to those issues after eight years of general neglect under President George W. Bush. "They've been very open to the dialogue," says Michael Guest, senior counselor at the Council for Global Equality, a coalition founded in 2008 to work for LGBT rights around the world.

Guest notes that the Obama administration decided in March to support a United Nations petition sponsored by France and the Netherlands calling for decriminalization of homosexual conduct. The Bush administration had taken no position on the resolution, now supported by 67 countries. Guest served as ambassador to Romania in the second Bush administration until his resignation in 2007 over the lack of spousal benefits and privileges for his partner.

In her speech, Clinton promised to give increased attention to violence against the LGBT community in the State Department's annual country-by-country reports on human rights. The most recent report, published in February and compiled during the Bush administration, includes what Guest calls

increase of $234 million, according to an analysis by Freedom House. "To their credit, they actually kept democracy and human rights levels up," says Windsor.[8]

Windsor says U.S. support for pro-democracy groups is important because of the resistance by authoritarian countries to outside aid. "Over the last three to four years, there's been a backlash by governments to make sure that no 'color revolution' occurs in their own country," she says, referring to the pro-democracy "Orange Revolution" in Ukraine and "Rose Revolution" in Georgia.

"We think neither the Bush administration nor the Obama administration has fully stood up for the right to cross-border help to fulfill human rights," Windsor continues.

the most detailed listing of LGBT rights violations to date. Among the incidents in 2008 noted were the murder of a transgender activist in Honduras, imprisonment in Egypt of men suspected of being HIV-positive and extensive discrimination in India against gays and lesbians in education and employment.[4]

The United States raised the issue of violence and rights violations against LGBT persons on Oct. 8 at a meeting of the Organization for Security and Co-operation in Europe, a regionwide human rights forum. Earlier, a U.S. representative had noted concern about the refusal in some countries to grant permits for pro-LGBT "pride" parades. Guest says increased U.S. attention to documenting LGBT issues is important because problems often go unreported. "LGBT communities in many countries are extremely marginalized, and social and cultural norms are such that nobody complains," he says.

Long also applauds the administration's statements on LGBT rights but says more concrete actions are needed. "What we're still looking for is action at the embassy level in countries where egregious things are going on," he says.

As one example, Long points to Uganda, where legislation was introduced in parliament in early October to tighten an existing prohibition on homosexual conduct by making any advocacy of or information about homosexuality a crime.[5] Long notes that Uganda received substantial funding under the Bush administration's AIDS initiative. "It will be a test of the Obama administration to see if it uses its leverage to oppose this bill, which would

LGBT activists in Tegucigalpa, Honduras, protest the murder of a transgender activist on May 15, 2009. Secretary of State Hillary Clinton has promised to give increased attention to violence against the LGBT community.

AFP/Getty Images/Orlando Sierra

be devastating to gays and lesbians," he says.

In its report on the Iraq killings, Human Rights Watch calls on the United States and U.S.-led multinational forces in Iraq to assist Iraqi authorities in investigating the killings and vetting and training Iraqi police on human rights issues with "no exceptions for sexual orientation and gender expression or identity." Long sees no action thus far on either of the recommendations. "It's not clear the embassy has done anything," he says.

— Kenneth Jost

[1] "They Want Us Exterminated," Human Rights Watch, August 2009, www.hrw.org/en/reports/2009/08/16/they-want-us-exterminated. The report does not identify the victim and uses a pseudonym for his partner.

[2] See Donald G. McNeil Jr., "Senegal: Where AIDS Efforts Are Often Praised, Prison for Counselors Is a Surprise," *The New York Times,* Jan. 20, 2009, p. D6.

[3] The full text is on the State Department's Web site: www.state.gov/secretary/rm/2009a/09/129164.htm. The one-paragraph reference drew coverage only in LGBT media. See Rex Wockner, "Clinton Says U.S. Will Fight Anti-Gay Violence Worldwide," *Windy City Times* (Chicago), Sept. 23, 2009.

[4] "2008 Country Reports on Human Rights Practices," U.S. State Department, Feb. 25, 2009, www.state.gov/g/drl/rls/hrrpt/2008/index.htm. See also "U.S. Government Documents Trend of Severe Human Rights Abuse Against LGBT People," Council for Global Equality, February 2009, www.globalequality.org/storage/cfge/documents/dos_human_rights_report_2008_analysis.pdf.

[5] See "Rights Groups Challenge Uganda's New Same-Sex Proposal," Voice of America English Service, Oct. 16, 2009.

In Egypt, a U.S. embassy official insisted in response to criticism from Egyptian activists that U.S. support continues. "We may have changed tactics, but our commitment to democracy and human rights promotion in Egypt is steadfast," an embassy official said in an e-mailed response to a reporter's questions.[9] But Carothers says human rights issues generally are getting only limited

attention as the administration deals with other major foreign policy problems in Iraq, Iran and Afghanistan.

"They have been very busy with the major crises on their hands and have neither articulated nor begun to implement any kind of broad approach on human rights," Carothers says. "These are really pressing, and human rights seems to be of secondary concern."

Was President Obama right to have the United States join the United Nations Human Rights Council?

When a Danish newspaper published a full page of satirical depictions of the Prophet Muhammad in 2005, Muslim leaders around the world denounced the publication as a defamation of Islam. Many called on the Danish government to take legal action against the newspaper. A Danish prosecutor found no basis for proceeding against the newspaper, however. And many leaders and commentators in Europe and the United States criticized the Muslim response as a threat to freedom of expression.

The dispute exemplified the tension between many Muslims and much of the rest of the world over how to reconcile free speech with freedom of religion. Now, the United States and predominantly Muslim Egypt have joined in sponsoring a broad U.N. reaffirmation of freedom of expression that condemns religious intolerance but significantly omits any legal sanctions for criticizing religion or specific faiths.

The freedom of expression resolution, adopted Oct. 2 by consensus by the United Nations Human Rights Council, marked the first significant accomplishment by the United States since the Obama administration's decision to join the still-new U.N. forum. The Bush administration had refused to join the council after it was created in 2006 to replace the U.N. Commission on Human Rights, which was widely criticized as weak and ideologically polarized.[10]

Many human rights advocates say the passage of the freedom of expression resolution demonstrates the Obama administration was right to join the council. "The United States was successful in reaching out to Egypt," says Neil Hicks, senior adviser on U.N. issues for Human Rights First. By omitting any reference to defamation of religion, the resolution means that "there will no longer be an effort to weaken protection of freedom of expression in the name of protecting religion," Hicks says.

Other human rights advocates, however, are troubled by passages in the resolution critical of the rising incidence of religious intolerance and stereotyping. The resolution has "some very good language and some problematic language," says Paula Schriefer, director of advocacy at Freedom House, who follows U.N. issues.

"There's some question whether this foray has been completely successful."

Hicks acknowledges the resolution is only "a step in the right direction" and may not end the dispute. Like most human rights advocates, however, including Freedom House, Hicks applauds the U.S. decision to participate in the council. "Our hope is that with U.S. membership there will be a concerted effort to stand up for democratic values in the council," Hicks says. "We're waiting for that to happen."

Some conservative human rights watchers, however, say the United States should have stayed out. "It was a token of the Bush administration's devotion to human rights that it would refuse to wade into this cesspool," says Johns Hopkins fellow Muravchik. "It is a great pity that the Obama administration has reversed that."

To join the council, the United States won election by 167 of the 192 members of the U.N. General Assembly in balloting in May. Among the 14 other countries elected were five with checkered human rights records, including two major powers, China and Russia; the regional power Saudi Arabia; and two smaller countries, Cameroon and Cuba.[11]

The U.N. Commission on Human Rights, the predecessor forum, had drawn criticism for being open to membership by — and domination by — human rights violators. In an effort to remedy the problem, membership in the new council requires an absolute majority of votes from the General Assembly rather than election from a regional bloc.

Proponents say the council is also stronger because all U.N. members will be subject to a "universal periodic review" of their records on rights issues, with council members up for review first. The commission had no procedure for reviewing human rights conditions in every country, Hicks says.

Supporters say membership by human rights violators is inevitable, but U.S. membership will strengthen the democratic bloc within the council. "Without United States leadership, other democratic countries rarely stand up effectively for human rights," says Human Rights Watch's Malinowski. "And repressive countries tend to band together quite effectively."

Mandelbaum at Johns Hopkins faults both the council and its predecessor for an anti-Israel bias. "They spend all their time persecuting the only country in the Middle East that takes human rights seriously: Israel," he says. Israel, which is not a member of the council, strongly criticized a report commissioned by the council that accused Israeli forces of human rights abuses during the invasion of Gaza launched in December 2008. (*See sidebar, p. 270.*)

Hicks agrees that the U.N. rights bodies have been guilty of "overconcentration on the Israeli-Palestinian situation," but he says that council actions adopting country-specific resolutions on Myanmar and Congo this year have shown some signs of reduced geographic-bloc voting.

In any event, most human rights experts applaud the Obama administration's decision to join the council. "The United States goes into these things recognizing that the council is not a perfect body," says UCLA's Kaye. "Rather than sitting outside and complaining, it's now inside the tent."

BACKGROUND

'Unalienable' Rights

As the first of the United States' founding documents, the Declaration of Independence affirmed a belief in the "unalienable" human rights of "life, liberty, and the pursuit of happiness" and the democratic principle of "consent of the governed." Those beliefs have remained central American ideals ever since. In the 20th century, the United States put its military and diplomatic might behind efforts to promote democracy and human rights — with limited success after World War I, somewhat more after World War II. Human rights remained a talking point during the Cold War but often took a back seat to geopolitics in the conflicts with two communist powers: the Soviet Union and China.[12]

The American Revolution succeeded in part because of aid from France. The young Republic turned a deaf ear in the 1820s, however, to pleas for help in the Greek war of independence. Then-Secretary of State John Quincy Adams said the United States was a "well-wisher to the freedom and independence of others," but "champion and vindicator only of her own." In the century's two major external wars — with Mexico (1846-1848) and Spain (1898) — the United States claimed to be spreading democracy, but the conflicts were aimed, in fact, at continental expansion and imperial conquest, respectively.[13]

As an emergent global power, the United States entered World War I with an explicit goal to "make the world safe for democracy." President Woodrow Wilson envisioned a postwar order founded on national self-determination with peace maintained by the League of Nations. With the United States out after the Senate's refusal to ratify the Versailles Treaty, the League was weakened from birth. The newly independent nations of Central and Eastern Europe mutated into dictatorships in the 1920s and '30s. And an isolationist-minded United States did nothing during the Spanish Civil War to prevent Francisco Franco's fascists from ousting a democratic government.

World War II brought a renewed commitment to human rights and democracy from the United States. Before the U.S. entry into the war, President Franklin D. Roosevelt in January 1941 identified four freedoms — freedom of speech and expression, freedom of religion, freedom from want and freedom from fear — as fundamental to people "everywhere in the world." Roosevelt's major wartime partner, British Prime Minister Winston Churchill, vowed in October 1942 that the war would end with "the enthronement of human rights." Like Wilson before him, Roosevelt envisioned a postwar order of national self-determination, including decolonization by wartime allies Britain and France. Decolonization proceeded only slowly over the next two decades, however. And the postwar settlement with the Soviet Union, an ally in the war, left Moscow in effective control of Eastern Europe.

As the war ended, the United States took the lead role in establishing an institutional and legal infrastructure intended to preserve the peace while promoting human rights. The charter of the newly created United Nations declared the goal of promoting "human rights and fundamental freedoms for all." As a member of the U.S. delegation, Eleanor Roosevelt, the late president's widow, helped create and became the first head of the U.N. Commission on Human Rights. And the commission organized the drafting of the Universal Declaration of Human Rights, adopted by the U.N. General Assembly on Dec. 10, 1948. The treaty's 30 articles detail individual rights that are to serve "as a common standard of achievement for all peoples and all nations."

Hopes for a worldwide flourishing of human rights fell victim to the Cold War. As UCLA's Kaye points out, the ideological conflict with the Soviet Union forced the

United States to struggle between devotion to human rights and pursuit of other geopolitical interests. Republican and Democratic presidents alike often resolved the conflict by supporting U.S. allies despite poor records on human rights and democracy. During the Chinese civil war, U.S. support for the Nationalist leader Chiang Kai-shek failed to prevent the communist takeover in 1949, which made Asia — like Europe — a major locus of ideological conflict with the United States and its allies.

A combination of ideological and economic interests led the United States during this period to organize coups that replaced leftist, democratically elected governments with right-wing U.S. allies in such countries as Iran (1953), Guatemala (1954) and Chile (1973). After the French defeat in Vietnam in 1954, the United States divided the nation rather than allow an election likely to have been won by the communist leader Ho Chi Minh. The United States did nothing, however, when Hungarians revolted against the communist government in 1956 or when Czechoslovakians rose up against their communist rulers in 1968. By then, the United States was bogged down in the Vietnam War, which ended in 1975 with the country unified under communist rule.

Rights Commitments

The end of the Vietnam War coincided with other developments that helped give human rights new prominence both domestically and internationally. The Soviet Union and its Eastern European satellites joined with the United States and Western Europe in 1975 in the historic Helsinki Accords, which committed all signatories to respect for human rights. In the United States, President Carter's election and four years in office left a lasting legacy of human rights as a central theme in U.S. foreign policy for future presidents, Republicans and Democrats alike. Then in the 1990s the fall of the Soviet Union and the end of the Cold War allowed human rights to be given greater priority in comparison to other national interests in the formation of U.S. foreign policy.

The Helsinki Accords — technically, the Final Act of the Conference on Security and Co-operation in Europe — were signed by the United States, Canada, the Soviet Union and all European countries but two (Albania and Andorra). They committed all of the countries to "respect for human rights and fundamental freedoms, including the freedom of thought, conscience, religion or belief."

In signing the agreement, the Soviet Union won the West's recognition of postwar borders, but with the proviso that they could be changed by peaceful means. The Soviet Union and the West remained at odds over how to define rights, but the accords spawned the creation of "Helsinki watch" monitoring groups that helped focus attention on alleged abuses.

Democrat Carter won election over Republican Gerald R. Ford in 1976 largely because of Ford's pardon of former President Richard M. Nixon for the Watergate scandal. In keeping with his moralistic approach to domestic and foreign issues alike, Carter promised in his campaign to make human rights a centerpiece of U.S. foreign policy. He institutionalized that commitment in his first year in office by creating in the State Department the Bureau of Human Rights and Humanitarian Affairs (now, the Bureau of Human Rights, Democracy and Labor). With the 30th anniversary of the Universal Declaration of Human Rights in 1978, Carter vowed again to make human rights central to U.S. policy as long as he was president. In the next year, Secretary of State Warren Christopher told a congressional committee that the United States had contributed to the atmosphere that enabled civilian regimes to replace military rulers in several countries and release political prisoners in some others.

With the election of the conservative Republican Ronald Reagan in 1980, rights issues became a sharp partisan divide in the United States. Democrats criticized Reagan for a renewed hard line in relations with the Soviet Union and for support of right-wing, rights-abusing regimes in El Salvador and Guatemala and right-wing rebels in Nicaragua. Under Reagan, however, U.S. aid to democratic movements abroad was institutionalized with the establishment of the National Endowment for Democracy as a publicly funded, privately operated entity. And by his second term Reagan was being credited with a turnaround on human rights exemplified by the U.S. backing of the successful ouster of two authoritarian U.S. allies: Ferdinand Marcos in the Philippines and Jean-Claude Duvalier in Haiti.

The dissolution of the Soviet Union and the ouster of communist regimes throughout Eastern Europe came with stunning suddenness during the presidency of George H. W. Bush. Reagan's admirers credit the downfall to his hard-line stance, but they and less-partisan observers also say the communist regimes failed because of the failure of communism itself. Whatever the causes, the events opened the door to opportunities for democratization and liberalization. Two decades later, Russia remains under critical scrutiny on rights issues, but many of the Eastern European countries are credited with successful transitions to democratic, rights-respecting governments.

Despite the easing of East-West tensions and a professed commitment to human rights, President Clinton was seen by rights advocates as falling short in some actions — for example, in delinking rights and trade with China and moving slowly to confront the humanitarian crises in the Rwanda conflict and in the wars in the former Yugoslavia. UCLA professor Kaye notes, however, that Democrat Clinton had to contend with a Republican-controlled House for six of his eight years in office and a GOP-controlled Senate for four.

The 1990s saw great progress, however, in the institutionalization of rights machinery at the United Nations, beginning in 1993 with the creation of the position of High Commissioner for Human Rights. Despite continuing controversy for its alleged anti-Israel bias, the Commission on Human Rights became an invaluable source of information by increasing the use of so-called special rapporteurs to investigate and report on conditions in individual countries and in broad areas such as arbitrary detention, child prostitution and violence against women. The U.N. Security Council also approved the creation of war crimes tribunals for the Balkan and Rwandan conflicts, even as a U.N.-sponsored conference was drafting a treaty to create a permanent International Criminal Court (ICC). Concerned with possible prosecution of U.S. service members, however, the United States was one of seven countries to vote against approval of the treaty in the U.N. General Assembly in 1998.

Rights Dichotomies

President Bush's record on human rights was sharply disputed during his eight years in the White House and remains sharply disputed today. Bush's admirers say the wars in Afghanistan and Iraq brought human rights improvements in both countries; critics say rights conditions in both countries continue to be unsatisfactory. The opposing camps similarly disagree on the detention and interrogation policies that Bush adopted in his "war on terror." Even Bush's critics concede, however, that his administration took positive steps on some human right fronts unconnected with the post-9/11 events.

Palestinian youths throw stones at Israeli soldiers near the West Bank town of Hebron on Oct. 12, 2009. The United States has opposed a U.N. Human Rights Council report that accuses Israel of targeting Palestinian civilians in Gaza.

Bush adopted an aggressive legal strategy after the Sept. 11, 2001, attacks on the United States to apprehend, detain and interrogate suspected al Qaeda members and sympathizers. Most notably, he claimed that the Geneva Conventions did not apply to the "enemy combatants" rounded up in Afghanistan and elsewhere and that they could be held at the Guantánamo Bay Naval Base in Cuba outside jurisdiction of federal courts. Both claims stirred strong opposition from European allies and from human rights groups within and outside the United States. Both claims were also rejected by the Supreme Court, which held in a series of cases that the Guantánamo detainees were protected by the Geneva Conventions' so-called Common Article 3 and that they could use federal habeas corpus petitions to challenge the legality of their imprisonment.

Bush mixed national security objectives with human rights goals in the wars both in Afghanistan and in Iraq. Admirers see human rights gains. "There are free elections in Iraq," says Johns Hopkins professor Mandelbaum. "Women go to school in Afghanistan."

In its most recent annual report issued in February 2009, however, Human Rights Watch is sharply critical of rights conditions in each. In Iraq, the government — described as resting on a narrow ethnic and sectarian base — is blamed for widespread torture and abuse of detainees. The report says girls and women are subject to gender-based violence; gays and lesbians are also subject to violence "by state and non-state actors." In Afghanistan, the government — described as weak and riddled with corruption — is faulted for taking no action on a justice-and-reconciliation plan adopted in 2006. Education for girls continues to lag, the report says, because of violence in some regions and social pressures elsewhere.

While criticizing Bush for taking "backward" steps on the war on terror, UCLA's Kaye says his presidency should not be viewed "as purely a dark period" on human rights issues. As one example, he notes the administration's decision in 2004 to accuse the Sudanese government of genocide in the rebellious province of Darfur. The administration also contributed to an international peacekeeping force and opposed a suspension of the ICC warrant against Sudan's president, Omar Hassan al-Bashir, for allegedly overseeing genocide in Darfur. Kaye also praises Bush for expanding U.S. programs to combat HIV/AIDS abroad. Bush won congressional approval for a $15 billion anti-AIDS initiative in 2003; as it was set to expire in 2008 he signed a five-year, $48 billion expansion. Kaye also gives Bush credit for tackling other global issues, such as human trafficking.

The Bush administration had less interest, however, in international human rights treaties. Most notably, the administration strongly opposed ratification of the treaty creating the ICC. Clinton had signed the treaty in 2000 but deferred asking the Senate to ratify it until after the court was in operation. Once the court began operations in 2002, however, Bush said he would not ask for ratification unless U.S. service members were exempted from possible prosecutions. Kaye notes that Bush also did not push for U.S. action on other international human rights covenants, including the Convention on the Rights of the Child and the Convention on the Elimination of All Forms of Discrimination Against Women. In its report, Human Rights Watch also cites the U.S. opposition to the U.N. Human Rights Council as an example of the Bush administration's "arrogant approach to multilateral institutions."

During his campaign, Obama strongly criticized the Bush administration's anti-terrorism policies as having lowered respect for the United States around the world. In his acceptance speech at the Democratic National Convention on Aug. 27, 2008, he promised to "restore our moral standing." He also vowed to "build new partnerships to defeat the threats of the 21st century: terrorism

and nuclear proliferation, poverty and genocide, climate change and disease."

As president, Obama moved quickly to redeem one of his promises by reversing some of Bush's anti-terror policies in his first week in office. He scrapped legal opinions that had questioned the applicability of the Geneva Conventions to suspected terrorists, shuttered the Central Intelligence Agency's secret prisons and set a one-year deadline for closing the Guantánamo prison camp.

In a series of foreign policy addresses from June through September, Obama also sought to reengage with the international community on a wide range of issues, including democracy and human rights. In his June 4 speech in Cairo, Obama pointedly underlined for the Muslim world the importance of religious tolerance and women's rights. In Ghana on July 11, he faulted post-colonial Africa for too much corruption and too little good governance. A few days earlier in Moscow, however, Obama steered clear of any direct criticism of Russia's restrictions on political freedoms. And his Sept. 23 speech to the U.N. General Assembly included only a single paragraph on democracy — but with the significant admission that the United States "has too often been selective in its promotion of democracy."

CURRENT SITUATION
Rights Policies in Flux

The Obama administration shows signs of becoming more active on international human rights issues, but it continues to draw mixed reactions from human rights groups and experts.

In the weeks since Obama's address to the U.N. General Assembly, the administration has unveiled a new strategy aimed at easing the humanitarian crisis in the Sudanese province of Darfur and implementing the 2005 peace accord between the country's predominantly Arab North and Christian and animist South. The administration has also strongly protested the Sept. 28 massacre and mass rapes of political protesters in the West African nation of Guinea, called for investigation of possible abuses during Sri Lanka's now-ended civil war and protested the arrest of a prominent human rights lawyer in Syria.

UCLA professor Kaye applauds the new Sudan policy for use of "benchmarks" to judge the government's compliance with the requested actions, but he adds, "The jury's still out." He says the statements on Guinea, Sri Lanka and Syria are "important signals" of the administration's human rights policy, but more action is needed. "One should hope that the statements of opposition and outrage are followed up by diplomatic moves," he says.

Johns Hopkins fellow Muravchik questions what he calls "the softer line" toward the Sudan government. Like Kaye, he views the U.S. stances on Guinea, Sri Lanka and Syria as unexceptional. The United States has "nothing at stake in Guinea or Sri Lanka," Muravchik says, "and issuing a protest about the arrest of a human rights lawyer is a fairly routine and mild thing to do."

The Sudan policy, announced by Clinton on Oct. 19, represents a conscious effort to find a balance between a hard-line approach emphasizing punitive sanctions and a refusal to deal with Sudanese President Bashir and a more conciliatory stance combining positive incentives and engagement with Bashir's government.[14]

The six-year-long crisis in Darfur — part of the turmoil in Africa's largest country spanning more than two decades — has defied peacekeeping and mediation efforts by the international community. Government-aided militias are blamed for killing at least 350,000 people; more than 2.4 million people have been displaced, most of them living in refugee camps that depend on international humanitarian groups for food and other supplies. In his campaign, Obama had called for strong sanctions against Bashir's government.

Darfur advocacy groups are voicing guarded optimism about the new approach. Jerry Fowler, president of the Washington-based Save Darfur Coalition, said the policy was similar to the "balance of incentives and pressures" that the group had been calling for. But he said the policy would not succeed without "substantial presidential leadership."

From a critical perspective, however, Bret Stephens, a *Wall Street Journal* columnist, mocked the administration's "menu of incentives and disincentives" in the policy. "It's the kind of menu Mr. Bashir will languidly pick his way through till he dies comfortably in his bed," Stephens wrote.[15]

On Guinea, Clinton registered a strong protest over the killing of more than 150 demonstrators in the capital of Conakry opposing the military government of Capt. Moussa "Dadis" Camara. There were also reports of dozens of rapes — including mass rapes and sexual mutilation of the victims — by government soldiers. Clinton on Oct. 7 denounced the brutality and violence as "criminality of the greatest degree" and called on Camara to step down. She also dispatched William Fitzgerald, deputy assistant secretary of state for African affairs, to Guinea to deliver the protest.[16]

The State Department's report on Sri Lanka, issued on Oct. 22, detailed alleged atrocities by both sides in the now-ended insurgency by a militant Tamil group seeking to create a separate homeland on the South Asian island nation. The report, requested by Congress, described as credible allegations that the government had targeted civilians and that the Tamil United Liberation Front had recruited children for the fighting. The report called for a full investigation by the government. "A very important part of any reconciliation process is accountability," State Department spokesman Ian Kelly said.[17]

On Syria, the administration joined Britain, France and international human rights groups in calling for the release of the prominent lawyer and former judge Haitham Maleh, who has been jailed since his Oct. 14 arrest. Maleh, 78, has opposed Syria's Baathist government and called for lifting the state of emergency it imposed after taking power in 1963. The arrest is "the latest Syrian action in a two-year crackdown on lawyers and civil society activists," the State Department said.[18]

The flurry of new statements "doesn't change the picture much," says Muravchik. "It's always true that any U.S. administration will be on the side of human rights if there is no cost to it in the coin of other U.S. foreign policy goals," he explains. "The problem that every administration faces is that insofar as we use some of our political influence and capital to press for human rights, we necessarily create frictions with governments that abuse human rights that make it harder for us to do other kinds of business with them."

Rights Treaties in Limbo

The Obama administration is signaling support for ratifying two long-pending United Nations-sponsored treaties on women's rights and children's rights, but Senate action is in doubt because of continued opposition from social conservatives and others.

The United States is all but alone in failing to join the two treaties: the Convention on the Elimination of All Discrimination Against Women and the Convention

AT ISSUE

Does President Obama deserve the Nobel Peace Prize for 2009?

YES
Ben Cohen
Editor, TheDailyBanter.com

NO
Erick Erickson
Editor-in-Chief, RedState.Com

Written for *CQ Researcher*, Oct. 25, 2009

Although Obama has governed as a centrist, one can't help but think that he is turning a very heavy ship ever so slowly leftwards, and that deep down, his heart lies far further to the left than he would like to let on. There is little doubt that Obama would, if he could, enact the extension of equal rights to gays, end the war in Iraq and Afghanistan, reconcile the Israelis and Palestinians and seriously reform the financial system.

The truth is, however, that a country taken over by special interests cannot be turned around quickly.

It is true that Obama has largely failed to deliver on all the above. But then again, he has only been in power for 11 months. And there has been progress — the engagement with the Middle East, multilateralism as the first option rather than the last, substantially increased unemployment benefits, cheaper student loans, a commitment (on paper at least) to reducing carbon dioxide emissions and a rebranding of America abroad.

Does this warrant a Nobel Peace Prize? Yes, and here's why.

The United States became a feared and despised state under the rule of the George W. Bush administration. The brazen disregard for global opinion, the trampling of international law and the overt environmental destruction were hallmarks of a presidency determined to project American power at all costs. With one election, the world forgave — and almost forgot — the tragic Bush years as a young, black president who spoke of hope rather than hatred, and cooperation rather than force, swept into power.

This monumental shift cannot and must not be underestimated.

Obama's Peace Prize was not necessarily given to him for what he has accomplished. It was given to him for what he can accomplish. As South African Archbishop Desmond Tutu put it:

"It is an award that speaks to the promise of President Obama's message of hope."

Hope will not fix the environment, stop the wars in Afghanistan and Iraq or prevent bankers from stealing all of our money.

Obama can certainly do better, much better than he is doing now. But it is too early to cast judgment, and he deserves time to make the changes he promised.

Obama has won the most prestigious prize for contributions to humanity in the world.

Now he must earn it.

Written for *CQ Researcher*, Oct. 26, 2009

In July 2006, speaking to schoolchildren, Betty Williams, the Nobel Peace Prize winner from Northern Ireland, said she would "love to kill George W. Bush." This year's recipient, Barack Obama, has yet to encounter a problem for which blaming Bush is not a solution. He fits the Nobel Peace Prize mold, which by and large is determined by a committee that runs an affirmative-action program giving preference to those people who view world peace as an absence of American influence — extra points to Americans who hate the American ideal.

Like Al Gore and Jimmy Carter before him, Barack Obama has done nothing to further peace in our time but has repudiated strong American leadership. The Nobel committee, possessed by the spirit of former British Prime Minister Neville Chamberlain, has descended to farcically awarding prizes for prospective peace that will never come and global warming fixes that will never work, but will make Al Gore a very rich man.

The Peace Prize long ago ceased to have any relevance to anyone outside the left. Awarding the prize to Yasser Arafat, who had the blood of thousands on his hands, was akin to awarding a safe-driving certificate to Ted Kennedy. The only thing the prize now stands for is approval from the anti-American European left. We should hope the president of the United States would pause to consider that, but as he did not, we can be sure he agrees.

In fact, in Barack Obama's short tenure as president he has done his best to apologize for perceived American abuses of power and arrogance, backpedaled on key issues of national security and flirted with some of the most kleptocratic, tyrannical regimes in modern history. Siding with tyrants over the democracy-loving people of Honduras, giving lip service to freedom as Iranians were gunned down in the streets of Tehran and coddling up to our Chinese bankers have ingratiated the man with those who have always been offended by the last 10 words of "The Star Spangled Banner." If that merits a peace prize, most Americans would probably prefer war.

The prospective peace the Nobel committee hopes for will not come. It is as illusory as the pot of gold at the end of the rainbow. Barack Obama's vanity will, however, compel him to pursue it. We can be sure his peace will be America's loss.

on the Rights of the Child. Besides the United States, only six other countries have failed to ratify the treaty on sex discrimination: Iran, Nauru, Palau, Somalia, Sudan and Tonga. Somalia is the only other country not to have approved the children's rights charter.[19]

The United States signed both treaties during Democratic administrations, but Republican opposition in Congress — fueled by opposition from social conservatives — has prevented the Senate ratification needed to give the treaties force of law. Now, the Obama administration says it wants both treaties ratified, but it has not set a timetable for moving on either one.

Social conservatives say both treaties pose threats to traditional family roles in the United States and to states' prerogatives on social issues. Some critics also question the treaties' practical effect since the signatories include any number of countries with poor human rights records. But human rights groups and other social welfare advocates say U.S. support for the treaties is important both symbolically and in practice. But they reject warnings that the treaties would impinge on private family arrangements.

The treaty on women's rights — sometimes known by the acronym CEDAW — was completed in 1979 and signed by the United States the next year while Carter was president. The Senate Foreign Relations Committee held hearings on the treaty in 1988, 1990, 1994 and 2002.

President Clinton submitted the treaty for ratification in 1994 with reservations on some issues including paid maternity leave and combat assignments for women. In the face of GOP opposition, Clinton never pressed for a Senate floor vote. Under Democratic control, the Foreign Relations Committee again recommended ratification in 2002, but the Bush administration opposed the treaty, and no floor vote was held.

In her confirmation hearing, U.N. Ambassador Rice said the administration considered the women's rights treaty "a priority." The treaty was included in May on a list of those recommended for action, but no action has been taken. Conservative groups continue to denounce the treaty. "It's the Equal Rights Amendment on steroids," says Wendy Wright, head of Concerned Women for America. Among other provisions, opponents complain of one that calls for nations to work to eliminate "stereotyped roles for men and women."[20]

The Reagan and George H. W. Bush administrations played a part in negotiating the children's rights pact but never signed it because of concern about its impact on U.S. law. The Clinton administration signed the treaty in 1995, but did not seek Senate ratification. The George W. Bush administration actively opposed the treaty.

Obama voiced concern during his campaign about the U.S. failure, along with Somalia, to approve the treaty. In a classroom session with schoolchildren in New York City in June, Rice said officials are actively discussing "when and how it might be possible to join." Again, no concrete action has been taken.

Conservative groups strongly oppose the pact. Stephen Groves, a fellow at the Heritage Foundation, a conservative think tank in Washington, says the treaty would give a U.N. body "a say over how children in American should be raised, educated or disciplined."[21]

The Obama administration's receptiveness to multilateral rights accords is viewed as a positive by human rights groups, but Human Rights Watch's Washington director Malinowski says political considerations still shape the ratification strategies. "They're rightly starting with the ones on which there's the most consensus," he says. Johns Hopkins fellow Muravchik questions the value of the charters. "I wouldn't say they are empty exercises, but their importance is quite secondary," he says.

On a more contentious issue, Human Rights Watch is urging the administration to move away from Bush's strong opposition to the ICC and instead "develop a constructive relationship" with the tribunal. Without joining the court, the group says the United States can lend assistance to investigations and prosecutions. It also wants the administration to oppose provisions passed by Congress in 2002 that, among other things, prohibited U.S. participation in peacekeeping missions unless U.S. service members were granted immunity from possible war crime prosecutions before the tribunal. So far, the administration has backed the ICC's prosecution of Sudan's President Bashir but has not outlined a general policy toward the court.

OUTLOOK

Waiting for Results

When President Obama arrives in Beijing in mid-November, he will be seeking to enlist China's help in dealing with some of the United States' most pressing issues, including nuclear proliferation, climate change and the global economic slowdown. Despite a newly published report by the joint Congressional-Executive Commission criticizing China for increased repression in some areas, however, U.S. experts expect human rights to be low on the agenda for Obama's visit.

"Elevating human rights . . . is not going to serve U.S. interests at this point," says Elizabeth Economy, director of Asia studies for the Council on Foreign Relations, a New York-based think tank.

The administration's critics, particularly partisan conservatives, accuse Obama of an across-the-board downgrading of human rights. Administration officials, however, depict the president as fully committed to promoting human rights abroad.

"The president's policy on these issues is clear," State Department legal adviser Koh told reporters at a Sept. 29 briefing in Geneva during a U.N. Human Rights Council session. "He promotes human rights through engagement. He promotes human rights through diplomacy. He promotes human rights through efforts to find common ground. And he's prepared to do this in both bilateral and multilateral settings."

Some experts see logic in the administration's apparent preference for engagement over confrontation but still warn about the risks of a perceived weakening of U.S. opposition to abusive practices. Obama "believes that solving foreign policy problems requires engaging with America's adversaries and ending the lecturing (and hectoring) tone of his predecessor," writes James Goldgeier, a senior fellow with the Council on Foreign Relations and a professor of political science and international affairs at George Washington University.

The strategy "might seem to make sense," Goldgeier continues. "Unfortunately, it sends a signal to repressive regimes that no one is going to call them to account for their human rights violations. And those fighting for freedom in their home countries may soon worry that the United States is no longer their champion."[22]

Johns Hopkins professor Mandelbaum is less convinced that the administration has merely shifted tactics on human rights issues without reducing their priority as a foreign policy goal. "No administration wants to say that it is downgrading human rights, so of course that's what they would say," Mandelbaum remarks. "Maybe they'll turn out to be correct."

Some of the administration's tactical choices are evidently open to debate, such as the decision to defer Obama's meeting with the Dalai Lama until after the China trip. Economy calls it a mistake. "The Dalai Lama is a global leader," she says. "Deciding to meet with him is unrelated to the China issue."

But Douglas Paal, a China expert at the Carnegie Endowment for International Peace who was on the National Security Council staff under Presidents Reagan and George H. W. Bush, calls the decision "a reasonable choice." "Tibet is at the head of China's core interests," he says. "Taking note of that, the administration doesn't want to have a debate about meeting with the Dalai Lama."

In a detailed report published on Oct. 16, the Congressional-Executive Commission on China finds increased repression in Tibet and the predominantly Uighur Xinjiang province along with increased harassment of human rights lawyers and advocates throughout the country. On Tibet, the report recommends that the United States urge China to open a dialogue with the Dalai Lama. It also calls on the government to increase aid to nongovernmental organizations (NGOs) for programs to aid Tibetans.[23]

In other sections, the report similarly urges a mix of government-to-government pressure along with concrete steps by the U.S. government and NGOs. The commission, created in 2000, includes nine senators, nine House members and five executive branch appointees. The Obama administration's seats on the commission are vacant; the administration has been slow in filling many executive branch slots.

With a full plate of major international crises and a challenging domestic agenda, the Obama administration is understandably hard-pressed to find time and resources to devote to human rights issues that — as in Sudan — present difficult and complex policy choices. Clinton, however, took time in August for a weeklong trip to Africa that included meetings with rape victims and visiting a refugee camp in the war-torn Democratic Republic of the Congo.[24] And in a visit to Russia in October, the secretary of state used a speech to university students to urge Moscow to open the political system. As *The New York Times'* reporter noted, "Mrs. Clinton spoke far more forcefully about human rights and the rule of law than she did on a trip to China earlier this year."[25]

With U.S. influence on other nations' internal policies necessarily limited, the likely impact of Clinton's Africa tour or Moscow speech is easily doubted. Human rights groups, however, believe the United States has made a difference in the past. Now, they are waiting with some impatience and skepticism to see whether the Obama administration will devote enough time, attention and resources to make a difference again.

"I keep hearing from the administration an interest in focusing on results," says Human Rights First Executive Director Massimino. "That's how I think they ought to be judged."

NOTES

1. Quoted in "Dalai Lama Shrugs Off Apparent Snub by Obama," Reuters, Oct. 8, 2009. For earlier coverage, see John Pomfret, "Obama's Meeting With the Dalai Lama Is Delayed," *The Washington Post*, Oct. 5, 2009, p. A1. The story notes that since 1991 three U.S. presidents — George H. W. Bush, Bill Clinton, and George W. Bush — have had a total of 10 meetings with the Dalai Lama at the White House; all were private photo opportunities except the Congressional Medal of Freedom ceremony in 2007. For background on China and Tibet, see Thomas J. Billitteri, "Human Rights in China," *CQ Researcher*, July 25, 2008, pp. 601-624; Brian Beary, "Separatist Movements," *CQ Global Researcher*, April 2008, pp. 85-114.

2. The official press release is at http://nobel prize.org/nobel_prizes/peace/laureates/2009/press.html.

3. For previous coverage, see Peter Katel, "Exporting Democracy," *CQ Researcher*, April 1, 2005, pp. 269-292; and in *Editorial Research Reports*: Kenneth Jost, "Human Rights," Nov. 13, 1998, pp. 977-1000; Mary H. Cooper, "Human Rights in the 1980s," July 19, 1985, pp. 537-556; and Richard C. Schroeder, "Human Rights Policy," May 18, 1979, pp. 361-380.

4. See Arch Puddington, "Freedom in the World 2009: Setbacks and Resilience," Freedom House, July

2009, www.freedomhouse.org/template.cfm?page=130&year=2009. Puddington is Freedom House's director of research.

5. Clinton is quoted in "Clinton: human rights can't interfere with other crises," CNN, Feb. 22, 2009; Amnesty International's statement can be found at www.amnestyusa.org/document.php?id=ENGUSA 20090220001&rss=iar#. For coverage, see Mark Landler, "Clinton Paints China Policy With a Green Hue," *The New York Times*, Feb. 22, 2009, p. A8.

6. Jamie Glazov, "Obama's Human Rights Disaster," *FrontPageMagazine.com*, Aug. 25, 2009, http://frontpagemag.com/readArticle.spx?ARTID=36042.

7. The text of the president's address in Cairo can be found on the White House Web site: www.white-house.gov/the_press_office/Remarks-by-the-President-at-Cairo-University-6-04-09/. For analysis, see Peter Baker, "Following a Different Map to a Similar Destination," *The New York Times*, June 9, 2009, p. A10. The text of Obama's and Mubarak's Aug. 18 remarks to reporters is on the White House Web site: www.whitehouse.gov/the_press_office/Remarks-by-President-Obama-and-President-Mubarak-of-Egypt-during-press-availability/.

8. "Making Its Mark: An Analysis of the Obama Administration FY2010 Budget for Democracy and Human Rights," Freedom House, July 2009, www .freedomhouse.org/uploads/FY2010Budget Analysis.pdf. For figures on Egypt, see Sudarsan Raghavan, "Egyptian Reform Activists Say U.S. Commitment Is Waning," *The Washington Post*, Oct. 9, 2009, p. A14.

9. Quoted in *ibid.*

10. The text of the resolution can be found on the U.N. Council on Human Rights' Web site: www2.ohchr .org/english/bodies/hrcouncil/12session/docs/A_ HRC_RES_12_16_AEV.pdf. For coverage of the council's action, see Frank Jordans, "UN rights body approves US-Egypt free speech text," The Associated Press, Oct. 2, 2009. For background, see Warren Hoge, "As U.S. Dissents, U.N. Approves a New Council on Rights Abuse," *The New York Times*, March 16, 2006, p. A3.

11. See Neil MacFarquhar, "U.S. Joins Rights Panel After Vote in the U.N.," *The New York Times*, May 13, 2009, p. A5. The other countries elected to the council were Bangladesh, Djibouti, Jordan, Kyrgyzstan, Mauritius, Mexico, Nigeria, Senegal and Uruguay.

12. Background drawn from previous *CQ Researcher* reports, footnote 3. See also Robert L. Maddex (ed.), *International Encyclopedia of Human Rights: Freedoms, Abuses, and Remedies* (2000).

13. Adams quoted in Joshua Muravchik, *Exporting Democracy: Fulfilling America's Destiny* (1991), p. 19.

14. For the State Department's background paper, see www.state.gov/r/pa/prs/ps/2009/oct/130676.htm. For background, see Karen Foerstel, "Crisis in Darfur," *CQ Global Researcher*, September 2008, pp. 243-270.

15. Bret Stephens, "Does Obama Believe in Human Rights?" *The Wall Street Journal*, Oct. 20, 32009, p. A19.

16. "Clinton: Violence in Guinea 'Criminal,' " The Associated Press, Oct. 7, 2009.

17. "Report to Congress on Incidents During the Recent Conflict in Sri Lanka," U.S. Department of State, Oct. 22, 2009, www.state.gov/documents/organization/131025.pdf. For coverage, see "U.S. Details Possible Sri Lanka Civil War Abuses," Reuters, Oct. 7, 2009.

18. "U.S. Says Syria Should Release 78-Year-Old Dissident," Reuters, Oct. 24, 2009.

19. Background drawn from two Congressional Research Service reports, both by Luisa Blanchfield: "The United Nations Convention on the Elimination of All Forms of Discrimination Against Women," Aug. 7, 2009, http://assets.opencrs.com/rpts/R40750_20090807.pdf; "The United Nations Convention on the Rights of the Child: Background and Policy Issues," Aug. 5, 2009, http://assets.opencrs.com/rpts/R40484_20090805.pdf.

20. Wright quoted in David Crary, "Discord likely over ratifying women's rights pact," The Associated Press, March 7, 2009.

21. Quoted in Robert Kiener, "Rescuing Children," *CQ Global Researcher*, October 2009, p. 265.

22. See "Critics say Obama is punting on human rights. Agree or disagree," *The Arena*, www.politico.com/arena/archive/obama-human-rights.html. The online forum hosted by *Politico* included comments from eight other experts and political activists.

23. "Congressional-Executive Commission on China," Annual Report 2009, Oct. 10, 2009, www.cecc.gov/pages/annualRpt/annualRpt09/CECCannRpt2009.pdf.

24. See Jeffrey Gettleman, "A Flash of Pique After a Long Week in a Continent Full of Troubles," *The New York Times*, Aug. 13, 2009, p. A8.

25. Mark Landler, "In Russia, Clinton Urges Russia to Open Its Political System," *The New York Times*, Oct. 15, 2009, p. A6.

BIBLIOGRAPHY

Books

Muravchik, Joshua, *Exporting Democracy: Fulfilling America's Destiny*, AEI (American Enterprise Institute) Press, 1991.
With the Cold War ending, a leading neoconservative author laid out the case for an active U.S. role in promoting democracy in other countries. Includes notes.

Traub, James, *The Freedom Agenda: Why America Must Spread Democracy (Just Not the Way George Bush Did)*, Farrar Straus and Giroux, 2008.
As George W. Bush's presidency was ending, journalist Traub argued that aid to civil-society organizations focused on political liberalization, economic modernization and social welfare is the best way for the United States to promote democracy abroad. Includes six-page note on sources.

Articles

Bolton, John, "Israel, the U.S., and the Goldstone Report," *The Wall Street Journal*, Oct. 19, 2009, p. A19.
The former U.S. ambassador to the United Nations argues that the U.N. Human Rights Council's approval of the report by South African jurist Richard Goldstone critical of Israel's conduct during the Gaza war shows that the Obama administration made a mistake in joining the body and should now withdraw.

Carothers, Thomas, "The Democracy Crusade Myth," The *National Interest online*, July 1, 2007, www.nationalinterest.org/PrinterFriendly.aspx?id= 14826.

A leading democratization expert at the Carnegie Endowment for International Peace says that despite pro-democracy rhetoric, the Bush administration actually gave traditional security and economic interests priority over promoting democracy abroad.

Krauthammer, Charles, "Three Cheers for the Bush Doctrine," *Time*, March 14, 2005, p. 28.

The conservative columnist argues that President Bush's plan for democratization has sparked free elections in numerous countries.

Kristof, Nicholas D., "What to Do About Darfur," *The New York Review of Books*, July 2, 2009, www .nybooks.com/articles/22771.

The New York Times foreign affairs columnist, in reviewing several books on the crisis in Sudan's Darfur province, calls the Obama administration's approach to the crisis inadequate but only a start. The article was written before the administration's announcement in October of a new "carrots and sticks" policy toward Sudan aimed at easing the Darfur crisis and fully implementing the 2006 accord that ended the Sudanese civil war.

Risen, Clay, "Does Human Rights Talk Matter?" *The New Republic*, Feb. 24, 2009, www.tnr.com/blog/ the-plank/does-human-rights-talk-matter.

The article argues that Secretary of State Hillary Rodham Clinton gave a green light to rights abusers throughout the world with her statement that China's human rights violations would not interfere with U.S.-China relations. Risen is a freelance writer and managing editor of *Democracy: A Journal of Ideas*.

Reports and Studies

"Annual Report 2009," *Congressional-Executive Commission on China*, Oct. 10, 2009, www.cecc.gov/

pages/annualRpt/annualRpt09/CECCannRpt2009 .pdf.

A commission established to monitor human rights and the rule of law in China finds that the country's continued use of repression undermines its stated international commitments to create a more open society. The 468-page report calls on the U.S. government to monitor Chinese progress in turning the principles outlined in the National Human Rights Action Plan of 2009 into tangible results.

"2008 Country Reports on Human Rights Practices," *U.S. Department of State*, Feb. 25, 2009, www.state .gov/g/drl/rls/hrrpt/2008/index.htm.

The State Department's congressionally mandated country reports on human rights practices points to three overarching trends during 2008: "a growing worldwide demand for greater personal and political freedom; governmental efforts to push back on those freedoms, and further confirmation that human rights flourish best in participatory democracies with vibrant civil societies."

"Freedom in the World 2009," *Freedom House*, July 2009, www.freedomhouse.org/template.cfm?page= 363&year=2009.

The organization's annual survey, covering 193 countries and 16 territories, finds a third consecutive yearly decline in global freedom. In an overview, the group's research director says the United States and other democracies face "serious challenges" in confronting "a forceful reaction" by authoritarian governments against democratic reformers and outside assistance for democratization.

"World Report 2009," *Human Rights Watch*, www .hrw.ort/world-report-2009.

The group's 19th annual review, covering human rights practices in more than 90 countries, opens with an essay by Executive Director Kenneth Roth arguing that intergovernmental discussions of human rights have recently been dominated by "human rights spoilers" — countries and leaders opposed to enforcement of human rights.

For More Information

Council on Foreign Relations, 58 East 68th St., New York, NY 10065; (212) 434-9400; www.cfr.org. Nonprofit organization that operates a think tank, sponsors task forces, and publishes *Foreign Affairs*, a leading journal of global politics.

Council for Global Equality, 1220 L St., N.W., Suite 100-450, Washington, DC 20005-4018; (202) 719-0511; www.globalequality.org. Brings together international human rights activists, foreign policy experts, LGBT leaders, philanthropists and corporate officials to encourage a strong American voice on human rights concerns impacting LGBT communities worldwide.

Freedom House, 1301 Connecticut Ave., N.W., 6th Floor, Washington, DC 20036; (202) 296-5101; www .freedomhouse.org. Works to advance the worldwide expansion of political and economic freedom through international programs and publications, including annual country reports.

Heritage Foundation, 214 Massachusetts Ave., N.E., Washington, DC 20002; (202) 546-4400; www.heritage.org. Public policy research institute promoting conservative positions on free enterprise, limited government and a strong national defense.

Human Rights First, 333 Seventh Ave., 13th Floor, New York, NY 10001-5108; (212) 845-5200; www.humanrightsfirst .org. Nonprofit international human rights organization promoting laws and policies that advance universal rights and freedoms.

Human Rights Watch, 350 Fifth Ave., 34th floor, New York, NY 10118-3299; (212)-290-4700; www.hrw.org. Leading independent organization dedicated to defending human rights around the world through objective investigations of abuses and strategic, targeted advocacy.

12

The Taj Mahal Hotel in Mumbai burns last November during attacks by Islamic militants throughout the city — India's financial capital — that killed 173 people. Afterwards, New York City's police commissioner noted chilling parallels between the two huge metropolises.

From *CQ Researcher*,
February 13, 2009.

Homeland Security

Is America Safe From Terrorism Today?

Peter Katel

The attackers struck in the last days of November 2008. With terrifying precision, shooters in five two-man teams moved from target to target, unleashing lethal bursts of automatic weapons fire in the train station, an upscale restaurant, two luxury hotels and a Jewish cultural center.

By the time the terrorists had been killed or captured three days later, 173 people had been slain.[1]

The massacre occurred in Mumbai, India, but 7,800 miles away, New York City Police Commissioner Raymond W. Kelly couldn't help but notice some troubling parallels. Mumbai, he told the Senate Homeland Security Committee in January, is "the country's financial capital, a densely populated, multi-cultural metropolis and a hub for the media and entertainment industries. Obviously, these are also descriptions of New York City."

In the post-9/11 world, Kelly's job is to make such connections. But among Americans in general, beset by foreclosures, job layoffs and other manifestations of the global economic meltdown, terrorism fears have diminished in the years since the Sept. 11, 2001, attacks on the World Trade Center and Pentagon.

"There may be a false sense of security in the United States because we haven't been attacked in seven years," says Bruce Hoffman, a professor at Georgetown University's School of Foreign Service and former scholar-in-residence for counterterrorism at the Central Intelligence Agency (CIA).

Indeed, while the Mumbai attacks seem as distant from the United States as South Asia itself, Hoffman and others view Mumbai as a wake-up call for the United States.

Inside the Department of Homeland Security

After the Sept. 11, 2001, terrorist attacks, Congress created the Department of Homeland Security in an effort to reassure the American public and improve intelligence gathering and processing. The DHS employs some 200,000 people in two-dozen separate agencies, most culled from other departments. But many major intelligence agencies remain outside the new department, leading to criticism the DHS left untouched the biggest problem revealed by 9/11: The inability of U.S. intelligence services, notably the CIA and FBI, to share and digest collected intelligence.

Agencies That Moved to the Department of Homeland Security
(Departments where agencies were previously located are in parentheses.)

Border and Transportation Security
U.S. Customs Service (Treasury)
Bureau of Citizenship and Immigration Services (Justice)
Federal Protective Service (General Services Administration)
Transportation Security Administration (Transportation)
Federal Law Enforcement Training Center (Treasury)
Animal and Plant Health Inspection Service (Agriculture, part transferred)
Office for Domestic Preparedness (Justice)

Emergency Preparedness and Response
Federal Emergency Management Agency (formerly independent)
Strategic National Stockpile and the National Disaster Medical System (Health and Human Services)
Nuclear Incident Response Team (Energy)
Domestic Emergency Support Teams (Justice)
National Domestic Preparedness Office (FBI)

Information Analysis and Infrastructure Protection
Critical Infrastructures Office (Commerce)
Federal Computer Incident Response Center (General Services Administration)
National Communications System (Defense)
National Infrastructure Protection Center (FBI)
Energy Security and Assurance Program (Energy)

Science and Technology
Chemical, Biological, and Radiological Countermeasures Program (Energy)
Environmental Measures Laboratory (Energy)
National Biological Warfare Defense Analysis Center (Defense)
Plum Island Animal Disease Center (Agriculture)

Citizenship and Immigration Services

Bureau of Citizenship and Immigration Services (Justice)

Coast Guard (Transportation)

Secret Service (Treasury)

Source: Department of Homeland Security

The attacks have been linked to Lashkar-e-Taiba (LeT), or the "Army of the Pure," a Pakistani group with deep connections to Pakistan's intelligence service. LeT seeks to force India to cede Kashmir to Pakistan, which, like Kashmir, is majority Muslim. The group shares longstanding ties with Osama bin Laden's jihadist group al Qaeda, which carried out the 9/11 attacks.[2]

While the daily fear that gripped Americans after Sept. 11 may have faded, the nation nonetheless has remained on high alert ever since, its security infrastructure extensively strengthened.

Creation of the Department of Homeland Security (DHS) the year after the attacks reflected officials' certainty that further terrorist strikes were imminent. Since then, increasingly intense airport screenings provide constant reminders of danger, along with warnings by terrorism experts that the United States' 361 ports and long borders leave the nation vulnerable.

"America's margin of safety against a WMD (weapon of mass destruction) attack is shrinking," a blue-ribbon congressional commission reported in December, pointing specifically at Pakistan and the jihadist groups flourishing there. "Were one to map terrorism and weapons of mass destruction today, all roads would intersect in Pakistan. . . . Trends in South Asia, if left unchecked, will increase the odds that al Qaeda will successfully develop and use a nuclear device or biological weapon against the United States or its allies."[3]

Bin Laden is doing his best to keep fears alive. Five days before Barack

Obama's Jan. 20 inauguration, a recording released by bin Laden said the new president was "inheriting two wars, in which he is not able to continue, and we are on our way to open other fronts, God willing."[4]

Thought to be holed up in the mountainous tribal-ruled belt of northwestern Pakistan, bin Laden and his top commanders — notably Ayman al-Zawahiri, an Egyptian doctor who is considered al Qaeda's second-in-command — remain America's No. 1 counterterrorism targets. As Defense Secretary Robert Gates told the Senate Armed Services Committee in January: "We will go after al Qaeda wherever al Qaeda is."[5]

Still, some veteran terrorism analysts say bin Laden's network no longer commands the funds, communications facilities nor technical expertise necessary to plan and carry out a major attack in the United States.

Marc Sageman, a former CIA officer in Pakistan, notes that the London subway and bus attacks in 2005 mark the last effective al Qaeda action outside Asia or Africa.[6] "There has not been a single fatality from al Qaeda or an al Qaeda-linked group in the West since July 7, 2005," Sageman, now a consultant to the NYPD's counterterrorism division, told a Washington conference sponsored by the Cato Institute think tank in January.

Another longtime expert on al Qaeda, Peter Bergen, noted recently that intensive investigations since 9/11 failed to uncover a single al Qaeda "sleeper cell" in the United States or any operatives on immediate missions. "While a small-bore attack may be organized by a[n a]l Qaeda wannabe at some point, a catastrophic, mass-casualty assault along the lines of 9/11 is no longer plausible," said Bergen, a journalist and a fellow at the nonpartisan New America Foundation, who interviewed bin Laden in 1997.[7]

John Mueller, an Ohio State University political scientist, has been arguing for several years that U.S. officials have vastly exaggerated the extent of terrorism danger to the United States. "It's looking more and more that 9/11 was an outlier," says Mueller, author of a 2006 book on terrorism. "Even if you assume that

Security-Related Agencies Not Included in the Department of Homeland Security
Central Intelligence Agency
National Security Agency
Department of Defense
Defense Intelligence Agency
Northern Command
Department of Health and Human Services
National Institutes of Health
Centers for Disease Control and Prevention
Department of the Interior
National Park Service Police
Bureau of Land Management Police
Department of Justice
Federal Bureau of Investigation
Department of State
Bureau of Consular Affairs
Department of Transportation
Federal Aviation Administration
Department of Treasury
Bureau of Alcohol, Tobacco, Firearms, and Explosives

Source: Donald F. Kettl, *System Under Stress: Homeland Security and American Politics,* 2nd ed., CQ Press, 2007

U.S. protection measures are 90 percent effective, that would mean that some al Qaeda agents would have been caught entering the United States. The fact that the government can't find any means that al Qaeda isn't trying."[8]

Even experts who question the need for some security procedures call Mueller's position extreme. Al Qaeda and its allies "would kill you if they could," says James Jay Carafano, director of the conservative Heritage Foundation's Kathryn and Shelby Cullom Davis Institute for International Studies. Minimizing terrorism threats would be risky, he argues. "If you get a cold and just ignore it, then you get pneumonia and die."

However, experiments conducted last year by journalist Jeffrey Goldberg suggest that domestic aviation security, at least, wouldn't stop terrorists. Goldberg got on a flight from Minneapolis-St. Paul to Washington with a forged boarding pass, no driver's license and a coat (in summertime) over an Osama bin Laden t-shirt. A security supervisor let Goldberg through. " 'All right, you can go,' " he said, pointing me to the X-ray line. " 'But let this be a lesson for you.' "[9]

Transportation Security Administration (TSA) Director Kip Hawley previously told one of Goldberg's key sources, security guru Bruce Schneier, that the agency's intelligence service effectively spots potentially dangerous passengers before they reach airports. "Our intel operation works closely with other international and domestic agencies," Hawley told Schneier.[10]

Other intelligence experts argue for paying close attention to the shared jihadist roots and operational ties between al Qaeda and LeT, the apparent Mumbai attack mastermind. "Bin Laden was an early supporter of the group and provided some of the initial funding," writes Bruce Riedel, a former CIA expert on Pakistan now at the Brookings Institution think tank. He has noted that the first major al Qaeda operative arrested after 9/11, Abu Zubayda, was nabbed in an LeT safe house in Islamabad.[11]

Riedel, author of a recent book on al Qaeda, predicts that Mumbai sets a pattern for future attacks.[12] "I think this will become a role model for terrorists around the world," he told the German news magazine *Der Spiegel*. "You will see the copycat phenomenon where others will try to imitate what has just happened in Mumbai."[13]

Some say it's an easy model to adapt. "In Mumbai, the terrorists demonstrated that with simple tactics and low-tech weapons they can produce vastly disproportionate results," Brian M. Jenkins, a terrorism analyst at the RAND Corporation think tank, told the Senate Homeland Security Committee. Their weapons, he noted, amounted essentially to a 1940s-era arsenal — rifles, pistols and grenades.[14]

By attacking a non-aviation transportation hub, the attackers reinforced another warning by many terrorism analysts — jihadists' adaptability. "I think what Homeland Security has done well up to this point is to prepare defenses to respond to the last attack," says Roger Cressey, transnational threat director for the National Security Council during the Clinton administration. "If you look at TSA, it's more focused on aviation than on any other element of transportation."

Many other terrorism experts point to al Qaeda's apparent obsessiveness about aviation and highly symbolic targets. Sept. 11 provided the clearest example. In addition to the hijackers aiming at the World Trade Center and Pentagon a fourth plane apparently had targeted the Capitol or White House. It crashed in Shanksville, Pa., after passengers rushed the cockpit.[15]

In fact, jihadists had tried toppling the towers once before, exploding a bomb in the garage in 1993. After fast police work rolled up nearly the entire network of conspirators, counterterrorism expert Hoffman warned that the danger hadn't passed.

"The fact there haven't been any more attacks doesn't mean we're out of the woods," he said. "Terrorism doesn't work in a predictable fashion." He was speaking in 1994, seven years before 9/11.

As counterterrorism experts and lawmakers seek to keep America safe, here are some of the questions they are debating:

Does al Qaeda remain a danger within the United States?

Even before the Sept. 11 attacks, the small group of al Qaeda leaders around Osama bin Laden had become the prime target of U.S. counterterrorism efforts. They remain so today, with many in the national-security community convinced that as long as al Qaeda exists, it's plotting attacks on U.S. soil.

Along with many in the military and intelligence communities, Defense Secretary Gates sees current U.S military efforts in Afghanistan as countering another 9/11. "My own personal view is that our primary goal is to prevent Afghanistan from being used as a base for terrorists and extremists to attack the United States and our allies," Gates told the Senate Armed Services Committee in late January.[16]

In this view, al Qaeda's track record — going back to the U.S.-supported war against the Soviet occupation of Afghanistan during the 1980s — reveals a battle-hardened, highly trained and imaginative leadership that should never be underestimated.

A clear indication that al Qaeda may be down but not out came with the arrests of 24 Britons in 2006 for plotting to blow up transatlantic airliners in midflight to the United States, using small bombs filled with explosive liquid. In the end, only eight were put on trial and three convicted — of conspiracy to commit murder, not of more serious charges of trying to mount a massive suicide attack. Still, authorities in both countries maintained they had foiled a serious plot, which included preparation of "martyrdom videos" by some defendants.[17]

All of the defendants were Muslims, six of them Pakistani, and counterterrorism officials said some had gotten training in Pakistan from an al Qaeda explosives expert.[18]

The bin Laden group's ability to keep operating in its Pakistani sanctuary is the key to the continuing danger it poses, intelligence professionals say. In November, then-CIA Director Michael Hayden told foreign-policy specialists that al Qaeda was still the intelligence agency's main target. "Al Qaeda, operating from its safe haven in Pakistan's tribal areas, remains the most clear and present danger to the safety of the United States," Hayden said. "If there is a major strike against this country, it will bear the fingerprints of al Qaeda."[19]

Hayden and others who share his view acknowledge that bin Laden's organization now has far less freedom in its presumed location in Pakistan than it did before late 2001, when it enjoyed the hospitality of Afghanistan's Taliban government.

The constant targeting of the group by the United States — which has a $25 million bounty on bin Laden — combined with help from European, Asian and some Middle Eastern allies, is limiting action by al Qaeda, some counterterrorism experts say. "It's more difficult to travel, more difficult to cross borders," says P. J. Crowley, a former National Security Council staffer who is homeland security director at the Center for American Progress, a think tank with close ties to the Obama administration. "In the late 1990s they had training capability in Afghanistan, and they've lost that."

Despite the apparent difficulty of operating outside the Pakistani tribal area, Crowley says enough legal traffic exists between Pakistan and Pakistani immigrants in Europe to give cover to al Qaeda operatives. "When you compare the United States to Europe, the ongoing risk of an attack is even higher in Europe."

But a member of two congressional commissions on terrorism and WMD argues that Europe is a bridge to the United States on which holders of Western European passports can travel easily. "If it's in Europe's living room, then it's on our doorstep," says former Rep. Timothy J. Roemer, D-Ind., who served on the 9/11 Commission convened after the attacks and on the recent Commission on the Prevention of Weapons of Mass Destruction Proliferation and Terrorism. He is now president of the Center for National Policy think tank.

At the WMD commission, Roemer recalls, "When we talked to our intelligence people in the United States,

A U.S. Customs and Border Protection officer at the Port of Newark, N.J., uses a hand-held radiation detector to check a shipping container that was stopped for further inspection after it passed through a radiation detector. Some terrorism experts say poor security at U.S. ports leaves the nation vulnerable to terrorism.

they continued to say al Qaeda has become stronger since 9/11 and that the threat to the homeland radiates from the Pakistani border area."

The Heritage Foundation's Carafano argues that al Qaeda is suffering the effects of unrelenting targeting by the United States. "Are they directing operations in the methodical way that they did before 9/11?" he asks. "There's zero evidence of that."

A former career U.S. Army officer, Carafano acknowledges al Qaeda may be capable of inspiring or encouraging terrorist acts in the United States. But al Qaeda made its reputation with spectacular, coordinated operations in different locations — such as the bombings of two U.S. embassies in Africa and the 9/11 attacks, which involved the hijacking of four airliners. "The question is, can they do a terrorist attack in a systematic way? That is real terror," Carafano says. "They don't have the capacity to do that. A little splinter cell will do something, and five seconds later they're going to get rolled up."

Nevertheless, an old spy-world dictum holds that there's no way to know what you don't know. "From my point of view, the lesson of 9/11 is the price of complacency," says Georgetown's Hoffman. "We knew there was a threat from al Qaeda before 9/11. We deluded ourselves into thinking it was an overseas threat and couldn't possibly come here."

On Feb. 10, in a sign that worries about terrorism continue, the government of Saudi Arabia asked Interpol, the international police force based in Lyon, France, to issue an unprecedented global alert to apprehend 85 fugitives suspected of ties to al Qaeda.

Is the Department of Homeland Security set up effectively to spot potential threats?

The huge and diverse department wins little praise for organization. Its constituent elements range from the entire Customs, Border Patrol and immigration-control forces to the Coast Guard, Secret Service and Federal Emergency Management Agency (FEMA).

"I voted against it," says Roemer. "I believed that we were cobbling together a 20th-century Frankenstein for 21st-century threats."

Roemer's criticism reflects a widely shared view among security professionals. But forcing the department to reverse course would waste time and energy better spent improving the department's operations, they say. "We really don't have the choice to go backwards — reorganizing, rearranging and dismantling," Roemer says.

Security experts readily volunteer suggestions for improvements, such as the need for more sharing of intelligence between DHS and other counterterrorism agencies. "We need . . . the new secretary to really push hard on that," RAND terrorism expert Jenkins told lawmakers, arguing that restrictions on access to information within the government remain stuck in the Cold War era. "We are now dealing with nebulous networks, fast-moving developments, and we have to come up with a lot more streamlined processing for moving intelligence and information around in the system."[20]

In simple bureaucratic terms, structure is an issue for new Homeland Security Secretary Janet Napolitano, not only because of the large number of agencies pulled into the new department but also because of those that were left out. (*See charts, pp. 290–291.*) Agencies outside DHS include the CIA, FBI and National Security Agency — the three biggest counterterrorism agencies and the ones that were at the center of the debate that gave rise to the department's creation.[21]

Following Sept. 11, officials learned that intelligence and law-enforcement agencies had picked up indications

of a terrorist plot but hadn't fully compared notes. As a result, intelligence experts hadn't "connected the dots" pointing to 9/11. "The importance of integrated, all-source analysis cannot be overstated," the 9/11 Commission said in its landmark 2004 report. "Without it, it is not possible to 'connect the dots.' "[22]

By 2004, the DHS had already been created. The move followed a policy reversal by the Bush administration, which had resisted early pressure to create a new Cabinet department for domestic security.

The few federal terrorism charges the government did file, however, were brought by the Justice Department. Homeland Security became known largely for airport security and for the disastrous FEMA response to Hurricane Katrina in 2005.[23]

"The sheer complexity of creating and unifying such a wide-ranging operation remains an enormous problem," says Donald F. Kettl, a University of Pennsylvania political scientist and the author of a book on homeland security.

Indeed, he says, although the department's range of responsibilities vastly increased, the "dot-collecting" agencies remained unconnected. "There are important pieces of the apparatus that are not included," he says. "The main problem that the department was set up to cure is left unanswered."

Although many experts share Kettl's concern, some think the new Obama administration can offset the department's built-in shortcomings.

Cressey, the former White House counterterrorism official, expects Secretary Napolitano and her staff to zero in on DHS structural problems. Presently, he says, at least 22 senior officials report directly to her. "That's insane, it's unworkable," he says, pointing to the Pentagon as a model of how to set up a massive department.

Cressey adds that any reorganization would have to be precise and detailed, so as to do no harm. "The Secret Service and Customs are working reasonably well, as is the Coast Guard," he says. "You don't want to screw up any agency within the department that is successfully executing its mission."

But Crowley at the Center for American Progress argues that, while modest reforms are possible, the department suffers from deep structural and managerial flaws.

He cites a New Year's Day episode in which a group of American Muslim travelers were forced off a

Washington-to-Orlando flight because a passenger became alarmed.[24] "TSA says there are 20 layers of security," he says. "There should have been points within the system where someone could say, 'Hey there's no real threat here. The layer that alarmed was the 20th, and least reliable. The way the system reacted, it didn't seem to trust the other 19 layers; it just defaulted to the maximum response."

Is the United States focusing anti-terrorism resources in the right places?

Former President George W. Bush and his senior officials have credited the security measures they put into effect after 9/11 with preventing further attacks on the United States. "We'll leave behind a vastly upgraded network of homeland defenses," Bush said at the Army War College in Carlisle, Pa., shortly before leaving office. "Federal, state and local law enforcement officers are working together more closely than ever before. The number of border patrol agents has doubled since 2001. Our airports and seaports have bolstered screening procedures."[25]

Bush made oblique mention of missile strikes launched from unmanned aircraft onto reported al Qaeda and Taliban targets in Pakistan. "With weapons like the Predator drone in our arsenal, our troops can conduct precision strikes on terrorists in hard-to-reach areas while sparing innocent life," he said. (Obama has ordered the strikes continued, and government officials say they are crippling al Qaeda and its fellow jihadists.)[26]

For his part, former Vice President Dick Cheney put special emphasis on warrantless monitoring of phone calls and e-mail. "I think what the National Security Agency did . . . working with the CIA at the direction of the president, was masterfully done," Cheney told CBS's "Face the Nation" about two weeks before leaving office. "I think it provided crucial intelligence for us. It's one of the main reasons we've been successful in defending the country against further attacks."[27]

Critics of the monitoring program say the government would have been able to obtain warrants quickly if the eavesdropping had been important. Others insist that the absence — so far — of a sequel to 9/11 reflects terrorists' weakness more than it does tougher security measures.

The intelligence effort does get a back-handed compliment from the leading skeptic on counter-terrorism

A Port Authority policeman guards the Holland Tunnel linking New York City and New Jersey following reports in July 2006 that jihadists had planned to bomb the tunnel and other New York landmarks, including the United Nations.

programs. "If there's nothing to find, then intelligence-gathering is a waste," says Mueller of Ohio State University. "But it probably makes more sense than trying to protect everything, because there's an infinite number of targets."

As for tighter port and border controls, security skeptics say tougher inspections at official crossings, higher fences and more patrolling to keep out illegal crossers may simply deter foreigners from entering the United States to find jobs. But, these experts add, U.S. borders remain open to savvy and determined operators. "If you have any doubt about terrorists' ability to bring a bomb to an American city, remember, they could always hide it in a bale of marijuana, which we know comes to [every] American city," Graham Allison, director of the Belfer Center for Science and International Affairs at Harvard's Kennedy School of Government, told the House Armed Services Committee in January.[28]

Less than two weeks later, *The New York Times* reported that Mexican marijuana exporters have "routinely transported industrial-sized loads of marijuana" over the border — and under it, using tunnels.[29]

The security weakness Allison pointed to stems from a lack of strategic focus, argues Center for National Policy President Roemer, who served with Allison on the WMD Commission. "If you focus on everything, you

Getty Images/Scott Olson

Former Gov. Janet Napolitano, D-Ariz., the new secretary of Homeland Security, is expected to focus on structural problems at the huge agency, including developing better information-sharing with the CIA, FBI and National Security Agency.

focus on nothing," Roemer says. Specifically, he questions whether the drive to assemble "watch lists" of terrorism suspects has produced valid results.

Meanwhile, other problem areas have been neglected, Roemer says. "What about nuclear security, biosecurity, cybersecurity? These are things we should have looked at two years ago, on which we've done precious little."

Even so, other experts argue, the continuing emphasis on airline security reflects attention to jihadists' targeting preferences. "If you were advising a terrorist group, you'd tell them, 'The one area the government pays attention to is aviation.' Yet they keep going for it," says Daniel Byman, director of the Security Studies Program at Georgetown.

Byman, a former 9/11 Commission staffer, says jihadists have focused on airliners for good reason, at least from their point of view. "It's a highly symbolic target, and an attack on one is seen as having a huge psychological effect."

While many experts agree, some analysts argue that airport procedures may look more imposing and rigorous than they are. "Somebody smart and determined is

going to be able to defeat the process, I have a feeling," says Kettl of the University of Pennsylvania. "Can someone get a bomb on a plane? Probably." He acknowledges, however, that breaking into a cockpit has become far more difficult.

"The underlying and more important issue" about airport security, he says, "is that it gives citizens a feeling they have a free pass — that at bottom the government is in control, and we don't have to worry."

BACKGROUND

Mideast Conflict

Conflict between Israel and Palestinians emerged as a U.S. security issue in the 1960s, but only in retrospect. Sirhan Sirhan, the gunman who assassinated New York Sen. Robert F. Kennedy, D-N.Y., in 1968, was a Jerusalem-born Arab angered at Kennedy's support for Israel during the Six-Day War of 1967. "My only connection with Robert Kennedy was his sole support of Israel and his deliberate attempt to send . . . 50 bombers to Israel to obviously do harm to the Palestinians," Sirhan told British journalist David Frost 20 years later.[30]

At the time of the assassination in a Los Angeles hotel kitchen, however, Sirhan was generally described as mentally ill rather than politically motivated. His legal defense, in fact, was that he was incapable of premeditated killing. Only in recent years has his act come to be seen as a harbinger of political violence in the Middle East.

A year after Kennedy's death, terrorists indisputably targeting Israel hijacked a Tel Aviv-bound TWA airliner from Los Angeles. A man and a woman from the Che Guevara Commando Unit of the Popular Front for the Liberation of Palestine boarded in Rome. Apparently believing Israeli Ambassador to the United States Yitzhak Rabin was aboard, the hijackers eventually forced the plane to land in Syria. No passengers were killed.[31]

Further hijackings, as well as bombings and other attacks, mostly in Western Europe, in the 1970s and '80s, were rooted in the Middle East. The most notorious was the seizure of Israeli athletes at the 1972 Olympic Games in Munich by Palestinian gunmen. All 11 hostages and five of eight gunmen were killed, most of them in a failed rescue attempt.[32]

The next year, Palestine Liberation Organization (PLO) gunmen kidnapped two U.S. diplomats and a Belgian envoy in Khartoum, Sudan. The attackers demanded the release of Sirhan and hundreds of other Palestinians imprisoned elsewhere. The U.S. refused to negotiate, and the three were executed.[33]

Subsequently, PLO leader Yasser Arafat secretly pledged to the United States to refrain from violence outside of Israel. But other Middle East groups adopted similar tactics.

In April 1983, a suicide bomber from an organization named Islamic Jihad killed 63 people at the U.S. Embassy in Beirut, Lebanon, where President Ronald Reagan had deployed 1,200 Marines to help enforce a cease-fire in a civil war. No retaliation was attempted. Then, in October, a suicide truck-bomber blew up the U.S. peacekeepers' barracks in Beirut, killing 241 Marines. U.S. intelligence blamed Hezbollah, a Lebanese militia organized largely by Iran.[34]

The backdrop was the 1982 Israeli invasion of Lebanon. Iran's radical religious rulers — newly in power after the 1979 overthrow of the shah (king), a close U.S. ally who was friendly to Israel — saw Hezbollah as a force to challenge both those foes.

A deadly event in the region's biggest country had its own connection to Israel and the United States. In 1981, Islamist members of the Egyptian army assassinated President Anwar Sadat in retaliation for his signing of a peace treaty with Israel — a move the United States had supported. A young Islamist doctor played a minor role in the assassination conspiracy — Ayman al-Zawahiri, who would later become bin Laden's chief strategist.[35]

On U.S. Soil

The violence spawned by the Mideast conflict hit U.S. soil with full force in 1993. On Feb. 26 of that year, a powerful truck bomb detonated in the basement parking lot beneath the World Trade Center in New York, killing six people. Police quickly discovered a terrorist cell of recent immigrants, mostly Palestinians, who had come to the United States from Egypt, Jordan and other Middle Eastern countries.

The bombers turned out to be more zealous than competent. The operative who rented the Ryder van that carried the fertilizer bomb reported the vehicle stolen so he could claim his deposit. The FBI — which had traced the van to the rental agency — arrested him and then nabbed most of his comrades.[36]

But the mastermind, Ramzi Yousef, a Kuwaiti national of Pakistani descent, had fled. Schooled in explosives at a training camp in Afghanistan — during the Taliban's rule — Yousef was the key link between the 1993 bombing and the 9/11 attack eight years later.

He was captured in Pakistan in 1995, tried and convicted in the United States and sentenced to life plus 240 years in prison; his co-conspirators received 240-year sentences.[37]

The trade center bombing investigation revealed another jihadist plot — to bomb New York landmarks including the United Nations and the Holland and Lincoln tunnels. The nine so-called "landmarks" defendants were all convicted and sentenced to terms ranging from 11 years (for a cooperating witness) to life. In a third related case, a man convicted of conspiracy to murder Meir Kahane, a violently anti-Arab Israeli-American rabbi who was assassinated in a New York hotel in 1990, received a life sentence.[38]

Except for two U.S.-born, non-Arab converts to Islam, all of those convicted in the 1993 trade center bombing and the related conspiracies were immigrants from Egypt and other Middle Eastern countries.

But even as prosecutors prepared the cases against these conspirators, a white American ex-GI triggered the explosion that was — until Sept. 11, 2001 — the most destructive act of terrorism on U.S. soil.

Timothy McVeigh, a veteran of the 1991 Persian Gulf War devoted to neo-Nazi ideology, blew up the Alfred P. Murrah Federal Building in Oklahoma City on April 19, 1995. McVeigh was arrested in a traffic stop shortly after his ammonia-fertilizer bomb, packed into a van, exploded in front of the building, killing 168 people, including 19 children. Convicted of murder and conspiracy, he was executed on June 11, 2001.[39]

The bombing sparked a wave of concern about homegrown extremists. Law enforcement agencies and journalists zeroed in on the "militia" movement — loosely coordinated bands of white men inclined to survivalism, gun rights and, typically, far-right politics. They constituted "a secretive, paranoid and profoundly alienated political subculture that may now constitute a threat to law and order," *Newsweek* said.[40]

But the movement dwindled after the Oklahoma bombing, though right-wing extremists were involved in a later, smaller-scale bombing and several murders. One of the most notorious was the 1999 shooting of three children and two adults at the North Valley Jewish Community Center near Los Angeles (all survived), followed by the murder of a Filipino-American postman. The lone shooter, Buford O. Furrow Jr., a member of the neo-Nazi Aryan Nation, pleaded guilty to murder and other charges and was sentenced to life in prison.[41]

Al Qaeda

As the threat posed by domestic far-right extremists waned, bin Laden turned to U.S. targets in Africa and the Mideast.

In 1998, al Qaeda operatives simultaneously bombed the U.S. embassies in Nairobi, Kenya, and Dar es Salaam, Tanzania, killing at least 220 people and wounding more than 4,000 others, the vast majority of them local nationals.[42]

Then, in 2000, an al Qaeda suicide team in a small, inflatable boat filled with explosives pulled up beside the *USS Cole*, an American warship, in the port of Aden, in Yemen and blew a hole in the ship's side, killing 17 crew members.

In retaliation, the Clinton administration, which had been tracking bin Laden's moves, launched cruise missiles against al Qaeda training camps in Afghanistan, from Navy warships in the Arabian Sea. But bin Laden had left one of the camps.[43]

Even before the attack on the *Cole*, some counterterrorism officials — as well as government researchers relying on open-source materials — had been trying to draw more high-level attention to bin Laden. By September 1999, the Library of Congress warned in a non-classified report commissioned by an unnamed government agency (apparently the CIA): "Al-Qaida poses the most serious terrorist threat to U.S. security interests."[44]

Citing Washington as a likely prime target for a "spectacular" attack, the report said: "Suicide bomber(s) belonging to al-Qaida's Martyrdom Battalion could crash-land an aircraft packed with high explosives (C-4 and semtex) into the Pentagon, the Headquarters of the Central Intelligence Agency, or the White House."[45]

The authors of the dead-on analysis couldn't have known it at the time, but only months earlier, bin Laden had approved a new attack on the World Trade Center planned by Khalid Shaikh Muhammed, the uncle of

Ramzi Yousef. The attackers would use hijacked airliners as flying bombs.

In the aftermath of the attack on the *Cole*, U.S. officials and nongovernmental terrorism experts repeatedly warned Americans to prepare for more. In May 2002, for instance, administration officials told reporters that al Qaeda operatives had stepped up the pace of their communications, in a probable prelude to an attack.[46]

Days later, Vice President Cheney, appearing on NBC's "Meet the Press," said future attacks were "not a matter of if, but when." And over the next two days, FBI Director Robert S. Mueller said that suicide bomber attacks in the United States were "inevitable," while Defense Secretary Donald H. Rumsfeld spoke of terrorists acquiring weapons of mass destruction.[47]

Instead, the years following the Sept. 11 strike would see jihadist terrorists strike at Westerners (or Jews) in non-U.S. locations, including Madrid, London, Bali and Casablanca, as well as the recent assault in Mumbai.

With one exception, no attacks by Islamist militants were launched within the United States. Richard C. Reid, a British citizen, tried to light the fuse of a small but powerful bomb concealed in his shoe, while aboard a Paris to Miami flight in December 2001. Passengers and crew managed to extinguish the fuse. Reid, a convert to Islam, pleaded guilty while declaring his allegiance to bin Laden and was sentenced to life in prison.[48]

In early 2009, a half-dozen Miami men went on trial for the third time, after two mistrials, on charges of plotting religiously inspired terrorism. Their trial follows a half-dozen similar trials around the country that produced mixed outcomes. None of those accused carried out a successful attack.

The one terrifying attack that did occur following Sept. 11 had no Qaeda connection. Three weeks after Sept. 11, envelopes containing spores of the deadly lung disease anthrax were mailed to political and media figures. The anthrax — accompanied by threatening notes in the name of Islam — killed five people and sickened 17. Al Qaeda or a similar organization was widely presumed to be the sender, though none claimed responsibility.

The FBI soon pointed, instead, to a scientist at the military's main biodefense laboratory in Fort Detrick, Md. No charges were ever filed against the scientist, Steven J. Hatfill, whom FBI officials had called a "person of interest." Then, in July 2008 — after agreeing to pay Hatfill $4.6 million to settle a lawsuit he filed alleging violations of the

CHRONOLOGY

1960s-1980s *Anti-American terrorism spawned by Arab-Israeli conflict spreads through the Mideast and Europe, barely touching U.S.*

1968 Palestinian immigrant Sirhan Sirhan assassinates Sen. Robert F. Kennedy, D-N.Y., for supporting Israel.

1973 Palestine Liberation Organization gunmen in Sudan kill two U.S. diplomats and a Belgian after U.S. refuses to free Sirhan.

1979 Soviet Union invades Afghanistan, prompting millionaire Saudi exile Osama bin Laden to join anti-Soviet jihad.

1981 Jihadists arrested after assassination of Egyptian President Anwar Sadat include Ayman al-Zawahiri, who heads for Afghanistan after he is freed.

1983 Islamic Jihad organization blows up U.S. Embassy in Beirut, Lebanon, in retaliation for U.S. intervention in civil war, killing 63. . . . Six months later, another bomb, apparently planted by Hezbollah, destroys U.S. Marine barracks and kills 241.

1990s *Mideast terrorism hits U.S. soil, while far-right extremists escalate their violence.*

1990 Anti-Arab Rabbi Meir Kahane is assassinated in New York by a Palestinian immigrant.

1993 A mostly Mideast immigrant cell detonates a truck bomb under New York's World Trade Center, killing six. . . . Investigation leads to discovery of related conspiracy to blow up New York landmarks.

1995 Far-right extremist Timothy McVeigh bombs Oklahoma City federal building, killing 168 and prompting worries about domestic terrorism.

1998 Al Qaeda operatives bomb two U.S. embassies in Africa, killing 220.

1999 Library of Congress report warns that al Qaeda could crash an airplane into the Pentagon.

2000s *Al Qaeda becomes primary target of U.S. counterterrorism operations even before 9/11.*

2000 Al Qaeda suicide bombers hit *USS Cole* in Yemen, killing 17 and prompting retaliatory U.S. missile strikes, which miss Osama bin Laden.

2001 Nearly 3,000 die in Sept. 11 attacks on World Trade Center and the Pentagon and the crash of a fourth hijacked plane in Shanksville, Pa. . . . Anthrax-filled envelopes are sent to media organizations and political figures, killing five. . . . President George W. Bush forms homeland security office. . . . Richard Reid tries detonating a shoe bomb on a Paris-Miami flight.

2002 Administration warns that new al Qaeda attacks are imminent. . . . Congress creates new Cabinet-level Department of Homeland Security. . . . Jose Padilla is arrested as "enemy combatant," accused of plotting to detonate a "dirty bomb."

2003 Homeland Security Secretary Tom Ridge advises Americans to stock up on protective equipment including duct tape, provoking widespread ridicule.

2004 9/11 Commission documents government's failure to "connect the dots" and respond to intelligence warnings before the attacks. . . . Spain-based jihadists bomb Madrid commuter trains, killing 191.

2005 British-based jihadists bomb London subway and bus system, killing 52.

2006 FBI charge seven men in Miami's Liberty City neighborhood, with conspiracy to destroy Chicago's Sears Tower and other targets. . . . British charge alleged jihadists with plotting to detonate liquid bombs on airliners.

2007 First trial of Miami terrorism defendants ends in mistrial; one defendant is acquitted.

2008 Padilla is sentenced to 17 years. . . . Five Muslim immigrants convicted of plot to kill U.S. soldiers at Fort Dix, N.J. . . . Terrorist assault in Mumbai, India, kills 173, alarms U.S. officials.

2009 Osama bin Laden predicts continuing economic meltdown in U.S. . . . President Barack Obama orders continued rocket and missile attacks on al Qaeda sites in Pakistan. . . . Obama weighs merging homeland security and national security councils.

Commission Warns of Bioterrorism Threat

But skeptic says terrorist groups don't have the know-how.

Immediately after the Sept. 11, 2001, attacks, U.S. intelligence operatives and officials who'd been tracking the al Qaeda terrorist group for years didn't doubt for a second. "I knew immediately this was [Osama] bin Laden," former CIA Director George J. Tenet told CBS News six years later. "There was no doubt what had happened." But no such certainty accompanied a deadly anthrax attack that was launched soon after 9/11.[1]

Arguably, it posed an even scarier future than the 9/11 attacks. Finding unknown enemies is far tougher than tracking down foes who, ultimately, announce themselves, as bin Laden eventually did.

And stopping the spread of a disease or infection poses a bigger challenge than looking for survivors of a bombing. For one thing, no cures exist yet for some disease agents, including the Ebola virus. Nevertheless, the extent to which terrorists are capable of deploying bioweapons is a subject of sharp debate.[2]

Controversy also surrounds the 2001 anthrax case. The government's only suspect killed himself last year without leaving a confession, but FBI officials say they're confident that Bruce E. Ivins, a career microbiologist at the U.S. Army's biodefense laboratory at Fort Detrick, Md., mailed the envelopes filled with powdered anthrax spores that killed five people and sickened 17 others in September and October of 2001.

But before announcing that conclusion, the FBI had spent years building a case against Mark Hatfill, another

Fort Detrick scientist. And officials concede that the evidence concerning Ivins isn't absolutely conclusive.

Far from it, some independent scientists say. Microbiologist Richard O. Spertzel told *The New York Times* last year he's unpersuaded that Ivins had transformed anthrax spores into a weapon by drying them. But if he did, Spertzel said, and "an individual can make that kind of product, just by drying it, we are in deep trouble as a nation and a world."[3]

Independently, a congressional panel announced in late 2008 that trouble looms. "Unless the world community acts decisively and with great urgency, it is more likely than not that a weapon of mass destruction will be used in a terrorist attack somewhere in the world by the end of 2013," said the Commission on the Prevention of Weapons of Mass Destruction Proliferation and Terrorism. "The Commission further believes that terrorists are more likely to be able to obtain and use a biological weapon than a nuclear weapon."[4]

While the commission conceded that highly specialized knowledge and equipment would be indispensable to mount a bioattack, it noted that trained biologists are relatively numerous. "Terrorists are trying to upgrade their capabilities and could do so by recruiting skilled scientists," the commission said.[5]

Meanwhile, the Government Accountability Office (GAO) reported in late 2008 that security is sub-par at two of the five U.S. laboratories authorized to handle deadly

Privacy Act — the FBI reported that it had been closing in on another Fort Detrick scientist, Bruce E. Ivins. Aware that arrest was imminent, Ivins committed suicide.[49]

FBI officials say circumstantial and scientific evidence make Ivins's guilt clear. Some of his colleagues and other scientists dispute that conclusion. And officials concede the absence of definitive proof.[50]

Homeland Security

With expectations of new attacks running high after 9/11, President Bush created a presidential office of homeland security nine days after the attacks. Some Democratic lawmakers, and even some of his own

Cabinet members, argued for a new agency dedicated to ensuring domestic security. But Bush, who portrayed himself as a small-government conservative, resisted the idea. A crisis, however severe, shouldn't automatically prompt major government expansion, he held.[51]

Bush chose Pennsylvania Gov. Tom Ridge, a Republican, to coordinate the work of 40 government agencies with counter-terrorism responsibilities. They included the FBI, Central Intelligence Agency and Centers for Disease Control and Prevention as well as the Federal Aviation Administration (FAA).

But nine months later, events forced a new, more radical approach. Minnesota FBI agent Colleen Rowley pathogens, the WMD commission said. The two insecure facilities were at Georgia State University in Atlanta and the Southwest Foundation for Biomedical Research in San Antonio, Texas.[6]

No one questions that advanced science can provide lethal weapons to people who want to wreak death and destruction. But it's not as clear that a biological assault on the United States looms in the near future.

Milton Leitenberg, senior research scholar at the University of Maryland's Center for International and Security Studies, cites evidence that terrorist groups lag far behind the scientific curve. Pointing to the 2001 anthrax attack, Leitenberg asked a recent conference held by the Cato Institute think tank, "What does this have to do with what a terrorist group could do, and how soon they could do that?" Answering his own question, he replied, "Next to nothing. What we've found so far is that those people have been abysmally ignorant of how to read the technical, professional literature. What is on jihadi Web sites comes from American poisoners' handbooks sold here at gun shows, which can't make anything. What it would make is just garbage."

He reached that conclusion following an exhaustive study of the evidence left by al Qaeda operatives in Afghanistan — the same evidence that some experts have cited as a sign of the growing danger of a biological weapon attack. In a study published by the U.S. Army War College, Leitenberg said the evidence shows, in fact, that U.S. officials' public voicing of alarm at terrorists armed with bioweapons prompted al Qaeda's interest in the first place.

Computer disks with writings by Ayman al-Zawahiri, al Qaeda's second-in-command, show him remarking that "the enemy drew our attention to" the possibility of deploying bioweapons. Leitenberg traces the source to a 1997 press conference by then-Defense Secretary William S. Cohen, who held up a five-pound bag of sugar to show how small a quantity of anthrax spores it would take to cause mass fatalities.

"An edifice of institutes, programs, conferences and publicists has grown up which continue the exaggeration and scare-mongering," Leitenberg wrote. "This persistent exaggeration is not benign: It is almost certainly the single greatest factor in provoking interest in BW [biological warfare] among terrorist groups."[7]

Bioweapons could become a menace in the future, Leitenberg told the conference. But for the foreseeable future, naturally occurring epidemics pose a far bigger danger. HIV, tuberculosis and malaria kill 5 million people a year, he said. And bioterrorism? "Zero."

[1] Quoted in Daniel Schorn, "George Tenet: At the Center of the Storm," CBS News, April 27, 2007, www.cbsnews.com/stories/2007/04/25/60minutes/main2728375_page2.shtml.

[2] See "World at Risk: The Report of the Commission on the Prevention of WMD Proliferation and Terrorism," December 2006, p. 3, www.preventwmd.gov/report/.

[3] Quoted in Eric Lichtblau and Nicholas Wade, "F.B.I. Details Anthrax Case, But Doubts Remain," *The New York Times*, Aug. 18, 2008, www.nytimes.com/2008/08/19/us/19anthrax.html?pagewanted=all.

[4] See "World at Risk," *op. cit.*, pp. xv, 74-75.

[5] *Ibid.*, p. 11.

[6] *Ibid.*, pp. 3-4. For the GAO report, see "Biosafety Laboratories: Perimeter Security Assessment of the Nation's Five BSL-4 Laboratories," Government Accountability Office, September 2008, www.gao.gov/new.items/d081092.pdf.

[7] See Milton Leitenberg, "Assessing the Biological Weapons and Bioterrorism Threat: U.S. Army War College, December 2005, pp. 35, 89, www.cissm.umd.edu/papers/files/assessing_bw_threat.pdf.

told the Senate Judiciary Committee that her bosses had responded lackadaisically to her urgent requests — shortly before Sept. 11 — for a warrant to search the computer of Zacarias Moussaoui, whom she suspected of training to fly a hijacked plane.

Bush concluded that the explosive testimony would renew calls to create a new department that wouldn't fail to connect the dots next time. The administration's Homeland Security Department bill proposed unifying 22 government agencies, but not including the two of the most critical counterterrorism organizations — the FBI and CIA (nor the National Security Agency, which monitors communications). Administration officials argued that their front-line work shouldn't be slowed by reorganization tasks.

If the criteria for inclusion in the new department seemed unclear, so did its very mission. Ridge, who was quickly confirmed as the department's first director, contributed to the confusion when he announced in 2003 that the department's duties would include hunting down sexual predators who operated through the Web.

The connection to counterterrorism seemed distant, at best. But the episode reflected senior officials' belief that the post-Sept. 11 sense of emergency that gave rise to the department wouldn't last.

Critics Question Constant Terrorism Warnings

Security expert dismisses airport screening as "Security theater."

When Americans go to the airport, they might as well be going to a Broadway show, says security expert and skeptic Bruce Schneier. To describe the protective measures Americans encounter all too often, he coined the term "security theater" — "security primarily designed to make us feel safer, but not actually safer."

His prime example: airport security searches.

"Banning box cutters since 9/11, or taking off our shoes since ["shoe bomber"] Richard Reid, has not made us any safer," he wrote two years ago on his influential blog. "And a long-term prohibition against liquid carry-ons won't make us safer, either. It's not just that there are ways around the rules, it's that focusing on tactics is a losing proposition. It's easy to defend against what the terrorists planned last time, but it's shortsighted. If we spend billions fielding liquid-analysis machines in airports, and the terrorists use solid explosives, we've wasted our money."[1]

The founder of a computer-security company and now chief technology security officer of BT (British Telecom), Schneier writes and speaks in bolder tones than most others in the field. But some of his arguments are gaining ground.

Donald F. Kettl, a University of Pennsylvania political scientist and homeland security specialist, notes that widespread ridicule of airport screening — he calls it "screening theater" — reflects its low level of credibility.

Kettl acknowledges, however, that insiders have told him the security system did prevent some terrorist incidents — a point suggested by Transportation Security Administration Director Kip Hawley.

Nonetheless, what the public sees of security measures has done little to inspire confidence — even when confidence might be warranted — critics say.

The ridicule ended a Homeland Security Department effort to extend security beyond airports and elsewhere, Kettl notes. Gov. Tom Ridge, R-Pa., the first Homeland Security secretary, had suggested in 2003 that citizens stock up on duct tape and other supplies in case of disaster. "It created enormous amounts of laughter, but it was basic advice about how to prepare," Kettl says. "In some ways, it was not bad advice."

Still, in a climate dominated by warnings of imminent terrorist strikes, Ridge's small-scale advice to everyday citizens seemed mostly to inspire late-night TV comedians.

Paradoxically, critics say, government warnings may exaggerate terrorists' power. The vast size of the United States makes a tiny enemy such as al Qaeda incapable of inflicting death and destruction on a national scale, many experts note. But trying to stop attacks nationwide can wind up causing more damage than the strike itself, says John Mueller, an Ohio State University political scientist who argues that the government has exaggerated the extent of danger from terrorism. "Fear is costly in terms of overreaction expenditures like the war in Iraq," he says.

Other critics say the stoking of fear has left citizens feeling there is little they can do if disaster does strike. "Washington has been sounding the alarm about apocalyptic terrorist groups while providing the American people with no meaningful guidance on how to deal with the threats they pose or the consequences of a successful attack," wrote Stephen E. Flynn,

Indeed, other non-terrorism-related missions were built into the new agency. The inclusion of the Border Patrol and the Immigration and Naturalization Service (now Immigration and Customs Enforcement) meant considerable focus on illegal immigration. And with FEMA now included in the new department, Homeland Security was also responsible for natural disaster response — a responsibility that became a handicap, as the botched response to Hurricane Katrina demonstrated in 2005.

The Katrina disaster validated a 2003 Congressional Research Service report. Homeland Security's color-coded "threat level" indicator was one of eight separate disaster warning systems, the CRS noted, for catastrophes including severe weather, chemical and biological contamination from government stockpiles and presidential alerts. All of the systems operated independently.

And the department's notifications to state and local officials about threat-level changes followed a a senior counterterrorism fellow at the Council on Foreign Relations think tank and former Coast Guard officer.[2]

Given the impossibility of guaranteeing there will be no attacks in a nation as big as the United States, Flynn says, citizen helplessness is especially troubling in a society that has grown dependent on instantly available goods and services.

"The United States is becoming a brittle nation," Flynn wrote. "An increasingly urbanized and suburbanized population has embraced just-in-time lifestyles tethered to ATM machines and 24-hour stores that provide instant access to cash, food and gas. When the power goes out and these modern conveniences fail, Americans are incapacitated. Meanwhile, two decades of taxpayer rebellion have stripped away the means necessary for government workers to provide help during emergencies."[3]

In addition, Flynn told a recent security conference, the federal government's capabilities have also eroded. He cited a program to issue machine-readable credentials, after background investigations, to 1.5 million workers at U.S. ports. The card is being issued, but scanning machines aren't available yet, Flynn said. The Transportation Security Administration is scheduling card-reader tests for early 2009.[4]

A program involving truck drivers, who are among the port workers required to carry the cards, won rare praise from

A traveler at Chicago's O'Hare Airport dons disposable booties after taking off her shoes for a security check.

Schneier. Highway Watch was a 2005 Homeland Security project to train truckers to look for dangerous or suspicious activities or conditions. "This program has a lot of features I like in security systems: It's dynamic . . . it relies on trained people paying attention and it's not focused on a specific threat," Schneier wrote.[5]

But the program didn't survive. "The U.S. Department of Homeland Security has elected to fund another trucking security program," says an undated announcement on the program's Web site. "We will continuously provide updates on this site as to the future of the program as developments occur."[6]

[1] See Bruce Schneier, "Last Week's Terrorism Arrests," "Schneier on Security" blog, Aug. 13, 2006, www.schneier.com/blog/archives/2006/08/terrorism_ secur.html.

[2] See Stephen E. Flynn, "America the Resilient: Defying Terrorism and Mitigating Natural Disasters," *Foreign Affairs*, March-April, 2008, www.foreignaffairs.org/20080301faessay87201-p0/stephen-e-flynn/america-the-resilient.html.

[3] *Ibid.*

[4] "TWIC Pilot Test," Transportation Security Administration, undated, www.tsa.dhs.gov/what_we_do/layers/twic/pilot_test.shtm.

[5] "Truckers Watching the Highway," Schneier blog, *op. cit.*, Dec. 8, 2005, www.schneier.com/blog/archives/2005/12/truckers_watchi.html.

[6] "Highway Watch," Homeland Security Department, undated, www.highwaywatch.com.

mid-20th-century tempo. The police chief in Portland, Maine, for example, told congressional researchers he'd learn of changes from CNN eight hours before hearing from the agency.

The exclusion of the FBI and CIA aroused considerable criticism when the Bush administration and lawmakers were hammering out the legislation creating the department. "I am concerned that this is a damage-control document that was more designed to divert the nation's

focus from the problems at the CIA and FBI than intelligently reorganize our security bureaus," Rep. John Conyers Jr., D-Mich., said in June 2002.[52]

But many security professionals argued that integrating foreign intelligence and domestic counterterrorism into one agency would be a mistake — as would separating counterterrorism from law enforcement. "There is a real benefit to keeping the counterterrorism and domestic spying aspects housed in an agency that understands what it means to operate within the rule of law," an anonymous official told *The Washington Post.*[53]

CURRENT SITUATION

Testing Time

President Obama is spending his early days in office under the shadow of expectations that terrorists will test him in the near future. "Presidents Bill Clinton and George W. Bush and U.K. Prime Minister Gordon Brown share at least one sobering experience: Each saw a major domestic terrorist attack by al Qaeda and its allies during his first year in office," two think tanks closely tied to the new administration reported last year in drawing up domestic security advice.[54]

The Center for American Progress Action Fund and Third Way, a new think tank, issued that reminder in the course of advising the new president to streamline the domestic security decision-making process.

The 1993 World Trade Center bombing occurred about a month after Clinton took office. Bush had been president only nine months when the 9/11 attackers struck. And Brown had been prime minister for four weeks when a small group of immigrant doctors from the Middle East and an engineer from India tried to detonate home-made car bombs in London and Glasgow in June 2007.[55]

Once terrorists strike, no one in the White House would have time to refine organizational structure, the think tanks said, arguing that Obama should fold his domestic counterterrorism staff into the National Security Council (NSC), which traditionally deals with foreign policy matters. "Homeland security should not be viewed as distinct from national security," they said. "In today's globalized world . . . it is difficult to envision where homeland security ends and national security begins."

Some caution that the focus on the jihadist threat may lead to neglect of danger close to home — far-right extremists enraged by an African-American in the White House. Mark Potok, an expert on hate groups at the Southern Poverty Law Center, says that Obama's election electrified the white-supremacist movement. "Two of the larger groups had their servers crash as a result of all the traffic they got," says Potok, director of the group's Intelligence Project. "Will that translate into actual new members? It certainly could."

New membership wouldn't guarantee violence, though the possibility would increase. Fred Burton, a former State Department counterterrorism director, questions whether the FBI and other law-enforcement agencies have kept up their monitoring of the far right. "I see that as a challenge," he says. "Historically, the FBI has not been very nimble in shifts of emphasis." Burton is vice president for counterterrorism and corporate security at Stratfor, a consulting and analysis firm in Austin, Texas.

Still, the overwhelming focus for terrorism experts remains the jihadist movement. The creation of a separate Homeland Security Council may reflect the fears that prevailed at that time of al Qaeda "sleeper cells" that could spring into action at any time.

Obama shows signs of heeding the calls for a new approach. As his top counterterrorism adviser, he appointed an ex-career CIA official with extensive experience abroad. John O. Brennan was chief of staff to then-CIA Director George J. Tenet in 1999-2001 and head of the National Counterterrorism Center in 2004-2005, having served previously as the agency's station chief in Saudi Arabia.

White House staffers told reporters that Obama hadn't yet decided whether to merge the president's domestic security and national security staffs, which would be a departure from the setup under the Bush administration. But during the administration's first weeks, all indications were that the merger would be ordered. Even some Bush administration veterans endorsed the plan.

C. Stewart Verdery, a former deputy Homeland Security secretary under Bush, said his department had found getting attention from NSC difficult. "You want your issues considered," he told *The New York Times.* "You don't want to be off in some second bucket."[56]

Bush's last Homeland Security director, Kenneth Wainstein, conceded shortly before Bush left office that the logic behind the operation he had supervised was open to question. "When you look at the organization chart, you see it's not the cleanest org chart around," he told a Washington think tank recently.[57]

Not all Bush officials approve of the merger idea, however. His national security adviser, Stephen J. Hadley, reportedly has advised his successors against the plan, on the grounds that it would lessen attention to some important matters.[58]

For Hadley, in particular, the issue cuts deep, especially in the context of a brand-new administration. As deputy national security adviser before 9/11, he and his then-boss,

Is the chance of a nuclear terrorist attack virtually nonexistent?

YES — John Mueller
Political Science Professor,
Ohio State University

Excerpted from Cato Institute conference presentation, Jan. 12, 2009

The chances of a terrorist group getting nuclear weapons are almost vanishingly small. You're a terrorist, OK, and you have to find highly enriched uranium. The scientist working for you may be incompetent. You're going to have to use criminals to get it out of the country. You're probably going to have to kill them once they've done what they've done. They may think of that and decide not to cooperate.

Building the bomb is difficult; you have to get the precise blueprints and a lot of expensive equipment. And you have to get scientists and engineers who are willing to give up their lives for the project, because there's going to be an international effort to try to find them after the bomb is discovered or blown up.

Then you have to get it across an international border and get it to Times Square. You have to find somebody in the country who is technologically capable of getting it to the goal and then setting it off.

People say it would be difficult but not impossible. I agree. Leaning very heavily in favor of the terrorists, difficult but not impossible means one chance in three of being successful [or] about one chance in three-and-a-half billion. I'm willing to say I'm off by factor of 1,000 — so, one chance in three-and-a-half million. You're putting everything, including your life, at stake for a gamble of one-in-three-and-a-half million.

An atomic bomb going off in [Washington, D.C.] would be a horrific disaster. Therefore, even if the probability is very low you still have to worry about it. The question is, how low does a probability have to get before you stop worrying about it?

We don't get along all that well with the Russians. They could easily kill 40 million to 50 million Americans if they worked at it, and we don't worry about that. It must be that the probability even of that horrific catastrophe has gotten so low that it has passed out of our consideration.

Al Qaeda is the only terrorist group that seems to want to attack the United States. It's about 150 people running around Afghanistan and Pakistan. Then there's the leaderless jihadis who are connecting on the Internet. The idea that these guys could make a nuclear weapon — come on. They can't even figure out each others' chatroom codes half the time.

NO — Jim Walsh
Senior Research Associate, Security Studies
Program, Massachusetts Institute of
Technology

Excerpted from Cato Institute conference presentation, Jan. 12, 2009

I think it's somewhere between nearly impossible and inevitable that there will be a nuclear terrorist attack. We're working in a world of uncertainty. This is a classic, low-probability, high-consequence event.

How much risk can we tolerate? I find John's statistical estimate of the likelihood of a nuclear attack unpersuasive. If I got up before 9/11 and said, there are 20 obstacles to carrying out [an attack] — what happens if they went and said they wanted to learn how to fly a plane but not land it, certainly they would be caught, and so on. I could have made it sound highly improbable. Is it one chance in a hundred?

What if I went to the Environmental Protection Agency or the Food and Drug Administration and said there's a one-in-one-hundred chance that this chemical is going to kill you. You think they'd allow it? I don't think so.

John thinks that we'll notice when uranium is missing. I doubt that if we don't have a baseline inventory that tells us how much uranium there is. He says non-state actors can't get detailed blueprints needed for bomb construction. The International Atomic Energy Agency says those blueprints are still floating around. I do worry about countries that have nuclear weapons today. And I think we should worry about them as much as we worry about those that might get them in the future.

The other question to be addressed is, what action should we take? John's argument is, the probability is low so we don't have to worry about it. I think it's odd to say we should wait until the terrorists have more capability before we do something. Better to do something now, when the risk is low and we have the time to be successful. The paradox is that for all the alarmism, we haven't done much about the problem. We have moved ever so modestly to lock down nuclear materials.

I think most terrorists are not interested in nuclear weapons. I'm underwhelmed by al Qaeda's technical capability. John's implicit notion is that al Qaeda is the only possible candidate for nuclear terrorism. I worry about al Qaeda 4.0 — kids in Europe who go to good schools 20 years from now or types of terrorists we don't even imagine. In the 1970s we thought it was all ideological — we did not see the terrorists that we have today.

Video and podcasts of the conference are accessible at: http://cato.org/events/counterterrorism/index.html.

A canine officer patrols San Francisco International Airport on July 3, 2007, the start of the Independence Day holiday. Creation of the Department of Homeland Security after the 9/11 attacks, along with stepped up airport security, reflected officials' near-certainty that further terrorist strikes were imminent.

National Security Adviser Condoleezza Rice, had failed to take effective action on a drumbeat of intelligence reports that a spectacular attack appeared imminent. "Hadley told us that before 9/11, he and Rice did not feel they had the job of coordinating domestic agencies," the 9/11 commission reported in 2004. "There was a clear disparity in the levels of response to foreign versus domestic threats. . . . Far less was done domestically."[59]

Back to Court

As the Obama administration was getting under way, federal prosecutors in Miami were starting up the third trial of a group of Miami men whom the government has depicted as terrorists in training. Jury selection began in late January.

The "Liberty City Six," named for the impoverished African-American district where the defendants lived, had seen two previous attempts to send them to prison end in mistrials. One of their codefendants was acquitted in 2007, at the group's first trial.

Jurors and defense lawyers have belittled the government's determination to win convictions on charges of conspiring to provide material support to a foreign terrorist organization — al Qaeda — and to destroy Chicago's Sears Tower and other buildings. The group of penniless construction workers did have a leader who had talked of jihad to a government

informant who was wired for recording. But they had no explosives, no connection to al Qaeda and no weapons beyond a samurai sword. "There was really nothing that indicated that this was a real threat," Jeffrey Agron, jury foreman at the first trial, told *The New York Times*.[60]

The Miami trial is the last of a series of terrorism-related cases brought by the Justice Department under the Bush administration, with mixed results. As with the Liberty City group, initial charges tended to be announced in the gravest terms. Attorney General Alberto Gonzales said in announcing indictments against the men in 2006 that they were "homegrown terrorists." He also conceded that they "posed no immediate threat."[61]

Gonzales's predecessor, John Ashcroft, set the standard for such announcements. In the middle of a 2002 trip to Russia, the then-attorney general said that authorities had arrested Brooklyn-born Jose Padilla, designating him an "enemy combatant," on charges that he was plotting with al Qaeda to detonate a radiological "dirty bomb" in the United States.[62]

After nearly five years of litigation concerning the limits of presidential power to order an American citizen indefinitely detained, the Justice Department backed down from its position before the case reached the Supreme Court. Prosecutors then charged him in civilian court, dropping the "dirty bomb" allegation because it was based on interrogation evidence that wouldn't have been admissible in court. He was convicted of conspiracy and support for terrorism and sentenced in 2008 to 17 years in prison — though prosecutors had argued for a life sentence.[63]

Sentencing is scheduled later this year for five Muslim immigrants who were convicted in December 2008 of planning to kill soldiers at Fort Dix, N.J. The convicted men, all longtime residents of the United States with no military training, had tried to buy assault weapons and had spoken about jihad to a government informant. Their lawyers said the men, mostly in their 20s, hadn't been serious, though they had practiced at a firing range.[64]

"The word should go out to any other would-be terrorists of the homegrown variety that the United States will find you, infiltrate your group, prosecute you and send you to prison for a very long time," Ralph J. Marra Jr., the acting U.S. attorney for New Jersey, said after the men were convicted.[65]

As Marra suggested, and as Miami's Liberty City case also shows, the Justice Department aggressively deployed informants to gather evidence against young men who spoke of mounting attacks.

A trial outcome elsewhere in the country may also have encouraged Miami prosecutors to pursue a third trial in the Liberty City case. In November 2008, federal prosecutors in Dallas won convictions in a second trial against five directors of a Muslim charity, the Holy Land Foundation for Relief and Development. The men were found guilty of channeling millions of dollars to Hamas, the Palestinian organization that governs the Gaza Strip and that the United States classifies as a terrorist group. Sentencing is pending.[66]

For supporters of the Bush administration approach, the overall results will discourage would-be jihadists in the United States. "It is a very aggressive counterterrorism effort, and it seems to be working," James Lewis, a senior fellow at the Center for Strategic and International Studies, told the *Los Angeles Times*.[67]

Critics charge, though, that the administration hyped small-fry braggarts into deadly jihadists. In the Liberty City trials, said Bruce Winick, a University of Miami law professor who has been following the case, "A government informant got a bunch of guys together to swear a loyalty oath to al Qaeda. It's [a] B-movie, really, more than a criminal case."[68]

OUTLOOK
The Next Generation

Whatever else Osama bin Laden did to the United States, he altered the perspective of the political and governing class. The number of books, reports and conferences on terrorism and America's vulnerabilities seems to remain on the increase.

To some extent, of course, the rate of publication and of conference-holding has been accelerated in 2008 and early 2009 by the coming to power of a new president, and the possibility that al Qaeda would want to greet him with a major attack of some kind.

But during the first weeks, at least, of the Obama administration, no terrorist strike had occurred.

For some terrorism experts, the absence of attacks following 9/11 — despite nearly universal predictions — served as a lesson. "I was clearly wrong," says Byman at Georgetown University's Security Studies Program.

Heavy pressure on al Qaeda in its Pakistani redoubt is the main force working against its undoubted desire to mount a sequel to the 2001 attacks.

"It's difficult for them to do sophisticated long-term attacks," Byman says. "So local resources are important. In Europe, where they have local resources, they hit." Small groups of al Qaeda wannabes might conceivably make attempts in the United States, he acknowledges. "They can certainly kill, but I would be surprised if they could pull off anything on the scale of al Qaeda."

Whatever bin Laden's organization may have gained in global notoriety, and — in some circles — prestige, as a result of 9/11, that recognition also brought the continuing U.S. counterattack that lately has taken the form of deadly airstrikes in Pakistan. And the battle-hardened, lifelong jihadists who formed the core of the group are no longer as numerous, leaving a new wave of young, European Muslims from immigrant families who can be more easily dealt with, says ex-CIA officer Sageman, a psychiatrist by training.

"Our main goal should be the prevention of radicalization of the next generation — to take the glory out of terrorism," he told the Cato conference in January. "That's the main reason people want to become terrorists. It's to become like the Terminator. If you look at the transcripts of what they talk about when we bug their apartments, they talk about the Terminator, about Rambo" — the movie action heroes.

Ways to lessen the alienation that puts young Muslims in a Terminator frame of mind would be a smaller U.S. presence in the Middle East, Sageman said. That reasoning is consistent with Obama's vow to pull out of Iraq, to promote Israel-Palestinian peace and to build friendlier relations with the Muslim world in general.

Some others in the counterterrorism world speak in similar terms. Cressey, the Clinton-era National Security Council veteran, says, "After you've eliminated the core that has the terrorist capability, how do you ensure over the long term that fewer people are interested in choosing terrorism to express their grievances? That's the challenge for the Obama administration, one that he understands."

Even so, some who've examined U.S. vulnerabilities observe that bin Laden's recent threat amounted to more than violence, however terrifying that violence was. In the pre-inauguration message, bin Laden gloried in the U.S. economic meltdown. "This talk about weakness and recession of the American ascendancy as well as the collapse of its economy, is not a talk of hopes, but testimonies given by leaders themselves which they couldn't conceal any longer," bin Laden said in his Jan. 15 recording.[69]

Roemer, the former member of the 9/11 and WMD commissions, implicitly acknowledges that bin Laden's analysis was grounded in reality. "A decade from now, will our greatest threat be something that al Qaeda has done to us, or something that we've done to ourselves?" Roemer asks. "Will it be an al Qaeda attack on one of our cities, or our failure to have addressed a 51 percent dropout rate in inner-city schools or investing in and protecting the energy grid?"

Bin Laden, Roemer says, knows how to exploit his enemy's responses. "He has an economic strategy — bleed America, make us spend money on wars. He can win by bleeding us to death economically, in effect having us do to ourselves what he couldn't do. We can't allow that. Our economic security priority has to be elevated, and the fear card cannot be played."

NOTES

1. Extensive media coverage of the attacks includes Eric Schmitt, Somini Sengupta and Jane Perlez, "U.S. and India See Link to Militants in Pakistan," *The New York Times*, Dec. 2, 2008, www.nytimes.com/2008/12/03/world/asia/03 mumbai.html?scp=105&sq=mumbaiattack&st=cse. Also see K. Alan Kronstadt, "Terrorist Attacks in Mumbai, India, and Implications for U.S. Interests," Congressional Research Service, Dec. 19, 2008, www.fas.org/sgp/crs/terror/R40087.pdf.

2. *Ibid.* Also see "Lashkar-e-Taiba denies role in Mumbai attacks," Reuters, Nov. 27, 2008, http://in.reuters.com/article/topNews/idINIndia-36740420081127.

3. See "World at Risk: The Report of the Commission on the Prevention of WMD Proliferation and Terrorism," December 2006, pp. xv-xxii, 74-75, www.preventwmd.gov/report/.

4. See "English Translation of Osama bin Laden's 'Call for Jihad to Stop Aggression Against Gaza,' " Worldanalysis.net, Jan. 15, 2009, http://worldanalysis.net/modules/article/view.article.php?129/c40.

5. See "Senate Armed Services Committee Holds Hearing on Challenges Facing the Defense Department," *CQ Congressional Transcripts*, Jan. 27, 2009.

6. For background, see Peter Katel, "Global Jihad," *CQ Researcher*, Oct. 14, 2005, pp. 857-880.

7. See Peter Bergen, "Safe at Home," *The New York Times*, Dec. 14, 2008, p. W10.

8. Mueller's book is *Overblown: How Politicians and the Terrorism Industry Inflate National Security Threats and Why We Believe Them* (2006).

9. Jeffrey Goldberg, "The Things He Carried," *The Atlantic*, November 2008, www.theatlantic.com/doc/200811/airport-security.

10. Bruce Schneier, "Interview with Kip Hawley," blog, July 30, 2007, www.schneier.com/ interview-hawley.html.

11. Bruce Riedel, "Terrorism in India and the Global Jihad," Brookings Institution, Nov. 30, 2008, www.brookings.edu/articles/2008/1130_india_terrorism_riedel.aspx.

12. Bruce Riedel, *The Search for Al Qaeda: Its Leadership, Ideology, and Future* (2008).

13. Quoted in " 'A Nightmare We Cannot Afford in the 21st Century,' " *Spiegel Online International*, Dec. 8, 2008, www.spiegel.de/international/world/0,1518,595148,00.html.

14. "Senate Homeland Security and Governmental Affairs Committee Holds Hearing on 'Lessons From the Mumbai Terrorist Attacks," *CQ Transcripts*, Jan. 28, 2009.

15. Passengers on the fourth hijacked plane thwarted the attack on Washington when they learned via cell phones about the other attacks and forced the plane down in Shanksville, Pa.

16. "Senate Armed Services Committee. . . .," *op. cit.*

17. Janet Stobart and Sebastian Rotella, "3 in Britain convicted of conspiracy," *Los Angeles Times*, Sept. 9, 2008, p. A3; John F. Burns and Elaine Sciolino, "No One Convicted of Terror Plot to Bomb Planes," *The New York Times*, Sept. 9, 2008, p. A1.

18. *Ibid.*

19. "CIA Director Hayden — State of al Qaeda Today," Atlantic Council of the United States, Nov. 13, 2008, www.acus.org/event_blog/cia-director-event.

20. "Senate Homeland Security . . . Mumbai Attacks," *op. cit.*

21. Donald F. Kettl, *System Under Stress: Homeland Security and American Politics* (2007).

22. The 9/11 Commission Report," National Commission on Terrorist Attacks Upon the United States (2004), p. 408, www.9-11commission.gov/report/911Report.pdf.

23. *Ibid.* For background see Pamela M. Prah, "Disaster Preparedness," *CQ Researcher*, Nov. 18, 2005, pp. 981-1004.

24. Amy Gardner, "9 Muslim Passengers Removed From Jet," *The Washington Post*, Jan. 2, 2009, p. B1, and Cynthia Dizikes, "Muslim families are taken off flight," *Los Angeles Times*, Jan. 3, 2009, p. A10.

25. "Bush Remarks on Security at U.S. Army War College," America.gov, Dec. 17, 2008, www.america .gov/st/texttrans-english/2008/December/2008 1217171510xjsnommis0.0446741.html.

26. *Ibid.* Also see Tom Gjelten, "U.S. Officials: Al-Qaida Leadership Cadre 'Decimated,' " National Public Radio, Feb. 3, 2009, www.npr.org/templates/story/story.php?storyId=100195353.

27. "Face the Nation," CBS News, Jan. 4, 2009, www .cbsnews.com/htdocs/pdf/FTN_010409.pdf.

28. "House Armed Services Committee Holds Hearing on Preventing Weapons of Mass Destruction and Terrorism," *CQ Transcripts*, Jan. 22, 2009. For background, see Pamela M. Prah, "Port Security," *CQ Researcher*, April 21, 2006, pp. 385-408.

29. Solomon Moore, "Border Proves No Obstacle for Mexican Cartels," *The New York Times*, Feb. 2, 2009, p. A1.

30. Quoted in Sasha Issenberg, "Slaying gave US a first taste of Mideast terror," *The Boston Globe*, June 5, 2008, www.boston.com/news/nation/washington/articles/2008/06/05/slaying_gave_us_a_first_taste_of_mideast_terror/?page=full.

31. Unless otherwise indicated, material in this subsection is drawn from Timothy Naftali, *Blind Spot: The Secret History of American Counterterrorism* (2005), pp. 35-41.

32. Matthew Davis, "Athens 2004 remembers Munich 1972," BBC News, Aug. 20, 2004, http://news.bbc .co.uk/2/hi/europe/3581866.stm.

33. Naftali, *op. cit.*, pp. 68-73.

34. *Ibid.*, pp. 130-135. For background, see Peter Katel, "Middle East Tensions," *CQ Researcher*, Oct. 27, 2006, pp. 889-912. Riedel, *The Search for Al Qaeda*, *op. cit.*, pp. 16-21.

36. Naftali, *op. cit.*, pp. 231-234.

37. Benjamin Weiser, "Mastermind Gets Life for Bombing of Trade Center," *The New York Times*, Jan. 9, 1998, p. A1; John J. Goldman, "2 Found Guilty in Bombing of Trade Center," *Los Angeles Times*, Nov. 13, 1997, p. A1.

38. Joseph P. Fried, "Sheik Sentenced to Life in Prison in Bombing Plot," *The New York Times*, Jan. 18, 1996, p. A1.

39. "Defiant McVeigh dies in silence," BBC News, June 11, 2001, http://news.bbc.co.uk/1/hi/world/americas/1382602.stm.

40. Tom Morganthau, "The View From the Far Right," *Newsweek*, May 1, 1995, www.newsweek.com/id/103757/page/1.

41. James Sterngold, "Supremacist Who Killed Postal Worker Avoids Death Sentence," *The New York Times*, Jan. 24, 2001, http://query. nytimes.com/gst/fullpage.html?res=9F0CEED61E3CF937A15752C0A9679C8B63.

42. "Report of the Accountability Review Boards on the Embassy Bombings in Nairobi and Dar es Salaam on Aug. 7, 1998," www.state.gov/www/regions/africa/accountability_report.html.

43. Unless otherwise indicated, material in this subsection is drawn from the 9/11 Commission report, *op. cit.*, p. 134, www.9-11commission.gov/report/911Report.pdf.

44. Quoted in Bruce Maxwell, *Homeland Security: A Documentary History* (2004), p. 182. For full report, see Rex A. Hudson, *The Sociology and Psychology of Terrorism: Who Becomes a Terrorist and Why?* (September 1999), Library of Congress, www.loc .gov/rr/frd/pdf-files/Soc_Psych_of_Terrorism.pdf.

45. *Ibid.*

46. Ronald Brownstein, "Terror Warnings Offer Cautionary Tale," *Los Angeles Times*, May 23, 2002, p. A10.

47. Quoted in *ibid.*

48. Pam Belluck, "Unrepentant Shoe Bomber Is Given a Life Sentence For Trying to Blow Up Jet," *The New York Times*, Jan. 31, 2003.

49. Scott Shane and Eric Lichtblau, "Scientist's Suicide Linked to Anthrax Inquiry," *The New York Times*, Aug. 2, 2008, www.nytimes.com/2008/08/02/washington/02anthrax.html?scp=1&sq="BruceIvins"anthrax&st=cse.

50. Scott Shane, "Portrait Emerges of Anthrax Suspect's Troubled Life," *The New York Times*, Jan. 3, 2009, www.nytimes.com/2009/01/04/us/04anthrax.html?scp=3&sq="BruceIvins"anthrax&st=cse.

51. Unless otherwise indicated, this subsection is drawn from Kettl, *op. cit.*

52. Quoted in Elisabeth Bumiller with Alison Mitchell, "Bush Predicts Turf War in Creation of New Department," *The New York Times*, June 8, 2002, p. A11.

53. Quoted in Jim VandeHei and Dan Eggen, "Hill Eyes Shifting Parts of FBI, CIA," *The Washington Post*, June 13, 2002, p. A1.

54. "Homeland Security Presidential Transition Initiative," Center for American Progress Action Fund, and Third Way, November 2008, p. 1, www.americanprogressaction.org/issues/2008/pdf/homeland_security_transition.pdf.

55. For background on the London-Glasgow bombing attempts, see Sebastian Rotella, "Unusual duo at center of British case," *Los Angeles Times*, July 7, 2007, p. A5. Also see Sarah Glazer, "Radical Islam in Europe," *CQ Global Researcher*, November 2007.

56. Peter Baker, "Obama is Reported Set to Revise Counterterrorism Efforts," *The New York Times*, Jan. 8, 2009, p. A22.

57. Quoted in Eileen Sullivan and Pamela Hess, "Obama plans to overhaul counterterrorism apparatus," The Associated Press, Jan. 8, 2009, www.google.com/hostednews/ap/article/ALeqM5iOLjTMSexoKymgOZO2ed0Q-4PicQD95J469O0.

58. *Ibid.*

59. The 9/11 Commission report, *op. cit.*, p. 263.

60. Damien Cave, "After 2 Mistrials, Prosecutors Try Again to Prove Jihad Plot," *The New York Times*, Jan. 27, 2009, p. A22.

61. Quoted in Scott Shane and Andrea Zarate, "F.B.I. Killed Plot in Talking Stage, A Top Aide Says," *The New York Times*, June 24, 2006, p. A1.

62. Quoted in Dan Eggen and Susan Schmidt, "'Dirty Bomb' Plot Uncovered, U.S. Says," *The Washington Post*, June 11, 2002, p. A1.

63. Peter Woriskey and Dan Eggen, "Judge Sentences Padilla to 17 Years, Cites His Detention," *The Washington Post*, Jan. 23, 2008, p. A1; Carol J. Williams, "Arrested in '02, 'dirty bomb' suspect Padilla to be tried," *Los Angeles Times*, April 16, 2007, p. A8.

64. Julian E. Barnes, "Five in N.J. convicted of plot to kill soldiers," *Los Angeles Times*, Dec. 23, 2008, p. A8.

65. Quoted in *ibid.*

66. Gretel C. Kovach, "Five Convicted in Terrorism Financing Trial," *The New York Times*, Nov. 24, 2008, www.nytimes.com/2008/11/25/us/25charity.html?ref=us.

67. Barnes, *op. cit.*

68. Quoted in Cave, *op. cit.*

69. "English Translation of Osama bin Laden's Call for Jihad. . . .," *op. cit.*

BIBLIOGRAPHY

Books

Ervin, Clark Kent, *Open Target: Where America is Vulnerable to Attack*, Palgrave MacMillan, 2006.
An ex-inspector general of the Department of Homeland Security exposes what he argues are grave deficiencies in the department, as well as their consequences for the country.

Kettl, Donald F., *System Under Stress: Homeland Security and American Politics*, CQ Press, 2007.
The electoral and bureaucratic politics involved in the creation of the Department of Homeland Security are analyzed by a University of Pennsylvania political scientist.

Mueller, John, *Overblown: How Politicians and the Terrorism Industry Inflate National Security Threats, and Why We Believe Them, Free Press,* **2006.**
An Ohio State University political scientist issues a stinging indictment of what he deems to be a chronic exaggeration of terrorism dangers.

Naftali, Timothy, *Blind Spot: The Secret History of American Counterterrorism, Basic Books,* **2005.**
Decades of U.S. anti-terrorism work predating 9/11 are examined by a historian who now directs the National Archives' Richard Nixon Presidential Library and Museum.

Riedel, Bruce, *The Search for Al Qaeda: Its Leadership, Ideology, and Future, Brookings Institution,* **2008.**
A former CIA expert examines al Qaeda's capacity to strike.

Sageman, Marc, *Leaderless Jihad: Terror Networks in the 21st Century, University of Pennsylvania,* **2008.**
A former CIA officer examines the spread of jihadist doctrine beyond the original al Qaeda organization.

Articles

Burton, Fred, and Ben West, "From the New York Landmarks to the Mumbai Attack," *Stratfor,* **Dec. 3, 2008, www.stratfor.com/weekly/20081203_new_york_landmarks_plot_mumbai_attack.**
Intelligence analysts trace the Mumbai attacks to a thwarted 1993 plot to attack sites in New York.

Gorman, Siobhan, and Susan Schmidt, "Officials Worry Attacks in Mumbai Could Spur Copycats in the West," *The Wall Street Journal,* **Dec. 11, 2008, online. wsj.com/article/SB122895354114996367.html.**
Experts worry that the low-tech but deadly assault on Mumbai could appeal to would-be jihadists outside Asia.

Hoffman, Bruce, "The Myth of Grass-Roots Terrorism: Why Osama bin Laden Still Matters," *Foreign Affairs,* **May-June, 2008; and Sageman, Marc, and Bruce Hoffman, "Does Osama Still Call the Shots?"** *Foreign Affairs,* **July-August, 2008.**
Experts debate the future of jihadist terrorism.

Johnson, Carrie, "Bad Economy May Fuel Hate Groups, Experts Warn," *The Washington Post,* **Jan. 11, 2009, p. A4.**

An economic meltdown is a classic stimulus to right-wing extremism — a historical precedent that has terrorism experts on guard.

Johnson, Carrie, and Walter Pincus, "Few Clear Wins in U.S. Anti-Terror Cases," *The Washington Post,* **April 21, 2008, p. A1.**
Correspondents chronicle the mixed results of post-9/11 terrorism trials.

Weiner, Tim, "The Kashmir Connection: A Puzzle," *The New York Times,* **Dec. 6, 2008, query.nytimes .com/gst/fullpage.html?res=9D05E6D91438F934A3 5751C1A96E9C8B63.**
A *New York Times* correspondent and author of a history of the CIA reports on evidence of possible ties between al Qaeda and the Pakistani group Lashkar-e-Taiba.

Reports and Studies

"Biosafety Laboratories: Perimeter Security Assessment of the Nation's Five BSL-4 Laboratories," *Government Accountability Office,* **September 2008, www.gao.gov/new. items/d081092.pdf.**
Congressional staffers have discovered lax security in two laboratories authorized to work with deadly pathogens.

"Planning Guidance for Response to a Nuclear Detonation," *Homeland Security Council,* **Jan. 16, 2009, www.afrri.usuhs .mil/outreach/pdf/planning-guidance.pdf.**
A White House agency advises city and county officials as well as emergency responders on how to prepare for the first three days following a nuclear explosion.

Benjamin, Daniel, "Strategic Counterterrorism," *Brookings Institution,* **October, 2008, www.brookings .edu/papers/2008/10_terrorism_benjamin.aspx.**
A former Clinton-era counterterrorism specialist critiques the Bush administration's military approach to fighting terrorists.

Randol, Mark A., "Homeland Security Intelligence: Perceptions, Statutory Definitions, and Approaches," *Congressional Research Service,* **Jan. 14, 2009, fas. org/sgp/crs/intel/RL33616.pdf.**
A writer for Congress's analytical arm examines options for restructuring domestic intelligence on terrorism.

For More Information

America's War Against Terrorism, World Trade Center/ Pentagon Terrorism and the Aftermath, 203 Hatcher Graduate Library, University of Michigan Library; www.lib .umich.edu/govdocs/usterror.html. Administers a massive archive on major terrorism-related issues.

Counterterrorism Blog; http://counterterrorismblog.org. A content-rich site with plentiful links to documents and news reports.

Homeland Security Watch; www.hlswatch.com. A Washington-based blog that follows daily events at the Homeland Security Department.

In Case of Emergency, Read Blog; http://incaseofemergencyblog.com. A blog by an author writing a book on citizen preparedness for disasters, with links to documents and reports on related events.

Jihadica, www.jihadica.com. International blog by military intellectuals tracking developments in the Sunni jihadist world via blog posts, with links to primary sources, many in Arabic.

National Consortium for the Study of Terrorism and Responses to Terrorism (START), 3300 Symons Hall, University of Maryland, College Park, MD 20742; (301) 405-6600; www.start.umd.edu. A Homeland Security Department-funded think tank that runs an enormous database of terrorist incidents since 1970.

Senate Committee on Homeland Security and Governmental Affairs, 340 Dirksen Senate Office Building, Washington, DC 20510; (202) 224-2627; http://hsgac.senate.gov/public/index.cfm?Fuseaction=Home.Home. A valuable source of information on hearings and reports.

13

Port Security

Are New Anti-Terrorism Measures Adequate?

Pamela M. Prah

The Port of Los Angeles is the busiest of the nation's 361 seaports. Many security experts say the government and private industry aren't doing enough to prevent terrorists from smuggling a "dirty bomb" or other weapon of mass destruction into the United States in a container.

From *CQ Researcher*,
April 21, 2006.

A truck driver in Indonesia picks up a shipment of designer sneakers made for a big U.S. firm. But before delivering the load to a port in Jakarta, he stops to let al Qaeda members stash a radioactive bomb inside the sealed container. The "dirty bomb" is encased in lead to avoid radiation-detection equipment used at many ports.

U.S. Customs officers based in Jakarta, however, neither open the container nor screen it for radioactivity because the Indonesian shipper and the big-name U.S. sneaker firm are on the government's list of "trusted" companies. When the container arrives at its destination — a warehouse in Chicago — terrorists detonate the bomb. The radioactive blast causes several deaths, devastating environmental damage and potentially long-term health risks.

Retired Coast Guard Cmdr. Stephen Flynn recently described that chilling, hypothetical scenario to congressional committees in calling for tighter port security. A former security specialist for presidents George H.W. Bush and Bill Clinton, Flynn, now a senior fellow at the Council on Foreign Relations, says the story is not all that far-fetched.

Indeed, the Department of Homeland Security (DHS) found numerous security breaches at foreign and U.S. ports that could easily allow terrorists to smuggle weapons of mass destruction (WMD) into the United States, according to The Associated Press. The three-year study, yet to be released, reportedly found that

U.S. Port Security Spans the Globe

U.S. Customs inspects suspicious containers in 44 foreign seaports as part of its Container Security Initiative (CSI). By the end of 2007, the program is slated to operate in 58 ports and cover 85 percent of U.S.-bound maritime cargo. In addition, the Department of Energy's Megaports program to combat nuclear smuggling operates radiation-detection equipment at five major foreign seaports, with another seven slated to be added. Other U.S. programs in 36 countries — primarily in the former Soviet Union and Eastern Europe — guard against smuggling of nuclear materials.

U.S. Port Security Operations Overseas

Sources: U.S. Customs; Government Accountability Office, 2006

sealed shipping containers could be opened en route to the United States without detection.[1]

More than 11 million containers entered the 361 U.S. ports in 2005 from more than 100 countries, and container traffic is expected to grow by some 10 percent each year in the future.

In addition to health and environmental havoc, a dirty bomb exploding at a U.S. port would cause "staggering economic damage," said Sen. Susan Collins, R-Maine, chairwoman of the Senate Homeland Security and Governmental Affairs Committee. As a security precaution, officials likely would immediately shut down all

U.S. ports, she said, and imports would come to a grinding halt for several days, creating a container-ship backup that would take months to untangle.

Supplies of imported food, medicine, raw materials and consumer goods from bananas to computers to toys would quickly run out, costing the economy an estimated $58 billion, according to the consulting firm Booz Allen Hamilton.[2] A Congressional Budget Office report likened the economic impact to the aftermath of the Sept. 11, 2001, terrorist attacks or Hurricane Katrina.[3]

The Bush administration insists its efforts to beef up port security are on track.[4] "I'd be the first person to tell you we have more work to do, but . . . a lot of work has been done," Homeland Security Secretary Michael Chertoff told the Heritage Foundation on March 20.[5]

But others are skeptical. "The ports are not secure," warned former Gov. Thomas Kean, R-N.J., co-leader of the bipartisan investigation of the Sept. 11 terrorist attacks known as the 9/11 Commission.[6] "You and I can walk today into the port of New York . . . and get into areas where people shouldn't get." The commission last December graded the administration on port security and gave it a "D" for failing to screen more cargo.[7]

New government studies show U.S. port security programs are highly vulnerable to terrorists. Only 5 percent of the estimated 11.3 million containers arriving at American ports last year were either physically inspected by Customs agents or screened with X-ray-like imaging machines capable of detecting unusually dense objects, such as a dirty bomb encased in lead that would elude radiation detectors. Ports overseas are even more vulnerable: Only 2.8 percent of containers destined for the United States were screened for radiation in 2005, and only about one-third of 1 percent were X-rayed.[8]

"This is a massive blind spot," said Sen. Norm Coleman, R-Minn., chairman of the Senate Homeland Security Committee's Permanent Subcommittee on Investigations, noting that more than 60 percent of U.S. ports lack basic radiation detectors. In addition to lax seaport security, federal investigators in late 2005 passed through Canadian and Mexican border checkpoints into Texas and Washington carrying enough radioactive material to make two dirty bombs.[9]

Moreover, if terrorists did attack a U.S. port today, the response likely would be poorly coordinated, according to a recent Department of Justice report. Lack of preparedness and interagency squabbling between the Coast Guard and FBI could result in a "potentially disastrous" delay, it said. "[N]one of the FBI's intelligence reports [has] assessed the threat and risk of terrorists smuggling a WMD in a shipping

Largest U.S. Ports Have Foreign Partners

The Port of Los Angeles, busiest of the nation's 361 ports, has corporate partners from five nations. Terminals at four of the nation's five biggest ports are operated by foreign-owned firms.

Foreign Operating Partners at the Five Biggest U.S. Ports 2005

Port Location	Foreign Partners	Total TEUs*
Los Angeles	Japan, Denmark, Singapore, China, Taiwan	4.9 million
Long Beach	Hong Kong, China, Japan, South Korea	4.4 million
New York	Denmark, Hong Kong, United Kingdom	3.4 million
Charleston	Denmark, Japan	1.5 million
Savannah	None; operated by Georgia Ports Authority	1.5 million

* The standard unit of measure for container capacity is the TEU (for "twenty-foot equivalent unit"). U.S. shippers typically use 40-foot containers, which are counted as two TEUs of cargo.

Sources: U.S. Transportation Maritime Administration and American Association of Port Authorities, 2006

container aboard a cargo ship," the 117-page report said. And while both the Coast Guard and the FBI now have specialized anti-terror SWAT teams, during a mock terrorist strike on a ferry in Connecticut last year the FBI "repeatedly blocked the Coast Guard's efforts, saying the FBI was the lead federal agency," the report said.[10]

Policing sea shipments entering the country is a massive, multi-agency job. The Coast Guard and U.S. Customs and Borders Protection (CBP), formerly Customs, oversee anti-terrorism efforts at ports, while state and local governments administer 126 "port authorities" that either handle day-to-day port operations themselves or hire private operating companies. Local governments also provide law enforcement. The Port Authority of New York and New Jersey's 1,600-member police department, for instance, is one of the nation's largest police organizations.

Some critics say the federal government has radically overhauled airport security since 9/11 but paid scant attention to seaports. The administration, however, says the system of "layered security" it has developed since 9/11 focuses on identifying threats overseas before they reach the United States. "Our nation's ports in the global supply chain are far safer today than they were before the

A truck passes through a portal radiation-detection system that scans cargo for nuclear materials at a port in Hong Kong, one of two that is testing enhanced security operations.

terrorist attacks of Sept. 11," Jayson Ahern, assistant commissioner for CBP field operations, told lawmakers in March. Nearly 200 Customs agents are stationed in 44 foreign ports looking for suspicious U.S.-bound cargo, he noted.[11]

Nevertheless, national outrage erupted when reports surfaced in February that an Arab-owned company, Dubai Ports World, planned to take over terminal operations at six U.S. ports, "When you read in the paper that a foreign company may run a terminal at a port near the 9/11 attack, people get afraid," said Republican Sen. Lindsey Graham of South Carolina.[12]

Not long after a poll showed that an overwhelming majority — 66 percent — of Americans opposed the deal, Dubai Ports World agreed to have U.S. firms run the disputed U.S. terminals.[13] Only 9 percent of respondents thought port security is "a lot better" since Sept. 11, while 34 percent felt airports were safer.

But security experts say concern about an Arab-owned company running major U.S. ports missed the more important security threat. "The maximum danger to the United States is where cargo is loaded on its way to our shores, not where the cargo is offloaded. By then it will be too late," says Daniel Goure, former director of the Pentagon's Office of Strategic Competitiveness and now vice president of the conservative Lexington Institute think tank.

DHS Secretary Chertoff claims federal authorities screen "100 percent" of containers entering the United

States, but critics point out that often simply means inspectors have looked at the paperwork — a ship's manifest that lists its cargo — which security experts say is unreliable.

Flynn wants the United States to replicate a security program being tested in Hong Kong that requires every container entering the port to undergo scanning and radiation detection. (*See sidebar, p. 324.*) "This is not a pie-in-the-sky idea," he says, claiming such a system would cost only $10 to $25 per container. The Bush administration says the concept is good but that the technology is unproven and the program untested.

Critics also say the Coast Guard and Customs are overburdened and underfunded. Since 9/11, for example, the number of hours the Coast Guard patrols U.S. waters each week has increased by 1,220 percent, but its funding has not dramatically increased.[14] (*See graph, p. 330.*) Others complain that the administration is overdue on drafting new rules requiring background checks and proper identification for those with access to U.S. ports.

Meanwhile on Capitol Hill, proposals are pending to toughen rules for screening U.S.-bound containers and to increase funding for port security. As Congress debates beefing up port security, here are some questions people are asking:

Are U.S. ports secure?

The Bush administration says it has implemented numerous port-security measures since 9/11, but critics say neither port personnel nor the thousands of cargo containers that arrive daily are properly screened.

For instance, three times in 2005 a 24-year-old man from Stockton, Calif., snuck into Oakland's port and stowed away on ships traveling to Los Angeles, Long Beach and Taiwan. "Isn't that a suggestion that, at least at Oakland, we have a real problem?" asked Rep. Dan Lungren, R-Calif., chairman of the House Homeland Security Subcommittee on Economic Security, Infrastructure Protection and Cybersecurity.[15]

Subcommittee member Jane Harman, D-Calif., added that twice last year illegal Chinese immigrants were found inside shipping containers at the port of Los Angeles, but it "could have been terrorists or the components for a radiological bomb" instead.[16]

Others point out that the administration still hasn't instituted the Transportation Worker Identification

Credential, known as TWIC, mandated by the Maritime Transportation Security Act of 2002. The law required anyone with port access to be identified using biometric information such as fingerprints or iris scans, following extensive background checks.

"We still don't know whether it's an American or a foreign operator who is on our docks," said Noel Cunningham, a security consultant and former director of operations and emergency management for the Port of Los Angeles. The current system of relying on drivers' licenses and employee IDs is "just not acceptable," he said.[17]

The Government Accountability Office (GAO) last year blamed bureaucratic obstacles for some of the TWIC delays. The Transportation Security Administration (TSA), created after the 9/11 attacks, initially envisioned TWIC-style IDs at all airports, seaports and railroad terminals beginning in August 2004. But implementation was delayed when the agency was moved in 2003 from the Department of Transportation to the newly created Department of Homeland Security, the GAO said.[18]

In the meantime, port operators have spent "hundreds of millions of dollars" on new security measures — such as fencing, lighting and video surveillance — says Kurt Nagle, president and chief executive officer of the American Association of Port Authorities. But the operators have been reluctant to develop new ID programs, he says, because of the impending TWIC program.

Homeland Security Secretary Chertoff admitted on March 20 that TWIC "has languished for too long" and promised to start it within months.[19]

The International Longshore and Warehouse Union (ILWU), among others, wants all workers with port access — including non-union truckers — covered by TWIC so union members won't be held to higher standards than other workers. The unions also fear that TWIC background checks may cost union members their jobs because of past criminal convictions unrelated to terrorism. "We want a fair process," says ILWU Legislative Director Lindsay McLaughlin.

The ILWU and other transportation unions say some aspects of port security have deteriorated since 9/11. "Real security measures have yet to be implemented and our ports remain extremely vulnerable," the AFL-CIO's Transportation Trades Department said in a March 23

statement asking the government to step up enforcement and provide more funding for security.

For example, some terminal operators replaced guards with cameras to make sure container seals have not been broken, but the image resolution is often too low to tell, McLaughlin says. In addition, not all terminal operators are ensuring that containers marked "empty" are actually empty, he says, and regulations requiring hazardous cargo to be properly documented and separated from other cargo are often ignored.

"Our port security is full of holes that need to be fixed," McLaughlin says.

Others say the United States should be inspecting more than just 5 percent of the incoming cargo. "Five percent . . . is unacceptable given the threats we face," Sen. Frank Lautenberg, D-N.J., told the Senate Permanent Subcommittee on Investigations on March 28. He called for inspections or scans of all arriving containers.

Customs spokesman John Mohan acknowledges the 5 percent figure may sound low but says those inspections follow a 100 percent screening before all goods leave foreign ports. Carriers must provide manifest information electronically at least 24 hours before containers are loaded onto a vessel, Mohan explains. Customs then checks the information against databases and watch lists maintained by the DHS's National Targeting Center to determine if the cargo poses a threat.

In addition to the 24-hour Customs rule, the Coast Guard requires that all international vessels file "notices of arrival" 96 hours before arriving in a U.S. port.

The Lexington Institute's Goure is not concerned that less than 10 percent of the cargo entering the United States is actually inspected. "You don't want to have to inspect more than just a small fraction," he says, lauding the administration's strategy of "pushing the borders out" to track and inspect more cargo while it's still overseas.

But critics say federal authorities have no way of knowing if the information on the shipping inventories is accurate. The 24-hour rule is a good start, says Christopher Koch, president and chief executive officer of the World Shipping Council, but authorities should also demand more details — better cargo descriptions, names of the sellers and buyers of the goods, point of origin, name of the broker and name and address of the business that "stuffed," or loaded, the container.

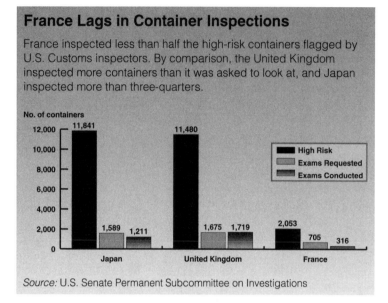

France Lags in Container Inspections

France inspected less than half the high-risk containers flagged by U.S. Customs inspectors. By comparison, the United Kingdom inspected more containers than it was asked to look at, and Japan inspected more than three-quarters.

No. of containers

Source: U.S. Senate Permanent Subcommittee on Investigations

to dock nearby, giving terrorists access to the bigger ships.

Security experts also fear that terrorists could:

- Seize a large cargo ship and crash into a bridge or waterfront refinery;
- Sink a cargo ship in a major shipping channel, blocking traffic;
- Blow up a large ship carrying volatile fuel;
- Attack an oil tanker, disrupting world oil markets and causing serious environmental damage; or
- Seize a cruise ship and threaten to kill the passengers if demands are not met.

The Bush administration also touts its 180 new "radiation portal monitors" that now screen incoming cargo for nuclear and radiological materials. Before 9/11, no such monitors were used, Customs' Ahern told a Senate Homeland security panel on March 28. Currently, radiation monitors scan 37 percent of arriving international cargo, but the goal is 98 percent by December 2007, said DHS Assistant Secretary Stewart Baker.[20] Customs also has deployed 12,400 hand-held radiation-detection devices.

The radiation-screening equipment is promising technology, Koch says, but the devices often set of false alarms. Bananas, broccoli and kitty litter, for example, set off the equipment because they contain potassium.

"The technology is conceptually attractive," Koch says, "but a real-world evaluation of the technology . . . is clearly needed."

But cargo screening is not the only security problem. Ports are attractive terrorist targets for several reasons, according to John F. Frittelli, a transportation specialist at the Congressional Research Service and author of the 2003 book, *Port and Maritime Security, Background and Issues.*[21] The thousands of trucks serving U.S. ports every day provide opportunities for terrorists to sneak themselves or dangerous materials inside. And the hundreds of cargo ships are easy targets for fast-moving boats. In addition, many ports allow fishing and recreational boats

Should foreign firms be barred from operating cargo terminals in U.S. ports?

The proposed lease of six U.S. port facilities to Dubai Ports World, a company based in the United Arab Emirates (UAE), was blocked after it triggered a furor in the United States. Critics said foreign-owned firms — particularly those with ties to terrorists — should be barred from controlling such crucial infrastructure as ports, which provide access to the rest of the country. The 9/11 Commission's Kean said the Dubai deal "doesn't make any sense," noting that two of the 9/11 hijackers came from the UAE and that terrorists' money has been laundered through Dubai.[22]

Some of the deal's staunchest opponents were lawmakers from New York, which suffered grievously on Sept. 11 and whose port — the country's third largest — would have been operated by Dubai Ports under the deal. "Outsourcing the operations of our largest ports to a country with a dubious record on terrorism is a homeland security and commerce accident waiting to happen," said Sen. Charles E. Schumer, D-N.Y. Along with Sen. Hillary Rodham Clinton, D-N.Y., and Rep. Peter King, R-N.Y., Schumer introduced legislation blocking the deal.[23]

The Bush administration and others, however, point out that foreign companies already run many U.S. port facilities without compromising security. In fact, a British company — the Peninsular and Oriental Steam Navigation Co. — had already been operating the six terminals in question. Dubai Ports World had planned to take over the operations at the six terminals (in New York, Miami, Newark, Philadelphia, New Orleans and Baltimore) once it bought Peninsular.

In response to the public outcry, however, Dubai Ports World promised that once its purchase of Peninsular and Oriental was finalized, as it was in March, the company would lease the six U.S. terminals to an American company. It is still seeking bids from U.S. firms for those terminals.

A terminal operator leases terminal space from a state or local port authority only to load and unload cargo. The port authorities own, manage and maintain the physical infrastructure of a port, such as the docks and piers. Customs agents check cargo, and the Coast Guard oversees security. The arrangement is similar to those at U.S. airports, where foreign airlines may lease a terminal, but security is still the TSA's responsibility.

About 80 percent of U.S. ports lease some or all of their terminals to third-party operators, including foreign firms. For instance, companies from China, Denmark, Japan, Singapore and Taiwan operate more than 80 percent of the terminals at the Port of Los Angeles, the nation's largest. (*See chart, p. 315.*)

The presence of so many foreign terminal operators, said Homeland Security adviser Frances Fragos Townsend, means there is little difference between a British firm running a terminal and a UAE firm.[24] Assistant Homeland Security Secretary Baker told the Senate Banking, Housing and Urban Affairs Committee in March that a terminal operator — whether foreign or domestic — does not have "a unique insight into the breadth and depth of [Department of Homeland Security] security measures" nor can a terminal operator with ill intent get access "to inside information to avoid or evade DHS scrutiny."[25]

But critics weren't convinced. "For a port manager to run the ports, they have to interface with our security forces," Rep. King said. "They have to work with the Coast Guard, they have to work with all the local authorities, which means they are within our defense perimeter. They know exactly what is being done as far as security, so they can easily infiltrate, they can easily take advantage of that."[26]

But James Jay Carafano, a senior fellow for national security at the Heritage Foundation, told the House Armed Services panel that terrorists "don't need to buy a $7 billion company to penetrate maritime." Instead, they can just take cues from smugglers, he said. "The Mafia doesn't buy FedEx to smuggle. The Mafia makes low-level penetrations."[27]

Flynn and other security experts insist that foreign operation of port terminals doesn't make those ports more vulnerable. "We need to know what's in the box more than we need to know who is moving them around a container yard," Flynn said.[28]

At one point, President Bush implied that those questioning the Dubai deal were racist and only concerned because the firm is Arab. "It sends a terrible signal to friends around the world that it's OK for a company from one country to manage the port, but not a country that plays by the rules," he said.[29]

Arsalan T. Iftikhar, national legal director of the Council on American-Islamic Relations in Washington, was more direct. The outcry over the Dubai Ports World deal, he said, "was nothing more than knee-jerk, xenophobic and political 'cherry-picking' by certain political leaders seeking to bolster their national security platform in a midterm election year." (*See "At Issue," p. 329.*)

But some of the president's staunchest supporters rejected the racism accusations, insisting their concerns were based on the UAE's past involvement in supporting international terrorists. "I don't believe you can treat the United Arab Emirates the same as you treat Great Britain," King, chairman of the House Homeland Security Committee, told NBC's "Meet the Press."[30]

The UAE was one of three countries that openly supported the Taliban in the 1990s, opponents of the deal noted. "Their track record is terrifying," said Rep. Duncan Hunter, R-Calif., chairman of the House Armed Services Committee.[31] Other critics pointed out that when the Pakistani nuclear scientist A.Q. Khan wanted to sell black-market nuclear-weapons materials to Iran and North Korea, he used UAE middlemen and smuggled the contraband in shipping containers through Dubai.[32]

Opponents also stressed that Dubai Ports World is not simply a company located in the UAE but is owned by the government itself.

However, the Bush administration and others say the UAE is now a trustworthy and important U.S. ally. It

Cargo containers are stacked high on the deck of a vessel at the Port of Los Angeles. Critics of port security say only 5 percent of the 11 million containers that arrived in the United States in 2005 were inspected.

allows the United States and its allies to dock 131 war-ships and 590 military command ships in its ports, said Sen. Ted Stevens, R-Alaska, chairman of the Senate Commerce, Science and Transportation Committee. Sen. John McCain, R-Ariz., agreed, noting that the UAE hosts the U.S. Air Force at Al Dhafra, the UAE air-warfare and fighter-training center, and that the UAE government has worked to stop terrorist money-laundering. "We are dealing with a friend and an ally on this issue."[33]

Goure of the Lexington Institute called Schumer, Clinton and King "the axis of idiocy," charging that they had "totally misconstrued the issue for pure political gain."

The rising xenophobia and anti-Arab sentiment, he said, echoes concerns raised by some Americans when the Japanese bought Lincoln Center in New York City and other U.S. properties in the 1990s. "It's this weird notion that if they buy [U.S. facilities] that it means they're stronger and we're weaker. None of this makes a rat's ass difference," he says. The biggest danger "is at the port of embarkation, where cargo is loaded on its way to our shores, not where the cargo is offloaded."

Is the administration doing enough to improve port security abroad?

Homeland-security experts and the Bush administration agree that oversight of foreign ports is key to ensuring that U.S. ports are safe, but some experts say the

administration's post-9/11 efforts to improve overseas port security fall short.

Customs launched two programs in 2002 aimed at preventing terrorists from smuggling dangerous materi-als into the United States from foreign ports: The Container Security Initiative (CSI) and the Customs-Trade Partnership Against Terrorism (C-TPAT). The CSI posts U.S. Customs agents at foreign ports, where they can target and screen U.S.-bound shipments deemed "high risk" by the United States. Participating ports must install radiation-detecting equipment. The 44 foreign ports currently participating in CSI handle about 75 per-cent of the containers entering the United States. By the end of the year, the administration expects 50 ports to be participating, covering 82 percent of the U.S.-bound cargo, Customs' Ahern said.

However, GAO investigators found that only 17.5 percent of containers that U.S. officials tagged as "high-risk" were given follow-up inspections by U.S. officials overseas.[34] Some of the foreign host countries have either been "unwilling or unable to share their intelligence" with U.S. officials, and the radiation-detection equipment var-ies widely from country to country, the Senate Permanent Subcommittee on Investigations reported in March. Moreover, investigators said, Customs agents cannot force suspicious containers to be opened. Ports in France, for example, refused to inspect about 60 percent of the cargo deemed high-risk by U.S. agents. (*See graph, p. 318.*)

Equally troubling, says Sen. Carl Levin D-Mich., ranking Democrat on the Senate Homeland Security investigations panel, Customs relies on cargo manifests — which security experts say are undependable — to identify "high-risk containers." The system has never been tested or validated, Levin adds.

The U.S. government uses a computerized model known as the Automated Targeting System to determine which containers might be "high risk." But as Flynn's nightmare scenario involving Indonesian-made sneakers shows, the CSI program doesn't take into account the many stops foreign-made products — even those from "trusted" shippers — can make between the factory and the ship. "All a terrorist organization need do is find a single weak link within a trusted shipper's complex sup-ply chain, such as a poorly paid truck driver taking a container from a remote factory to a loading port," Flynn said in March.

Nearly 10,000 businesses have applied to take part in C-TPAT, the other major Customs initiative. It promises companies fewer inspections if they agree to voluntarily beef up their security measures. Thus far, Customs has reviewed the security plans of 5,800 firms but has validated only 1,545 of the plans. Ahern told the House Homeland Security Committee in March he is "not happy" with the agency's progress in checking the plans but hopes to have 65 percent of the applications reviewed by year's end.[35]

GAO concluded last year, however, that C-TPAT does not necessarily improve security because U.S. officials do not check to see if companies are doing what they promised in their security plans.[36]

However, C-TPAT can be a good investment for businesses. After toymaker Hasbro spent $200,000 to join the program in 2002 and get its plan validated, its inspections dropped from 7.6 percent of all containers in 2001 to 0.66 percent in 2003. That saved the company more than a half a million dollars in inspection costs, says Rep. Lungren, who has proposed legislation to expand the program.

Henry H. Willis, an analyst at the RAND Corporation, says the government has no way to ensure that CSI and C-TPAT work. The World Shipping Council's Koch agrees, noting that because both programs are voluntary, "It's hard to measure their effectiveness." Nevertheless, he insists, they are "absolutely valuable" and should be expanded.

Critics also worry that Customs won't have enough time or manpower to follow up and make sure that companies involved in C-TPAT continue to use top-of-the-line security procedures. Today Customs has 88 specialists on staff to review and monitor companies' security plans. Another 40 are to join the agency by late spring, Ahern told Coleman's panel.

Some experts say the two programs give a false sense of security because terrorists can figure out which shipments inspectors routinely designate as low risk. "Because name-brand companies like Wal-Mart and General Motors are widely known to be considered low-risk, terrorists need only to stake out their shipment routes and exploit the weakest points to introduce a weapon of mass destruction," wrote Flynn and Lawrence M. Wein, a faculty member at Stanford University's Center for International Security and Cooperation.[37]

"A terrorist cell posing as a legal shipping company for more than two years or a terrorist truck driver hauling goods from a well-known shipper can also be confident of being perceived as low risk," Wein and Flynn wrote. The entire program, Flynn testified, relies on the honor system.

The Bush administration in 2003 also launched Megaports, a Department of Energy program designed to prevent nuclear materials from entering the United States. Under the program, the United States has installed radiation-detection systems in ports in Greece, the Bahamas, Sri Lanka, the Netherlands and Spain and is working on installation arrangements with Belgium, China, the U.A.E., Honduras, Israel, Oman, the Philippines, Singapore and Thailand. The administration hopes to work out deals with 21 other countries, David G. Huizenga, deputy assistant secretary of the agency, testified during a March 28 hearing by the Senate Homeland Security and Governmental Affairs Subcommittee on Investigations.

But GAO investigators warned that corruption is a "pervasive problem" in some countries that received radiation-detection equipment. Border-security authorities in those countries turned off the devices or ignored alarms, GAO's director of Natural Resources and Environment, Gene Aloise, said during the same March 28 Senate hearing.

Lawmakers also worry that there are too many federal agencies with jurisdiction over port security, creating problems of coordination and overlapping responsibilities. The agencies include Customs, the Coast Guard, the Transportation Security Administration and the Domestic Nuclear Detection Office — all within the DHS — plus the departments of State, Transportation and Defense.

However, insists Vayl Oxford, director of the Nuclear Detection Office, the groups now have a "daily dialogue" that didn't exist before 9/11. "It's a great step forward," he told Coleman.

BACKGROUND

Taxes and Smugglers

For decades, port security meant preventing thieves — including organized crime — from stealing cargo. For

CHRONOLOGY

1700s-1950s *The two federal agencies responsible for port security — Customs and the Coast Guard — are created early in the nation's history, primarily to collect taxes.*

1789 The Customs Service is created and a year later the Revenue Cutter Service, which is renamed the Coast Guard in 1915.

1917 German saboteurs attack an ammunition depot near New York Harbor prompting passage of the Espionage Act giving the Coast Guard authority over U.S. waters.

Dec. 7, 1941 The U.S. naval base at Pearl Harbor, Hawaii, is attacked by the Japanese, forcing the United States into World War II. During the war, airplanes and blimps patrol U.S. ports and coastlines for German and Japanese submarines.

1950 Congress amends the Espionage Act, expanding the Coast Guard's authority to harbors, ports and waterfront facilities.

1960s-1990s *Coast Guard's focus shifts to enforcing environmental and safety standards, intercepting illegal drugs and helping Cuban refugees.*

1980 Coast Guard launches the so-called Mariel boatlift to assist the 125,000 Cubans — including many prisoners and mental patients — who had suddenly been released by Cuban President Fidel Castro and were trying to reach U.S. shores in 1,700 overcrowded boats.

2000s *Following the Sept. 11, 2001, terrorist attacks, the Coast Guard launches the largest port-security operation since World War II, and Customs tightens scrutiny overseas of U.S.-bound cargo.*

January 2002 Container Security Initiative allows U.S. Custom agents at foreign ports to screen high-risk containers bound for the United States. . . . Customs-Trade Partnership Against Terrorism promises fewer Customs inspections for companies that voluntarily beef up security.

October 2002 The consulting firm Booz Allen Hamilton estimates that the detonation of a radioactive, or "dirty

bomb," at a U.S. port could force all American ports to be shut down for 12 days, at a cost of $58 billion.

Nov. 25, 2002 President George W. Bush signs the Maritime Transportation Security Act requiring the nation's 361 commercial seaports to develop anti-terrorism plans and an ID system for port workers.

Nov. 20, 2003 Congress creates the Department of Homeland Security, which absorbs Customs, Border Patrol and the Coast Guard.

July 1, 2004 A security regime for international shipping approved in 2002 by the International Maritime Organization, a branch of the United Nations, goes into effect. The requirements parallel the United States' Maritime Transportation Security Act of 2002 by requiring ports and shipping companies to review their operations to prevent terrorists from infiltrating the maritime sector.

May 2005 Congressional investigators find that only 17.5 percent of the cargo identified by U.S. officials overseas as high risk is being properly inspected and examined.

September 2005 President Bush issues the National Strategy for Maritime Security.

Dec. 5, 2005 The 9/11 Commission issues a "report card" faulting U.S. efforts to improve cargo screening and security at critical infrastructure.

February 2006 Arab-owned Dubai Ports World announces controversial plans to run terminals at six U.S. ports, prompting hearings and proposals to block foreigners from operating U.S. ports and to improve port security.

March 2006 Senate investigators find that port inspectors overseas screen less than 3 percent of U.S.-bound containers for radiation. The Bush administration promises to install 620 radiation devices at the top U.S. ports by December 2007.

April 2006 Department of Homeland Security Secretary Michael Chertoff inspects Hong Kong's pilot program for screening all containers with radiation and scanning detectors.

the government, it meant collecting taxes, or duties, on imported goods and looking for smuggled goods or drugs.

Customs and the Coast Guard were established — primarily to collect taxes — shortly after the United States became a country. The Tariff Act of July 4, 1789, allowed the government to collect duties on imported goods to raise money and pay off debts. Four weeks later, on July 31, 1789, Congress created the Customs Service to collect those taxes at ports of entry.[38]

Customs collections funded the country's expansion — including purchases of Louisiana, Oregon, Florida and Alaska — and for building the nation's lighthouses, the military and naval academies and Washington, D.C.

The Coast Guard's history is more complicated because it involves several independent but overlapping federal agencies.[39] The Revenue Cutter Service, created in 1790, officially became the Coast Guard in 1915. It primarily ensures that tariffs are paid, ships are protected from pirates and that neither products nor humans are smuggled into the country. Intercepting "contraband" — whether it be slaves, narcotics or, during Prohibition, liquor — has been the Coast Guard's most challenging responsibility.

The Sept. 11 terrorist attacks were not the first foreign attacks on the United States that resulted in new laws to protect U.S. waterways. In 1916, during World War I, German agents in 1916 blew up ammunition stored on an island near New York Harbor that was bound for the Allied powers in Europe.[40] The next year, after the United States entered the war, Congress passed the Espionage Act of 1917, giving the Coast Guard authority over U.S. waters.[41]

During World War I, uniformed Customs intelligence officers were responsible for security and operations support for port and federal/military activities and formed a special intelligence bureau at the Port of New York. In World War II, the Coast Guard was not only involved in every major invasion abroad but also rescued more than 1,500 survivors of torpedo attacks in areas adjacent to the United States.

In the early 1960s, the Coast Guard's focus shifted to helping refugees fleeing Cuba after communist Fidel Castro took power in 1959. The assistance ended in 1965, when the United States imposed new restrictions on Cuban immigration, but it restarted with the 1980 "Mariel boatlift." The effort to help 125,000 Cubans trying to

Homeland Security Secretary Michael Chertoff (front right) tours a port in Hong Kong that is operating a pilot program to show cargo can be screened with both radiation-detection and X-ray-type machines without disrupting trade.

reach U.S. shores in 1,700 overcrowded boats was the largest Coast Guard operation ever undertaken in peacetime.[42] In the 1970s the Coast Guard and Customs launched drug-interdiction efforts in the "war on drugs" that continue today.

War on Terror

Experts say the "war on terrorism" is fundamentally different from the "war on drugs." Drug smugglers seek secret routes that can be used repeatedly, which allows federal agencies to look for patterns of behavior by the smugglers. Terrorists, on the other hand, prize methods that have never been used and likely will be used only once, explained transportation specialist Frittelli.[43]

One of the earliest maritime terrorist attacks occurred in 1985, but not in the United States, Frittelli points out. Palestinian terrorists seized the *Achille Lauro* cruise ship in the Mediterranean and demanded that Israel release 50 Arab prisoners. To demonstrate their resolve, the attackers shot and killed a wheelchair-bound Jewish-American passenger, Leon Klinghoffer, and threw his body overboard. And in 2000, suicide bombers rammed a small boat filled with explosives into the destroyer *USS Cole* during a refueling stop in Aden, Yemen, killing 17 U.S. sailors.[44]

Does Hong Kong Have the Answer?

Some security experts think a pilot port security program in Hong Kong may represent the "Holy Grail" of modern port security technology.

Since March 2005, all containers entering two Hong Kong ports have been scanned for both radiation and large, dense objects that — according to the shipper's cargo manifest — don't seem to belong in the shipment. Digital images of the containers' contents are then stored in a database.

The Hong Kong initiative is "a true model of where we might be able to go" with port security, says Stephen E. Flynn, a senior fellow at the Council on Foreign Relations and former Coast Guard commander. The density scanning is particularly important, he explains, because radiation sensors would not detect a radioactive "dirty bomb" wrapped in lead. But gamma-ray (similar to X-rays) machines single out unusually dense objects.

The program is funded by the Container Terminal Operators Association of Hong Kong and Hutchison Port Holdings, one of the world's largest port operators, and receives no government funding. Shipping companies and terminal operators say they support the program because it might prevent a terrorist event that could shut down port operations for days or weeks, costing billions of dollars, said Hutchison Senior Vice President Gary Gilbert.[1] If the

program were mandated worldwide, Gilbert said, it would not only deter terrorism but also provide a way for investigators to track shipments to their port of origin if there is an incident, possibly avoiding an entire maritime shutdown.

Shippers and the Bush administration call the Hong Kong initiative a good start but not a panacea. "The technology is not totally proven," Michael Jackson, deputy secretary of the Department of Homeland Security (DHS), told the House Homeland Security Committee on April 4. "We need to do more testing."

Christopher Koch, president and CEO of the World Shipping Council, concurs, noting that today's radiation devices cannot distinguish between deadly radiation and low-level, natural radiation emitted by such products as kitty litter and bananas. The result would be countless "nuisance alarms," he says.

Moreover, said Jayson Ahern, assistant commissioner for field operations at U.S. Customs and Border Protection, the Hong Kong screening operation has been "completely oversold. It is not doing 100 percent of the containers."[2]

Jackson also complains that so far no one is reviewing the images of the container contents being collected. The images are "basically going onto a disk and being stored," he said.

After the 9/11 attackers brought terrorism to U.S. shores, however, the Coast Guard created the largest port-security operation since World War II, according to Frittelli. The Coast Guard now maintains "security zones" around waterside facilities, Navy vessels and cruise and cargo ships entering or leaving ports. Coast Guard cutters and aircraft have been diverted from other assignments to patrol the new security zones as well as coastal waters.

In addition to CSI and C-TPAT — the two anti-terrorism port programs launched by Customs after 9/11 — Congress created the new Transportation Security Administration with a mandate to develop an ID and background-check program for all transportation workers, including dock workers.

But the Maritime Transportation Security Act signed by President Bush in November 2002 was the first legislation devoted to port security, requiring U.S. ports to

develop "security and incident-response plans." Since then the Coast Guard has reviewed and approved security plans for 3,200 maritime facilities in the nation's ports.[45]

The Coast Guard also has completed security checks at all 55 U.S. ports the federal government deems "strategic" due to their economic or military importance. For example, during Operation Desert Storm in 1991 about 90 percent of military equipment and supplies was shipped through "strategic" ports.[46] If those ports were attacked, "not only could massive civilian casualties be sustained, but the Defense Department could also lose precious cargo and time and be forced to rely heavily on its overburdened airlift capabilities," according to a 2002 GAO report.[47]

The 2002 law also required vessels to install special tracking devices that transmit a unique identifying signal to a receiver located at the port and to other ships in the area. The system relies on global positioning systems,

But shippers point out that it's only a pilot program, designed to show that the technology exists to scan for both radiation and density. There were never plans to analyze the data, says Alison Williams, a spokeswoman at SAIC, the San Diego-based company that provides the screening machines. Instead, the objective was designed to show that accurate screening information could be collected without impeding the flow of commerce, she says.

The program is still working on its other objective: to show the U.S. government that if the system were deployed in foreign terminals the database could be useful, Williams says. "There have been a number of U.S. delegations to see the system in operation in Hong Kong, but there still is not a definitive statement from DHS" regarding the program, she says. Nevertheless, the operators have agreed to continue running it while DHS studies the system.

DHS Secretary Michael Chertoff visited the project on April 1 and calls it "very innovative," says DHS spokesman Russ Knocke. "He wanted to see the pilot firsthand to see if there are any elements that could be applicable here," he says, adding that not analyzing the data is a concern.

Several lawmakers have advocated that all U.S.-bound containers be screened or inspected, but many do not spell out whether they mean screening for radiation, density or both.

For the program to work worldwide, Flynn says Customs would need 400 agents reviewing the images.

Currently, Customs has 80 agents stationed abroad, designated to look for suspicious cargo bound for the United States as part of a voluntary program called the Customs-Trade Partnership Against Terrorism, but the agency says another 40 agents are to be posted to that program by May.[3]

Meanwhile, the question of who would pay for such a global screening system remains unanswered. At an April 3 Senate forum, Hutchison's Gilbert suggested that taxpayers pay for the personnel to examine the data and shippers pay for the technology. Clark Kent Ervin, former DHS inspector general and now a homeland security expert at the Aspen Institute, endorsed an even split for the cost of new radiation monitors.[4]

But Knocke warns that "technology alone for supply-chain security is not the only solution. What's needed, he says, is "a combination of personnel, technology, private-sector participation, business practices and the layered security defense that we have throughout the container supply chain."

---

[1] Pamela Hess, "Pilot port security program data unused," United Press International, April 4, 2006.

[2] Transcript of House Homeland Security Subcommittee on Economic Security, Infrastructure Protection and Cybersecurity Hearing on Port Security, March 16, 2006.

[3] House Homeland Security Subcommittee, *op. cit.*

[4] Tim Starks "Experts Recommend Increased Port Security," *CQ Today*, April 3, 2006.

digital communication equipment and other technology to provide port officials and other vessels nearby with a vessel's identity, position, speed and course. Such a system aims to provide an "early warning" if a vessel is in a location where it shouldn't be. The system is operational in 12 major U.S. ports, but all ports nationwide are scheduled to have it eventually.

Last September President Bush issued a blueprint for improving port security, called the National Strategy for Maritime Security.[48] The 30-page plan calls for beefing up existing programs but does not propose any new initiatives. It dovetails with eight "supporting" plans, such as the International Outreach and Coordination Strategy and the Maritime Infrastructure Recovery Plan.

U.S. Coast Guard Commandant Admiral Thomas Collins said the strategy builds on the nation's "layered defense as the government and private-sector improve their coordination during maritime incidents."[49]

But Flynn of the Council on Foreign Relations says all of the plans and activity "should not be confused with real capability." He told a Senate Homeland Security panel on March 28 that the administration's approach on port security has been piecemeal, "with each agency pursuing its signature program or programs with little regard for other initiatives."

CURRENT SITUATION

The Fast Track

In the wake of the controversial Dubai Ports World deal, the administration is fast-tracking several port-security initiatives that had been languishing for years, including installing more radiation-detection devices in U.S. ports and issuing the first-ever identification cards for port workers. And lawmakers on Capitol Hill

The Revolutionary, Versatile Shipping Container

Gone are the days when burly longshoremen wielding lethal-looking metal hooks unloaded cargo from ships — bundle by bundle and crate by crate — storing it in warehouses to await loading onto trucks.

Today, more than 90 percent of the world's cargo moves in standard-sized containers stacked like children's blocks on ships as long as football fields. When the ships dock, the containers are loaded directly onto freight cars or trucks by giant gantry cranes, which inspired the robotic creatures in George Lucas's film, "The Empire Strikes Back."

More than 11 million containers arrived in U.S. ports in 2005, with 12 million expected this year, says Christopher Koch, president of the World Shipping Council. A typical container today is 20-, 40- or 45-feet long and can be equipped with special technologies such as refrigeration units or hanger systems for clothing. A 40-foot container can hold 4,403 VCRs, 267,000 video games or 10,000 pairs of shoes, according to the American Association of Port Authorities.

The ease with which containers can be moved around helped foster the rapid globalization of international trade by reducing both labor costs and transport time.[1] Today a standard container with 32 tons of cargo can be shipped from China to the United States for as little as $2,000.[2]

"The world has become dependent upon the box — and the box, in return, has changed the world," German filmmaker Thomas Greh said in a Web site posting about his 2004 documentary film, "The Container Story."

The re-release of Greh's documentary coincides with the 50th anniversary of the first container shipped — in 1956, from Newark, N.J., bound for Houston.[3] Containers were invented by a North Carolina farmer's son, Malcolm McLean, who had started his own trucking company during the Great Depression. Frustrated by the inefficiency of the dockside loading and unloading process, McLean asked himself, "Wouldn't it be great if my [tractor] trailer could simply be lifted up and placed on the ship?"[4]

McLean eventually died a very rich man, having sold his Sea-Land shipping business for $160 million in 1969. But, while he and the world's consumers benefited from containers, others did not. As the first container ship left Newark harbor, International Longshoremen's Association official Freddy Fields was asked how he liked the new ship. "I'd like to sink that sonofabitch," Fields replied.[5]

Unsuccessful longshoremen's strikes followed the introduction of containers. As shipping costs plummeted, so did dockworkers' jobs. Containers and other new technologies slashed the number of West Coast longshoremen's jobs from more than 100,000 in the 1970s to 10,500 today.[6]

Intermodal shipping containers — as they're technically called — are nearly indestructible and typically last for decades. McLean probably never imagined his invention would one day be recycled as temporary offices, living quarters, schools and medical facilities in remote locations.

"Construction companies often own their own containers and ship supplies, tools and equipment to job sites in a container. Then they use the empty container as an office while the project is ongoing," says construction supervisor Tom Koch, who has worked in container "offices" on projects in Guam and Tajikistan. "When the project is finished, they load all the equipment back into the container and ship it home."

Some companies donate their old containers. In the 1990s Coca-Cola donated a container to Soweto's Nanto primary school in South Africa, which leased it out to a convenience store operator. Thousands of donated containers have been converted into schools, community centers,

finally are getting traction on a flurry of port-security proposals.

"The controversy focused much-needed attention on the issue of port security," said Sen. Collins on March 21, when she was named "Port Person of the Year" by the American Association of Port Authorities.[50]

Democrats, however, quickly seized on the Ports World controversy as a potential election-year issue and began pushing for more money for port security. "If the Republicans are now deciding to get on board, then we welcome them, because for so long they have been on a sinking ship, basically saying that our ports are homes, even restaurants and beauty salons in Africa.[7] Seattle architects Robert Humble and Joel Egan have turned old shipping containers into modular homes, designed a mobile medical unit for Doctors Without Borders and a base camp in rural Siberia for Earth Corps, which is helping to develop ecotourism at Lake Baikal.[8]

The windowless containers have also reportedly been used for more nefarious purposes — such as places to secretly torture prisoners in Afghanistan or Iraq.[9] "Around Iraq, in the back of a Humvee or in a shipping container, there's no camera," an Army interrogator told a documentary filmmaker. "And there's no one looking over your shoulder, so you can do anything you want."[10]

Since containers are large enough for people to live in, they are sometimes used to smuggle large groups of illegal immigrants with enough food and water for a long sea journey. In April, 22 illegal Chinese immigrants were found inside a sealed cargo container at Seattle's Harbor Island.[11]

And while sealed shipping containers have dramatically reduced the amount of pilferage that once occurred during shipments, security experts worry that terrorists could sneak a radioactive "dirty bomb" into a locked shipping container bound for the United States. Pakistani nuclear scientist A.Q. Khan, for example, confessed in 2004 that he smuggled nuclear-weapons materials to Libya, Iran and North Korea in containers.[12]

Food, water and makeshift toilets are among the debris left behind after 22 Chinese immigrants arrived in Seattle after 15 days in a 40-foot container.

[1] Marc Levinson, *The Box: How the Shipping Container Made the World Smaller and The World Economy Bigger* (2006).

[2] Christian Caryl, "The Box Is King," *Newsweek International*, April 10, 2006.

[3] www.containerstory.com.

[4] Quoted from "Who Made America?" PBS, www.pbs.org/wgbh/theymadeamerica/whomade/mclean_hi.html.

[5] *Ibid.*

[6] From David Bacon and Freda Coodin, "Bush Threatens West Coast Dockers' Right to Strike," *Labor Notes*, September 2002.

[7] Michael Wines, "Africans find a refuge in cast-off 'big boxes,'" *The New York Times*, Aug. 8, 2004.

[8] See www.cargotecture.com/contact.html.

[9] See Michael Ignatieff, "Lesser Evils," *The New York Times Magazine*, May 2, 2004, p. 46.

[10] Alessandra Stanley, "The Slow Rise of Abuse That Shocked the Nation," *The New York Times*, Oct. 18, 2005, p. E5.

[11] Lornet Turnbull, "Stowaways say each paid $10,000," *The Seattle Times*, April 12, 2006.

[12] For background, see Mary H. Cooper, "Nuclear Proliferation and Terrorism," *CQ Researcher*, April 2, 2004, pp. 297-320.

secure," said Rep. Bennie Thompson of Mississippi, ranking Democrat on the House Homeland Security Committee.[51]

In March Congress received three separate GAO reports showing weaknesses in the country's port defenses. Among the findings:

- U.S. port operators are delaying deployment of radiation portal monitors, fearing they will slow shipping.[52]
- DHS plans to buy "advanced" radiation portal monitors that will cost between $330,000 and $460,000 apiece without really knowing if they

Inspection Technology at Work

U.S. Customs inspectors cut off a padlock in order to examine a shipping container in Jersey City (top). Inspectors also use X-ray-type devices and radiation detectors when inspecting containers. A Department of Homeland Security inspector inside a mobile scanning unit at the Port of Los Angeles examines X-ray images of a shipping container (bottom).

work better than the existing devices costing $49,000 to $60,000.[53]

- Customs officers are not required to verify that shippers of radiological material actually obtained required licenses, and Customs lacks access to Nuclear Regulatory Commission (NRC) data that could authenticate a license.[54]

Ahern told Sen. Coleman's March 28 Homeland Security hearing that Customs is working hard to improve

its programs. In addition to being able to screen 98 percent of inbound containers for radiation by December 2007, the agency plans to deploy 60 mobile radiation portal monitors in seaports by the end of 2006, he says. GAO investigators caution, however, that the schedule is ambitious.

Ahern also promised to establish new procedures so Customs officials do not get fooled by fake documents, as they did during GAO's recent undercover sting operation at Mexican and Canadian border crossings. Investigators were allowed to bring radioactive material into the United States after producing fake documents showing they had an NRC license. The GAO had downloaded examples of the documents they needed on the Internet and used off-the-shelf computer software to create copies.

DHS Deputy Secretary Jackson says ID cards for port workers are a "very high priority" and that the department plans to issue them in "months, not years." Both the TSA and the Coast Guard are working on regulations, he explained, and in late March the administration published a notice seeking firms with the technological background to run certain parts of the program.

But some on Capitol Hill complain that the administration is not acting quickly enough. A House Homeland Security panel on March 30 approved the first piece of port-security legislation since the Dubai Ports World dustup. The bipartisan SAFE Port Act, proposed by California Reps. Lungren and Harman, would require the DHS to develop timelines for installing radiation equipment in ports and launching the TWIC program. It would also establish procedures for restoring port operations in the event of an attack and improving the CSI and C-TPAT programs.

On March 30, Lungren's Subcommittee on Economic Security, Infrastructure Protection and Cybersecurity approved the measure, increasing to $821 million the amount of federal funds set aside each year for port security — including a $20 million increase earmarked for speeding up the TWIC identification cards.[55]

Democrats were defeated in efforts to include amendments requiring full inspection of every cargo container and increasing the number of port inspectors by 1,600 over four years. The full House is expected to vote on the measure in May.

A similar bill in the Senate, introduced by Collins and Sen. Patty Murray, D-Wash., would provide quicker processing, or "green lanes," to shippers who meet strict

Is it racist to ban Arab companies from operating U.S. ports?

YES
Arsalan T. Iftikhar
National Legal Director, Council on American-Islamic Relations

Written for *CQ Researcher*, April 2006

Unfortunately, the whole Dubai Ports World fiasco was nothing more than knee-jerk, xenophobic and political "cherry-picking" by political leaders seeking to bolster their national-security platform in a midterm election year.

Although these leaders have now become the self-anointed vanguards of our port security, their disingenuous arguments that port "security" being outsourced to an Arab company would somehow put that security at risk is based on nothing more than anti-Muslim, anti-Arab sentiment that is, unfortunately, becoming pervasive within the Washington Beltway.

Note that none of these elected officials gave a bloody hoot while Dubai Ports World was being fully vetted and blessed by the Committee on Foreign Investment in the United States (CFIUS), which includes representatives from the departments of Treasury, Defense and Homeland Security.

The *Wall Street Journal* editorial board took the naysayers to task by questioning why these politicians "believe Dubai Ports World has been insufficiently vetted for the task at hand. So far, none of the critics provided any evidence that the administration hasn't done its due diligence."

Another insincere argument advanced by these politicians is that we as Americans cannot outsource port "security" to an Arab Muslim nation. The editorial board at the *Los Angeles Times* found this argument to be equally as vapid. "The notion that the Bush administration is farming out port 'security' to hostile Arab nations is alarmist nonsense. Dubai Ports World would be managing the commercial activities of these U.S. ports, not securing them," wrote the *Times*.

Nonetheless, these "superhawks" still do not believe that an Arab and Muslim company has the moral equilibrium to merely hire longshoremen, many of whom are red-blooded Americans and card-carrying members of the AFL-CIO.

This is where xenophobia takes over. Baltimore Mayor Martin O'Malley asked: "Do we want to turn over the port of Baltimore, home of the 'Star-Spangled Banner,' to the United Arab Emirates? Not so long as I'm mayor."

The knee-jerk rhetoric was so eloquently epitomized by Sen. Charles Schumer, D-N.Y., who said: "Let's say skinheads had bought a company to take over our port. . . . I think the outcry would have been the same."

When jingoistic references to our national anthem and silly comparisons of Arabs to skinheads become political talking points, you know racism and xenophobia cannot be far behind.

NO
U.S. Rep. Duncan Hunter, R-Calif.
Chairman, House Armed Services Committee

Written for *CQ Researcher*, April 2006

We're in an age that unites terrorism and technology. So we must critically examine America's vulnerabilities, especially those in our infrastructure — such as in our ports and power plants — where disasters would paralyze commerce or imperil populations.

Unfortunately, there's no perfect protection against attack. Therefore, vigilance is paramount — especially regarding who controls our nation's critical infrastructure. That is why I introduced legislation to ensure that critical national-security assets remain in the hands of reliable, American-controlled companies.

The proposed legislation would require the secretary of Defense to maintain a list of assets so vital that their destruction would cripple our ability to maintain national security, economic security or public safety. Further, American citizens must control sensitive or classified aspects of the national-defense critical infrastructure. Appropriate U.S. authorities must also search 100 percent of inbound cargo.

Ensuring American control of key U.S. assets isn't new. For example, businesses that perform classified defense work must have an American CEO and outside directors who are U.S. citizens who cannot be removed except with Department of Defense permission. In domestic airlines, U.S. citizens must comprise top management. Indeed, many foreign investments in the United States leave U.S. management intact. Despite what critics say about the economic impact of such measures, America has long been foreign investment's favorite destination — perhaps because we ensure a safe, stable society.

National security, not simple economic opportunity, comes first. The Committee on Foreign Investment in the United States (CFIUS) apparently forgot this when it OK'd the deal to shift major port terminal operations to government-controlled Dubai Ports World, overlooking facts like these: In 2003, over U.S. protests, customs officials in the United Arab Emirates allowed Dubai to transship 66 high-speed electrical switches, which can be used to detonate nuclear weapons. Dubai also rejected U.S. requests to inspect containers holding the switches.

Yet, Dubai's track record somehow passed muster at CFIUS, which let the president down. Accordingly, my legislation mandates the administration be notified of mergers, acquisitions or takeovers being reviewed by CFIUS.

The drive to globalization shouldn't dupe us into letting down our guard regarding critical American assets and infrastructure. If that makes me a protectionist, as critics say, I'll say it again: America is worth protecting.

Port Security Funding Has Increased

Federal funding for port security has increased by more than 600 percent since the terrorist attacks on Sept. 11, 2001, to about $1.6 billion in 2005 says the Bush administration (top). But U.S. port authorities complain that in the past three years they received only 19 percent of the $3.8 billion in federal grants they requested to upgrade security infrastructure, such as lighting, fencing and security cameras (bottom).

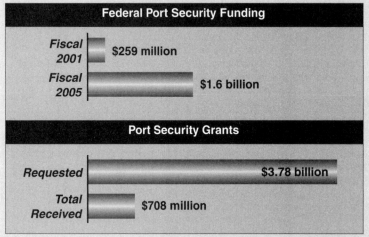

Federal Port Security Funding

Fiscal 2001 — $259 million

Fiscal 2005 — $1.6 billion

Port Security Grants

Requested — $3.78 billion

Total Received — $708 million

Sources: Department of Homeland Security (top); American Association of Port Authorities

security requirements along with $400 million in security grants. Collins's committee has held a hearing on the measure and expects to vote on it in April.

Lungren stresses that neither his bill nor Collins's is "an afterthought" to the recent Dubai Ports World controversy and that their efforts began months before the deal made headlines.

Homeland Security Deputy Secretary Jackson declined on April 5 to endorse the Collins and Lungren measures but said nonetheless that he looked forward to the "passage of bipartisan legislation that will strengthen our work in the maritime domain." It was the first time DHS has supported any of the pending legislation to beef up port security.

Meanwhile, a larger transportation bill approved by the Senate Commerce, Science and Transportation Committee in late February would authorize random inspections of cargo entering the United States and provide $729 million annually for port security. In April, the House Transportation and Infrastructure Committee approved a bill that would require greater oversight of transfers of ownership or operation of port facilities and limit a port terminal's top security post to U.S. citizens. (*See "At Issue," p. 329.*)

Money Matters

Port facilities may soon see more federal dollars. A Senate panel in April earmarked an additional $648 million for port security in an emergency fiscal 2006 budget package to help finance the war in Iraq. The additional funding includes $227 million for port-security grants, $211 million for Customs to purchase 60 additional cargo-container inspection systems, $23 million for 50 additional Customs port inspectors, $23 million for the Coast Guard to triple the number of port-security plan specialists, $32 million for Customs to hire 85 container-security specialists and $132 million to deploy more than 300 additional radiation portal monitors at U.S. seaports.[56]

The full Senate is scheduled to take up the emergency bill after the Easter recess. The House in March narrowly rejected, 208-210, an amendment that would have added $825 million for port security to the emergency measure.

As for fiscal 2007, many proposed measures increase money for port security. In recent years Democrats had tried repeatedly to increase spending on port security, but Republicans had blocked them. This year, however, key Republicans in both chambers have called for more funding.

"Regrettably, the administration's budget shortchanges port security," said Collins, who wants a separate stream of federal funds for port security rather than the administration's approach, which folds in money for ports with all other transportation projects.[57]

The administration points out that funding for port security has increased more than 600 percent since 9/11. The Department of Homeland Security spent $1.6 billion on port security in fiscal 2005, compared to $259 million before 2001. Overall, the federal government will spend $2.8 billion this year on port security, including the Department of Energy's Megaports program, says Jackson.[58]

But critics say that amount falls short. The Coast Guard has estimated the cost of installing adequate port-security measures at $5.4 billion.[59] "While billions of homeland-security dollars have been allocated to airports, first responders and research and development, only a modest amount has been made available for port security," says Nagle of the Association of Port Authorities.

Rep. Harman estimates that $9 of every $10 spent on transportation security since 9/11 has gone to airports. "We have severely underfunded ports," she said on April 4.

Unions also insist that more federal funds are needed, among other things, to teach workers how to recognize a security breach and how to evacuate during an emergency. Unions also want access to the security plans that port operators are required to write but are not required to share with unions, says McLaughlin of the International Longshore and Warehouse Union.

Meanwhile, proposed immigration reform — if it passes — might also result in additional Customs agents, money and equipment. The Senate left for its Easter break without wrapping up work on how to deal with the highly charged issue of illegal immigration. Tucked into comprehensive immigration legislation proposed by Senate Majority Leader Bill Frist, R-Tenn. — already included in a House-passed version — is language that would add more maritime border security and technology. But prospects are mixed on whether Congress will pass a bill this year.

Finally, none of the pending measures to bar foreign, government-owned companies from controlling U.S. ports has passed. Several measures also would overhaul the process by which mergers and acquisitions of American companies by foreigners are reviewed by the Committee on Foreign Investment in the United States (CFIUS), the interagency panel that approved Dubai Ports World's lease proposal.

A Senate panel in April approved a measure that would retain Treasury as the lead agency of CFIUS but make the process more transparent. Another measure, proposed by Collins, would create a new panel headed by DHS to review transactions with national-security concerns.

Security expert and former Coast Guard commander Stephen Flynn of the Council on Foreign Relations tells a congressional committee that the United States has not done enough since the terrorist attacks of Sept. 11, 2001, to beef up port security.

OUTLOOK

'Time Is of the Essence'

Security experts hope intensified port-security concerns will force Congress and the Bush administration to give ports the same protection that airports received after 9/11.

"The hullabaloo surrounding the Dubai Ports World deal injected a sense of urgency into the need for important port-security reform," says Rep. Lungren.

Rep. Harman calls the House Homeland Security panel's quick approval of the SAFE Port Act "nothing short of a miracle." It shows that "Congress is appropriately focused" after years of giving short shrift to port security. "Time is of the essence."

Sen. Murray of Washington state likewise says immediate action by Congress is needed. "Let's make the changes now, on our terms, before there's a deadly incident."

Meanwhile, there is wide agreement that it will take more time and money to completely secure the ports. "We have a long way to go to make this a reality," says Collins.

Regardless of what Congress does, the administration plans to continue relying on voluntary compliance by private companies via the C-TPAT program and by foreign governments under the CSI and Megaports programs. It also plans to continue looking for new and better screening technologies. "I am convinced that we can make great progress in the near term," says DHS Deputy Secretary Jackson.

DHS Secretary Chertoff expects that by year's end two-thirds of the containers entering the United States will be screened for radiation either overseas or in this country. But he also stresses that his department won't be consumed by port mania: "My job is not to go from protecting the ports to protecting the railroads to protecting this and protecting that, following along as the media focuses in fits and starts on the particular news of the day."[60]

Experts like Flynn of the Council on Foreign Relations, however, worry that the current attention on ports will fade and little will change. "Should terrorists strike in a major U.S. seaport today, Americans, I believe, will experience a post-Katrina sense of dismay and frustration at how little the federal government has been investing to effectively safeguard this critical national-security and economic-security asset," he says.

Sen. Coleman agrees: "If we think that the terrorists are going to ignore our vulnerabilities and not find the kinks in our supply chain, we are mistaken."

Some lawmakers fear it will take more than good intentions to get the government to act. Rep. Gene Taylor of Mississippi, a former member of the Coast Guard Reserve and ranking Democrat on the House Armed Services Committee, said in March, "It's going to take a 9/11-type maritime-industry-based disaster for our country to do what we should be doing."[61]

NOTES

1. Ted Bridis, "Port Security Lapses Raise Fears of Attacks," The Associated Press, March 12, 2006.

2. Booz Allen Hamilton, "Port Security War Game, Implications for U.S. Supply Chains," 2002.

3. Congressional Budget Office, "The Economic Costs of Disruptions in Container Shipments," March 29, 2006.

4. For background, see Martin Kady II, "Homeland Security," *CQ Researcher*, Sept. 12, 2003, pp. 749-772; and Patrick Marshall, "Policing the Borders," *CQ Researcher*, Feb. 22, 2002, pp. 145-168.

5. Remarks of Homeland Security Secretary Michael Chertoff at the Heritage Foundation, March 20, 2006.

6. Transcript, MSNBC, "Hardball with Chris Matthews," Feb. 27, 2006; www.msnbc.msn.com/id/11605058/.

7. "Final Report on 9/11 Commission Recommendations," Dec. 5, 2005, www.9-11pdp.org/press/2005-12-05_report.pdf.

8. Senate Permanent Subcommittee on Investigations, Committee on Homeland Security and Governmental Affairs, "An Assessment of U.S. Efforts to Secure the Global Supply Chain," March 30, 2006.

9. Government Accountability Office, "Border Security: Investigators Successfully Transported Radioactive Sources Across Our Nation's Borders at Selected Locations," March 2006.

10. Department of Justice, Office of the Inspector General Audit Division, "The Federal Bureau of Investigation's Efforts to Protect the Nation's Seaports," March 2006; www.usdoj.gov/oig/reports/FBI/a0626/final.pdf.

11. Transcript, House Homeland Security Subcommittee on Economic Security, Infrastructure Protection and Cybersecurity Hearing on Port Security, March 16, 2006.

12. Transcript, CBS News, "Face the Nation," Feb. 26, 2006.

13. According to a March *USA Today*/CNN/Gallup Poll, www.usatoday.com/news/polls/2006-03-02-poll.htm#ports.

14. Government Accountability Office, "Maritime Security, Enhancements Made, But Implementation and Sustainability Remain Key Challenges," May 17, 2005, p. 12.

15. Transcript of March 16, 2006, hearing, *op. cit.*

16. *Ibid.*

17. *Ibid.*

18. Government Accountability Office, May 17, 2005, *op. cit.*, p. 20-21.

19. Chertoff remarks, Heritage Foundation, *op. cit.*

20. Prepared testimony of Homeland Security Assistant Secretary Stewart Baker before the House Coast Guard and Maritime Transportation Subcommittee, March 9, 2006.

21. John F. Frittelli, *Port and Maritime Security, Background and Issues*, Novinka Books, 2003.

22. Transcript, Fox News, "Hannity & Co.," March 1, 2006.

23. Press releases, Sen. Charles E. Schumer, Feb. 16 and 26, 2006.

24. Transcript, White House press briefing of Assistant to the President for Homeland Security and Counterterrorism Frances Fragos Townsend, Feb. 23, 2006; www.whitehouse.gov/news/releases/2006/02/20060223-5.html.

25. Transcript, Senate Banking, Housing and Urban Affairs Committee hearing, March 2, 2005.

26. "Meet the Press," Feb. 26, 2006.

27. Transcript, House Armed Service Committee Hearing on Dubai Purchase of U.S. Port Facilities, March 2, 2006.

28. *Ibid.*

29. White House transcript, "President Discusses Port Security," Feb. 21, 2006; www.whitehouse.gov/news/releases/2006/02/20060221-2.html.

30. "Meet the Press," *op. cit.*

31. Press release, Rep. Duncan Hunter, March 2, 2006.

32. For background, see Mary H. Cooper, "Nuclear Proliferation and Terrorism," *CQ Researcher*, April 2, 2004, p. 297-320.

33. Transcript, Senate Commerce, Science and Transportation Committee Hearing on U.S Port Security, Feb. 28, 2005.

34. Government Accountability Office, "Container Security, A Flexible Staffing Model and Minimum Equipment Requirements Would Improve Overseas Targeting and Inspection Efforts," April 2005.

35. March 16, 2006 transcript, *op. cit.*

36. Government Accountability Office, "Cargo Security, Partnership Program Grants, Importers Reduced Scrutiny with Limited Assurance of Improved Security," March 2005.

37. Lawrence M. Wein and Stephen E. Flynn, "Think Inside the Box," *The New York Times*, Nov. 29, 2005, p. A27.

38. Background on Customs from "U.S. Customs Service, Over 200 Years of History," www.cbp.gov/xp/cgov/toolbox/about/history/history.xml.

39. U.S. Coast Guard History, www.uscg.mil/hq/g-cp/history/h_USCGhistory.html.

40. The site of the 1916 incident, known as the "Black Tom Island explosion," is today a portion of Liberty State Park.

41. Carmela Karnoutsos, "Jersey City, Past and Present Web Site Project," New Jersey City University, 2004; www.njcu.edu/programs/jchistory/About.htm.

42. For background, see "Refugee Policy," *Editorial Research Reports*, May 30, 1980, available at CQ Electronic Library, *CQ Researcher Plus Archive*, http://library.cqpress.com.

43. John F. Frittelli, *Port and Maritime Security, Background and Issues* (2003).

44. For background, see David Masci, "War on Terrorism," *CQ Researcher*, Oct. 12, 2001, pp. 817-848.

45. Baker testimony, March 9, 2006, *op. cit.*

46. Frittelli, *op. cit.*, p. 50.

47. General Accounting Office (now the Government Accountability Office), "Combating Terrorism, Actions Needed to Improve Force Protection for DOD Deployments Through Domestic Seaports," October 2002.

48. www.whitehouse.gov/homeland/maritime-security.html#intro.

49. Press release, Department of Homeland Security, "National Strategy for Maritime Security Supporting Plans Announced," Oct. 26, 2005.

50. Press release, American Association of Port Authorities, March 22, 2006.

51. "Ports Deal News Tracker," *The Wall Street Journal*, March 16, 2006.

52. Government Accountability Office, "Combating Nuclear Smuggling: Corruption, Maintenance and Coordination Problems Challenge U.S. Efforts to Provide Radiation Detection Equipment to Other Countries," March 2006.

53. Government Accountability Office, "Combating Nuclear Smuggling: DHS Has Made Progress Deploying Radiation Detection Equipment at U.S. Ports of Entry, But Concerns Remain," March 2006.

54. Government Accountability Office, "Border Security," March 2006, *op. cit.*

55. Tim Starks, "House Panel OKs $821 Million for Beefed Up Port Security," *CQ Weekly Report*, April 3, 2006, p. 924.

56. Press release, Senate Appropriations Committee, "Appropriations Committee Reports Supplemental Bill," April 4, 2006.

57. John M. Donnelly and Tim Starks, "A Plethora of Port Security Bills," *CQ Weekly*, March 6, 2006, p. 604.

58. From testimony before the House Homeland Security Committee on April 4, 2006.

59. Memo of House Subcommittee on Coast Guard and Maritime Transportation Hearing on Foreign Operations of U.S. Port Facilities, March 9, 2006.

60. Chertoff speech before Heritage Foundation, *op. cit.*

61. House Armed Services Committee hearing, March 2, 2006, *op. cit.*

BIBLIOGRAPHY

Books

Flynn, Stephen, *America the Vulnerable, How Our Government Is Failing to Protect Us From Terrorism*, *HarperCollins*, in cooperation with the Council on Foreign Relations, 2004.
A former Coast Guard commander concludes that while the Bush administration has waged an aggressive war against terrorists abroad it has neglected to protect critical U.S. infrastructure, including ports.

Frittelli, John F., *et al.*, *Port and Maritime Security, Background and Issues*, *Novinka Books*, 2003.
Experts on security at the Library of Congress's Congressional Research Service give a concise history of maritime security and lay out the key issues facing Congress, including funding levels.

Articles

Bridis, Ted, "Port Security Lapses Raise Fears of Attacks," *The Associated Press*, March 12, 2006.
A Department of Homeland Security study slated for release this fall finds that cargo containers can be opened secretly and that there are serious security lapses at foreign and American ports, aboard ships and on trucks and trains.

Carafano, James Jay, "The Administration Misses an Opportunity," *The Heritage Foundation*, March 2, 2006.
A former director of Military Studies at the Army's Center of Military History says the Bush administration should have used the Dubai deal to explain how ports can be made more secure, which includes providing more funds to the Coast Guard and Customs.

Cohen, William S., and James M. Loy, "Fact, Not Fear," *The Wall Street Journal*, Feb. 28, 2006.
The former Defense secretary and the former administrator of the Transportation Security Administration say Congress should not let the "inflamed rhetoric" over the Dubai port deal distract them from the more important task of identifying "the substantial gaps that exist in our current port security system."

Goure, Daniel, "Right Issue — Wrong Port," *Lexington Institute*, Feb. 28, 2006.
A military expert says Americans should be most concerned about the ports where cargo is loaded, not where it arrives and is unloaded.

Plummer, Anne, "Hill Scrutiny of Ports Deal Intensifies," and Donnelly, John, and Tim Starks, "A Plethora of Port Security Bills," *CQ Weekly*, March 6, 2006, pp. 603-604.
Two analyses of the dispute over the proposed Dubai Ports World deal outline the various proposed port security bills.

Wein, Lawrence, and Stephen E. Flynn, "Think Inside the Box," *The New York Times*, Nov. 29, 2005, p. A27.
A management professor and faculty member of Stanford's Center for International Security and Cooperation (Wein) and a senior fellow at the Council on Foreign Relations argue that President Bush's border security reform and immigration proposals won't protect the country from what the authors say is the gravest risk: the possibility that a ship, truck or train will import a 40-foot cargo container in which terrorists have hidden a "dirty bomb."

Reports and Studies

"An Assessment of U.S. Efforts to Secure the Global Supply Chain," *Senate Permanent Subcommittee on*

Investigations, Committee on Homeland Security and Governmental Affairs, **March 30, 2006.**
Senate investigators find that only 2.8 percent of containers destined for the United States in 2005 were screened overseas with radiation detectors, while less than 1 percent (0.38 percent) were screened with X-ray-type imaging technology.

"Combating Nuclear Smuggling: Corruption, Maintenance and Coordination Problems Challenge U.S. Efforts to Provide Radiation Detection Equipment to Other Countries," and "Combating Nuclear Smuggling: DHS Has Made Progress Deploying Radiation Detection Equipment at U.S. Ports of Entry, But Concerns Remain," both *Government Accountability Office*, **March 2006.**
A series of reports by the congressional watchdog agency finds U.S. seaport operators have delayed deployment of radiation-detection equipment, fearing that corrupt border security officials overseas could compromise the effectiveness of the devices given to foreign ports by the United States.

"The Economic Costs of Disruptions in Container Shipments," *Congressional Budget Office*, **March 29, 2006.**
Congressional investigators estimate that an unexpected shutdown of the ports of Los Angles and Long Beach could cost up to $150 million a day.

"Port Security War Game, Implications for U.S Supply Chains," *Booz Allen Hamilton Inc.*, **2002.**
The consulting firm concludes after a two-day "war game" involving government and private industry that a dirty bomb delivered at a U.S. seaport could force the government to shut down all U.S. ports for up to 12 days at a cost of $58 billion.

Willis, Henry H., and David S. Ortiz, "Evaluating the Security of the Global Containerized Supply Chain," *RAND*, **2004.**
The authors lay out the challenges of trying to keep cargo secure while en route to U.S. ports.

For More Information

American Association of Port Authorities, 1010 Duke St., Alexandria, VA 22314; (703) 684-5700; www.aapa-ports .org. Represents more than 150 port authorities in the United States, Canada, the Caribbean and Latin America.

Council on Foreign Relations, 58 East 68th St., New York, NY 10021; (212) 434-9400; www.cfr.org. A non-partisan think tank that has long been concerned about port security.

International Longshore and Warehouse Union, AFL-CIO, 1188 Franklin St., 4th Floor, San Francisco, CA 94109; (415) 775-0533; www.ilwu.org. Represents 42,000 workers, primarily on the West Coast.

U.S. Coast Guard, 2100 Second St., S.W., Washington, DC 20593; (202) 267-1587; www.uscg.mil. A Department of Homeland Security (DHS) agency that plays a lead role in patrolling waters in and around U.S. ports.

U.S. Customs and Border Protection, 1300 Pennsylvania Ave., N.W., Washington, DC 20229; (202) 354-1000; www .cbp.gov. A DHS agency that screens cargo and cargo manifests at home and in foreign ports for dangerous materials.

U.S. Department of Homeland Security, Washington, DC 20528; (202) 282-8000; www.dhs.gov. The Cabinet-level department with overall responsibility for protecting U.S. ports.

World Shipping Council, 1015 15th St., N.W., Suite 450, Washington, DC 20005; (202) 589-1230; www.world shipping.org. A trade group representing more than 40 shipping companies, including the largest container lines.

A Customs Service agent inspects the seal on a cargo container in the port of Miami. Agents monitor more than 6 million containers of cargo brought to U.S. ports yearly by 7,500 foreign-flag ships. About 2 percent are x-rayed or physically inspected.

14

Policing the Borders

Can the United States Guard Against Terrorists?

Patrick Marshall

Foreign visitors to the United States are expected to fill out their entry forms accurately. When Khalid Al Midhair and Nawaq Alhamzi arrived, they noted they would be staying at an unspecified Marriott Hotel in New York City.

Shortly before the Sept. 11 terrorist attacks, the two Arab men were identified as potential terrorists, but when FBI agents went looking for them the addresses proved bogus. Midhair and Alhamzi eventually surfaced — they were among the hijackers on the American Airlines plane that slammed into the Pentagon.[1]

In the wake of the attacks, whatever comfort Americans took from the two oceans buffering them from the rest of the world suddenly vanished. As the deaths of more than 3,000 people tragically underscored, America is as vulnerable to terrorists as any country in the Middle East or Europe.

What had gone so wrong? Why had 19 Arab men with terrorist ties been allowed into the country? How had all of them managed to carry box cutters aboard commercial airliners? And why hadn't the CIA, FBI and other government intelligence agencies been able to track down those that had been identified?

The attacks put the nation on high alert. Airports shut down; ships with potentially dangerous cargo, such as liquefied natural gas, were blocked from ports; National Guardsmen patrolled power plants, reservoirs, borders, airports and major bridges. Greyhound even stopped running buses.[2]

Then, without warning, anthrax-tainted letters began arriving at government and news organization offices around the country, eventually killing two postal workers.

From *CQ Researcher*, February 22, 2002.

Illegal Apprehensions Dropped After Sept. 11

The number of illegal aliens apprehended by U.S. Border Patrol agents along the 2,000-mile Southwest border with Mexico plummeted 45 percent after the terrorist attacks. Officials say increased patrol efforts help account for the drop, as well as the depressed U.S. economy and increased optimism in Mexico.

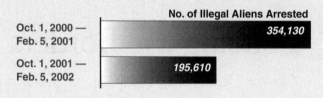

No. of Illegal Aliens Arrested

Oct. 1, 2000 —
Feb. 5, 2001   **354,130**

Oct. 1, 2001 —
Feb. 5, 2002   **195,610**

Source: Immigration and Naturalization Service

Soon afterward, more sweeping responses were ordered. President Bush formed a new Homeland Security Office to find answers and coordinate a response. Legislators summoned experts from the responsible agencies and quickly passed legislation giving police agencies more power to fight terrorism. And the administration started the process of funneling more money to border-security agencies.

Debate still rages over how best to reduce threats to the nation's security, but experts agree that border security is one of the keys. The task is massive. In addition to policing the nation's 7,500-mile-long borders with Mexico and Canada, agents from the Customs Service and Immigration and Naturalization Service (INS) must monitor the 11 million trucks and 2.2 million rail cars that enter the United States every year, plus 7,500 foreign-flag ships that make 51,000 calls in U.S. ports.

The job includes responsibility for the more than 31 million non-citizens who enter the country each year — who are supposed to notify the INS when their visas expire or when they change addresses, jobs or schools.

It's an uphill battle, in the view of Stephen E. Flynn, a senior fellow in the National Security Studies Program at the Council on Foreign Relations and a commander in the U.S. Coast Guard.

"As Americans now contemplate the road ahead, they need to accept three unpleasant facts," he wrote recently. "First, there will continue to be anti-American terrorists with global reach for the foreseeable future."[3]

Secondly, "These terrorists will have access to the means — including chemical and biological weapons — to carry out catastrophic attacks on U.S. soil.

"And third, the economic and societal disruption created by both the Sept. 11 attacks and the subsequent anthrax mailings will provide grist for the terrorist mill."

But many experts say the U.S. must also focus on border security in other nations. "All of us are thinking about a more layered approach to the border," says an official at the Office of Homeland Security, who asked that his name not be used. "Before, we were working with a paradigm based on the war against drugs: If drugs reached the border, that was OK, because if we found the drugs at the border and confiscated them, they didn't get to the end user.

"But today we have the threat of weapons of mass destruction reaching our borders. As soon as they get close to our borders they can be harmful. That's one of the reasons we need to push our borders out" and work with border security in other nations.

To bolster border security, anti-terrorism experts have called for several immediate improvements, including:

- better intelligence gathering on visa applicants;
- increased data-sharing among federal agencies;
- closer scrutiny of incoming cargo;
- stronger security measures at the borders; and
- computer tracking of immigrants and visa holders after they've arrived in the United States.

President Bush's 2003 budget proposes about $11 billion for border security, including $380 million for the INS to build a state-of-the-art visa-tracking system, and an increase of $619 million for the Customs Service's inspection budget.

But experts disagree over which steps would be the most cost-effective and the least disruptive to trade and Americans' daily lives.

"How much should we spend, and how many liberties should we curtail, in an attempt to stop terrorists?" asks Sam Francis, a syndicated columnist who has written extensively on domestic terrorism. "Congress is going to have to look at some of the proposed systems, and they're going have to answer that question. At this point, there's just a lot of chest thumping. Nobody wants to be seen as soft on terrorism."

Dennis McBride, president of the Potomac Institute for Policy Studies in Arlington, Va., says, "Basically, we need a cost analysis of where we're putting our assets. This is a war, and we have to take a warlike approach and be systematic."

Flynn argues that the goal of such an assessment should be keeping America's infrastructure functioning rather than preventing all terrorist acts. "It is inevitable that we will have breaches of security," he explains. "When we do the postmortem, it is important that we see the event as a result of a correctable security feature, not the absence of security."

On Sept. 11, Flynn notes, "we assumed that we had no credible airport security anywhere, and so we grounded all flights and basically had to go back to square one." The goal should be to strengthen the system enough so [the entire system] doesn't have to shut down when a terrorist incident occurs, he says.

Security officials say they generally feel confident that the government has responded well to the terrorism challenge up to this point, but largely through efforts that will be very difficult to maintain without dedicating additional resources.

"Since Sept. 11, there have been some huge efforts by the border agencies to improve our security, but it's not sustainable," says the Office of Homeland Security official. "For starters, the Customs and INS agents on the borders are burning out. That's why the president has asked for the additional funds."

Meanwhile, civil liberties advocates warn that certain proposed security measures — such as instituting a national ID card and enforcing immigration laws by targeting certain ethnic groups — would undermine some of Americans' most cherished civil liberties.[4] (*See "At Issue," p. 351.*)

As policy-makers discuss how to protect America's borders, here are some of the key questions they are asking:

Can the United States track foreign visitors effectively?

When Americans learned that 13 of the 19 terrorists involved in the Sept. 11 attacks had entered the country legally and that three of them had overstayed their visas,

A gamma-ray imaging device scans a truck passing through U.S. Customs at the U.S.-Mexico border crossing in Laredo, Texas. Unlike older technologies using x-rays, the new technology uses low radiation doses and doesn't require a special enclosure. Trucks are scanned for contraband, mis-manifested cargo, explosives and weapons.

the public immediately wanted to know how visas are issued by the State Department and then monitored by the INS after the visa holder enters the United States.

"What went wrong in the issuance of valid visas that permitted these 13 terrorists to legally enter the United States?" Sen. Dianne Feinstein, D-Calif., asked Mary Ryan, assistant secretary of State for consular affairs, during Senate hearings last October. "Or do you view their entry as acceptable risk?"[5]

"We had no information on them whatsoever from law enforcement or from intelligence," Ryan replied. "So they came in. They applied for visas. They were interviewed. And their stories were believed. Like most Americans, I was surprised at how much we learned about some of these terrorists in the immediate aftermath of the Sept. 11 atrocities. And the question in my own mind is, 'Why didn't we know that before Sept. 11?' "

Ryan's question was rhetorical. Her department knows very well why they didn't have the information they needed to filter out the terrorists before granting them visas: Federal agencies, such as the CIA and the FBI, didn't share the information they have about visa applicants.

"We have had a struggle with the law enforcement and intelligence communities in getting information," Ryan complained. "I've tried, we've tried in the Bureau of Consular Affairs . . . to get . . . information from the FBI. We were constantly told we were not a law-enforcement agency, and so they couldn't give it to us. Other agencies fear compromise of sources and methods."[6]

Indeed, many intelligence experts argue that the FBI and the CIA might have been able to thwart the Sept. 11 attacks had they worked together more closely. The critics blame the lack of cooperation on several factors, including U.S. laws — especially grand jury secrecy laws — that prevent the FBI from sharing information with the CIA and other intelligence agencies.

Just six weeks after the attacks, however, Congress revamped some of the secrecy laws. A sweeping new anti-terrorism bill — the USA Patriot Act — now allows the FBI to share secret grand jury evidence with the CIA and other agencies dealing with national security without first obtaining a court order (*see p. 352*).[7]

Attorney General John D. Ashcroft says the new law "takes down some of the walls" between the FBI, the CIA and the INS. "We are working very aggressively to coordinate our informational capabilities so [agencies] in one part of the government that have information can make that information available to, and valuable to, others," Ashcroft said after the Patriot Act was signed on Oct. 26.[8]

There have been other changes since the attacks. Law enforcement and intelligence agencies have nearly tripled their contributions to the database used by consular officials to screen visa applicants, according to the Bureau for Consular Affairs. The database contains an estimated 5.7 million records on aliens in or applying to enter the United States, generated primarily from visa applications and supplemental information from other federal agencies. The information is now being shared with the INS, the agency that decides whether to admit visa holders to the United States.

In addition to the tens of millions of legal visa holders in the United States, the INS estimates that 6 million to 7 million people are in the country illegally, 41 percent of whom have overstayed their visas. At a minimum, that would mean tracking some 2.4 million people.

Some critics of the visa system say that even when agencies have had all the information they need about applicants, the criteria for granting visas and permitting entry to the United States are too loose. Currently, individuals can be denied visas for a variety of reasons, from having a contagious disease or a criminal record to having committed or planned to commit a terrorist act.

However, once inside the United States, visa holders are not monitored unless they are under investigation by a federal law-enforcement agency, such as the FBI or the Drug Enforcement Administration. But because one of the Sept. 11 attackers was in the country on an expired student visa, many have called for stricter monitoring.

"The State Department needs to be given sweeping authority to keep out anyone who belongs to the 'Death to America Club,' " says Mark Krikorian, executive director of the Center for Immigration Studies, an immigration policy think tank. "If you're an enemy of America, I'm not really interested in whether you've killed anybody or not — you have no business being here."

However, others see serious problems with the current procedure for putting foreigners on a "lookout list" of individuals who should be denied admission.

"We're concerned that people might be put on the list not because of involvement in a terrorist group but because of their political views or because their government just doesn't like that person," says Timothy Edgar, legislative counsel at the American Civil Liberties Union (ACLU). "That happened back in the Cold War days, when we had grounds of inadmissibility based on being a member of the Communist Party or advocating communism and so forth. [Such practices] interfere with American citizens' right to hear that person."

The INS faces challenges even more daunting than those facing the State Department. Due to limited resources and, some critics say, poor planning, even if the agency had good information about dangerous individuals headed for our borders, the service would be hard-pressed to prevent them from entering the country or to track and deport those who do get in.

"On Sept. 10," notes Flynn of the Council on Foreign Relations, "just over 300 U.S. Border Patrol agents supported by a single analyst were assigned the job of detecting and intercepting illegal border crossings along the entire, vast 4,000-mile land and water border with Canada."*

---

* Of the Immigration and Naturalization Service's 9,824 Border Patrol agents, 9,500 are assigned to the U.S.-Mexico border.

While patrols have been beefed up significantly since Sept. 11, no one seriously believes any number of border agents can prevent a determined terrorist from entering the United States. What's more, recent experience has shown that even when the Border Patrol catches a criminal alien, he may be released because of lack of data coordination between agencies.

Such was the infamous case of the "Railway Killer," a rail-hopping Mexican named Angel Maturino Resendiz, alias Rafael Resendez-Ramirez, who eventually confessed to murdering at least eight people along railway lines in three Southwestern states. When Maturino was still at large, Houston police had contacted the INS about him, but the agency failed to put an alert for him in the Border Patrol's primary database. Thus, when he was caught trying to enter the United States in El Paso, Border Patrol agents didn't know he was wanted for murder and sent him back to Mexico. A few days later, he re-entered the country and murdered again. He eventually surrendered in 1999.

Congress responded to the incident by ordering the government to merge the fingerprint files of the FBI and the INS, but the two databases still are not linked.

And that wasn't the first time Congress had ordered better tracking of alien entries and exits. In the Illegal Immigration Reform and Immigrant Responsibility Act of 1996, lawmakers mandated that a computerized system be established for tracking aliens whose visas have expired. But after border-area business groups complained it might delay cross-border shoppers, Congress never appropriated enough money for it and later watered it down so it doesn't apply to most land-border entries into the United States (*see p. 349*).

Glenn Fine, inspector general of the Department of Justice, found that the INS had not properly managed another entry and exit system mandated by Congress, despite having spent $31 million on the pilot program.

As a result, Fine told a congressional hearing recently, the INS is virtually incapable of tracking those who overstay their visas and has no way to apprehend them. "Our review found that the principal INS system for tracking these overstays, the non-immigrant information system, was not producing reliable data, either in the aggregate or on individuals," Fine said. "We also found that the INS had no specific enforcement program to identify,

locate, apprehend and remove overstays, and that using the INS data was of little use for locating them."[9]

James Ziglar, who was appointed INS commissioner two months before the hearing and only a month before the Sept. 11 attacks, admitted the agency has many holes to plug, but said they've been trying.

"There are lots of things that we need to change, but the idea that this organization is sitting around and doesn't care and hasn't been approaching these problems is not true," Ziglar told senators.

Can the United States keep weapons of mass destruction out of the country?

Keeping terrorists out of the United States is only half the battle; they also must be prevented from bringing in lethal biological agents or other weapons. For the U.S. Customs Service, the Treasury Department agency that handles property searches at the borders, the challenge is at least as daunting as the challenge facing the INS.

Part of the challenge is understaffing. For example, observes Flynn of the Council on Foreign Relations, the number of customs inspectors on the U.S.-Canadian border was reduced by about 25 percent from 1985 to 2000, even as trade between the two nations increased from $116.3 billion to $409.8 billion.[10]

The Customs Service also faces serious challenges in monitoring America's ports. "At many ports, access is virtually uncontrolled," F. Amanda DeBusk, a former member of the Interagency Commission on Crime and Security in U.S. Seaports, told a Senate hearing last December.[11]

"Access is overseen by contract security personnel, who, like airport baggage screeners, receive low wages and little training," said Argent Acosta, a customs official in New Orleans."[12] And the ranks of customs agents at the ports are just as decimated as they are along the borders, he pointed out.

"Despite the huge increases in trade since I started with customs in 1970, the number of customs inspectors at the Port of New Orleans has dropped from approximately 103 in 1970 to 29 this year," Acosta said, pointing out that with its current staff, the service is only capable of inspecting about 2 percent of the 600,000 cargo containers that come into the nation's seaports each day.

U.S. Customs Commissioner Robert C. Bonner later took issue with Acosta's use of the 2 percent figure, saying

AFP Photo/Jeff Kowalsky

More than 3 million vehicles a year pass U.S. Customs before driving through the Detroit-Windsor tunnel at the Canada-U.S. border crossing. Customs agents nationwide annually monitor more than 11 million trucks and 2.2 million rail cars crossing the borders.

it was unfair to use the "startling statistic" without explaining the complex process used by customs inspectors to carefully target which shipments to inspect among the $1.2 trillion in goods processed by the service each year.

"An effective border strategy requires a thoughtful approach that relies only in part on physical examinations of cargo," Bonner said in a Feb. 16 *Washington Post* Op-Ed article.

The service also combines "good intelligence, advance-arrival information, state-of-the-art inspection technology, strong industry-government partnerships, a well-trained work force and sophisticated systems to exchange and analyze mountains of data," Bonner said.

"We follow a complex process that requires far more than mere physical examination to prevent terrorists or their weapons from entering the United States," he said.[13]

But the agency had warned earlier that it was woefully understaffed and underfunded. According to a February 2001 study, in order to meet its mission requirements, the service said it needed an additional

14,777 positions — mostly inspectors — over its fiscal 1998 base of 19,428 positions.[14]

And it is not just lack of manpower that hampers the Customs Service, critics say. Like the INS, the service lacks information about land and sea shipments because it has inadequate databases and outdated equipment.

"The world may be well into the electronic age, but the U.S. Customs Service is still struggling with paper-based systems," Flynn wrote. "For years, its proposed [data-modernization] projects have run aground on the twin shoals of flat federal budgets and industry disputes over the timing, format and quantity of data it should provide to customs in advance."[15]

Last April, the Customs Service received the seed money to start modernizing its database, but completion is years away. In the interim, according to Flynn, "inspectors will have to rely on only the bluntest of data-management tools."[16]

Customs Service officials are optimistic, despite the challenges. While conceding that the current system "is clearly on overload," Deputy Assistant Commissioner John Heinrich says the situation is improving rapidly. Besides increasing staffing since Sept. 11, Heinrich says, all ports of entry on the northern border — many of which were frequently unstaffed before Sept. 11 — are being "hardened," or made more secure.

And new technology will extend the range of existing personnel. "We're going to install new gates and extensive video systems so that remotely we can see what is happening at ports of entry after they've been closed [for the night] and the gates have been shut," Heinrich says.

In addition, the purchase of new x-ray and gamma-ray detectors will make it possible to examine more containers with fewer inspectors, he says.

"The deployment of this additional technology . . . will enable us to examine in a matter of minutes an entire 40-foot container or an entire truckload of merchandise," Heinrich says. "Had we used simple, backbreaking labor, the time would be two to three hours."

In fact, Heinrich promises, at some ports inspectors will be able to increase by a factor of two or three the amount of "high-risk" cargo they can inspect from questionable shippers or lax foreign ports.

Flynn agrees that things have improved since Sept. 11, but he warns that there is still "virtually no security" at many ports, and that land entry points are similarly porous. If there were a terrorist incident at a port, he warns, it could lead to a "tremendously costly" shutdown of all ports, as it did for aviation on Sept. 11.

Most of the measures implemented since Sept. 11 have been too narrowly focused, Flynn says. "Ultimately," he says, "we need to go toward a point of origin and bring security to what we call the supply chain," by beefing up the security measures in place in other countries that ship to the United States.

Kim E. Petersen, executive director of the Maritime Security Council, an industry group, agrees.

"It was erroneous for the Office of Homeland Defense to consider U.S. ports as the first line of defense against weapons of mass destruction," Petersen says. "The fact is, our first line of defense must be the ports of origin [because] we haven't been that good about identifying problem [domestic] ports."

Petersen argues that industry and the government need to work together to establish minimum-security standards for foreign ports, including tougher requirements for cargo manifest reporting and inspection. "If a particular port is identified as noncompliant, then, just as the Federal Aviation Administration does now, the U.S. government would impose sanctions up to and including a prohibition of shipments coming directly from that port," Petersen says.

"Otherwise, we're at the mercy of shipments coming into the United States," he continues. "In the case of a weapon of mass destruction, we won't discover it until it actually exists within our ports, and that is an unacceptable risk."

Customs officials say they agree with the concept. Heinrich says such a program would require "deploying our own officers as analysts in foreign countries, sharing of technology that we're using here and working closely with those governments to identify cargo shipments before they actually are placed on the vessel."

But Heinrich concedes that it won't happen overnight. "It will be two to three years before we can say with certainty that the threat has been reduced about as significantly as we can expect," he says.

And while many of the proposed measures may be costly, Petersen points out that in addition to increased security, they will provide across-the-board benefits to ports, shippers and the nation's economy.

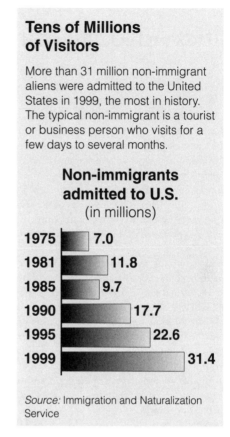

Tens of Millions of Visitors

More than 31 million non-immigrant aliens were admitted to the United States in 1999, the most in history. The typical non-immigrant is a tourist or business person who visits for a few days to several months.

Non-immigrants admitted to U.S.
(in millions)

Year	Millions
1975	7.0
1981	11.8
1985	9.7
1990	17.7
1995	22.6
1999	31.4

Source: Immigration and Naturalization Service

"These very same measures would also help prevent theft of cargo and other crimes," he says. "Literally tens of billions of dollars are lost worldwide through cargo theft. It would be cost-effective for many ports to enact these measures, and I expect they'll be far more receptive than many people suppose."

Should lawmakers create a new border security agency?

President Bush created the Office of Homeland Security and tapped then-Gov. Tom Ridge, R-Pa., to develop and coordinate a comprehensive national strategy against terrorist attacks. Without a congressional mandate, however, policy experts say the office largely depends upon presidential coattails for influence, because it has no direct authority over any of the agencies involved in protecting the borders and very little experience in dealing with the issues.

Critics Advocate Immigration Limits

Critics of U.S. immigration policy argue that the Sept. 11 terrorist attacks tragically proved that the country needs to clamp down on legal as well as illegal immigration.

"The numbers of immigrants are such that the government has lost the capacity to monitor who is here, and under what conditions," says Daniel Stein, executive director of the Federation for American Immigration Reform. "The numbers are too high. The exploded numbers of the aliens fighting to stay in the country have hamstrung the whole enforcement apparatus of the Immigration and Naturalization Service" (INS).

In fact, according to INS figures, the number of legal immigrants has been steadily falling. From an all-time high of more than 1.5 million in 1990, the number dropped to 646,568 in 1999, the most recent year for which totals are available.[1] At the same time, however, non-immigrant visitors, such as tourists, business people and students, rose sharply. In 1999, 31.4 million visitors were admitted, compared with 17.6 million in 1990.

The number of immigrants isn't the critics' only concern. Some argue that immigrant communities in the United States offer a haven for terrorists.

"Immigrant sub-cultures, not just Islamic or Arabic but many different cultures, provide comfort and anonymity for potential terrorists," says political columnist Sam Francis. "Obviously, most of the people in the subculture communities are not terrorists, and most of them are not sympathetic with terrorists. But the community itself provides cover and a kind of sanctuary for terrorists."

Mark Krikorian, executive director of the Center for Immigration Studies, agrees. "Immigrant communities serve as the sea within which terrorist fish swim," he says, much as Italian communities in major U.S. cities once served as "incubators" for the Mafia. It was only when immigration from Italy was reduced, Krikorian says, that people in the communities began to assimilate into the broader American society. "The Mafia lost the incubator they benefited from and the FBI was, little by little, able to penetrate the group," Krikorian says.

Krikorian argues that lower levels of immigration today would have a similar impact. "Today, Muslim communities form unwitting cover for terrorists, and promoting the assimilation of the recent immigrants in these communities can only make it more difficult for terrorists who operate in these communities to use them as hosts," he says. "A reduction in immigration is naturally going to allow assimilation to operate more thoroughly, and that will have national-security benefits."

But civil liberties advocates reject proposals that single people out by race or national origin, and especially those that target legal immigrants for special attention. "We had a terrible legacy in this country of discriminatory immigration policy," says Timothy Edgar, legislative counsel for the American Civil Liberties Union. "It would be a huge mistake for this country to assume we're going to come up with a list of pariah countries in the Islamic world that can't get access to the United States."

In fact, Edgar says, terrorists don't always come from a specific country or group of countries. For example, he says, recent terrorist incidents have involved an American — Oklahoma City bomber Timothy McVeigh — and a man from Great Britain, Richard Reid, who was recently arrested on board a U.S. airliner after trying to ignite explosives in his shoes.

Edgar suspects other motives lie behind suggestions to reduce legal immigration. "I think the basic impetus behind some of these proposals has nothing to do with enforcing immigration laws," he says. "It stems from a vague anxiety that immigrants are more likely to be dangerous."

Judith Golub, senior director for advocacy for the American Immigration Lawyers Association, agrees. "We are a nation of immigrants," she says. "The only way to enhance our security is to target only those who plan to do us harm, and those are terrorists, not immigrants."

[1] *1998 Statistical Yearbook of the Immigration and Naturalization Service*, Department of Justice, November 2000, p. 19.

"Let's face it, Tom Ridge's office is brand new," said INS Commissioner Ziglar. "They are still getting organized, and they don't have anybody over there who are experts on immigration, customs [or] border enforcement. That's why they necessarily have to rely on us."[17]

Ridge acknowledges the problem and has proposed combining the agencies responsible for border enforcement. "There may be some fusion of these agencies," he said. "We need to change our border strategy so there is only one face greeting people, instead of the way it is now

Policing the Borders — at a Glance

- Of the 9,824 Immigration and Naturalization Service (INS) Border Patrol agents, 9,500 are assigned to the U.S.-Mexico border.

- INS agents arrested 1.2 million people who tried to enter the United States illegally last year. For every one person arrested, an estimated three more enter the United States undetected.

- There are 300 official ports of entry into the United States, but only 5,113 INS immigration inspectors. Last year they made more than a half-billion inspections at all border crossings.

- The 1,977 INS special agents posted worldwide are authorized to arrest non-citizen criminals and also investigate alien-smuggling cases, counterfeit immigration documents, foreign-based organized-crime syndicates and gang activities.

- The INS has 2,618 adjudication officers to consider petitions for immigration benefits. Last year, 7.3 million applications for immigration benefits were filed — not counting a half-million citizenship applications.

- About 640 INS deportation officers are responsible for tracking 314,000 aliens who have ignored deportation orders.

- The INS has 371 asylum officers who process more than 66,000 requests for asylum each year.

- The Customs Service collected $24 billion in duties, excise taxes, fees and penalties on imported and exported goods and services in fiscal 2000.

- The Customs Service has 7,562 inspectors, 588 canine enforcement officers and 1,030 import specialists.

- Customs agents inspected cargo (including 5.7 million seagoing containers) on 964,447 aircraft, 11.2 million trucks, 2.3 million rail cars and 214,610 vessels in fiscal 2001.

where one agency looks in the trunk and another looks in the back seat. But I know my colleagues resist this consolidation."[18]

Indeed, the president's 2003 budget proposals did not include such a request. "The administration is convinced that we basically have a very good system," says McBride of the Potomac Institute. "They give me no reason to think that they want to re-examine our philosophy of security."

However, the Bush administration has proposed restructuring the INS so that its enforcement functions are separate from its visa and other administrative functions.

But House Judiciary Committee Chairman James Sensenbrenner Jr., R-Wis., says the INS restructuring plan is inadequate. "It does not go far enough for the rescue mission that is needed — both on the enforcement side and the immigration-services side," Sensenbrenner said at a Nov. 14 press conference. "I fear this proposal will follow its administrative-restructuring predecessors in making little impact and possibly making things worse at the agency. We must remember that the current INS is the direct product of previous INS administrative-restructuring efforts."[19]

Instead, Sensenbrenner wants to abolish the INS and create an Agency for Immigration Services. Besides dividing enforcement functions from service functions, his proposed legislation would raise the agency's profile by putting an associate attorney general for immigration affairs at its helm, a position higher than the current INS commissioner.

Rep. Tom Tancredo, R-Colo., says Sensenbrenner's plan doesn't go far enough.

"There's something big-time wrong with the INS," Tancredo says and calls for an entirely new agency with broader responsibilities. Tancredo has introduced a bill to combine the responsibilities of the INS, the Customs Service, the Coast Guard and other agencies into a new National Border Security Agency.

"Right now, you can go to an entry point on the border and look at lines of cars coming in, each to a different station. Each of those stations might be manned by a different agency," Tancredo explains. "People sit in the hills around the portal with binoculars, trying to figure out which agency is manning which station. If they're smuggling drugs, they'll pick one line, and if they're smuggling people they'll pick a different line. That's how goofy it is.

"You could dump a zillion dollars into this system, and it would all be sucked up by inefficiency," he continues. "We should not add more money to this. The problem is lack of coordination, lack of a single line of authority and lack of direction."

But Tancredo is not hopeful about the prospects for his bill.

"When you're fighting the chairman of the committee, the president of the United States and all the agencies, I'd say the chances are slim to none," Tancredo says.

But, he warns, "If we don't do anything to shore up our borders and something else happens as a result of that inability or inaction, then we're not just responsible, we're culpable."

BACKGROUND

Open-Door Policy

Border control meant two things to the newly independent American colonies: repelling invading armies and enforcing duties on imported goods.

The threat of invasion was of real but limited concern. For a European army to invade meant assembling a mighty fleet, and the only country at the time capable of doing that was England, which was licking its wounds following its defeat in the American war for independence. Thus, the new nation's primary military concern was policing the borders against Indian raids — deadly nuisances, to be sure, but not ultimately threatening to the country's security.

More of a threat was the nation's impending bankruptcy. On July 4, 1789, in an effort to put the country on a firmer financial footing, Congress passed the Tariff Act, which authorized the collection of duties on imported goods. A few weeks later, lawmakers passed legislation creating the U.S. Customs Service to collect the duties. In its first year, the service was the primary source of revenue for the federal government, collecting more than $2 million.

For nearly 125 years, customs funded virtually the entire government, and paid for the nation's early growth and infrastructure. The territories of Louisiana and Oregon, Florida and Alaska were purchased; the National Road from Cumberland, Maryland, to Wheeling, West Virginia, was constructed; and, the Transcontinental Railroad stretched from sea-to-sea. Customs collections built the nation's lighthouses; the military and naval academies; and the City of Washington. The new nation that once teetered on the edge of bankruptcy was now solvent. By 1835, customs revenues alone had reduced the national debt to zero!

In addition to collecting duties from law-abiding importers, the Customs Service — along with the Coast Guard and other agencies — apprehended smugglers trying to evade duties or smuggle illegal goods into, or out of, the country. During the War of 1812, for example, American profiteers took cattle to Canada illegally to sell to British troops. But because of the long and mostly unguarded land border, customs officers barely made a dent in the illegal cattle trade.

The young country was just about as hungry for workers as it was for revenue, so immigration control was not an issue. Indeed, getting to the New World was still a relatively expensive proposition, which meant that hordes of uneducated people from the Old World did not threaten to flood the gates. For the most part, new arrivals were either relatively affluent immigrants or indentured workers and slaves. Laws restricting immigration were not seen as necessary. In 1793, in fact, President George Washington announced an open-door immigration policy.

While Congress wouldn't restrict immigration for almost 100 years, it was only five years until lawmakers, worried that radical supporters of the French Revolution might agitate in the United States, passed the four Alien and Sedition Acts of 1798. The controversial laws — later largely overturned — required a 14-year residency before immigrants could become citizens; allowed the president to expel aliens in the event of war or when they represented a threat to security; and made it a crime — for citizens as well as for aliens — to criticize the government.

Despite the new concerns, the government didn't begin recording the names of newcomers until 1819, when the Steerage Act required ship captains bringing immigrants to submit passenger lists to the Customs Service.

Federal Controls

The Immigration Act of 1875 marked the real beginning of federal controls on immigration. Among other things, the act prohibited the importation of Asian laborers

C H R O N O L O G Y

1875-1892 *Labor unrest and concern about an influx of Asians spur restrictive policies.*

1875 The Immigration Act of 1875 imposes the first significant federal controls on immigration, mainly by prohibiting new Asian laborers.

1882 The Immigration Act of 1882 sets a 50-cents per immigrant head tax. The first of several Chinese Exclusion Acts limits Chinese immigration. Similar legislation in 1884 and 1888 bars ethnic Chinese.

Jan. 1, 1892 Ellis Island in New York Harbor becomes the primary entry point for immigrants.

1917-1930 *Postwar fears of foreign agitators trigger immigration backlash.*

1917 The Immigration Act of 1917 imposes the first literacy test on immigrants and a head tax on Canadian and Mexican immigrants.

1921 The 1921 Emergency Immigration Restriction Act establishes the first quotas on the number of people admitted from each country or region.

1924 Congress creates the U.S. Border Patrol. The 1924 Immigration Act sets new quotas on immigrants from specific countries.

1940-1965 *Cold War politics influences immigration policy.*

1940 The Immigration and Naturalization Service is transferred to the Department of Justice. The Alien Registration Act requires all aliens — visitors as well as immigrants — to register and anyone over 14 to be fingerprinted.

1950 Internal Security Act includes political "subversives" among the list of excludable aliens.

1952 Influenced by Cold War political concerns, the Immigration and Nationality Act sets pro-Europeans immigration quotas.

1965 The 1965 Amendments to the Immigration and Nationality Act replaces the immigration quota system with ceilings on the number of entrants from the Eastern and Western Hemisphere.

1980-2000 *High immigration levels spur calls for restriction.*

1986 Immigration Reform and Control Act sanctions employers who knowingly hire illegal aliens.

1990 The Immigration Act of 1990 significantly increases the number of immigrants allowed into the country and prohibits exclusion because of beliefs, statements or associations.

1996 The Illegal Immigration Reform and Responsibility Act of 1996 provides increased funding for the Border Patrol, tougher penalties for illegal entry and added grounds for excluding aliens.

2001-2002 *Terrorism on American soil causes tighter border security.*

Sept. 11, 2001 Terrorists crash two airliners into the World Trade Center and one into the Pentagon; a fourth crashes in a Pennsylvania field.

Oct. 8, 2001 President Bush creates the Office of Homeland Security.

Oct. 26, 2001 Bush signs the USA Patriot Act allowing the FBI to share secret grand jury evidence with the CIA and other agencies without first obtaining a court order.

Dec. 19, 2001 The House passes by voice vote the Enhanced Border Security and Visa Reform Act, strengthening the foreign-student tracking system and once again requiring an automated entry-and-exit tracking system for all non-citizens entering and exiting the country, except for Canadian nationals. It also requires all visas and passports of immigrants and visitors to be tamper-resistant, machine-readable and contain biometric identifiers, such as fingerprints. It bars visas for anyone from countries that sponsor terrorism and authorizes 2,000 more INS inspectors and investigative personnel over the next five years.

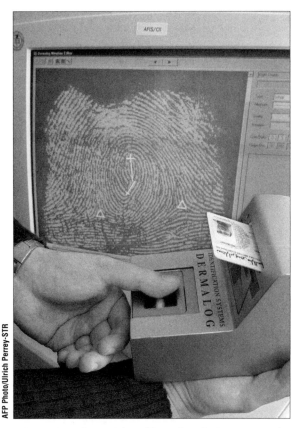

A fingerprint reader made by a German firm checks a passenger's thumbprint against the print on his passport. Legislation passed by the House would require that visas and other identification documents issued by the U.S. and other countries contain such "biometric" information.

without their consent and barred convicted felons and prostitutes from entering the country.

In 1882, Congress passed the first major restriction on immigration, the Chinese Exclusion Act. The law established a head tax of 50 cents per immigrant and banned "lunatics" and other individuals who might become public charges. Over the next 10 years, virtually all legislation related to immigration focused on controlling the flow of Chinese "coolie" labor. Subsequent Exclusion Acts in 1884 and 1888 progressively expanded the restrictions from Chinese nationals to all individuals of Chinese extraction.

By 1891, anti-Catholic sentiment, coupled with business interests' concern that radical immigrants were behind the nation's rising labor activism, spurred passage of the Immigration Act. While the act extended exclusion of immigrants to the indigent and those with contagious diseases, it also created a superintendent of immigration in the Department of the Treasury. Soon after, the office was transformed into the Bureau of Immigration, the predecessor of the INS, with orders to deny entry to paupers, polygamists, the insane and persons with contagious diseases.

Until well after the turn of the century, immigration was generally easy to control since transportation was still relatively costly, and there were few entry points to the United States. The main public concern was not terrorists or criminals, but mass influxes of uneducated workers. On Jan. 1, 1892, the primary entry point for immigrants became Ellis Island. Sitting in the middle of New York Harbor, the facility was easy to control.

The only potentially uncontrollable area at the turn of the century was the long border with Mexico, which became a conduit for illegal Chinese laborers and Europeans who feared rejection at Ellis Island. Mounted guards were assigned to patrol the southern border, but the new patrol initially consisted of only a few dozen men and was not particularly effective.

World War I marked a turning point for America as a world power, and for U.S. concerns about immigration. The war's end brought special worries about the threat of radicalism, particularly after the Russian Revolution in 1917. The high levels of immigration from poorer Eastern and Southern European countries just before the war were cut dramatically during the war, and afterward, by restrictive — some would say racist — immigration legislation. The Immigration Act of 1917 imposed a literacy test intended to turn back some of the new, more impoverished immigrants, barred Asian immigrants from permanent residency and, for the first time, imposed a head tax on immigrants from Canada and Mexico.

Two major pieces of legislation in the 1920s — the 1921 Emergency Immigration Restriction Act and the 1924 Immigration Act — for the first time established quotas on immigrants from specific countries and regions. The new caps helped spark an immediate increase in illegal immigrants, which in turn prompted Congress to pass legislation creating the U.S. Border Patrol in 1924.

Growing Concern

World War II marked another turning point in U.S. immigration policy. In 1940, as part of a new wartime focus on controlling immigration, Congress transferred the INS to the Department of Justice. At the same time, the new Alien Registration Act required all aliens — visitors as well as immigrants — to register with the government. Those over 14 years of age had to be fingerprinted. Members or former members of prohibited organizations (especially communist organizations) were excluded from the country.

In 1965, amid charges that immigration quotas were biased against non-whites, lawmakers eliminated the system of visa quotas based on an applicant's country of origin. Instead, they set a ceiling on entrants from the Eastern Hemisphere and the Western Hemisphere, with a maximum of 20,000 visas to be granted per year to applicants from any single country.

Illegal aliens were the primary target of the sweeping 1986 Immigration Reform and Control Act. For the first time, both civil and criminal penalties were set for employers who knowingly hired illegal aliens. Largely as a tradeoff for the new penalties, however, Congress raised the official ceiling to 540,000 legal immigrants annually.

The 1986 law represented a response to public concerns over growing levels of both legal and illegal immigration. Between 1940 and 1991, legal immigration rose from 70,756 to a high of 1.8 million.[20] Expulsion of illegal aliens also increased over the same period by a factor of about 10.[21]

The number of foreign visitors also increased dramatically, rising from 6.3 million in 1975 to 11.8 million in 1981 and 1982. In 1999, there were more than 31 million non-immigrant arrivals.[22]

Public opinion polls throughout the 1980s and '90s showed a clear preference for restricting immigration. "Strong and increasingly well-organized public support for new restrictions on both legal and illegal immigration, coupled with Republican victories in both the House and the Senate in 1994, signaled that the immigration policy debate in the United States would likely be entering a new era of restrictionism," writes Debra L. DeLaet, a professor of political science at Drake University in Des Moines, Iowa. "Indeed, within two years, the new Republican Congress pushed through two significant pieces of legislation designed to reduce immigration to the United States."[23]

Sweeping New Laws

The Welfare Reform Act of 1996 denied federal benefits to legal and illegal immigrants. That same year, the Illegal Immigration Reform and Responsibility Act provided increased funding for the Border Patrol, increased penalties for illegal entry and added to the list of grounds for excluding aliens.

The new legislation also ordered the attorney general to develop within two years a computerized database showing when non-citizens enter and exit the country, so the INS could track visitors who had overstayed their visas.

Canadian officials and American merchants along both the northern and southern borders quickly attacked the tracking provision, saying it would disrupt America's ever-increasing cross-border traffic and trade with Mexico and Canada. The opponents convinced border-state lawmakers to try to gut the provision. And some lawmakers from northern-border states, like Michigan, where the automobile industry depends on just-in-time delivery of parts and materials from Canadian plants, wanted to repeal it altogether.

Then Sen. Spencer Abraham, R-Mich., currently Secretary of Energy — was among those who tried to get the tracking system scrapped. Abraham, who was chairman of the Senate Immigration Subcommittee, said the law would create 24-hour backups at U.S.-Canada bridges. "That would be unbearable, and the border would be effectively closed," Abraham said.[24]

In the end, Congress did not repeal the law but delayed its implementation for 30 months. But the issue remained contentious, especially since the country was experiencing a robust economy with unprecedented high employment. Employers were anxious to get as many immigrant workers into the country as possible.

"There was a general reluctance to enforce the laws regarding visa over-stays," remembers Daniel Stein, executive director of the Federation for American Immigration Reform (FAIR), which lobbies for tougher immigration controls.

Then in May 2000, Congress passed a compromise bill that fundamentally changed the tracking program by prohibiting the INS from requiring individuals to obtain any new documentation as part of the automated entry and exit system. In essence, it exempted Canadians — who do not need visas to drive across the border — from the bill's requirements. Congress also refused to fund creation of the database. Critics say the measure prevented the entry-exit tracking system from being

U.S. Targets Mideast 'Absconders'

The Justice Department in late January ordered anti-terrorism officials to target Middle Easterners who have ignored deportation orders, according to a confidential memo obtained by *The Washington Post*.

Out of the estimated 314,000 so-called absconders at large in the United States, federal officials are targeting approximately 6,000 individuals from countries on the list as being hospitable to Al Qaeda, the terrorist organization headed by Osama bin Laden.

Special apprehension teams of agents from the Federal Bureau of Investigation, the Immigration and Naturalization Service and other agencies are being assembled, according to the *Post*. Absconders who are picked up will be detained and interviewed, and the memo directs investigators to encourage absconders to cooperate by referring to rewards being offered and the possibility of obtaining S Visas, which are given to immigrants who provide information to authorities that is helpful in criminal investigations.[1]

According to the memo, the government already has compiled a database of information gathered from recent interviews with thousands of Middle Eastern men who were invited to come forth voluntarily after the Sept. 11 attacks. Information gleaned from those apprehended and interrogated for failure to respond to deportation proceedings will be added to the database.

"We can't go after 314,000 people at a time, so it only makes sense to prioritize them in a way that makes sense from a law-enforcement perspective," a senior Justice Department official told the *Post*. "If we didn't do this, then we should be criticized."[2]

Meanwhile the administration is drawing criticism for targeting those from Middle Eastern countries.

"It's a fishing expedition," says Timothy Edgar, legislative counsel of the American Civil Liberties Union. "This is the biggest racial-profiling effort on the part of the government in decades."

Edgar says that the people who will be arrested and detained will be people for whom there is no indication that they are involved in terrorism. "It has become clear that it has nothing to do with enforcing immigration laws and has everything to do with selectively providing a pretext to aggressively investigate, interrogate and prosecute people based solely on their national origin," he says. "You really have to question whether this is the right use of limited government resources. This is a real blunderbuss approach."

But columnist Sam Francis argues that citizens should be more concerned about Americans' civil liberties than those of illegal aliens. "Frankly, we've allowed immigration to get out of control at this point," he says. "The result is that we're facing potential restrictions on our own civil liberties to control the situation. I don't think that's a good thing. I'd rather control immigration and have our civil liberties more secure."

[1] Dan Eggen, "Deportee Sweep Will Start With Mideast Focus," *The Washington Post*, Feb. 8, 2002, p. A1.

[2] *Ibid.*

properly implemented at the nation's land border entry ports.

"They tried to gut it without formally repealing it," Krikorian says. That is particularly true for traffic coming in from Canada, where, he says, liberal asylum procedures make the country a haven for terrorists.

But lawmakers from northern and southern states were happy. "The implementation of this system would have resulted in intolerable traffic delays and congestion at our borders," said Rep. Solomon Ortiz, D-Texas, then chairman of the Congressional Border Caucus.[25]

Political science Professor DeLaet concluded that "proposals for a computerized national registry database, a national identification card and stronger border control

and enforcement measures are likely to be significant issues in the perennial debate [over] U.S. immigration policy."[26]

CURRENT SITUATION

Administration Action

When security officials sought to provide a higher state of security at land border crossings following the Sept. 11 attacks, massive traffic delays occurred. Long delays at the Canadian border in inspecting trucks carrying auto parts, for example, caused the temporary shutdown of assembly plants in Detroit. And the bureaucratic

Should driver's licenses be linked to a national database and used as ID cards?

YES Daniel Stein
*Executive Director, Federation
for American Immigration Reform*

Written for the *CQ Researcher*, February 2002

There was a time in this country when most of us were born, lived and died in the same town where everybody knew us. We went to church with the local shopkeeper, bowled with the local bank president and called the cop on the beat by his first name. In that America, our face was all the identification we needed.

We don't live in that world anymore. Our ability to function in today's world depends upon being able to identify ourselves with a high degree of certainty to complete strangers.

Because we no longer know the people we deal with, we have come to rely on the government to vouch for our identity. The merchant who takes your check may not know you, but your driver's license assures him that the state knows who you are. In order for our society and economy to function efficiently, the information the state has must be reliable and accessible.

Mobility is not restricted to decent, upstanding people. The terrorists who murdered some 3,000 people on Sept. 11 succeeded in part because no database exists in the United States that can differentiate between people who belong here and those who do not.

These 19 terrorists were able to obtain Social Security numbers and driver's licenses (many issued under aliases) because there was no way to verify that they were illegally in the United States.

Identity fraud and identity theft are problems for law enforcement and an impediment to commerce. We need to correct the serious flaws in our identity process that endanger people's physical and economic security.

That must begin with the Social Security Administration confirming that applicants for an ID number are legally present in the United States and that the identity given is not an alias.

States could then rely on the Social Security number when issuing the second important identity document — the driver's license. Adding biometric information and including it on a common database used by all 50 states would create a high degree of certainty that a driver's license truly is a reliable form of identification. That's why the recent proposal developed by the American Association of Motor Vehicle Administrators deserves federal and state support.

We are already using these documents to identify ourselves. With the addition of technological features, we could close many of the loopholes that terrorists and other criminals use to their advantage, without any intrusion into the lives of law-abiding Americans.

NO Katie Corrigan
*Legislative Counsel,
American Civil Liberties Union*

Written for the *CQ Researcher*, February 2002

The recent proposal put forward by the American Association of Motor Vehicle Administrators to standardize driver's licenses nationwide and link state licensing databases into one giant integrated information bank is nothing less than a de facto national ID. Regardless of recent protestations that this plan is nothing like a national ID scheme, clearly this is a case of "if it walks like a duck and quacks like a duck, it must be a duck."

Considered side by side, the motor vehicle proposal and a national ID scheme are nearly identical. Each would require the establishment of a giant information bank accessible nationwide, and each would deploy a universal identification card of standard design across the country. Furthermore, the motor vehicle proposal and a national ID scheme also have exactly the same problems, including, most crucially, that they would both be ineffective in the fight against identify theft and terrorism.

Not only would the actual card be built upon a shaky foundation of easily forged or stolen documentation (Social Security cards, birth certificates), but a card touted as tamper-proof, especially one with biometric identifiers, could lead our nation to a false sense of security and would actually exacerbate the problem of identity theft. Consider the consequences if a thief steals someone's name and then walks around with an ID containing the stolen name with the thief's fingerprint. How difficult would it be for the victim to reclaim his identity?

The very idea of a national ID — or the standardized driver's license — should be anathema to a free society. One of the first principles of American democracy is the idea that we have the right to be immune from intrusive government — that we have the "right to be left alone."

That's why such a broad array of organizations signed onto a letter to the White House opposing the proposal. In addition to the ACLU, signatories included the Eagle Forum and Free Congress Foundation, as well as privacy groups, consumer-advocacy groups and conferences of state legislators from both sides of the political aisle.

Since Sept. 11, the United States has been engaged in widespread reflection on what it is about this country that we defend and celebrate. While civil libertarians want security as much as anybody else, we do not believe we must sacrifice our freedom to secure our safety. And in the final analysis, a national ID scheme of any form will guarantee us neither freedom nor safety.

difficulties encountered in deploying National Guard troops to help with the job contributed to the problem of overlapping agency roles and jurisdictions.

Since Sept. 11, all federal agencies dealing with border security have shifted their primary missions. The Customs Service — which previously focused on collecting duties and interdicting contraband and drugs — now is focusing on preventing terrorists from smuggling chemical, biological or nuclear weapons or their components into the country in cargo, postal shipments or personal luggage.

The INS, whose primary mission was to manage the flow of immigrants and visitors to the United States, is under pressure to institute organizational reforms that will keep terrorists out of the country, improve databases, improve integration with other agency databases and separate its service and enforcement functions.

As part of the $2.2 billion increase in border-security spending requested by the Bush administration, the INS enforcement budget would be increased by $1.2 billion, $380 million of which is earmarked to implement the non-citizen entry-exit tracking system mandated in 1996. In addition, the administration wants to increase the Customs Service budget by $619 million, and the Coast Guard's security-related budget by $282 million.

Immigration reform groups complain that the budget does not beef up the agency's domestic-enforcement capabilities enough. "The administration is tinkering on the edges of the issue in a very lukewarm way," says Stein of FAIR.

FAIR and other immigration reform groups charge that the administration's border-protection policy is caught between two conflicting goals — one related to national security and one to politics. The administration wants to secure the borders against terrorists, while at the same time it wants to loosen immigration controls on Mexican immigrants, they say.

Before Sept. 11, Bush had indicated he would support an amnesty program for undocumented Mexicans already living and working in this country, a proposal sought by Mexican President Vicente Fox.[27] Fox had addressed a joint session of Congress on Sept. 5, and his visit was expected to spur liberalization of U.S. immigration laws.

"The president is trying to satisfy conflicting political objectives," Stein says. "You can't say you are a national-security president and then continue to support a system

whereby you don't know who is in the country. These are totally irreconcilable goals." Under the amnesty program, he says, "You never really find out who these people are."

Bush and congressional leaders have assured pro-immigrant groups that they will not abandon the move toward liberalizing immigration laws. The issue speaks to a growing Hispanic electorate whose votes are sought by both parties.[28]

Congress Responds

Just six weeks after the Sept. 11 terrorist attacks, Congress sent legislation to President Bush giving new powers to the government to fight terrorism. Included was broad, new authority allowing law enforcement officials to conduct searches and detain suspects, one of several requests made by Attorney General Ashcroft. The president signed the USA Patriot Act on Oct. 26.

Although the bill was tempered somewhat by more liberal members of Congress, especially Senate Judiciary Committee Chairman Patrick Leahy, D-Vt., it gave Ashcroft much of what he had asked for, including provisions that:

- Grant INS and State Department personnel access to the FBI's database and the Wanted Persons File for the purpose of checking the criminal history of a visa applicant;
- Give law enforcement the authority to conduct "secret searches" of a suspect's residence, including computer files;
- Allow the attorney general to detain any non-citizen believed to be a national security risk for up to seven days. After seven days, the government must charge the suspect or begin deportation proceedings;
- Allow authorities to track Internet communications (e-mail) as they do telephone calls;
- Broaden the grounds for excluding terrorists and aliens with ties to terrorist organizations; and,
- Direct the attorney general to implement fully and expand the foreign student tracking system.

Lawmakers are now considering legislation addressing several additional aspects of border protection. At least a dozen narrowly focused bills have been introduced, but the House has passed a comprehensive bill — HR 3525 — that would:

- Increase the number of border inspectors and provide more training;
- Improve technology and expand data-sharing among federal agencies;
- Remove the 45-minute time limit on INS inspections of people on incoming foreign flights;
- Restrict visas issued to individuals from countries designated as sponsors of international terrorism;
- Create terrorist "lookout committees" at U.S. embassies abroad;
- Tighten the student visa system by requiring schools to report to the government when foreign students do not report for class;
- Require that identification documents, such as passports and visas, issued by other countries contain "biometric information," such as fingerprints, by October 2003; and,
- Require airplanes and passenger ships arriving from other countries to provide passenger and crew lists to immigration officials before arrival.

The legislation passed by voice vote on Dec. 19, but it is blocked in committee in the Senate, where a similar bill has been negotiated — after much compromise — by Sens. Edward M. Kennedy, D-Mass., Sam Brownback, R-Kan., Jon Kyl, R-Ariz., and Feinstein. The law, which is strongly supported by the families of victims killed on Sept. 11, is expected to eventually pass the Senate and clear Congress.

The compromise bill contains the policy of exempting Mexicans and Canadians from the entry and exit visa system. "In the face of clear threats, they continue to take the short-range view, and they stall, stall, stall until the situation becomes intolerable," says a frustrated Stein, who charges that Congress is "capitulating to business interests" such as meatpackers and restaurant owners who resist "any kind of tightening of the labor market."

"It's maddening," he says. "Congress is constantly cheering the primacy of border commerce over the national security."

OUTLOOK

Civil Liberties

Ironically, notes Flynn of the Council on Foreign Relations, the tragic events of Sept. 11 revealed that America's economic and political openness and success also increased the nation's vulnerability. "For years, U.S. policy-makers, trade negotiators and business leaders have operated on the naive assumption that there was no downside to building frictionless global networks of international trade and travel," he writes. " 'Facilitation' was the order of the day.

"Inspectors and agents with responsibility for policing the flows of people and goods passing through those networks were seen as nuisances at best — and at worst, as barriers to competitiveness who should be marginalized, privatized or eliminated wherever possible."[29]

The laissez-faire mindset made it relatively easy for potential terrorists to gain access to the country and to operate inside our borders, notes Stein of FAIR.

"One miscreant can get into the country and wind up perpetrating the murder of millions of people," he warns. "We're in what appears to be a protracted clash of civilizations. As long as we have to deal with these real and present threats — and we probably will for the rest of our lives — the immigration issue will never be seen the same again."

How much are Americans willing to change the way they live and do business in order to protect themselves? Krikorian at the Center for Immigration Studies says that tracking the millions of visitors to the United States is crucial to the nation's security. The most effective, practical way to track them, he says, is through the use of a secure driver's license.

Going after foreign visitors who overstay their visas is "difficult and time-consuming," Krikorian says, "but it's possible and feasible."

But the ACLU's Edgar urges caution in taking steps that might erode Americans' constitutional rights. "The greatest concern, first of all, is preserving the privacy of everyone in the country, particularly American citizens, and insuring against a national ID proposal," Edgar says. "We're also concerned about the possibility of 'mission creep' — that once we create the infrastructure of a vast computer database to track immigrants, we would also be able to track citizens."

No matter what steps are taken, security experts warn that the nation faces an uphill battle. "One characteristic of terrorists is that they want to meet the challenge," says McBride of the Potomac Institute. "As you raise the bar — and all these [anti-terrorist] measures are going to raise the bar — we're going to attract a more serious contender. The more serious contender is not going to just take a building out. A more serious contender is going to do something more destructive, and that worries me a lot."

McBride says his one hope is that if we can raise the bar enough, the cost of undertaking a major terrorist action may be too high for individual terrorist groups. "Diplomatic and other approaches are going to reduce the probability of state sponsorship," McBride says. "That's the good news."

NOTES

1. Nancy San Martin, "INS System Simply Can't Keep Up with Immigrant Tracking," Knight Ridder Tribune Business News, Sept. 27, 2001.

2. David Masci and Kenneth Jost, "War on Terrorism," *The CQ Researcher*, Oct. 12, 2001, pp. 817-848.

3. Stephen E. Flynn, "America the Vulnerable," *Foreign Affairs*, Jan. 1, 2002.

4. David Masci and Patrick Marshall, "Civil Liberties in Wartime," *The CQ Researcher*, Dec. 14, 2001, pp. 1017-1040.

5. Senate Judiciary Subcommittee on Technology, Terrorism and Government Information hearing on "Technological Help for Border Security," Oct. 12, 2001.

6. *Ibid.*

7. For background, see Brian Hansen, "Intelligence Reforms," *The CQ Researcher*, Jan. 25, 2002, pp. 49-72.

8. *Ibid.*

9. Senate Judiciary Subcommittee on Technology, Terrorism and Government Information, *op. cit.*

10. Flynn, *op. cit.*

11. Testimony before Senate Committee on Government Affairs hearing on "Weak Links: Assessing the Vulnerability of U.S. Ports and Whether the Government is Adequately Structured to Safeguard Them," Dec. 6, 2001.

12. *Ibid.*

13. Robert C. Bonner, "The Customs Patrol," *The Washington Post*, Feb. 16, 2002.

14. "U.S. Customs Service Resource Allocation Model Fact Sheet," February 2001, http://www.customs.gov/about/pdf/ram1.pdf.

15. Flynn, *op. cit.*

16. *Ibid.*

17. Joel Brinkley and Philip Shenon, "Ridge Facing Major Doubts on His Ability," *The New York Times*, Feb. 7, 2002.

18. *Ibid.*

19. http://www.house.gov/judiciary/news111401b.htm

20. *1998 Statistical Yearbook of the Immigration and Naturalization Service*, Department of Justice, November 2000, p. 15.

21. *Ibid.*, p. 212.

22. *Ibid.*, p. 122.

23. Debra L. DeLaet, *U.S. Immigration Policy in an Age of Rights* (2000), p. 103.

24. Quoted in Catherine Strong, "Congress must undo controversial border provision slipped into a massive 1996 bill," The Associated Press, Oct. 4, 1998.

25. Quoted in Gary Martin, "Tracking plan gets House OK; INS system to follow foreigners' entries, exits," *San Antonio Express-News*, May 26, 2000.

26. *Ibid.*, p. 116.

27. For background, see David Masci, "U.S.-Mexico Relations," *The CQ Researcher*, Nov. 9, 2001, pp. 921-944.

28. For background, see David Masci, "Hispanic-Americans' New Clout," *The CQ Researcher*, Sept. 18, 1998, pp. 809-832.

29. Flynn, *op. cit.*

BIBLIOGRAPHY

Books

Borjas, George J., *Heaven's Door: Immigration Policy and the American Economy*, Princeton University Press, 1999.

A professor of public policy at the John F. Kennedy School of Government at Harvard University offers a thorough and insightful discussion of immigration's economic impact on the United States and how economic issues frame the overall debate over immigration policy.

DeLaet, Debra L., *U.S. Immigration Policy in an Age of Rights*, Praeger, 2000.
A professor of political science offers a cogent historical discussion of the development of immigration policy, including an examination of the impact of immigration policies on civil rights and, conversely, the impact of civil rights concerns on immigration policy.

Gimpel, James G., and James R. Edwards Jr., *The Congressional Politics of Immigration Reform*, Allyn and Bacon, 1999.
Gimpel, a professor of government at the University of Maryland, and Edwards, a former congressional staffer, have produced a detailed history of immigration legislation in Congress.

Mills, Nicolaus, ed., *Arguing Immigration: The Debate Over the Changing Face of America*, Touchstone, 1994.
This collection of essays by academicians, policy-makers and social commentators largely focuses on whether Americans should welcome immigrants or not, with additional contributions on such topics as the debate over a national ID card.

Reimers, David M., *Unwelcome Strangers: American Identity and the Turn Against Socialism*, Columbia University Press, 1998.
A professor of history at New York University explores the arguments of groups that advocate restrictions on immigration levels.

Articles

Brinkley, Joel, and Philip Shenon, "Ridge Facing Major Doubts on His Ability," *The New York Times*, Feb. 7, 2002.
Two reporters offer a number of interviews with key players to substantiate the argument that Tom Ridge, head of the Office of Homeland Security, faces an uphill battle in fulfilling his mandate to coordinate federal anti-terrorism policies among more than a dozen federal, state and local agencies.

Corn, David, "Ridge on the Ledge," *The Nation*, Nov. 19, 2001, p. 19.
Will the Homeland Security chief be an effective overseer or another spinner?

Eggen, Dan, "Deportee Sweep Will Start With Mideast Focus," *The Washington Post*, Feb. 8, 2002.
Eggen relates the contents of a confidential Justice Department memo obtained by the *Post* that details a plan to round up Middle Easterners who have ignored deportation orders.

Flynn, Stephen E., "America the Vulnerable," *Foreign Affairs*, January 1, 2002.
A senior fellow in the National Security Studies Program at the Council on Foreign Relations critiques the administration's responses to the terrorist attacks on Sept. 11. He urges the government to select future measures with a view not to preventing all future attacks — a goal he says is impossible — but to minimizing the disruption that will occur after an attack.

Waller, Douglas, "A Toothless Tiger? Bureaucratic barriers could thwart Tom Ridge's chance to be an effective antiterror czar," *Time*, Oct. 15, 2001, p. 78.
In the three weeks since Bush tapped Ridge to head his new Office of Homeland Security, the unified front against terrorism has started to develop some cracks.

Reports and Studies

***1998 Statistical Yearbook of the Immigration and Naturalization Service*, Department of Justice, November 2000.**
This 294-page annual report offers a wealth of statistical information on current and historical levels of immigration and INS actions.

Krouse, William J., and Raphael F. Perl, "Terrorism: Automated Lookout Systems and Border Security Options and Issues," *Congressional Research Service*, June 18, 2001.
This report examines options and issues related to tightening border security by improving the "lookout" systems employed by the State Department and the INS to exclude individuals known to be members or supporters of foreign terrorist organizations from entry into the United States.

"Report on Crime and Security in U.S. Seaports," Interagency Commission on Crime and Security in U.S. Seaports, fall 2000.
A commission established by President Clinton in April 2000, long before the terrorist attacks of Sept. 11, 2001, finds lax security measures in the United States.

For More Information

Alexis de Tocqueville Institution, 1446 E St., S.E., Washington, DC 20003; (202) 548-0006; www.adti.net. A public policy think tank that seeks to increase public understanding of the cultural and economic benefits of immigration.

American Immigration Lawyers Association, 918 F St. N.W., Washington, DC 20004; (202) 216-2400; www.aila .org. Founded in 1946, the AILA includes over 7,800 attorneys and law professors who practice and teach immigration law. The related American Immigration Legal Foundation "promotes an alternative to the anti-immigrant messages produced by opponents of newcomers in America" through education and litigation.

Center for Immigration Studies, 1522 K St., N.W., Suite 820, Washington, DC 20005; (202) 466-8185; www.cis .org. The CIS is a nonpartisan, nonprofit research organization founded in 1985 devoted exclusively to studying the impact of immigration on the United States. CIS "seeks fewer immigrants but a warmer welcome for those admitted."

Federation for American Immigration Reform (FAIR), 1666 Connecticut Ave., N.W., Suite 400, Washington, DC 20009; (202) 328-7004; www.fairus.org. FAIR is a nonprofit public interest organization that lobbies in favor of strict limits on immigration.

Immigration History Research Center, http://www.ihrc .umn.edu/. An international resource on American immigration and ethnic history based at the University of Minnesota.

Lutheran Immigration and Refugee Service, 700 Light St., Baltimore, MD 21230; (410) 230-2700; www.lirs.org. Advocates for refugees and other migrants.

National Council of La Raza, 1111 19th St., N.W., Suite 1000, Washington, DC 20036; (202) 785-1670; www.nclr .org. Monitors legislation and lobbies on behalf of Latinos in the United States.

National Immigration Forum, 220 I St., N.E., Washington, DC 20002; (202) 544-0004; www.immigrationforum.org. Advocates pro-immigration policies.

National Immigration Law Center, 3435 Wilshire Blvd., Suite 2850, Los Angeles, CA 90010; (213) 639-3900; http:// www.nilc.org. NILC is a national support center that promotes the rights of low-income immigrants.

U.S. Customs and Border Protection, Office of Public Affairs, 1300 Pennsylvania Ave., N.W., Room 6.3D, Washington, DC 20229; (202) 927-8727; http://www.cbp.gov/. The Customs Service is the primary enforcement agency protecting the nation's borders. Part of the Department of Homeland Security, it is the only border agency with an extensive air, land and marine interdiction force.

U.S. Citizenship and Immigration Services, 425 I St., N.W., Suite 7100, Washington, DC 20536; (202) 514-1900; www.ins.usdoj.gov. The Department of Homeland Security agency that administers and enforces U.S. immigration and naturalization laws.

Interrogating the CIA

Should Its Role in Terrorism
Cases Be Reexamined?

Kenneth Jost

15

The CIA's questioning of accused al Qaeda terrorist Abd al-Rahim al-Nashiri may be among the cases ordered reexamined by Attorney General Eric H. Holder Jr. to see whether CIA operatives exceeded official interrogation guidelines. With al-Nashiri shackled, a CIA debriefer racked an unloaded pistol next to al-Nashiri's head. Later, he revved a power drill near a naked and hooded al-Nashiri.

From *CQ Researcher,*
September 25, 2009.

Abd al-Rahim al-Nashiri, the accused mastermind of the bombing of the *USS Cole* in October 2000, was captured by Central Intelligence Agency (CIA) operatives in the United Arab Emirates in November 2002 and taken to a secret CIA prison in Thailand. Immediately upon arrival, around Nov. 15, al-Nashiri — identified as the chief of operations in the Persian Gulf for the terrorist group al Qaeda — was subjected to one or more of the harsh measures that the CIA calls "enhanced interrogation techniques" and that human-rights advocates say can amount to torture.

Al-Nashiri continued to be harshly interrogated until Dec. 4 — including two instances of waterboarding, or simulated drowning, on his 12th day in custody — and then for another two weeks later in the month. By then, the agents deemed al-Nashiri to be "compliant" and turned him over to a "debriefer" from CIA headquarters.

By the end of the month, however, the debriefer — untrained in interrogation and not authorized to use any of the 10 enhanced techniques sanctioned by the CIA and the Justice Department under President George W. Bush — determined that al-Nashiri was "withholding" information. He decided, after consultation with an unnamed individual, to go beyond the approved interrogation methods. With al-Nashiri shackled, the debriefer entered the cell with an unloaded pistol and racked the weapon "once or twice" next to al-Nashiri's head. "Probably" on the same day, the debriefer entered the cell again and, with al-Nashiri naked and hooded, revved a power drill.

The debriefer made no report of the episode to CIA headquarters in Langley, Va., outside Washington. But CIA officers who

Interrogation Techniques Included Waterboarding

Ten "enhanced interrogation techniques" were approved by the Department of Justice for use by Central Intelligence Agency (CIA) interrogators. The legal memorandum approving the techniques, dated Aug. 1, 2002, was signed by Jay Bybee, assistant attorney general for the Office of Legal Counsel, and prepared by his deputy, John Yoo.

Attention grasp — Detainee is grasped with both hands, one hand on each side of collar opening, in "a controlled and quick motion," and in the same motion drawn toward interrogator.

Walling — Detainee is pulled forward and then "quickly and firmly" pushed into flexible false wall so that shoulder blades hit wall. Head and neck are supported with rolled towel to prevent whiplash.

Facial hold — Detainee's head is immobilized by interrogator placing open palm on either side of detainee's face; interrogator's fingertips "are kept well away from" detainee's eyes.

Facial or insult slap — With fingers "slightly spread apart," the interrogator's hand "makes contact with" area between tip of detainee's chin and bottom of corresponding earlobe.

Cramped confinement — Detainee is placed in confined space, typically a small or large box, usually dark; confinement can last up to two hours in small space, up to 18 hours in larger space.

Insects — "Harmless" insect is placed in confinement box with detainee.

Wall standing — Detainee stands about 4 to 5 feet from wall with feet spread to shoulder width, arms stretched out in front of him, and fingers resting on wall to support body weight. Not allowed to reposition hands or feet.

Stress positions — Detainee sits on floor with legs extended straight out in front of him with arms raised above head or kneels on floor while leaning back at 45-degree angle.

Sleep deprivation — "Will not exceed 11 days at a time."

Waterboarding — Detainee is bound to bench with feet elevated above head; head is immobilized and interrogator places cloth over detainee's mouth and nose while pouring water onto cloth in controlled manner. "Airflow is restricted for 20 to 40 seconds, and the technique produces the sensation of drowning and suffocation."

Source: CIA, Inspector General, "Special Review: Counterterrorism Detention and Interrogation Activities (September 2001-October 2003)," May 7, 2004.

2003 formally decided not to bring criminal charges and left any discipline up to the CIA.

Now, six years later, the case may be one of those that Attorney General Eric H. Holder Jr. has asked a respected career prosecutor to reexamine. On Aug. 24 Holder announced his decision to reopen cases in which CIA agents may have gone beyond official guidelines, just as the agency was itself releasing under court order a 158-page report documenting more than a dozen instances of possible abuse over the first two years of the CIA's controversial interrogation program. The other "unauthorized" techniques described in the report included a staged mock execution, a threat to sexually abuse a detainee's mother, a threat to kill another's children and the choking of another prisoner to the point of losing consciousness.[1]

The IG's report — first released in May 2008 but with much heavier redactions than in the new version — was part of the latest batch of documents on the Bush administration's treatment of suspected terrorists unearthed by two Freedom of Information Act (FOIA) lawsuits filed by the American Civil Liberties Union (ACLU) beginning in 2004. ACLU officials are praising Holder's decision to reopen the cases against CIA agents but say more needs to be done. The latest information "further underscores the need for a comprehensive investigation into the torture of detainees and those who authorized it," says Jameel Jaffer, director of the ACLU's National Security Project.[2]

President Obama decided on Jan. 22 — his second full day in office — to bar the use of waterboarding or any of the other enhanced techniques by CIA or military interrogators. "We believe we can abide by a rule that

arrived in January heard of the incident and reported it to Langley, prompting an investigation by the CIA's inspector general (IG), John Helgerson, and a referral to the Justice Department for possible prosecution. After review by prosecutors in the U.S. attorney's office in Alexandria, Va., however, the government in September

CIA Report Evaluates Interrogation Techniques

Here are major conclusions from a May 2004 report by the Central Intelligence Agency's inspector general on counterterrorism and interrogation activities from September 2001 through October 2003:

- Program provided intelligence that helped identify and apprehend terrorists and warned of planned terrorist attacks on U.S., other countries.
- Office of General Counsel "worked closely" with Justice Department to determine legality of "enhanced interrogation techniques" (EITs) and also "consulted" with White House and National Security Council regarding techniques.
- Justice Department legal opinion "consists of finely detailed analysis" to support conclusion that EITs, "properly" carried out, would not constitute torture; opinion did not address whether practices were consistent with U.S. voluntary undertaking to prevent "cruel, inhuman or degrading" treatment.
- A number of agency officers are concerned that they "may be vulnerable" to legal action in the United States or abroad and that the U.S. government "will not stand behind them."
- Officers are concerned that future public revelation of the program is "inevitable" and "will seriously damage" reputations of personnel, agency.
- Agency "generally" provided "good guidance and support" to officers using EITs, in particular at "these [redacted] foreign locations."

- Agency in early months of program "failed to provide adequate guidance, staffing, guidance and support" to agents involved in interrogation at [redacted location(s)].
- "Unauthorized, improvised, inhumane, and undocumented detention and interrogation techniques were used [redacted] referred to the Department of Justice (DoJ) for potential prosecution."
- Agency "failed to issue in a timely manner comprehensive written guidelines for detention and interrogation activities."
- "Such written guidance as does exist . . . is inadequate."
- Waterboarding was used during interrogation of two detainees "in a manner inconsistent with" the Justice Department's legal opinion; one key al Qaeda terrorist [Khalid Shaikh Mohammed] was subjected to waterboarding 183 times and denied sleep for 180 hours. In this and another instance, "the technique of application and volume of water used differed from the DoJ opinion."
- CIA's Office of Medical Services provided "comprehensive medical attention," but did not issue formal medical guidelines until April 2003.
- EITs may have been applied "without justification" in some instances based not on analytical assessments but on agents' "presumptions" about individual's knowledge.
- Agency faces "potentially serious long-term political and legal challenges" because of use of EITs and government's inability to decide what it will ultimately do with detainees.

Source: "Counterterrorism Detention and Interrogation Activities," Office of Inspector General, Central Intelligence Agency, May 7, 2004

says, we don't torture, but we can effectively obtain the intelligence we need," Obama said in a White House ceremony on Jan. 22 attended by a group of former military officers assembled by human-rights groups. He also promised to close the prison camp at the Guantánamo Bay Naval Base in Cuba within one year.[3]

Republicans and national security-minded conservatives immediately began attacking the Obama policies, with former Vice President Dick Cheney assuming the highest-profile role among the critics. Cheney is continuing his attacks on the president since Holder's decision to reopen the CIA cases. He calls Holder's action "political" and credits use of the harsh methods with

preventing any attacks on the United States following the Sept. 11, 2001, attacks.

"My sort of overwhelming view is that the enhanced interrogation techniques were absolutely essential in saving thousands of American lives and preventing further attacks against the United States," Cheney said on "Fox News Sunday" on Aug. 30. "I think they were directly responsible for the fact that for eight years we had no further mass casualty attacks against the United States."[4]

Seven former CIA directors raised the stakes in the controversy with a letter on Sept. 18 asking Obama to reverse Holder's decision to reopen the investigations. The group, including CIA directors in Republican and Democratic administrations, said the investigation of previously closed cases was unfair to the officers involved, would "seriously damage" other officers' willingness to "take risks to protect the country" and would damage the ability to obtain cooperation from foreign intelligence agencies.

Obama rebuffed the suggestion in an appearance on one of several Sunday talk shows on Sept. 20. "I appreciate the former CIA directors wanting to look after an institution that they helped to build," he told host Bob Schieffer on the CBS program "Face the Nation." "But I continue to believe that nobody's above the law. And I want to make sure that, as president of the United States, I'm not asserting in some way that my decisions overrule the decisions of prosecutors who are there to uphold the law."

At the same time, *The Washington Post* reported that the investigation may be narrower than once thought, with perhaps only two or three cases being seriously considered for possible indictments. *The Post* based the story on two unnamed sources who were described as having been briefed on the investigation.[5]

In the Jan. 22 session, Obama appointed an interagency task force to be headed by Holder to recommend new policies on interrogation and detainee transfers. The task force's recommendations announced by Holder on Aug. 24 reaffirmed Obama's decision to bar any interrogation techniques other than those outlined in the latest version of the *U.S. Army Field Manual.* The manual — revised in 2006 by the Bush administration after the disclosure of abuses of Iraqi prisoners by U.S. military personnel at the Abu Ghraib prison outside Baghdad — details 17 different techniques of interrogation and bars any use of physical force or degrading treatment against prisoners. (*See story, p. 363.*)

Holder said the task force, including members of the intelligence community, was unanimous in concluding that the manual provides "adequate and effective means of conducting interrogations." Obama accepted the task force's further recommendation to take interrogation of so-called high-value detainees away from the CIA and assign the responsibility to a new group comprising specially trained experts from several agencies that will be housed at the FBI and overseen by the National Security Council.[6]

Obama also drew sharp criticism earlier for revoking and then directing the Justice Department to release controversial legal opinions from its Office of Legal Counsel (OLC) that concluded the CIA's enhanced interrogation techniques were legal and did not constitute torture under U.S. or international law. The release of the memos in the ACLU's FOIA suit — with the most graphic description until then of the CIA's harsh techniques — came after a strong plea by CIA Director Leon Panetta to withhold or heavily edit the documents. Instead, the memos were released on April 16 with few redactions.

In releasing the memos, however, Obama appeared to rule out prosecutions of CIA operatives who conducted interrogations according to the techniques he was ordering discarded. "It is our intention," Obama said in the April 16 statement, "to assure those who carried out their duties relying in good faith upon legal advice from the Department of Justice that they will not be subject to prosecution."[7]

At the same time, Obama reiterated his opposition to a broad reexamination of the Bush administration's counterterrorism policies. Obama described the events as "a dark and painful chapter in our history," but added, "Nothing will be gained by spending our time and energy laying blame for the past."

Nevertheless, some lawmakers and many civil liberties and human-rights groups continue to press for a full investigation of the Bush policies either by a special congressional committee or a bipartisan, independent commission comparable to the commission that reexamined events leading up to the 9/11 terrorist attacks. "An independent commission would take a broader look at the policies that have troubled so many people and look at how we can avoid going in that direction again," says Virginia Sloan, president and founder of the bipartisan Constitution Project.

Meanwhile, Obama is making only slow progress toward meeting his goal of closing the Guantánamo prison camp by Jan. 20, 2010. The review of individual cases is moving slowly, other countries are reluctant to accept transferred detainees and Republican politicians are opposing relocating any of the detainees to U.S. soil.

The national security issues complicate Obama's political standing as he tries to move the country out of the economic doldrums and push an ambitious domestic agenda through Congress.

Here are some of the questions being debated:

Should CIA agents be prosecuted for exceeding interrogation guidelines?

Abdul Wali, an Afghan farmer, turned himself in to U.S. authorities in June 2003 after learning he had been implicated in rocket attacks on the U.S. military base at Asadabad, near the Pakistani border. But David Passaro, a former Special Forces medic working on contract as a CIA interrogator, got angry when Wali was unable to answer his questions.

Witnesses said the enraged Passaro repeatedly struck Wali with a foot-long flashlight and his fists and kicked him in the groin while wearing combat boots. Wali died two days later. Today, Passaro is serving time in a federal prison after a federal jury in North Carolina convicted him in August 2006 of assault.[8]

The CIA itself referred Passaro's case to the Justice Department for possible prosecution, and then CIA Director Michael Hayden stressed after the verdict that Passaro's conduct was "neither authorized nor condoned" by the agency. The agency also referred other cases to the Justice Department, but career prosecutors in the U.S. attorney's office in Alexandria decided not to bring criminal charges in any of the others.

Attorney General Holder's Aug. 24 decision to designate John Durham, a career federal prosecutor from Connecticut, to take a second look at those cases is drawing heavy criticism from the intelligence community, including high-ranking CIA officials from Democratic and Republican administrations.

Jeffrey Smith, the CIA's general counsel for two years under President Bill Clinton, warns that prosecutions could set a "dangerous precedent" of using criminal law to settle policy differences at the expense of career officials. And former CIA Inspector General Helgerson says a successful prosecution would be "very difficult" because of the Justice Department's approval of the interrogation program. "I do not believe there was any criminal intent among those involved," Helgerson told *The Washington Post* after the release of his 2004 report on interrogation practices.[9]

In his television interview, Cheney cited the previous investigations, including the prosecution of Passaro, as evidence of a political motivation in Holder's action. Robert Alt, a senior legal fellow with the conservative Heritage Foundation, also notes that any prosecution

Former Vice President Dick Cheney harshly criticizes President Obama's decision to bar waterboarding and other enhanced techniques used by CIA and military interrogators. Cheney labels Attorney General Eric Holder's decision to reopen the CIA interrogation cases "political" and credits the harsh methods with preventing any attacks on the United States following the Sept. 11, 2001, attacks.

would face substantial legal hurdles, including the five-year statute of limitations for most federal offenses. "When you put all that together and you hear the howl from the political left about the need for more action, it begins to look political," says Alt, deputy director of Heritage's Center for Legal and Judicial Studies.

Civil liberties and human-rights advocates defend Holder's action in part by criticizing what they describe as the Bush administration's politicization of the Justice Department. "I'm not convinced that those prosecutors had access to all the facts," says Elisa Massimino, chief executive officer and executive director of Human Rights First. "I'm not convinced that they were operating in the appropriate legal framework to make those decisions."

ACLU lawyer Alex Abdo notes that Holder has only asked for a review of the cases and would have to decide later whether to bring any prosecutions. A legal fellow with the ACLU's National Security Project, Adabo dismisses accusations of political motivations. "The question of whether the law was broken is strictly a legal question, not a political one," he says.

Cheney also warned of the effect the decision is having on the morale of CIA officers. "We ask those people to do some very difficult things. Sometimes, they put their own lives at risk," Cheney said in the Fox News interview.

"And if they are now going to be subject to being investigated and prosecuted by the next administration, nobody's going to sign up for those kinds of missions."

Massimino counters that CIA morale suffered because the agency was given the assignment to interrogate the high-value detainees using legally questionable tactics that Cheney famously characterized shortly after the 9/11 attacks as "the dark side."

"There were a lot of people at the CIA who were devastated by the idea that they were the agency that would go to what Vice President Cheney called the dark side, that they were the agency that would violate the law," Massimino says. "People who are concerned about the morale, where were those people when there was pressure on people at the agency to go beyond the law? Why didn't they stand up then for the morale of the intelligence officers who are trying to serve their country honorably?"

Cheney and other critics also warn that the review of the CIA cases is merely a first step toward possible criminal investigations against others in the Bush administration involved in the interrogation policies, including Justice Department lawyers who sanctioned the enhanced interrogation techniques. Many critics "will not be satisfied until they see former Bush administration officials paraded in orange jump suits," says Alt.

In fact, the ACLU and Human Rights First are among the groups pressing for broader inquiries. "Given what's on the public record, we should be investigating attorneys in the Department of Justice and other senior officials who were the architects of the CIA's enhanced interrogation program," says Abdo.

Should the CIA be allowed to use "enhanced interrogation techniques" when questioning "high-value" detainees?

With Democratic majorities in both chambers, Congress in 2008 moved to prohibit any of the "enhanced interrogation techniques" that CIA operatives had been using against selected "high-value" detainees. But President Bush vetoed the measure, saying the harsh measures were needed to overcome resistance techniques learned by al Qaeda members during training.

"It is vitally important," Bush said in the March 8, 2008, veto message, "that the Central Intelligence Agency be allowed to maintain a separate and classified interrogation program."[10]

In his Jan. 22 executive order, President Obama accomplished what Congress had sought by limiting all interrogations to those practices authorized in the *U.S. Army Field Manual*.[11] Seven months later, Holder announced that the task force Obama had appointed to review the policy reaffirmed the president's decision. "The task force concluded that the *Army Field Manual* provides appropriate guidance on interrogation for military interrogators and that no additional or different guidance was necessary for other agencies," Holder said.

Despite Obama's decision, the debate over the legality and effectiveness of the CIA interrogation program is continuing. Cheney and other defenders of the practices say the CIA interrogations produced valuable intelligence after proper review and approval by the Justice Department. As evidence, they point to the CIA inspector general's bottom-line conclusion that the agency's interrogations provided "actionable intelligence" that helped identify and apprehend terrorists and warned of planned terrorist attacks against the United States or other countries.

In his interview, Cheney said that two of the most valuable al Qaeda detainees — Khalid Shaikh Mohammed and Abu Zubaydah — provided information only after being subjected to some of the enhanced interrogation techniques (EITs). "The evidence is overwhelming that the EITs were crucial in getting them to cooperate," he said.

Critics of the practices reject the now-repudiated Justice Department advisories that said the techniques did not constitute torture as defined by U.S. law. They also question whether the enhanced techniques were necessary to obtain information from detainees. As evidence, they point to the caveat in the CIA inspector general's report that the effectiveness of the techniques in eliciting information that would not have been obtained otherwise "cannot be so easily measured."[12]

"What the report doesn't say and doesn't conclude is that torture was responsible for the information that was obtained or that the intelligence could not have been obtained without torture," says ACLU lawyer Abdo.

After years of secrecy, the operational details of the CIA interrogation program are now coming to light with the release of the inspector general's report and a second document: a Dec. 30, 2004, description of the program for the

Army Prohibits Force in Questioning Prisoners

The U.S. Army's 384-page field manual on "human intelligence (HUMINT) collection" details more than a dozen "approaches" to questioning an enemy prisoner of war (EPW) or detainee, none entailing physical force, coercion or threat of violence. The manual, as revised in September 2006, included specific prohibitions against abusive practices documented at the Abu Ghraib prison in Iraq, including forced nudity and use of military dogs to harass or intimidate prisoners. Here are the approaches listed in the manual:

Direct approach: HUMINT collector "asks direct questions." Effective 90 percent of time during World War II, 95 percent of time in Operation Desert Storm in Iraq (1991); preliminary studies indicate "dramatically less successful" in Afghanistan (2001-2002) and Iraq (2003).

Incentive approach: HUMINT collector "may use incentives to enhance rapport and to reward the source for cooperation and truthfulness." May not state or imply that basic rights under international, national law are contingent on cooperation.

Emotional approaches: HUMINT collector "can often identify dominant emotions that motivate the EPW/detainee." These approaches are:

Emotional love approach: HUMINT collector "focuses on the anxiety felt by the source . . . , his isolation from those he loves, and his feelings of helplessness." Has "a chance of success" if source can be shown what he can do to improve the situation of the object of his emotion: family, homeland, comrades.

Emotional hate approach: HUMINT collector must "build on [source's hate] so the emotion overrides the source's rational side." Hate may be directed to his country's regime, immediate superiors, officers in general or fellow soldiers.

Emotional fear-up approach: HUMINT collector "identifies a preexisting fear or creates a fear" within source and "links" elimination or reduction of fear to source's cooperation. Must be "extremely careful" not to threaten or coerce source.

Emotional fear-down approach: HUMINT collector "mitigates existing fear in exchange for" source's cooperation.

Emotional-pride and ego-up approach: HUMINT collector "exploits a source's low self-esteem" by flattery. "This should produce positive feelings on the part of the source," who "will eventually reveal pertinent information to solicit more favorable comments. . . ."

Emotional-pride and ego-down approach: HUMINT collector attacks ego or self-image of source, who in defense "reveals information to justify or rationalize his actions."

Emotional-futility: HUMINT collector convinces source that resistance is futile.

Other approaches: Most "require considerable time and resources." They are:

We Know All: HUMINT collector "subtly" convinces source that questioning is perfunctory because information is already known.

File and Dossier: HUMINT collector prepares dossier with all known information about source and uses the file to convey impression that source is only confirming information already known.

Establish Your Identity: HUMINT collector accuses source of being "infamous individual" wanted on more serious charges; source then attempts to establish his true identity in an effort to clear himself.

Repetition: HUMINT collector repeats question and answer several times; source then answers "fully and truthfully . . . to gain relief from the monotony. . . ."

Rapid Fire: HUMINT collector asks rapid-fire questions to confuse source, who "will tend to contradict himself" and then be caught in inconsistencies.

Silent: HUMINT collector says nothing, looks squarely at source and waits for source to break eye contact.

Change of Scenery: Source is removed from "intimidating" atmosphere to "setting where he feels more comfortable speaking."

Mutt and Jeff: Requires two HUMINT collectors, both "convincing actors." One adopts formal, unsympathetic stance ("bad cop"); the second gains source's confidence by scolding colleague's stance ("good cop"). No violence or threats may be used.

False Flag: Goal is to trick detainee into cooperating by convincing him he is being interrogated by non-U.S. forces; use must be approved by superiors; no "implied or explicit threats" that non-cooperation will result in harsh treatment by non-U.S. entities.

Source: U.S. Department of the Army, *Human Intelligence Collection Operations*, September 2006, www.army.mil/institution/armypublicaffairs/pdf/fm2-22-3.pdf.

Justice Department written by an unidentified lawyer. The 19-page background paper — written after the Bush administration's decision in 2003 to discontinue use of waterboarding — groups the techniques then in use into three categories: "conditioning techniques," including nudity, sleep deprivation and "dietary manipulation"; "corrective techniques," including facial slap, abdominal slap, facial hold and attention grasp; and "coercive techniques," including "walling," water dousing, stress positions, wall standing and cramped confinement.

The paper describes the use of the techniques sequentially from less to more severe. The objective, the paper says, is to place the detainee in "a state of learned helplessness and dependence conducive to the collection of intelligence in a predictable, reliable, and sustainable manner."

The Justice Department memos in August 2002 concluded the techniques did not constitute torture under applicable federal law, which prohibits actions "under the color of law intended to inflict severe physical or mental pain or suffering." In his Fox News interview, Cheney stressed the Justice Department's approval of the enhanced techniques, but also agreed to a question from host Chris Wallace that he was "comfortable" with the program even when interrogators went beyond the authorized practices. Cheney has also been reported to be planning to write in his forthcoming memoir that he disagreed with Bush's decision to discontinue use of waterboarding.[13]

Today, waterboarding has few vocal defenders, but the legal status of the other harsh interrogation techniques remains a subject of dispute. "Most of the techniques fall pretty clearly on the legal side of the torture line," says Alt at the Heritage Foundation. "Most fall into the category of mind games, which is what interrogation is."

But the ACLU's Abdo says the techniques "in combination" amounted "either to torture or cruel, inhuman and degrading treatment, both of which are prohibited by international law as well as our own laws." The prohibition against inhuman treatment was added by the Detainee Treatment Act of 2005, enacted after the Justice Department memo and the period covered by the CIA inspector general's report.

For now, the legal debate is moot, since the Obama administration decided to limit interrogation to the non-coercive techniques permitted under the *Army Field Manual.* The White House asked that the interrogation issue be kept out of a pending bill to reauthorize intelligence activities.

As for the debate on the need for the techniques or their effectiveness, Benjamin Wittes, a Brookings Institution senior fellow who has studied the interrogation of post-9/11 detainees, says the answer may be unknowable.

"It's very hard to do a controlled experiment," Wittes says. "The CIA wasn't trying to do a controlled experiment. They were trying to get actionable intelligence and save lives."

Should Congress authorize an in-depth investigation of past detention and interrogation practices?

A little more than a year after the Sept. 11 terrorist attacks, Congress in November 2002 passed legislation to create an independent, bipartisan commission to examine why the government had failed to prevent the attacks and what could be done to guard against future attacks. President Bush reluctantly agreed to the measure, which Democrats in Congress had pushed with strong backing from many of the families of the nearly 3,000 people killed in the attacks.

The commission's report, issued in July 2004, identified a host of intelligence failures under Bush as well as President Clinton that underestimated the threat posed by al Qaeda and missed clues to the group's plan to hijack airplanes and crash them into landmark buildings in the United States. The commission recommended a number of steps to guard against future attacks, including the creation of a new national intelligence director with authority over both the CIA and FBI. That step was one of several that were eventually adopted.[14]

A coalition of 18 civil liberties and human-rights advocates is pressing for a similar investigation of the Bush administration's detention and interrogation policies. "We can't entirely move forward unless we look back and find out what happened," says Sloan of the Constitution Project. "The American people don't know what was done in their name, and we're entitled to know."[15]

Sloan approves of Obama's decision to change detention and interrogation policies but says a broad inquiry is needed for Congress to consider legislative changes.

"That's an executive branch decision that the president has made, but another president could change that," she says.

Proposals for an independent commission have support among some Democratic lawmakers, including House Speaker Nancy Pelosi, D-Calif. But Pelosi's counterpart, Senate Majority Leader Harry Reid, D-Nev., prefers investigations by individual congressional committees. Republican lawmakers generally oppose any look back as unnecessary and politically motivated. "I don't see what we're going to learn that congressional leaders didn't already know," House Minority Leader John Boehner of Ohio remarked in April.[16]

For his part, President Obama has generally opposed any broad inquiry into the Bush administration policies. "We should be looking forward, not backwards," Obama said in an April 21 news conference, five days after release of the Justice Department memo. But he went on to indicate a preference for an independent commission over congressional committees as a forum for any investigation. "I think it's very important for the American people to feel as if this is not being dealt with to provide one side or another political advantage but rather is being done in order to learn some lessons so that we move forward in an effective way," he said.

Conservatives echo the concerns about political recriminations from any broad investigation. "Part of the question is whether it's needed to get at the truth or whether it becomes a political rehashing," says the Heritage Foundation's Alt. "Given the time that has elapsed, one wonders whether it's not simply an attempt to criminalize or vilify differences with the past administration."

ACLU lawyer Abdo counters that a broad investigation is needed to compile "an accurate historical record of what took place during the last eight years." The ACLU favors a select congressional committee for that purpose. "It's unlikely that anybody could compile as accurate and comprehensive a record as Congress," he says.

Sloan says the coalition has a "slight preference" for an independent commission over congressional inquiries. "So much in Congress gets politicized and bogged down," she says. "We thought a commission that would be independent of that kind of politics would be better."

Whatever forum might be used for an investigation, Sloan says Congress should use the results to draft

CIA Director Leon Panetta warns that "exceptionally grave damage" to national security could result — including exposing individual CIA officers to "grave risk" — if additional documents about the CIA detention and interrogation program are released under a Freedom of Information Act request by the American Civil Liberties Union and other groups. President Obama opposes a broad reexamination of the Bush administration's counterterrorism policies.

legislation. "If you don't have laws, then you're leaving things to the discretion of the executive branch," she says, "and that seems to be what got us into trouble in the first place."

BACKGROUND

Eliciting the Truth

The use of coercive interrogation techniques dates to ancient times, and so too the debate over their value in eliciting the truth. In the Western world, pain has been wielded as an instrument of judicial interrogation by the ancient Greeks and Romans, European monarchs and 20th-century dictators. For several centuries, the Roman Catholic Church inflicted pain on presumed heretics to educe confessions. Throughout, some have argued that — apart from moral considerations — coercion is an inefficient technique that often produces unreliable information from subjects willing to say anything to stop the pain.[17]

CHRONOLOGY

Cold War *Central Intelligence Agency established, given covert roles in propaganda, subversion; disclosures of CIA operations often bring controversy.*

1947 National Security Act of 1947 establishes CIA to collect and analyze intelligence; mandate expanded next year to include covert propaganda, support for anti-communist movements.

1950s CIA's MKUltra program experiments with interrogation techniques using hypnosis, drugs and physical coercion; terminated in late 1960s, records destroyed in 1973.

1963 Secret CIA manual — *Kubark counterintelligence interrogation-July 1963* — details "coercive" interrogation techniques.

Mid-to-late 1960s Widespread torture carried out by South Vietnamese forces in Operation Phoenix, CIA-designed counterinsurgency program.

1960s-1970s CIA-trained and funded police forces in Latin America are accused of abuse, torture.

1983 Secret CIA "Human Resource Exploitation Training Manual" details non-physical methods for coercive interrogation: "debility, disorientation and dread."

1997 CIA declassifies interrogation manuals in response to threatened Freedom of Information Act suit by *Baltimore Sun*.

2001-Present *CIA given lead role in interrogating "high-value" terrorism suspects after Sept. 11 attacks; gains permission for "enhanced" techniques that critics say amount to torture.*

September 2001 Vice President Dick Cheney says U.S. will have to "work the dark side" to combat al Qaeda (Sept. 16); President George W. Bush signs order directing CIA to interrogate "high-value" detainees (Sept. 17).

Fall-winter 2001-2002 CIA arranges to hold future detainees in secret prisons overseas.

March 2002 Abu Zubaydah, purported adviser to Osama bin Laden, captured in Pakistan; CIA proposes using "enhanced interrogation techniques."

2002 Justice Department approves use of 10 "enhanced" CIA interrogation techniques. . . . Abd al-Rahim al-Nashiri, accused mastermind of *USS Cole* bombing, captured, taken to secret prison in Thailand, subjected to waterboarding; later threatened with pistol, power drill.

2003 CIA inspector general opens investigation of interrogation practices (January), later refers some cases to Justice Department for prosecution. . . . Khalid Shaikh Mohammed (KSM), alleged architect of 9/11 attacks, captured in Pakistan (March), waterboarded 183 times; dispute continues about value of information elicited by enhanced techniques.

April-May 2004 Photos of abuse of Iraqi prisoners in U.S. military prison outside Baghdad provoke outcry in U.S., around world. . . . CIA report questions implementation of interrogation program; notes agents' concern about potential backlash if disclosed.

November-December 2005 *Washington Post* publishes first detailed story on CIA secret prisons. . . . CIA destroys 92 videotapes of interrogation of KSM, others. . . . Detainee Treatment Act prohibits "cruel, inhuman or degrading" treatment by military, but not CIA, interrogators.

August 2006 CIA contractor David Passaro convicted of assault in death of Afghan farmer Abdul Wali after interrogation in June 2003; later given prison term. . . . Bush orders 14 remaining "high-value" detainees in CIA prisons transferred to Guantánamo Bay Naval Base, Cuba.

March 2008 Bush vetoes bill passed by Congress barring enhanced interrogation techniques by CIA; says techniques vital to war on terror.

2009 President Obama bars enhanced interrogation techniques, orders CIA prisons closed; promises closure of Guantánamo within one year. . . . Obama declassifies Justice Department memos approving use of enhanced interrogation techniques; rules out prosecution of agents who followed guidelines. . . . CIA inspector general's report declassified in August, yields detailed picture of CIA interrogation program. . . . Attorney General Eric H. Holder Jr. asks career prosecutor to review CIA interrogation cases where agents exceeded guidelines; move brings strong criticism from Republicans, conservatives and former CIA officials.

'Extraordinary Rendition' of Terrorists Challenged

Detainees say they were abducted and tortured.

The Obama administration continues to invoke a "state secrets" privilege to block a federal lawsuit seeking damages from a CIA-contractor airline for transporting prisoners to foreign countries where they were allegedly tortured.

The two-year-old lawsuit in a federal appeals court in California is one of several American Civil Liberties Union (ACLU) efforts to challenge the practice known as "extraordinary rendition." Under President George W. Bush, the Central Intelligence Agency (CIA) was accused of transferring suspected terrorists, often apprehended in foreign countries under questionable circumstances, to countries known to abuse or torture prisoners.

The Obama administration has continued to hand over suspected terrorists to other countries but is vowing to prevent abuses against U.S.-captured detainees by more frequent inspection of foreign prison facilities. ACLU lawyers say those efforts are inadequate because prisoners held in other countries are unlikely to report abuse to visiting U.S. monitors.[1]

Meanwhile, Justice Department lawyers are asking the federal appeals court in San Francisco to reconsider its April 28 decision to allow five former or current detainees to pursue a lawsuit charging Jeppesen Dataplans, a Bay-area airline, with knowingly assisting the CIA in forcibly transporting them to other countries to be tortured. A federal judge in San Jose had granted the government's motion to dismiss the suit on "state secrets" grounds, a privilege the government can use to limit evidence or even throw out a suit altogether if state secrets might be disclosed. However, the 9th U.S. Circuit Court of Appeals overturned that decision.

In rejecting the privilege for now, the three-judge panel said the subject of the suit — the agreement between the government and the airline, a Boeing subsidiary — was not secret. The ruling, which the government now wants the full appeals court to hear, left the question open as to whether the government can invoke the privilege in regard to specific evidence as the case proceeds.[2]

The lead plaintiff in the case, Ethiopian-born British citizen Binyam Mohamed, was arrested by Pakistani authorities in 2002,

Khaled el-Masri, a German citizen, says he was abducted and tortured by the CIA.

Getty Images/Suedwest Presse/Volkmar Koenneke

turned over to U.S. authorities and transferred to Morocco. He claims he was tortured during 18 months of captivity there before being transferred to U.S. facilities in Afghanistan and then in Guantánamo Bay, Cuba. He was finally released in February 2009.

Of the other four plaintiffs, two remain in prison, one in Egypt, one in Italy; two others have been released.

The ACLU filed a similar suit in 2005 on behalf of Khaled el-Masri, a German citizen who said he was abducted in Macedonia and taken to a secret CIA prison in Afghanistan where he was tortured. El-Masri was eventually released without charges; he was apparently confused with a suspected terrorist with a similar name.

The federal appeals court in Richmond, Va., cited the state secrets privilege in dismissing el-Masri's earlier suit against former CIA Director George Tenet and three CIA-contractor airlines; the Supreme Court declined to hear el-Masri's appeal in October 2007. The ACLU is now asking the Inter-American Commission on Human Rights to hear the case; the government has two months from the Aug. 27 filing to respond.

Attorney General Eric Holder announced on Sept. 23 new limits on the use of the state secrets privilege. It will be invoked only to prevent "genuine and significant harm" to national security or foreign policy, Holder said, and not to conceal violations of law or prevent embarrassment to the government. The policy was described as applying to cases after Oct. 1 — apparently ruling out any direct effect on the *Jeppesen* case.[3]

---

[1] See David Johnston, "Renditions to Continue, but With Better Oversight, U.S. Says," *The New York Times*, Aug. 25, 2009, p. A8.

[2] The decision is *Mohamed v. Jeppesen Dataplan, Inc.*, 08-15693 (9th Cir. 2009), as amended Aug. 31, 2009, www.ca9.uscourts.gov/datastore/opinions/2009/08/31/08-15693.pdf. See Bob Egelko, "U.S. fights rendition suit against Bay Area firm;" *San Francisco Chronicle*, Aug. 10, 2009, p. C1.

[3] See Department of Justice, "Attorney General Establishes New State Secrets Policies and Procedures," Sept. 23, 2009, www.usdoj.gov/opa/pr/2009/September/09-ag-1013.html. For advance coverage, see Carrie Johnson, "Obama to Set Higher Bar for Keeping State Secrets," *The Washington Post*, Sept. 23, 2009, p. A1.

As University of Wisconsin history professor Alfred W. McCoy notes, torture was practiced by the ancient Greeks on slaves and by the Romans on slaves and freemen alike. The third-century Roman jurist Ulpian defined *quaestio* (torture) as "the torment and suffering of the body in order to elicit the truth," but recognized its limitations. Some people have "such strength of body and soul" that there is "no means of obtaining the truth from them," he wrote, while others "are so susceptible to pain that they will tell any lie rather than suffer it."[18]

Torture fell out of use in Christian Europe during the first millennium, but resurfaced among civil and ecclesiastical authorities by the 12th and 13th centuries. The Catholic Church's "inquisitions" aimed at suppressing heretical movements took on torture as an instrument of interrogation under a papal bull issued by Pope Innocent IV in 1252. One of the techniques used by the Italian Inquisition was to suspend the subject by rope in five degrees of escalating severity — hence, the modern term "third degree." Church manuals prescribed techniques of interrogation. In one, Nicholas Eymerich, 14th-century inquisitor general of Aragon, cataloged 10 techniques of "evasion and deception" by heretics; he went on to specify methods for interrogators to counter them that entailed physical intimidation as well as psychological manipulation.

Civil authorities in Europe also used torture from medieval times into the 18th and 19th centuries both as coercive interrogation and public punishment. England's King Henry VIII and Queen Elizabeth I both used torture against their opponents; the Tower of London housed a rack and other instruments of torture. In Paris, the Bourbon kings confined prisoners in the Bastille under torture-like conditions.

Legal acceptance of torture began to recede with its abolition by Prussia in 1754. Ten years later, the Italian penal reformer Cesare Beccaria denounced torture as "a sure route for the acquittal of robust ruffians and the conviction of weak innocents." By the late 19th century, the French author Victor Hugo felt justified in declaring that torture "has ceased to exist." The widespread use of torture by such 20th-century dictatorial regimes as the Soviet Union and Nazi Germany, however, proved the reports of its demise to be exaggerated.

The United States has no acknowledged experience with legally sanctioned torture, but coercive interrogation was a widespread if unacknowledged law enforcement practice as late as the mid-20th century. "Our police, with no legal sanction, employ duress, threat, bullying, a vast amount of moderate physical abuse and a certain degree of outright torture," the author and social critic Ernest Jerome Hopkins wrote in 1931.[19] In a succession of cases beginning in 1936 and continuing through the 1950s, the Supreme Court began throwing out convictions based on confessions that police secured either by physical or psychological coercion. Frustrated with the case-by-case adjudications, the court in 1966 laid down the famous Miranda rule requiring police to notify suspects of their rights. Chief Justice Earl Warren, a former district attorney, stressed that the rule was aimed at preventing the use of physical beatings or incommunicado interrogation to coerce confessions from suspects in custody.[20]

World War II gave the United States its first sustained experience with interrogating wartime captives. Far removed from the battlefield, the government built two special detention centers in the United States to interrogate German and Japanese prisoners. The two facilities — Fort Hunt, in Northern Virginia near Washington, D.C., and Camp Tracy, near Stockton, Calif. — were kept secret during and for decades after the war. During the war, the military even delayed or avoided telling the International Committee of the Red Cross about the camps — a violation of the Geneva Conventions. Interrogators emphasized rapport-building instead of coercion. "I never laid hands on anyone," one of the Fort Hunt veterans told a *Washington Post* reporter in 2007. But the interrogators also gathered intelligence by secretly monitoring and recording the prisoners' cellblock conversations.[21]

Mind Control

The Cold War between the United States and two communist states — the Soviet Union and China — featured the use of interrogation on both sides for multiple purposes. The principals used interrogation to gather intelligence and to create propaganda. They also fostered the use of interrogation by proxy states to suppress or intimidate domestic opposition. The CIA was a prime player in secretly developing techniques of interrogation in the 1950s and '60s that became intensely controversial when publicly disclosed in later decades.[22]

The CIA was created in 1947, and the next year given a broad congressional charter to collect and analyze intelligence and carry out covert operations overseas without disclosing its budget, staffing or other information. As the new agency was taking shape, the nations of the world were also laying the foundations of a new framework of international law, including the Universal Declaration of Human Rights in 1948 and the rewritten and expanded Geneva Conventions in 1949. Included in the fourth Geneva Convention regarding treatment of civilians was a new provision that barred the use of "physical or mental coercion" for any purpose, including "to obtain information from them or third parties." The official commentators described the provision, Article 31, as "an important step forward in international law."

Despite this international law prohibition, the CIA worked over the course of two decades to develop new interrogation techniques using hypnosis, drugs and various forms of physical discomfort. The initiatives stemmed in part from information about the use of hypnosis, drugs and electroshock by Nazi interrogators during World War II. They gained urgency from the belief that the Soviet and Chinese regimes had developed mind-control techniques that — whether applied to Soviet citizens in the Stalinist-era "show trials" or to U.S. prisoners in the Korean War — could induce the subjects to say almost anything the interrogators wanted them to say. Edward Hunter, a journalist secretly on the CIA's payroll, gave a frightening name to the techniques with his 1951 book *Brainwashing in Red China.*[23]

In his critical account, University of Wisconsin history professor McCoy chronicles a secret program code named MKUltra, whose findings and techniques

Terrorism Suspects Transferred from Secret Sites

Fourteen "high-value" terrorism suspects were transferred from secret CIA sites to the prison camp at the Guantánamo Bay Naval Base in Cuba in September 2006. Five have been charged with helping plan the Sept. 11 terrorist attacks on the United States; the government is deciding whether to continue prosecuting them in special military tribunals or move the trials to a regular federal court. Formal charges have not been brought against the other nine detainees. The now disbanded combatant status review tribunals at Guantánamo confirmed their status as "enemy combatants."

Here are the 14 "high-value" detainees and the role the government alleges they played in terrorism:

The five 9/11 detainees — *Each defendant is charged with conspiracy and a number of separate offenses including murder in violation of the law of war, attacking civilians, destruction of property in violation of the law of war and terrorism.*

Khalid Shaykh Muhammad: principal al Qaeda operative directing 9/11 attacks.

Walid Bin Attash: linked indirectly to the 1998 U.S. Embassy bombings in Tanzania and Kenya and the *USS Cole* bombing in 2000.

Ramzi Bin al-Shibh: coordinator of 9/11 attacks.

Mustafa al-Hawsawi: linked to detailed computer records of al Qaeda members, finances.

Ammar al-Baluchi: linked to arrangements for 9/11 attacks.

The other nine high-value detainees yet to be charged are:

Ahmed Khalfan Ghailani: linked to bombing of U.S. Embassy in Tanzania.

Mohd Farik bin Amin ("Zubair"): arranged financing for bombing of J. W. Marriott Hotel in Jakarta, Indonesia, in 2003.

Al Nashiri, Abd Al Rahim Hussein Mohammed: linked to *Cole* bombing.

Bashir bin Lap ("Lillie"): linked to planning of bombing of J. W. Marriott Hotel.

Rjduan bin Isomuddiiu ("Hambali"): linked to bombings in Indonesia, efforts to topple Malaysian government.

Zayn al Abidin Muhammad Husayn ("Abu Zubaydah"): Head of al Qaeda training camps in Afghanistan; diary entries include unacted-on plans for attacks within United States.

Guleed Hassan Ahmed: al Qaeda cell leader in Djibouti.

Majid Khan: linked to alleged al Qaeda money-laundering plot.

Abu Faraj al-Libi: deputy to al Qaeda's 3rd in command.

Source: Combatant Status Review Tribunals/Administrative Review Boards, U.S. Department of Defense, Oct. 17, 2007; accessed online on Sept. 21, 2009.
Note: The DOD's name spellings are used; variations are often used in the news media.

were later codified in a 1963 manual called *Kubark*. The program used human subjects in experiments with the newly discovered hallucinogen LSD and with such sensory-deprivation techniques as isolation in a cramped box or water tank. Drug-induced interrogation proved to be a blind alley, but sensory deprivation proved more efficacious in inducing a state of helplessness in the subjects. McCoy describes the CIA's discovery of "no-touch torture" as "the first real revolution in the cruel science of pain in centuries."

The official directing the program was Richard Helms, assistant deputy director of operations in the 1950s and later the director of the CIA from 1966 to 1973. In one of his final acts in office, Helms directed the destruction of all documents pertaining to the program — in advance of imminent journalistic and congressional investigations of the agency.

By then, however, the CIA had come under intense criticism for its role in a counterinsurgency program in the Vietnam War known as Operation Phoenix. The CIA-designed program as carried out by the South Vietnamese entailed the use of outright torture, including beatings and electric shocks; the South Vietnamese attributed nearly 41,000 deaths to the program. In hearings on his nomination to succeed Helms as CIA director in 1973, William Colby, who had served as the CIA's chief of pacification in Vietnam, told the Senate Foreign Relations Committee he was aware of reports of abuse but had instructed CIA personnel not to participate.[24]

McCoy depicts the CIA as guilty of "propagating torture" also through a program in the 1960s and '70s that funneled aid to police forces in pro-American governments. The program was housed in the Office of Public Safety in the Agency for International Development (U.S. AID), but was headed by a former CIA official and operated in what McCoy describes as "close coordination with the agency's intelligence mission." Latin American countries sent police recruits to a clandestine academy in Washington for training. A report by what was then the General Accounting Office (GAO) in 1976 acknowledged allegations that the academy "taught or encouraged the use of torture," but made no formal finding on the claims. Amnesty International, however, claimed to have documented widespread torture by police in at least two dozen countries that had received aid under the program.

Allegations of CIA complicity in torture were renewed in the 1980s — notably, in Latin America. A *New York*

Times report on the CIA's role in counterinsurgency in Honduras in 1988 prompted a closed-door hearing by the Senate Intelligence Committee that disclosed to lawmakers — but not the public — a CIA instructional manual on interrogation used in at least seven Latin American countries in the 1980s. *The Human Resource Exploitation Training Manual*, adapting methods outlined in *Kubark* two decades earlier, cautioned against physical torture in favor of non-physical coercive techniques: "debility, disorientation, and dread." The 1983 manual suggests, among other techniques, "persistent manipulation of time," "disrupting sleep schedules" and "serving meals at odd times." The CIA declassified and released both manuals in 1997 in response to the threat of a Freedom of Information Act suit by *The Baltimore Sun*.[25]

'Using Any Means'

Within weeks of the 9/11 attacks, the CIA was tasked with helping capture and then interrogate high-ranking officials in the al Qaeda terrorist network despite the agency's lack of recent experience in questioning adversaries. Some "high-value" detainees were kept in secret prisons and questioned using the "enhanced" techniques approved by the Justice Department despite concerns among some operatives about the reaction to their eventual disclosure. With information leaking out, the Bush administration eventually discarded the harsh measures and in September 2006 transferred the remaining 14 detainees from CIA prisons to Guantánamo. Even with the Obama administration's change in policy, however, some Bush officials and supporters of the former administration continue to defend both the legality and effectiveness of the interrogations.[26]

Vice President Cheney set the mood for the administration's war on terror with his statement on NBC's "Meet the Press" on Sept. 16, 2001, that the government would "have to work through sort of the dark side if you will. . . . It's going to be vital for us to use any means at our disposal, basically, to achieve our objective," Cheney said.[27] Against that backdrop, the CIA seemed the logical choice for any off-the-books counterterrorism work. And the agency had an interest in restoring its reputation after a major pre-9/11 failure: The CIA had failed to notify domestic law enforcement of the entry into the United States of two known al Qaeda operatives who later became two of the 9/11 hijackers.

As journalist Jane Mayer relates in her sharply critical book, *The Dark Side*, the agency had focused on where to house high-value detainees in late 2001 and early 2002, before it even had anyone in custody. Guantánamo, chosen to hold those captured by the military in Afghanistan, was rejected as too visible; a suggestion to use perpetually circumnavigating aircraft was rejected as impractical. Eventually, friendly governments were asked and agreed to provide secret sites for the detainees transported under the so-called "extraordinary rendition" program. Thailand, Lithuania, Poland and Romania were later identified, but none acknowledged their role.

Meanwhile, the agency had turned to a retired military psychologist, John Mitchell, to prepare a paper on al Qaeda's resistance techniques. Mitchell and his partner and fellow psychologist John Bruce Jessen had served in the Air Force in a program called Survival, Evasion, Resistance, Escape (SERE) that trained U.S. service members in countering coercive techniques that an adversary might employ. As the CIA inspector general's report notes, the pair "developed a list of new and more aggressive EITs that they recommended for use in interrogations."[28]

The capture of the senior al Qaeda operative Abu Zubaydah in Pakistan in late March 2002 provided the template for the CIA's enhanced interrogations. Zubaydah, an al Qaeda veteran believed to be personally close to Osama bin Laden, was captured in a joint raid by FBI, CIA and Pakistani law-enforcement and intelligence officers outside Faisalabad. With the badly wounded Zubaydah in custody, the FBI team was pushed aside by a CIA team headed by Mitchell. The measures used on Zubaydah, including being confined in a coffin-like box and water-boarded, formed the basis of the Aug. 2, 2002, Office of Legal Counsel opinion sanctioning a total of 10 enhanced techniques. The memo carried the signature of Jay Bybee, who had the rank of assistant attorney general as head of the office, but was actually written by his deputy, John Yoo, a soft-spoken but hard-edged proponent of expansive presidential power on leave from the University of California's Berkeley Law School.

According to later information, Nashiri became the second detainee to be waterboarded following his capture in November 2002. The inspector general's investigation of the program began in January 2003; the report is ambiguous as to whether the account of Nashiri's treatment was the catalyst. Even with the internal probe going on, however, CIA interrogators conducted the most extensive use of coercive measures two months later after the capture of the highest-value detainee: Khalid Shaikh Mohammed.

The self-described mastermind of the 9/11 hijackings, KSM, as he came to be known, was captured on March 1, 2003, in Rawalpindi, Pakistan, thanks to a $25 million reward paid to an informant. The inspector general's report states that he was waterboarded 183 times, but the remainder of the account of his treatment is redacted in the version released in August. Mohammed himself later described being kept naked for more than a month, chained to a wall in a painful crouch, subjected alternately to extreme heat or cold and doused with water. Mohammed's interrogation is the focal point of the dispute over the need or effectiveness of these coercive measures. Supporters say KSM provided invaluable information but only after use of the enhanced techniques. Opponents say he was glad to boast of his role in al Qaeda but also deliberately fed false information to his interrogators.

As some in the agency had feared, the details of the CIA interrogations slowly leaked out, but only after pictures of abuses of Iraqi prisoners by U.S. military personnel at Abu Ghraib prison gained worldwide attention in April and May 2004. It also was revealed that leaders of the congressional intelligence oversight committees, who had been secretly briefed on the CIA's activities, had raised no public objections.

By 2005, CIA and military interrogators were being publicly implicated in deaths of detainees in Afghanistan and Iraq. In the most notorious case, Manadel al-Jamadi, an Iraqi suspected in the bombing of a Red Cross office in Baghdad, died in November 2003 during interrogation by Navy SEALS and a CIA interrogator. An image of Jamadi's ice-packed corpse with a smiling U.S. service member standing over it was among the Abu Ghraib photos published in 2004. In February 2005, The Associated Press reported that Jamadi died while hung from his wrists — a technique dubbed "Palestinian hanging." In October, the ACLU reported that documents obtained in Freedom of Information Act litigation showed at least 44 detainees' deaths during interrogation, with 21 of those classified in official autopsies as homicides. A report by the group Human Rights First published in February 2006 raised the number of deaths to 100, with 34 classified as homicides.[29]

The controversies spawned by the Abu Ghraib photographs and detainees' deaths helped drive Congress to pass the Detainee Treatment Act of 2005, with a ban on "cruel, inhuman or degrading treatment" of detainees. The provision was written by Sen. John McCain, the Arizona Republican who was held by North Vietnam as a prisoner of war for five years, and reluctantly accepted by President Bush. But the ban applied only to military interrogators, not to the CIA.

Meanwhile, *The Washington Post* had published in November 2005 a well-informed story on the CIA's secret prisons and its program of "extraordinary renditions."[30] Unbeknownst to the public at the time, the International Committee for the Red Cross (ICRC), officially designated under the Geneva Conventions to monitor wartime captives, was denied any access to the detainees despite repeatedly expressing concerns about their whereabouts. ICRC monitors were first allowed to visit the detainees in October 2006, after their transfers to Guantánamo. In a confidential report written in February 2007 and disclosed by author-journalist Mark Danner in March 2009, the ICRC described the prisoners' allegations of their treatment as amounting to "torture and/or cruel, inhuman or degrading treatment."[31]

Bush's decision in September 2006 to transfer the high-value detainees to Guantánamo symbolized the retreat on the issue. But the prisoners were still kept separate from other detainees. And through the end of the administration, both Bush and Cheney continued to defend the interrogation program as the key to having prevented al Qaeda from any subsequent attacks on U.S. soil.

CURRENT SITUATION

Fighting Over Disclosure

The Obama administration is continuing to resist disclosure of some details of the CIA's interrogation program, even after disavowing the harsh measures used on some "high-value" detainees and shutting down the secret prisons once used to hold them.

The administration is invoking national security and other grounds in federal court filings to block release of hundreds of documents that the ACLU and other civil liberties and veterans' groups are seeking from the CIA through Freedom of Information Act (FOIA) litigation.*

The documents withheld include President George W. Bush's original Sept. 17, 2001, order authorizing the CIA's detention and interrogation program and scores of messages between CIA headquarters and field operatives on implementation of the program. Also being withheld are some documents pertaining to the CIA's destruction of 92 videotapes of the interrogations in November 2005 and the contents of the tapes.[32]

John Durham, a career federal prosecutor in Connecticut, was designated in 2008 by Attorney General Michael Mukasey to conduct an independent investigation of the destruction of the tapes; Durham was then chosen by Attorney General Holder to review the cases involving CIA interrogation of detainees.

President Obama has declassified and ordered the release of some of the documents sought in the litigation, including the CIA inspector general's critical May 2004 report on the program. In court filings, however, CIA Director Panetta and an agency FOIA officer are warning that further releases could do "exceptionally grave damage" to national security, endanger cooperation with foreign intelligence services and expose individual CIA officers to "grave risk."

The legal scrapping on the CIA issues is playing out in front of a federal judge in New York City, Alvin Hellerstein, who previously chastised the Bush administration for its "glacial pace" in responding to the ACLU litigation. Hellerstein is scheduled to hear arguments on Sept. 30 on the ACLU's objections to some redactions in three Justice Department memos released on April 16 and to the withholding of the documents pertaining to the destruction of the videotapes.[33]

Meanwhile, in a separate part of the FOIA litigation, the government is asking the Supreme Court to block the release of photographs of abuse of prisoners held by the military in seven facilities in Afghanistan and Iraq. The New York-based 2nd U.S. Circuit Court of Appeals ruled in September 2008 in favor of the ACLU's FOIA request for the photographs, which are in addition to photographs already released of prisoners at Abu Ghraib being abused.

The Justice Department originally decided not to appeal, but in May Obama said that release of the photos could harm U.S. service members abroad by inflaming

---

* Other plaintiffs in the litigation are the Center for Constitutional Rights, Physicians for Human Rights, Veterans for Common Sense and Veterans for Peace.

AT ISSUE

Did harsh CIA interrogations amount to torture?

YES   David Kaye
Executive Director, UCLA School of Law International Human Rights Program

Written for *CQ Researcher*, September 2009

Senior officials in the Bush administration initiated and authorized a policy of harsh treatment of terrorism suspects held by the United States. Recent documents released by the Obama administration — some only released under court orders — demonstrate that CIA interrogation techniques included waterboarding, extensive sleep deprivation, forced confinement in extremely small spaces, threats with handguns and power drills, threats against the lives and well-being of detainees' family members, severe stress positions, "walling" detainees by slamming them against fixed spaces during interrogations, forced standing and shackling, exposure to cold and other forms of torture or cruel, inhuman or degrading treatment.

In my opinion, these techniques constituted torture or, at a minimum, cruel or inhuman treatment prohibited by U.S. law.

Since the United States had long been at the forefront of objecting to torture under any circumstance, it should not be a surprise that the U.S. government, prior to 2001, had joined many treaties that prohibit torture — including the 1949 Geneva Conventions, the 1966 International Covenant on Civil and Political Rights and the 1984 Convention Against Torture — and enacted domestic laws criminalizing it. The anti-torture statute in the U.S. Code prohibits acts "specifically intended to inflict severe physical or mental pain or suffering," defining such mental pain or suffering as, among other things, "the threat of imminent death." The War Crimes Act similarly prohibits torture and cruel or inhuman treatment (such as "serious physical abuse"). Neither permits any sort of exceptional circumstance to justify torture.

As a bipartisan report of the Senate Armed Services Committee underscored last year, the Justice Department under President Bush distorted the meaning of these criminal laws beyond recognition, approving harsh techniques that the United States has condemned in other contexts. Many of the abuses noted above are prohibited under any good-faith reading of U.S. law, some plainly constituting torture. Take waterboarding, which creates a profound sensation of drowning and imminent death: Even one application amounts to the kind of physical and mental abuse prohibited by U.S. law, but interrogators applied it 83 times to one detainee and 183 times to another, according to the CIA inspector general.

While the argument against prosecuting CIA agents for these acts may be understandable, the argument that these techniques are permitted by U.S. law is simply wrong. As we consider the kind of detention policy our country deserves, defining our past conduct in the proper terms — that is to say, recognizing it as torture, cruel and inhumane — is an important step forward.

NO   Jeffrey F. Addicott
Director, Center for Terrorism Law, St. Mary's University School of Law

From testimony submitted to Senate Judiciary Subcommittee on Administrative Oversight and the Courts, May 13, 2009.

In the context of the Department of Justice legal memorandums that approved certain CIA enhanced interrogation techniques, the issue is whether they amounted to "torture" — especially the use of "waterboarding" on high-value al-Qaeda detainees.

Since the detainees are not entitled to prisoner of war status, international law does not forbid interrogation. By its very nature, even the most reasonable interrogation process places the detainee in emotional duress and causes stress to his being — both physical and mental. Allegations of "torture" roll off the tongue with ease. Recognizing that not every alleged incident of interrogation or mistreatment necessarily satisfies the legal definition of torture, it is imperative that one view such allegations with a clear understanding of the applicable legal standards set out in law and judicial precedent.

In this manner, allegations or claims of illegal interrogation practices can be properly measured as falling above or below a particular legal threshold. In my legal opinion, the so-called CIA enhanced interrogation practices approved by the Department of Justice in several detailed legal memorandums did not constitute torture under international law or U.S. domestic law.

The 1984 U.N. Convention Against Torture and Other Cruel, Inhuman or Degrading Treatment or Punishment is the primary international agreement governing torture. It defines torture as:

"[A]ny act by which severe pain or suffering, whether physical or mental, is intentionally inflicted on a person for such purposes as obtaining . . . information or a confession."

Even the worst of the CIA techniques — waterboarding — would not constitute torture under the Torture Convention. (CIA waterboarding lasted no more than 40 seconds and appears similar to what we have done hundreds of times to our own military special-operations soldiers in training courses.)

As foreboding as the term enhanced interrogation techniques may sound, responsible debate must revolve around legal case law associated with interpreting the Torture Convention and not simply cases that use the word torture.

For example, in *Ireland v. United Kingdom*, the European Court of Human Rights ruled by a sweeping vote of 13-3 that certain British interrogation techniques used against suspected Irish terrorists — which included wall-standing for up to 30 hours and subjection to loud noises — were not torture. If the British techniques were deemed not to constitute torture by this leading court, then even the worst of the American interrogation techniques fell far below what the British interrogators practiced.

anti-American sentiment. The government is arguing the photographs fall within the Freedom of Information Act's exemption for "information compiled for law enforcement purposes" that "could reasonably be expected to endanger the life or physical safety of any individual." In its ruling, the appeals court said the government's use of the exemption was too broad.[34]

In the CIA case, the government's legal arguments are based on four other exemptions from the information act, which protect classified information, information specifically exempted by other statutes, attorney-client communications and personnel and medical files. In broader terms, the CIA's most recent court filing, on Aug. 31, warns that further disclosures regarding the interrogation program are "reasonably likely to degrade the [U.S. government's] ability to effectively question terrorist detainees." In addition, the agency says that disclosure of cooperation from other countries "would damage the CIA's relations with these foreign governments and could cause them to cease cooperating with the CIA on such matters."

ACLU lawyers call the administration's stance in the litigation inconsistent with President Obama's past criticisms of the Bush administration's policies. "It's disappointing that the government continues to withhold these vital documents that would fill in the remaining gaps in the public record," says ACLU legal fellow Abdo.

From the opposite side, the administration has faced pressure from within the CIA and from past CIA directors to limit disclosures. Former CIA Director Hayden was one of four past heads of the agency who contacted the White House in April to urge the president not to release the Justice Department memos approving use of the enhanced interrogation techniques. Appearing on "Fox News Sunday" at the time, Hayden said the disclosures were making it "more difficult for CIA officers to defend the nation."[35]

Human-rights advocates, however, say the public needs still more information about the detention and interrogation programs. "We've learned a lot," says John Sifton, a human-rights investigator and attorney in New York City. But, he adds, "there's still a lot of things that are unclear."[36]

Meanwhile, the ACLU filed a new FOIA suit in federal court in New York City on Sept. 22 seeking records from the Pentagon and the CIA on prisoners held at Bagram Air Force Base in Afghanistan. In announcing the suit, ACLU staff attorney Melissa Goodman described Bagram

as "the new Guantánamo," but complained that the public "is still in the dark" about basic facts about the facility, including the number of prisoners and rules and conditions of confinement. The ACLU said that the Defense Department had identified a list of prisoners, but declined to release it on national security and privacy grounds.[37]

Getting to Trial?

The government is weighing its next move in the trial of the five CIA "high-value" detainees charged with helping plan the Sept. 11 attacks. In question is whether to continue prosecuting them in special military tribunals or move the trial to a regular federal court.

Justice Department attorneys disclosed the pending decision in court filings on Sept. 16 that opposed a motion by one of the detainees, Ramzi bin al-Shibh, seeking to bar all proceedings before the military commission already convened at Guantánamo to try the five. While opposing the motion, the lawyers also filed a new motion asking the military judges to temporarily stay the proceedings in order for the government to decide by mid-November whether to shift the trial to a civilian federal court.

The lawyers noted that Congress is currently considering changes to the Military Commissions Act, the 2006 law that added new procedural safeguards to the military commissions set up by the Bush administration in order to comply with a Supreme Court decision.[38] In addition, the lawyers pointed to "upcoming decisions" on the forum for the trial that would be made within 60 days by Attorney General Holder in consultation with Defense Secretary Robert Gates.[39]

The requested continuance — which the military judge granted on Sept. 21 — is the third delay since January in the government's highest-profile proceeding against detainees rounded up in other countries by the Bush administration. The lead defendant is Khalid Shaikh Mohammed, the accused chief planner of the 9/11 attacks and one of three CIA detainees known to have been waterboarded.

The trial was thrown into disarray on Dec. 8 when all five defendants said they wanted to plead guilty to the broad conspiracy charges filed against them in February 2008. The proceedings were put on hold, however, to allow the tribunal time to determine whether bin al-Sibh and a second defendant, Mustafa Ahmed al-Hawsawi, were mentally competent to decide to proceed without an attorney. Mohammed and two others had already been granted permission to represent themselves.

President Obama moved to put all the military commissions on hold after taking office in January as part of his promise to close Guantánamo within a year. He tasked Holder with deciding how to proceed against what were then the camp's remaining 241 prisoners. Since then, 14 inmates have been transferred to other countries and about 80 others approved for resettlement.

Bin al-Shibh has been described as the coordinator of the 9/11 attacks. Al-Hawsawi is alleged to have assisted, another of the defendants, Ali Abd al-Aziz Ali, in handling financial arrangements for the hijackers. Aziz Ali, also known as Ammar al-Baluchi, is a nephew of Mohammed and allegedly acted as his lieutenant for the operation. The fifth defendant, Waleed bin Attash, also known as Khallad, is alleged to have helped select and train some of the hijackers.

A sixth defendant, Mohammed al-Qahtani, was originally charged, but his case was dismissed in May 2008 without explanation. Al-Qahtani has been identified as the "twentieth hijacker" in the attacks because he tried to enter the United States before Sept. 11 but was denied entry. In January 2009, the presiding military judge, Susan Crawford, said she dismissed charges against al-Qahtani because she concluded he had been tortured at Guantánamo.[40]

The five remaining defendants are among 14 detainees from CIA sites who were transferred to Guantánamo in September 2006. The government has not brought formal charges against the other nine, who are challenging their detentions in federal habeas corpus proceedings. All nine were given hearings before the now disbanded combatant status review tribunals at Guantánamo, which confirmed their status as "enemy combatants."

As part of its Freedom of Information Act litigation, the ACLU obtained redacted transcripts in June of some of those proceedings, including testimony by Mohammed and three others that they had been tortured or abused while in U.S. custody. Transcripts released during the Bush administration had deleted all references to abuse, the ACLU said. The transcripts quote Mohammed as saying he used to "make up stories" for CIA interrogators after being tortured. Al Nashiri, one of the waterboarded detainees, said that interrogators would "drown me in water."[41]

ACLU lawyers favor shutting down the military commissions altogether. "We have said from the beginning that these are illegitimate proceedings," says Denny LeBoeuf, head of the John Adams Project, a joint venture with the National Association of Criminal Defense Lawyers that is providing attorneys for detainees in the 9/11 and other capital cases.

LeBoeuf says that any evidence obtained by torture will not be allowed in either the military commissions or in federal courts, but that other evidence will be admissible. "There'll be civilian lawyers, there'll be military lawyers and they'll argue about what evidence should be admitted." In the end, she adds, "some people will get convicted."

OUTLOOK
Change and Continuity

Four days after releasing details of the harsh interrogation measures used by the CIA against suspected terrorists, President Obama visited the agency's headquarters on a politically sensitive morale-boosting mission.

"Don't be discouraged by what's happened in the last few weeks," Obama told the assembled employees on April 20. The government's willingness to acknowledge "serious mistakes" and "move forward," Obama said, "is precisely why I am proud to be president of the United States, and that's why you should be proud to be members of the CIA."[42]

Four months later, Obama's attorney general undercut the president's efforts to reassure CIA employees by asking a federal prosecutor to investigate agency operatives who may have gone beyond the "enhanced interrogation techniques" that the Justice Department authorized. "Morale at the agency is down to minus 50," said A. B. "Buzzy" Krongard, the third-ranking CIA official at the time of the use of harsh interrogation practices.[43]

"The agency feared this day would come," says Amy Zegart, a professor of public policy at UCLA who has studied intelligence agencies' role in counterterrorism.."They did everything that was legally authorized by the Department of Justice and politically sanctioned by the White House. And now they feel they're being hung out to dry."

Some human-rights advocates are applauding Holder's decision to refer the CIA interrogation cases for further investigation. "It's important for the United States to be able to return to a system of operating under law," says Human Rights First executive director Massimino.

Many want Holder to go further. Human-rights investigator Sifton calls for an investigation of "any and all violations of law that took place in connection with the detention and interrogation program," including possible obstruction of justice by officials at the Justice Department and White House up to and including Vice President Cheney and President Bush. "No one wants to go after low-level CIA officers," Sifton says. "That's not accountability. That's scapegoating."

Others, however, disagree with Holder's decision. "I'm opposed to prosecutions," says Joseph Marguiles, a veteran human-rights advocate who is representing Abu Zabaydah. Like other human-rights advocates, however, Marguiles strongly favors a full investigation by a congressional committee or independent commission.

Among the new proposals to emerge in that regard is a suggestion by Fred Hiatt, editorial page editor of the *Post*, for a "truth commission" to be chaired by two retired Supreme Court justices: Sandra Day O'Connor and David H. Souter. "A fair-minded commission," Hiatt wrote on Aug. 30, "could help the nation come to grips with its past and show the world that America is serious about doing so."[44]

The prospects for a full-blown investigation of that sort, however, appear to be dim. "I don't get any sense that the Obama administration is willing to see this full discussion take place," says Marguiles. "In fact, there's every indication they don't want it to take place." For her part, Zegart doubts that an investigation could produce a "sober" assessment in what she calls "this partisan, poisonous atmosphere."

National-security law expert Robert Chesney at the University of Texas Law School in Austin says Obama has tried to navigate the political shoals with measured steps in revising the Bush administration's counterterrorism policies. Obama has scrapped the "enhanced interrogation techniques" but continues to defend the power to detain enemy combatants with limited judicial review. He has changed review procedures at the prison camp at Bagram Air Force base in Afghanistan, but continues to oppose habeas corpus rights for the detainees there. The government is also continuing to invoke the state-secrets privilege in such cases as one in federal court in California seeking to hold CIA-contractor airlines liable for their role in transporting detainees to other countries.

"People are going to find what they want to find," says Chesney, who served this summer with the task force that Obama created on detention policy. "If they want to see continuity [with the Bush policies], they are going to see continuity. If they want to see change, they're going to see change."

The CIA's role in future interrogations remains to be worked out with the new high-value detainee information group that Obama created and placed under the FBI instead of the CIA. The plans call for interagency cooperation, but Zegart calls the plan a "terrible idea." "Since when did interagency processes work well in intelligence?" she asks.

In his visit to Langley, however, Obama tried his best to reassure the agency that it is still needed in dealing with terrorist threats. "We're going to have to operate smarter and more effectively than ever," Obama said in closing. "So I'm going to be relying on you, and the American people are going to rely on you."

NOTES

1. "Special Review: Counterterrorism Detention and Interrogation Activities (September 2001-October 2003)," Inspector General, Central Intelligence Agency, May 7, 2004, http://luxmedia.vo.llnwd.net/o10/clients/aclu/IG_Report.pdf. For coverage, see these stories by Peter Finn, Jory Warrick and Julie Tate in *The Washington Post*: "CIA Report Calls Oversight of Early Interrogations Poor," Aug. 25, 2009, p. A1; "CIA Releases Its Instructions on Breaking a Detainee's Will," Aug. 26, 2009, p. A1.

2. For background on the ACLU litigation, see Scott Shane, "A.C.L.U. Lawyers Mine Documents for Truth," *The New York Times*, Aug. 30, 2009, sec. 1, p. 4. The ACLU maintains a comprehensive archive of documents in the litigation: www.aclu.org/safefree/torture/index.html. For a compilation of some of the documents and a narrative overview, see Jameel Jeffer and Amrit Singh, *Administration of Torture: A Documentary Record from Washington to Abu Ghraib and Beyond* (2007).

3. For background, see these *CQ Researcher* reports: Kenneth Jost, "Closing Guantánamo," Feb. 27, 2009, pp. 177-200; Kenneth Jost and the *CQ*

Researcher Staff, "The Obama Presidency," Jan. 30, 2009, pp. 73-104; Peter Katel and Kenneth Jost, "Treatment of Detainees," Aug. 25, 2006, pp. 673-696. See also Seth Stern, "Torture Debate," *CQ Global Researcher*, September 2007, pp. 211-236.

4. For transcript, see www.foxnews.com/story/0,2933,544522,00.html. For coverage of comments from others, see Rachel L. Swarns, "Cheney Offers Sharp Defense of C.I.A. Tactics," *The New York Times*, Aug. 31, 2009, p. A1.

5. See Carrie Johnson, Jerry Markon and Julie Tate, "Inquiry Into CIA Practices Narrow," *The Washington Post*, Sept. 19, 2009, p. A1. The full text of the letter can be found on RealPolitics.com: www.realclearpolitics.com/politics_nation/cialetter0918.pdf. For Obama's reply, see CBS "Face the Nation," Sept. 20, 2009, www.cbsnews.com/stories/2009/09/20/ftn/main5324077.shtml?tag=cbsnewsTwoColUpperPromoArea.

6. "Special Task Force on Interrogations and Transfer Policies Issues Its Recommendations to the President," Department of Justice, Aug. 24, 2009, www.usdoj.gov/opa/pr/2009/August/09-ag-835.html. For coverage, see Anne E. Kornblut, "New Unit to Question Key Terror Suspects," *The Washington Post*, Aug. 24, 2009, p. A1.

7. See "Statement of President Barack Obama on Release of OLC Memos," April 16, 2009, www.whitehouse.gov/the_press_office/Statement-of-President-Barack-Obama-on-Release-of-OLC-Memos/. For coverage, see Mark Mazzetti and Scott Shane, "Memos Spell Out Brutal Mode of C.I.A. Interrogation," *The New York Times*, April 17, 2009, p. A1.

8. Estes Thompson, "Ex-CIA Contractor Guilty in Afghan Death," The Associated Press, Aug. 18, 2006. Passaro was convicted of assault with a dangerous weapon and assault with intent to inflict serious injury. He was sentenced in 2007 to eight-and-a-half-years in prison, but the 4th U.S. Circuit Court of Appeals on Aug. 10, 2009, ordered resentencing on the ground that Judge Terence Boyle had not justified a sentence longer than recommended under the federal sentencing guidelines.

9. See Jeffrey H. Smith, "CIA Accountability," *The Washington Post*, Aug. 24, 2009, p. A15; Walter Pincus

and Jory Warrick, "Ex-Intelligence Officials Cite Low Spirits at CIA," *ibid.*, Aug. 30, 2009, p. A2.

10. The veto message appears in the *Congressional Record* on March 10, 2008: http://fas.org/irp/congress/2008_cr/veto.html. For coverage, see Steven Lee Myers, "Bush Vetoes Bill on C.I.A. Tactics, Affirming Legacy," *The New York Times*, March 9, 2008, p. A1.

11. "Executive Order — Ensuring Lawful Interrogations," Jan. 22, 2009, www.whitehouse.gov/the_press_office/EnsuringLawfulInterrogations/.

12. "Special Review," *op. cit.*, p. 100.

13. Barton Gellman, "Cheney Uncloaks His Frustration With Bush," *The Washington Post*, Aug. 13, 2009, p. A1.

14. *The 9/11 Commission Report: Final Report of the National Commission on Terrorist Attacks Upon the United States*, 2004. For background, see Kenneth Jost, "Re-examining 9/11," *CQ Researcher*, June 4, 2004, pp. 493-516.

15. Other groups include Amnesty International USA, Human Rights First, Human Rights Watch, Open Society Institute, Physicians for Human Rights and the Rutherford Institute. For a complete list, see www.commissiononaccountability.org/.

16. Quoted in Bennett Roth, "Democrats Split on Interrogation Inquiry," *CQ Weekly*, April 27, 2009, p. 978.

17. Background drawn from Alfred W. McCoy, *A Question of Torture: CIA Interrogation, from the Cold War to the War on Terror* (2006), pp. 16-20; Pauletta Otis, "Educing Information: The Right Initiative at the Right Time by the Right People," in Intelligence Science Board, "Educing Information: Interrogation: Science and Art; Foundations for the Future: Phase 1 Report," December 2006, pp. xv-xx. See also Stern, *op. cit.*; David Masci, "Torture," *CQ Researcher*, April 18, 2003, pp. 345-368.

18. McCoy, *op. cit.*, p. 16.

19. Ernest Jerome Hopkins, *Our Lawless Police* (1931), quoted in Richard A. Leo, "From Coercion To Deception: The Changing Nature of Police Interrogation in America," *Crime, Law and Social Change*, Vol. 18 (1992), p. 35.

20. The decision is *Miranda v. Arizona*, 384 U.S. 436 (1966).

21. Petula Dvorak, "Fort Hunt's Quiet Men Break Silence on WWII," *The Washington Post*, Oct. 6, 2007, p. A1; Roni Gehlke, "New book out about Byron's Camp Tracy," *Contra Costa* (Calif.) *Times*, July 8, 2009. The referenced book is Alexander Corbin, *The History of Camp Tracy: Japanese WWII POWs and the Future of Strategic Interrogation* (2009).

22. For background, see McCoy, *op. cit.*, chs. 2 & 3; Laura L. Finley, "The Central Intelligence Agency and Torture," in *The Torture and Prisoner Abuse Debate* (2008).

23. McCoy, *op. cit.*, pp. 24-25.

24. *Ibid.*, pp. 68-69.

25. See Gary Cohn, Ginger Thompson and Mark Matthews, "Torture was taught by CIA," *The Baltimore Sun*, Jan. 27, 1997.

26. Background drawn from Jane Mayer, *The Dark Side: How the War on Terror Turned Into a War on American Ideals* (2008). See also "Special Review," *op. cit.* Approximately 100 prisoners were held at the secret CIA sites at one time or another.

27. Quoted in Mayer, *op. cit.*, pp. 9-10.

28. "Special Review," p. 13; the report does not identify Mitchell and Jessen by name. See also Mayer, *op. cit.*, pp. 157-158.

29. See Seth Hettena, "Iraqi Died While Hung From Wrists," The Associated Press, Feb. 17, 2005; "U.S. Operatives Killed Detainees During Interrogations in Afghanistan and Iraq, CIA, Navy Seals and Military Intelligence Personnel Implicated," American Civil Liberties Union, Oct. 24, 2005, www.aclu.org/intlhumanrights/gen/21236prs 20051024.html; Human Rights First, "Command's Responsibility: Detainee Deaths in U.S. Custody in Iraq and Afghanistan," February 2006, www.human-rightsfirst.org/us_law/etn/dic/exec-sum.aspx. For an account of Jamadi's interrogation and death, see Mayer, *op. cit.*, pp. 238-258. Mark Swanner, the CIA interrogator, has denied any wrongdoing; Mayer said the agency's inspector general referred the case to the Justice Department "for possible criminality," but no charges were brought.

30. Dana Priest, "CIA Holds Terror Suspects in Secret Prisons," *The Washington Post*, Nov. 2, 2005, p. A1. Priest won a Pulitzer Prize for her reporting on the sites.

31. Mark Danner, "U.S. Torture: Voices from the Black Sites," *New York Review of Books*, April 9, 2009. The ICRC keeps its reports confidential to preserve its impartiality with individual governments. After Danner obtained the report, the *New York Review* posted the complete document on its Web site: www.nybooks.com/icrc-report.pdf.

32. See Mark Mazzetti, "U.S. Says CIA Destroyed 92 Tapes of Interrogations," *The New York Times*, March 3, 2009, p. A16.

33. The consolidated cases are *American Civil Liberties Union v. Department of Defense*, 04 Civ. 4151, and *American Civil Liberties Union v. Department of Justice*, 05-9620. For coverage of Panetta's declaration, see R. Jeffrey Smith, "CIA Urges Judge to Keep Bush-Era Documents Sealed," *The Washington Post*, June 9, 2009, p. A1.

34. The Supreme Court case is *U.S. Defense Department v. American Civil Liberties Union*, 09-160. For coverage, including links to the government's petition and the lower court ruling, see Lyle Denniston, "Transparency in wartime at issue," SCOTUSBlog, Aug. 24, 2009, www.scotusblog.com/wp/transparency-in-wartime-at-issue/. See also Adam Liptak, "Obama's About-Face on Detainee Photos Leads to Supreme Court," *The New York Times*, Sept. 15, 2009, p. A13.

35. "Fox News Sunday," April 19, 2009, www.foxnews.com/story/0,2933,517158,00.html.

36. See John Sifton, "What's Missing from the CIA Docs," *The Daily Beast*, Aug. 25, 2009, www.thedailybeast.com/blogs-and-stories/2009-08-25/whats-missing-from-the-cia-docs/.

37. The case is *ACLU v. Department of Defense*, 09 CV 8071 (S.D.N.Y.) For background, see Bagram FOIA (8/13/2009), www.aclu.org/safefree/detention/40715res20090813.html.

38. The decision is *Hamdan v. Rumsfeld*, 548 U.S. 557 (2006). For an account, see Kenneth Jost, *The Supreme Court Yearbook 2005-2006*.

39. For coverage, including a link to the government's filing, see Lyle Denniston, "Decision soon on 9/11 trials," SCOTUSBlog, Sept. 16, 2009, www.scotusblog.com/wp/decision-soon-on-911-trials/. See also David Johnston, "U.S. Seeking 3rd Delay on Guantánamo Cases," *The New York Times*, Sept. 17, 2009, p. A17, from which some background has been drawn.

40. Bob Woodward, "Detainee Tortured, U.S. Official," *The Washington Post*, Jan. 14, 2009, p. A1.

41. See "Newly Released Detainee Statements Provide More Evidence of CIA Torture Program," June 15, 2009, www.aclu.org/safefree/torture/39868prs20090615.html. For coverage, see Julian E. Barnes and Greg Miller, "Detainee says he lied to the CIA," *Los Angeles Times*, June 16, 2009, p. A1.

42. The text of the speech is on the CIA's Web site: www.cia.gov/news-information/speeches-testimony/president-obama-at-cia.html. For coverage, see Peter Baker and Scott Shane, "Pressure Grows to Investigate Interrogations," *The New York Times*, April 21, 2009, p. A1.

43. See Pincus and Warrick, *op. cit.*, p. A2.

44. Fred Hiatt, "Time for a Souter-O'Connor Commission," *The Washington Post*, Aug. 30, 2009, p. A21.

BIBLIOGRAPHY

Books

Finley, Laura L., *The Torture and Prisoner Abuse Debate, Greenwood Press*, 2008.
The book, part of Greenwood's "Historical Guides to Controversial Issues in America," includes chapters on the origins of torture, the CIA and torture and abusive interrogations and detentions in Afghanistan and Iraq and at Guantánamo. Finley teaches in the women's studies department at Florida Atlantic University. Includes chapter notes, seven-page bibliography.

Mayer, Jane, *The Dark Side: How the War on Terror Turned Into a War on American Ideals, Doubleday*, 2008.
The book details the origins and implementation of harsh interrogation practices by military and CIA interrogators after Sept. 11 and strongly criticizes the practices on legal, moral and pragmatic grounds. Mayer is an author and staff writer for *The New Yorker.* Includes notes, bibliography.

McCoy, Alfred W., *A Question of Torture: CIA Interrogation, from the Cold War to the War on Terror, Metropolitan Books*, 2006.
A professor of history at the University of Wisconsin traces the history of the CIA's controversial interrogation practices. Includes notes, 23-page bibliography.

Wittes, Benjamin, *Law and the Long War: The Future of Justice in the Age of Terror, Penguin*, 2008.
A leading researcher on national security argues for legislation to authorize administrative detention of suspected enemy combatants and some methods of interrogation at least for the CIA beyond those authorized in the *U.S. Army Field Manual.* Wittes is a research fellow at the Brookings Institution and a member of the Hoover Institution's National Security Task Force. His paper co-authored with Stuart Taylor Jr., "Looking Forward, Not Backward: Refining American Interrogation Law," is being published in *Legislating the War on Terror: An Agenda for Reform* (Brookings, 2009).

Articles

Herman, Arthur, "The Gitmo Myth and the Torture Canard," *Commentary*, June 2009, www.commentarymagazine.com/viewarticle.cfm/the-gitmo-myth-and-the-torture-canard-15154?search=1.
The historian and longtime *Commentary* contributor argues that reports of abusive interrogation by the military and CIA have been exaggerated, part of a "Gitmo myth" created to "ruin the Bush administration" and "blacken" the United States' reputation.

Sullivan, Andrew, "Dear President Bush," *The Atlantic*, October 2009, p. 78, www.theatlantic.com/doc/200910/bush-torture.
The well-known author-journalist lays out a searing critique of detention and interrogation practices by the military and the CIA and asks former President George W. Bush to support "a full accounting and report from an independent body."

Reports and Studies

"Educing Information: Interrogation: Science and Art; Foundations for the Future: Phase 1 Report," *Intelligence Science Board NDIC Press,* **December 2006, www1.umn.edu/humanrts/OathBetrayed/ Intelligence%20Science%20Board%202006.pdf.**
The official advisory body at the National Defense Intelligence College laments the limited knowledge about the efficacy of specific interrogation techniques and recommends scientific studies on the questions. Includes introductory essays, 10 scientific papers and annotated bibliography.

"Inquiry Into the Treatment of Detainees in U.S. Custody," *Senate Armed Services Committee,* **Nov. 20, 2008, as declassified April 20, 2009, http://graphics8 .nytimes.com/packages/images/nytint/docs/report-by- the-senate-armed-services-committee-on-detainee-treat- ment/original.pdf.**
The report provides the most thorough accounting to date of the harsh interrogation practices approved at the highest levels of the Bush administration.

Bibliographic Note

The Bush administration's "war on terror" has already produced a number of accounts, some from participants, others from journalists. In his memoir, *At the Center of the Storm: My Years at the CIA* (HarperCollins, 2007), former CIA Director George Tenet writes boastfully of the agency's interrogation of "high-value" detainees. In *The Terror Presidency: Law and Judgment Inside the Bush Administration* (W.W. Norton, 2007), Jack L. Goldsmith, former head of the Justice Department's Office of Legal Counsel, writes of his role in rescinding OLC memos approving "enhanced-interrogation techniques."

Two journalist authors published books in 2006 detailing what was then known about CIA interrogations: Ron Suskind, *The One Percent Doctrine: Deep Inside America's Pursuit of Its Enemies Since 9/11* (Simon & Schuster), and James Risen, *State of War: The Secret History of the CIA and the Bush Administration.* (Thorndike Press).

For More Information

American Civil Liberties Union, 125 Broad St., 18th Floor, New York, NY 10004; (212) 607-3300; www.aclu.org. Works to defend and preserve individual rights and liberties guaranteed by the Constitution.

Constitution Project, 1200 18th St., N.W., Suite 1000, Washington, DC 20036; (202) 580-6920; www.constitutionproject.org. Promotes bipartisan dialogue to reach consensus on difficult legal and constitutional issues.

Heritage Foundation, 214 Massachusetts Ave., N.E., Washington, DC 20002; (202) 546-4400; www.heritage .org. Public policy research institute promoting conservative

positions on free enterprise, limited government and a strong national defense.

Human Rights First, 333 Seventh Ave., 13th Floor, New York, NY 10001; (212) 845-5200; www.humanrightsfirst.org. Nonprofit international human-rights organization promoting laws and policies that advance universal rights and freedoms.

National Security Archive, The George Washington University, 2130 H St., N.W., Washington, DC 20037; (202) 994-7000; www.gwu.edu/~nsarchiv. Non-governmental research institute serving as a repository for government documents relating to national security and intelligence.

16

Torture Debate

Is the U.S. War on Terror Legitimizing Torture?

Seth Stern

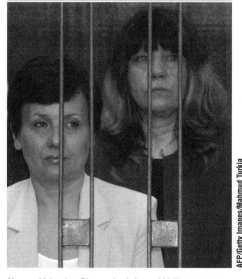

Nurses Valentina Siropoulu, left, and Valia Cherveniashlka are among six Bulgarian medical workers who were tortured while imprisoned for eight years in Libya on charges they infected hundreds of Libyan children with HIV-AIDS. They were released in August. About 160 countries torture prisoners, despite six international treaties banning the practice.

From *CQ Global Researcher*, September 2007.

I t is called, simply, waterboarding. A prisoner is strapped to a board with his feet above his head, his mouth and nose covered, usually with cloth or cellophane. Water is then poured over his face, inducing gagging and a terrifying sense of drowning.

The U.S. government — which has been accused of using waterboarding on detainees it suspects are terrorists — denies that it practices torture or cruel, inhuman or degrading treatment. The Central Intelligence Agency (CIA) says it must use what it calls "enhanced interrogation techniques" — to obtain critical information from "enemy combatants" in the war on terrorism.[1] But human rights advocates say waterboarding and other abusive interrogation tactics are prohibited by international law.

To be sure, the United States is far from the worst offender when it comes to mistreating prisoners. Even human rights advocates who complain the most bitterly about the tactics used in America's war on terror say they don't compare to those utilized by the world's worst human rights abusers.

"Nothing the administration has done can compare in its scale to what happens every day to victims of cruel dictatorships around the world," Tom Malinowski, Human Rights Watch's Washington advocacy director, told the U.S. Senate Foreign Relations Committee on July 26. "The United States is not Sudan or Cuba or North Korea."[2]

Indeed, about 160 countries practice torture today, according to human rights groups and the U.S. State Department.[3] In July, for example, six Bulgarian medical workers freed after eight years in a Libyan prison said they had been tortured. "We were treated like

381

Torture Still in Use Throughout the World

Some 160 countries practice torture, according to a 2005 survey of incidents reported by the U.S. Department of State and Amnesty International. Besides using torture to solicit information, some countries use it to punish or intimidate dissidents, separatists, insurgents and religious minorities. The Council of Europe accuses the U.S. Central Intelligence Agency (CIA) of using its rendition program to send kidnapped terror suspects to be interrogated in 11 cities — all in countries that practice torture.

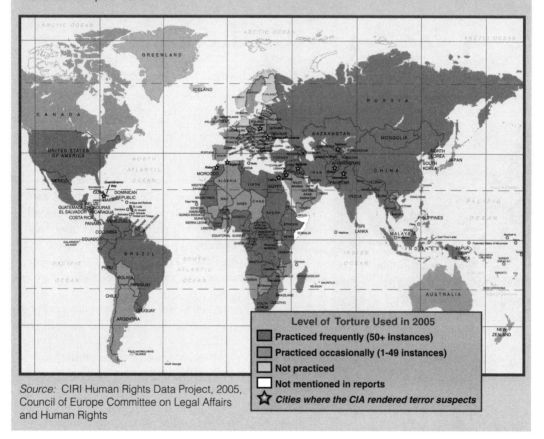

Level of Torture Used in 2005
- Practiced frequently (50+ instances)
- Practiced occasionally (1-49 instances)
- Not practiced
- Not mentioned in reports
- ☆ *Cities where the CIA rendered terror suspects*

Source: CIRI Human Rights Data Project, 2005, Council of Europe Committee on Legal Affairs and Human Rights

animals," said Ashraf al-Hazouz, one of the prisoners, who had been accused of deliberately infecting Libyan children with the HIV-AIDS virus. Hazouz said the Libyans attached electrodes to his genitals and feet, unleashed attack dogs on him and tied his hands and legs to a metal bar, spinning him "like a chicken on a rotisserie."[4]

While other countries' abuse methods may seem more abhorrent, human rights advocates worldwide complain angrily that America's detention and interrogation practices in the post-9/11 war on terror have lowered the bar for torturers worldwide, giving habitual abusers a new justification for their behavior.

America's detention policies since Sept. 11, 2001, "are a gift to dictators everywhere" who "use America's poor example to shield themselves from international criticism and pressure," Malinowski said. Abusive governments now routinely "justify their own, long-standing practices of systematically violating basic human rights norms" by arguing that they — like the

United States — must use torture to deal with the threat of international terrorism.[5]

U.S. counterterrorism policies that anger allies and human rights activists include the indefinite detentions — without a guaranteed trial or right to counsel — of hundreds of alleged terrorists at Guantánamo Bay, Cuba, beginning shortly after 9/11. Then in April 2004 CBS's "60 Minutes II" televised explosive photographs that circulated around the world portraying harsh interrogation methods that reportedly had migrated from Guantánamo to the U.S.-run Abu Ghraib military prison near Baghdad. A year later *The Washington Post* revealed that the CIA was operating so-called "black sites" — secret prisons in Eastern Europe and Southeast Asia where detainees were subjected to extreme interrogation methods, allegedly including waterboarding.[6] Finally, news that the United States was kidnapping terror suspects from foreign locations and transporting them to interrogation sites in third countries with reputations for practicing torture — a tactic known as extraordinary rendition — triggered further global outrage.[7]

By adopting such measures, the United States has lost its moral authority to condemn torture and human rights abuses in other countries, say critics. "It's a very bad precedent for people to be able to say 'the U.S. — the biggest democracy promoter in the world — has to use it, why can't we?' " says physician Bhogendra Sharma, president of the Center for Victims of Torture in Nepal, which treats victims tortured by both the Nepalese government and Maoist guerrillas.

Severe Torture Still Used by Many Nations

According to the U.S. State Department and Human Rights Watch, the following nations are among those condoning widespread and particularly severe forms of torture:

 China: Prison guards are forbidden from using torture, but former detainees report the use of electric shock, beatings and shackles. Among those targeted for abuse are adherents of the outlawed Falun Gong spiritual movement, Tibetans and Muslim Uighur prisoners.

 Egypt: Government interrogators from the State Security Investigations arm of the Ministry of the Interior regularly torture suspected Islamic militants, including prisoners transferred to Egypt by the United States. Victims were kicked, burned with cigarettes, shackled, forcibly stripped, beaten with water hoses and dragged on the floor.

 Indonesia: Security officers in Aceh Province systematically torture suspected supporters of the armed Free Aceh movement, using beatings, cigarette burning and electric shock.

 Iran: Political prisoners are subjected to sensory deprivation known as "white torture" — they are held in all-white cells with no windows, with prison clothes and even meals all in white.

 Morocco: Terrorism suspects detained after a May 2003 attack in Casablanca were subjected to torture and mistreatment, including severe beatings.

 Nepal: Both government security personnel and Maoist rebels employ torture, including beating the soles of victims' feet, submersion in water and sexual humiliation.

 Nigeria: Armed robbery and murder suspects are subjected to beatings with batons, horse whips, iron bars and cables.

 North Korea: Captors routinely tortured and mistreated prisoners using electric shock, prolonged periods of exposure, humiliations such as public nakedness, being hung by the wrists and forcing mothers recently repatriated from China to watch the infanticide of their newborn infants.

 Russia: Russian security forces conducting so-called anti-terror operations in Chechnya mutilate victims and dump their bodies on the sides of roads.

 Uganda: Government security forces in unregistered detention facilities torture prisoners with caning and severe beatings and by inflicting pain to the genitals.

 Uzbekistan: Police, prison guards and members of the National Security Service routinely employ suffocation, electric shock, deprivation of food and water and sexual abuse. Prison regulations in 2005 permitted beatings under medical supervision.

Sources: "Human Rights Watch's 2007 World Report;" U.S. State Department "2006 Country Reports on Human Rights Practices"

Few American ambassadors today "dare to protest another government's harsh interrogations, detentions without trial, or even 'disappearances,' knowing how easily an interlocutor could turn the tables and cite U.S. misconduct as an excuse for his government's own abuses," said a 2007 Human Rights Watch (HRW) report.[8]

Sarah Leah Whitson, HRW's director for the Middle East and North Africa, says when she visits officials in those regions to discuss their use of torture, their first reply now is often, "What about the United States? Go talk to the U.S. government."

The worldwide anger triggered by America's post-9/11 detention and interrogation policies stems not only from the perception that notorious governments now feel free to continue torturing prisoners. It also stems from widespread perceptions that:

- The United States' overwhelming military and technological superiority have made it arrogant, immune from having to abide by international norms.
- America's pervasive cultural influence has, since 9/11, "normalized" torture by spreading the concept across the globe that torture works and can be legally or morally justified.
- The United States has squandered its historic position as the world's leader in the fight against human rights abuses, opening itself to charges of being a hypocrite.

When the U.S. State Department released its annual report on human rights violators in 2005, both China and Russia said the United States has its own abuses to explain. "Unfortunately, [the report] once again gives us reason to say that double standards are a characteristic of the American approach to such an important theme," said a statement issued by the Russian foreign ministry. "Characteristically off-screen is the ambiguous record of the United States itself."[9]

Disappointment over U.S. tactics has been widespread. *El Tiempo*, a leading newspaper in Bogotá, Colombia, editorialized in 2005: "It seems incredible that these kind of un-civilizing backward steps are coming from a country which declares itself a defender of Western values and which has been so on more than one occasion."[10]

A 2006 survey of 26,000 people in 25 countries found that 67 percent disapproved of U.S. treatment of detainees in Guantánamo and other prisons. Some of the highest disapproval rates were among America's closest allies in Europe — which have suffered their own terrorist attacks since 9/11 — and Middle Eastern allies such as Lebanon and Egypt, who fear the growing influence of Islamic extremists.[11]

But the 9/11 attacks did more than raise the profile of the torture debate in the United States. An Australian law professor has become one of the world's most vocal advocates for "life-saving compassionate torture," which he says is justified if it elicits crucial information needed to prevent future terrorist attacks and save innocent lives. (*See "At Issue," p. 399.*)

But critics of that argument point out that torture is not only used to extract life-saving information from terrorists but also to punish political dissidents, suspected criminals — who sometimes are innocent — and religious minorities. China, for instance, tortures members of the Falun Gong spiritual movement, Tibetan dissidents and Muslims from the Uighur region, according to Human Rights Watch.

In Iraq — where former leader Saddam Hussein was notorious for torturing political enemies — the U.S. occupation has not curbed the prevalence of torture by government agents or insurgents. In fact, say human rights advocates, the level of torture perpetrated by the Shiite-dominated Iraqi government and affiliated militias reportedly has escalated as the country has descended into civil strife. (*See sidebar, p. 388.*)

Despite the damage done to America's reputation by its counterterrorism tactics, President Bush in July said he was authorizing the CIA to reopen its overseas black sites. Bush had announced last September that the use of secret prisons had been suspended and that the prisoners were being transferred to Guantánamo. That decision was prompted by the U.S. Supreme Court's ruling that all U.S. detainees, including those held by the CIA, were covered by the Geneva Conventions' guidelines for the treatment of wartime detainees.

The administration said in July 2007 the CIA would comply with the conventions in its treatment of prisoners at the sites. But Bush's new order did not ban waterboarding or any other controversial interrogation techniques and gave interrogators wide latitude if their purpose is to gather intelligence needed to prevent terrorist attacks.[12]

The Bush administration and its supporters argue the United States is operating within the confines of U.S. and international law and that aggressive interrogation methods are needed to protect against future terrorist attacks. "These are dangerous men with unparalleled knowledge about terrorist networks and their plans for new attacks," President Bush said in 2006. "The security of our nation and the lives of our citizens depend on our ability to learn what these terrorists know."[13]

With America seen as abandoning its role as the world's ethical standard-bearer, human rights groups complain that the European Union (EU) has not stepped up to fill the void. The EU has dragged its feet in questioning U.S. interrogation policies, say critics, and some EU countries have secretly allowed U.S. aircraft to use their airports for rendition flights. Some renditions involved innocent citizens who were tortured in countries long known to abuse prisoners, such as Egypt and Syria. Besides generating outrage among close U.S. allies such as Canada, the incidents have led to prosecutions in Germany and Italy of Americans allegedly involved in the renditions.

As the Bush administration continues to defend itself against global criticism of its counterterrorism policies, these are some of the questions being asked:

Is torture effective?

Advocates and opponents of torture and other coercive techniques can look at the same evidence about their effectiveness and come to very different conclusions.

Take the case of Khalid Shaikh Mohammed, a senior al Qaeda operative and the alleged principal architect of

Views Differ on U.S. Interrogation Tactics

A wide gulf exists between Americans' and Europeans' views of how the United States treats terrorism suspects. Americans are almost evenly split on whether the United States uses torture, but three-quarters of Germans and nearly two-thirds of Britons believe it does. And while just over half of Americans think U.S. detention policies are legal, 85 percent of Germans and 65 percent of Britons think they are illegal.

Source: "American and International Opinion on the Rights of Terrorism Suspects, International Questionnaire," WorldPublicOpinion.org, June 2006

the 9/11 attacks. He was captured in Pakistan in 2003 and interrogated by U.S. intelligence agents — reportedly using waterboarding — before being transferred to military custody at Guantánamo.[14] In a military hearing in March 2007 the Defense Department released a transcript of his confession in which he took credit for 31 different terrorist operations, including planning the

Vann Nath, one of only seven people to survive the Khmer Rouge's infamous Tuol Sleng prison, looks at a photo of Kaing Guek Eav, who ran the murderous regime's security service. Eav was recently found living in Cambodia as a born-again Christian. He was indicted by a U.N.-backed tribunal in July for his role in the torture and deaths of 14,000 men, women and children at the facility. His trial is expected to begin in 2008.

9/11 attacks in the United States and the beheading of *Wall Street Journal* reporter Daniel Pearl.

CIA Director Michael Hayden cited coercive interrogation techniques employed against detainees such as Mohammed (dubbed K.S.M. by intelligence agents) as an "irreplaceable" tool that helped yield information that has helped disrupt several terrorist plots since 9/11. "K.S.M. is the poster boy for using tough but legal tactics," said Michael Sheehan, a former State Department counterterrorism official. "He's the reason these techniques exist."[15]

But opponents of aggressive interrogation techniques, like Col. Dwight Sullivan, head defense lawyer at the Office of Military Commissions, cite Mohammed's serial confessions as "a textbook example of why we shouldn't allow coercive methods."[16]

Some intelligence experts doubt the veracity of portions of Mohammed's information. For one thing they don't think a single operative — even one as high ranking as he — could have been involved in 31 separate terrorist plots. And those intimately associated with the Pearl case are highly skeptical that Mohammed himself murdered Pearl, as he claimed.

"My old colleagues say with 100-percent certainty that it was not K.S.M. who killed Pearl," former CIA officer Robert Baer told *New Yorker* writer Jane Mayer. And Special Agent Randall Bennett, who oversaw security at the U.S. consulate in Karachi when Pearl was killed, said "K.S.M.'s name never came up" during his interviews with those convicted in 2002 of the murder.[17]

Skeptics of torture's effectiveness say most people — to end their suffering — will provide false information. For instance, a torture victim deprived of his clothes will feel so "ashamed and humiliated and cold," said retired FBI counterterrorism agent Dan Coleman, "he'll tell you anything you want to hear to get his clothing back. There's no value in it."[18]

Others say torture doesn't work against zealots. "People who are committed to their ideology or religion . . . would rather die than speak up," says Sharma at the Center for Victims of Torture in Nepal.

Both opponents and supporters of coercive interrogation methods, however, agree torture is useful for other purposes. Many countries use torture to punish dissidents, separatists or guerrillas and to intimidate others from joining such groups. "The real purpose of torture is oppression of one or the other kind, to send a signal to anyone who is an opponent that there is a very, very grave risk," says Sune Segal, head of communications for the Copenhagen-based International Rehabilitation Council for Torture Victims, which collaborates with 131 treatment centers around the world. "It's not about soliciting information."

Underlying the debate is the fact that little scientific evidence exists about whether torture works. A recent Intelligence Science Board study concluded that "virtually none" of the limited number of techniques used by U.S. personnel in recent decades "are based on scientific research or have even been subjected to scientific or systematic inquiry or evaluation."[19]

Darius Rejali, a political science professor at Reed College in Portland, Ore., says regimes that employ torture aren't likely to divulge their findings, and torturers themselves have very little incentive to boast about their work, which is punishable under international law. "Torture travels by back routes," Rejali says. "There's rarely training, so there is no particular mechanism for determining whether it works."

Experienced interrogators who have talked about their work say pain and coercion are often counterproductive. John Rothrock, who as a U.S. Air Force captain in Vietnam headed a combat interrogation team, said he didn't know "any professional intelligence officers of my generation who would think this is a good idea."[20]

Experts say the most effective interrogations require a trained interrogator. Coleman says he learned to build a rapport with even the worst suspects rather than trying to intimidate them. He would patiently work to build a relationship in which the target of his interrogation would begin to trust him and ultimately share information.

You try to "get them to the point, in the intelligence world, where they commit treason," he said.[21]

Is torture ever justified?

Australian law Professor Mirko Bagaric at Deakin University in Melbourne prompted a vigorous public debate in May 2005 when he suggested that torture is sometimes morally justified.

"Given the choice between inflicting a relatively small level of harm on a wrongdoer and saving an innocent person, it is verging on moral indecency to prefer the interests of the wrongdoer," Bagaric wrote in *The Age*, a leading daily paper in Melbourne. Such cases are analogous to a situation in which a wrongdoer threatens to kill a hostage unless his demands are met, he said. "In such a case, it is not only permissible but desirable for police to shoot (and kill) the wrongdoer if they get a 'clear shot.' "[22]

In the United States, Harvard Law Professor Alan Dershowitz has argued that the legal system should adjust to the reality that if it could prevent a catastrophic terrorist attack that could kill millions, interrogators will probably torture a suspect whether or not it's legal. In emergencies, he contends, courts should issue "torture warrants" to interrogators trying to prevent such attacks.

"A formal, visible, accountable and centralized system is somewhat easier to control than an ad hoc, off-the-books and under-the-radar-screen non-system," Dershowitz wrote.[23]

Those who justify torture in certain situations usually invoke a hypothetical "ticking time bomb" scenario in which interrogators torture a suspect to obtain information that can help prevent an imminent attack. Twenty-five years ago, long before the rise of Islamist terrorists, philosophy Professor Michael Levin of the City University of New York hypothesized a similar scenario in *Newsweek*.

"Suppose a terrorist has hidden a bomb on Manhattan Island, which will detonate at noon on 4 July. . . . Suppose, further, that he is caught at 10 a.m. that fateful day, but — preferring death to failure — won't disclose where the bomb is. . . . If the only way to save those lives is to subject the terrorist to the most excruciating possible pain, what grounds can there be for not doing so?"[24]

But opponents of torture say such perfect "ticking time bomb" scenarios occur in the movies, but rarely in real life. Interrogators usually aren't positive they have captured the one person with knowledge of a real plot. And even if they torture such a suspect, it usually won't prevent the attack because his accomplices will proceed without him, critics say.

"I was in the Army for 25 years, and I talked to lots of military people who had been in lots of wars. I talked to lots of people in law enforcement," says James Jay Carafano, a fellow at the conservative Heritage Foundation. "I've never yet ever found anyone that's ever confronted the ticking time bomb scenario. That's not the moral dilemma that people normally face."[25]

"The United States is a nation of laws," says Sen. Patrick J. Leahy, a Vermont Democrat who chairs the Senate Judiciary Committee, "and I categorically reject the view that torture, even in such compelling circumstances, can be justified." Even if harsh interrogation techniques do not rise to the level of torture, he said, they are probably illegal under international laws that prohibit cruel, inhumane or degrading treatment of prisoners.

Law professors and philosophers widely agree that torture is always immoral and should not be legalized. Once torture is allowed in extreme circumstances, they point out, it quickly spreads to less urgent situations. "It has a tendency to just proliferate," says Raimond Gaita, a professor of moral philosophy at King's College in London.

Torture Has Escalated in Iraq

Saddam's brutal legacy survives.

The fall of Saddam Hussein and more than four years of U.S. occupation have done little to curb torture in Iraq. In fact, the level of torture perpetrated by government personnel and militias reportedly has escalated as the country has descended into what many consider a civil war.

The use of torture in Iraq is "totally out of hand," said Manfred Nowak, a U.N. official appointed to study torture around the world, and "many people say it is worse than it had been in the times of Saddam Hussein."[1]

Bodies brought to the Baghdad morgue often bear signs of acid-induced injuries, broken limbs and wounds caused by power drills and nails, said U.N. investigators.[2] The torture is mostly being perpetrated by the largely Shiite ministries of the Interior and Defense as well as by private Shiite militias, according to Sarah Leah Whitson, Human Rights Watch's program director for the Middle East and North Africa.

"The torture committed in the Ministry of Interior facilities we documented is certainly comparable to torture and abuse that's been recorded in the Baath prisons prior to the war," says Whitson.

In 2006 U.S. and Iraqi troops discovered a secret Baghdad prison run by the Interior Ministry, known as Site 4, where some of the more than 1,400 prisoners were found to have been subjected to systematic abuse.

Human rights advocates say the widespread use of torture is being fueled by the breakdown of law and order and the continued employment of officials who previously used torture during Saddam's regime. The weakened Iraqi central government has been unable to rein in the abuse of prisoners in these facilities, despite promises to do so. There has been less documented evidence of torture by Sunni insurgents, Whitson points out. Sunnis usually execute their victims, often by beheading.

A January 2005 report by Human Rights Watch found that police, jailers and intelligence agents — many of whom had similar jobs under Saddam — were "committing systematic torture and other abuses." Despite being "in the throes of a significant insurgency" in which thousands of police officers and civilians are being killed, the report said, "no government — not Saddam Hussein's, not the occupying powers and not the Iraqi interim government — can justify ill-treatment of persons in custody in the name of security."[3]

The government of Iraqi Prime Minister Nuri Kamal al-Maliki has been slow to respond to reports of torture by governmental personnel, say human rights advocates. The Iraqi government "made all kinds of promises and commitments to investigate and review" allegations of torture in 2005, Whitson says, but since then the Interior Ministry "has only gone further outside control of the government," as war and sectarian violence have escalated. "There's not a commitment to making this issue a priority."

When British and Iraqi special forces raided the office of an Iraqi government intelligence agency in the southern city of Basra in March 2007, they found prisoners exhibiting signs of torture. Al-Maliki condemned the raid, but not the abuse it uncovered.[4]

Torture has continued since the start of the U.S. military occupation in Iraq. A 2004 report by the International Committee of the Red Cross found that after Saddam's fall Iraqi authorities beat detainees with cables, kicked them in the genitals and hung them by handcuffs from iron bars of cell windows for several hours at a time.[5]

Torture is also being employed in Kurdistan, a semi-autonomous region in northern Iraq that is the most stable part of the country. Human Rights Watch reported in July 2007 that detainees accused of anti-government activities were subjected to torture and other mistreatment.[6]

The torturers are security forces and personnel at detention facilities operated by the two major Kurdish political parties — the Kurdistan Democratic Party and the Patriotic Union of Kurdistan — which operate outside control of the region's government, the report said. Detainees have been beaten, put in stress positions and handcuffed for several days at a time.

Nonetheless, the abuses in Kurdistan do not equal those occurring elsewhere in Iraq. "Certainly the situation in mainland Iraq is much worse," says Whitson.

[1] BBC News, "Iraq Torture 'worse than Saddam,'" Sept. 21, 2006.

[2] *Ibid.*

[3] Doug Struck, "Torture in Iraq Still Routine, Report Says," *The Washington Post,* Jan. 25, 2005, p. A10.

[4] Kirk Semple, "Basra Raid Finds Dozens Detained by Iraqi Unit," *The New York Times,* March 5, 2007.

[5] "Report of the International Committee of the Red Cross on the Treatment by the Coalition Forces of Prisoners of War and Other Protected Persons by the Geneva Conventions in Iraq During Arrest, Internment and Interrogation," February 2004, www.globalsecurity.org/military/library/report/2004/icrc_report_iraq_feb2004.pdf.

[6] "Caught in the Whirlwind: Torture and Denial of Due Process by the Kurdistan Security Forces," Human Rights Watch, July 3, 2007, http://hrw.org/reports/2007/kurdistan0707/.

He cites the experience of Israel, which authorized coercive interrogation techniques in 1987 in limited circumstances. But interrogators in the field used more aggressive techniques with more suspects than intended.

Eitan Felner, former director of the Israeli Information Center for Human Rights in the Occupied Territories, writes the lesson of Israel's experience is "the fallacy of believing — as some influential American opinion-makers do today — that it is possible to legitimize the use of torture to thwart terrorist attacks and at the same time restrict its use to exceptional cases."[26]

Instead, torture should remain illegal and interrogators faced with the time-bomb scenario should be in the same legal position as someone who commits civil disobedience, say opponents. "Anyone who thinks an act of torture is justified should have . . . to convince a group of peers in a public trial that all necessary conditions for a morally permissible act were indeed satisfied," writes Henry Shue, a professor of politics and international relations at the University of Oxford.[27]

Human Rights advocates say that — while not explicitly endorsing torture — U.S. policies have changed the dialogue about torture around world. "It used to be these things were automatically bad," says Jumana Musa, advocacy director for Amnesty USA. "Now, there's a cost-benefit analysis and the notion that this isn't really that bad."

Have U.S. attitudes toward torture changed?

Some prominent American politicians and some soldiers, albeit anonymously, have recently endorsed torture as a way to prevent terrorist attacks or save lives.

At a May 2007 GOP presidential debate, Rudolph W. Giuliani, the mayor of New York during the Sept. 11 terror attacks, said if elected president he would advise interrogators "to use every method they could think of" to prevent an imminent catastrophic terror attack. Other candidates were even more explicit, embracing torture with an openness that would have been unheard of before 9/11. California Rep. Duncan Hunter said he would tell the Defense secretary: "Get the information," while Colorado Rep. Tom Tancredo endorsed waterboarding.[28]

Some U.S. military personnel who have served in Iraq express similar attitudes. More than a third of the 1,700 American soldiers and Marines who responded to a 2006 survey said torture would be acceptable if it helped save the life of a fellow soldier or helped get information, and 10 percent admitted to using force against Iraqi civilians or damaging their property when it wasn't necessary.[29]

But many top U.S. military leaders, interrogators and veterans denounce torture as ineffective and say it will only make it more likely that American captives will be tortured in the future. Sen. John McCain, R-Ariz., who was tortured while a prisoner of war in Vietnam, has spoken out forcefully against torture and led the 2005 effort in Congress to limit the kinds of interrogation methods U.S. military personnel can use.

"We've sent a message to the world that the United States is not like the terrorists. [W]e are a nation that upholds values and standards of behavior and treatment of all people, no matter how evil or bad they are," McCain said. Furthermore, he added, disavowing torture will "help us enormously in winning the war for the hearts and minds of people throughout the world in the war on terror."[30]

A 2006 public opinion survey by the University of Maryland's Program on International Policy Attitudes (PIPA) suggests that most Americans reject the use of torture. The PIPA poll found that 75 percent of Americans agreed that terror detainees had "the right not to be tortured." Fifty-seven percent said the United States should not be permitted to send terror suspects to countries known to torture, and 73 percent said government officials who engage in or order torture should be punished. Fifty-eight percent of Americans said torture was impermissible under any circumstances — about the same percentage as those in countries like Ukraine, Turkey and Kenya — but lower than the percentages in Australia, Canada and France.[31]

Some critics fear that since 9/11 U.S. television shows and movies have changed the way torture is portrayed, making torture more palatable to Americans and the rest of the world.

"It used to be the bad guys who used these techniques," says David Danzig of Human Rights First, a New York-based advocacy group that works to combat genocide, torture and human rights abuses. "You saw it infrequently — an average of four or five times a year — and when you did see it, it was space aliens or Nazis doing it, and it almost never worked. Now it's often the heroes who are using these techniques."

Getty Images/The Washington Post

An American soldier threatens an Iraqi detainee with an attack dog in one of the graphic Abu Ghraib prison abuse photos that shocked the world in 2004. Human rights advocates worldwide say America's harsh post-9/11 detention and interrogation practices lowered the bar for torturers worldwide. Twelve low-level U.S. military personnel have since been convicted for their roles in the abuse, which an Army investigation described as "sadistic, blatant and wanton criminal" abuse.

The number of instances of torture portrayed on television jumped from almost none in 1996 to 228 in 2003, according to the Parents Television Council.[32]

Fox Television's "24" has come to symbolize that almost tectonic shift in TV's treatment of torture. The hero of the show — which debuted two months after 9/11 — is Jack Bauer, a member of a unit charged with preventing catastrophic terrorist attacks, including nuclear and poison gas attacks on American cities such as Los Angeles. Bauer and his comrades have been shown using electrical wires, heart defibrillators, physical assaults and chemical injections to obtain information vital to preventing the attacks.[33]

The show's creator has insisted he is not trying to present a realistic — or glamorized — view of torture and that Bauer is portrayed as paying a high psychological price for using torture.[34]

But critics say the show — enormously popular in the United States and throughout the world — is changing how American citizens and soldiers view torture. "The biggest lie that has gained currency through television is that torture is an acceptable weapon for the 'good guys' to use if the stakes are high enough. . . . It is a lie," wrote John McCarthy, a journalist who was held hostage in

Lebanon in the late 1980s. He accused the entertainment industry of "minimizing the true horrors of torture by failing to show the very profound impact it has on victims' lives."[35]

The show "leaves a message with junior soldiers that it's OK to cross the line in order to gather intelligence and save lives," said Danzig.

Senior American military officials were so worried about the show's impact that Brig. Gen. Patrick Finnegan, dean of the United States Military Academy, and top FBI and military interrogators visited the set in 2006. Finnegan told the show's creators it gives U.S. military personnel the wrong idea and has hurt America's image abroad by suggesting the United States condones torture.[36]

The show's impact on world opinion of Americans has been the subject of numerous debates — both in the United States and abroad — including a 2006 panel discussion at the Heritage Foundation. The show reinforces a world view of Americans as people who succeed by "breaking the law, by torturing people, by circumventing the chain of command," said David Heyman, director of Homeland Security at the nonpartisan Center for Strategic and International Studies, which focuses on security issues.[37]

Carafano, the Heritage fellow, said the program "just sort of confirms [the] prejudice" of those "who think ill of us" already.[38]

The show was also debated in June at a conference of North American and European judges in Ottawa, Canada. U.S. Supreme Court Justice Antonin Scalia argued that government agents should have more latitude in times of crisis. "Jack Bauer saved Los Angeles," said Scalia. "He saved hundreds of thousands of lives."[39]

Scalia's comments sparked heated retorts from the other judges and a subsequent *Globe and Mail* editorial. "Jack Bauer is a creation of wishful thinking. . . . He personifies the wish to be free of moral and legal constraints. . . . That's why constitutions exist; it's so tempting when fighting perceived evil to call for Jack Bauer." But, left unchecked, the commentary concluded, "Jack Bauer will poison liberty's fount."[40]

The popular TV program, however, doesn't seem to have clouded the vision of a group of American high school students invited to the White House in June to receive the prestigious Presidential Scholar award. They handed President Bush a handwritten letter urging him to halt "violations of the human rights" of terror suspects. "We do not want America to represent torture," said the letter.[41]

BACKGROUND

Ancient Practice

Torture has been embraced by some of the world's most enlightened civilizations. Egyptian wall paintings and friezes depict scenes of horrific treatment of enemies.[42] In ancient Greece, slaves and foreigners could be tortured lawfully but free citizens could not. The same held true in ancient Rome, where free citizens could only be tortured in cases of treason. Slaves could be beaten, whipped, stretched on the rack or burned with hot irons — as long they were not permanently injured or killed.[43]

The use of torture in Europe expanded in the 13th century after Italian city-states began to require stricter proof of guilt in criminal trials. Before that, guilt or innocence was proven by combat or endurance trials in which God was expected to favor the innocent.[44] Under the reforms, defendants could only be found guilty if two witnesses testified against them or the accused confessed to the crime. When there were no witnesses, torture was used to produce confessions, a practice that would persist for the next 500 years in Europe.

Torture was also used to punish prisoners in public spectacles, often attended by cheering crowds. In the technique known as "pressing to plead" weights were piled on the prisoner's body, crushing him until he confessed — or died. Victims were also stretched on a device called the rack — sometimes until their bones were pulled out of their sockets. Britain's King Henry VIII used torture against those who challenged his position as head of the Church of England. Queen Elizabeth I employed torture against those suspected of treason.

Particularly brutal torture methods gained religious sanction during the inquisitions conducted by the Roman Catholic Church to stamp out heresy. In 1252, Pope Innocent IV formally authorized the use of torture against heretics. In Spain for instance, victims were bound to a turning wheel as various body parts — the soles of their feet or the eyes — were brought closer and closer to a fire. In Italy, victims were suspended by their arms — tied behind their backs — from a pulley attached to a beam. The "strappado," as it was called,

THE RACK.

AFP/Getty Images/Hulton Archive

Cuthbert Simpson, a Protestant martyr, suffers on the rack in the Tower of London in 1563. Torture has been used over the centuries to solicit information and to punish political and religious dissenters.

was then repeatedly jerked to increase the pain. Weights sometimes were attached to the victim's feet to increase the agony, often fracturing bones and tearing limbs from the body.[45]

In the early 17th century, some Europeans tried to regulate torture. Dutch legal scholar Johannes Voet, for instance, argued that torture should only be used when there are "grave presumptions" against the accused. He also suggested that the youngest member of any group of defendants be tortured first, because the youngest was thought most likely to talk.[46]

In 1754 Prussia became the first modern European state to abolish torture. Ten years later, in his seminal book *On Crimes and Punishments*, Italian philosopher and penal reformer Cesare Beccaria denounced torture as "a sure route for the acquittal of robust ruffians and the conviction of weak innocents." The book reflected emerging Enlightenment-era ideals about individual rights and the proper limits on punishment.[47] Within a century, most of Europe had banned torture, in part because convictions without eyewitness testimony or confessions were increasingly allowed, reducing the need for torture. But torture continued to thrive in Africa, Asia and the Middle East. In 1852, for example, leaders of an outlawed religious group in Persia — modern-day Iran — were "made into candlesticks" — with holes dug into their flesh into which lighted candles were inserted.[48]

CHRONOLOGY

1700s *Torture is banned in Europe.*

1754 Prussia becomes first European state to abolish torture; other European countries soon follow suit.

1900-1950 *Torture re-emerges, then is prohibited.*

1917 Russian Revolution gives birth to communism, which will foster totalitarian regimes that will torture perceived enemies of the state.

1933 Nazis take over Germany and soon begin torturing civilian prisoners.

1948 U.N. adopts Universal Declaration of Human Rights banning torture.

1949 Geneva Conventions ban all use of "mutilation, cruel treatment and torture" of prisoners of war.

1950s-1960s *Torture continues, despite international ban.*

1954 France tortures thousands of Algerians during Algeria's war for independence.

1961 Amnesty International is founded after two Portuguese students are jailed for seven years for toasting freedom.

1970s-1990s *Democracies — as well as authoritarian regimes — continue to torture.*

1971 British interrogators use the "five techniques" against Irish Republican Army suspects. European Court of Human Rights calls the methods illegal.

1975 Khmer Rouge takes over Cambodia and soon begins torturing and murdering thousands of detainees.

1978 Human Rights Watch is founded.

1987 Israel authorizes use of aggressive interrogation techniques during widespread Palestinian unrest.

1999 Israel's Supreme Court bans torture and abusive interrogation methods.

2000s-Present *Rise of Islamic terrorist attacks sparks increasing use of torture.*

2001 Muslim terrorists kill 3,000 in Sept. 11 attacks. . . . Hundreds of Muslims are detained in the United States and Afghanistan. . . . Fox Television's "24" begins showing U.S. agents using torture.

2002 First "enemy combatants" captured in Afghanistan arrive at Guantánamo naval base in Cuba. President Bush says they will be treated humanely, but that they are not protected by Geneva Conventions. . . . In September Syrian-born Canadian Maher Arar is detained during a stopover in New York and is sent to Syria for interrogation, where he is tortured.

March 30, 2004 U.S. Supreme Court rules Alien Tort Claims Act can be used to sue human rights abusers.

April 27, 2004 CBS News's "60 Minutes II" airs photographs of U.S. troops abusing prisoners at Abu Ghraib prison in Iraq.

November 2005 *Washington Post* reports the CIA detains terror suspects in secret prisons where detainees allegedly are subjected to coercive interrogation techniques. . . . U.S. government insists it does not torture. Congress passes Detainee Treatment Act, prohibiting torture and mistreatment of prisoners but limiting detainees' rights to challenge their detentions.

2006 On June 29, Supreme Court rules U.S. detainees are subject to the Geneva Conventions. . . . Military Commissions Act authorizes new courtroom procedures for enemy combatants but allows greater flexibility for CIA interrogations.

2007 A German court orders 13 U.S. intelligence agents arrested for their alleged role in rendering a German citizen to Afghanistan. . . . Canada apologizes to Arar for allowing him to be taken to Syria. . . . In July, President Bush authorizes the CIA to reopen secret overseas prisons. . . . International war crimes tribunal in Cambodia indicts former Khmer Rouge leader Kaing Guek Eav for the torture and murder of thousands of prisoners. . . . Libya admits it tortured Bulgarian medical personnel imprisoned for eight years.

Careful Training Creates Soldiers Who Torture

Most defy sadistic stereotype.

Torturers are made, not born. That was the finding of a Greek psychology professor who studied the military regime that came to power in Greece after a 1967 coup.

Until it fell in 1974, the dictatorship carefully trained soldiers to gather information and squelch dissent through torture. That's when Professor Mika Haritos-Fatouros tried to understand how the soldiers had been turned into torturers. In one of the most in-depth studies of torturers ever conducted, she interviewed 16 former soldiers and reviewed the testimony of 21 others and their victims.[1]

Many of her interviewees defy the stereotype of sadistic men who take pleasure in abuse. Haritos-Fatouros found that the torturers were simply plucked from the ranks of ordinary soldiers and trained. One, from a farm family, was a 33-year-old high school teacher married with two children by the time Haritos-Fatouros interviewed him. But for 18 months he had tortured prisoners and ordered others to do so.

The army sought young recruits from rural, conservative families who were physically healthy, of normal intelligence, conformist in nature and compliant. They underwent three months of intensive "training," during which they were broken down physically and mentally — a process that began almost before they arrived at the training facility. The abuse of the torturers-in-training intensified during the subsequent weeks as they were allowed little sleep and ordered to run or hop everywhere they went.

The aim "was to minimize all resistance by instilling in the cadets the habit of obeying without question an order without logic," Haritos-Fatouros wrote.[2] In short, they were programmed to blindly obey authority and dehumanize their victims.

Gradually, they were desensitized to torture. First, they participated in group beatings. One of the torturers said the first time he participated in a group beating he went to his cousin's house and cried. But it got easier each time, he said. Later, they ratcheted up to inflicting electric shocks and other serious abuse.

The underlying goal, Haritos-Fatouros concluded, was making the torturers believe they were "not, in fact, inflicting a savage and horrifying violation upon another human being."

"They brainwashed us," one torturer said. "It was only later we realized that what we did was inhuman. It was only after I finished my military service that it occurred to me that most of us beat up prisoners because we'd been beaten up ourselves."[3]

Another torturer told her, "When I tortured, basically, I felt it was my duty. A lot of the time I found myself repeating the phrases I'd heard in the lessons, like 'bloody communists' and so on. I think I became worse as time went on. I became more a part of the system. I believed in the whole system."[4]

Haritos-Fatouros's chilling conclusion: "We are all, under the right conditions, capable of becoming torturers."[5]

---

[1] Mika Haritos-Fatouros, *The Psychological Origins of Institutionalized Torture* (2003).

[2] *Ibid.*, p. 46.

[3] *Ibid.*, p. 95.

[4] *Ibid.*, p. 82.

[5] *Ibid.*, p. 229.

By 1874, French author Victor Hugo naively declared "torture has ceased to exist." But torture continued to be used against insurgents in Austria and Italy and against opponents of the Tsarist government in Russia.

Changing Norms

By the 20th century, social norms about punishment had changed; the upper classes no longer wanted to watch gruesome public spectacles. Torture sessions became secretive affairs, conducted in prison basements and detention centers.[49]

In the first half of the 20th century, torture was employed by totalitarian governments in countries such as Germany, Russia, Italy and Japan.[50] The Nazis tortured prisoners of war to get information and conducted horrific medical experiments on Jewish and Gypsy civilians in concentration camps. Japanese soldiers severely abused and tortured Allied prisoners.

After the horrors of World War II, torture and lesser forms of abuse known as cruel, inhumane and degrading treatment were outlawed by a series of treaties: the 1948

Universal Declaration of Human Rights, the Geneva Conventions of 1949 and the 1984 Convention Against Torture. (*See box, p. 396.*)

Torture persisted during the second half of the century, however, particularly in authoritarian countries. For instance, Soviet and Chinese communist regimes tortured political and religious dissidents. Cambodia's murderous Khmer Rouge military regime had a 42-page interrogation manual for use at its Tuol Sleng torture center during the 1970s.

Many repressive regimes were supported by the United States, which was fighting a proxy Cold War with the Soviet Union in developing countries like Vietnam, El Salvador and Guatemala. Because such governments were resisting socialist or communist insurgencies, the United States often provided them with guns, military aid and training, even though they were known to use torture.

In the 1970s, President Jimmy Carter broke with the past by announcing that the nation's foreign policy henceforth would be based on advancing human rights. Congress passed a law requiring the State Department to issue annual reports on the human rights records of any country that received U.S. economic or military aid.[51] Although the law remains on the books and the State Department continues to issue its annual human rights "country reports," the foreign policy focus on human rights faded under Carter's successor, Ronald Reagan, who placed fighting communism above protecting human rights.

Since the 1970s, however, greater scrutiny by Western governments, the U.N., the EU and human rights groups has prompted changes in how countries torture. Increasingly, methods were adopted that don't leave visible scars, such as beating the soles of feet, sleep deprivation, sexual humiliation and electric shock.

Democracies' Experience

It wasn't only communists and dictators who tortured captives after World War II. Democratic countries — including Great Britain, France and Israel — all used torture or other forms of abuse during the last half of the century, usually in response to what they viewed as imminent threats from religious or political dissidents.

But the democracies ended up alienating their own citizens as well as the occupied populations, according to

Christopher Einolf, a University of Richmond sociologist who has studied the history of torture. Torture also proved difficult to control once it was authorized.

For instance, France initiated an intensive counterinsurgency strategy — which included torture — in Algeria after the Algerian National Liberation Front began a terrorist bombing campaign in 1956 to force France to cede control of the colony. France's strategy sometimes is cited as evidence that torture works.[52]

But Rejali at Reed College says France succeeded in gathering information because informants voluntarily cooperated — not as a result of torture. And tortured suspects often gave their interrogators the names of rival insurgents, dead militants or old hiding places rather than good information, he says.

Lou DiMarco, a retired U.S. Army lieutenant colonel who teaches at the Command and General Staff College, Fort Leavenworth, Kan., contends the French experience in Algeria also proves the difficulty of controlling torture. "In Algeria, officially condoned torture quickly escalated to prolonged abuse, which resulted in permanent physical and psychological damage as well as death," he wrote.[53]

Similarly, the British, facing a spike in Irish Republican Army (IRA) violence in Northern Ireland in 1971, turned to aggressive interrogation techniques, including the "five techniques" — a combination of hooding, noise bombardment, food and sleep deprivation and forced standing. Individually, any one of these techniques could be painful, but taken together, "they induced a state of psychosis, a temporary madness with long-lasting after-effects," wrote John Conroy in his book, *Unspeakable Acts, Ordinary People: The Dynamics of Torture.*[54]

Tom Parker, a former British counterterrorism agent, says extreme interrogation methods had "huge" adverse consequences for Britain: They alienated Ireland — not a natural ally of the IRA — and enabled Ireland to successfully challenge British interrogation methods in the European Court of Human Rights.

Israel approved similar methods in 1987 after its security services were found to be using illegal interrogation techniques on Palestinian detainees in the occupied territories. Officials felt it would be better to allow a few psychological methods and "moderate physical pressure." But coercive methods proved hard to regulate and keep under control.[55]

In 1999, Israel's Supreme Court outlawed such techniques as cruel and inhuman treatment.

Post-9/11 Crackdown

After the 9/11 attacks, aggressive interrogation of suspects became a key — and highly controversial — part of U.S. antiterrorism strategy. On Nov. 13, 2001, President Bush signed an executive order allowing the military to detain and try "enemy combatants" outside the United States.

Defense Secretary Donald H. Rumsfeld announced the next month that enemy combatants detained in Afghanistan would be transferred to Guantánamo. In February 2002 Bush said the United States would treat the detainees humanely but did not consider them legitimate prisoners of war protected by the Geneva Conventions, which ban torture and "cruel, inhuman and degrading treatment."

U.S. interrogators used the same harsh methods designed to train American personnel to resist torture if captured. The so-called "Survival, Evasion, Resistance and Escape" (SERE) techniques included physical and mental pressure ("stress and duress") and sleep deprivation.

Rumsfeld formally approved many of these techniques in December 2002, including prolonged standing, use of dogs and the removal of clothing; he later rescinded approval for some of the methods.[56] Mohammed al-Qhatani — the alleged 20th 9/11 hijacker who had been captured along the Pakistani-Afghan border — says he was interrogated for 20-hour stretches, forced to stand naked while being menaced by dogs and barred from praying during Ramadan unless he drank water, which Islam forbids during Ramadan's fasting periods. The Pentagon said such techniques were designed to "prevent future attacks on America."[57]

But some within the administration disapproved. In July 2004 Alberto J. Mora, the Navy's general counsel, warned in a 22-page memo that circumventing the Geneva Conventions was an invitation for U.S. interrogators to abuse prisoners.[58]

His prediction was prescient. SERE techniques apparently migrated to U.S. facilities in Afghanistan and Iraq, where they were reportedly employed by inadequately trained and unsupervised personnel. What began as "a set of special treatments" had become routine, wrote Tony Lagouranis, a former Army interrogator in Iraq.[59]

In late 2003 American military personnel at Abu Ghraib prison committed the abuses that generated the most public outrage, thanks to graphic photographs taken by the soldiers involved that eventually were circulated by news media around the world. An Army investigation later detailed "sadistic, blatant and wanton criminal" abuse that included beating detainees with a broom handle, threatening male detainees with rape, sodomizing another with a chemical light stick and frightening them with dogs.[60] Twelve U.S. military personnel have since been convicted for their roles in the abuse.

Mistreatment of Iraqi detainees was not just limited to Abu Ghraib. A military jury convicted Chief Warrant Officer Lewis Welshofer of negligent homicide after an interrogation in a facility in western Iraq in which he put a sleeping bag over the head of Iraqi Gen. Abed Hamed Mowhoush, sat on his chest and covered the general's mouth while asking him questions. American civilian contractors working alongside CIA and military interrogators in Iraq have also been accused of mistreating detainees.

Ever since the 9/11 attacks, a furious legal debate, both inside and outside the Bush administration, has examined the kinds of coercive interrogation methods the military and CIA can employ and the extent to which the United States must abide by international law. In 2005 Congress sought to limit the use by U.S. personnel of cruel, inhumane and degrading treatment in the Detainee Treatment Act.[61]

Then in 2006 the Supreme Court ruled that all prisoners held by the United States — including those in CIA custody — were subject to Common Article 3 of the Geneva Conventions, which outlaws torture or cruel and inhuman treatment of wartime detainees. (*See box, p. 396.*)[62] Later that year Congress passed another bill, the Military Commissions Act, endorsed by the Bush administration. It limited military interrogators to techniques that would be detailed in an updated *Army Field Manual.* The law did not specify, however, which interrogation methods CIA personnel can use — an omission designed to provide flexibility for interrogators at secret CIA facilities where "high value" prisoners are interrogated.

When *The Washington Post* revealed in 2005 that the CIA was operating secret prisons in eight countries in Eastern Europe, Thailand and Afghanistan, the administration had at first refused to confirm the story.[63] In 2006 Bush finally acknowledged the facilities existed, pointing out that, "Questioning the detainees in this program has given us information that has saved innocent lives by

Five International Treaties Ban Torture

Torture has been banned by international treaties since 1948. Key provisions include:

Universal Declaration of Human Rights (1948)

No one shall be subjected to torture or to cruel, inhuman or degrading treatment or punishment.

Adopted by U.N. General Assembly on Dec. 10, 1948, www.un.org/en/documents/udhr/index.shtml.

Third Geneva Convention, Common Article 3 (1949)

Regarding the treatment of civilians and prisoners of war, "the following acts are and shall remain prohibited at any time:

    (a) violence to life and person, in particular murder of all kinds, mutilation, cruel treatment and torture;
    (b) taking of hostages;
    (c) outrages upon personal dignity, in particular humiliating and degrading treatment . . ."

Adopted on Aug. 12, 1949, by the Diplomatic Conference for the Establishment of International Conventions for the Protection of Victims of War, held in Geneva, Switzerland; effective Oct. 21, 1950, www.icrc.org/ihl.nsf/7c4d08d9b287a42141256739003e636b/6fef854a3517b75ac125641e004a9e68.

International Covenant on Civil and Political Rights (1966)

Article 7
No one shall be subjected to torture or to cruel, inhuman or degrading treatment or punishment. In particular, no one shall be subjected without his free consent to medical or scientific experimentation.

Article 10
All persons deprived of their liberty shall be treated with humanity and with respect for the inherent dignity of the human person.

Adopted the U.N. General Assembly on Dec. 16, 1966, and opened for signature and ratification; became effective on March 23, 1976, www2.ohchr.org/english/law/ccpr.htm.

helping us stop new attacks — here in the United States and across the world."[64]

In 2007, Human Rights Watch and *The Post* detailed the experience of one former CIA detainee — Marwan Jabour, a Palestinian accused of being an al-Qaeda paymaster — who spent two years in a CIA-operated prison.

Jabour says he was kept naked for the first three months of his detention in Afghanistan. The lights were kept on 24 hours a day, and when loud music wasn't blasted through speakers into his cell, white noise buzzed in the background. And while he was frequently threatened with physical abuse, he says he was never beaten during 45 interrogations. He was also deprived of sleep and left for hours in painful positions. He was ultimately transferred to Jordanian and then Israeli custody, where a judge ordered his release in September 2006.[65]

CIA detainees also reportedly have been subjected to waterboarding and had their food spiked with drugs to loosen their inhibitions about speaking.[66]

The United States did not allow the International Committee of the Red Cross (ICRC) to visit the CIA's detainees until 2006. A subsequent ICRC report based on interviews with 15 former CIA detainees concluded that the detention and interrogation methods used at the "black sites" were tantamount to torture, according to confidential sources quoted in *The New Yorker.*[67]

The United States has strongly denied the ICRC's conclusions and claims the program is closely monitored by agency lawyers. "The CIA's interrogations were nothing like Abu Ghraib or Guantánamo," said Robert Grenier, a former head of the CIA's Counterterrorism Center. "They were very, very regimented. Very meticulous." The program is "completely legal."[68]

Unlike the CIA's secret prisons, the agency's use of so-called "extraordinary renditions" predated the 9/11 attacks. The first terror suspects were rendered to Egypt in the mid-1990s.[69] But the practice expanded greatly after 9/11, with up to 150 people sent to countries such as Morocco, Syria and Egypt between 2001 and 2005. Many, like Abu Omar — an imam with alleged links to terrorist groups — were snatched off the street. Omar, an Egyptian refugee, was kidnapped from Milan

Protocol Additional to the Geneva Conventions of Aug. 12, 1949, relating to the Protection of Victims of International Armed Conflicts (1977)

Article 75: Fundamental guarantees

1. ". . . persons who are in the power of a Party to the conflict . . . shall be treated humanely in all circumstances and shall enjoy, as a minimum, the protection provided by this Article without any adverse distinction based upon race, colour, sex, language, religion or belief, political or other opinion, national or social origin, wealth, birth or other status, or on any other similar criteria. Each Party shall respect the person, honour, convictions and religious practices of all such persons.

2. The following acts are and shall remain prohibited at any time and in any place whatsoever, whether committed by civilian or by military agents:

    (a) Violence to the life, health, or physical or mental well-being of persons, in particular:
        (i)   Murder;
        (ii) Torture of all kinds, whether physical or mental;
        (iii) Corporal punishment; and
        (iv) Mutilation;

    (b) Outrages upon personal dignity, in particular humiliating and degrading treatment, enforced prostitution and any form of indecent assault;
    (c) The taking of hostages;
    (d) Collective punishments; and
    (e) Threats to commit any of the foregoing acts."

Adopted by the Diplomatic Conference on the Reaffirmation and Development of International Humanitarian Law applicable in Armed Conflicts on June 8, 1977; became effective on Dec. 7, 1979, www.icrc.org/ihl.nsf/7c4d08d9b287a42141256739003e636b/f6c8b9fee14a77fdc125641e0052b079.

Convention Against Torture and Other Cruel, Inhuman or Degrading Treatment or Punishment (1984)

Article 1

". . . the term 'torture' means any act by which severe pain or suffering, whether physical or mental, is intentionally inflicted on a person for such purposes as obtaining from him or a third person information or a confession, punishing him for an act he or a third person has committed or is suspected of having committed, or intimidating or coercing him or a third person, or for any reason based on discrimination of any kind, . . .

Article 2

1. Each State Party shall take effective legislative, administrative, judicial or other measures to prevent acts of torture in any territory under its jurisdiction.
2. No exceptional circumstances whatsoever, whether a state of war or a threat of war, internal political instability or any other public emergency, may be invoked as a justification of torture.
3. An order from a superior officer or a public authority may not be invoked as a justification of torture.

Article 3

1. No State Party shall expel, return ("refouler") or extradite a person to another State where there are substantial grounds for believing that he would be in danger of being subjected to torture.
2. For the purpose of determining whether there are such grounds, the competent authorities shall take into account all relevant considerations including, where applicable, the existence in the State concerned of a consistent pattern of gross, flagrant or mass violations of human rights."

Adopted by the U.N. General Assembly on Dec. 10, 1984, and opened for signature and ratification; became effective on June 26, 1987, www2.ohchr.org/english/law/cat.htm.

in February 2003 and sent to Egypt where he says he was tortured for four years before being released in 2007.[70]

U.S. officials have repeatedly insisted the United States does not send detainees to countries where they believe or know they'll be tortured.[71] But such declarations ring hollow for human rights advocates like Malinowski. "The

administration says that it does not render people to torture," he told the Senate Foreign Relations Committee. "But the only safeguard it appears to have obtained in these cases was a promise from the receiving state that it would not mistreat the rendered prisoners. Such promises, coming from countries like Egypt and Syria and Uzbekistan where torture is routine, are unverifiable and utterly

AP Photo/Jonathan Hayward

Syrian-born Canadian citizen Maher Arar was picked up by the CIA in 2002 at John F. Kennedy International Airport in New York and taken to Syria, where he was imprisoned for a year and tortured with electric cables. He was later cleared of any links to terrorism. Human rights advocates say the CIA's so-called extraordinary rendition program "outsources" torture to countries known to abuse prisoners. The U.S. Justice Department said Syria had assured the United States it would not torture Arar.

untrustworthy. I seriously doubt that anyone in the administration actually believed them."[72]

Renditions usually require the complicity of the countries where the suspects are grabbed. A 2006 report by the Council of Europe's Parliamentary Assembly tried to identify all the member countries that have allowed rendition flights to cross their airspace or land at their airports.[73]

One was the Czech Republic, which reportedly allowed three different jets to land at Prague's Ruzyne Airport during at least 20 different rendition flights, triggering anger from some Czechs. "No 'law enforcement,' 'intelligence,' or 'security' argument in support of torture can ever be anything but inhumane," wrote Gwendolyn Albert, director of the Czech League of Human Rights, in 2006 in *The Prague Post*.[74]

Former CIA operative Melissa Boyle Mahle condemns torture but has defended renditions and the need for absolute secrecy. "Renditions should be conducted in the shadows for optimal impact and should not, I must add, leave elephant-sized footprints so as to not embarrass our allies in Europe," she wrote in a 2005 blog entry. "During my career at the CIA, I was involved in these types of operations and know firsthand that they can save American lives."[75]

CURRENT SITUATION

Rendition Fallout

Kidnapping and shipping off allies' citizens to be harshly interrogated in foreign countries has strained relations with America's friends. Prosecutors in Germany and Italy are attempting to prosecute U.S. personnel for their role in renditions, and the rendition of Canadian citizen Maher Arar to Syria has chilled relations between Canada and the United States.

In Italy, the former chief of Italy's intelligence service is on trial for Omar's 2003 abduction in a case that threatens to ensnare top officials of the current and past Italian governments. A U.S. Air Force colonel and 25 CIA operatives also were indicted but are being tried in absentia because the United States has blocked their extradition.[76]

Similarly, a court in Munich ordered the arrest of 13 American intelligence operatives in January 2007 for their role in the kidnapping of a German citizen interrogated for five months at a secret prison in Afghanistan. But Germany, unlike Italy, does not allow trials in absentia, so an actual trial is unlikely because the United States will not extradite the defendants.[77]

Other European governments may be called to task for their role in U.S. renditions. Investigations have been initiated by Spain, and the Most Rev. John Neill — archbishop of Dublin — said the Irish government compromised itself by allowing rendition flights to land at Shannon Airport.

Meanwhile, on this side of the Atlantic, Canadian-U.S. relations are strained by the case of Syrian-born Canadian citizen Maher Arar. The McGill University graduate was returning to Canada from Tunisia in September 2002 when he landed at John F. Kennedy International Airport in New

Is torture ever justified?

YES
Mirko Bagaric
Professor of Law, Deakin University
Melbourne, Australia

Written for *CQ Global Researcher*, August 2007

Despite its pejorative overtone, we should never say never to torture. Torture is bad. Killing innocent people is worse. Some people are so depraved they combine these evils and torture innocent people to death. Khalid Shaikh Mohammed, who is still gloating about personally beheading American journalist Daniel Pearl with his "blessed right hand," is but just one exhibit.

Torture opponents must take responsibility for the murder of innocent people if they reject torture if it is the only way to save innocent lives. We are responsible not only for what we do but also for the things we can, but fail, to prevent.

Life-saving torture is not cruel. It is morally justifiable because the right to life of innocent people trumps the physical integrity of wrongdoers. Thus, torture has the same moral justification as other practices in which we sacrifice the interests of one person for the greater good. A close analogy is life-saving organ and tissue transplants. Kidney and bone marrow transplants inflict high levels of pain and discomfort on donors, but their pain is normally outweighed by the benefit to the recipient.

Such is the case with life-saving compassionate torture. The pain inflicted on the wrongdoer is manifestly outweighed by the benefit from the lives saved. The fact that wrongdoers don't consent to their mistreatment is irrelevant. Prisoners and enemy soldiers don't consent to being incarcerated or shot at, yet we're not about to empty our prisons or stop trying to kill enemy soldiers.

Most proponents of banning torture say it does not produce reliable information. Yet there are countless counter-examples. Israeli authorities claim to have foiled 90 terrorist attacks by using coercive interrogation. In more mundane situations, courts across the world routinely throw out confessions that are corroborated by objective evidence because they were only made because the criminals were beaten up.

It is also contended that life-saving torture will lead down the slippery slope of other cruel practices. This is an intellectually defeatist argument. It tries to move the debate from what is on the table (life-saving torture) to situations where torture is used for reasons of domination and punishment — which is never justifiable.

Fanatics who oppose torture in all cases are adopting their own form of extremism. It is well-intentioned, but extremism in all its manifestations can lead to catastrophic consequences. Cruelty that is motivated by misguided kindness hurts no less.

NO
Sune Segal
Head of Communications Unit, International
Rehabilitation Council for Torture Victims
Copenhagen, Denmark

Written for *CQ Global Researcher*, August 2007

Taking a utilitarian "greater good" approach in the wake of 9/11/2001, some scholars argue that torture is justified if used to prevent large-scale terror attacks. That argument rests on several flawed assumptions.

The claim that torture — or what is now euphemistically referred to as "enhanced interrogation techniques" — extracts reliable information is unfounded. The 2006 *U.S. Army Field Manual* states that "the use of force . . . yields unreliable results [and] may damage subsequent collection efforts." As laid out in a recent *Vanity Fair* article, it was humane treatment — not torture — of a detainee that led to the arrest of alleged 9/11 mastermind Khalid Shaikh Mohammed. In the same article, a U.S. Air Force Reserve colonel and expert in human-intelligence operations, drives home the point: "When [CIA psychologists argue that coercive interrogation] can make people talk, I have one question: 'About what?' "

But even if torture did "work," is it justified when a suspect is in custody and presumed to possess information about an imminent attack likely to kill thousands of people?

No, for several reasons. First, the above scenario assumes the person in custody has the pertinent information — a presumption that is never foolproof. Thus, by allowing torture there would be cases in which innocent detainees would be at risk of prolonged torture because they would not possess the desired information.

Second, it might be argued that mere circumstantial evidence suggesting the detainee is the right suspect is enough to justify torture or that torturing a relative into revealing the suspect's whereabouts is acceptable.

Third, if one form of torture — such as "waterboarding" — is allowed to preserve the "greater good," where do we go if it doesn't work? To breaking bones? Ripping out nails? Torturing the suspect's 5-year-old daughter?

Fourth, torture is not a momentary infliction of pain. In most cases the victim — innocent or guilty — is marked for life, as is the torturer. As a former CIA officer and friend of one of Mohammed's interrogators told *The New Yorker* in an Aug. 13, 2007, article: "[My friend] has horrible nightmares. . . . When you cross over that line, it's hard to come back. You lose your soul."

That's why we refrain from torture: to keep our souls intact. Torture is the hallmark of history's most abhorrent regimes and a violation of civilized values. Taking the "greater good" approach to torture is intellectually and morally bankrupt.

York during a stopover. U.S. immigration authorities detained him after seeing his name on a terrorist "watch" list.

After two weeks of questioning, he was flown to Jordan and then driven to Syria. During a yearlong detention by Syrian military intelligence, Arar says he was beaten with two-inch-thick electric cables. "Not even animals could withstand it," he said later.[78]

He was released in October 2003. A Canadian inquiry cleared Arar of any links to terrorism and said the Royal Canadian Mounted Police had given U.S. authorities erroneous information about him. Canada's prime minister apologized to Arar in January 2007 and announced an $8.9 million compensation package. Canada has also demanded an apology from the U.S. government and asked that Arar's name be removed from terrorist watch lists.[79]

U.S. federal courts have dismissed a lawsuit by Arar, and Attorney General Alberto R. Gonzales said Syria had assured the United States it would not torture Arar before he was sent there.

But Paul Cavalluzzo, a Toronto lawyer who led the government investigation of Arar's case, calls Gonzales's claim "graphic hypocrisy," pointing out that the U.S. State Department's own Web site lists Syria as one of the "worst offenders of torture."

"At one time, the United States was a beacon for the protection of human rights, whether internationally or domestically. Certainly, the Arar case was one example that lessened [that] view [among] Canadians."

Suing Torturers

Criminal prosecutions and civil lawsuits are pending against alleged torturers in several courts around the world.

In the United States, Iraqis claiming they were mistreated by American military personnel and private contractors are seeking redress under a little-used 18th-century law. The Alien Tort Claims Act, which originally targeted piracy, allows federal courts to hear claims by foreigners injured "in violation of the law of nations or a treaty of the United States."

In May 2007, the American Civil Liberties Union used the law to sue Jeppesen Dataplan Inc., a subsidiary of the Boeing Co., on behalf of three plaintiffs subjected to renditions. The company is accused of providing rendition flight services to the CIA. Two additional plaintiffs joined the suit in August.[80]

The law also was used in a class-action suit against Titan Corp. and CACI International Inc., military contractors that provided translators and interrogation services at Abu Ghraib. The suit asserts the two companies participated in a "scheme to torture, rape and in some instances, summarily execute plaintiffs." CACI called it a "malicious recitation of false statements and intentional distortions."[81]

The law was rarely used until the late 1970s, when human rights groups began suing abusive foreign officials. Since then it has been used to sue a Paraguayan police chief living in Brooklyn accused of torturing and killing a young man in Paraguay, an Ethiopian official, a Guatemalan defense minister and the self-proclaimed president of the Bosnian Serbs.

Advocates of such suits say they are important tools in holding abusers accountable. "It is truly a mechanism that provides for policing international human rights abuses where a criminal prosecution may not necessarily be feasible," says John M. Eubanks, a South Carolina lawyer involved in a suit that relies on the statute. The home countries of human rights abusers often lack legal systems that enable perpetrators to be held accountable.

"America is the only venue where they're going to be able to get their case heard," says Rachel Chambers, a British lawyer who has studied the statute.

Although the U.S. Supreme Court affirmed the use of the statute in 2004, legal experts disagree about just how much leeway the court left for future plaintiffs.[82]

Moreover, the statute can't provide redress in lawsuits against the U.S. government for the mistreatment of prisoners. The United States has successfully challenged such lawsuits by claiming sovereign immunity, a doctrine that protects governments against suits. The same defense has protected individuals sued in their official government capacity, according to Beth Stephens, a professor at Rutgers School of Law, in Camden, N.J. It is unclear how much protection private contractors such as CACI can claim for providing support services for interrogations.

Meanwhile, in Cambodia a U.N.-backed tribunal in July accused former Khmer Rouge leader Kaing Guek Eav of crimes against humanity for his role in the torture and deaths of 14,000 prisoners at Tuol Sleng. Only seven people who entered the prison emerged alive. The trial is expected to begin in 2008.[83]

And in Sierra Leone former Liberian President Charles Taylor is facing a U.N.-backed war-crimes tribunal for his role in financing and encouraging atrocities — including torture — committed during the civil war in neighboring Sierra Leone. The trial has been delayed until January 2008.[84]

The 'Black Sites'

In July, when President Bush authorized the CIA's secret prisons to be reopened, the executive order laid out the administration's position on how the "enhanced interrogation" program will fully comply "with the obligations of the United States under Common Article 3" of the Geneva Conventions, which bans "outrages upon personal dignity, in particular humiliating and degrading treatment."

The president's order said the United States would satisfy the conventions if the CIA's interrogation methods don't violate federal law or constitute "willful and outrageous acts of personal abuse done for the purpose of humiliating the individual in a manner so serious that any reasonable person, considering the circumstances would deem the acts to be beyond the bounds of human decency."

The language appears to allow abusive techniques if the purpose is to gather intelligence or prevent attacks, say critics. "The president has given the CIA carte blanche to engage in 'willful and outrageous acts of personal abuse,' " wrote former Marine Corps Commandant P. X. Kelley and Robert Turner, a former Reagan administration lawyer.[85]

Human rights advocates are troubled by the executive order's lack of an explicit ban on coercive interrogation techniques such as stress positions or extreme sleep deprivation, which military interrogators are explicitly barred from using in the latest *Army Field Manual*, issued in 2006.

Media reports suggested the Bush administration also has sought to maintain other methods, such as inducing hypothermia, forced standing and manipulating sound and light.[86]

"What we're left with is a history of these kinds of techniques having been authorized, no explicit prohibition and we don't know what the CIA is authorized to do," says Devon Chaffee, an attorney with Human Rights First. "This creates a real problematic precedent."

Human rights advocates worry that foreign governments may cite Bush's executive order to justify their own coercive interrogations. "What they did is lower the bar for anybody," says Musa, the advocacy director for Amnesty USA.

In August, the American Bar Association passed a resolution urging Congress to override the executive order.[87] Also that month, Democratic Sen. Ron Wyden of Oregon vowed to block President Bush's nominee to become the CIA's top lawyer. Wyden said he was concerned that the agency's senior deputy general counsel, John Rizzo, had not objected to a 2002 CIA memo authorizing interrogation techniques that stopped just short of inflicting enough pain to cause organ failure or death.

"I'm going to keep the hold [on Rizzo] until the detention and interrogation program is on firm footing, both in terms of effectiveness and legality," Wyden said.[88]

OUTLOOK
No Panaceas

Human rights advocates worry countries that have tortured in the past will feel more emboldened to do so in the future as a result of U.S. government policies.

"This is just empowering the dictators and torturing governments around the world," said Whitson of Human Rights Watch.

They also worry that China, a rising superpower, is an abuser itself and has proven willing to do business with countries with histories of abuse in Central Asia and Africa.

HRW Executive Director Kenneth Roth also complains that — as its membership swells and the difficulty of reaching consensus grows — the European Union appears unable or unwilling to act. "Its efforts to achieve consensus among its diverse membership have become so laborious that it yields a faint shadow of its potential," he says.

The future direction of U.S. interrogation policies could depend heavily on the outcome of the 2008 American presidential election, which will likely determine the fate of what has become the most important symbol of U.S. detention policies: the prison for enemy combatants at Guantánamo. All the Democratic presidential candidates say they would close the facility, according to a study of candidate positions by the Council on Foreign Relations.[89]

On the Republican side, only two candidates — Rep. Ron Paul, R-Texas, and Sen. McCain — have advocated shutting the facility, and neither has been among the leaders in the polls. Mitt Romney, the former Massachusetts governor who has been among the front-runners this summer, suggested doubling the size of Guantánamo if he became president.

But regardless of who wins the election, human rights advocates do not look to a new occupant of the White House as a panacea. Amnesty USA's Musa says new administrations are often skittish about radically changing course from predecessors' foreign policies.

"It's not the absolute cure for all ills," she says.

NOTES

1. See Jonathan S. Landay, "VP confirms use of waterboarding," *Chicago Tribune*, Oct. 27, 2006, p. C5; and "Interview of the Vice President by Scott Hennen, WDAY at Radio Day at the White House," www.whitehouse.gov/news/releases/2006/10/20061024-7.html. Also see John Crewdson, "Spilling Al Qaeda's secrets; 'Waterboarding' used on 9/11 mastermind, who eventually talked," *Chicago Tribune*, Dec. 28, 2005, p. C15. Also see Brian Ross and Richard Esposito, "CIA's Harsh Interrogation Techniques Described," ABC News, Nov. 18, 2005, www.abcnews.com.

2. Testimony by Tom Malinowski before Senate Committee on Foreign Relations, July 26, 2007.

3. David Cingranelli and David L. Richards, CIRI Human Rights Data Project, 2005, http://ciri.binghamton.edu/about.asp.

4. Quoted in Molly Moore, "Gaddafi's Son: Bulgarians Were Tortured," *The Washington Post*, Aug. 10, 2007, p. A8.

5. "In the Name of Security: Counterterrorism and Human Rights Abuses Under Malaysia's Internal Security Act," Human Rights Watch, http://hrw.org/reports/2004/malaysia0504/.

6. Dana Priest, "CIA Holds Terror Suspects in Secret Prisons," *The Washington Post*, Nov. 2, 2005, p. A1; also see Rosa Brooks, "The GOP's Torture Enthusiasts," *Los Angeles Times*, May 18, 2007, www.latimes.com/news/opinion/commentary/la-oe-brooks18may18,0,732795.column?coll=la-news-comment-opinions.

7. For background see Peter Katel and Kenneth Jost, "Treatment of Detainees," *CQ Researcher*, Aug. 25, 2006, pp. 673-696.

8. Kenneth Roth, "Filling the Leadership Void: Where is the European Union?" *World Report 2007*, Human Rights Watch.

9. Edward Cody, "China, Others Criticize U.S. Report on Rights: Double Standard at State Department Alleged," *The Washington Post*, March 4, 2005, p A14.

10. Lisa Haugaard, "Tarnished Image: Latin America Perceives the United States," Latin American Working Group, March 2006.

11. "World View of U.S. Role Goes from Bad to Worse," Program on International Policy Attitudes, January 2007, www.worldpublicopinion.org/pipa/pdf/jan07/BBC_USRole_Jan07_quaire.pdf.

12. See Karen DeYoung, "Bush Approves New CIA Methods," *The Washington Post*, July 21, 2007, p. A1.

13. See "President Discusses Creation of Military Commissions to Try Suspected Terrorists," Sept. 6, 2006, www.whitehouse.gov/news/releases/2006/09/20060906-3.html.

14. Crewdson, *op. cit.*

15. Jane Mayer, "The Black Sites," *The New Yorker*, Aug. 13, 2007, pp. 46-57.

16. *Ibid.*

17. *Ibid.*

18. Jane Mayer, "Outsourcing Torture," *The New Yorker*, Feb. 14, 2005, p. 106.

19. Intelligence Science Board, "Educing Information; Interrogation: Science and Art," Center for Strategic Intelligence Research, National Defense Intelligence College, December 2006, www.fas.org/irp/dni/educing.pdf.

20. Anne Applebaum, "The Torture Myth," *The Washington Post*, Jan. 12, 2005, p. A21.

21. Henry Schuster, "The Al Qaeda Hunter," CNN, http://edition.cnn.com/2005/US/03/02/schuster.column/index.html.

22. Mirko Bagaric, "A Case for Torture," *The Age*, May 17, 2005, www.theage.com.au/news/Opinion/A-case-for-torture/2005/05/16/1116095904947.html.

23. Alan Dershowitz, *Why Terrorism Works: Understanding the Threat, Responding to the Challenge*, Yale University Press, 2003, pp. 158-159.

24. Michael Levin, "The Case for Torture," *Newsweek*, June 7, 1982.

25. " '24' and America's Image in Fighting Terrorism," Heritage Foundation Symposium, June 30, 2006.

26. Eitan Felner, "Torture and Terrorism: Painful Lessons from Israel," in Kenneth Roth, *et al.*, eds., *Torture: Does it Make Us Safer? Is It Ever OK? A Human Rights Perspective* (2005).

27. Henry Shue, "Torture," in Sanford Levinson, ed., *Torture: A Collection* (2006), p. 58.

28. See Brooks, *op. cit.*

29. Humphrey Hawksley, "US Iraq Troops 'condone torture,' " BBC News, May 4, 2007, http://news.bbc.co.uk/2/hi/middle_east/6627055.stm.

30. "Bush, McCain Agree on Torture Ban," CNN, Dec. 15, 2005, www.cnn.com/2005/POLITICS/12/15/torture.bill/index.html.

31. "American and International Opinion on the Rights of Terrorism Suspects," Program on International Policy Attitudes, July 17, 2006, www.worldpublicopinion.org/pipa/pdf/jul06/TerrSuspect_Jul06_rpt.pdf.

32. Allison Hanes, "Prime time torture: A U.S. Brigadier-General voices concern about the message the show '24' might be sending to the public and impressionable recruits," *National Post*, March 19, 2007.

33. Evan Thomas, " '24' Versus the Real World," *Newsweek Online*, Sept. 22, 2006, www.msnbc.msn.com/id/14924664/site/newsweek/.

34. Jane Mayer, "Whatever It Takes," *The New Yorker*, Feb. 19, 2007, www.newyorker.com/reporting/2007/02/19/070219fa-fact_mayer?printable=true.

35. John McCarthy, "Television is making torture acceptable," *The Independent*, May 24, 2007, http://comment.independent.co.uk/commentators/article2578453.ece.

36. Mayer, Feb. 19, 2007, *ibid.*

37. Heritage symposium, *op. cit.*

38. *Ibid.*

39. Colin Freeze, "What would Jack Bauer do?," *Globe and Mail*, June 16, 2007, www.theglobeandmail.com/servlet/story/LAC.20070616.BAUER16/TPStory/TPNational/Television/.

40. "Don't Go to Bat for Jack Bauer," *Globe and Mail*, July 9, 2007, www.theglobeandmail.com/servlet/story/RTGAM.20070709.wxetorture09/BNStory/specialComment/home.

41. The Associated Press, "Scholars Urge Bush to Ban Use of Torture," *The Washington Post*, June 25, 2007, www.washingtonpost.com/wp-dyn/content/article/2007/06/25/AR2007062501437.html.

42. See David Masci, "Torture," *CQ Researcher*, April 18, 2003, pp. 345-368.

43. James Ross, "A History of Torture," in Roth, *op. cit.*

44. John Langbein, "The Legal History of Torture," in Levinson, *op. cit.*

45. Brian Innes, *The History of Torture* (1998), pp. 13, 43.

46. Roth, p. 8.

47. Ross, p. 12.

48. Darius M. Rejali, *Torture & Modernity: Self, Society, and State in Modern Iran* (1994), p. 11.

49. *Ibid.*, p. 13.

50. Christopher J. Einolf, "The Fall and Rise of Torture: A Comparative and Historical Analysis," *Sociological Theory* 25:2, June 2007.

51. For background, see R. C. Schroeder, "Human Rights Policy," in *Editorial Research Reports 1979* (Vol. I), available in *CQ Researcher Plus Archive*, http://library.cqpress.com. Also see "Foreign Aid: Human Rights Compromise," in *CQ Almanac*, 1977.

52. Darius Rejali, "Does Torture Work?" *Salon*, June 21, 2004, http://archive.salon.com/opinion/feature/2004/06/21/torture_algiers/index_np.html.

53. Lou DiMarco, "Losing the Moral Compass: Torture & Guerre Revolutionnaire in the Algerian War," *Parameters*, Summer 2006.

54. John Conroy, *Unspeakable Acts, Ordinary People: The Dynamics of Torture* (2001).

55. Miriam Gur-Arye, "Can the War against Terror Justify the Use of Force in Interrogations? Reflections in Light of the Israeli Experience," in Levinson, *op. cit.*, p. 185.

56. Jess Bravin and Greg Jaffe, "Rumsfeld Approved Methods for Guantánamo Interrogation," *The Wall Street Journal*, June 10, 2004.

57. Department of Defense press release, June 12, 2005, www.defenselink.mil/Releases/Release.aspx?ReleaseID=8583.

58. Jane Mayer, "The Memo," *The New Yorker*, Feb. 27, 2006, pp. 32-41.

59. Tony Lagouranis, *Fear Up Harsh: An Army Interrogator's Dark Journey Through Iraq* (2007), p. 93.

60. A summary of the Taguba report can be found at www.fas.org/irp/agency/dod/taguba.pdf.

61. "Bush Signs Defense Authorization Measure With Detainee Provision," *CQ Almanac 2005 Online Edition*, available at http://library.cqpress.com.

62. The case is *Hamdan v. Rumsfeld*, 126 S. Ct. 2749 (2006).

63. Priest, *op. cit.*

64. "President Discusses Creation of Military Commissions to Try Suspected Terrorists," *op. cit.*

65. Dafna Linzer and Julie Tate, "New Light Shed on CIA's 'Black Site' Prisons," *The Washington Post*, Feb. 28, 2007, p. A1.

66. Mark Bowden, "The Dark Art of Interrogation," *The Atlantic*, October 2003.

67. Mayer, Aug. 13, 2007, *op. cit.*

68. *Ibid.*

69. Mayer, Feb. 14, 2005, *op. cit.*

70. Ian Fisher and Elisabetta Povoledo, "Italy Braces for Legal Fight Over Secret CIA Program," *The New York Times*, June 8, 2007.

71. Jeffrey R. Smith, "Gonzales Defends Transfer of Detainees," *The Washington Post*, March 8, 2005, p. A3.

72. Malinowski testimony, *op. cit.*

73. Council of Europe Parliamentary Assembly, "Alleged secret detentions in Council of Europe member states, 2006," http://assembly.coe.int/CommitteeDocs/2006/20060606_Ejdoc162006PartII-FINAL.pdf.

74. Gwendolyn Albert, "With Impunity," *Prague Post*, April 12, 2006, www.praguepost.com/articles/2006/04/12/with-impunity.php.

75. http://melissamahlecommentary.blogspot.com/2005/12/cia-and-torture.html.

76. Elisabetta Povoledo, "Trial of CIA Operatives is delayed in Italy," *The International Herald Tribune*, June 18, 2007.

77. Jeffrey Fleishman, "Germany Orders Arrest of 13 CIA Operatives in Kidnapping of Khaled el-Masri" *Los Angeles Times*, Jan. 31, 2007.

78. Mayer, Feb. 14, 2005, *op. cit.*

79. "Arar Case Timeline," Canadian Broadcasting Company, www.cbc.ca/news/background/arar.

80. Christine Kearney, "Iraqi, Yemeni men join lawsuit over CIA flights," Reuters, Aug. 1, 2007.

81. Marie Beaudette, "Standing at the Floodgates," *Legal Times*, June 28, 2004.

82. The case is *Sosa v. Alvarez-Machain*, 2004, 542 U.S. 692 (2004).

83. Ian MacKinnon, "War crimes panel charges Khmer Rouge chief," *The Guardian*, Aug. 1, 2007.

84. "Taylor Trial Delayed until 2008," BBC News, Aug. 20, 2007, http://news.bbc.co.uk/2/hi/africa/6954627.stm.

85. P. X. Kelley and Robert F. Turner, "War Crimes and the White House," *The Washington Post*, July 26, 2007.

86. Thomas, *op. cit.*

87. Henry Weinstein, "ABA targets CIA methods, secret law," *Los Angeles Times*, Aug. 14, 2007.

88. The Associated Press, "Dem blocking Bush pick for CIA lawyer," MSNBC, Aug. 16, 2007, www.msnbc.msn.com/id/20294826.

89. "The Candidates on Military Tribunals and Guantánamo Bay," Council on Foreign Relations, July 17, 2007, www.cfr.org/publication/13816/.

BIBLIOGRAPHY

Books

Bagaric, Mirko, and Julie Clarke, *Torture: When the Unthinkable Is Morally Permissible,* **State University of New York Press,** 2007.
Bagaric, an Australian law professor, argues torture is sometimes morally justified and should be legally excusable.

Conroy, John, *Unspeakable Acts, Ordinary People: The Dynamics of Torture,* **Random House,** 2000.
A reporter examines the history of torture.

Dershowitz, Alan M., *Why Torture Works: Understanding the Threat, Responding to the Challenge,* **Yale University Press,** 2003.
A Harvard law professor argues that torture will be employed by interrogators, so courts should issue "torture warrants" to bring some legal oversight to the process.

Haritos-Fatouros, Mika, *The Psychological Origins of Institutionalized Torture,* **Routledge,** 2003.
A sociologist explores the indoctrination of Greek torturers during military rule of the country during the 1970s.

Lagouranis, Tony, *Fear Up Harsh: An Army Interrogator's Dark Journey Through Iraq,* **NAL Hardcover,** 2007.
A former U.S. Army interrogator describes the use of coercive techniques by American soldiers.

Levinson, Sanford, ed., *Torture: A Collection,* **Oxford University Press,** 2004.
Essays by academics and human rights advocates examine the historical, moral and political implications of torture.

Rejali, Darius, *Torture and Democracy,* **Princeton University Press,** 2007.
A Reed College professor and expert on torture traces its history from the 19th century through the U.S. occupation of Iraq.

Articles

"Torture in the Name of Freedom," *Der Spiegel,* Feb. 20, 2006, www.spiegel.de/international/spiegel/0,1518,401899,00.html.
The German news magazine concludes the United States is ceding its moral authority on the issue of torture.

Bowden, Mark, "The Dark Art of Interrogation," *The Atlantic Monthly,* October 2003, www.theatlantic.com/doc/200310/bowden.
An American journalist examines interrogation methods employed by U.S. personnel since the 9/11 terrorist attacks.

Einolf, Christopher J., "The Fall and Rise of Torture: A Comparative and Historical Analysis," *Sociological Theory,* June 2007, www.asanet.org/galleries/default-file/June07STFeature.pdf.
A University of Richmond sociology professor explains the continued prevalence of torture during the 20th century.

Mayer, Jane, "The Black Sites," *The New Yorker,* Aug. 13, 2007, p. 46, www.newyorker.com/reporting/2007/08/13/070813fa_fact_mayer.
A journalist examines the history of the CIA's secret "black site" prisons for high-value terror suspects.

Mayer, Jane, "Outsourcing Torture," *The New Yorker,* Feb. 14, 2005, www.newyorker.com/archive/2005/02/14/050214fa_fact6.
The reporter traces the history of the United States' "extraordinary rendition" policy.

Mayer, Jane, "Whatever It Takes," *The New Yorker,* Feb. 19, 2007, www.newyorker.com/reporting/2007/02/19/070219fa_fact_mayer.
The article examines the popular television show "24" and its role in "normalizing" perceptions of torture.

Ozdemir, Cem, "Beyond the Valley of the Wolves," *Der Spiegel,* Feb. 22, 2006, www.spiegel.de/international/0,1518,401565,00.html.
A Turkish member of parliament discusses a popular Turkish movie that depicts American soldiers mistreating Iraqi civilians.

Reports and Studies

"Alleged secret detentions and unlawful inter-state transfers involving Council of Europe member states," *Committee on Legal Affairs and Human Rights Council of Europe Parliamentary Assembly,* June 7, 2006, http://assembly.coe.int/CommitteeDocs/2006/20060606_Ejdoc162006PartII-FINAL.pdf.

An organization of European lawmakers examines the role of European governments in U.S. renditions.

"Educing Information, Interrogation: Science and Art," *Foundations for the Future Phase 1 Report, Intelligence Science Board,* **December 2006, www.fas .org/irp/dni/educing.pdf.**
Too little is known about which interrogation methods are effective.

"Tarnished Image: Latin America Perceives the United States," *Latin American Working Group,* **www.lawg .org/docs/tarnishedimage.pdf.**
A nonprofit group examines Latin American press coverage of U.S. policies, including its interrogation of detainees.

For More Information

Amnesty International USA, 5 Penn Plaza, New York, NY 10001; (212) 807-8400; www.amnestyusa.org. U.S.-affiliate of London-based international human rights organization.

Center for Victims of Torture, 717 East River Rd., Minneapolis, MN 55455; (612) 436-4800; www.cvt.org. Operates healing centers in Minneapolis-St. Paul and Liberia and Sierra Leone. Also trains religious leaders, teachers, caregivers and staff from other NGOs about the effects of torture and trauma.

Human Rights First, 333 Seventh Ave., 13th Floor, New York, NY 10001-5108; (212) 845-5200; www.human-rightsfirst.org. A New York-based advocacy group that combats genocide, torture and other human rights abuses; founded in 1978 as the Lawyers Committee for Human Rights.

Human Rights Watch, 350 Fifth Ave., 34th floor, New York, NY 10118-3299; (212) 290-4700; www.hrw.org. Advocates for human rights around the world.

International Rehabilitation Council for Torture Victims, Borgergade 13, P.O. Box 9049 DK-1022, Copenhagen K, Denmark; +45 33 76 06 00; www.irct.org. Umbrella organization for worldwide network of centers that treat torture victims.

Medical Foundation for the Care of Victims of Torture, 111 Isledon Rd., Islington, London N7 7JW, United Kingdom; (020) 7697 7777; www.torturecare.org.uk. Trains and provides medical personnel to aid victims of torture.

Office of the High Commissioner for Human Rights, 8-14 Ave. de la Paix, 1211 Geneva 10, Switzerland; (41-22) 917-9000; www.ohchr.org. United Nations agency that opposes human rights violations.

Treatment of Detainees

17

Are Suspected Terrorists Being Treated Unfairly?

Peter Katel and Kenneth Jost

Protesters call for changes in U.S. policies on the treatment of suspected terrorists during a Senate Armed Services Committee hearing on July 13, 2006.

Getty Images/Mark Wilson

From *CQ Researcher*,
August 25, 2006.

"**K**illers," President George W. Bush has called the prisoners being held by the United States at Guantánamo Bay — murderers of civilians who don't deserve to be treated under the international laws of war. "These are terrorists," Bush declared in 2002. "They know no countries."[1]

But the top lawyers from the Army, Navy, Air Force and Marines disagree with their commander in chief. When the Senate Armed Services Committee asked them on July 16 if Congress should endorse the controversial trial and detention system created by Bush for enemy combatants, they answered no — emphatically.

"Clearly, we need a change," declared Major Gen. Jack Rives judge advocate general of the Air Force. His colleagues agreed.

In fact, military attorneys have argued for the past several years against the administration's refusal to apply the Geneva Conventions to the war on terrorism. The conventions are the set of treaties governing military conduct in wartime, including the treatment of prisoners and civilians.

Until the Supreme Court ruled in late June, the Bush administration had maintained that the conventions did not apply to prisoners captured in Afghanistan and other battlefields in the war on terrorists. That led to the use of interrogation methods, such as threatening prisoners with guard dogs, near-drowning by "waterboarding," sleep deprivation and forcing prisoners into painful "stress positions."

For the past two years, the abuse of detainees held at Bagram Air Base, in Afghanistan, Abu Ghraib prison in Iraq and the U.S. Naval Station at Guantánamo Bay, Cuba, have generated international

Many Detainees Not Linked to Hostile Acts

More than half of the detainees at Guantánamo Bay have no history of hostile acts against the United States or its allies, according to an analysis of government data by lawyers for detainees (left). Nearly three-quarters of the detainees whom the U.S. government has characterized as "associated with" the al Qaeda terrorist network have not committed hostile acts against the United States or its allies.

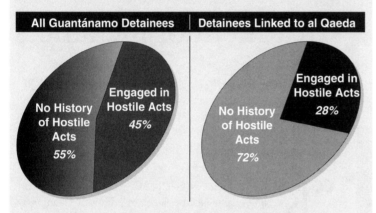

| All Guantánamo Detainees | Detainees Linked to al Qaeda |

All Guantánamo Detainees:
No History of Hostile Acts 55%
Engaged in Hostile Acts 45%

Detainees Linked to al Qaeda:
No History of Hostile Acts 72%
Engaged in Hostile Acts 28%

Source: "Report on Guantánamo Detainees, A Profile of 517 Detainees Through Analysis of Department of Defense Data," Seton Hall University School of Law

outrage. Yet military lawyers, politicians and other critics of U.S. policies had largely failed to get Bush and his top legal-affairs and military appointees to change policies on treatment of these prisoners, whom Bush defined as "unlawful combatants."[2]

In behind-the-scenes battles within the administration, military lawyers argued that the United States was violating the laws of warfare in seeming to condone abuse and torture of detainees. The lawyers also opposed the system of military courts proposed by Bush for war-on-terrorism prisoners at Guantánamo that denied many rights that the conventions grant even to irregular fighters who don't wear any country's uniform.[3]

"I'd only say I wish they'd taken our advice," says William H. Taft, IV, chief legal adviser to Secretary of State Colin Powell during President Bush's first term.[4]

Critics could be ignored or overruled — but not the U.S. Supreme Court.

In its landmark June 29 decision, the justices ruled, 5-3, that prisoners being held in the fight against the al Qaeda terrorist organization are entitled to the protections afforded by the Geneva Conventions. The suit challenging the administration was brought on behalf of Salim Ahmed Hamdan, a Yemeni prisoner at Guantánamo who was Osama bin Laden's driver.[5]

"We fought very hard to get him a fair trial," Hamdan's military-appointed lawyer, Navy Lt. Cmdr. Charles Swift, told the Senate Judiciary Committee. He argued that the military's existing court-martial system — rather than tribunals known as military commissions — would suit that aim perfectly.*

Military lawyers and their congressional supporters argue that American lives may depend on whether the United States upholds Geneva standards for all detainees. "We will have more wars, and there will be Americans who will be taken captive," Arizona Republican Sen. John McCain, who was tortured during his five-and-a-half years as a prisoner of war in North Vietnam, told the Senate Armed Services Committee. "If we somehow carve out exceptions to treaties . . . then it will make it very easy for our enemies to do the same in the case of American prisoners."

Sen. Saxby Chambliss, R-Ga., responded, "It certainly irritates me to no end to think that we have to continue to do what's right at all times when the enemy that we're fighting is going to be cruel and inhuman to American men and women who wear our uniform [if] they might fall into their hands."

While the Supreme Court did not address the government's right to hold war-on-terror prisoners "for the duration of active hostilities," it ruled that Bush had exceeded his authority in establishing the commissions. Only Congress has the power to decide that the standard military justice system couldn't be used, the court majority wrote. The decision leaves lawmakers with two basic options: require detainees to be tried under the

---

* The lawsuit, *Hamdan v. Rumsfeld,* has delayed trials of other alleged terrorists.

existing court-martial system, or bow to the administration's wishes and create a new, legal version of the commissions.[6]

Retaining the commissions would, in effect, undercut the high court's ruling that Common Article 3 of the Geneva Conventions covers Guantánamo detainees. The provision requires that a prisoner on trial — even someone not fighting for a specific nation — be judged by a "regularly constituted court" that provides "all judicial guarantees which are recognized as indispensable by civilized peoples." And it prohibits "humiliating and degrading treatment" and well as "cruel treatment and torture."[7]

The high court's reasoning didn't sit well with some lawmakers.

"Where I'm from in South Dakota," Republican Sen. John Thune told his Armed Services colleagues, "when you talk about humiliating or degrading or those types of terms, in applying them to terrorists . . . people in my state would [not] be real concerned that we might be infringing on [the terrorists'] sense of inferiority."

But Sen. Lindsey Graham, R-S.C., resisted any implication that critics of the commission system want to coddle terrorists. "All the people who are out there ranting and raving [that] having . . . some basic due process cripples us in the war effort, you're flat wrong," said Graham, a colonel in the Air Force Reserve and a judge on the Air Force Court of Criminal Appeals.[8]

The debate over whether the rules of traditional warfare apply in the war on terrorists began in the months following the 9/11 terrorist attacks on the World Trade Center and the Pentagon. Then-White House Counsel Alberto Gonzales summed up the administration's mindset in a Jan. 25, 2002, memo to Bush: "The war against terrorism is a new kind of war," wrote Gonzales, now the nation's attorney general. "The nature of the new war places a high premium on . . . the ability to quickly obtain information from captured terrorists and their sponsors in order to avoid further atrocities against

Where Are the Detainees?

About 14,000 detainees are being held by the United States, but the number fluctuates, especially following major offensives. Many prisoners captured in battle initially are held at bases in combat zones and are not included in the detainee figures below.

Locations of Detention Facilities	No. of Detainees
Afghanistan	
Bagram Air Force Base	500
Kandahar	100 to 200
Cuba	
Guantánamo Bay	450
Since the detention camp was opened, about 310 prisoners have been freed or transferred to their home countries or to other nations.	
Iraq	**12,800**
The majority of the prisoners captured in Iraq and Afghanistan are held at Abu Ghraib prison, Camp Bucca and various facilities around Baghdad airport.	
Other Locations	30
Human Rights Watch says more than two-dozen high-value detainees, sometimes called "ghost prisoners," are in CIA custody in undisclosed locations outside the United States.	

Sources: Department of Defense, Human Rights Watch

American civilians, and the need to try terrorists for war crimes."[9]

Taft and then-Secretary of State Powell were among a handful of officials who rejected Gonzales's approach.[10]

But Gonzales and other officials carried the day. At about the time he wrote his memo, the first prisoners were being shipped to Guantánamo. By mid-2006, the camp held about 450 detainees, according to the Department of Defense (DOD). The military itself conceded that some of the Guantánamo prisoners didn't belong there. The DOD says about 80 men have been released and another 230 transferred to their countries of origin, in most cases after Combatant Status Review Tribunals determined they hadn't fought the United States and had no other connections to terrorism, or did not pose a significant threat.[11]

The tribunals were set up after the Supreme Court ruled in 2004 that the Guantánamo prisoners could use habeas corpus petitions to challenge their detentions.[12]

That ruling landed the first major legal blow against the administration's detention policies. Only a month before, the scandal over prisoner abuses at Abu Ghraib had exploded, followed by leaked memos in which officials discussed how to avoid defining some interrogation methods as torture. By the end of 2004, the administration was forced to back down from a narrow definition of "torture" fashioned by a top Justice Department lawyer — that the term applied only to methods so extreme that they caused "organ failure" or the equivalent.[13]

Following that administration retreat, Congress at the end of 2005 passed the Detainee Treatment Act, sponsored by McCain, which prohibits "cruel, inhuman or degrading" treatment of any captive in American hands. A provision limiting court enforcement complicated the law's practical effect.[14]

The Supreme Court's *Hamdan* ruling further undermined the administration's detention and trial system for enemy fighters and terrorists. Captured in Afghanistan in 2001, Hamdan had acknowledged serving as a driver for al Qaeda leader Osama bin Laden. But the government charged him with participating in al Qaeda's conspiracy to kill Americans, which he denies.[15]

To the administration, Hamdan was exactly the kind of prisoner the new rules were designed to deal with — both an intelligence source and an alleged war criminal.

But military lawyers say Gonzales and other civilians blur the lines between intelligence gathering and war-crimes prosecution.

"That confusion has created all kinds of problems," says former Navy Judge Advocate General John D. Hutson, dean of Franklin Pierce Law Center in Manchester, N.H. For one thing, he argues, the administration hasn't distinguished among prisoners who clearly have valuable intelligence, those who had terrorist links but didn't possess any secrets and those who had neither.

But even an established connection to al Qaeda may mean less than the government alleges, according to Hutson. "Hamdan — we can pretend he was something else, but the reality is, he was a driver," Hutson says. "He is no more and no less a war criminal than Hitler's driver. To prosecute him for conspiracy is a very problematic proposition."

The charges against Hamdan have been described only in general terms, but an Air Force lawyer who works with the commission told *The New York Times* that the evidence, including photographs and Hamdan's statements to interrogators, added up to a "solid" case.[16]

As for other detainees, the Defense Department says they include former terrorist trainers, operatives and bomb makers who have provided "valuable insights" into al Qaeda methods and personnel.[17]

Meanwhile, the conflict over detention and trial has put military lawyers at odds with their civilian leaders. Swift, for example, told the Armed Services Committee the commissions' rules made a mockery of judicial fairness by allowing defendants to be kept out of the courtroom and barred from seeing at least some of the evidence against them.

To those who argue that following Geneva Convention rules would compromise America's defenses, Swift said: "Given the handcuffs put on its counsel, the accused is really the only one that can dispute the evidence against him. Without knowing what that evidence is, the accused is left undefended."

As the political, legal and military communities ponder how to treat prisoners, these are some of the major issues being debated:

Should Congress require wartime detainees to be treated according to the Geneva Conventions?

The *Hamdan* decision brought Congress face-to-face with a fundamental choice: Whether to create a system for imprisoning and trying detainees based on the Geneva Conventions.

The Supreme Court seemingly decided the issue when it rejected the administration's assertion that Common Article 3 of the conventions does not apply to Guantánamo detainees. "That reasoning is erroneous," the majority opinion said. "Common Article 3 . . . is applicable here."[18]

Moreover, military lawyers have testified that Common Article 3 has served as the minimum standard for decades on how troops must treat all prisoners. In fact, U.S. military personnel are required to meet an even higher threshold, treating all prisoners as uniformed prisoners of war representing a nation, Thomas J. Romig, a former Army judge advocate general, told the Senate Armed Services Committee. "And at that standard, you're never going to violate Common Article 3," he said.

Under the Geneva Conventions POWs must be allowed to keep their personal property, exercise and receive regular medical care. Common Article 3, on the other hand, imposes what military lawyers consider the bare essentials of how to treat an enemy, even a terrorist.[19]

But defining those bare essentials has become the biggest point of dispute between the administration and its critics.

"Common Article 3 is written in such generalities, it's almost like taking a blank piece of paper," says Andrew C. McCarthy, a former federal prosecutor who helped mount the case against the terrorists who tried to blow up the World Trade Center in 1993. " 'Judicial guarantees,' which are recognized as indispensable by civilized peoples — what does that mean? What does Common Article 3 tell you about whether you need to give terrorist defendants access to national-security secrets during trial? Is that indispensable to civilized peoples? Who knows?"

Variations on that theme have become a major feature of debates on detainee treatment. Daniel Dell'Orto, principal deputy general counsel at the Pentagon, told the House Armed Services Committee: "I don't want a soldier when he kicks down a door in a hut in Afghanistan searching for Osama bin Laden to have to worry about whether — when he does so and questions the individuals he finds inside, who may or may not be bin Laden's bodyguards, or even that individual himself — he's got to advise them of some rights before he takes a statement."

Former Navy Judge Advocate General Hutson says: "Yes, Common Article 3 is vague in some sense, I suppose, but life, and particularly law, are replete with vague terms: obscenity, probable cause, torture. If we need to explain what we believe those terms mean, then we should do it. We're just using vagueness as an excuse to avoid Common Article 3 and the Geneva Conventions."

But Hutson noted during an appearance before the Senate Armed Services Committee on July 13, "nobody — certainly not me" had argued that troops on a search mission should be required to give Miranda warnings.

As for how to define various terms in Common Article 3, Air Force Maj. Gen. Rives added that the provision has been incorporated into military law for more than 50 years with no objections raised.

Washington lawyer David B. Rivkin Jr., a former lawyer in the Reagan and George H.W. Bush administrations, zeroes in on Common Article 3's opening sentence, which specifies that it applies to conflicts occurring only

Top military lawyers, or judge advocate generals (JAGs), testify before a Senate Armed Services Committee hearing on military tribunals for Guantánamo Bay detainees, on July 13, 2006. From left: Maj. Gen. Scott C. Black (Army), Rear Adm. James E. McPherson (Navy), Maj. Gen. Jack L. Rives (Air Force), Brig. Gen. Kevin M. Sandkulher (Marine Corps) and former JAGs Thomas J. Romig (Army) and John D. Hutson (Navy).

Getty Images/Mark Wilson

in the countries that signed the convention. "Not every country has signed," Rivkin says, arguing that the restriction would make enforcement unmanageable. "So if you capture al Qaeda personnel in Afghanistan, which is a party to the Geneva Conventions, you have one set of rules, and if you make a capture in Somalia — I don't know if Somalia signed — then Common Article 3 doesn't apply. Does that make any sense?"

But Katherine Newell Bierman, a former Air Force captain who is now counterterrorism counsel for Human Rights Watch (HRW), says no such geographic limitation would exist if Congress simply adopted the protections of Common Article 3 in a statute.

Bierman notes that nothing in the provision requires every prisoner to be granted a trial. "But if you're going to sentence them, there has to be a fair trial," she says. What that means, she says, amounts to nothing more extravagant than giving the defendant a chance to defend himself, not forcing him to incriminate himself and ensuring he's not tortured — the elements of what an ordinary citizen would consider a fair trial.

Administration supporters insist that such seemingly simple notions of justice conflict with the plain reality that definitions of elementary matters vary widely from country to country. For instance, says Kris Kobach, a former Justice

Majority of Americans Support Detainees' Rights

A majority of Americans believe that terrorism suspects have widespread human rights, including the right not to be tortured.

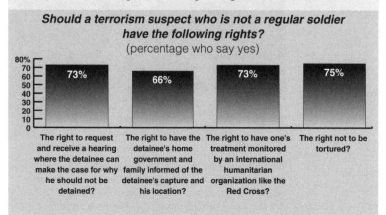

Should a terrorism suspect who is not a regular soldier have the following rights?
(percentage who say yes)

- 73% — The right to request and receive a hearing where the detainee can make the case for why he should not be detained?
- 66% — The right to have the detainee's home government and family informed of the detainee's capture and his location?
- 73% — The right to have one's treatment monitored by an international humanitarian organization like the Red Cross?
- 75% — The right not to be tortured?

Should the rules for treating detainees suspected of terrorist activities be the same for citizens and non-citizens?

- Should be the same: 63%
- Should not be the same: 33%

Should the U.S. military and intelligence agencies be permitted to secretly send terrorism suspects to other countries that use torture?

- Should: 37%
- Should not: 57%

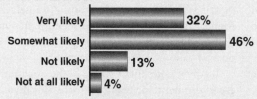

How likely is it that terrorism suspects being questioned in other countries will be tortured?

- Very likely: 32%
- Somewhat likely: 46%
- Not likely: 13%
- Not at all likely: 4%

Is it your impression that current U.S. policies at Guantánamo Bay are or are not legal, according to international treaties on the treatment of detainees?

- Are legal: 52%
- Are not legal: 38%

Source: WorldPublicOpinion.org, Program on International Policy Attitudes, University of Maryland

Department lawyer who now teaches at the University of Missouri School of Law, " 'Cruel and unusual punishment' can mean one thing in the United States, where we're trying to decide whether it's cruel to put someone to death by virtually pain-free lethal injection, whereas in another country the question is whether public caning is cruel. This is a war in which very different cultures are involved."

Should Common Article 3 apply to CIA prisoners held in undisclosed locations in other countries?

Although attention has focused on detainees held by the military, there is also concern about prisoners being held in secret by the Central Intelligence Agency (CIA). Human Rights Watch (HRW) says media reports indicate that 30 such "ghost" detainees are being held, including high-ranking alleged terrorists. Government officials have confirmed some of the detentions.[20]

Administration critics say flatly that prisoners of the United States should not be held incommunicado but should be put on trial if they're believed to have committed crimes. "Secret detention is the gateway to torture," said Reed Brody, a special counsel for HRW, arguing that the Geneva Conventions on both POWs and detained civilians require International Red Cross access to all prisoners.[21]

But administration advocates argue that the relevance of the conventions to CIA prisoners detained as terrorists isn't clear.

"We're testing our definitions," the University of Missouri's Kobach says. "We have two categories that we know: traditional soldiers who become

POWs when we capture them and garden-variety criminals who become defendants in civilian courts when we capture them. Terrorists fit somewhere in between. They're committing offenses against laws of war and terrorist acts that transcend normal criminal acts."

Kobach acknowledges that he could make the argument that even CIA prisoners are entitled to military trials, but he said that the *Hamdan* decision doesn't provide guidance on whether alleged terrorists who are not being held by the Defense Department should get the same treatment. One common factor with the Guantánamo prisoners is that they have all been apprehended by the U.S. military, he says. "If someone has been apprehended by a foreign government, it wouldn't necessarily flow that he should go to Guantánamo."

"Ghost" detainees took center stage in 2004 following the disclosure of photographs of detainees being abused at Abu Ghraib prison in Iraq. On Sept. 9 — some five months after the prison abuse came to light — an Army general told the Senate Armed Services Committee that "dozens, perhaps up to 100" CIA detainees had been imprisoned secretly.[22]

At least one CIA prisoner died in custody at Abu Ghraib, apparently from a rifle butt blow to the head while in custody. The injury went undiscovered because he didn't get a medical screening when brought to the prison, as did prisoners held by the military.[23]

"Water-boarding," a form of torture that simulates drowning, reportedly was used on Khalid Shaikh Muhammed, a Pakistani whom the government's "9/11 Commission" called the "principal architect" of the 9/11 attacks.[24] No trials have been reported scheduled for Shaikh Muhammed or for any other spy-agency prisoner.

"There's some interagency discussion about what you do with these people long term once their intelligence value has been fully exploited," a U.S. intelligence official told the *Los Angeles Times* in 2004. "The CIA is an intelligence collection and analysis organization. This isn't the bureau of prisons."[25]

Bierman of HRW says putting the alleged terrorists on trial would solve the problem. "Anybody subject to the laws of war — and all these people are subject — should be prosecuted in fair trials," she says. "Prosecuting these guys would be a step ahead of hiding them and torturing them. The whole idea of socking them away is

Former CIA contractor David A. Passaro (left) faces up to 11 years in prison after being convicted on Aug. 17, 2006, of beating Afghan farmer Abdul Wali (right) in June 2003 during questioning about rocket attacks at a remote base in Afghanistan; Wali died two days later.

AP Photo/WRAL-TV (left)/U.S. District Court

that these are people the law doesn't even reach. That is so fundamentally abhorrent to our values."

Rivkin agrees the status of CIA detainees should be "regularized." But his reasoning differs sharply from that of human-rights advocates. Creating a standard detention-and-trial process would cut down on lawsuits aimed at forcing disclosures of prisoners' whereabouts, he says. "Who needs that crap?"

That view flows out of Rivkin's analysis that even Common Article 3 doesn't require POW-style detention — with food parcels from the Red Cross, and notification to detainees' families of where they are being held, among other provisions. "No, you do not have to tell the world where they are," he says. "You don't have to give them rights to which they are not entitled. It's not bad to have people disoriented, and it's not useful to tell the bad guys who we've captured. Let them wonder if the guy is alive or dead."

But Eugene R. Fidell, president of the National Institute of Military Justice, argues that imposing the Common Article 3 standard even on intelligence agencies someday might protect captured CIA officers from extreme abuse.

Practicality aside, Fidell says that because Common Article 3 imposes a minimum set of standards, it must be the baseline for treatment of all detainees, regardless of who holds them. "You can't say, 'Anybody in uniform, fine,' but if the CIA is holding them, the sky's the limit" regarding abuse.

Should the U.S. outlaw "extraordinary rendition"?

Another variant of CIA detention — "extraordinary rendition" — came to light in 2004. The secret procedure involves the seizure of terrorism suspects, usually outside the United States, by U.S. intelligence agents, who ship them to countries reputed to use torture during interrogations.[26]

Ex-CIA officer Michael Scheuer told *The New Yorker's* Jane Mayer that extraordinary rendition began during the Clinton administration, when the threat from bin Laden and associated terrorists first arose. The program expanded after 9/11, when government lawyers created a loophole in a requirement that war-on-terrorism prisoners be treated humanely: Only the military had to comply, not intelligence agencies.[27]

On the CBS news program "60 Minutes II," Scheuer said that countries receiving the suspects were supposed to assure the United States that the prisoners wouldn't be tortured. But no one took the assurances seriously, he said. The bottom line, he said, was that "extraordinary rendition" had produced "very useful" information. Asked if he condoned the use of torture, he replied, "It's OK with me. I'm responsible for protecting Americans."[28]

Only a few "rendered" prisoners have emerged from foreign prisons. Khaled al-Masri, a German of Kuwaiti origin, and Maher Arar, a Canadian citizen from Syria, say they were released after managing to prove their innocence. Both sued the United States for allegedly violating their rights, but the suits were dismissed after government lawyers said the trials would expose official secrets.[29]

Rendition is a long-established procedure for turning wanted people over to governments asking for them, says former State Department adviser Taft. He says rendition can be carried out without violating any laws or policies against delivering people to torturers. If another country asks for a citizen to be sent back because he's wanted for questioning or trial, "Before we would transfer anybody in those circumstances, we ensure that we are confident that they will be treated properly," he says. He adds that he wasn't involved in any extraordinary rendition cases and knows nothing of them beyond media reports.

If the requesting country has a spotty human-rights record, the State Department can ask to see the prisoner routinely, Taft says. And some countries are off-limits. "I would think that for every person who is bundled off — there should be confidence they will not be treated improperly," he says. "I thought that was the process."

Advocates of the Bush administration approach to counterterrorism acknowledge that human-rights protections may not be assured for terrorism suspects — but they say imposing such a rule would be impractical. "This is one area where Congress is not particularly entitled to the right to oversight," Rivkin says. "It just gets too much into the regulation of foreign policy and intelligence operations."

The process by which American officials evaluate the trustworthiness of other countries' pledges not to mistreat suspects is "too delicate and imprecise to try to reduce to writing," Rivkin says.

But administration critics argue that the Supreme Court's *Hamdan* ruling left no wiggle room about standards for prisoner treatment. "The language of the decision guarantees minimum Geneva Convention Common Article 3 rights to all detainees," says Neal Katyal, Hamdan's co-counsel, a professor at Georgetown Law School. He argues, moreover, that military-justice standards demand humane treatment across the board.

Attorney General Gonzales told the House Judiciary Committee in April that the United States is committed by treaty to not sending people to countries where their human rights would be violated. The 1987 Convention Against Torture and Other Cruel, Inhuman or Degrading Treatment or Punishment, which the Senate ratified in 1990, commits the U.S. not to "expel, return or extradite a person to another State where there are substantial grounds for believing that he would be in danger of being subjected to torture."

But in practice U.S. observance of the treaty is a "farce," says Joseph Margulies, a professor at Northwestern University Law School who is among the lead lawyers for Guantánamo detainees challenging their confinement. He cites the U.S. reliance on declarations by other countries that they won't torture prisoners.

Even some hard-line administration supporters are troubled by the possibility that the United States might wink at the prohibition. If the government doesn't believe that the prohibition against torture should apply to accused terrorists sent to their home countries, ex-prosecutor McCarthy says, officials should say so publicly. "Or else, we should stop doing it."

CHRONOLOGY

1860s-1946 *Conflicts arise among the three branches of government over the treatment of captured enemy soldiers and spies and respect for civil liberties vs. national-security concerns.*

1861 President Abraham Lincoln suspends habeas corpus, defying the Supreme Court and setting the stage for military trials of hundreds of accused Confederate agents.

1866 U.S. Supreme Court orders release of a Confederate sympathizer who had been sentenced to death, on the grounds that martial law can't be applied outside theaters of war as long as civilian courts are functioning.

1942 Supreme Court upholds military tribunal convictions of eight German saboteurs; six are executed.

1946 Gen. Tomoyuki Yamashita is executed after a quick — and some say unfair — military commission trial finds him guilty of not stopping atrocities by Japanese troops in the Philippines.

1949-1971 *In the wake of World War II atrocities, greater protection is offered for prisoners and civilians.*

1949 Geneva Conventions are revised to apply prisoner of war (POW) standards to prisoners in conflicts that aren't wars between nation-states.

1950 Congress enacts the Uniform Code of Military Justice, which grants defendants rights equal to those enjoyed by defendants in civilian courts and adopts the standards of Geneva's Common Article 3. The provision requires prisoners on trial — even those not fighting for a specific nation — to be judged by a "regularly constituted court."

1966 U.S. military command in Vietnam grants POW status to captives from the Vietcong guerrilla army.

1971 The massacre of 400-500 Vietnamese civilians in the village of My Lai leads to courts-martial for two officers; one is convicted and one acquitted.

2000s *Attacks on the World Trade Center and the Pentagon on Sept. 11, 2001, prompt the Bush*

administration to set up controversial special courts to try accused terrorists and "unlawful combatants."

Nov. 13, 2001 President George W. Bush signs an executive order establishing military commissions to try accused members and supporters of the al Qaeda terrorist network.

2002 Two groups of Guantánamo detainees file habeas corpus petitions challenging their confinement.

July 2003 A military commission rules that Salim Ahmed Hamdan, a driver for Osama bin Laden captured in Afghanistan, is eligible for trial; he is later charged with conspiracy.

April 27, 2004 CBS News's "60 Minutes II" televises photographs of U.S. troops abusing prisoners at Abu Ghraib prison.

June 28, 2004 U.S. Supreme Court rules, in *Rasul v. Bush*, that Guantánamo prisoners can go to court to demand they be freed.

Oct. 21, 2004 The first in a stream of internal government documents concerning treatment of detainees are released to the American Civil Liberties Union by the government.

December 2005 Congress passes the Detainee Treatment Act, prohibiting torture and mistreatment of prisoners while limiting detainees' right to challenge their detentions.

June 29, 2006 Supreme Court rules in *Hamdan v. Rumsfeld* that the president exceeded his authority in establishing military commissions.

July 13, 2006 Top military legal officers tell congressional committees that lawmakers shouldn't endorse the administration's military commission system.

Aug. 2, 2006 Attorney General Alberto R. Gonzales argues that Congress shouldn't ban coerced testimony in military trials of accused terrorists.

Aug. 17, 2006 Former CIA contract interrogator David A. Passaro faces up to 11 years in prison after being convicted of beating Afghan farmer Abdul Wali, who died two days later.

Geneva Conventions Protect Prisoners

Warfare has changed radically since the first of four Geneva Conventions was adopted in 1864. Well-ordered lines of uniformed infantrymen with rifles at the ready have given way to vast, highly mobile armies and atomic weapons as well as terrorists and stateless paramilitary groups.

The changes have strained the international treaties governing the military's treatment of combatants and civilians.

The Bush administration says the Geneva Conventions don't cover prisoners captured during the wars in Afghanistan and Iraq. "In my judgment, this new paradigm [in warfare] renders obsolete Geneva's strict limitations on questioning of enemy prisoners," Attorney General Alberto Gonzales advised the president in 2002.[1]

Gary Solis, former director of the law of war program at the U.S. Military Academy at West Point, dismisses Gonzales's view. "The Geneva conventions do apply to today's warfare," says the retired Marine Corps lieutenant colonel. "You just have to have half a brain to apply them."

The U.S. Supreme Court also stepped into the debate, ruling on June 29, 2006, in *Hamdan v. Rumsfeld* that U.S. plans to prosecute Salim Ahmed Hamdan and other detainees being held at the U.S. Naval Station in Guantánamo Bay, Cuba, violated the conventions.

The conventions grew out of the horrors witnessed in 1859 by Henri Dunant, a Swiss merchant, after a battle between Austrian and French forces during the Austro-Sardinian War. After Dunant saw the more than 40,000 soldiers who had been left dead or dying on the battlefield near Solferino, Italy, he organized volunteers to help both sides.[2]

Dunant went on to found the International Committee for Relief to the Wounded, which later became the International Committee of the Red Cross (ICRC). In 1864, Dunant convinced the Swiss government to hold a diplomatic conference to lay down rules for the treatment of battlefield casualties.[3]

Ten European governments sent representatives to the conference and adopted the Geneva Convention for the Amelioration of the Condition of the Wounded in Armies in the Field, more commonly known as the first Geneva Convention.[4] It protects wounded soldiers on the battlefield and the medical personnel attending to them.[5]

The second convention, adopted in 1929, required prisoners of war to be humanely treated, properly fed and quartered in conditions comparable to those used by their captors.

And following the Holocaust and other atrocities committed against civilians in World War II, a third convention

---

A critic of the administration's overall detainee policy takes that reasoning even further. Former Navy JAG Hutson favors outlawing extraordinary rendition. But, he adds, "If you're going to torture, you ought to, at least, have the moral courage to do it yourself. Don't send them to Saudi Arabia. It's even worse to contract it out to have it done by someone else."

BACKGROUND

Laws of War

The Constitution designates the president as "commander in chief of the Army and Navy of the United States." But the power to "make rules concerning captures on land and water" is reserved for Congress. Throughout history,

Congress has passed laws governing trials before military courts or tribunals, but presidents or military commanders have sometimes skirted the required procedures.[30]

A full year before the Declaration of Independence, the Continental Congress in 1775 passed 69 "Articles of War" to regulate Army conduct. As commander in chief during the Revolutionary War, Gen. George Washington used the powers provided to convene tribunals to try suspected spies. In the most notable instance, Washington convened a board of 14 officers to try a captured British spy, Major John Andre, Gen. Benedict Arnold's infamous co-conspirator. The board found Andre guilty and recommended a death sentence, which Washington approved.

As a general in the War of 1812 and again in the first Seminole War (1817-1818), Andrew Jackson drew criticism for his broad view of his powers as a military commander.

was created in 1949, protecting non-combatants and their property from harm. Protections given to ground troops in the first convention were also extended to wounded and shipwrecked sailors.

"In 1949, we had a unity in the world that we hadn't seen before and we're not likely to see again," Solis says. "The world was united in its abhorrence of the actions of the Nazis and the Japanese."

In 1977, the conventions were amended with two additional protocols to cover the use of modern weapons and protect victims of internal conflicts.[6]

In 2005, another protocol was added permitting the use of a hollow, red diamond symbol in addition to the traditional cross and crescent emblems of the Red Cross. This protocol was instrumental in bringing Israel into the international humanitarian movement because Magen David Adom, Israel's rescue service, refused to work under the cross or crescent, the Red Cross symbol used in Muslim countries.[7]

The most controversial part of the conventions of late has been Common Article 3, which appears in each of the four conventions and was cited in the *Hamdan* case. It protects non-combatants from violence, cruel treatment, degradation and torture; prevents the taking of hostages; and ensures prisoners the right of a fair trial by a "regularly constituted court."[8]

The burden of enforcing the conventions falls on signatory nations and international organizations like the ICRC, which performs regular inspections of POW camps. The

conventions became federal law in the United States after they were signed and ratified by Congress.

Despite their role in dictating foreign policy today and their importance to domestic and international law, the Geneva Conventions (GC) are only as strong as the member nations want them to be.

"If you approach the GC's in such a way as to find loopholes, and to work around them, then you can do it," Solis says. "Geneva depends on the good will of those who adopt it. . . . No law is going to deter the lawless."

— *Nicholas Sohr*

[1] Gail Gibson, "Abuse scandal puts Gonzales in spotlight," *The Houston Chronicle*, May 23, 2004.

[2] Michael Tackett, "Abuses in Iraq highlight standards for treatment," *Chicago Tribune*, May 12, 2004.

[3] Maria Trombly, "A Brief History of the Laws of War," *Reference Guide to the Geneva Conventions*, July 31, 2006, www.genevaconventions.org.

[4] Tackett, *op. cit.*

[5] Office of the United Nations High Commissioner for Human Rights, www.ohchr.org/english/.

[6] For background, see Kenneth Jost, "International Law," *CQ Researcher*, Dec. 17, 2004, pp. 1049-1072, and David Masci, "Ethics of War," *CQ Researcher*, Dec. 13, 2002, pp. 1013-1032.

[7] Alexander G. Higgins, "Red Cross changes emblem," *The Seattle Times*, Dec. 8, 2005.

[8] For full text of Common Article 3, see "Protection of victims of non-international armed conflicts," International Committee of the Red Cross, Dec. 31, 1988. www.icrc.org/Web/Eng/siteeng0.nsf/iwpList104/6D73335C674B821DC1256B66005951D1.

(He was elected president in 1828.) In 1818, Jackson faced a censure motion in Congress for having two British subjects tried and sentenced to death for inciting the Creek Indians against the United States. Although the House of Representatives rejected the censure motion, House and Senate committees strongly criticized his actions.

During the Civil War and again during World War II, the Supreme Court was called on to resolve challenges to presidential orders for trials of enemy belligerents. The Civil War provoked intense conflicts over the use of military trials during wartime. To enable the military to summarily arrest Confederate spies and sympathizers, President Abraham Lincoln suspended habeas corpus shortly after the war broke out in April 1861. A month later, Chief Justice Roger B. Taney, in his role as a circuit

justice, ruled the action unconstitutional, but Lincoln ignored the decision. Over the next two years, hundreds of people suspected of aiding the secessionists were arrested and tried by ad hoc military tribunals, which sometimes ignored judicial orders to release the prisoners.

Congress passed a law sanctioning the suspension of habeas corpus in 1863 and adopted various rules for military tribunals, but their authority outside war zones remained doubtful. The Supreme Court dodged the issue in 1864, but after the war had ended, however, it ruled that martial law could not be imposed outside war theaters if civil courts were "open and their process unobstructed." The 1866 decision in *Ex parte Milligan* ordered the release of a prominent Southern sympathizer, Lambdin Milligan, who had been convicted of conspiracy by a military tribunal and sentenced to death.[31]

In the meantime, military tribunals had been used in two other high-profile cases: the May 1865 trial of the Lincoln assassination conspirators and the August 1865 trial of Capt. Henry Wirz, the Confederate commander of the notorious Andersonville prison camp in Americus, Ga., where nearly 13,000 prisoners died. Speedy convictions and executions resulted in both cases. Military tribunals continued to be used in the South during the early years of Reconstruction.[32]

Like Lincoln, President Franklin D. Roosevelt tested the limits of the president's powers during World War II. And, as in the Civil War, the Supreme Court erected no obstacle to Roosevelt's actions. In 1943 and 1944, the court upheld the curfew and then the internment of Japanese-Americans on the West Coast.[33] A more direct confrontation with the judiciary, however, came in 1942 with the trial of eight German saboteurs. They were speedily brought to trial before a military commission specially convened by Roosevelt that deviated from prescribed procedures in several respects.

The saboteurs, who had come ashore in June 1942 in Florida and New York from German submarines, were rounded up after one turned informant. Roosevelt's order creating a seven-member commission to try the men authorized the tribunal to admit any "probative" evidence and to recommend a death sentence by a two-thirds vote instead of the normal unanimous verdict.

Seven of the men filed habeas corpus petitions, but the Supreme Court — also departing from regular procedure — rejected their pleas in a summary order issued on July 31, only two days after hearing arguments in the case, known as *Ex parte Quirin*. The court issued a full opinion on Oct. 29 — after six of the men had been executed. The justices unanimously ruled that the offenses fell within the tribunal's jurisdiction. They also upheld the procedures used: Some justices said they complied with the Articles of War; others said the Articles did not apply.[34]

The court again blinked at departures from standard military procedures in its 1946 decision upholding the war-crimes conviction of Gen. Tomoyuki Yamashita, the Japanese commander in the Philippines. Rushed to trial in late October 1945 on charges of failing to prevent wartime atrocities, Yamashita was found guilty and sentenced on Dec. 7 to death by hanging.

Yamashita filed a habeas corpus petition, but the high court rejected his request on Feb. 2, 1946, upholding the military commission's jurisdiction and procedures. In stinging dissents, however, Justices Frank Murphy and Wiley Rutledge strongly attacked, among other things, the validity of the charges, the limited time for Yamashita to prepare a defense and the sufficiency of the evidence against him.[35] He was hanged on Feb. 23.

'Military Justice'

Two major legal reforms adopted after the war fundamentally changed the laws of war. The Geneva Conventions extended previous POW protections to combatants in conflicts other than those between nation-states. The Uniform Code of Military Justice (UCMJ), approved by Congress in 1950, brought civilian-like procedures and protections into a system previously focused on discipline and command authority.

The widespread atrocities committed during World War II against civilians, combatants and POWs led humanitarian groups to strengthen the protections for wartime captives initially established by the Geneva Convention of 1929. The resulting four accords — signed in Geneva in 1949 — outlined provisions for treating "the wounded and sick" on the battlefield or at sea, prisoners of war and civilians. Each accord also included Common Article 3, which extends basic protections against violence, humiliating or degrading treatment and summary punishment to non-traditional conflicts such as civil wars or conflicts in which at least one side is not a nation-state. The Senate ratified the four treaties in 1954.

One purpose of the UCMJ was to establish a uniform system of military justice for what were then three services: Army, Navy and Coast Guard. But it was also intended to respond to criticism of the Army and Navy justice systems as unfair to service members accused of offenses. Harvard law Professor Edmund Morgan, who headed the committee that drafted the proposed code, said it was designed to "provide full protection of the rights of persons subject to the code without undue interference with appropriate military discipline and the exercise of appropriate military functions." Morgan's draft was introduced in Congress in February 1949 and formed the principal basis for the final version approved by Congress in May 1950.[36]

Another development would become crucial to the present debate over detainees. U.S. law and the military code of conduct embraced Common Article 3, as the

Supreme Court majority noted in its *Hamdan* decision.[37]

However, the United States exceeded that minimum treatment threshold during the Vietnam War. In 1966, the U.S. Military Assistance Command in Vietnam ordered enemy captives to be granted prisoner of war status, even if they belonged to the guerrilla force known as the Vietcong (which fought alongside the regular North Vietnamese Army). Vietcong captured performing "terrorism, sabotage or spying" operations were classified as civilian defendants and were to be treated under the Geneva Conventions.[38]

Military justice also demands punishment for war crimes committed by one's own troops. In the Vietnamese hamlet of My Lai in 1968, U.S. soldiers massacred some 400-500 civilians. Lt. William Calley, the senior officer on scene, was convicted of murder and sentenced to life at hard labor, though the sentence was later reduced to 10 years, and Calley was freed on parole. Calley's commanding officer, Capt. Ernest Medina, was acquitted on charges of failing to control the troops under him because prosecutors couldn't prove that he knew what the soldiers were doing. Two other officers were acquitted of lesser charges.[39]

After Vietnam, new questions about detainees grew out of American support for U.N. "peacekeeping missions." In 1993, efforts by Special Operations troops to capture warlord Mohammed Farah Aidid in Mogadishu, Somalia, went terribly wrong. The U.S. action — depicted in the book and movie "Black Hawk Down" — led to the deaths of 18 Americans. One of the dead soldiers was dragged through the city.

The U.N.'s peacekeeper role in civil conflicts has turned the world organization into an enforcer of the international laws of war. U.N. tribunals have been established to try war-crimes cases arising from massacres during the 1990s and early 2000s in the former Yugoslavia, Rwanda and Sierra Leone. As the new century opened, military justice was coming to be seen as the leading source of law in regions torn by conflict involving irregular forces.[40]

'War on Terror'

Within weeks of the 9/11 terrorist attacks on the World Trade Center and the Pentagon, President Bush and other administration officials came to view the capture and detention of al Qaeda members and adherents as critical

Getty Images/Joshua Roberts

Georgetown University Law Professor Neal Katyal, left, and Navy Lt. Commander Charles Swift, lawyers for Guantánamo Bay detainee Salim Ahmed Hamdan, address the media following the Supreme Court's ruling against the Bush administration's proposed military tribunals on June 29, 2006. The court ruled the tribunals violate both American military law and the Geneva Conventions.

to the president's "war on terror." A month after the 9/11 attacks, an executive order signed by Bush on Nov. 13, 2001, calling for "enemy combatants" to be detained outside the United States and tried outside regular civilian or military courts, provoked immediate criticism and legal challenges. But the administration vigorously defended its plans and resisted changes, even after adverse court rulings.[41]

Bush's order directed that al Qaeda members, other terrorists and any others who had "harbored" them were to be "placed in the custody of the secretary of Defense," tried by military commissions to be created under newly written rules and regulations and denied any right to "seek the aid of" any U.S. court or international tribunal. Administration officials said the national terrorism emergency required special procedures, but the order drew immediate criticism from a variety of sources, including military lawyers, civil libertarians, constitutional scholars and members of Congress from both parties.

Late in December, Defense Secretary Donald H. Rumsfeld announced that detainees from Afghanistan would be transported to Guantánamo — "the least worst place," he called it — but that no trials would be held there. The Pentagon first issued procedures for the tribunals in March 2002 in so-called Order No. 1, with still no trial site specified. More detailed rules continued to come

Military Lawyers Endorse Geneva Rules

The sight of uniformed officers arguing that detainees deserve more legal rights may cause some observers to wonder if the military has gone soft. But retired Air Force Col. Katherine Newell Bierman is among those who argue that treating prisoners humanely — aside from being legally required — simply makes good sense militarily.

"It's common-sense war fighting," says Bierman, now counterterrorism counsel for the advocacy group Human Rights Watch. "If you don't have some control over how your people are behaving, you lose discipline."

For Bierman as well as many active-duty military lawyers, the Geneva Conventions provide that control.

"When we train Marines, and soldiers, sailors and airmen, when we talk about handling people that we grab or get on the battlefield, we're normally talking in context of the Geneva Conventions regarding prisoners of war," Brig. Gen. Kevin Sandkuhler, the Marine Corps' top legal officer, told the Senate Armed Services Committee in July.

Administration officials suggest the military attorneys are making the classic soldier's mistake of fighting today's war with yesterday's doctrines. Attorney General Alberto R. Gonzales, testifying at a later hearing, echoed Republican lawmakers' comments that Geneva language such as "humiliating and degrading treatment," aren't adequately defined. "I wonder, given the times that we currently live in and given this new enemy and this new kind of conflict, whether all of the provisions continue to make sense," Gonzales said, adding that he wasn't "in any way suggesting a retreat from the basic principles of Geneva, in terms of the humanitarian treatment."

In early 2006, recently retired generals began leveling attacks at Defense Secretary Donald H. Rumsfeld and, in some cases, at the Iraq war itself. "It speaks volumes that guys like me are speaking out from retirement about the leadership climate in the Department of Defense," said retired Maj. Gen. John Batiste, who led an infantry division in Iraq in 2004-2005. "I think we need a fresh start," he said.[1]

Another Iraq war veteran, retired Army Maj. Gen., Charles H. Swannack Jr., said Rumsfeld had "culpability" for abuse and torture at Abu Ghraib prison in Iraq.[2]

The attacks on Rumsfeld by retired generals, combined with criticism of the administration's detainee policy from military lawyers, led a noted constitutional scholar to remark half-jokingly that military-civilian relations had undergone a drastic change.

"For the first time in our nation's history, a military takeover of the government would move the country slightly to the left," Walter Dellinger quipped at a July 26 discussion of the *Hamdan* decision sponsored by the liberal

out through 2003, but the delays also reflected the administration's decision to give priority to interrogating detainees, not trying them.

With criticism of the procedures continuing, the administration in early 2002 also began facing court challenges. Two groups of Guantánamo detainees filed habeas corpus petitions in federal court in Washington, D.C., in February and May, generally denying involvement with al Qaeda and challenging their detention without trial or even charges. The administration argued not only that federal courts had no authority over Guantánamo since it was outside the United States but also that the president's war powers justified his actions. Two more habeas petitions were filed in June by two U.S. citizens — José Padilla and Yaser Hamdi — who were being held as enemy combatants, also without charges, at a naval brig in Charleston, S.C.

After lower-court proceedings, the cases reached the Supreme Court, which handed the administration limited but unmistakable setbacks on June 28, 2004. In the consolidated Guantánamo cases, the court ruled, 6-3, that federal courts could exercise jurisdiction over Guantánamo prisoners' challenges. The majority noted that unlike the situation that prompted a contrary ruling in 1950, the government had virtual control over the Guantánamo base.[42]

The ruling in *Rasul v. Bush* settled only the jurisdictional issue and left all other questions for further development in lower courts. In the *Hamdi* and *Padilla* cases, the court upheld the president's authority to detain a U.S. citizen

American Constitution Society for Law and Policy. Dellinger, now a professor at Duke University law school, was acting solicitor general under President Bill Clinton.

A conservative fellow panelist, a former lawyer during the Reagan and George H.W. Bush administrations, David B. Rivkin Jr., challenged military lawyers' oft-stated insistence that humane detention policies help assure civilized treatment of American military prisoners. "It is rubbish to talk about how our POWs will be mistreated" if the U.S. does not abide by the Geneva Conventions, he said, citing a consistent pattern of abuse and torture of U.S. POWs since World War II, including Korea and Vietnam. "The notion that the head cutters and the torturers are going to be motivated to behave better if we accord them Geneva treatment is laughable."

Meanwhile, criticism of administration detainee policies has emerged among civilians as well as the military. William H. Taft IV, a former legal adviser to Secretary of State Colin Powell, was among the first internal critics of prisoner policy when it was developed in 2001-2002. Powell himself warned then-Counsel to the President Gonzales that not applying Geneva Conventions standards to the detainees would "reverse over a century of U.S. policy and practice in supporting the Geneva Conventions and undermine the protections of the law of war for our troops, both in this specific conflict and in general."[3]

Another civilian critic, former Navy general counsel Alberto J. Mora, urged the administration to stop the mistreatment of prisoners at Guantánamo. "I was appalled by the whole thing," Mora told Jane Mayer of *The New Yorker* after resigning. "It was clearly abusive, and it was clearly contrary to everything we were ever taught about American values."[4]

Military lawyers, for their part, also cite professional pride in advocating adherence to the Geneva rules. "When we get a conviction, we can say forthrightly that we won because we had the best evidence — as opposed to, 'The [defendant] wasn't in the courtroom and didn't get to see any of the evidence against him,' " says Hardy Vieux, a former Navy JAG lawyer who serves on the board of the nonprofit National Institute of Military Justice.

Among institute members, virtually all of them former military lawyers, "We're unanimous" in supporting a return to Geneva Convention rules, says Vieux. "I don't know of a dissenting voice."

---

[1] Thomas E. Ricks, "Rumsfeld Rebuked by Retired Generals," *The Washington Post*, April 13, 2006, p. A1.

[2] Peter Spiegel, "Another Retired General Joins Battalion of Rumsfeld Critics," *Los Angeles Times*, April 14, 2006, p. A5.

[3] Quoted in Colin L. Powell, "Memorandum To: Counsel to the President; Assistant to the President for National Security Affairs," Jan. 26, 2002. See also, William H. Taft IV, "Memorandum, to: Counsel to the President," Feb. 2, 2002; The memos, along with other internal administration documents concerning U.S. policy toward detainees, are available at www.nytimes.com/ref/international/24MEMO-GUIDE.html.

[4] Jane Mayer, "The Memo; how an internal effort to ban the abuse and torture of detainees was thwarted," *The New Yorker*, Feb. 27, 2006, p. 32. Mora's 22-page memo to the Navy's inspector general is available at www.newyorker.com/images/pdfs/moramemo.pdf.

---

as an enemy combatant but also required some form of hearing before "a neutral decision-maker."[43]

In the meantime, Hamdan had been designated as eligible for trial by a military commission in July 2003, and a single charge of "conspiracy" was filed a year later, in July 2004.

The charging document accused Hamdan of "willingly and knowingly" joining al Qaeda in order to commit terrorism; it specified as "overt acts" his serving as bin Laden's driver, delivering weapons and receiving arms training. Hamdan's trial opened at Guantánamo on Aug. 28 — the first of the military commission proceedings — even as his lawyers were pressing his habeas corpus petition.

An initial ruling granting Hamdan's petition put the trial on hold while the government appealed. The federal appeals court in Washington reversed the ruling in July 2005. His lawyers then appealed to the Supreme Court, which heard his case in March 2006.

Congress then entered the picture by passing the Detainee Treatment Act, which Bush signed on Dec. 30, 2005. Although its anti-torture provision received most of the attention, the act also curtailed judicial review of the Guantánamo cases. In two sections, the law limited review of decisions by the Combatant Status Review Tribunals. The new law also barred federal courts from hearing habeas corpus petitions filed by the Guantánamo detainees, but it did not say whether that provision applied to pending cases such as Hamdan's.

In ruling in Hamdan's case on June 29, the court held that the Detainee Treatment Act did not eliminate the

President George W. Bush answers questions on the treatment of detainees at Guantánamo Bay during a joint press conference with Japanese Prime Minister Junichiro Koizumi at the White House on June 29, 2006, following the Supreme Court's rejection of the administration's trial and detention system.

court's jurisdiction over the case and that the military commissions established by Bush violated both the Uniform Code of Military Justice and the Geneva Conventions. In separate opinions, Justices John Paul Stevens and Anthony M. Kennedy faulted several departures in the tribunal rules from regular court-martial procedures, including provisions to exclude the accused from portions of a trial, to allow hearsay evidence and to use non-lawyer judges who would not be appointed by the judge advocate general. In a brief concurrence, Justice Stephen G. Breyer added, "Nothing prevents the president from returning to Congress to seek the authority he believes necessary."

CURRENT SITUATION

Allowing Coercion?

The Bush administration, Senate and House committees and military and civilian lawyers of all stripes are arguing over whether testimony obtained under duress should be allowed in military trials of alleged terrorists.

A series of congressional hearings in the weeks following the *Hamdan* decision have been marked by administration attempts to preserve military commissions as they were first established by presidential order. After bad reviews from lawmakers and military lawyers, administration officials have been proposing commissions modeled more

closely on courts-martial — but with permissive evidence rules that would allow coercive interrogations.[44]

"As we talk about whether or not coerced testimony should come in," Gonzales told the Senate Armed Services Committee on Aug. 2, "our thinking is that if it's reliable and if it's probative, as determined by a certified military judge, that it should come in. If you say that coerced testimony cannot come in, everyone is going to claim evidence has been coerced. Then we'll get into a fight with respect to every prosecution as to what is, in fact, coerced or what is not coerced."[45]

Maj. Gen. Scott C. Black, the Army's judge advocate general, opposed the use of coercion. "I don't believe that a statement that is obtained under coercive — under torture, certainly, and under coercive measures — should be admissible," he told the Senate Judiciary Committee on Aug. 2, 2006.[46]

On the same day, Attorney General Gonzales was explaining the administration's position. At a Senate Armed Services Committee hearing, Sen. McCain asked Gonzales if statements obtained through "illegal, inhumane treatment should be admissible."

After a long pause, Gonzales haltingly replied: "The concern that I would have about such a prohibition is, What does it mean? . . . If we could all reach agreement about the definition of cruel, inhumane and degrading treatment, then perhaps I could give you an answer. . . . Depending on your definition of something as degrading, such as insults, I would say that information should still come in."[47]

McCain called the proposal to use coercion a "radical departure" from standards of military conduct. And, he said, "We must remain a nation that is different from, and above, our enemies."

The exchanges showed that the question of whether torture or rough treatment is permissible remains very much alive, despite the Supreme Court's *Hamdan* decision, which ruled that Common Article 3 should apply to Guantánamo detainees. Even lawyers who support the Common Article 3 standard agreed that Congress isn't bound to uphold it.

"Sure, Congress could effectively disavow Common Article 3 by passing an inconsistent law," says military law expert Fidell. Constitutional scholar Laurence H. Tribe of Harvard Law School writes, however, that doing so would effectively require the United States to jettison all the other Geneva Conventions as well.

Should detainee trials before military commissions be based on courts-martial?

YES — Eugene R. Fidell
President, National Institute of Military Justice

From testimony before the
Senate Armed Services Committee, July 19, 2006

The National Institute of Military Justice believes that the highest priority for military justice is the achievement of public confidence in the administration of justice. The institute's basic approach is to strongly tilt military commissions in the direction of general courts-martial, our felony-level military court.

[T]here's no question that Congress cannot legislate every jot and tittle of the system . . . there is always going to be some presidential rulemaking. The president [should have the] power to depart from the Uniform Code of Military Justice (UCMJ) model [by stating] with particularity those facts that render it impracticable to follow the general court-martial model on any particular point — not a blanket presidential determination that general court-martial rules are impracticable across-the-board.

The president will not have satisfied the requirement if his justification is filled with vague generalities. Our proposal requires that Congress be notified of any determination of impracticability. Congress should stand ready to review determinations and intervene with legislation. And the president's determination that some rule is impracticable [would be] subject to judicial review for abuse of discretion or on the ground that it is contrary to law.

Congress could take certain things off the table — for example, the right to select your own uniformed defense counsel. Congress could conclude that that is part of the deluxe version of military justice that need not be extended to enemy combatants in the context of a military commission.

Congress might also conclude that some provisions are so critical to public confidence in the administration of justice that they should be placed beyond the president's power to make exceptions. Congress has already said that we don't want coerced testimony in a court-martial. I can't imagine that Congress would take a different position in a military commission.

"Public confidence in the administration of justice" is not another way of saying we have 100 percent assurance that every person who is charged will be convicted. Rather it is a shorthand way of summarizing all of those deeply held values that reflect the commitment of the Founders to due process of law and fundamental fairness. This sounds like an obvious proposition, but it bears repeating because there are those who believe the military commission system rules must ensure convictions. I believe they must ensure fairness. If that means some who are guilty may not ultimately be convicted, that is the price we pay for having a legal system.

NO — James J. Carafano
Senior Research Fellow, The Heritage Foundation

From testimony before the
Senate Armed Services Committee, July 19, 2006

President Bush was right to argue that the concerted effort to destroy the capacity of transnational groups who seek to turn terrorism into a global corporate enterprise ought to be viewed as a long war. The Uniform Code of Military Justice (UCMJ) is not at all appropriate for the long war [because it] puts the protection of the right of the individual foremost, and then adds in accommodations for national security and military necessity.

For example, the UCMJ requires informing servicemen suspected of a crime of their Miranda rights. The exercise of Miranda rights is impractical on the battlefield. Hearsay evidence is prohibited in a court-martial. On the battlefield, reliable hearsay may be the only kind of evidence that can be obtained about the specific activities of combatants. Likewise, overly lenient evidentiary rules make sense when trying a U.S. soldier for a theft committed on base, but not when someone is captured on the battlefield and is being tried for war crimes committed prior to capture, perhaps in another part of the world.

Rather than amend court-martial procedures to address security concerns, it would be preferable to draft military commissions that put the interests of national security first, and then amend them to ensure that equitable elements of due process are included in the procedures.

After Sept. 11, the Bush administration's critics framed a false debate that indicated citizens had a choice between being safe and being free, arguing that virtually every exercise of executive power is an infringement on liberties and human rights. The issue of the treatment of detainees at Guantánamo Bay has been framed in this manner. It is a false debate. Government has a dual responsibility to protect the individual and to protect the nation. The equitable exercise of both is guaranteed when the government exercises power in accordance with the rule of law.

In wartime it's the courts' job to interpret the war, it's the president's job to fight the war and essentially it's the Congress' job to provide the president the right kinds of instruments to do that.

If we respect the purposes of the Geneva Conventions and want to encourage rogue nations and terrorists to follow the laws of war, we must give humane treatment to unlawful combatants. However, we ought not to reward them with the exact same treatment we give our own honorable soldiers. Mimicking the UCMJ sends exactly the wrong signal.

"Unless Congress is prepared to step up to the plate and say it is knocking Geneva out of the park, Geneva should be deemed to remain in place and therefore binding," Tribe wrote to David Remes, a Washington lawyer representing Guantánamo detainees who are challenging their detention (*see below*).[48]

Even before details of the administration proposal began to filter into the press, officials had made clear their opposition to using military-justice standards in terrorism trials for non-citizens.

"Full application of court-martial rules would force the government either to drop prosecutions or to disclose intelligence information to our enemies in such a way as to compromise ongoing or future military operations, the identity of intelligence sources and the lives of many," Dell'Orto, the Pentagon deputy general counsel, told the House Judiciary Committee on July 12. "Military necessity demands a better way."

Administration critics argue that the practicalities of the matter run in the other direction. A congressionally approved version of the military commission would be held up by court challenges, they said. "If . . . after more litigation we find ourselves right back here in four or five more years after we've litigated, then what are we going to end up with?" Lt. Cmdr. Swift, Hamdan's lawyer, asked the Senate Judiciary Committee on July 11. "Neither side will ever get a fair trial, and both Mr. Hamdan and the United States deserve one."

Legally speaking, says Hamdan's co-counsel Katyal, objections that court-martial procedures are too protective of defendants' rights to function effectively in terrorism cases ring hollow. In fact, Katyal told Senate Armed Services members, courts-martial can be closed to keep national-security matters secret, witnesses' identities can be hidden and officers who act as juries can be required to possess security clearances.

Meanwhile, the administration is discussing the possibility of allowing detainees to face life imprisonment or death based on evidence that was never disclosed to the accused at trial.[49]

Beyond the arguments over commissions vs. courts-martial looms a debate over the extent of the president's power. For instance, last December when Bush signed the Detainee Treatment Act banning torture of prisoners in U.S. military custody, he included a "signing statement" that suggested he was not bound by it. Indeed, Gonzales

recently suggested that Bush might be inclined to retain his unilateral approach to terrorist crimes regardless of what Congress does.[50]

A July 18 exchange between Gonzales and Sen. Russell Feingold, D-Wis., made clear the president's views on the limits of congressional power. Feingold asked if Gonzales saw the Supreme Court as having ruled that "the president has to obey the statutes we write."

Gonzales replied: "Of course, we have an obligation to enforce the laws passed by the Congress. But the president also takes an oath, senator, to preserve, protect and defend the Constitution. And if, in fact, there are constitutional rights given to the president of the United States, he has an obligation to enforce those rights."

Other Prisoner Suits

Hamdan is only one of dozens of Guantánamo detainees who have challenged the United States' power to try or to hold them. While Hamdan awaits a government decision on what to do following the Supreme Court's June 29 decision, the rest of the lawsuits are pending in federal appeals court in Washington.

Lawyers for about 65 prisoners held as "unlawful combatants" — but not yet charged with a crime like Hamdan — have filed habeas corpus petitions seeking to have their detentions ruled illegal.

The prisoners argue that the government hasn't proved that any of them fought for al Qaeda or the Taliban. The government has cited decisions by Combatant Status Review Tribunals concluding that the prisoners involved had indeed been fighters. Shortly after the tribunals began, Army Maj. Gen. Geoffrey D. Miller, then in command at Guantánamo said, "I have found no innocent people" at the camp.[51]

During the tribunal hearings, which began in 2004, prisoners appearing before the panels of three military officers had neither lawyers — nor access to the evidence against them. Defense lawyer Remes calls the panels "pseudo-tribunals" designed to give a false impression that evidence had been fully and fairly evaluated in each detainee's case.

At the district court level, the habeas suits have produced contradictory rulings by the two judges who considered the cases. In January 2005, U.S. District Judge Richard J. Leon ruled that courts had little room to challenge the president's right to hold enemy prisoners." Any [judicial] role must be limited when, as here, there is an ongoing armed conflict and the individuals challenging their detention are non-resident aliens."[52]

Less than a month later, Judge Joyce Hens Green reached the opposite conclusion. "Although this nation unquestionably must take strong action under the leadership of the commander in chief to protect itself," she wrote, "that necessity cannot negate the existence of the most basic fundamental rights."[53]

The Guantánamo habeas suits began in 2004, two years after Hamdan's case began. Though *Hamdan* focused on the legality of the military commissions, the Supreme Court's June decision has become an issue in the habeas cases. The Court of Appeals for the District of Columbia Circuit has ordered lawyers on both sides to present written arguments on how the *Hamdan* decision affected the habeas cases.

Government lawyers argued that *Hamdan's* upholding of Common Article 3 wasn't relevant to the habeas prisoners. The Geneva Convention doesn't grant any rights that an individual can go to court to demand, the government said.[54]

Moreover, the prisoners' challenges now have to be started over in the appeals court, which has "exclusive jurisdiction" under the Detainee Treatment Act of 2005, the government lawyers argued.

The prisoners' lawyers maintained that the *Hamdan* decision makes clear that the prisoners can challenge their detentions on the grounds that they violate the Geneva Conventions. The Supreme Court ruled that the conventions can be enforced by American courts, the lawyers said. Remes says habeas litigation could drag on for years. If the appeals court does not rule soon, he warns, the U.S. Supreme Court may not be able to decide the cases until late 2007. "By that time," Remes says, "the men at Guantánamo will have been there for more than five-and-a-half years."

OUTLOOK

'Blistering Fight'

The uncertainty surrounding the future of the war on terrorists makes for hesitancy on all sides about predicting the fate of Guantánamo detainees, and of detainee policy in general.

"We're still in mid-chapter," says military-law expert Fidell. "Our national course in constitutional law is not yet finished."

Ex-prosecutor McCarthy says conflict could arise over whether Common Article 3 creates rights that people in U.S. custody can claim — as opposed to rights that a foreign government would demand for its detained citizens.

"Pro-international law people are arguing that the Supreme Court crossed the Rubicon and made provisions of a treaty judicially enforceable by individuals," McCarthy says. "People on my side of the fence say that the Supreme Court didn't address that issue." The dispute is likely to come to a head in a "blistering fight," he says.

Margulies, who represents some Guantánamo detainees, raises the question of whether Guantánamo prisoners taken in Afghanistan could be held even after combat ended there.

"Could Congress define the conflict in such a way that even if Afghanistan, a sovereign state, orders the United States to leave or the conflict moves to a different place, you can still hold a guy who's picked up in Afghanistan?" he asks. Margulies says the answer is no but acknowledges that others may differ.

Former Justice Department official Kobach agrees that the question of how to define the end of conflict is likely to wind up in court. "If 20 years from now we're still engaged in a worldwide battle against the same enemy organizations, a case might be brought arguing that the war itself is over and the detainees should be released," he says. "I don't think it will fly."

For all the cloudiness obscuring views of the future, advocates on all sides of the divide over how to fight terrorists speak unequivocally about the dangers of taking the wrong path.

Former Reagan and George H.W. Bush administration lawyer Rivkin argues that granting treatment decreed by the Geneva Conventions to terrorists and other "unlawful combatants" would be a major step down the wrong road. "We have a civilization that is besieged by a bunch of barbarians and bad people," he says. "We are dealing with a grave threat to everything, to civilized law and order, to democracy. Much of the rest of the world has abandoned the stigmatization and de-legitimization of unlawful combatants. For us to say, 'We're to treat everyone the same, everyone's going to get the gold standard, everyone's going to get courts-martial,' given where the rest of the world is, would just complete this transformation. It would be unimaginably bad."

Meanwhile, detainees' advocates worry about continued Republican dominance in Washington and its likely effect on Supreme Court makeup.

If 86-year-old Justice John Paul Stevens — a member of the *Hamdan* majority — stays on the bench through the end of the Bush presidency, and the next president is a Democrat, "The Supreme Court will probably not shift to the right," says detainee lawyer Remes."

But if Stevens retires soon and Bush gets to pick his successor, "The Guantánamo prisoners could be dead meat," Remes says. "You could have a Supreme Court majority that would uphold unlimited, unreviewable executive power. That would be a sad day for America."

NOTES

1. Quoted in Richard A. Serrano, "Officials Agree on Prisoners' Status," *Los Angeles Times*, Jan. 29, 2002, p. A9.

2. *Ibid.*; for Bush's definition of prisoners, see David E. Sanger, "President Defends Military Tribunals in Terrorist Cases," *The New York Times*, Nov. 30, 2001, p. A1.

3. A virtual library of books, reports and articles exists on treatment of detainees in the war on terrorists. Selected examples include, "Article 15-6 Investigation of the 800th Military Police Brigade," [Taguba Report on Abu Ghraib], 2004 [undated], www.fas .org/irp/agency/dod/taguba.pdf; Tim Golden, "In U.S. Reports, Brutal Details of 2 Afghan Inmates' Deaths," *The New York Times*, May 20, 2006, p. A1. For a response to critics of U.S. detention practices, see Kenneth Anderson, "An American Gulag? Human rights groups test the limits of moral equivalency," *The Weekly Standard*, Jan 13, 2005. A voluminous file of government documents involving interrogations was released to the American Civil Liberties Union and can be found at www.aclu.org/ safefree/torture/torturefoia.html#.

4. William H. Taft, IV, "Memorandum To: Counsel to the President," Feb. 2, 2002; Colin L. Powell, "Memorandum To: Counsel to the President;

Assistant to the President for National Security Affairs," Jan. 26, 2002. The memos, along with other internal administration documents concerning U.S. policy toward detainees, are available at www .nytimes.com/ref/international/24MEMO-GUIDE.html.

5. The case is *Hamdan v. Rumsfeld*, 05-184 (2006). For an analysis of the court decision, see Kenneth Jost, *Hamdan v. Rumsfeld*, CQ Electronic Library, *CQ Supreme Court Collection* (2006), at http://library .cqpress.com/scc/scyb05-421-18449-991165. Only eight justices participated in the decision; Chief Justice John Roberts recused himself.

6. *Ibid.*

7. "Geneva Convention relative to the treatment of prisoners of war," adopted Aug. 12, 1949, available at www.unhchr.ch/html/menu3/b/91.htm.

8. For background on Graham's career, see Maura Reynolds, "Senate Insider on Military Justice," *Los Angeles Times*, July 13, 2006, p. A20.

9. Alberto R. Gonzales, "Memorandum for the President," Jan. 25, 2002, p. 1. The memo is one of a series of internal Bush administration documents, some leaked and some officially released through a Freedom of Information Act lawsuit by the American Civil Liberties Union. The leaked documents are collected on Web sites of several research and news organizations, including *The New York Times*. See "A Guide to the Memos on Torture," [undated] www .nytimes.com/ref/international/24MEMO-GUIDE. html.

10. For detailed explanations of their opposition, see William H. Taft, IV, "Memorandum To: Counsel to the President," Feb. 2, 2002; Colin L. Powell, "Memorandum To: Counsel to the President; Assistant to the President for National Security Affairs," Jan. 26, 2002, www.nytimes.com/ref/ international/24MEMO-GUIDE.html.

11. The Defense Department maintains updated statistics and other information at the "Detainee Affairs" section of the Pentagon Web site, www.defenselink .mil/home/features/Detainee_Affairs. For a critical analysis of the tribunal rulings, see Mark Denbeaux, Joshua Denbeaux, *et al.*, "Report on Guantánamo Detainees," Seton Hall University School of Law,

Feb. 8, 2006, http://law.shu.edu/news/guantánamo_report_final_2_08_06.pdf.

12. The case was *Hamdi v. Rumsfeld*, 542 U.S. 547 (2004). The Pentagon announced formation of the tribunals about a week after the Supreme Court decision. See John Hendren, "Pentagon Sets Review of Detainees," *Los Angeles Times*, July 8, 2004, p. A13.

13. For the article that broke the Abu Ghraib story, see Seymour Hersh, "Torture at Abu Ghraib," *The New Yorker*, May 10, 2004, www.newyorker.com/fact/content/?040510fa_fact. For the "organ failure" definition, see "Memorandum for Alberto R. Gonzales, Counsel to the President," Aug. 1, 2002, http://fl1.findlaw.com/news.findlaw.com/nytimes/docs/doj/bybee80102mem.pdf. For the Supreme Court decision, see Charles Lane, "Justices Back Detainee Access to U.S. Courts," *The Washington Post*, June 29, 2004, p. A1. For the torture policy revision, see R. Jeffrey Smith and Dan Eggen, "Justice Expands 'Torture' Definition," *The Washington Post*, Dec. 31, 2004, p. A1.

14. For background on McCain, see "John McCain, CQ Politics in America Profile," CQ.com, updated April 2005.

15. For background on Hamdan, see Jonathan Mahler, "The Bush Administration vs. Salim Hamdan," *The New York Times Magazine*, Jan. 8, 2006, p. 44.

16. *Ibid.* The charge against Hamdan, undated and unsigned is available at www.defenselink.mil/news/Jul2004/d20040714hcc.pdf.

17. "Information from Guantánamo Detainees," JTF-GTMO (Joint Task Force-Guantánamo), March 4, 2005, www.defenselink.mil/news/Mar2005/d20050304info.pdf.

18. *Hamdan v. Rumsfeld*, Supreme Court, 548 U.S.__ (2006), pp. 67, 69.

19. "Relative to the Treatment of Prisoners of War, Geneva, 12 August 1949," [Geneva Convention III], http://www.globalissuesgroup.com/geneva/convention3.html; "Text of Geneva Conventions Article 3," The Associated Press, http://seattlepi.nwsource.com/national/1151AP_Guantánamo_Geneva_Conventions.html.

20. For an earlier, shorter list of CIA detainees, see "The United States 'Disappeared': The CIA's Long-Term 'Ghost Detainees,' Human Rights Watch, October 2004, www.hrw.org/backgrounder/usa/us1004. p. 37.

21. "U.S.: Investigate 'Ghost Detainees," Human Rights Watch, Sept. 10, 2004, press release, http://hrw.org/english/docs/2004/09/10/usint9338_txt.htm.

22. Gen. Paul J. Kern quoted in Eric Schmitt and Douglas Jehl, "Army Said C.I.A. Hid More Detainees Than It Claimed," *The New York Times*, Sept. 9, 2004, p. A1.

23. Douglas Jehl and David Johnston, "C.I.A. Expands Its Inquiry Into Interrogation Tactics," *The New York Times*, Aug. 28, 2004, p. A10.

24. For an account of "water-boarding" used on Shaikh Muhammed, see James Risen, David Johnston and Neil A. Lewis, "Harsh C.I.A. Methods Cited in Top Qaeda Interrogations," *The New York Times*, May 12, 2004, p. A1; for a characterization and account of Shaikh Muhammed's role in the 9/11 plot, see *The 9/11 Commission Report* (2004), pp. 145-180.

25. Quoted in Greg Miller, "It's a Tough Time to be the Intelligence Chief," *Los Angeles Times*, Feb. 20, 2004, p. A23.

26. For the first U.S. journalistic reports, see Jane Mayer, "Outsourcing Torture: the secret history of America's 'extraordinary rendition' program," *The New Yorker*, Feb. 14, 2005, p. 106; Craig Whitlock, "A Secret Deportation of Terror Suspects," *The Washington Post*, July 25, 2004, p. A1; Megan K. Stack and Bob Drogin, "Detainee Says U.S. Handed Him Over For Torture," *Los Angeles Times*, Jan. 13, 2004, p. A1.

27. *Ibid.*

28. "CIA Flying Suspects to Torture?" CBS's "60 Minutes II," March 6, 2005, partial transcript available at http://cbs5.com/minutes/sixtyminutes_story_065094819.html.

29. Scott Shane, "Invoking Secrets Privilege Becomes a More Popular Legal Tactic by the U.S.," *The New York Times*, June 4, 2006, p. A32.

30. Background drawn in part from Louis Fisher, *Military Tribunals and Presidential Power: American Revolution to the War on Terrorism* (2005). See also briefs by the following "friends of the court" in

Hamdan v. Rumsfeld: Military Historians; Former
Attorneys General; Citizens for Common Defense,
posted at www.hamdanvrumsfeld.com/briefs (last
visited July 2006).

31. The citation is 71 U.S. 2 (1866). The earlier decision is *Ex parte Vallandingham*, 68 U.S. 243
(1864).

32. Four of the eight Lincoln conspirators were sentenced to death and were hanged on July 7, 1865;
Wirz was hanged on Nov. 10, 1865.

33. The ruling in the curfew case is *Hirabayashi v. United
States*, 320 U.S. 81 (1943); the ruling in the internment case is *Korematsu v. United States*, 323 U.S.
214 (1944). For background, see David Masci,
"Reparations Movement," *CQ Researcher*, June 22,
2001, pp. 529-552.

34. The citation is 317 U.S. 1 (1942). For a full account,
see Louis Fisher, *Nazi Saboteurs on Trial: A Military
Tribunal and American Law* (2003). For background,
see C. E. Noyes, "Sabotage," *Editorial Research Reports,
1941* (Vol. I), available at *CQ Researcher Plus Archives*,
CQ Electronic Library, http://library.cqpress.com.

35. The decision is *In re Yamashita*, 327 U.S. 1 (1946).

36. See Edmund M. Morgan, "The Background of the
Uniform Code of Military Justice," *Military Law
Review*, Vol. 28 (April 1965).

37. *Hamdan v. Rumsfeld, op. cit.*, p. 68, n. 3.

38. For a summary of the Vietnam policy, see Jennifer
Elsea, "Treatment of 'Battlefield Detainees' in the
War on Terrorism," Congressional Research Service,
Sept. 17, 2003, pp. 31-32.

39. For a detailed account of the My Lai massacre and
aftermath, see Maj. Tony Raimondo, "The My Lai
Massacre: A Case Study," School of the Americas,
Fort Benning, Ga. [undated]; http://carlisle-www
.army.mil/usamhi/usarsa/HUMANRT/Human%
20Rights%202000/my-lai.htm. For legal details of
the *Medina* case, see Fisher, *op. cit., Military Tribunals
and Presidential Power*, pp. 153-153.

40. In establishing the tribunals, U.N. member states
aimed explicitly to restore or create the rule of law by
establishing accountability for war crimes and crimes
against humanity. The sites for the Rwanda, Sierra
Leone and former-Yugoslavia tribunals are: Rwanda,
http://69.94.11.53/default.htm; Sierra Leone, www
.sc-sl.org/; former Yugoslavia, www.un.org/icty/.

41. For an overview, see Fisher, *op. cit.*, pp. 168-252; for
Fisher's critical assessment, see pp. 253-260.

42. The earlier case is *Johnson v. Eisentrager*, 339 U.S.
763 (1950).

43. The decisions are *Rasul v. Bush*, 542 U.S. 466 (2004),
and *Hamdi v. Rumsfeld*, 542 U.S. 507 (2004). The
other U.S. citizen case, *Rumsfeld v. Padilla*, 542 U.S.
426 (2004), was dismissed on the grounds it had
been filed in the wrong federal court.

44. For reports on Senate hearings concerning the debate,
see R. Jeffrey Smith, "Top Military Lawyers Oppose
Plan for Special Courts," *The Washington Post*, Aug.
3, 2006, p. A11; and Kate Zernike, "White House
Asks Congress to Define War Crimes," *The New York
Times*, Aug. 3, 2006, p. A16.

45. Committee testimony, Aug. 2, 2006.

46. Smith, *op. cit.*

47. *Ibid.*

48. Tribe's July 11, 2006, letter, confirmed by his office,
was made available by Remes.

49. Jeffrey R. Smith, "On Prosecuting Detainees; Draft
Bill Waives Due Process for Enemy Combatants,"
The Washington Post, July 28, 2006, p. A23.

50. For background see Kenneth Jost, "Presidential
Power," *CQ Researcher*, Feb. 24, 2006, pp. 169-192.

51. Quoted in John Mintz, "Most at Guantánamo to Be
Freed or Sent Home, Officer Says," *The Washington
Post*, Oct. 6, 2004, p. A16. For a detailed look at the
tribunals' operation, see Neil A. Lewis, "Guantánamo
Prisoners Getting Their Day, but Hardly in Court,"
The New York Times, Nov. 8, 2004, p. A1.

52. Quoted in Charles Lane and John Mintz, "Detainees
Lose Bid For Release," *The Washington Post*, Jan. 20,
2005, p. A3.

53. Quoted in Neil A. Lewis, "Judge Extends Legal
Rights For Guantánamo Detainees," *The New York
Times*, Feb. 1, 2005, p. A12.

54. For an analysis of the government's claims, see Lyle
Denniston, "Government: Detainee cases must start
over," Scotusblog, Aug. 1, 2006 (includes a link to
government brief), www.scotusblog.com/movable-
type/archives/2006/08/government_deta_1.html.

BIBLIOGRAPHY

Books

Fisher, Louis, *Military Tribunals & Presidential Power: American Revolution to the War on Terrorism,* University of Kansas Press, 2005.
A specialist at the Library of Congress on the power relationships between the three branches of government closely examines the development of the president's wartime authority in legal matters.

Margulies, Joseph, *Guantánamo and the Abuse of Presidential Power,* Simon & Schuster, 2006.
A law professor at the MacArthur Justice Center at Northwestern University Law School provides a non-legalistic narrative of his experiences in representing Guantánamo detainees.

Saar, Erik, and Viveca Novack, *Inside the Wire: A Military Intelligence Soldier's Eyewitness Account of Life at Guantánamo,* Penguin Press, 2005.
Confusion, ignorance and bigotry plagued the ranks of the military personnel who supervised and interrogated Guantánamo detainees, according to Saar, a former translator and interrogator, and *Time* reporter Novack.

Yoo, John, *The Powers of War and Peace,* University of Chicago Press, 2005.
A former top Justice Department lawyer in 2001-2003 explains how the government's detention policy grew out of the government's belief that presidents have greater power during wartime. Now a law professor at the University of California at Berkeley, Yoo helped craft the policy.

Articles

Golden, Tim, "After Terror, a Secret Rewriting of Military Law," *The New York Times,* Oct. 24, 2004, p. A1.
An investigative reporter digs into the legal and political origins of the detention and trial system centered at Guantánamo Bay.

Mahler, Jonathan, "The Bush Administration vs. Salim Hamdan," *The New York Times Magazine,* Jan. 8, 2006, p. 44.
A New York-based journalist who is writing a book about Hamdan traveled to Yemen to speak to the family of the man at the center of the Supreme Court's latest ruling on detainees.

Mayer, Jane, "The Memo; How an internal effort to ban the abuse and torture of detainees was thwarted," *The New Yorker,* Feb. 27, 2006, p. 32.
A Washington-based staff writer for *The New Yorker* details how the Navy's top civilian lawyer — now resigned — tried and failed to have mistreatment of detainees prohibited.

Rivkin, David B., Jr., and Lee A. Casey, "The Gitmo Decision," "Targeting Illegal Combatants," "Misreading Hamdan v. Rumsfeld," "Bush hatred and constitutional reality," *The Washington Times,* July 11-July 14, 2006.
Conservative lawyers who served in the Reagan and George H.W. Bush administrations lay out legal and political arguments for the present administration's detainee policy.

Weisman, Jonathan, and Michael Abramowitz, "White House Shifts Tack on Tribunals," *The Washington Post,* July 20, 2006, p. A3.
Two reporters track the administration's re-embrace of a harder line concerning detainee treatment following the Supreme Court's Hamdan decision.

Reports and Studies

"JTF-GTMO [Joint Task Force-Guantánamo] Information on Detainees — Information From Guantánamo Detainees," Department of Defense, March 4, 2005.
Detainees have provided valuable information on matters ranging from terrorist support structures to bomb-making techniques to the identities of al Qaeda operatives, according to the Pentagon.

"Report on Torture and Cruel, Inhuman and Degrading Treatment of Prisoners at Guantánamo Bay, Cuba," Center for Constitutional Rights, July 2006.
The liberal group uses notes by lawyers for detainees, government documents, press accounts and other sources to depict what it views as a pattern of treatment that violates international treaties and U.S. law.

"Situation of detainees at Guantánamo Bay," Report of the Chairperson of the Working Group on Arbitrary Detention, United Nations, Feb. 15, 2006.

Legal and physical treatment of detainees violate international treaties that the United States has signed, the U.N. panel concluded.

Elsea, Jennifer, "Treatment of 'Battlefield Detainees' in the War on Terrorism," Congressional Research Service, Sept. 17, 2003.
The CRS dispassionately examines the controversy surrounding detainee treatment in light of history, recent litigation and options facing Congress.

Gardner, Nile, and James J. Carafano, "The UN's Guantánamo Folly: Why the United Nations Report is Not Credible," The Heritage Foundation, Feb. 27, 2006.
Conservative commentators argue that the U.N. report on detainees (above) is politically biased.

For More Information

American Civil Liberties Union, 125 Broad St., New York, NY 10004; www.aclu.org. Obtains and disseminates government documents on detention and litigates on behalf of detainees.

Center for Constitutional Rights, 666 Broadway, 7th Floor, New York, NY 10012; (212) 614-6464; http://ccrjustice.org/. Played a key role in the filing of habeas corpus lawsuits by Guantánamo detainees.

Department of Defense, Public Affairs, 1400 Defense Pentagon, Washington, DC 20301; (703) 428-0711; www.defenselink.mil/home/features/DetaineeAffairs. Provides information on detainees and related matters.

The Heritage Foundation, 214 Massachusetts Ave., N.E., Washington, DC 20002; (202) 546-4400; www.heritage.org. Supports the administration's approach to the detention and trial of prisoners in the war on terror.

MacArthur Justice Center, Northwestern University School of Law, 375 E. Chicago Ave., Chicago, IL 60611; (312) 503-1271; www.law.northwestern.edu/macarthur/. Has been active in representing Guantánamo detainees.

National Institute of Military Justice, 4801 Massachusetts Ave., N.W., Washington, DC 20016; (202) 274-4322; www.wcl.american.edu/nimj/. An organization of retired military lawyers that is participating in the debate on detainee treatment.

Prosecuting Terrorists

18

Should Suspected Terrorists Be Given Military or Civil Trials?

Kenneth Jost

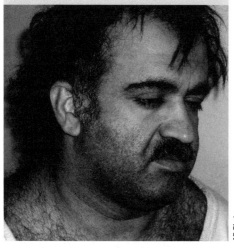

Republican lawmakers say al Qaeda terrorist Khalid Sheikh Mohammed, seen shortly after his capture in Pakistan in 2003, should be treated as an enemy combatant and tried in the military commissions established during the Bush administration. But administration officials and Democratic lawmakers say criminal prosecutions have produced hundreds of convictions since 9/11 compared to only three in the military system.

From *CQ Researcher*,
March 12, 2010.

H e has been described as Osama bin Laden's chief executive officer, the man who conceived the plan to crash hijacked airliners into buildings symbolic of America's political, military and financial power.

Some 18 months after the 9/11 attacks, Pakistani intelligence agents, working with the U.S. Central Intelligence Agency, captured Kuwait-born Khalid Sheikh Mohammed at an al Qaeda safe house in Rawalpindi. Rousted out of bed in the middle of the night, he looked like a street person — not the scion of a well-to-do Pakistani family once known for his expensive tastes and elegant dress.[1]

For the next three years, KSM — as U.S. officials and news media dubbed him — was held at a secret CIA site, reportedly in Poland, where interrogators waterboarded him 183 times in the first month of his captivity. In September 2006 he was transferred to the U.S. prison camp at the Guantánamo Bay naval base in Cuba, to be held awaiting trial.

The trial — on 2,973 counts of murder and other charges — began before a military judge on June 5, 2008, but was thrown into disarray six months later, when Mohammed announced that he and his four co-defendants wanted to plead guilty. A month later, the judge, Army Col. Stephen Henley, agreed to put the trial on hold in response to President Obama's decision, on his first full day in office, to suspend the military trials of all suspected "enemy combatants" being held at Guantánamo.

Now, a year after Obama's interim move, the proceedings against KSM remain in limbo thanks to the full-throttle controversy that erupted after Attorney General Eric Holder announced plans to try

Military Commissions Convicted Three

Three of the terrorism suspects who were detained at Guantánamo Bay — Ali Hamza Ahmad Suliman al Bahlul, Salim Ahmed Hamdan and David Hicks — have been convicted after trials before military commissions. Hicks, known as the "Australian Taliban," and Hamdan, identified as the driver for al Qaeda leader Osama bin Laden, have served their sentences already and been released to their home countries. Al Bahlul awaits a decision on his appeal to his life sentence before a U.S. military judge panel. Hamdan's appeal of his conviction is pending before the same panel; Hicks waived his right of appeal after pleading guilty.

Terrorists Convicted in Military Commissions at Guantánamo Bay

al Bahlul
Nationality: Yemeni
Conviction date: Nov. 3, 2008
Charges: 35 counts of solicitation to commit murder, conspiracy and providing material support for terrorism.
Current status: Sentenced to life in prison; appeal pending before panel of military judges; argued Jan. 26.

AFP/Getty Images

Hamdan
Nationality: Yemeni
Conviction date: Aug. 6, 2008
Charges: Providing material support for terrorism.
Current status: Returned to Yemen and released; appeal pending before panel of military judges; argued Jan. 26.

AFP/Getty Images

Hicks
Nationality: Australian
Conviction date: March 30, 2007
Charges: Providing material support for terrorism.
Current status: Returned to Australia and released

Getty Images

Source: News reports

the five alleged 9/11 conspirators in a federal court in New York City. In announcing his decision on Nov. 13, Holder said the defendants would "answer for their alleged crimes in a courthouse just blocks away from where the twin towers [of the World Trade Center] once stood."[2]

New York City Mayor Michael Bloomberg and Police Commissioner Raymond Kelly welcomed Holder's decision, but many New Yorkers expressed concerns about the costs and risks of a sensational trial in Lower Manhattan. Some families of 9/11 victims also voiced criticism, saying enemies of the United States deserved military tribunals, not civilian courts.

Holder faced a buzz saw of criticism when he appeared before the Senate Judiciary Committee a week later to defend his decision — which he said he made without consulting the White House. Sen. Jeff Sessions of Alabama, the committee's ranking Republican, called the decision "dangerous," "misguided" and "unnecessary."[3]

Criticism of the decision intensified — and became even more overtly politicized — after the Christmas Day arrest of Umar Farouk Abdulmutallab for the attempted bombing of a Northwest Airlines flight bound from Amsterdam to Detroit. Republican lawmakers and former GOP officials, including former Vice President Dick Cheney and former Attorney General Michael Mukasey, strongly criticized the decision to treat Abdulmutallab as a criminal suspect instead of as an enemy combatant. A major focus of the criticism was the decision to advise Abdulmutallab of his Miranda rights not long after his arrest. (*See sidebar, p. 442.*)

GOP lawmakers raised the stakes on the issue by introducing legislation in Congress to prohibit the use of any funds to try KSM in civilian courts. With administration officials and Democratic lawmakers making little headway in quieting the criticism, the White House let it be known in early February that Obama was personally reviewing the planned location for the trial as part of the broader issue of where and how to try the remaining prisoners at Guantánamo.[4]

The trials have been delayed by controversies that began immediately after President George W. Bush decided to use the base to house alleged enemy combatants captured in the Afghanistan war or rounded up from other locations. Instead of using civilian courts or regular military courts — courts-martial — Bush used his power as commander in chief to create military commissions to try the detainees, with fewer procedural rights than courts-martial.[5]

Critics, including a wide array of civil liberties and human rights organizations, denounced the military commissions as a second-class system of justice. They also lent their support to legal challenges filed by some of the prisoners that eventually resulted in Supreme Court decisions guaranteeing judicial review of their cases and forcing some changes in the rules for the commissions.

Because of the legal uncertainties, the military commissions did not produce their first conviction until March 2007 when David Hicks, the so-called Australian Taliban, pleaded guilty to providing material support for terrorism. Two other Guantánamo prisoners were convicted on material-support counts the next year: Salim Ahmed Hamdan, former driver to bin Laden, and Ali Hamza Ahmad Suliman al Bahlul, an al Qaeda filmmaker and propagandist. (*See box, p. 432.*)

Even as the Guantánamo cases moved at a glacial pace, the Bush administration was using federal courts to prosecute hundreds of individuals arrested in the United States on terrorism-related charges. Among the first was Richard Reid, the so-called shoe bomber, who was charged with attempting to blow up a commercial aircraft en route to the United States on Dec. 22, 2001. Reid, an admitted al Qaeda supporter, is now serving a life sentence.

At various points, Bush himself touted the administration's record of convicting hundreds of individuals in terrorism-related cases in criminal courts. In a budget document in 2008, the Justice Department put the number of convictions or guilty pleas at 319 out of 512 individuals prosecuted.[6]

Guidelines Adopted for Detainee Prosecutions

The Justice and Defense departments adopted broadly written guidelines in July 2009 to be used in deciding whether a Guantánamo detainee was to be tried in a civilian court or before a military tribunal. The protocol begins with "a presumption that, where feasible, referred cases will be prosecuted in" federal criminal courts. The two-page agreement lists three categories of factors to be considered in deciding whether "other compelling factors make it more appropriate to prosecute a case in a reformed military commission":

Strength of interest, including where the offense occurred, where the defendant was apprehended and which agency or agencies investigated the case.

Efficiency, including protection of intelligence sources, foreign policy concerns and "legal or evidentiary problems that might attend prosecution in the other jurisdiction."

Other prosecution considerations, including the charges that can be brought and the sentences that can be imposed in one or the other forum.

Source: "Determination of Guantánamo Cases Referred for Prosecution," July 20, 2009, www.justice.gov/opa/documents/taba-prel-rpt-dptf-072009.pdf

More recently, a report written for Human Rights First counted 195 convictions or guilty pleas in al Qaeda- or Taliban-related terrorism cases through July 2, 2009, along with 19 acquittals or dismissals. The report, written by two lawyers who had previously served as federal prosecutors in New York, concluded that the criminal justice system "is well-equipped to handle a broad variety of cases arising from terrorism" associated with al Qaeda or similar groups.[7] (*See sidebar, p. 444.*)

Despite that record, GOP lawmakers, ex-Bush administration officials and conservative experts and advocates are arguing strongly for the use of military commissions to try Abdulmutallab and, apparently, most of the prisoners held at Guantánamo. "Wartime alien enemy combatants should be tried by military commissions in the safety of Guantánamo Bay," says Andrew McCarthy, a contributing editor with *National Review Online* and former federal prosecutor.[8]

While in the U.S. attorney's office in Manhattan, McCarthy was lead prosecutor in the 1995 trial of Omar Abdel Rahman, the so-called Blind Sheik, along with nine others for plotting to blow up various civilian targets in the New York City area. Rahman was convicted of seditious conspiracy and is now serving a life sentence.[9]

Human rights advocates, however, say military commissions have failed to produce results while tarnishing the United States' image both at home and abroad. "The only choice should be trial in civilian courts," says Laura Olson, senior counsel for the rule of law program at the Washington-based Constitution Project. "They're both tougher and more reliable than military commissions."

The Obama administration says civilian trials are the presumptive forum for terrorism cases but is continuing the use of what it calls "reformed" military commissions for some cases. A protocol adopted jointly by the Justice and Defense departments in July 2009 says forum selection will depend on a number of factors, including the agency or agencies involved in the investigation and the charges and sentences available in one or the other forum. Holder designated several Guantánamo prisoners for trial by military commissions on the same day he announced the decision to try KSM in New York City. (*See box, p. 446.*)

Meanwhile, administration officials also are saying that 50 or more Guantánamo prisoners may be held indefinitely without trial because they cannot be prosecuted successfully but are too dangerous to release.[10] Conservatives say the prolonged detentions are justifiable as long as the United States is effectively at war with al Qaeda. Civil liberties advocates strongly disagree.

President Obama cheered human rights groups with his initial moves on counterterrorism policies, especially his pledge to close the Guantánamo prison camp within a year. Now that the deadline has been missed and other policies recalibrated, Obama is drawing some complaints from liberal advocacy groups along with sharp criticism from Republicans and conservative groups for the planned use of federal courts to try enemy combatants.

Here are some of the major issues the administration faces:

Should suspected terrorists be tried in civilian courts?

When the FBI got wind of a group of Yemeni Americans who had trained at an al Qaeda camp in 2001 and returned to their homes in the Buffalo, N.Y., suburb of Lackawanna, Bush administration's officials were divided on what to do.

Vice President Dick Cheney and Defense Secretary Donald Rumsfeld wanted to use troops to arrest the men and treat them as enemy combatants to be tried before a military commission. President Bush, however, sided with Attorney General John Ashcroft and FBI Director Robert Mueller, who favored using federal agents to arrest the men and trying them in a federal court.

In the end, the men were arrested without incident on Sept. 14, 2002, and over the next year pleaded guilty and received prison sentences ranging from seven to 10 years for supporting a foreign terrorist organization. They also cooperated with authorities in providing information about al Qaeda, and three of them testified in the 2008 military commission trial of the al Qaeda filmmaker Bahlul.[11]

Supporters of criminal prosecutions — including but not limited to human rights and civil liberties groups — say prosecutions such as the Lackawanna Six case prove civilian courts can mete out effective, tough justice in terrorism-related cases without shortchanging constitutional rights.

"The criminal justice system is reasonably well-equipped to handle most international terrorism cases," New York attorneys Richard B. Zabel and James J. Benjamin Jr. wrote in the Human Rights First report in May 2008. A year later, the two former federal prosecutors reiterated that civilian court prosecutions had generally led to "just, reliable results" without causing security breaches or other harms to national security.[12]

National security-minded critics and some non-ideological experts counter that the rights accorded defendants in the criminal justice system do pose potential obstacles to successful prosecutions in some terrorism cases. "Civilian trials should be a secondary option," says David Rivkin, a former Justice Department official in the Bush administration now affiliated with the hawkish Foundation for the Defense of Democracies. Among other problems, Rivkin says classified information is harder to protect in a civilian court than in a military commission despite a federal law, the Classified Information Procedure Act (CIPA), which limits disclosure in federal trials.

"The federal courts have some real limitations," agrees Benjamin Wittes, a research fellow at the Brookings Institution and author of several influential reports about war-on-terror policies. He cites as examples the beyond-a-reasonable-doubt standard used in criminal prosecutions and the stricter standard on use of evidence obtained under coercive interrogation. Still, Wittes adds, the problems are "not as big as conservatives claim."

Critics assailed the decision to try the 9/11 conspiracy case in New York City in particular as a security risk. Rivkin complains of "the logistical nightmare" that would be created by a trial in a major metropolitan area such as New York.

When Holder visited New York to discuss plans for the trial in December, however, a Justice Department spokesman declared, "We have a robust plan developed by both federal and local officials to ensure that these trials can be safely held in New York, and everyone is committed to doing that."[13]

Above any practical considerations, however, critics such as Rivkin say simply that criminal prosecutions signal a wrong approach in the nation's fight against al Qaeda. "This is a long and difficult war," he says. "It is essential for any administration to inculcate the notion that this is a real war. And it is utterly jarring in that context to take enemy combatants, particularly high-value ones, and treat them as common criminals."

Benjamin counters that the criminal justice system in fact amounts to one of the United States' most effective weapons in the war on terror. "We are at war," he says. "One of the unique features of this particular war is that many of the people on the other side are violating our criminal law. If we can develop the evidence and successfully put them away, why in the world would we foreclose ourselves from doing that?"

Should suspected terrorists be tried in military tribunals?

Attorney General Holder's decision to try seven Guantánamo detainees in military commissions represents only a modest step toward resolving the cases of the remaining prisoners there. (*See box, p. 446.*) But the trials, if completed, would more than double the number of cases resolved by military tribunals since President Bush authorized them less than two months after the 9/11 attacks.

Supporters say history, law and national security justify the use of military tribunals to try enemy combatants. They blame opponents for the legal controversies that have limited their use so far.

"The record has been underwhelming," concedes ex-Justice Department attorney Rivkin. "Why should we be surprised? There has been a concentrated effort from day one to litigate against them."

Human rights and civil liberties groups counter that the military tribunals were flawed from the outset and, despite some recent reforms, still have significant problems and will face additional legal challenges.

"They remain vulnerable to constitutional challenge," says Olson of the Constitution Project. "We're going to have to go through this litigation for years and years."

In contrast to the three men convicted so far by military commissions, the prisoners that Holder designated in his Nov. 13 announcement for trial by military commissions include figures alleged to have played significant roles in al Qaeda operations. They include Abd al Rahim al Nashiri, a Yemeni accused of plotting the October 2000 attack on the *USS Cole*, and Noor Uthman Mohammed, a Sudanese alleged to have assisted in running an al Qaeda training center in Afghanistan.

The accusations against some of the others, however, depict them as hardly more than al Qaeda foot soldiers. The group includes Omar Khadr, the youngest Guantánamo detainee, who was captured at age 15 after a firefight in Afghanistan. Now 23, the Canadian citizen faces a charge of providing support for terrorism by throwing a grenade that killed a U.S. soldier. The charge goes against the United Nations' position that children should not be prosecuted for war crimes.[14]

In announcing his decisions on the legal forum to be used, Holder gave no explanation of the reasons for designating some of the prisoners for trial by military commissions. But he did say that recent changes approved by Congress for the commissions "will ensure that commission trials are fair, effective and lawful." Those changes include limits on use of hearsay and coerced testimony and greater access for defendants to witnesses and evidence.

Despite the changes, human rights advocates continue to oppose use of the military commissions. "We don't quarrel with military justice," says Ben Winzer, a staff attorney with the American Civil Liberties Union's (ACLU) national security project. "The problem is that even the modified military commissions are being used to paper over weaknesses in the government's evidence."

"Most of the growing pains have been alleviated," counters Rivkin. "The solution now is to stand them up,

AFP/Getty Images/Don Emmert

Omar Abdel Rahman, the so-called Blind Sheik, was convicted in a civilian criminal trial in 1995 along with nine others for plotting to blow up various civilian targets in the New York City area. Rahman is now serving a life sentence. Andrew McCarthy, the then-lead prosecutor for the U.S. attorney's office, is now a contributing editor with *National Review Online*, a conservative publication. He now says, "Wartime alien enemy combatants should be tried by military commissions in the safety of Guantánamo Bay."

make them work, give them the right resources and get out of the way."

For his part, Brookings Institution expert Wittes says the military commissions "have significantly underperformed to date" and continue to face a host of practical and legal difficulties. "We worry that the military commissions will present issues of their own, particularly with respect to challenges to the lawfulness and integrity of the system itself," he says. "And the rules have been used so little that there are a lot of issues about how the system works."

Among the most important pending issues is the question whether material support of terrorism — a mainstay of criminal prosecutions — is an offense that

can be tried in a military tribunal. The review panel established to hear appeals from the military commissions currently has that issue under advisement after arguments in two cases in January.

"No one questions that these are crimes, but there are special rules that come into play when we start talking about what crimes military commissions can prosecute," says Stephen Vladeck, a law professor at American University in Washington. "I think there are far fewer cases in which the government realistically has a choice between civilian and military courts than we might think, if for no other reason than the jurisdiction of military commissions is actually tightly circumscribed by the Constitution."

Should some Guantánamo detainees be held indefinitely without trial?

In his first major speech on how to deal with the Guantánamo prisoners, President Obama called in May 2009 for "prolonged detention" for any detainees "who cannot be prosecuted yet who pose a clear danger to the American people." Obama said he would work with Congress to "construct a legitimate legal framework" for such cases, but added: "I am not going to release individuals who endanger the American people."[15]

In the nine months since, neither Congress nor the president has put any appreciable work into possible legislation on the issue. Now, administration officials are estimating 50 or more detainees will have to be held without trial, but they have not listed names or described procedures being used to designate individuals for that category.

The ACLU and other human rights groups immediately denounced Obama's remarks on the issue and continue to oppose detention without trial. The administration's conservative critics approve of holding some prisoners without trial but fault the administration for its efforts to transfer others to their home countries or other host nations because they might return to hostilities against the United States.

"The term is detention for the duration of hostilities," says Rivkin. "Those rules have been in place since time immemorial. They are not meant to punish anybody; they are designed to prevent someone from going back to the battlefield."

Rivkin says the policy of transferring prisoners to other countries — begun by the Bush administration and continued by Obama — amounts to "a revolving door" for terrorists. "We know for sure that they go back

Khalid Sheikh Mohammed and the 9/11 Attacks

Khalid Sheikh Mohammed, self-described mastermind of the Sept. 11 terrorist attacks, faces trial in federal court on 2,973 counts of murder and other charges along with his four co-defendants. Kuwait-born KSM first claimed to have organized the 9/11 attacks during interrogations in which he was waterboarded 183 times. In March 2007, at a hearing at the Guantánamo Bay prison, he said he was responsible for the attacks "from A to Z" — as well as for 30 other terrorist plots. The five co-defendants now face nine charges including conspiracy, terrorism, providing material support for terrorism and murder. Controversy erupted over Attorney General Eric Holder's plan to hold the trial in New York City, and the location of the trial is now being reconsidered. KSM's four co-defendants are:

• **Ramzi Bin al-Shibh (Yemen)** — Alleged "coordinator" of the attacks after he was denied a visa to enter the United States.

• **Walid bin Attash (Saudi Arabia)** — Charged with selecting and training several of the hijackers of the attacks.

• **Ali Abdul Aziz Ali (Pakistan)** — Allegedly helped hijackers obtain plane tickets, traveler's checks and hotel reservations. Also taught them the culture and customs of the West.

• **Mustafa Ahmed al-Hawsawi (Saudi Arabia)** — Allegedly an organizer and financier of the attacks.

to combat," Rivkin says. "This is the first war in human history where we cannot hold in custody a captured enemy. That's a hell of a way to run a war."

ACLU lawyer Winzer calls Obama's detention-without-trial proposal "an extraordinarily controversial statement in a country governed by the rule of law." Anyone "truly dangerous" should be and likely can be prosecuted, Winzer says. "Our material-support laws are so broad that if we don't have legitimate evidence to convict [detainees] under those laws, it's hard to accept that they are too dangerous to release."

Allegations that some of the released Guantánamo prisoners have returned to hostilities against the United States stem from studies released by the Pentagon during the Bush administration and sharply challenged by some human rights advocates. The final of three studies, released in January 2009 only one week before Bush was to leave office, claimed that 61 out of 517 detainees released had "returned to the battlefield."

But an examination of the evidence by Mark Denbeaux, a law professor at Seton Hall University in South Orange, N.J., and counsel to two Guantánamo detainees, depicts the Pentagon's count as largely unsubstantiated. In any event, Denbeaux says the Pentagon's count is exaggerated because it includes former prisoners who have done nothing more after their release than engage in propaganda against the United States.[16]

Supporters of detention without trial cite as authority the first of the Supreme Court's post-9/11 decisions,

Hamdi v. Rumsfeld.[17] In that 2004 ruling, a majority of the justices agreed that the legislation Congress passed in 2001 to authorize the Afghanistan war included authority for the detention of enemy combatants. In the main opinion, Justice Sandra Day O'Connor said a detainee was entitled to some opportunity to contest allegations against him, but did not specify what kind of procedure.

The court rulings appear to support the government's power "to hold people indefinitely without charge if they are associated with al Qaeda or the Taliban in the same way that a solider is associated with an army," says Benjamin, coauthor of the Human Rights First report. Law professor Vladeck agrees, but says the number of people in that category is likely to be "small."

Brookings Institution expert Wittes defends the practice "philosophically" but acknowledges practical problems, including public reaction both in the United States and abroad. "The first risk is that it's perceived as the least legitimate option, domestically or internationally," he says. "It's not the way you like to do business."

The evidence needed to justify detention has been the major issue in the dozens of habeas corpus petitions filed by Guantánamo prisoners. Federal district judges in Washington who have been hearing the cases have mostly decided against the government, according to a compilation coauthored by Wittes.[18]

Wittes has long urged Congress to enact legislation to define the scope of indefinite detention. In an unusual interview, three of the judges handling the cases agreed. "It should be Congress that decides a policy such as this," Judge Reggie Walton told the online news site *ProPublica*.[19]

But David Cole, a law professor at Georgetown University in Washington and prominent critic of the detention policies, disagrees. The issues, Cole says, "require careful case-by-case application of standards. It's a job for judges, not Congress."[20]

BACKGROUND

Power and Precedent

The United States faced the issue of how to deal with captured members or supporters of al Qaeda or the Taliban with no exact historical parallel as guidance. The use of military tribunals for saboteurs, spies or enemy sympathizers dated from the American Revolution but had been controversial in several instances, including during the Civil War and World War II. After World War II, military commissions became — in the words of Brookings expert Wittes — "a dead institution." The rise of international terrorism in the 1980s and '90s was met with military reprisals in some instances and a pair of notable U.S. prosecutions of Islamist extremists in the 1990s.[21]

As commander of the revolutionary army, Gen. George Washington convened military tribunals to try suspected spies — most notably, Major John André, Benedict Arnold's coconspirator, who was convicted, sentenced to death and hanged. During the War of 1812 and the First Seminole War (1817-1818). Gen. Andrew Jackson was criticized for expansive use of his powers as military commander — most notably, for having two British subjects put to death for inciting the Creek Indians against the United States. During the occupation of Mexico in the Mexican-American War, Gen. Winfield Scott established — without clear statutory authority — "military councils" to try Mexicans for a variety of offenses, including guerrilla warfare against U.S. troops.

The use of military tribunals by President Abraham Lincoln's administration during the Civil War provoked sharp criticism at the time and remains controversial today. Lincoln acted unilaterally to suspend the writ of habeas corpus in May 1861, defied Chief Justice Roger Taney's rebuke of the action and only belatedly got Congress to ratify his decision. More than 2,000 cases were tried by military commissions during the war and Reconstruction. Tribunals ignored some judicial orders to release prisoners.

Lincoln, however, overturned some decisions that he found too harsh. As the war continued, the Supreme Court turned aside one challenge to the military commissions, but in 1866 — with the war ended — held that military tribunals should not be used if civilian courts are operating.[22]

During World War II, President Franklin D. Roosevelt prevailed in three Supreme Court challenges to expansive use of his powers as commander in chief in domestic settings. Best known are the court's decisions in 1943 and 1944 upholding the wartime curfew on the West Coast and the internment of Japanese-Americans. Earlier, the court in 1942 had given summary approval to the convictions and death sentences of German saboteurs captured in June and tried the next month before hastily convened military commissions. Roosevelt's order convening the seven-member tribunals specified that the death penalty could be imposed by a two-thirds majority instead of the normal unanimous vote. The Supreme Court heard habeas corpus petitions filed by seven of the eight men but rejected their claims in a summary order in the case, *Ex parte Quirin*, on July 31. Six of the men had been executed before the justices issued their formal opinion on Oct. 29.[23]

International law governing wartime captives and domestic law governing military justice were both significantly reformed after World War II in ways that cast doubt on the previous ad hoc nature of military commissions. The Geneva Conventions — signed in 1949 and ratified by the Senate in 1954 — strengthened previous protections for wartime captives by, among other things, prohibiting summary punishment even for combatants in non-traditional conflicts such as civil wars. The Uniform Code of Military Justice, approved by Congress in 1950, brought civilian-like procedures into a system previously built on command and discipline. The United States went beyond the requirements of the Geneva Conventions in the Vietnam War by giving full prisoner-of-war status to enemy captives, whether they belonged to the regular North Vietnamese army or the guerrilla Vietcong.

International terrorism grew from a sporadic problem for the United States in the 1970s to a major concern in the 1980s and '90s. The results of foreign prosecutions in two of the major incidents in the '80s left many Americans disappointed. An Italian jury imposed a 30-year sentence in 1987 on Magid al-Molqi after the Palestinian confessed to the murder of U.S. citizen Leon Klinghoffer during the 1985 hijacking of the cruise ship *Achille Lauro*; the prosecution had sought a life term. The bombing of

Pan Am Flight 103 over Scotland in 1988 — and the deaths of 189 Americans among the 270 victims — resulted in the long-delayed trial of Abdel Basset Ali al-Megrahi, former head of the Libyan secret service. Megrahi was indicted in 1991 in the United States and Scotland, extradited only after protracted diplomatic negotiations and convicted and sentenced to life imprisonment in 2001. He was released on humanitarian grounds in 2009, suffering from purportedly terminal pancreatic cancer.

Two prosecutions in the United States stemming from the 1993 bombing of the World Trade Center produced seemingly stronger verdicts. Omar Abdel Rahman, the so-called Blind Sheik, was convicted in federal court in New York City along with nine others in 1995 for conspiracy to carry out a campaign of bombings and assassinations within the United States. Abdel Rahman is now serving a 240-year prison sentence. Two years later, Ramzi Ahmed Yousef was convicted on charges of masterminding the 1993 bombing and given a life sentence. Even after the second verdict, however, questions remained about whether the plot had been sponsored by a foreign state or international organization.[24]

Challenge and Response

The Bush administration responded to the 9/11 attacks by declaring an all-out war on terrorism that combined separate strategies of detaining captured "enemy combatants" at Guantánamo outside normal legal processes and prosecuting hundreds of individuals in federal courts on terrorism-related charges. The improvised system of military tribunals at Guantánamo drew political and legal challenges that stalled their work, resulting in only three convictions late in Bush's time in office. Meanwhile, criminal cases proceeded in federal courts with relatively few setbacks and little hindrance from criticism by some civil libertarians of overly aggressive prosecutions.[25]

Even as the Guantánamo military tribunals were being formed, the administration was initiating criminal prosecutions in other al Qaeda or Taliban-related cases. In the most important, the government indicted Zacarias Moussaoui, sometimes called the 20th hijacker, on Dec. 11, 2001, on conspiracy counts related to the 9/11 attacks. The prosecution dragged on for more than four years, extended by Moussaoui's courtroom dramatics and a fight over access to classified information that ended with a ruling largely favorable to the government. The trial ended on May 3, 2006, after a jury that had deliberated for

seven days imposed a life sentence instead of the death penalty — apparently rejecting the government's view of Moussaoui as a central figure in the 9/11 attacks.

Two other early prosecutions ended more quickly. British citizen Richard Reid, the so-called shoe bomber, was charged in a federal criminal complaint on Dec. 24, 2001, two days after his failed explosive attack on American Airlines Flight 63. In January, Attorney General John Ashcroft announced that U.S. citizen John Walker Lindh, the so-called American Taliban captured in Afghanistan, would be tried in a civilian court in the United States. Both men entered guilty pleas in 2002; Lindh was given a 20-year sentence while Reid was sentenced in January 2003 to life in prison.

The government started two other early cases in the criminal justice system and moved them into the military system only to return later to civilian courts. Ali Saleh Kahlah al-Marri, a Qatari student attending college in Illinois, was detained as a material witness in December 2001 and indicted two months later on credit-card charges. Bush's decision in 2003 to designate him as an enemy combatant led to a protracted appeal that the Obama administration resolved in 2009 by indicting al-Marri on a single count of conspiracy to provide material support for terrorism. In a similar vein, U.S. citizen José Padilla was arrested at the Chicago airport on May 8, 2002, on suspicion of plotting a radioactive attack; designated an enemy combatant a month later and then indicted after drawn-out legal challenges that reached the Supreme Court. Padilla was convicted of terrorism conspiracy charges and given a 17-year prison sentence; al-Marri drew 15 years after pleading guilty.

Meanwhile, the military tribunals had been stymied by a succession of legal challenges before the Supreme Court and responses by the administration and Congress to the justices' rulings. In the pivotal decision in Hamdan's case, the court ruled in June 2006 that the military commissions as then constituted were illegal because the president had not shown a need to depart from established rules of military justice.[26] Reconstituted under the Military Commissions Act of 2006, the tribunals finally produced their first conviction in March 2007 when the Australian Hicks pleaded guilty to a single material-support count. Under a plea agreement and with credit for time served, he was allowed to return to Australia to serve the remaining nine months of a seven-year sentence.

Two more convictions followed in 2008, both after trials. Hamdan was convicted in August of conspiracy

CHRONOLOGY

1970s-2000 *International terrorism era begins, with attacks on civilian aircraft, facilities; prosecutions in foreign, U.S. courts get mixed results.*

1988 Bombing of Pan Am Flight 103 over Scotland kills 270, including 189 Americans; Scottish court later convicts and sentences to life former head of Libyan secret service; ill with cancer, he was released from Scottish jail in 2009.

1995 Civilian court convicts Omar Abdel Rahman and nine others for conspiring to blow up World Trade Center, other sites, in 1993.

1997 Ramzi Ahmed Yousef draws life sentence after 1997 conviction in civilian court for masterminding 1993 trade center bombing.

2000-Present *Al Qaeda launches 9/11 attacks; Bush, Obama administrations prosecute terrorism cases mainly in civilian courts.*

September-October 2001 Nearly 3,000 killed in al Qaeda's Sept. 11 attacks. . . . Congress on Sept. 14 gives president authority to use force against those responsible for attacks.

November-December 2001 President George W. Bush on Nov. 13 authorizes military commissions to try enemy combatants captured in Afghanistan, elsewhere. . . . U.S. Naval Base at Guantánamo Bay is chosen as site to hold detainees. . . . Zacarias Moussaoui indicted in federal court in Virginia on Dec. 11 for conspiracy in 9/11 attacks. . . . "Shoe bomber" Richard Reid arrested Dec. 21 for failed attack on American Airlines Flight 63.

2002 First of about 800 prisoners arrive in Guantánamo; first of scores of habeas corpus cases filed by detainees by mid-spring. . . . José Padilla arrested at Chicago airport May 8 in alleged radioactive bomb plot; case transferred to military courts. . . . John Walker Lindh, "American Taliban," sentenced Oct. 4 by a civilian court to 20 years in prison.

2003 Federal judge in Boston sentences Reid to life in prison on Jan. 31.

2004 Supreme Court rules June 28 that U.S. citizens can be held as enemy combatants but must be afforded hearing before "neutral decisionmaker" (*Hamdi v. Rumsfeld*); on

same day, court rules Guantánamo detainees may use habeas corpus to challenge captivity (*Rasul v. Bush*).

2006 Moussaoui is given life sentence May 3. . . . Supreme Court rules June 29 that military commissions improperly depart from requirements of U.S. military law and Geneva Conventions (*Hamdan v. Rumsfeld*). . . . Congress passes Military Commissions Act of 2006 in September to remedy defects.

2007 First conviction in military commission: Australian David Hicks sentenced on March 30 to nine months after guilty plea to material support for terrorism. . . . Padilla convicted in federal court Aug. 16 on material support counts; later sentenced to 17 years.

2008 Supreme Court reaffirms June 12 habeas corpus rights for Guantánamo detainees (*Boumediene v. Bush*). . . . Two more convictions of terrorists in military commissions: Hamdan convicted on material support counts Aug. 6, sentenced to a seven-and-a-half-year term; al Qaeda propagandist Ali Hamza al Bahlul convicted Nov. 3, given life sentence.

January-June 2009 President Obama pledges to close Guantánamo within a year, suspends military commissions pending review (Jan. 21). . . . Obama in major speech says some detainees to be held indefinitely without trial (May 21).

July-December 2009 Defense and Justice departments agree on protocol to choose civilian or military court (July 20). . . . Military Commission Act of 2009 improves defendants' protections (October). Attorney General Eric Holder announces plan to try Khalid Sheikh Mohammed (KSM), four others in federal court in Manhattan for 9/11 conspiracy (Nov. 13); other alleged terrorists designated for military commissions; plan for N.Y. trial widely criticized. . . . Umar Farouk Abdulmutallab arrested Dec. 25 in failed bombing of Northwest Flight 253; decision to prosecute in civilian court criticized, defended.

2010 Administration mulls change of plans for KSM trial. . . . U.S. appeals court backs broad definition of enemy combatant in first substantive appellate-level decision in Guantánamo habeas corpus cases (Jan. 5). . . . Military review panel weighs arguments on use of "material support of terrorism" charge in military commissions (Jan. 26).

and material support but acquitted of more serious charges and given an unexpectedly light sentence of 61 months. With credit for time served, he was transferred to his native Yemen in late November to serve the last month of his term. Earlier, a military tribunal on Nov. 3 had convicted Bahlul of a total of 35 terrorism-related counts after the former al Qaeda propaganda chief essentially boycotted the proceedings. The panel returned the verdict in the morning and then deliberated for an hour before sentencing the Yemeni native to life imprisonment.

As the Bush administration neared an end, the Justice Department issued a fact-sheet on the seventh anniversary of the 9/11 attacks touting its "considerable success in America's federal courtrooms of identifying, prosecuting and incarcerating terrorists and would-be terrorists." The report listed the Padilla and Moussaoui cases among eight "notable" prosecutions in recent years. It also briefly noted the department's cooperation with the Defense Department in developing procedures for the military commissions, defending against challenges to the system and jointly bringing charges against KSM and other high-value detainees.[27]

In an important post-election setback, however, a federal judge in Washington ruled on Nov. 20, 2008, in favor of five of the six Algerians whose habeas corpus petitions had led to the Supreme Court decision guaranteeing judicial review for Guantánamo detainees. Judge Richard Leon said the government had failed to present sufficient evidence to show that the six men, arrested in Bosnia in January 2002, had planned to travel to Afghanistan to fight against the United States. He found sufficient evidence, however, that one of the prisoners had acted as a facilitator for al Qaeda. Three of the five were returned to Bosnia in December; two others were transferred to France in May and November 2009.[28]

Change and Continuity

In his first days in office, President Obama began fulfilling his campaign pledge to change the Bush administration's legal policies in the war on terror. Obama's high-profile decisions to set a deadline for closing Guantánamo, shut down the secret CIA prisons and prohibit enhanced interrogation techniques drew support from Democrats and liberals and sharp criticism from Republicans and conservatives. By year's end, the roles were reversed, with support from the right and criticism from the left of Obama's decision to continue use of military tribunals

and claim the power to detain suspected terrorists indefinitely without trial. Meanwhile, the government was continuing to win significant terrorism-related convictions in federal courts but suffering setbacks in many habeas corpus cases brought by Guantánamo prisoners.

Even with the Guantánamo and interrogation policies under attack, the Justice Department was achieving some significant successes in prosecutions that carried over from the Bush administration. The new administration side-stepped a Supreme Court test of the power to detain U.S. residents by transferring al-Marri to civilian courts in late February and securing his guilty plea in April. Also in April, Wesam al-Delaema, an Iraqi-born Dutch citizen, was given a 25-year prison sentence for planting roadside bombs aimed at U.S. troops in his native country. Al-Delaema had fought extradition from the Netherlands and was to be returned there to serve what was expected to be a reduced sentence. The case marked the first successful prosecution for terrorist offenses against U.S. forces in Iraq.

In May, the government won convictions — after two prior mistrials — in its case against the so-called Liberty City Six (originally, Seven), who were charged with plotting to blow up the Sears Tower in Chicago and selected federal buildings. The jury in Miami convicted five of the men but acquitted a sixth. On the same day, a federal jury in New York City convicted Oussama Kassir, a Lebanese-born Swede, of attempting to establish a terrorist training camp in Oregon. Material-support charges were the major counts in both cases. Kassir was sentenced to life in September; of the six defendants in the Miami case, sentences handed down on Nov. 20 ranged from 84 to 162 months.

By summer, the Justice Department conceded that it would be late with an interim report on closing Guantánamo. In acknowledging the delay in a background briefing on July 20 — the eve of the due date for the report — administration officials claimed some progress in resettling some of the detainees but confirmed expectations to hold some of the prisoners indefinitely. The administration did release the two-page protocol from the Defense and Justice departments on prosecuting Guantánamo cases, with its stated "presumption" in favor of civilian prosecutions "where feasible." The memo outlined a variety of factors to consider in choosing between civilian courts or "reformed" military

The Case Against the 'Christmas Day' Bomber

Critics say prosecutors mishandled Abdulmutallab's arrest.

Caught in the act of trying to bomb a Northwest Airlines aircraft, Umar Farouk Abdulmutallab would appear to offer prosecutors a slam dunk under any of several terrorism-related charges. Indeed, there were dozens of witnesses to his capture.

But the case against the baby-faced Nigerian-born, Yemeni-trained al Qaeda supporter became enmeshed in post-9/11 American politics almost immediately after his Christmas Day flight landed in Detroit.[1]

President Obama invited the subsequent criticism by initially labeling Abdulmutallab as "an isolated extremist" on Dec. 26 before learning of his training in al Qaeda camps in Yemen and history of extreme Islamist views. Homeland Security Secretary Janet Napolitano compounded the administration's political problems by saying on Dec. 27 that Abdulmutallab's capture showed that "the system worked" — a statement she quickly worked hard to explain away, given that a U.S. airliner had nearly been bombed.

The administration also faced criticism for intelligence analysts' failure to block Abdulmutallab from ever boarding a U.S.-bound aircraft after having received a warning from the suspect's father, a prominent Nigerian banker, of his son's radicalization. Obama moved to stanch the criticism by commissioning and quickly releasing a review of the intelligence agencies' "failure to connect the dots" and by ordering other steps, including a tightening of airline security procedures.

The politicization of the case intensified, however, with a broadside from former Vice President Dick Cheney sharply attacking the administration's decision to treat Abdulmutallab as a criminal suspect instead of an enemy combatant to be tried in a military tribunal. Obama "is trying to pretend we are not at war," Cheney told *Politico*, the Washington-based, all-politics newspaper.

"He seems to think if he has a low-key response to an attempt to blow up an airliner and kill hundreds of people, we won't be at war. He seems to think if he gives terrorists the rights of Americans, lets them lawyer up and reads them their Miranda rights, we won't be at war."[2]

White House press secretary Robert Gibbs responded promptly by accusing Cheney of playing "the typical Washington game of pointing fingers and making political hay." But the response did nothing to stop Republican politicians and conservative commentators from keeping up a drumbeat of criticism for several weeks into the new year, focused in particular on the decision to advise Abdulmutallab of his right to remain silent and to confer with a lawyer.

The criticism appears to have been based in part on an erroneous understanding of when FBI agents advised the 21-year-old Abdulmutallab of his Miranda rights. For weeks, critics said he had been "Mirandized" within 55 minutes of his arrest. Only in mid-February did the administration release a detailed, materially different timeline.[3]

The administration's account showed that Abdulmutallab was questioned for 55 minutes and

commissions. With Guantánamo dominating the coverage, the memo drew little attention.[29]

Meanwhile, federal judges in Washington, D.C., were giving mixed verdicts as more of the long-delayed habeas corpus cases by Guantánamo detainees reached decision stage.[30] In the first of the rulings after Obama took office, Judge Leon ruled on Jan. 28 that evidence of serving as a cook for al Qaeda was sufficient to hold a prisoner for "material support" of terrorism. In 14 cases over the next year, however, the government lost more — eight — than it won (six). In five of the cases granting habeas corpus, judges found the government's

evidence either insufficient or unreliable. In one, the judge specifically found the government's evidence had been obtained by torture or under the taint of prior torture. In the two other cases, one of the detainees was found to have been expelled from al Qaeda, while the other was no longer a threat because he was cooperating with U.S. authorities.

In order to prevent leaks, Holder made his decision to try KSM in a federal court with little advance notice to New York City officials. He explained later to the Senate Judiciary Committee that a federal court trial would give the government "the greatest opportunity to provided some information about his rights before being taken away for surgery. When he returned after the four-hour procedure — a total of nine hours after his arrest — Abdulmutallab declined to answer further questions.

Without regard to the precise timing, critics said Abdulmutallab should have been treated outside the criminal justice system to maximize his value as a source of intelligence. Former Attorney General Michael B. Mukasey said the administration had "no compulsion" to treat Abdulmutallab as a criminal defendant "and every reason to treat him as an intelligence asset to be exploited promptly." The administration claimed that Abdulmutallab did begin providing actionable intelligence after family members were brought to the United States from Nigeria, but Mukasey said the five-week time lag meant that "possibly useful information" was lost.[4]

Administration supporters noted, however, that the Bush administration handled all suspected terrorists arrested in the United States as criminal defendants with the concomitant necessity to advise them of their Miranda rights. The administration's defense was substantiated by John Ashcroft, Mukasey's predecessor as attorney general. "When you have a person in the criminal justice system, you Mirandize them," Ashcroft told a reporter for *Huffington Post* when questioned at the conservative Tea Party Conference in Washington in mid-February.[5]

U.S. Marshals Service via Getty Images

Umar Farouk Abdulmutallab, a 23-year-old Nigerian, is charged with attempting to blow up a Northwest Airlines flight as it was landing in Detroit last Christmas Day.

Administration critics appeared to say little about the precise charges brought against Abdulmutallab. He was initially charged in a criminal complaint Dec. 26 with two counts: attempting to blow up and placing an explosive device aboard a U.S. aircraft. Two weeks later, a federal grand jury in Detroit returned a more detailed indictment charging him with attempted use of a weapon of mass destruction and attempted murder of 269 people. If convicted, he faces a life sentence plus 90 years in prison. No trial date is set.

— Kenneth Jost

[1] Some background drawn from a well-documented Wikipedia entry: http://en.wikipedia.org/wiki/Umar_Farouk_Abdulmutallab.

[2] Mike Allen, "Dick Cheney: Barack Obama 'trying to pretend,'" *Politico*, Dec. 30, 2009, www.politico.com/news/stories/1209/31054.html, cited in Philip Elliott, "White House Hits Back at Cheney Criticism," The Associated Press, Dec. 30, 2009.

[3] Walter Pincus, "Bomb suspect was read Miranda rights nine hours after arrest," *The Washington Post*, Feb. 15, 2010, p. A6.

[4] Michael B. Mukasey, "Where the U.S. went wrong on Abdulmutallab," *The Washington Post*, Feb. 12, 2010, p. A27.

[5] Ryan Grim, "Ashcroft: 'When You Have a Person in the Criminal Justice System, You Mirandize Them,'" *Huffington Post*, Feb. 19, 2010, www.huffingtonpost.com/2010/02/19/ashcroft-when-you-have-a_n_469384.html.

present the strongest case in the best forum." The explanation left Republicans, conservatives and many New Yorkers unconvinced of the benefits, dismayed at the potential costs and appalled at the idea of according full legal rights to a self-proclaimed enemy of the United States. Civil liberties and human rights groups applauded the decision while giving little attention to Holder's simultaneous move to try the alleged *USS Cole* plotter and others in military commissions that the groups had called for abolishing.

The political attacks over the administration's handling of Abdulmutallab's case added to the pressure against trying KSM in New York City. Behind the scenes, Justice Department officials were looking for alternate, more remote sites for a possible civilian trial. And by February Holder was being deliberately ambiguous about whether the case would be tried in a civilian court at all.

"At the end of the day, wherever this case is tried, in whatever forum, what we have to ensure is that it's done as transparently as possible and with adherence to all the rules," Holder said on Feb. 11.[31] "If we do that, I'm not sure the location or even the forum is as important as what the world sees in that proceeding."

Material-Support Law Called Anti-Terror "Weapon of Choice"

Critics say the broadly written law criminalizes lawful speech.

Oussama Kassir never took up arms against U.S. forces in Afghanistan and never carried out a terrorist attack against Americans in the United States or abroad. But he is serving a life prison sentence today after a federal court jury in New York City found him guilty of attempting to establish a jihadist training camp in Oregon and distributing terrorist training materials over the Internet.

To put Kassir behind bars, federal prosecutors used a broadly written law that makes it a crime to provide "material support" — broadly defined — to any group designated by the government as a "terrorist organization." The law, first passed in 1994 and amended several times since, accounts for roughly half of the al Qaeda-related terrorism convictions since 2001, according to a study by two ex-prosecutors written for the Washington-based group Human Rights First.[1]

The material-support law is "the anti-terror weapon of choice for prosecutors," says Stephen Vladeck, a law professor at American University in Washington, D.C. "It's a lot easier to prove that a defendant provided material support to a designated terrorist organization than to prove that they actually committed a terrorist act."

Kassir, a Lebanese-born Swedish citizen, was convicted on May 12, 2009, after a three-week trial. The evidence showed he came to the United States in 1999 and bought a parcel of land in Oregon with plans to take advantage of lax U.S. gun laws to train Muslim recruits in assembling and disassembling AK-47 rifles. He also established six different Web sites and posted materials about how to make bombs and poisons.

The defense denied that Kassir conspired to train recruits and claimed the Web sites contained only readily available information. The jury deliberated less than a day before returning guilty verdicts on a total of 11 counts. U.S. District Judge John Keenan sentenced him to life imprisonment on Sept. 15.[2]

On the same day as the Kassir verdict, a federal court jury in Miami returned guilty verdicts against five of the so-called "Liberty City Six," who had been charged with plotting to blow up the Sears Tower in Chicago and selected federal buildings. In the Human Rights First report, New York lawyers Richard Zabel and James J. Benjamin Jr. note that the trial shows the importance of the material-support charge because prosecutors won convictions against only two defendants on an explosives charge and against only one defendant for seditious conspiracy.

Zabel and Benjamin, who both served in the U.S. attorney's office in New York City, say the material-support law has similarly been used to convict defendants for such actions as providing broadcasting services to a terrorist organization's television station or traveling to Pakistan for training in a jihadist camp. The law was also invoked against Lynne Stewart, a well-known defense lawyer, for transmitting messages to her terrorism-case client, Omar Abdel Rahman, the "Blind Sheik."

The law defines material support to include not only financial contributions but also any "property" or "service," including "personnel" and "training, expert advice or assistance." Medicine and religious materials are exempted.

CURRENT SITUATION

Watching Appeals

Lawyers for the government and for Guantánamo detainees are watching the federal appeals court in Washington and a specially created military appeals panel for the next major developments on the rules for prosecuting terrorism cases.

The government scored a major victory in early January when the U.S. Circuit Court of Appeals for the District of Columbia decisively backed the government's power to detain a low-level member of a pro-Taliban brigade captured during the Afghanistan war and held at Guantánamo for more than eight years.

Later in the month, the U.S. Court of Military Commission Review heard arguments on Jan. 26 from two

Some civil liberties and humanitarian groups contend the law sweeps too broadly. Material support is defined "so expansively and vaguely as to criminalize pure speech furthering lawful, nonviolent ends," the bipartisan Constitution Project says in a recent report. The report recommends amending the law to exempt "pure speech" unless intended to further illegal conduct. It also calls for giving groups the opportunity to contest designation as a terrorist organization.[3]

Appellate courts have generally upheld broad readings of the statute. In a decision in December 2007, however, the San Francisco-based U.S. Court of Appeals for the Ninth Circuit ruled that some of the law's terms — "training," "service," and "expert advice or assistance" — were impermissibly vague or overbroad.

The ruling came in a suit filed originally in 1998 by the Humanitarian Law Project on behalf of individuals or U.S.-based groups that sought to provide assistance to two designated terrorist organizations: the Kurdistan Workers' Party in Turkey or the Liberation Tigers of Tamil Eelam in Sri Lanka. The plaintiffs claimed they wanted to counsel both groups on use of international law and nonviolent conflict resolution.

The Supreme Court agreed to hear the government's appeal of the case as well as the plaintiffs' cross-appeal of the part of the ruling that upheld a broad construction of the term "personnel." The case was argued on Feb. 23; a decision is due by the end of June.[4]

Meanwhile, a military appeals panel is weighing challenges to the use of material-support counts in military commission proceedings. The United States Court of Military Commission Review heard arguments on Jan. 26 in appeals by two of the three men convicted so far in military commissions: Salim Ahmed Hamdan, former driver

Oussama Kassir is serving a life sentence after a federal court jury in New York City found him guilty last year of attempting to establish a jihadist training camp in Oregon and distributing terrorist training materials over the Internet.

for al Qaeda leader Osama bin Laden, and al Qaeda filmmaker and propagandist Ali Hamza Ahmad Suliman al Bahlul.

Hamdan, who was freed in late 2008 after about seven-and-a-half years in captivity, and al Bahlul, who was sentenced to life imprisonment, both contend that material support for terrorism is outside the military tribunals' jurisdiction because it is not a traditional war crime. The cases were argued before separate three-judge panels, which gave no indication when rulings would be expected.[5]

— *Kenneth Jost*

[1] Richard B. Zabel and James J. Benjamin Jr., "In Pursuit of Justice: Prosecuting Terrorism Cases in the Federal Courts," Human Rights First, May 2008, p. 32, www.humanrightsfirst .info/pdf/080521-USLS-pursuit-justice.pdf. See also by same authors "In Pursuit of Justice: Prosecuting Terrorism Cases in the Federal Courts: 2009 Update and Recent Developments," July 2009, www .humanrightsfirst.org/pdf/090723-LS-in-pursuit-justice-09-update.pdf .Background drawn from both reports.

[2] The press release by the U.S. Attorney for the Southern District of New York can be found at www.humanrightsfirst.org/pdf/090723-LS-in-pursuit-justice-09-update.pdf. See also "Man convicted in NY of trying to start terror camp," The Associated Press, May 12, 2009.

[3] "Reforming the Material Support Laws: Constitutional Concerns Presented by Prohibitions on Material Support to 'Terrorist Organizations,' " Constitution Project, Nov. 17, 2009, www.constitutionproject .org/manage/file/355.pdf.

[4] The case is *Holder v. Humanitarian Law Project*, 08-1498. For materials on the case, including links to news coverage, see SCOTUSWiki, www .scotuswiki.com/index.php?title=Holder_v._Humanitarian_Law_Project.

[5] Material in Bahlul's case can be found at www.defense.gov/news/ CMCRHAMZA.html/; materials in Hamdan's case at www.defense .gov/news/commissionsHamdan.html.

of the men convicted so far in the military tribunals challenging the government's power to prosecute material support for terrorism in military instead of civilian courts. Separate three-judge panels convened to hear the appeals by al Qaeda propagandist Bahlul and former bin Laden driver Hamdan gave no indication when they would rule on the cases.

With several other habeas corpus cases pending before the D.C. Circuit, the appeals court is likely to determine

both the direction and the pace of the next stage of the litigation from Guantánamo prisoners, according to Brookings Institution scholar Wittes.

If other judges follow the lead of the conservative-dominated panel in the Jan. 5 decision, many of the outstanding issues regarding the government's power to hold enemy combatants could be resolved quickly, Wittes says. But different rulings by panels in other cases could

Cole Bombing Case, Six Others Set for Tribunals

Abd al Rahim al Nashiri, the alleged mastermind of the October 2000 suicide attack on the *USS Cole*, is one of seven Guantánamo detainees designated by Attorney General Eric Holder for trial by military commissions. Seventeen U.S. sailors were killed in the attack on the warship as it lay docked in Aden, Yemen.

The Saudi-born al-Nashiri, now 45, allegedly served as al Qaeda's chief of operations in the Arabian peninsula before his capture in the United Arab Emirates in November 2002. He was held in a secret CIA prison (reportedly in Thailand) until being brought to Guantánamo in 2006.

The CIA has confirmed that al-Nashiri was waterboarded. He claims that he falsely confessed to the *Cole* attack and six other terrorist incidents as a result. It is also reported that he was the target of a mock execution by CIA interrogators.

The six other prisoners designated for trial by military commissions are:

- **Ahmed al Darbi (Saudi Arabia)** — Accused of plotting to bomb oil tankers in the Strait of Hormuz.
- **Mohammed Kamin (Afghanistan)** — Charged with planting mines in Afghanistan.
- **Omar Khadr (Canada)** — Accused of killing a U.S. soldier with a grenade in Afghanistan in 2002; Khadr was 15 at the time.
- **Noor Uthman Mohammed (Sudan)** — Charged with assisting in running al Qaeda training center.
- **Obaidullah (Afghanistan)** — Charged with possessing anti-tank mines.
- **Ibrahim al Qosi (Sudan)** — Accused of acting as Osama bin Laden's bodyguard, paymaster and supply chief.

add to what he calls the "cacophony" surrounding the habeas corpus cases and force the Supreme Court to intervene to resolve the conflicts.

The appeals court's decision rejected a habeas corpus petition by Ghaleb Nassar Al-Bihani, a Yemeni native who served as a cook for a Taliban brigade. He argued that he should be released because the war against the Taliban has ended and, in any event, that he was essentially a civilian contractor instead of a combatant.

In a 25-page opinion, Judge Janice Rogers Brown rejected both arguments. Brown, a strongly conservative judge appointed by President George W. Bush, said Bihani's admitted actions of accompanying the brigade to the battlefield, carrying a weapon and retreating and surrendering with the brigade showed that he was "both part of and substantially supported enemy forces."

As for the status of the war, Brown said, it was up to Congress or the president to decide whether the conflict had ended, not the courts. In a significant passage, Brown also said that U.S. instead of international law determined the president's authority to hold enemy combatants. "The international laws of war as a whole have not been implemented domestically by Congress and are therefore not a source of authority for U.S. courts," Brown wrote.

Judge Brett Kavanaugh, another Bush-appointed conservative, joined Brown's opinion. Judge Stephen Williams, who was appointed by President Ronald Reagan, agreed on the result but distanced himself from Brown's comments on the impact of international law. He noted that Brown's "dictum" — the legal term for a passage unnecessary to the decision in the case —"goes well beyond what the government has argued in the case."[32]

Wittes says the ruling is "a huge development if it stands." The appellate panel, he says, was "signaling" to the federal district court judges in Washington handling habeas corpus cases to "lighten up" on the government. District court judges have ruled against the government in somewhat over half of the cases decided so far.

The appeals court for the military commissions was created by the 2006 law overhauling the rules for the tribunals, but it had no cases to review until after Hamdan's and Bahlul's convictions in 2008.

In their appeals, both men claim that their convictions for material support for terrorism were improper because the offense is not a traditional war crime prosecutable in a military court. Bahlul also argues that the First Amendment bars prosecuting him for producing a video documentary for al Qaeda that recounts the bombing of

Should terrorism suspects ordinarily be tried in civilian courts?

YES
Laura Olson
Senior Counsel, Rule of Law Program
Constitution Project

Written for *CQ Researcher*, March 2010

Civilian courts are the proper forum for trying terrorism cases. Trial in our traditional federal courts is a proven and reliable way to provide justice, while ensuring our national security. This is in stark contrast to the new military commissions that were re-created for the third time in the Military Commissions Act (MCA) of 2009. Like their predecessors, these new commissions remain vulnerable to constitutional challenge.

We should not place some of the most important terrorism trials, and arguably the most important criminal trials, in our nation's history in the untested and uncertain military commissions system.

Since 2001, trials in federal criminal courts have resulted in nearly 200 convictions of terrorism suspects, compared to only three low-level convictions in the military commissions. Two of those three are now free in their home countries. This record demonstrates that prosecutions in our traditional federal courts are tough on terrorists.

To date, the rules to accompany the MCA of 2009 remain to be approved. Therefore, military commission judges are without guidance on how to proceed with these cases. Meanwhile, our traditional federal courts move ahead, applying long-established rules on procedure and evidence. For example, the Classified Information Procedures Act (CIPA) elaborates the procedures by which federal courts admit evidence while protecting national security information from improper disclosure. The MCA of 2009 incorporates CIPA procedures on dealing with classified information into the military commissions system, but military judges have little or no experience with these procedures. Federal judges have worked with CIPA for the last 30 years.

Our Constitution provides a safe and effective way to prosecute terrorism suspects. In fact, Ahmed Kfalfan Ghailani, a former Guantánamo detainee, is now being held in New York City for his trial in federal court there. The judge has issued a protective order on all classified information, and there have been no reports of any increased safety risks or expenses associated with this trial.

I agree with the nearly 140 former diplomats, military officials, federal judges and prosecutors and members of Congress, as well as bar leaders, national-security and foreign-policy experts, and family members of the 9/11 attacks that signed Beyond Guantánamo: A Bipartisan Declaration. This unique and bipartisan group is in favor of trying terrorism suspects in our traditional federal courts. Federal trials are the only way to ensure swift and constitutional trials of terrorism suspects.

NO
Sen. John McCain, R-Ariz.

From statement in support of the Enemy Belligerent Interrogation, Detention and Prosecution Act, March 4, 2010

This legislation seeks to ensure that the mistakes made during the apprehension of the Christmas Day bomber, such as reading him a Miranda warning, will never happen again and put Americans' security at risk.

Specifically, this bill would require unprivileged enemy belligerents suspected of engaging in hostilities against the U.S. to be held in military custody and interrogated for their intelligence value by a "high-value detainee" interagency team established by the president. This interagency team of experts in national security, terrorism, intelligence, interrogation and law enforcement will have the protection of U.S. civilians and civilian facilities as their paramount responsibility. . . .

A key provision of this bill is that it would prohibit a suspected enemy belligerent from being provided with a Miranda warning and being told he has a right to a lawyer and a right to refuse to cooperate. I believe that an overwhelming majority of Americans agree that when we capture a terrorist who is suspected of carrying out or planning an attack intended to kill hundreds if not thousands of innocent civilians, our focus must be on gaining all the information possible to prevent that attack or any that may follow from occurring. . . . Additionally, the legislation would authorize detention of enemy belligerents without criminal charges for the duration of the hostilities consistent with standards under the law of war which have been recognized by the Supreme Court.

Importantly, if a decision is made to hold a criminal trial after the necessary intelligence information is obtained, the bill mandates trial by military commission, where we are best able to protect U.S. national security interests, including sensitive classified sources and methods, as well as the place and the people involved in the trial itself.

The vast majority of Americans understand that what happened with the Christmas Day bomber was a near catastrophe that was only prevented by sheer luck and the courage of a few of the passengers and crew. A wide majority of Americans also realize that allowing a terrorist to be interrogated for only 50 minutes before he is given a Miranda warning and told he can obtain a lawyer and stop cooperating is not sufficient. . . .

We must ensure that the broad range of expertise that is available within our government is brought to bear on such high-value detainees. This bill mandates such coordination and places the proper focus on getting intelligence to stop an attack, rather than allowing law enforcement and preparing a case for a civilian criminal trial to drive our response.

FEMA News Photo/WireImage/Andrea Booher

Controversy erupted after Attorney General Eric Holder announced plans to try the five alleged 9/11 conspirators in a federal court "just blocks away from where the twin towers [of the World Trade Center] once stood." New York City Mayor Michael Bloomberg and Police Commissioner Raymond Kelly welcomed Holder's decision, but many New Yorkers expressed concern about the costs and risks of a sensational trial in Lower Manhattan.

the *USS Cole* and calls for others to join a jihad against the United States.

The government counters by citing cases from the Civil War and World War II to argue that providing support to unlawful enemy combatants has been prosecutable in military courts even if the term "material support for terrorism" was not used. As to Bahlul's free-speech argument, the government contends that the First Amendment does not apply to enemy "propaganda."[33]

Bahlul is also challenging the life sentence imposed in November 2008; Hamdan was freed later that month after being credited with the seven years he had already been held at Guantánamo.

Wittes says the government has "a big uphill climb" on the material-support issue. He notes that in the Supreme Court's 2006 decision in Hamdan's case, four of the justices questioned whether military tribunals could try a conspiracy charge, another of the generally phrased offenses the government has used in terrorism cases. Material support for terrorism would be harder to justify, he says.

Wittes adds that it is important to resolve the issue quickly if the military commissions are to be used in other cases. "What you don't want to happen is to have a whole lot of people sentenced in military commissions and then find out that the charges are invalid," he says.

Making a Deal?

The Obama administration may be on the verge of deciding to try Khalid Sheikh Mohammed and four other alleged 9/11 conspirators in a military tribunal in an effort to gain Republican support for closing the Guantánamo prison camp.

Administration officials are reportedly near to recommending that Obama reverse Attorney General Holder's Nov. 13 decision to hold the 9/11 conspiracy trial in federal court in hopes of securing support for closing Guantánamo from an influential Republican senator, South Carolina's Lindsey Graham.[34]

Graham, a former military lawyer, has strongly advocated use of military tribunals for detainees held at Guantánamo but has not joined other Republicans in attacking Obama's pledge to close the facility. GOP lawmakers have been pushing legislative proposals to block use of funds for closing Guantánamo or for holding the 9/11 conspiracy trial in federal court.

The administration's possible reversal on the KSM trial is drawing a heated response from civil liberties and human rights groups. The decision would "strike a blow to American values and the rule of law and undermine America's credibility," according to the ACLU.

Elisa Massimino, president and CEO of Human Rights First, says failure to support Holder's decision would set "a dangerous precedent for future national security policy."

In the wake of the strong criticism of holding the KSM trial in New York City, Justice Department lawyers and others had been reported to be holding onto the plan for a federal court trial, but in a different location. Among the sites reported to have been under consideration were somewhere else in southern New York, Northern Virginia and western Pennsylvania.[35]

Any of those sites would satisfy the constitutional requirement that trial of a federal criminal case be held in "the district wherein the crime shall have been committed." Besides the World Trade Center in New York City, the 9/11 hijackers also crashed a plane into the Pentagon in Northern Virginia and into a rural location in western Pennsylvania.

Graham, first elected to the Senate in 2002, argued during the Bush administration for a greater role for Congress in defining detention policies. Since Obama's election, he is widely reported to have formed a working relationship on several issues with White House chief of staff Rahm Emanuel, a former colleague in the House of Representatives. Emanuel was described in a flattering profile in *The Washington Post* and elsewhere as having disagreed with Obama's pledge to close Guantánamo and with Holder's decision to try KSM in federal court.[36]

Beyond the KSM trial and Guantánamo issue, Graham is continuing to call for congressional legislation to govern the handling of detention issues. "I want Congress and the administration to come up with a detainee policy that will be accepted by courts and so that the international community will understand that no one is in jail by an arbitrary exercise of executive power," Graham told *The New York Times*.[37]

As outlined, the legislation would authorize holding terrorism suspects inside the United States without charging them with a crime or advising them of Miranda rights; establish standards for choosing between military or civilian court for prosecution; and authorize indefinite detention under standards subject to judicial review. Civil liberties and human rights groups remain opposed to indefinite-detention proposals.

Administration officials were quoted in news accounts as saying Obama hopes to have the KSM trial issue resolved before he begins a trip to Asia on March 18. But officials quoted in *The Washington Post* cautioned against expecting a "grand bargain" with Graham on the full range of detention issues in the near future.

OUTLOOK

Bringing Justice to Bear

When he defended the administration's decision to try Khalid Sheikh Mohammed in a civilian court, deputy national intelligence director John Brennan made clear that he expected the trial would be fair and just, but the result certain and severe.

"I'm confident that he's going to have the full weight of American justice," Brennan said on NBC's "Meet the Press" on Feb. 7. Asked by host David Gregory whether Mohammed would be executed, Brennan initially skirted the question but eventually concluded, "I'm convinced and confident that Mr. Khalid Sheikh Mohammed is going to meet his day in justice and before his maker."[38]

Despite the assurance from Brennan, Attorney General Holder and other administration officials, Americans apparently lack the same confidence in the federal court system. An ABC/*Washington Post* poll conducted in late February showed Americans favoring military over civilian trials for terrorism suspects by a margin of 55 percent to 39 percent. In a similar poll in the fall, Americans showed a statistically insignificant preference for military trials: 48 percent to 47 percent.[39]

A survey by Democratic pollsters similarly finds a majority of respondents opposed to Obama's policy on interrogation and prosecution of terrorism suspects (51 percent to 44 percent). But the survey, conducted in late February for the Democratic groups Democracy Corps and Third Way, also found majority approval of Obama's handling of "national security" (57 percent to 40 percent) and "fighting terrorism" (54 percent to 41 percent).

In a memo, leaders of the two organizations advise Obama to move the issue away from "civilian" versus "military" trials. Instead, they say the administration should "place the debate over terrorism suspects into the broader context of tough actions and significant results."[40]

Even before the memo's release, civil liberties and human rights groups were following the strategy in public lobbying of Obama as the administration was weighing where to hold the KSM trial. In a March 5 conference call for reporters arranged by Human Rights First, three retired military officers all depicted the military commissions as an unproven forum for prosecuting terrorists. "This is not ready for prime time," said Human Rights First President Massimino.

The ACLU followed with a full-page ad in the Sunday edition of *The New York Times* that compared the 300 terrorism cases "successfully handled" in the criminal justice system to "only three" in military commissions. "Our criminal justice system will resolve these cases more quickly and more credibly than the military commissions," the March 7 ad stated.

Meanwhile, former prosecutor McCarthy conceded in a speech sponsored by a college-affiliated center in Washington, "I don't think the military commission system performed well. By and large, the civilian system has performed well."

Speaking March 5 at the Kirby Center for Constitutional Studies and Citizenship at Hillsdale College in Michigan, McCarthy nevertheless reiterated that discovery procedures available to defendants argued against use of criminal prosecutions. "When you're at war, you can't be telling the enemy your most sensitive national intelligence," the *National Review* columnist said. Massimino noted, however, that a new military commissions law passed in 2009 dictates that defendants are to have access to evidence "comparable" to that provided in civilian courts.

The White House now says a decision on the KSM trial is "weeks" away. On Capitol Hill, Sen. Graham is continuing to push for a deal that would swap Republican support for closing Guantánamo for the administration's agreement to try KSM and other high-level terrorism suspects in military commissions. But Graham has yet to gain any public support for the plan from GOP colleagues.

McCarthy mocks Graham's proposed deal. He says the White House has already "stood down" on the military commissions issues and is only deferring a decision in hopes of getting GOP support for closing Guantánamo. "It makes no sense to horse-trade when Obama was being pushed toward military commissions by reality," McCarthy writes.[41]

Fellow conservative Rivkin also expects military commissions to become the norm for terrorism suspects. "My hope is that we'll come to our senses," he says. The current policies "are not consonant with the traditional law-of-war architecture, and they're not consistent with prevailing in this war."

Liberal groups continue to strongly oppose use of military commissions, but acknowledge congressional politics may determine decision-making. "There's no question that Congress has been trying to hold hostage the president's national security agenda," Massimino says.

For his part, former Assistant U.S. Attorney Benjamin doubts that military commissions will prove as useful as conservatives expect. "It would be great if the military commissions develop into a forum that works," he says. "But I have my doubts about how quickly or how smoothly that will happen."

NOTES

1. Some background information drawn from Farhan Bokhari, *et al.*, "The CEO of al-Qaeda," *Financial Times*, Feb. 15, 2003. See also the Wikipedia entry on Khalid Sheikh Mohammed and sources cited there, http://en.wikipedia.org/wiki/Khalid_Sheikh_Mohammed.

2. Quoted in Devlin Barnett, "NYC trial of 9/11 suspects faces legal risks," The Associated Press, Nov. 14, 2009. For Holder's prepared remarks, see U.S. Department of Justice, "Attorney General Announces Forum Decisions for Guantánamo Detainees," Nov. 13, 2009, www.justice.gov/ag/speeches/2009/ag-speech-091113.html.

3. Quoted in Carrie Johnson, "Holder Answers to 9/11 Relatives About Trials in U.S.," *The Washington Post*, Nov. 19, 2009, p. A3. See also Charlie Savage, "Holder Defends Decision to Use U.S. Court for 9/11 Trial," *The New York Times*, Nov. 19, 2009, p. A18.

4. See Anne E. Kornblut and Carrie Johnson, "Obama to help pick location of terror trial," *The Washington Post*, Feb. 12, 2010, p. A1.

5. For background, see these *CQ Researcher* reports: Kenneth Jost, "Closing Guantánamo," Feb. 27, 2009, pp. 177-200; Peter Katel and Kenneth Jost, "Treatment of Detainees," Aug. 25, 2006, pp. 673-696; and Kenneth Jost, "Civil Liberties Debates," Oct. 24, 2003, pp. 893-916.

6. "FY 2009 Budget and Performance Summary: Part One: Summary of Request and Performance," U.S. Department of Justice, www.justice.gov/jmd/2009summary/html/004_budget_highlights.htm. See also Mark Hosenball, "Terror Prosecution Statistics Criticized by GOP Were Originally Touted by Bush Administration," *Declassified* blog, Feb. 9, 2010, http://blog.newsweek.com/blogs/declassified/archive/2010/02/09/terror-prosecution-statistics-criticized-by-gop-were-originally-touted-by-bush-administration.aspx.

7. Richard B. Zabel and James J. Benjamin Jr., "In Pursuit of Justice: Prosecuting Terrorism Cases in the Federal Courts: 2009 Update and Recent Developments," Human Rights First, July 2009,

www.humanrightsfirst.org/pdf/090723-LS-in-pur-suit-justice-09-update.pdf. See also by the same authors, "In Pursuit of Justice: Prosecuting Terrorism Cases in the Federal Courts," Human Rights First, May 2008, www.humanrightsfirst.info/pdf/080521-USLS-pursuit-justice.pdf.

8. Andy McCarthy, "No Civilian Trial — In NYC or Anywhere Else," *Conservative Blog Watch*, Jan. 30, 2010, www.conservativeblogwatch.com/2010/01/30/no-civilian-trial-in-nyc-or-anywhere-by-an-dy-mccarthy.

9. See Benjamin Weiser, "A Top Terrorism Prosecutor Turns Critic of Civilian Trials," *The New York Times*, Feb. 20, 2010, p. A1.

10. See Del Quentin Wilber, " '08 habeas ruling may snag Obama plans," *The Washington Post*, Feb. 13, 2010, p. A2.

11. The defendants and their respective sentences were Mukhtar Al-Bakri and Yahya Goba (10 years each), Sahim Alwan (9-1/2 years), Shafal Mosed and Yaseinn Taher (eight years each) and Faysal Galab (seven years). For a full account, see Matthew Purdy and Lowell Bergman, "Where the Trail Led: Between Evidence and Suspicion, Unclear Danger: The Lackawanna Terror Case," *The New York Times*, Oct. 12, 2003, sec. 1, p. 1. See also Lou Michel, "Lackawanna officials say troops in city was bad idea," *Buffalo News*, July 26, 2009, p. A1.

12. *In Pursuit of Justice, op. cit.*, p. 2; *In Pursuit of Justice: 2009 Update, op. cit.*, p. 2.

13. Quoted in Bruce Golding, "Holder tours federal courthouse ahead of 9/11 terror trial," *The New York Post*, Dec. 9, 2009.

14. See Peter Finn, "The boy from the battlefield," *The Washington Post*, Feb. 10, 2010, p. A1.

15. "Remarks by the President on National Security," National Archives, May 21, 2009, www.whitehouse.gov/the_press_office/Remarks-by-the-President-On-National-Security-5-21-09/. For coverage, see Sheryl Gay Stolberg, "Obama Would Move Some Terror Detainees to U.S.," *The New York Times*, May 22, 2009, p. A1.

16. Department of Defense comments on the study are at www.defense.gov/Transcripts/Transcript

.aspx?TranscriptID=4340. See also Joseph Williams and Bryan Bender, "Obama Changes US Course on Treatment of Detainees," *The Boston Globe*, Jan. 23, 2009, p. A1. See Mark Denbeaux, Joshua Denbeaux and R. David Gratz, "Released Guantánamo Detainees and the Department of Defense: Propaganda by the Numbers?," Jan. 15, 2009, http://law.shu.edu/publications/GuantánamoReports/propaganda_numbers_11509.pdf.

17. The case is 542 U.S. 507 (2004). For an account, see Kenneth Jost, *Supreme Court Yearbook 2003-2004*, CQ Press.

18. Benjamin Wittes, Robert Chesney and Rabea Benhalim, "The Emerging Law of Detention: The Guantánamo Habeas Cases as Lawmaking," Brookings Institution, Jan. 22, 2010, www.brookings.edu/papers/2010/0122_Guantánamo_wittes_chesney.aspx. See Benjamin Wittes and Robert Chesney, "Piecemeal detainee policy," *The Washington Post*, Jan. 27, 2010, p. A17.

19. Chisun Lee, "Judges Urge Congress to Act on Indefinite Detention," *ProPublica*, Jan. 22, 2010, www.propublica.org/feature/judges-urge-congress-to-act-on-indefinite-terrorism-detentions-122. Walton, an appointee of President George W. Bush, was joined in the interview by Chief Judge Royce Lamberth, an appointee of President Ronald Reagan, and Judge Ricardo Urbina, an appointee of President Bill Clinton.

20. David Cole, "Detainees: still a matter for judges," *The Washington Post*, Feb. 9, 2010, p. A16.

21. Background drawn in part from Jennifer K. Elsea, "Terrorism and the Law of War: Trying Terrorists as War Criminals before Military Commissions," Congressional Research Service, Dec. 11, 2001, www.fas.org/irp/crs/RL31191.pdf. See also Louis Fisher, *Military Tribunals and Presidential Power: American Revolution to the War on Terrorism* (2005). Wittes's quote is from his book *Law and the Long War: The Future of Justice in the Age of Terror* (2008), p. 42.

22. The decision is *Ex parte Milligan*, 71 U.S. 2 (1866). *The New York Times'* contemporaneous account is reprinted in Kenneth Jost, *The New York Times on the Supreme Court 1857-2006* (2009), CQ Press, pp. 58-59.

23. The citation is 317 U.S. 1 (1942). The opinion was issued on Oct. 29, almost three months after the July 31 decision. The rulings on the curfew and internments are *Hirabayashi v. United States*, 320 U.S. 81 (1943), and *Korematsu v. United States*, 323 U.S. 214 (1944).

24. Joseph P. Fried, "Sheik Sentenced to Life in Prison in Bombing Plot," *The New York Times*, Jan. 18, 1996, p. A1, and Christopher S. Wren, "Jury Convicts 3 in a Conspiracy to Bomb Airliners," *The New York Times*, Sept. 6, 1996, p. A1. See also Benjamin Weiser, "Judge Upholds Conviction in '93 Bombing," *The New York Times*, April 5, 2003, p. A1.

25. Accounts drawn from *Pursuit of Justice* (2008), *op. cit.*, supplemented by Wikipedia entries or contemporaneous news coverage.

26. The decision is *Hamdan v. Rumsfeld*, 548 U.S. 557 (2006). For an account, see Kenneth Jost, *Supreme Court Yearbook 2005-2006*, CQ Press.

27. U.S. Department of Justice, "Fact Sheet: Justice Department Counter-Terrorism Efforts Since 9/11," Sept. 11, 2008, www.justice.gov/opa/pr/2008/September/08-nsd-807.html.

28. The Supreme Court decision is *Boumediene v. Bush*, 553 U.S. — — (2008). For an account, see Kenneth Jost, *Supreme Court Yearbook 2007-2008*, CQ Press. For Leon's decision granting habeas corpus to five of the six prisoners, see "Emerging Law of Detention," *op. cit.*, p. 99; William Glaberson, "Judge Declares Five Detainees Held Illegally," *The New York Times*, Nov. 21, 2008, p. A1.

29. See Peter Finn, "Report on U.S. Detention Policy Will Be Delayed," *The Washington Post*, July 21, 2009, p. A2.

30. For summaries of individual cases, see "Emerging Law of Detention," *op. cit.*, appendix II, pp. 88-105.

31. Quoted in Kornblut and Johnson, *op. cit.*

32. The decision is *Al Bihani v. Obama*, D.C. Cir., Jan. 5, 2010, http://pacer.cadc.uscourts.gov/docs/common/opinions/201001/09-5051-1223587.pdf. For coverage, see Del Quentin Wilber, "Court upholds ruling to detain Yemeni suspect," *The Washington Post*, Jan. 6, 2010, p. A3.

33. Material in Bahlul's case can be found at www.defense.gov/news/CMCRHAMZA.html/; materials

in Hamdan's case had not been posted by the deadline for this report.

34. See Anne E. Kornblut and Peter Finn, "Obama aides near reversal on 9/11 trial," *The Washington Post*, March 5, 2010, p. A1; Charlie Savage, "Senator Proposes Deal on Handling of Detainees," *The New York Times*, March 4, 2010, p. A12.

35. Richard A. Serrano, "Experts make case for N.Y. terror trial," *Los Angeles Times*, March 3, 2010, p. A12.

36. Jason Horwitz, "Obama's 'enforcer' may also be his voice of reason," *The Washington Post*, March 2, 2010, p. A1.

37. Savage, *op. cit.* (March 4).

38. Transcript: www.msnbc.msn.com/id/35270673/ns/meet_the_press//.

39. http://blogs.abcnews.com/thenumbers/2010/03/911-and-military-tribunals.html

40. "The Politics of National Security: A Wake-Up Call," Democracy Corps/Third Way, March 8, 2010, www.democracycorps.com/strategy/2010/03/the-politics-of-national-security-a-wake-up-call/?section=Analysis. The memo was signed by Stanley B. Greenberg, James Carville and Jeremy Rosner of Democracy Corps, and Jon Cowan, Matt Bennett and Andy Johnson of Third Way.

41. Andrew McCarthy, "Hold the Champagne on Military Commissions — It's a Head Fake," *The Corner*, March 5, 2010, http://corner.nationalreview.com.

BIBLIOGRAPHY

Books

Fisher, Louis, *Military Tribunals and Presidential Power: American Revolution to the War on Terrorism, University of Kansas Press*, 2005.
The veteran separation-of-powers specialist at the Library of Congress examines the development of the president's wartime authority in legal matters. Includes chapter notes, 10-page bibliography and list of cases.

Wittes, Benjamin, *Law and the Long War: The Future of Justice in the Age of Terror, Penguin Press*, 2008.
A leading researcher on national security at the Brookings Institution provides a critical examination of detention and interrogation policies along with his arguments for

Congress to pass legislation to authorize administrative detention of suspected enemy combatants and to create a national security court to try terrorism cases. Includes detailed notes. Wittes is also editor of *Legislating the War on Terror: An Agenda for Reform* (Brookings, 2009).

Yoo, John, *War by Other Means: An Insider's Account of the War on Terror*, Kaplan, 2005.

Yoo, a law professor at the University of California-Berkeley who served as deputy assistant attorney general for the Office of Legal Counsel during the George W. Bush administration, provides a combative account of his role in detention and interrogation policies and a strong argument for presidential wartime powers vis-à-vis Congress and the courts. Includes detailed notes. Yoo's other books include *Crisis and Command: The History of Executive Power from Washington to George W. Bush* (Kaplan, 2009); and *The Powers of War and Peace: Foreign Affairs and the Constitution after 9/11* (University of Chicago* (2005).

Articles

Mayer, Jane, "The Trial," *The New Yorker*, Feb. 5, 2010, www.newyorker.com/reporting/2010/02/15/100215fa_fact_mayer.

The magazine's prolific staff writer details the legal reasoning behind, and political implications of, Attorney General Eric Holder's decision to prosecute Khalid Sheikh Mohammed and four other alleged 9/11 conspirators in a civilian court instead of a military tribunal.

Reports and Studies

Elsea, Jennifer K., "Comparison of Rights in Military Commission Trials and Trials in Federal Criminal Courts," *Congressional Research Service*, Nov. 19, 2009, http://assets.opencrs.com/rpts/R40932_20091119.pdf.

The 23-page report provides a side-by-side comparison of the rights accorded to defendants respectively in federal criminal courts under general federal law or in military commissions under the Military Commissions Act of 2009. Elsea, a legislative attorney with CRS, also wrote two previous reports on military commissions: "The Military Commissions Act of 2006 (MCA): Background and Proposed Amendments" (Sept. 8, 2009), http://assets.opencrs.com/rpts/R40752_20090908.pdf; and "Terrorism and the Law of War: Trying Terrorists as War Criminals before Military Commissions" (Dec. 11, 2001), www.fas.org/irp/crs/RL31191.pdf.

Laguardia, Francesca, Terrorist Trial Report Card: September 11, 2001-September 11, 2009, *Center on Law and Security, New York University School of Law*, January 2010, www.lawandsecurity.org/publications/TTRCFinalJan14.pdf.

The series of reports studies data from federal terrorism prosecutions in the post-9/11 years and analyzes trends in the government's legal strategies.

Wittes, Benjamin, Robert Chesney and Rabea Benhalim, "The Emerging Law of Detention: The Guantánamo Habeas Cases as Lawmaking," *Brookings Institution*, Jan. 22, 2010, www.brookings.edu/papers/2010/0122_guantanamo_wittes_chesney.aspx.

The comprehensive report examines and identifies unsettled issues in decisions by federal courts in Washington, D.C., in several dozen habeas corpus cases filed by Guantánamo detainees. Wittes is a senior scholar and Benhalim a legal fellow at Brookings; Chesney is a law professor at the University of Texas-Austin.

Zabel, Richard B., and James J. Benjamin Jr., "In Pursuit of Justice: Prosecuting Terrorism Cases in the Federal Courts: 2009 Update and Recent Developments," *Human Rights First*, July 2009, www.humanrightsfirst.org/pdf/090723-LS-in-pursuit-justice-09-update.pdf.

The 70-page report by two New York City lawyers who formerly served as federal prosecutors finds federal courts to have a "track record of serving as an effective and fair tool for incapacitating terrorists." The report updates the authors' original, 171-page report, "In Pursuit of Justice: Prosecuting Terrorism Cases in the Federal Courts" (May 2008), www.humanrightsfirst.info/pdf/080521-USLS-pursuit-justice.pdf.

On the Web

Two newspapers — *The New York Times* and *The Miami Herald* — maintain Web sites with comprehensive information on Guantánamo detainees: **http://projects.nytimes.com/guantanamo** and **www.miamiherald.com/guantanamo**/. The Pentagon maintains a Web site on military commissions: **www.defense.gov/news/courtofmilitarycommissionreview.html**.

For More Information

American Civil Liberties Union, 125 Broad St., 18th Floor, New York, NY 10004; (212) 549-2500; www.aclu.org. Advocates for individual rights and federal civilian trials for suspected terrorists.

Brookings Institution, 1775 Massachusetts Ave., N.W., Washington, DC 20036; (202) 797-6000; www.brookings .edu. Public policy think tank focusing on foreign policy and governance.

Constitution Project, 1200 18th St., N.W., Suite 1000, Washington, DC 20036; (202) 580-6920; www.constitutionproject.org. Promotes bipartisan consensus on significant constitutional and legal issues.

Foundation for Defense of Democracies, P.O. Box 33249, Washington, DC 20033; (202) 207-0190; www.defend democracy.org. Nonpartisan policy institute dedicated to promoting pluralism, defending democratic values and opposing ideologies that threaten democracy.

Human Rights First, 333 Seventh Ave., 13th Floor, New York, NY 10001; (212) 845 5200; www.humanrightsfirst .org. Advocates for the U.S. government's full participation in international human rights laws.

National Institute of Military Justice, Washington College of Law, American University, 4801 Massachusetts Ave., N.W., Washington, DC 20016; (202) 274-4322; www.wcl.american .edu/nimj. Promotes the fair administration of justice in the military system.

Supporting researchers for more than 40 years

Research methods have always been at the core of SAGE's publishing program. Founder Sara Miller McCune published SAGE's first methods book, *Public Policy Evaluation*, in 1970. Soon after, she launched the *Quantitative Applications in the Social Sciences* series—affectionately known as the "little green books."

Always at the forefront of developing and supporting new approaches in methods, SAGE published early groundbreaking texts and journals in the fields of qualitative methods and evaluation.

Today, more than 40 years and two million little green books later, SAGE continues to push the boundaries with a growing list of more than 1,200 research methods books, journals, and reference works across the social, behavioral, and health sciences. Its imprints—Pine Forge Press, home of innovative textbooks in sociology, and Corwin, publisher of PreK–12 resources for teachers and administrators—broaden SAGE's range of offerings in methods. SAGE further extended its impact in 2008 when it acquired CQ Press and its best-selling and highly respected political science research methods list.

From qualitative, quantitative, and mixed methods to evaluation, SAGE is the essential resource for academics and practitioners looking for the latest methods by leading scholars.

For more information, visit **www.sagepub.com**.